GUNS

ILLUSTRATED®
2008 40th Anniversary Edition

Edited by
Ken Ramage

© 2007
by Krause Publications

Published by

Gun Digest Books

An imprint of F+W Publications
700 East State Street • Iola, WI 54990-0001
715-445-2214 • 888-457-2873
www.gundigestbooks.com

Our toll-free number to place an order or obtain
a free catalog is (800) 258-0929.

Manuscripts, contributions and inquiries, including first class return postage, should be sent to the
GUNS ILLUSTRATED Editorial Offices, Gun Digest Books, 700 E. State Street, Iola, WI 54990-0001.
All materials recieved will receive reasonable care, but we will not be responsible for their safe return.
Material accepted is subject to our requirements for editing and revisions. Author payment covers all
rights and title to the accepted material, including photos, drawings and other illustrations.
Payment is at our current rates.

CAUTION: Technical data presented here, particularly technical data on handloading and on firearms
adjustment and alteration, inevitably reflects individual experience with particular equipment and
components under specific circumstances the reader cannot duplicate exactly. Such data presentations
therefore should be used for guidance only and with caution. Gun Digest Books accepts no
responsibility for results obtained using these data.

ISSN 0072-9078

ISBN 13: 978-0-89689-533-1
ISBN 10: 0-89689-533-5

Designed by Patsy Howell & Tom Nelsen

Edited by Ken Ramage

Printed in the United States of America

GUNS ILLUSTRATED Staff

EDITOR
Ken Ramage

CONTRIBUTING EDITORS

Holt Bodinson – Ammunition, Ballistics & Components
J. W. "Doc" Carlson – Blackpowder Review
John Haviland – Shotgun Review
John Malloy – Handguns Today: Autoloaders

Layne Simpson – Rifle Review
Larry S. Sterett – Handloading Update
John Taffin – Handguns Today: Six-guns & Others

ABOUT THE COVERS

Handguns keep getting better and better. Our front and back covers show interesting examples from several of our leading manufacturers.

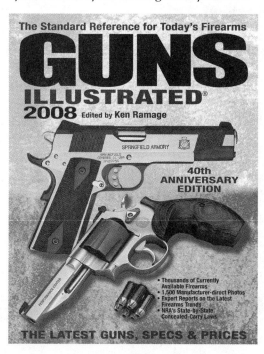

THE FRONT COVER:

Springfield Armory's full-size 1911 Loaded 45 ACP pistol (#PX9154LP) incorporates a number of features that previously were obtainable only from a custom gunsmith.

There are several versions in the Springfield 1911 family, but this particular version features black stainless steel, front and rear cocking serrations, a flared ejection port, an ambidextrous thumb safety and a number of other desirable features. Visit www.springfield-armory.com for full details.

Smith & Wesson is best known for its revolvers, and this Model 646 Performance Center Revolver is an excellent example of their work.

Made of frosted finish stainless steel, except for the titanium cylinder, the Model 646 is chambered for the 40 S&W cartridge. Because the 40 S&W is rimless, 'moon clips are needed to properly position the cartridges for firing and extraction. Two sets of half-moon clips come with the gun, plus a cartridge extraction tool. Sights are designed around the proven Patridge format and include a micrometer click-adjustable square-notch rear sight. The Altamount wood grips are fitted to the round-butt L-frame. Visit www.smith-wesson.

THE BACK COVER:

The Four-Inch Redhawk, from Sturm, Ruger & Co., is one of two big-bore snubbies Ruger introduced in 2007. Chambered for the 44 Magnum cartridge, this 6-shot stainless steel revolver is equipped with Hogue rubber finger-grooved grips with a pebbled texture for a more secure hold.

This new version of the Redhawk is designed for those who need a powerful firearm in a nicely portable package. For more details, visit www.ruger-firearms.com.

The Taurus Judge revolver, chambered for the 45 Colt/.410 shotshell, is a five-shot, corrosion-resistant pistol that can perform a number of useful functions.

Live in snake country or have to deal with agricultural vermin? This is your pistol. Load it with the widely available .410 shotshell and worry no more.

Need protection from larger critters, including the two-legged kind? This is your pistol. Fill the cylinder with the 45 Colt cartridge or the .410 shotshell that carries either the slug or the multiple-ball payload.

The Judge is available in several versions: blued or stainless steel *(shown)* and your choice of a 6- or 3-inch barrel *(shown)*. Sights are simple and effective, consisting of a square notch in the rear of the frame and a light-gathering front sight. The "Ribber" grips provide a secure hold. Visit www.taurususa.com.

CONTENTS

PAGE 13

PAGE 30

PAGE 42

PAGE 44

PAGE 51

PAGE 67

The new Stoeger Cougar is almost identical to the original Italian-made pistol, but it is made in Turkey. It's offered in 9mm and 40 S&W. The 40-caliber magazine holds 11 rounds and the 9mm magazine carries 15. Barrel length for either 9 or 40 is 3.6 inches, and overall length is 7 inches. Weight is about 32 ounces.

HANDGUN NEWS:

AUTOLOADING PISTOLS

by John Malloy

Sometimes, history seems to repeat itself.

Over a century ago, in the aftermath of the Spanish-American War, U. S. forces found that their standard sidearm, the 38 Long Colt revolver, lacked stopping power. It had been considered adequate for "civilized" warfare. However, it would not reliably stop fanatical Muslim attackers in the Philippines. Such adversaries sought heavenly reward by killing infidels, even if it meant their own death.

The situation led to the Thompson/LaGarde handgun tests of 1904. The findings were that no caliber smaller than 45 should be considered. Tests were scheduled for 1906, then postponed. The tests began in 1907, and after four years of extensive

testing that began in 1907, the Colt 45 ACP pistol was adopted in 1911. It served well—through World War I, World War II, Korea and Vietnam. Then, our leaders decided to use a cartridge common with our allies, and a 9mm pistol was adopted in 1985.

Recently, in the absence of "civilized" warfare, our soldiers had to once again face fanatical Muslim attackers, ones who do not mind dying as long as they can kill their targets. There has been a reevaluation of the role of the military sidearm. The 45 is being reconsidered as a military pistol. Tests were scheduled for 2006, and then postponed. At the time of this writing, military testing has been postponed indefinitely, but private development continues.

A number of companies, among them Beretta, FNH USA, Glock, Heckler & Koch, Sigarms, Smith & Wesson and Taurus, have introduced 45 ACP pistols in forms that could meet modern military specifications. Such pistols may have polymer frames, double-action trigger mechanisms, relatively large magazine capacity, grips that can fit a number of hand

A compact version of the Armalite AR-24, the AR-24k, was introduced at the January 2007 SHOT Show.

sizes and accessory rails. At any rate, the 45 ACP cartridge is getting a lot of attention for civilian, law enforcement and military use. Reportedly, some military combat units received small quantities of such modern new 45s. Others, again reportedly, acquired 1911s from storage, and seemed satisfied to have the nearly-century-old design available.

Here at home, the 1911 has never been more popular. More companies are making 1911s than ever before, many beginning just in the last few years. New 1911 models by established companies are essentially variations on the basic design—an effort to provide a 1911 to suit everyone's taste.

Of course, there is much more going on than just 1911s and 45s. The field of polymer-frame police service pistols in 9mm and 40 S&W—which also suit civilian self-protection—has expanded recently.

Polymer pistols continue to grow in popularity, but some new ones, such as the new Armalite and Sphinx pistols, use forged steel frames.

There are some completely new designs. Both the EAA FCP pistol and the Hogue Avenger are centerfire autoloaders that do not use a moving slide.

New countries have recently become important in the world of autoloading handguns. Turkey, in particular, now makes pistols for companies such as Armalite, Bernardelli, Stoeger and Tristar.

The 22-caliber handgun, often just taken for granted, continues to be of interest for training, hunting and target shooting. Almost everyone can use another 22 pistol, and a number of companies are ready to provide them. New versions of proven designs are available this year.

Because pistol-caliber carbines are seldom reported along with traditional hunting rifles, we'll continue to cover them here. On the other hand, rifle-caliber semiautomatic pistols interest a lot of people. For the most part, these long-range pistols have been based on the AR-15 design. Now, new ones based on the AK-47 are being offered by Century International.

Some politicians do not like such guns, and politics continues to influence the world of autoloading handguns. Certain politicians do not like any guns, but do not like semiautomatic pistols in particular.

The future is not very clear following the November 2006 takeover of Congress by Democrats. Not all Democrats are anti-gun, of course, but a number of anti-gun members of Congress are now in positions of great power. Our first loss was John Bolton, the outspoken representative of the United States in the United Nations. He held firm against attempts to use the UN to weaken the right of Americans to keep and bear arms. The Democratic leadership made it plain he would not be confirmed, and soon, he was out. The UN now plans to produce new global gun-control proposals in September 2008, shortly before our next presidential election.

When the new Democrat-controlled Congress convened in January 2007, four anti-gun bills were proposed before the month was out. Whether or not enough anti-gun votes exist to pass any such bills is in question, but the handwriting is on the wall—we can expect more restrictive firearms bills to be introduced.

Already, many new pistols come with mechanical changes made to placate the implacable politicians who do not like autoloaders. Loaded chamber indicators and magazine disconnectors appear on many new guns.

An accessory option that many shooters prefer now consists of grip-mounted laser sighting devices. Some are available as standard equipment on autoloading pistols.

With all that as background, let's take a look at what the individual companies are doing:

Armalite

Armalite, a rifle manufacturer, is now in the pistol business. The AR-24 pistol, announced last year, is a reality. The new Armalite pistol is a 9mm, and is made in Turkey (by Sarsilmaz) of forged parts that are CNC-machined. The barrel has cut rifling. The trigger system is conventional double action, that is, first shot is double action and succeeding shots single action. The basic mechanism is similar to that of the CZ-75.

Four variants are available. First is the standard AR-24, a full-size pistol with fixed sights, 15-round magazine, and a weight of 35 ounces. Second is the AR-24K, a compact version with a 13-round magazine, weighing 33 ounces. There are also "C" variants of both, variants that have adjustable rear sights. Actually the term "fixed sights" for the standard models is not quite correct, as even the front sights are adjustable for windage—they are dovetailed and held by setscrews.

A 45 ACP prototype is in the works. Plans are to name it the AR-26, and it will use a larger frame. A 40 S&W version is also planned later, probably on the larger frame. The Armalite 45 was planned for a 2007 introduction.

Armscor

Armscor may not be a familiar name to some American shooters, but the Philippine company makes a lot of pistols. For U. S. sales, Armscor 1911-type pistols are branded with the Rock Island Armory name. Various configurations of RIA 1911 pistols are available in 45 ACP, 40 S&W, 38 Super and 9mm.

New this year is the MAP series of pistols, based on the CZ 75 pattern. The parts are made by Tanfoglio of Italy and the guns are assembled in the United States.

Automag / AMT

Recall that the AMT and AutoMag lines became associated with High Standard a few years ago, under the umbrella of the Crusader Group. By last year, the AMT BackUp pistols and the AutoMag II pistols

The short rail on the Beretta Storm Subcompact's frame gives the pistol a stubby appearance, seen as Malloy gets off some aimed shots with the little pistol.

in 22 Winchester Magnum Rimfire (22 WMR) were in production.

Now, in the AutoMag line, a new caliber—17 Hornady Magnum Rimfire (17 HMR)—is being offered, and two previous chamberings—30 Carbine and 45 Winchester Magnum—have been reintroduced in appropriately larger pistols. The AutoMag II is in 17 HMR and 22 WMR, the AutoMag III is in 30 Carbine. The 45 Winchester Magnum appears in the Auto Mag IV.

Avenger

A new semiautomatic pistol design, which has a fixed barrel and does not use a reciprocating slide, has been introduced by Hogue Grips. The pistol, of European design, will be marketed as the Avenger. (See HOGUE)

Benelli

Benelli USA is importing the Cougar pistol in 9mm and 40 S&W under the Stoeger tradename. The Stoeger Cougar is similar to the original rotating-barrel Cougar pistol introduced by Beretta a decade or so ago. (See STOEGER)

Beretta

The Beretta Storm PX4 entered into production last year as Beretta's new polymer-frame service pistol. It was designed as a modular system, with interchangeable backstraps to create an individual fit for a shooter. The PX4 was available in 9mm and 40 S&W.

Now, several new variants have been introduced. The original PX4 was shortened from muzzle and butt. The original rotating barrel locking system was not suitable for the shorter pistol, so a tilting-barrel system was used. With its 3-inch barrel, the new Storm Sub-Compact measures about 5 x 6 inches and weighs 26 ounces. Calibers remain 9mm and 40 S&W. With the short staggered-column magazines, the 9 holds 13, with 10 for the 40. A patented "Sure Grip" magazine extender flips down to form a rest for the lower finger of larger hands. There is room on the shortened frame for a tiny little rail, so lasers, lights and other accessories can still be hung on the Sub-Compact.

The new PX4 Storm in 45 ACP had been anticipated, and the new 45 shows that the Storm design can be maximized as well as minimized. The PX4 45 uses the original rotating-barrel locking system, and has a 10-round staggered-column magazine.

A variation of the Storm 45 is the PX4 Storm SD (Special Duty) pistol. Designed to meet SOCOM (Special Operations Command) military specifications, the SD version as introduced offers a corrosion-resistant finish and special sights. It comes in a Tactical Carrying Case, with one 9-round and two 10-round magazines, a cleaning kit and other items.

Commercial production for the new variants was scheduled for summer 2007.

Beretta also planned to make limited runs of regular-line pistols with special enhancements during 2007. The pistols included the Model 3032 Tomcat, the Model 21 Bobcat, the M9 and the Model 92FS. Embellishments were to be special laser grips, two-tone finishes, high polish and pro-shop enhancements.

Browning

Browning seems determined to tweak its popular Buck Mark 22-caliber pistol line to provide variants to please every potential shooter.

For 2007, three new Buck Mark "Plus" pistols carrying the "UDX" code were introduced, all with the recently-introduced trim grip-frame option.

The Buck Mark Plus UDX has walnut ambidextrous "Ultragrip DX" grips and has a "slabside" 5.5-inch barrel and a matte blue finish. Sights are adjustable rear and fiber-optic front.

The Buck Mark Plus Rosewood UDX is similar, but has rosewood grips.

The Buck Mark Plus Stainless Black Laminated UDX differs by having a stainless barrel and slide, and it comes with black laminated grips.

Bul

The BUL Transmark firm was begun in Israel in 1990 as a company involved with shooting ranges. It soon became a maker of polymer-frame large-capacity 1911-type pistols, which were designated as BUL M-5. Many of the pistols were supplied to other companies and sold under other names.

Now, BUL is branching out. For the first time, the company is offering a steel-frame single-column 45 of more traditional 1911 design. Made in full-size and "commander" sizes, the new Buls still retain the M-5 model number, but are designated the M-5 Classic Government and the M-5 Classic Commander. Both versions come standard with a single-column 8-round magazine.

Even a greater departure in terms of mechanism is the new BUL Cherokee pistol line.

The standard Cherokee Compact is a conventional double-action pistol with a trigger mechanism reminiscent of that of the CZ 75. With its 3.7-inch barrel, the pistol is designated a compact, but the grip still holds a 17-round staggered-column magazine.

Another variant, called the G. Cherokee Compact, is basically similar, but has a slightly larger grip backstrap. The extra dimensions allow the attachment of a special telescoping shoulder stock.

Another Browning Buck Mark Plus is this variant with stainless-steel slide and barrel, and black laminated UDX grips.

Full-size Cherokee variants are also available with 4.4-inch barrels. They are also made in standard and "G" versions.

All Cherokee variants have a forward rail that will accommodate lights, lasers and other accessories.

Bushmaster

The Bushmaster Carbon 15 9mm pistols, built on lightweight AR-15 style lower and upper receivers, have new handguards available this year. The new parts are ceramic and are ventilated for better heat control.

Chrome-lined barrels are also now offered on the Carbon 15 pistols.

Century

The line between pistols and carbines continues to waver. We have become used to long-range 223-caliber pistols built on the AR-15 action. Now, Century International Arms is offering long-range pistols built on the AK-47 action. The new AK-style pistols, cataloged as "Champion" pistols, are newly-made in Romania and are offered in three models.

The HG1844-N is in the traditional 7.62 x 39mm chambering, and comes with a 30-round magazine. The HG1845-N is chambered for the 223 round, and also is fitted with a 30-shot magazine. For those who like inexpensive plinking with a big gun feel, the HG1846-N Champion is in 22 LR and uses a modified action that utilizes a 10-round magazine.

Colt

With the spread of legal concealed carry in the 1990s, Colt had introduced the Series 90 "Defender", a short, light 45. New for 2007, Colt offered a new small 45. There seems to be no doubt as to the intended market, as the new pistol is named the Colt "Concealed Carry" model.

The Concealed Carry 45 has an aluminum-alloy frame with a beveled magazine well. With its 3-inch barrel, it weighs only 25 ounces. Length is 6.75 inches. Its shortened serrated grip frame holds a special magazine that still offers the 7-round capacity of the full-size 1911. Thus,

the small new Colt is a 7 + 1 pistol.

Grips are slim "big diamond" wood grips. The long trigger and burr hammer are skeletonized, and the grip safety tang is extended. The entire pistol is finished a matte black. The sights are definitely snag-free—the sighting system is a channel along the top of the slide, in the style of pocket pistols of years past. The front slide treatment is different from that of previous Colts—instead of a scallop, the front of the slide is slightly narrowed along the entire front portion.

CZ

The subcompact CZ 2075 RAMI pistol has gained acceptance since its introduction several years ago.

Now, a new variant, the RAMI "P," has been added. The new pistol, offered in the 9mm and 40 S&W chamberings of the original, traded the aluminum alloy frame of the original for a new polymer frame. The slide was also lightened, and internal parts have been redesigned to reduce weight. With a 3-inch barrel, the little pistol weighs about 23 ounces. Magazine capacity is 8 for the 40, and 10 for the

9mm. An extended 14-round magazine is also available for the 9mm.

Two existing CZ models, the CZ 75B and the CZ P-01, are now available factory-equipped with Crimson Trace LaserGrips.

Detonics

All Detonics USA pistol models are offered in the 45 ACP chambering. In addition, the original compact CombatMaster was planned for a number of additional calibers. Now, all these extra chamberings are available. The CombatMaster can now be had in 45 ACP, 40 S&W, 357 SIG, 38 Super and 9mm Luger.

There have been subtle changes in Detonics magazines to match the recoil characteristics of the different calibers and different models.

EAA

European American Armory has had great success with its Tanfoglio-made Witness pistol line. Now, the Witness FCP pistol promises to be one of the most unusual ever offered. Three prototypes were displayed at

Too bad, but this is the only picture we have of EAA's new Witness FCP (Fast Cycling Pistol). EAA model Marisa Matthews holds the new pistol, which has a fixed "slide" and only four moving parts. The wire on this prototype shows the location of the "tube chamber" that holds the cartridge.

the January 2007 SHOT Show.

The FCP (think "Fast Cycling Pistol") uses a Witness polymer frame and some similar firing mechanism parts. What looks like the slide, however, is immobile, fixed in place. The rear portion forms a standing breech and the forward part houses a fixed 4-inch barrel. The barrel has no chamber. A large port occupies the space between the standing breech and the rear of the barrel. A special "tube chamber," containing a loaded cartridge, can be inserted to fill this space, with additional loaded chambers in a magazine below.

The FCP pistol can only be fired double-action, as nothing reciprocates to cock the hammer. When the cartridge in the tube chamber is fired, the bullet goes through the bore. Some gas from that shot is diverted back to expel the chamber (with its contained empty cartridge case) out the port. Another loaded chamber is immediately pushed up into firing position.

The tube chambers are reusable, and can be reloaded with new cartridges. The prototypes were all in 45 ACP. Other chamberings in the offing include 38 Special, 38 Super, 380, 9mm and 40 S&W.

EAA designers apparently have a sense of humor. Because the ejection of the tube chambers can be either right or left, one of the prototypes was made with a left-side ejection port. This configuration allowed the front and rear sights to be mounted on the right side of the "slide," instead of on the top. Thus, the "shooting sideways" method employed by TV bad guys could be used. The shooter could use the sights, and the tube chambers would eject straight down.

Ed Brown

Ed Brown Products adds a new model and a new limited edition to its line of 1911-style 45 automatics.

The new Special Forces model, announced last year, is now a production gun. It is a 5-inch "government" size pistol with 7+1 capacity. Front and rear grip straps have "chainlink" pattern checkering, and the pistol is finished with GEN III severe-use coating. Novak 3-dot

Ed Brown Products has introduced its Sheriff Jim Wilson limited edition 45 to honor lawman/writer Wilson.

night sights are fitted. The long trigger and commander-style hammer are skeletonized. The grip safety and frame have been modified to provide a higher and deeper hold. Cocobolo "big diamond" grips are furnished.

The Sheriff Jim Wilson limited edition pistol was designed to honor lawman/writer Sheriff Jim Wilson. Useful as well as decorative, the pistol incorporates some of Wilson's ideas about pistols used for serious purposes. The pistol is a 5-inch Government model, with a deeply-grooved arched mainspring housing and a front grip strap with 25 lines per inch checkering. The Novak sights consist of a black rear sight teamed with a dovetailed Tritium night sight. Smooth "Tru-Ivory" grip panels and Wilson's signature in the right side of the slide make the pistol a distinctive one.

Firestorm

Last year, this report was forced to record that the Firestorm 1911-style 45 pistols were no longer available. They had been made by Llama/Gabilondo in Spain, and with the demise of that company, the manufacture of the moderately-priced pistols came to a halt.

Now, the importer, SGS, has found a new supplier. The new Firestorm 1911 45s will be made in the Philippines and promise to be of true 1911 military-specification design. Samples for BATF approval were expected early in 2007, with production guns anticipated within the first half of that year. Once the mil-spec pistols become established, deluxe models, high-capacity variants and additional calibers are anticipated.

A new Firestorm 22 LR pistol with a 6-inch barrel is also being offered now.

FNH USA

New 45 ACP pistols joined FNH USA's line of semiautomatic handguns in 2007. Similar in general design to the previous FNP-9 and FNP-40 pistols, the new FNP-45 line comprises several variants.

The FNP-45 has a conventional double-action trigger system. The high-capacity black polymer frame comes with interchangeable backstrap inserts and an integral accessory rail. The slide is stainless steel. It is available in matte stainless finish, or with a black Melonite coating. The staggered-column magazine holds 14 rounds. However, 10-shot models are available for those who live under more-restrictive government controls. With a 4.5-inch barrel, the FNP-45 weighs about 33 ounces.

The FNP-45 USG is a special variant made for submission for consideration for United States military forces. Differences include a sand-colored frame, a lanyard ring and a 15-round magazine.

The new FNP-45 pistols can be readily distinguished visually from their smaller-caliber brethren. The base of the magazine on the earlier guns is parallel to the line of the slide. The new 45 has a magazine base that is perpendicular to the grip, and at a noticeable angle to the slide line.

FNH's Five-seveN pistol, in 5.7 x 28mm, is now offered with a C-More sight system. These are snag-free 3-dot sights, available either with or without Tritium elements, and are now available as optional accessories. Plans seem to be to offer them as standard items later.

The interesting PS 90 carbine—for the same 5.7 x 28 cartridge—has a new variant. The original PS 90 had "designated" optics that were mounted as a more-or-less permanent part of the firearm. Now, the new PS 90 TR (Triple-Rail) carbine has rails to allow mounting other sights and accessories, as the user chooses. Colors are black or green.

Glock

Glock introduced a new 45 ACP pistol in 2007. The new 45, in a way, sort of breaks Glock's tradition of sequentially numbering new models. The original Glock 45, the Model 21, was introduced some years ago, and Glock numbers now go up to 39. This new 45 is introduced as the Glock Model 21 SF, with the "SF" standing for "Short Frame." The 21SF is brand new, and was not in the Glock 2007 catalog in the early part of the year.

The pistol has a full-size barrel and slide, but a smaller frame. It offers what has been described as a "subtle but noticeable" different feel. The Glock 21 has been used in limited numbers by U. S. special forces in combat zones. Reports from the troops using them were favorable, but it was felt that the grip was too large for some shooters. Glock reshaped the frame and installed a new trigger mechanism housing. Most other parts remain the same. One new innovation introduced with the SF is a true ambidextrous magazine release. The 21 SF uses the same 13-round magazines as the original Model 21.

HK

Heckler & Koch has based most of its current line of pistols on its USP (Universal Selfloading Pistol) design, which allows a number of different mechanical and caliber variations. After getting used to HK pistols having "USP" in their model designations, it is something of a surprise that the new 45-caliber offering for 2007 was named, simply, the HK45.

The new HK45 reportedly was developed for potential U. S. military use. It can be made in a number of double-action and single-action variants. A mechanical internal recoil-reduction system was designed to improve control during rapid fire.

Two basic variants are offered. The standard HK45 has a 4.5-inch barrel and weighs about 28 ounces, and uses a 10-round magazine. A smaller version, the HK45C has a 3.9-inch barrel and tips the scales at 25 ounces. It uses an 8-round magazine. Both variants have replaceable grip panels. Both variants can be fitted with threaded barrels for use with sound suppressors.

Heckler & Koch also plans to offer the 9mm P30 pistol, based on a German customs pistol. Both rear *and side* grip panels can be changed for a very individualized grip feel. The P30 has a decocker control on the left rear of the slide.

Hi-Point

Has the long-awaited Hi-Point 45 ACP carbine become a reality yet? The 9mm and 40 S&W carbines have proved popular, and it seemed logical to bring out a 45-caliber version.

As of January 2007, a Hi-Point representative said the 45 carbine was still under development. They want it to be right before it is introduced. However, availability before the end of 2007 was anticipated.

Hogue

The prototype of a new pistol, the Hogue Avenger, was displayed at the January 2007 SHOT Show. Hogue, the grip company, plans to offer the European-designed pistol.

Dedicated readers of this publication may recall that in the 1997 edition, a new pistol called the Ultramatic was introduced by an Austrian firm. It looked a bit like a 1911, but had a fixed barrel and fixed "slide" and an internal reciprocating bolt. The bolt movement was retarded by two side-mounted locking studs. By the 1999 edition, both the company and the guns were called Wolf Sporting Pistols. However, by the following 2000 edition, the pistols had faded out of the publication.

The design had many good features, but the locking and recoil spring systems were complex, with a lot of parts. It did some good shooting, but had some problems, and soon was gone.

During the early days, I photographed Peter Spielberger, a young man with the company, holding an Ultramatic pistol. Many years later, Spielberger rethought the design. He realized that some of the original features, such as the fixed barrel, and the non-moving sights that were always in alignment with the barrel, were good. He set about, with computer assistance, to create new spring and locking systems. The present design uses a pivoting locking wedge that locks into a recess in the top of the fixed "slide." The locking wedge controls the rearward movement of the internal bolt. The locking wedge is prevented from opening too soon by a delay block that must be cammed out of the way. The resulting

The Hogue Avenger, a new design, has a fixed barrel and sights that remain aligned with the barrel during shooting (left view).

Kahr's new compact polymer-frame 45, the PM45, holds 5+1 rounds and weighs about 19 ounces (angled view).

Kahr's new polymer-frame 45, the TP45, has a 4.3-inch barrel and weighs about 22 ounces (left view).

mechanism is relatively simple, works well and reduces muzzle rise. The fixed, non-moving barrel and non-moving sights always stay in alignment with each other for good inherent accuracy.

Spielberger wisely refrained from reinventing the wheel for the bottom part of the pistol. The frame and trigger mechanism are straight 1911! Using the 1911 design for the lower half of the new pistol means that the Avenger can be made as a complete pistol or as a conversion unit for existing 1911 frames.

Spielberger was at the Hogue display at the January 2007 SHOT Show. So, over a decade later, I was able to take another picture of him (with his hair somewhat grayer now), holding the new pistol. Hogue will market it as the Avenger by Hogue. Limited production was scheduled for early 2007.

Iver Johnson

The new Iver Johnson 1911-style pistols, in 45 ACP and 22 LR calibers, and 22 LR conversion kits were announced year before last. Production of the 22 conversion kits began before pistol production. The production of the 45 pistol was scheduled for early 2007, while production of the 22 version was anticipated by mid-2007. Both calibers will be available in standard (Raven Series) and deluxe (Eagle Target Series) versions. The deluxe variants will be made with adjustable sights and other niceties.

Kahr

Kahr introduced its new polymer 45 last year, and this year expands its big-bore polymer line with two more 45s. Both are double-action-only, with black polymer frames and matte stainless-steel slides.

The TP45 has a 7-shot magazine, a 4-inch barrel, and weighs about 23 ounces. The PM45 is smaller. With a 3.14-inch barrel and a 5-round magazine; it weighs about 19 ounces. Either pistol can be had with Tritium night sights.

Recall that Kahr now owns the Auto-Ordnance and Thompson firearms lines. In the Thompson line, Kahr offers two new 45 ACP Thompson long guns. The early Thompsons might be considered the first of the pistol-caliber carbines. For 2007, models with detachable buttstocks were made available, for the first time in many decades. The Thompson 1927A-1 Deluxe has a finned 16.5-inch barrel (18 inches with compensator). Thus, even with the buttstock detached, the gun measures 31.5 inches long, and the feds do not consider it a "short-barrel rifle."

However, some people are willing to jump through the necessary hoops and cough up the extra money to have an authentic semiautomatic look-alike of the original Tommy Gun. For them, there is now the Thompson 1927A-1 SBR (Short Barrel Rifle.) Its 10.5-inch finned barrel (12 inches with compensator) gives it an overall length of 25.5

inches with the buttstock removed.

Both these new Thompson carbines will take either the 50-round drum or the 30-round box magazines.

Kimber

Kimber has evolved into one of the largest makers of 1911-type pistols. This year, three new series of 1911-style autoloaders have been introduced.

The Covert series of 45 ACP carry pistols comes from the Kimber Custom Shop. The series is composed of three models. The full-size variant, the Custom Covert II, has a 5-inch barrel and 7 + 1 capacity, and weighs 31 ounces. The 4-inch Pro Covert II has a bushingless bull barrel. Grip is full-size with 7-round magazine capacity, and the pistol weighs 28 ounces. Both the Custom Covert and Pro Covert have lanyard loops at the butt. The smallest Covert, the Ultra Covert II, has a 3-inch barrel and weighs 25 ounces. The frame of each Covert is Desert Tan, and the matte black slides are topped with 3-dot night sights. Each Covert pistol has camo-pattern Crimson Trace LaserGrips.

The Aegis is a series designed for 1911 lovers who somehow, for whatever reason, prefer the 9mm chambering. The Ultra Aegis II has a 3-inch barrel, the Pro Aegis II has a 4-inch barrel, and the Custom Aegis II is a full-size 5-inch version. Like the Covert series, the Aegis pistols have machined aluminum frames. Each Aegis has wide slide serrations, a spurless hammer and thin rosewood grips. Weights are about the same as for the Covert series. By the way, "Aegis" comes from the Greek, and means a shield or protection.

The SuperAmerica will be made in limited numbers. It is a full-size blued pistol, and the slide has scroll engraving inside a gold-filled border. It will come in a wooden case with a special Kimber knife. Both pistol and knife have grips made of mammoth ivory.

NAA

Grip-mounted lasers are gaining popularity on large-size pistols. Downsizing this trend, North American Arms will offer Crimson Trace LaserGrips on their little Guardian pistols. The first ones to wear the new grips will be the larger-frame 380 and 32 NAA versions, with the smaller 32 ACP and 25 NAA coming later. Availability was anticipated during 2007.

Para-Ordnance

Para-Ordnance has become one of the largest makers of 1911-type pistols. One can get the hint of this by looking at their 2007 catalog. On the cover, a large picture of a Para pistol overlies 51 small images of other pistols made by the company. Consider that Para makes traditional single-action and LDA (light double action) versions, offers single-column and staggered-column magazines with capacities of 6, 7, 8, 9, 10, 12, 13, 14, 15, 16 and 18

rounds, makes frames of carbon steel, stainless steel and aluminum alloy, offers barrel lengths of 3, 3.5, 4.25 and 5 inches, and can furnish pistols chambered for 9mm, 38 Super, 40 S&W, 45 GAP and 45 ACP. Small wonder that the company offers a lot of variations.

Some of Para's new offerings:

The Big Hawg can be considered the big brother of the Warthog and other compact pistols in Para's "Hawg" series. Since the small ones were well-received, why not a full-size model? The Big Hawg is a full 5-inch barrel 45 with a wide aluminum alloy frame and 14 + 1 capacity. The big pistol weighs only 28 ounces.

The Covert Black Slim Hawg is a 6 + 1 capacity 45 with a 3-inch barrel. It weighs 24 ounces.

The Carry GAP is a 6 + 1 steel-frame variant with a steel frame and 3-inch barrel, weighing 29 ounces. It is an LDA pistol chambered for the 45 G.A.P. cartridge. The grip is smaller because of the shorter cartridge.

The CCO GAP is a similar pistol with a 3.5-inch barrel and 7 + 1 capacity. Also for the 45 GAP, it weighs 31 ounces.

Because they are making the smaller grip frame, why then not make a smaller-grip 9mm? The Carry 9 is an 8 + 1 9mm pistol with a 3-inch barrel, weighing 24 ounces.

The 1911 Stainless SSP is a full-size classic single-column 8 + 1 45 ACP pistol in stainless steel.

The 1911 Limited is a similar pistol gussied up with special grips and a

striking black/stainless slide treatment.

Para seems determined to make a 1911 to suit just about any shooter's requirements.

Rock River

Accessory rails are becoming popular, and Rock River Arms has made a variant of their forged and machined frames which now includes a frame rail. This frame is used on the new 1911-style "Tactical Pistol" that appeared for the first time in the company's 2007 lineup. The Tactical Pistol is guaranteed to shoot 2.5-inch groups at 50 yards with specific factory ammunition.

Rohrbaugh

Rohrbaugh is the little company that came out of nowhere a few years ago with the smallest and lightest all-metal 9mm pistol. Just a little bit larger than a 3x5 index card, the Rohrbaugh R9 weighed in at 12.8 ounces. In 2005, the Rohrbaugh pistol was awarded the NRA "Golden Bullseye" award as handgun of the year. For 2007, the line expanded to include a new finish and a new chambering.

An all-black variant is now available as the "Stealth" R9. The slides are coated with "Diamond Black," which reduces friction as well as glare.

A light 9mm will kick, even as a locked-breech pistol. So, Rohrbaugh has

A palm-size pistol doesn't have much room for the components of a laser sight, but North American Arms is offering Crimson Trace LaserGrips on its little pistols.

Rock River Arms is now offering its Tactical Pistol, a full-size 45 with a machined frame rail.

The Ruger 22/45 MK III Hunter has a 4.5-inch fluted stainless-steel barrel (right view).

introduced a version in 380 ACP. This variant gives a useful power level with reduced recoil.

Ruger

Ruger has introduced a shorter version of its 22-caliber 22/45 Mark III Hunter pistol. The new 4.5-inch barrel Hunter pistol has a slim polymer grip with the angle and feel of the 1911. The receiver and barrel are stainless steel. Sights are an adjustable "V" rear and a "HiViz" fiber-optic front sight. If a scope is desired, the receiver is already drilled and tapped for a scope base—which is included with the pistol. Also included with each new Hunter are two 10-round magazines.

Sarsilmaz

The Turkish Sarsilmaz company, well-known as a shotgun maker, has come to the attention of American pistol shooters recently. The firm is making pistols which are sold under the names of several other companies.

Two new pistols were introduced under the Sarsilmaz name in January 2007. The 45-caliber Kilinc pistol is an enlargement of the steel-frame 9mm Kilinc pistol (a CZ 75 design) made for the Turkish military forces. Production models of the new 45 were scheduled to be offered by the end of 2007.

A new pistol, the Vatoz, is being designed for the Turkish army. It will be in the standard 9mm chambering, and will have a new light alloy frame. Early specimens were displayed at the 2007 SHOT Show.

Sigarms

45 ACP pistols are prominent in Sigarms' new offerings this year.

Sigarms is a relative newcomer to the world of 1911 pistols, but its 1911-type Revolution pistols have sixteen entries in the 2007 catalog. The latest is the Revolution Compact C3. The striking-looking pistol has a black anodized alloy frame under a stainless steel slide and controls. Rosewood grips complete the package. With its 4-inch barrel, the C3 weighs about 29 ounces.

The 45-caliber P220 was introduced back in the mid 1970s. It took a back seat to 9mm offerings when the "wondernine" era took off in the 1980s. Now, times have changed, and the P220 has moved up to the driver's seat. Most of SIG's new offerings are variants of the P220.

The P220 Super Match has had the barrel extended to 5 inches. It has a two-tone appearance, with a black beavertail frame and a stainless-steel slide. Grips are SIG custom wood panels. A factory test target comes with each pistol to prove its accuracy.

The P220 Combat is a 45 designed to meet military standards. It has an earth-tone frame, Picatinny rail and night sights. A variant, the P220 Combat TB, has a threaded barrel that can accept a sound suppressor. Unlike some of the pistols designed for military consideration, the Sigarms P220 Combat uses a single-column magazine. The standard magazine holds 8 rounds. An extended 10-shot magazine, which protrudes below the bottom of the grip, is also available.

The P220 Compact is the same general size as the compact P245 but has a new shape. The frame has a beavertail tang, and the 6-round magazine has an extended base. Several variants are made, and in 2007, it replaces the P245.

The P220 Carry Elite is an 8 + 1 compact pistol with a full-size frame and shorter 3.9-inch barrel of the Compact. It features the Sigarms short reset trigger (SRT).

A fundraising pistol for the group known as "Concerns of Police Survivors (C.O.P.S.)," is a special P226 designated the COPS model. For every pistol

The Sigarms 1911 Revolution Compact C3 pistol has a two-tone finish and rosewood grips (right view).

The new Sigarms P220 Combat 45 (right view).

S&W's new M&P Compact is shortened to match its 3.5-inch barrel. This one is an M&P 9c, the 9mm compact.

sold, Sigarms will contribute to the fund to help the families of slain police officers.

Smith & Wesson

S&W's Military & Police (M&P) polymer-frame autoloaders in 40 and 9mm were well-received. Now a 45 ACP version, the Smith & Wesson M&P45, has been added. The new 45 was offered in all-black or earth-tone variants. The earth-tone pistol, which apparently was designed with an eye to military contracts, has an additional ambidextrous manual safety. All M&P45 pistols have a 4.5-inch barrel,

with three interchangeable grips. An accessory rail is on the forward part of the frame. Weight is just under 30 ounces.

The M&P series was expanded to use the 45 cartridge, but the 9mm variant was also downsized into a compact version. The new M&P9 Compact has a 3.5-inch barrel and comes with either a 10-round or 12-round magazine. The smaller polymer-frame pistol weighs about 22 ounces. The stainless-steel barrel and slide are coated with black Melonite. Three interchangeable grip sizes allow the shooter to fit the smaller gun to a particular hand.

The Smith & Wesson Performance Center offers the 45 ACP Model 945. When S&W introduced its 45-caliber double-action autoloader, the Model 645, much pistol competition was dominated by 1911-type pistols. Long before the company gave in and brought out its own 1911, S&W made a number of attempts to create a better competition pistol. The present Model 945 is a sort of hybrid

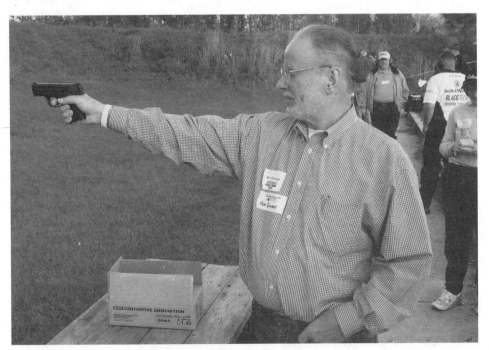

Ken Ramage, the Editor-in-Chief of this publication, tries out the Smith & Wesson M&P 9c, the new 9mm compact version of the company's M&P line.

Robert Malloy, the writer's brother, shoots the new S&W 45-caliber M&P pistol in its earth-tone military configuration.

of 1911 and earlier S&W 45 features. Some think the resultant pistol is better than the 1911. Whatever the comparison, I can agree that the 945 is a very good-shooting pistol. I had a chance to shoot one recently, and it was exceptionally accurate.

Sphinx

The Sphinx, a Swiss-made pistol based on the CZ 75 with a number of modifications, has been available as a top-end 9mm. Now, it is available in a larger version, in 45 ACP chambering.

The Sphinx design differs from the basic CZ 75 in a number of aspects. Perhaps most noticeable is that the operating frame and the grip frame are machined as two separate pieces. All parts are CNC-machined. A full slide-length frame and integral accessory rail put weight forward to reduce muzzle rise.

The new Sphinx 45 is a heavy pistol, weighing in at about 43 ounces. It should appeal to those who have admired the workmanship of the Sphinx, but wanted a 45.

*Middle:
The new
Smith & Wesson
M&P 45 is available
in military-style
configuration, with
manual safety,
accessory rail and
earth-tone frame.*

*Right: The S&W Model 945,
available as a Performance
Center gun, is a hybrid of
1911 and early S&W 45
features. Malloy shot this
handsome specimen and
was impressed with its
accuracy.*

Springfield

The 45 ACP chambering in Springfield's XD line was introduced last year. This year, the company introduced the 45 ACP XD Compact. The new XD Compact seems designed to help people who can't quite decide what size pistol they want. The new XD Compact comes in a 4-inch barrel version, with a 5-incher anticipated in the near future.

Springfield's Laura Lewsader displays the company's new small-grip 1911, the Springfield EMP in 9mm chambering.

The Compact has had about three-quarters of an inch trimmed off the grip to match the length of a 10-shot magazine. However, two magazines are furnished with each pistol—a ten-shot "concealment" magazine that ends at the base of the grip, and a 13-round "service model" magazine that has an extension of the grip at the base. Springfield calls this the "Mag X-Tension." Each pistol comes with special "XD Gear" items—a polymer belt holster, magazine loader and double magazine pouch.

Also new is the Springfield EMP (Enhanced Micro Pistol), a nice-looking little 9mm 1911-type pistol. The small-grip 9mm has a two-tone appearance, with dark frame and stainless-steel slide. Rosewood grips set off the colors of the metal.

STI

STI International makes 1911-type pistols and offers over 25 different models in multiple calibers. New for 2007 were five different variants.

The Escort is a compact-length pistol with a commander-size frame. Weighing about 23 ounces, this is the lightest pistol in the STI line. In 45

ACP, it has a 3-inch ramped bull barrel with a fully supported chamber. The frame is forged aluminum.

The Guardian is a commander-frame 45 with a 3.9-inch supported ramped barrel. The Guardian comes with redwood grips and weighs about 32 ounces.

The Legend is a big pistol with a modular steel/polymer frame that holds a long staggered-column magazine. The barrel is a 5-inch supported bull barrel. The hard chrome slide has a black "Legend" inlay and distinctive "Sabertooth" cocking serrations. Weight is 38 ounces. An adjustable rear sight and Dawson fiber-optic front sight are fitted. The Legend is

*The STI Escort is a 45
with a shortened slide
and 3.4-inch barrel.*

STI's new Guardian is a compact 45 with a 3.9-inch bull barrel.

STI's Sentinel is a 5-inch barrel, single-column 1911, available in 9mm, 40 or 45.

available in 9mm, 40 S&W and 45 ACP.

The Sentinel is a full-size 5-inch 1911 pistol available in 9mm, 40 and 45. Thick rosewood grips are fitted to the blued, matte-finish frame. Adjustable rear sight and competition front sight are fitted. The gun is suitable, out-of-the-box, for IPSC or IDPA competition.

The Spartan is a basic Parkerized 5-inch 1911-type pistol. It has a traditional barrel bushing and uncheckered frame, but comes with a number of enhancements. The Spartan

has a high-ride beavertail grip safety and front and rear slide serrations. It weighs 35 ounces, and has adjustable rear and fiber-optic front sights fitted.

Stoeger

The new Stoeger Cougar may look familiar to many shooters. The design was introduced as the Beretta Cougar in the mid-1990s. As introduced, the Cougar was a fairly compact, aluminum-frame pistol of locked breech/rotating

barrel design. The trigger mechanism was conventional double action.

The new Stoeger Cougar is almost identical to the original Italian-made pistol, but it is made in Turkey, imported by Benelli, and marketed under the Stoeger name. Pistols are offered in 9mm and 40 S&W. The 40-caliber magazine holds 11 rounds and the 9mm magazine carries 15. Niceties such as 3-dot sights and ambidextrous safety/decocking levers come standard. Barrel length for either 9 or 40 is 3.6 inches, and overall length is 7 inches. Weight is about 32 ounces.

Taurus

As did a number of other manufacturers, Taurus designed a 45-caliber pistol to meet SOCOM requirements for the Joint Combat Pistol trials. With the postponement of the trials, Taurus decided to introduce the pistol to the commercial and law enforcement markets. The new 24/7 OSS pistol is now offered in 40 S&W and 9mm, as well as 45 ACP. It has an interesting single action/double action (SA/DA) trigger system. It fires normally from SA mode. However, in case of a misfire, the mechanism changes to DA mode to permit additional strikes to the primer.

The 24/7 OSS comes in two versions. The "DS" model can be carried in SA "cocked and locked" condition, with the manual safety on. The striker can be released safely by pushing up on the safety lever. Then it switches to DA mode. The "D" model is double action only, with a decocker.

Barrel length for any 24/7 OSS variant is 5.25 inches. Capacity is 17 + 1 for the 9mm, 15 + 1 for

The 24/7 PRO from Taurus also comes in a 4-inch barrel variant, with frame rail and ribber grip.

The Taurus Millennium PRO 3.25-inch compact is vailable in an all-black finish. This is a 40 S&W version with 10+1 capacity.

The compact Millennium PRO is offered with a 3.25-inch barrel. This variant is a 12+1 9mm with a titanium slide.

The Taurus PT 1911 45 is also available with an integral frame accessory rail.

Taurus PT 24/7 PRO pistols come with a 3.3-inch barrel option. This version has a frame rail.

The new Taurus PT 1911 45 is offered in blue (shown) or stainless steel.

This new 45-caliber Taurus PT 24/7 OSS pistol is the "DS" version, which has a unique single action/double action trigger mechanism.

the 40 and 12 + 1 for the 45.

I cannot verify the story, but if it is true, some people at Taurus have a sense of humor. The "OSS" model designation, which calls to mind the clandestine WWII organization that became the CIA, is said to stand for "O-Six Submission." That tongue-in-cheek designation simply meant it was made to submit for government tests in 2006.

Beside the military-type 24/7 OSS, 24/7 Pro pistols are now offered. Similar in some mechanical features to the 24/7 OSS, the 24/7 Pro pistols are made in 3.33-inch and 4-inch barrel lengths as well as 5.2 inches. They have more "civilian" features such as ribbed rubber

("ribber") grips.

Some of the same engineering has been applied to the smaller Millennium Pro series with 3.25-inch barrels. Caliber offerings should suit nearly everyone—32 ACP, 380, 9mm, 40 S&W and 45 ACP. Weights vary from 16 to 22 ounces, depending on caliber and magazine capacity.

Taurus created a stir a few years ago when the company announced they would offer a 1911-type pistol. Now the Taurus 1911 is available.

Barrel length is the traditional 5 inches. Capacity is 8 + 1. The Taurus 1911 is available in 45 ACP only and offers blued (Model 1911B) and stainless-steel (Model 1911SS) finishes. Versions with integral Picatinny rail on the frame forward extension, and versions with aluminum frames were planned for late 2007. A Novak Custom variant is also in the works. Interestingly, each Taurus 1911 pistol has the serial number not only on the frame, but on the slide and barrel. If you buy several, you don't have to worry about mixing the parts while cleaning.

The new Tisas 45 ACP pistol was introduced at the 2007 SHOT Show. The new 45 has unusual wood grips that extend forward on the frame.

Thompson

Perhaps no other firearm outline is as recognizable as that of a Thompson. The original 45 ACP Thompson submachine guns and semiautomatic carbines of the 1920s can perhaps be considered the first of the pistol-caliber carbines. They continue to have an appeal all these decades later. Kahr Arms, the current manufacturer, offers two new variants this year. (See KAHR)

Tristar

Tristar Sporting Arms imports a line of shotguns and replica Sharps rifles. New for 2007, a line of Turkish-made "Tisas" pistols will be imported.

The pistols are conventional double action, with staggered-column magazines and ambidextrous decockers. Most are expected to be offered in 9mm, but one 45 was on display at the Tristar exhibit at the January 2007 SHOT Show.

Uselton

Uselton's new pistol offering is the "Slant Six" pistol, a small 1911-type 45. It has a semi-bobtail "slant" grip treatment and a 6-round magazine.

Rick Uselton promotes exotic looks in his pistols, and displayed one with crocodile-skin grip panels—inlaid into Cocobolo wood—at the January 2007 SHOT Show. In the works are grips with inlays of ostrich, elephant, alligator and shark skins.

Uselton race guns are planned. They will be double-column 1911s with 19 + 1 capacity. The "Desert Storm" pistol will be a full-size 5-inch 1911 with a ceramic coating finish.

U. S. Firearms

Recall that U. S. Firearms made its reputation building replicas of historic Colt revolvers. Then, a few years ago, the company started adding early Colt semiautomatic pistols, and the early 45 ACP, 38 Super and 22 Ace pistols are now in their line. Now, USFA will reintroduce the Colt Woodsman, the historic first-ever 22-caliber autoloading pistol, which was invented by John M. Browning. The version they are planning is the "first generation" pistol initially made by Colt in 1915. The company is serious about its intention to produce the early Woodsman, but no date has been set for production.

Volquartsen

The acceptance of the little 17 Mach 2 cartridge has brought about the production of a number of rifles and also handguns, both autoloaders and revolvers, in that caliber. Owners of 22 LR pistols may have wondered if their guns could be converted to the new little 17. For Ruger owners, Volquartsen has an answer with its new Mach 2 conversion kit. The kit is suitable for Ruger Mark II and Mark III pistols. The "drop-in" kit includes a barreled receiver, with mated bolt and other necessary parts.

Postscript

More interesting autoloading handguns are available now than ever before. If you have held off, consider buying a new pistol, perhaps several. Give yourself a chance to try out new ideas—or new versions of old classics—this year. And, because autoloaders are liable to come under fire during the present Congress, take someone new with you to the range to try the guns out. The more people that understand guns, know how to handle them, and enjoy shooting them, the less the chance that anti-gun politicians can have their way. ✸

For those who like the authentic "Tommy Gun" look and don't mind extra regulation, the 1927A1 Thompson semiautomatic carbine is available as a "short barrel rifle." It has the new detachable stock and can use either box or drum magazines.

SIXGUNS & OTHERS

by John Taffin

As this is written we are commemorating two very important six-gun anniversaries. The first cartridge-firing revolver, appearing 150 years ago, was the Smith & Wesson Model #1 chambered in 22 rimfire, also a new development. While this little seven-shot Tip-Up is long gone, the 22 remains our most popular cartridge. The Model #1 would evolve into the Model #2, Model #3, the Double Action Model, the Military & Police; then, 100 years ago, those evolutionary models would lead to the first N-frame, the New Century or 1st Model Hand Ejector, or as it is more affectionately known, the Triple-Lock chambered in 44 Special which a half century later would become the Smith & Wesson 44 Magnum.

I intend to shoot a lot of 22s this year to not only celebrate the cartridge's 150th anniversary, but also because they are so enjoyable. I started off the year celebrating the 44 Special by purchasing a 2nd Generation 7½-inch, ivory-stocked Colt Single Action Army 44 Special insuring more good shooting. It won't be alone as we shall see looking at the offerings for six-gunners this year.

A Dream Come True

Since this is the 100th anniversary of the 44 Special it is altogether fitting to see a museum dedicated to the person who not only did the most to popularize the 44 Special but also highly influenced the development of the 44 Magnum. From 1929 until 1955 Elmer Keith was the leading advocate of 44 Special six-guns. When he received the new 44 Magnum from Smith & Wesson in early 1956, he retired his 44 Specials and carried a 44 Magnum virtually daily from then on. In 1981 Elmer Keith suffered a stroke and died in 1984. He left a rich legacy to all shooters as well as a large collection of firearms and game trophies.

In November 2005 a friend of Ted Keith's, Al Marion, heard Cabela's planned to open a new store in Boise, Idaho and he had an idea. He contacted Jeff Montgomery of Cabela's who happens to be in charge of all the taxidermy displays at all Cabela's stores, and outlined his idea. Jeff caught the vision and, subsequently, Cabela's would do what no one else had been able to do, establish a true Elmer Keith Museum. Part of the museum is Elmer Keith sitting at his desk in front of his ancient typewriter in his office. When a button is pushed,

he turns around in his chair, moves his arm with his ever-present cigar, and talks to those who are present. I used his writings to put together the seven-minute presentation.

My second job was to write the descriptions of the nearly 60 handguns, rifles and shotguns on display and then help place them in the glass cases. One side of the museum has all the six-guns while the other displays the rifles. I chose the #5 SAA 44 Special as the centerpiece of the handgun display so it would be the first thing anyone would see. On each side of it I placed two of his other most used six-guns. On one side of the #5 we have the King Custom 44 Special Colt Single Action with a 7½-inch barrel and custom sights; on the other side rests Keith's most used 44 Magnum, a 4-inch pre-29 with ivory grips carved in his favorite longhorn pattern.

I always wondered how Keith could shoot his heavy 44 Magnum load consisting of his 250-grain #429421 bullet over 22 grains of #2400. I found out the first time I handled his six-guns while serving on the Museum Board. The carving of the grip filled in the natural crease in the hand, doing much to help moderate felt recoil. All three of these famous six-guns are stocked with ivory and the #5 is fully engraved,

Taffin shooting the AWA octagon-barreled Ultimate 1873.

while the other two working guns are the standard case-hardened/blue finish of a Colt Single Action and the old Smith & Wesson Bright Blue, heavily worn thus showing a lot of daily use. Other six-guns include two other 44 Special Colt Single Actions as well as several 44 Magnum Smith & Wesson and Ruger revolvers; his matched pair of 4-inch S&W 41 Magnums; a fully engraved and ivory-stocked S&W Model 1917, very rare examples of the factory 5-inch 1950 Target 44 Special and S&W 44 Magnum, and his only semi-automatic, an old 1911. Until Keith's stroke, Salmon, Idaho was the six-gunner's Mecca; now all roads lead to Cabela's in Boise, Idaho.

AWA-USA

AWA does not import complete firearms but rather parts that are finished and assembled into complete firearms in AWA's Florida facility. Originally, American Western Arms offered two basic Colt replicas, the standard model Longhorn and the top-of-the-line Peacekeeper which boasted a factory-tuned action, 11-degree forcing cone, 1st Generation-style cylinder flutes and bone/charcoal case-hardened frame. I have one of these Peacekeepers, a 45 Colt 4¾-inch single-action six-gun that has been in use for several years with nary

a problem. The Longhorn and the Peacekeeper models are now gone, replaced by the Classic 1873 and the Ultimate 1873. The standard model is finished in high-polish bluing and has one-piece walnut stocks; all springs are Wolff, and the trigger pull—out of the box—is 3½ to 4 pounds. The finish of the Classic 1873 can be upgraded to blue/bone & charcoal color-case, or nickel—or even hard chrome. Polymer ivory stocks are also available.

The top-of-the-line six-gun from AWA-USA is the Ultimate, which offers many options, including a coil mainspring. Chamberings available are 32-20, 38-40, 44-40, 357 Magnum and 45 Colt, in standard barrel lengths of 4¾, 5½ and 7½ inches. The standard finish is high-polish blue, with the same finish options as the Classic to include the frame being finished in bone and charcoal color case-hardening by Doug Turnbull Restoration. Standard stocks are one-piece walnut, polymer ivory or two-piece black checkered grips as well as the full gamut of A, B, C, or D engraving. A third offering is the Ultimate Octagon, which is the same six-gun as the Ultimate but with an octagon barrel. I have two of these from the Custom Shop, one 7½ inches and the other 10 inches; both are 44-40s with extra cylinders chambered in 44 Special, and they have consecutive serial numbers.

There is no way I can pass up a good 44 Special, let alone one with an extra 44-40 cylinder. Both have proven to be excellent-shooting six-guns.

The final offering from AWA is the Lightning Bolt, based on Steve "Josh Randall" McQueen's Mare's Leg as used in the TV series "Wanted Dead Or Alive." As far as I know AWA was the first to offer a replica of the Colt Lightning and they have now pistol-ized it. The Lightning Bolt uses the basic pump action; however, it is not a rifle but ATF-classified as a handgun. Barrel length is 12 inches, magazine capacity is five rounds and it is available with round or octagon barrels, several finish options as on their six-guns, and chambered in 45 Colt, 38 Special, 38-40 and 44-40.

Charter

Charter Arms Bulldogs have been tremendously important to me and mine. Three times in my life I have really needed a firearm. Once, when I was a teenager, it was just the sudden appearance of a 7½-inch 45 Colt that protected me from a whole lot of trouble. A Charter Arms 44 Special Bulldog was involved the other two times, and in both cases my family was present and in possible danger had that 44 Special Bulldog not been in my hand. Over the past four decades I have carried a Bulldog in my boot top, in my pocket and somewhere in a vehicle when

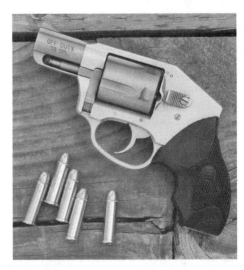

The Charter Arms Undercover offered in 38 Special is also now available in 32 Magnum.

traveling; it has been on innumerable camping and hiking trips. It is one of my most-used firearms, although it is very seldom fired and hardly ever brought out to show someone as an example of a great 44 Special.

One Bulldog, a stainless steel version, rests in the main bathroom medicine cabinet; another stainless steel Bulldog 44 is in the bathroom off my reloading room. One house gun can be pretty worthless if it's in one spot and I'm in the other when it is needed. Can you think of any place one can be more vulnerable in the house if trouble begins than the bathroom? My wife used to do quite a bit of fishing—both fly and otherwise—and always seemed to fall in at least once every trip. It didn't take me long to realize the gun of choice in her vest should be a stainless Bulldog.

The newest 44 Special from Charter Arms is the Bulldog Pug. The Pug is the same basic design as the two original Bulldogs, with differences. The barrel length is now 2½ inches and the ejector rod is now enclosed. This means it is no longer possible to pull forward on the ejector rod to release the cylinder so the cylinder latch release may not be removed. Another change is the grip design. The Bulldog Pug is fitted with finger-groove rubber grips that are quite narrow, very comfortable for shooting and also mate well with the satin matte stainless steel frame. The sights are the same: easy-to-see square rear notch; the front sight is now a ramp-style rather than the post of the originals. This Bulldog Pug not only shoots closer to point of aim than the other two, it also has proven quite accurate in its own right.

A second gun from Charter Arms is the appropriately named Off Duty. This 2-inch barreled, five-shot, double-action-only 38 Special weighs only 12 ounces with its aluminum frame and boot grip-style rubber stocks. The ejector rod is also enclosed on this little pocket pistol and the sights are the same easy-to-see square style as found on all Charter Arms revolvers. Charter now offers the Undercoverette in 32 Magnum for those unable to handle the recoil of the 38 Special, as well as the Southpaw, a left-handed version of the Undercover 38 with a cylinder that swings out to the right.

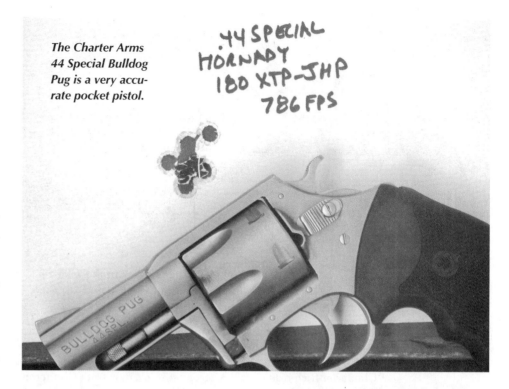

The Charter Arms 44 Special Bulldog Pug is a very accurate pocket pistol.

Cimarron

The Richards Conversion, the improved Richard-Mason Conversion and the 1871-72 Open-Top all served as transition revolvers from the 1860 Army to the Colt Single Action Army. For those who wish to shoot such revolvers, all three have been available as replicas for quite some time, most being chambered in 44 Colt. This cartridge, in both its original and modern version, has a smaller rim than the 44 Russian as the cylinder of the converted 1860 Army is not large enough to accept the larger rim of the Russian without overlapping. Now thanks to Cimarron Firearms we have the newest version of the Richards Conversion, the Richards II, which not only has room for the larger diameter rims, but the frame and cylinder have been made larger to accept the 45 Colt. It is also available in 44 Colt, 44

Cimarron now offers the 1858 Remington in 45 Colt.

Cimarron Arms 1871-72 Open-Top is offered in such chamberings as 44 Special, 44 Russian and 44 Colt.

Another fancy six-gun from Cimarron is this engraved and silver-plated 1871-72 Open-Top.

Special and 38 Special. The 45 Colt Cimarron Richards II is an all-steel revolver without the brass trigger guard of the original. Mainframe, hammer, breech plate and loading gate are all case-colored, with the balance of the revolver being finished in a nicely polished deep blue black. The grip frame is the comfortable 1860 Army very well fitted with one-piece walnut stocks with good grain. It loads the same as any traditional single action— that is, the hammer is placed on half-

cock to allow the cylinder to rotate and opening the loading gate accesses the chambers for loading or unloading.

A second 45 Colt new from Cimarron this year is the Remington 44 New Army percussion revolver conversion in 45 Colt. Once again it was necessary to increase the size of the cylinder to be able to place six 45 Colt chambers in the cylinder. This conversion is quite different from the Richards II. The breech plate/loading gate is somewhat of a double saddle construction; that is, it slides into place and clips over both sides of the top strap and both sides of the mainframe. When the

cylinder is removed, the breech plate can also be removed without tools and the percussion cylinder, which is supplied with this Cimarron Cartridge Conversion, placed in the frame. This conversion also follows the original in that the bullet seater is maintained and the top of the forepart is notched to hold the ejector rod in place. For loading or unloading, the bullet seater is unlatched, the ejector rod is rotated 180 degrees and is then ready for punching out empty cartridges.

The third new revolver from Cimarron is the "Man with No Name" patterned after a six-gun often used by Clint Eastwood's movie characters. Based on the 1851 Colt Navy, this conversion is not the same as the other two as the breech plate is an integral machined part of the frame and not a separate piece. The barrel and bullet seater assembly are traditional 1851 Navy with the cylinder accessed by a loading gate; however, there is no ejector rod for removing cartridges. I did not find this a problem as it is chambered in 38 Long Colt/38 Special and fired cartridges are easily removed and will often fall out of their own accord when the barrel is pointed skywards.

The finish is a cylinder and barrel nicely polished deep blue black; the mainframe, hammer, and bullet seater are case-colored; while the grip frame— both back strap and trigger guard—are brass. One-piece walnut stocks, which in this case have exceptional grain, are available in plain smooth wood, with the silver rattlesnake on the right grip.

Cimarron Firearms has come a long way since Mike Harvey first purchased a little import company known as Allen Firearms. I was the first to write up Cimarron too many years ago and I have been well pleased to see the continued upgrading of Italian replicas due in no small part to the efforts of Mike Harvey. Not only has the quality improved significantly, but it has gone hand-in-hand with a higher level of authenticity. The Cimarron catalog contains replicas of nearly every Colt and Remington single action offered in the last half of the 19th century. Replicas of the traditional Colt-style single action are offered as the Model P in all the standard barrel lengths and blued/case-colored, nickel-plated, and

Cimarron's 1851 Navy "Man With No Name" 38 conversion.

even stainless steel. Custom engraved versions include replicas based on the fully engraved single actions of General Patton and Col. Theodore Roosevelt. One of my favorites is the "Wyatt Earp," a 10-inch Buntline Special complete with identifying medallion on the grip as seen in the movie "Tombstone." It is offered in both the antiqued traditional finish and regular blue/case-color.

Colt

I'm sitting at my desk looking through a Colt catalog. There are double-action revolvers: Python, Detective Special, Cobra, Agent, Diamondback, Trooper, Official Police and Lawman; and single-action revolvers, Single Action Army, New Frontier, Buntline Special, Peacemaker 22, and New Frontier 22. Another section has Colt Percussion Revolvers, the Third Model Dragoon and the 1851 Navy. We finally come to the section on Colt Center Fire Automatics and we find the Gold Cup National Match, Government Model, Combat Commander, Lightweight Commander, Woodsman Match Target, Woodsman, Targetsman, and Huntsman. I sigh as I put the 1975 Colt catalog back in my file.

Every single revolver save one is long gone from the production line at Colt. That is the downside. The upside is not only does the Single Action Army remain as Colt's only six-gun, the word I hear from shooters all across the country is Colt is doing an excellent job with their current 3rd Generation Single Actions. They are available in the three standard barrel lengths of 4¾-, 5½-, and 7½-inches, nickel or blued/case-colored finish and chambered for 32-20, 38-40, 44-40, 38 Special, 357 Magnum and 45 Colt. There are many grand traditional single-action six-guns out there... but only one can say it is a genuine Colt.

Freedom Arms

The first factory-produced Freedom Arms 454 left the Star Valley, Wyoming factory in 1983. When I discovered Freedom Arms in late 1985, they were building a whole lot more guns than they could sell. One of the reasons was the fear factor.

Most gun writers did not want to shoot the 454. At the time I was just really getting started as a freelancer for the major publications and I called Wayne Baker and was pleasantly surprised to find he would trust me with a test gun. I subsequently purchased that 10½-inch revolver and it is as tight today as it was 25 years ago; a Freedom Arms revolver has the precision of the finest crafted machinery while at the same time having the strength of a bank vault. They are built of the finest materials obtainable and with tight as possible tolerances. They do not shoot loose.

As sales of the 454 increased, Freedom Arms branched out into other chamberings such as the 44 Magnum, 357 Magnum, 41 Magnum, 50 Action Express and even 22 Long Rifle. Both the 357 and 44 Magnum Silhouette Models became very popular among the top shooters. Next came the really big six-guns or—as far as Freedom Arms goes—five-shooters in 475 Linebaugh. Once the 475 Linebaugh in a Freedom Arms revolver was reality, Bob Baker could take a serious look at the 500. To chamber such a cartridge in the Freedom Arms cylinder would necessitate cutting into the ratchet at the back of the cylinder as well as reducing the rim diameter significantly to fit a Freedom Arms cylinder. The result was a cartridge headspacing

on a belt rather than the cartridge rim... and the 500 Wyoming Express Model 83 was born. Factory-chambered 500 WE revolvers are now available in three barrel lengths, the Perfect Packin' Pistol candidate 4¾-inch as well as 6- and 7½-inch versions, and if one has an older Model 83 chambered in 50 Action Express a new cylinder can be fitted in 500 Wyoming Express.

In 1997 Freedom Arms introduced their "90% gun," the smaller—and thus easier packin', easier-shooting Model 97. The 90% comes from the fact that they are about 9/10ths the size of the original Freedom Arms Model 83. The first Model 97 six-guns offered were just that, true six-guns with six-shot cylinders in 357 Magnum and offered with either fixed or adjustable sights. In 1998, the Model 97 arrived as a five-shot 45 Colt. This is the most compact single-action 45 Colt ever factory-produced. The 45 Colt Model 97 from Freedom Arms is one ounce lighter than a 5½-inch Colt SAA at 38 ounces, two ounces lighter than the same barrel length in the Colt New Frontier.

The 357 Magnum and 45 Colt were only the beginning. The Model 97 is now also available in 41 Magnum and 44 Special with five-shot cylinders, and as true six-guns in 17 HMR, 22 LR/22 Magnum, and 32 Magnum/32-20. The Model 97 is a thoroughly modern six-

Two versions of the Freedom Arms 500 Wyoming Express.

The six-shot Freedom Arms Model 97 is offered in 22/22 Magnum, 32 Magnum/32-20 and 357 Magnum.

gun made of stainless steel, factory custom hand-fitted parts, extremely close tolerances and a modern transfer-bar action. Unlike the Model 83, which has a safety that must be engaged by placing the hammer in the safety notch, the Model 97 has an automatic safety that places a bar of steel between the hammer and the firing pin when it is lowered. With either model I prefer to carry them with the hammer down on an empty chamber.

This year Freedom Arms is offering several new custom touches such as fluted cylinders and 9mm auxiliary cylinders for the Model 97, as well as dovetail front sights for fixed-sight revolvers. These sights can be adjusted in the dovetail for windage and feature interchangeable blades of differing heights allowing fixed-sighted six-guns to be sighted in perfectly for each individual shooter.

Ruger

For some reason Ruger has always seemed to have an aversion for placing short barrels on 44 Magnum revolvers. The original 44 Flat-Top came standard with the shortest length being 6½ inches. I had mine cut to 4⅝ inches in the late 1950s and Ruger made up

a special 4⅝-inch Blackhawk 44 for Elmer Keith but it would never be cataloged. The 7½-inch Ruger Super Blackhawk 44 arrived in 1959 and it would be into the 1990s before it would be offered with a short barrel.

The same held true for the Redhawk until now. The Redhawk arrived in 1979 with a 7½-inch barrel, and a 5½-inch barrel was added later. Wanting an easier-to-pack 44 that would handle heavyweight bulleted loads I had my local gunsmith cut the barrel to 4 inches, install a black front sight on a ramp base, and slightly round-butt the grip frame and

Ruger's 44 Magnum Packin' Pistols, the 4-inch Redhawk and 2¾-inch Alaskan.

factory stocks. My "new" Perfect Packin' Pistol 44 Redhawk carried easily in an Idaho Leather pancake holster and handled standard 44 Magnum loads with ease; however, with heavyweight bullets at 1300-1400 fps, even the modified factory grip frame and grips left something to be desired— in my hands, at least.

Now Ruger is finally offering a 4-inch 44 Magnum Redhawk and they have fitted it with stocks which handle recoil much better than the original factory offering. It is all stainless steel as the original, with a massive six-shot cylinder, and a solid frame with no sideplate. There are two major changes in addition to the obvious shorter barrel. Instead of the interchangeable front sight system, the 4-inch Redhawk has a pinned-in ramp front sight with a red insert matched up with a white outline rear blade. The stocks, instead of the standard factory wood grips, are hand-filling finger-grooved Hogue rubber grips, which are much more comfortable when firing heavy 44 Magnum loads. The surface of these Hogue grips also offer a more secure feeling, thanks to their pebble-grained but non-punishing surface, than offered by the original smooth wood grips. Those grips, matched with the strength of the Redhawk and the stainless-steel construction, result in a Perfect Packin' Pistol for hard outdoor use. For my use the holster of choice is by Rob Leahy of Simply Rugged; it is a pancake style which can be worn strong-side or crossdraw and is designed to fit tightly and cover most of the six-gun except for the grip, providing easy access and security without resorting to security straps.

When I first wrote about the Super Redhawk nearly 20 years ago I said it should be a natural for the touch of custom six-gunsmiths. By chopping the barrel of the Super Redhawk off flush with the frame, milling off the scope recesses and fitting a front sight, the Super Redhawk would become an easily carried snub-nosed 44 Magnum. I never heard of any gunsmith doing such a project; however, this is exactly what Ruger did to come up with the Alaskan chambered in 454 Casull a few years back. Then the 480 Ruger chambering was added to the Alaskan and now the third big bore has arrived with the addition of the 44 Magnum version of the Super Redhawk Alaskan giving 44 Magnum six-gunners two choices for easy packin' while at the same time providing as much comfort as possible when firing heavy loads. To aid in this the 44 Alaskan is also fitted with Hogue soft rubber stocks. It also carries easily and securely in a pancake-style holster by Simply Rugged with six cartridge loops sewn on the holster itself making six-gun and holster a compact survival kit.

In 2005 Ruger issued the 50th Anniversary Model of the original 357 Blackhawk complete with flat-top frame and Micro rear sight, but with the New Model action. They followed up in 2006 with the same style 50th Anniversary Model of the original 44 Blackhawk. Someone at Ruger was thinking ahead and set aside 357

Ruger's 44 Magnum Alaskan packs easily in a Simply Rugged pancake holster.

Blackhawks and has now mated them up with 44 Blackhawks with the same serial numbers and they are offered as a Special Anniversary pair in a glass-topped wooden box. Both of these commemorative six-guns have a steel version of the original XR3 grip frame shaped and sized just like the Colt SAA and also checkered hard rubber grips with the black Ruger eagle medallion. Good lookin' and shootin' six-guns.

Ruger produced approximately three quarters of a million Colt SAA-styled Vaqueros in just over 10 years; the original run of Colt Single Actions from 1873 to 1941 numbered about

357,000. The Vaquero was made to look much like a Colt but was slightly larger in frame size, being built on the Ruger New Model 44 Super Blackhawk frame. A few years ago Ruger dropped the Vaquero and replaced it with the New Vaquero that is basically the same size as the Colt Single Action Army. New Vaqueros are now offered in both blue and stainless versions in 357 Magnum and 45 Colt with the latter available in consecutively numbered, highly polished stainless steel 5½-inch Cowboy Pairs engraved in a Western scroll pattern, fitted with simulated ivory grips and in a glass-topped wooden presentation case.

Smith & Wesson

In late December 1955 Smith & Wesson called Elmer Keith to inform him his dream had come true and one of the first production 44 Magnum revolvers was on the way to the man directly responsible for it finally becoming reality. Keith had been asking for a new revolver and a new cartridge, a "44 Special Magnum" loaded with a 250-grain hard-cast bullet of his design at 1,200 fps. What he got was the Smith & Wesson 44 Magnum, for which Keith used his hard-cast 250-grain bullet over what was to become known as

Ruger's Anniversary Models, the 44 Magnum and 357 Magnum Blackhawks are available as a matched set with the same serial numbers.

the Keith Load: 22.0 grains of #2400. At 1,400+ fps it is still a good load.

It was very difficult to find 44 Magnums on gun shelves in those early days. The first one I ever saw, in late 1956, was a 4-inch version at the Shell's Gun and Archery Farm. Three of us teenagers hung out there

Smith & Wesson reaches into the past for inspiration for the 44 Special Model 21 (top) and 45 Model 22 (middle) and 45 Model 1917 (bottom).

regularly and when the 4-inch 44 Magnum arrived, it was not sold but rather rented six shots at a time. All three of us paid our money, all three of us shot six rounds—and all three of us lied! The recoil was brutal in our young hands, which had never shot anything heavier than a 1911 45 ACP or a 45 Colt. We all looked at each other and said, "That's not bad!" We all lied. It would take several years, custom stocks and much practice before any of us could really handle the Smith & Wesson 44 Magnum.

With its beautiful S&W Bright Blue finish, tight tolerances and superbly smooth action, the S&W 44 Magnum began a new chapter in the book of six-gunning power. In 1957 the 44 Magnum became the Model 29 when S&W decided model numbers were better than such great titles as "38/44 Heavy Duty," "Combat Magnum," "Highway Patrolman," and "Chiefs Special." In 1968 the diamond center was dropped from the S&W stocks; by 1982 both the pinned barrel and recessed case heads were gone and then the profile disappeared with the use of heavy under-lugged barrels and round-butt grip frames. In 1999 Smith & Wesson unceremoniously dumped the Model 29. How could such a thing happen? I've never really forgiven Smith and Wesson for that, I'm still smarting from 1957 and 1968. However the Model 29 is now back in its 21st century form. No, it is not the original 44 Magnum of 1956; however, it is a Model 29 complete with the original 6½-inch barrel that was dropped in 1979 in favor of the 6-inch length. I never could understand that one, either!

In 2006 S&W offered the 50th Anniversary Model of the original Smith & Wesson 44 Magnum with a blued finish not quite as bright as the fabled Bright Blue finish of 50 years ago—almost, but not quite. The sights are the same white outline rear and red ramp front as on the original, and the barrel length is also the original 6½ inches—not the 6-inch barrel found on S&W 44s since 1979. The hammer and trigger are the original checkered

and serrated style while the stocks are somewhat like the originals with the diamond around the grip screw holes and slightly thinner in overall feel and tapered quite a bit to the top of the grip frame. The grip frame itself is square-butt, not round-butt, and original 44 Magnum stocks will also fit. So we do have the original grip frame and barrel length—but missing is the pinned barrel, cylinder recessed for case heads, and the firing pin is now mounted in the frame instead of on the hammer. It also has the internal lock found on all Smith & Wesson revolvers and comes in a lockable, padded plastic case. Taking crucial measurements of this Anniversary Model 44 Magnum we find cylinder throats are a uniform 0.429-inch, and, all-in-all, it is a harmonious blending of 1956 and 2006 that results in a good-shooting, good-looking six-gun. Of even greater import is the fact it is now a standard catalog item, and also available beautifully finished in bright nickel.

All arguments as to which is the most powerful revolver ended in 2003 with Smith & Wesson's introduction of the X-Frame Model 500 chambered in the 500 S&W Magnum with the capability of a 440-grain bullet launched from an 8⅜-inch barrel at nearly 1,700 fps. No one could argue which was the most powerful pistol now. Then, just as they did in 1964 with the 41 Magnum coming 10 years after the 44 Magnum, Smith & Wesson backed up. This time it only took two years to take a step down the ladder. Using the same basic X-Frame as on the Model 500 revolver, Smith & Wesson introduced the Model 460 XVR chambered in 460 S&W Magnum; it

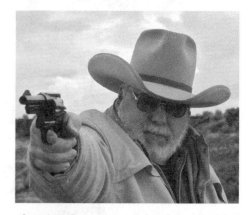

Shooting the resurrected N-frame Smith & Wesson.

was time to drop back and put a little more enjoyment in shooting while still maintaining extreme power. Even in the 4½-pound Model 500, the recoil with the full-house 440-grain bullet is brutal. With full-house loads the 460 is almost comfortable.

The original barrel lengths were 8⅜ inches, plus a compensator, and both models were soon offered in 4-inch plus compensator versions. Now Smith & Wesson is offering Emergency Survival Kits packed in a waterproof case containing a firestarter, saw, folding knife, whistle, signal mirror, compass, two space blankets and the choice of a 2¾-inch 460 with bright yellow rubber stocks, or the bright orange-stocked 500 S&W revolver. For wandering from the beaten path the other things may go in a backpack but the six-gun belongs in a good holster on the hip.

The N-frame may no longer be the largest used by Smith & Wesson but several other most interesting N-frame six-guns are offered this year. The stainless steel, eight-shot Performance Center Model 627-5 comes in a padded, locking aluminum case with three full moon clips and two sets of grips. Shooters have a choice of wooden finger groove grips or the Hogue MonoGrip. The latter is pebble-grained and finger-grooved, and it fits my hand much better than the wooden option. With its eight-shot cylinder and slab-sided under-lugged barrel, the Model 627-5 weighs 42 ounces, making it very comfortable to shoot with all factory 357 Magnum loads—including 180s—tried. Smith & Wesson pioneered the use of scandium and titanium, super strong lightweight metals, in developing the 340Sc and 360 SC J-frame 357 Magnums. These still remain as two of the easiest-packin' and hardest-shootin' pocket pistols. Now Smith & Wesson has carried the scandium and titanium theme even further by offering the eight-shot 357 Magnum Model 327 with a black scandium alloy frame and a 2-inch Lothar-Walther button-rifled barrel.

This Perfectly Portable Packin' Pistol does not carry as easy as my 10-ounce J-frame 340Sc, but at 19½ ounces it is hardly noticeable when carried in a waist belt holster. With its short stubby barrel and eight-shot cylinder it is every bit as serious looking—maybe

Smith & Wesson has resurrected the Model 29 in both blue and nickel finishes.

even more so—as the original 3½-inch 357 Magnum. The Model 327 is basically built on the same platform as the Model 627. In addition to having a shorter barrel and being constructed of lighter materials than the Model 627, it also has fixed sights with a square notch rear sight and a fluorescent red front sight.

Going up in bore size, we find the 44 Magnum Mountain Gun is back with a 4-inch tapered barrel, blued finish and finger-groove wooden stocks and the 44 Magnum is also found in a 3-inch Model 29 blued with the old-style Magna stocks. Before the arrival of Magna stocks in 1935, Smith & Wesson's six-guns came with small stocks that did not extend up to the top of the frame. This year Smith & Wesson reaches back in history to resurrect this style of six-gun with the 5½-inch 45 ACP/45 Auto Rim Model 1917 complete with the old-style stocks and lanyard rings; the blued Model 21 in 44 Special and Model 22 in 45 ACP/Auto Rim are now equipped with the same style stocks and 4-inch barrels.

The Smith & Wesson Holding Co. now owns Thompson/Center so it is quite appropriate to find the single-shot Encore chambered in both the 460 and 500 S&W Magnums. These are available in factory barrels, and SSK Industries offers a large line of custom barrels for both the G2 Contender as well as the Encore, including 460 and 500 barrels for the latter. G2s are available in blued or stainless steel with wood or rubber stocks and forearms, mostly with 14-inch barrels and offered in many chamberings from 17 Mach II up to and including the 45-70, with such excellent hunting cartridges as the 30-30, 375 JDJ and 44 Magnum in-between. There is not much, if anything, as far as hunting is concerned which cannot be handled with the 375 JDJ. The stronger-actioned Encore is fitted with a 15-inch barrel and also offered in blue or stainless with wooden or rubber grips and forearms. Chamberings include the 22-250, 25-06, 270 Winchester, 30-06 and two of my favorites—308 Winchester and 7-08 Remington. The do-it-all 375 JDJ is also offered in the Encore for those who prefer a heavier single-shot pistol.

STI International

As this is written, and paraphrasing Rooster Cogburn, "The Texican is long on promise and short on production." Hopefully, by the time you read

STI's latest is the Texican 45 Colt single-action revolver.

Taurus offers the lightweight, five-shot Tracker in several calibers.

Taurus offers the Raging Bull in this stainless 454 Casull as well as 41 Magnum, 44 Magnum and 480 Ruger.

action revolver in 2005. Taurus is offering the Gaucho in four finishes: all blue, blue with a case-colored frame and hammer, and polished or matte stainless steel; barrel lengths of 5½ and 7½ inches in both 357 Magnum and 45 Colt. Metal-to-metal fit on the Gaucho is excellent as is grip-to-metal fit. There is no overhang or undercutting on the grips and they all fit tightly with no movement whatsoever. Taken overall, the fit and finish of the Gaucho is at least equal to—and in some cases much better than—that found on more expensive guns. Grips are very comfortable checkered black plastic, sights are the typical single-action style with a square-notch rear sight cut into the top of the frame and the traditionally styled Colt-type front sight; the cylinder base pin is held in by the spring-loaded-style catch.

Although fitted with a transfer bar safety, the action of the Gaucho is the standard four-position single-action style with the hammer all the way down or the use of three notches in the hammer, the ill-named "safety" notch, a half-cock notch and the full-cock notch. The cylinder can only be rotated for loading and unloading with the hammer set at half-cock. In addition to the transfer bar safety, the Gaucho also has a key

this, I will have one for testing. I can say the picture looks awfully good. STI, normally known for their 1911 semi-automatic pistols, enters the six-gunnin' scene with the blued and case-colored Texican which they describe thusly: "Proudly made in the USA, the Texican sets itself apart from the other single-action revolvers. All Texican parts are either ultra-high speed or electron discharge-machined from chrome-moly steel forgings or bar stock (no castings) to dimensions measured in ten thousands of an inch, then precisely installed, achieving an exactness of fit and smoothness of function not found in custom revolvers at twice the price of the Texican." Stay tuned.

Taurus

Taurus, long known for economically-priced, very smoothly working, good trigger double-action revolvers, introduced their first single-

Remington replicas from Uberti include the Model 1875 (top) and the Model 1890 (bottom).

lock safety found in the back of the hammer just above the backstrap.

Taurus has a very large lineup of double-action revolvers, Trackers, Hunter Models, probably at least four dozen concealable revolvers, and the very popular Raging Bulls. I have carried a Taurus Model 85 UltraLite fitted with Crimson Trace laser grips in my jacket pocket for many years. The Raging Bull is offered in stainless steel or blue in 41 Magnum, 44 Magnum, 454 Casull and 480 Ruger. All Taurus double-action revolvers are also fitted with the safety lock Taurus security system in the back of the hammer.

USFA's Rodeo is a matte finish version of their standard Single Action.

Uberti

Uberti is the leading producer of replica single-action six-guns. They are owned by Beretta, from whom we get the Stampede, and the Laramie through Benelli. The three major manufacturers of single-action six-guns in the latter part of the 19th century were Colt, Remington and Smith & Wesson. Colt-style Ubertis include the traditional Single Action in blued steel or stainless steel, the Richards Conversion, Richards-Mason Conversion and the 1871-72 Open Top. Remington copies include the 1875 and 1890. In Smith & Wesson replicas we have the Model #3 Russian, the Schofield and the Laramie—which is patterned after the New Model #3 Target Model. Uberti also supplies most of the replica single actions offered by Cimarron, Navy Arms and Taylor & Co.

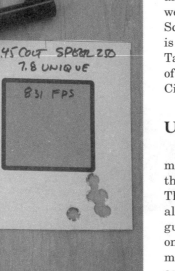

USFA

If ever there was a gun catalog made to fill a six-gunner's dreams it is the one from United States Firearms. This relatively new company markets all-American made single-action six-guns inspired by history and produced on totally up-to-date machinery, maintaining tight tolerances. They are not inexpensive, however they are as good as, or better than, the Single Actions produced prior to World War II. The same options offered 100 years ago are still available from USFA. Finishes include all blue, blue and case-colored, nickel—and even a "modern" finish making the brand-new revolver look like it has gone through 100 years of hard use.

Standard chamberings include 32-20, 38-40, 44-40, 38 Special, 44 Special and 45 Colt with others such as 38 Long Colt, 41 Long Colt, 44 Colt and 44 Russian also available with the same style caliber markings as found 100 years ago.

Uberti/Beretta's Stampede has proven to be an excellent shooting revolver.

Uberti's Top Break No. 3 New Model Russian with 6-1/2-inch barrel.

USFA even offers their single action chambered in 44 Colt.

It may look like an antique but it is simply a new USFA Single Action made to look 100 years old.

USFA also offers a replica of the famous Sears six-gun.

Beautifully engraved versions, such as the famous Sears and Theodore Roosevelt single actions, are also available. Many styles of engraving as well as custom stocks in wood, stag, pearl, and ivory may be ordered. This year USFA commemorates the 100th anniversary of the birth of Marion Michael Morrison—better known as John Wayne—with a replica of the six-gun he used in

so many great western movies.

USFA's Flat-Top Target Model takes us back to the target-shooting days in the 1890s and USFA has also resurrected the Bisley Model, which began as a Target Model in the 1890s and soon found favor as an everyday working gun, especially for those who had trouble reaching the hammer on the standard Single Action. Also new this year are two

special military-style offerings. One is chambered in 30 Carbine and the other is the 5½-inch Lend-Lease Model chambered in 45 ACP; both versions are fitted with lanyard loops.

One of the most interesting single actions ever offered by Colt was the short-barreled, ejector-less Sheriff's Model. I even owned one once. It was chambered in 41 Long Colt and I paid $35 for it; I wish I still had it but it went in one of my teenage trades. It didn't have much finish left; however, it functioned fine and would be worth a whole lot more than $35 today. In the early 1960s Colt resurrected the Sheriff's Model (only available through Centennial Arms) as a special run of 3-inch 45 Colt Single Actions. Even though I couldn't understand why less gun cost more money, $15 more than the already too-expensive standard Single Action, I really wanted one. They were beautiful little six-guns, even looked very serious; however, for me it was not to be.

Thanks to USFA, totally American-made Sheriff's Models are now available with a choice of caliber, barrel length and finish. Mine is a 45 Colt with a 2½-inch barrel and beautifully nickel-plated. Grips are checkered hard rubber with a "US" molded into the top part and are perfectly fitted to the frame and, as with all Sheriff's Models, the USFA version has the "blackpowder" frame; that is, the base pin is held in place by a screw through the front of the frame.

Several years ago USFA introduced the Rodeo, which was nothing more than a matte-finished model allowing a significant savings in price. This year they are offering the Cowboy in full-blue chambered in 38 Special and 45 Colt and fitted with brown—not black—rubber stocks. Jim Finch, who does custom gunsmithing as Long Hunter Shooting Supply, takes the Rodeo one step further as the LHSS/USFA Rodeo. USFA ships specially LH-prefixed serial numbered Rodeos directly to Finch who gives them his custom touches. Finch's Rodeos are available in both 38 Special and 45 Colt and the choice of either a 4¾- or 5½-inch barrel. Finch makes the fixed sights of the standard Rodeo more usable by widening the rear

USFA's Flat-Top Target takes us back to the target-shooting days of the 1890s.

One of the special engraved six-guns offered by USFA is this replica of Theodore Roosevelt's 44-40 Frontier Six-Shooter.

They don't come much nicer-looking than this, USFA's Single Action. (left and right).

notch from 0.108- to 0.140-inch and serrating the backside of the front sight. The forcing cone is opened to 11 degrees, the square corners of the trigger are radiused and polished, and the trigger pull is set at a crisp creep-free three pounds. To eliminate drag marks on the sides of the hammer, it is relieved .007-inch on each side where it rides in the hammer slot and, if desired, is polished and jeweled. The flat hand spring is replaced by drilling the frame for a Ruger-style coil spring, the main spring is replaced with a Lee's Gunslinger spring for smooth cocking and a fast hammer drop, while a Lee's Gunslinger wire spring replaces the trigger and bolt spring. The Rodeo is a six-gun ready for hard duty without worrying about scratching a beautiful finish.

Dan Wesson's six-shot revolver, the Alaskan Guide Model in 445.

Wesson Firearms

Dan Wesson has a long up-and-down history since their beginning in the 1970s. Dan Wesson himself had radical ideas including interchangeable barrels, an interchangeable front sight system, and a grip stud instead of a grip frame allowing a great choice of grip styles and sizes. The Dan Wesson 357 Magnum was an early favorite among long-range silhouetters and it was followed by the large-frame 44 Magnum and then stretched-frame 357, 375, 414, and 445 SuperMags—which are the forerunners of the 460 and 500 S&W Magnums.

After Dan Wesson's death the family took over the business, lost it, got it back again, and then in the mid-1990s had to close the doors. The company was purchased by Bob Serva, moved, upgraded with all-new machinery and Wesson Firearms began producing the large-frame Dan Wesson revolvers once again. In the early part of the 21st century, Wesson Firearms began producing a large line of quality 1911s and the company was then purchased by CZ. Today revolver production is limited, with only two models currently cataloged.

Wesson was the first to offer a revolver aimed at those who wander among the large bears as the Alaskan Guide Model in 445. This rubber-stocked, short-barreled, compensated six-shot revolver remains in production as does the stainless steel standard model 445 SuperMag. Today's Dan Wesson revolvers are the finest ever built under the Wesson name. They also maintain the excellent accuracy for which Dan Wesson firearms are noted.

I ended last year's report talking of the 44s I expected to be shooting all year and also announced my working on a new book. It is appropriate that in this centennial celebration of the 44 Special *The Gun Digest Book Of The 44* is now available. It covers not only the 44 Special and 44 Magnum but all 44s—from the 44 percussion six-guns to the 44 Henry, 44 S&W American, 44 Colt, 44-40, 44 AutoMag, 444 Marlin and 445 SuperMags—and the guns and loads that go along with them. May you enjoy my labor of love. ✹

Sako's Model 85 Hunter in action

RIFLES TODAY:

RIFLE REVIEW

by Layne Simpson

For no reason other than the fact that I wanted to kick off this column with something clever or thought-provoking rather than going right into the business at hand, I decided to exercise your brain with a short quiz. Answer all of them correctly and you may be qualified to become the next editor of GUN DIGEST. Answer at least one and you have the potential of becoming the star of your own television show. The answers are at the end of this report.

1. How did the Weatherby Mark V rifle come by its name?

2. What animal inspired John Nosler to develop his world-famous Partition bullet?

3. How many different bullet diameters are required to load the following cartridges?

218 Bee, 219 Zipper, 220 Swift, 221 Fireball, 222 Remington, 223 Remington, 224 Weatherby Magnum, 225 Winchester

4. What famous rifle was once offered in "African," "Alaskan" and "Westerner" versions and what were their

This Anschutz rifle is being built to commemorate the 150th anniversary of the company.

chamberings?

5. Townsend Whelen developed the 35 Whelen cartridge, correct?

6. In what year was the Remington Model 700 introduced?

7. What rifle was called "the bolt-action with a lever" in its advertisements?

8. Which company was first to introduce a big-game rifle with a synthetic stock?

9. Are the many gunwriters who have proclaimed the 204 Ruger as our fastest commercial cartridge preaching gospel or spouting hot air?

10. What invention that converted the 1903 Springfield rifle to semiautomatic operation came too late to be used in World War I and who invented it?

Now that you have answered each question correctly, it is time to take a brief look at what's new for 2007.

Anschutz

The circa-1856 logo of company founder Julias Gottfried Anschutz can be found on the trigger guard of the special-edition Model 1710 DHB Classic and that, along with a few other details such as the circa-1901 Germania logo engraved on the 23-inch stainless steel barrel and special carving on the walnut buttstock, serves to commemorate the 150th anniversary of the Anschutz company. Other things worth noting are select-grade walnut with cut checkering, gold-plated trigger, oversized bolt handle knob and match-dimensioned 22 Long Rifle chamber.

This Anschutz rifle, in addition to being quite colorful, is built for the pressure-cooker world of world-class competitive shooting.

Benelli's R1 Rifle Comfor Tech– 30-06 Springfield with Realtree APG HD.

Benelli USA

Due to its gas operation, the R1 autoloading rifle was comfortable to shoot to begin with and it is even more so now that it wears the same ComforTech synthetic stock design that was first seen on Benelli shotguns. Available in black or camo, the stock has interchangeable soft comb inserts, *regular* for use with open sights or low-mounted scopes and *high* for elevating the eye to the same height as a scope with a large objective lens. Interchangeable recoil pads of various thicknesses offer three options in length of pull: 13⅝ inches, 14 inches and 14⅜ inches. A newcomer to the lineup of top-quality reproductions made by Uberti is a carbine version of the Model 1874 Sharps in 45-70 Government. Already available with 30-, 32- and 34-inch barrels, you can now buy one with a 22-inch barrel. It, and the equally new Hunter with 28-inch barrel, are quite plain and this makes them more affordable than other Sharps reproductions imported by Benelli.

Beretta USA

Beretta is not just about great shotguns, the company also imports very nice rifles made by the Italian firm of Uberti. One of the latest is called Gold Rush and it is a reproduction of the Colt Lightning pump gun in 357 Magnum or 45 Colt. Several variants are available, rifle with 24-inch barrel, carbine with 20-inch barrel and both of those in Deluxe Grade with fancy wood, jeweled hammer, case-colored receiver and gold-plated medallion in the stock. Equally interesting is the Stampede Buntline Carbine, a single-action Colt reproduction with a shoulder stock and 18-inch barrel. Said to be a copy of the guns given to Wyatt Earp and Batt Masterson during the 1870s, it is in 45 Colt and can be bought singly or in a matched pair with 1876 Philadelphia Centennial engraving.

Browning

The BLR Lightweight is now available in a takedown version in both curved-grip and straight-grip styles. Flip down a lever on the bottom of the receiver and the barrel with the forearm still attached can be removed from the receiver. An optional mount can be used to attach a long eye relief scope to the barrel rather than the receiver. Barrel lengths are 20, 22 and 25 inches depending on the caliber and your options there cover anything anyone would want to do with a lever-action rifle. To name but a few of the 14 available chamberings: 22-250, 7mm-08, 358 Winchester, 450 Marlin, 270 Winchester, 270 WSM, 323 WSM and 300 WSM. Nominal weight ranges from 6½ to 7¾ pounds depending on barrel and receiver length and caliber.

Continuing on with quick-shooting rifles, the BAR autoloader in both ShorTrac and LongTrac versions is now available with its ejection port located where left-hand shooters have long wanted it to be. Nine different chamberings are available from 243 Winchester to 300 Winchester Magnum. Right-hand versions of both rifles are also available with a Mossy Oak Break-Up camo skin.

My favorite Browning big-game rifle? That's an easy question to answer––the A-Bolt Mountain Ti. Mine is in 300 WSM and outfitted with a Zeiss 3-9X scope, a nylon carrying sling and three cartridges in its magazine it weighs only 7½ pounds. I like a lot about that rifle not the least of which are its accuracy, reliability, durability and the feel of the Dura Touch finish on its synthetic stock. Other chambering options are 243 Winchester, 7mm-08, 308, 270 WSM and 323 WSM.

Last year Browning brought back a new rifle with the old T-Bolt name and this year it is available in two versions, Standard with straight-comb stock and lightweight barrel and the new Target/Varmint with Monte Carlo-style stock and heavier barrel. Both barrels are 22 inches long and overall weights are 4¾ and 5½ pounds. Very nice and quite accurate to boot.

Chaparral Arms

Reproductions of Winchester rifles that won the West are now as abundant as fleas on a stray coon dog and Chaparral Arms adds Models 1866, 1873 and 1896 to the list. The '66 and '73 are available with 19-inch round or 24-inch octagon barrel in 38 Special, 38-40, 44-40 and 45 Colt while you can buy the '76 with a 22-, 26- or 28-inch octagon barrel in 40-60, 45-60 or 45-75 caliber.

Chiappa Firearms

This company's reproduction of the Winchester Model 92 is one of the finest I have examined lately. Barrel length options are 16, 20 and 24 inches and calibers include 38 Special, 38 Special/357 Magnum, 38-50, 44-40 and 45 Colt. Of particular interest to me are the cased takedown model with 20-inch barrel and the Trapper model with a 16-inch barrel.

CZ USA

The CZ527 American is now available with its bolt handle over on the side of left-hand shooters. For now it is available only in 223 Remington but other options will surely follow.

Ed Brown Custom Rifles

The new Gen III finish resists wear and rusting much better than bluing and is now standard on all rifles from Ed Brown Custom. Seven models of various weights are now available, Damara (6.2 lbs), Savanna (7.5 lbs), Compact Varmint (8.75 lbs), Bushveld (8.5 lbs), Express (9 lbs), Marine (10 lbs) and Tactical (11.25 lbs). All the popular chamberings are there plus a few that should be more popular than they are such as the 17 Remington, 6mm Remington, 6.5-284 Norma, 340 Weatherby Magnum and 416 Remington Magnum.

Harrington & Richardson

One of the more interesting new members of the Handi-Rifle family is the Survivor––its 20-inch barrel accepts both the .410 shotshell and the 45 Colt cartridge. The barrel is fully rifled for the 45 Colt and for .410 slug loads but it also has screw-in chokes for use with .410 shot loads. Swinging the recoil pad to the side reveals enough room inside the oversized synthetic buttstock to stow a compass, matches, fishing line, a photo of Faith Hill and other survival gear. The Survivor weighs six pounds and when taken down it carries nicely inside a backpack or when strapped to a packframe.

Henry Rifles

Henry rifles are manufactured in Brooklyn, New York of all places and they build lever-actions in 17 HMR, 22 LR, 22 WMR, 357 Magnum, 44 Magnum and 45 Colt. As rumor has it, the 30-30 Winchester is just around the corner. The guys and gals at Henry also turn out slide-action hammer guns in 22 LR and 22 WMR, as well as a mini single-shot bolt-gun that has managed to win its place in the hearts of kids, alongside the Chipmunk and the Cricket. Last but certainly not least is a survival rifle in 22 LR that stows in its own hollow buttstock and even floats like Ivory soap when dropped overboard. Many years ago it was called the Armalite AR-7 Explorer.

Iver Johnson Arms, Inc.

The M-1 Carbine from Iver Johnson is now available in three versions––all wood, wood stock with metal handguard and synthetic stock. They say all parts will interchange with the original American-built carbine. Many years ago I bought the real McCoy through the NRA and if memory serves correctly, it cost me the princely sum of $17.50 and war-surplus ammo was only slightly more expensive than dirt. Sure wish I had kept it because the M-1 Carbine is a fun little gun.

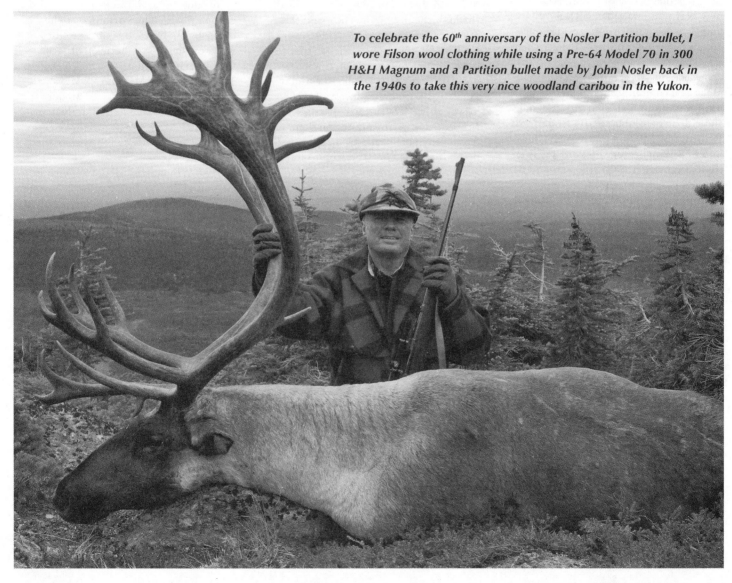

To celebrate the 60th anniversary of the Nosler Partition bullet, I wore Filson wool clothing while using a Pre-64 Model 70 in 300 H&H Magnum and a Partition bullet made by John Nosler back in the 1940s to take this very nice woodland caribou in the Yukon.

Kimber

The action of the Kimber Model 8400 Standard Classic has been stretched just enough to allow it to accept several new chamberings including 25-06, 270 Winchester and 30-06. The magnum version is available in 300 Winchester and 338 Winchester. Latest version is a safari-style rifle in 375 H&H Magnum replete with express-style rear sight. With the exception of a couple of minor·details the pre-production African rifle I examined had all the right things in all the right places.

Legacy Sports International

Howa rifles are now available wearing Hogue overmolded stocks in olive drab or black with chambering options ranging from 223 Remington to 338 Winchester Magnum. Also new is the Axiom stock with a pull-length adjustment range of 11½ to 15½ inches and a built-in Knoxx shock absorber that soaks up 70 percent of the recoil, or so its maker claims. The stock is a combination of machined aluminum and molded synthetic and the rifle is available in 204 Ruger, 223 Remington, 22-250, 243 Winchester and 308 Winchester. Just as new is a lightweight mountain rifle rated at 6¼ pounds in calibers ranging from 223 Remington to 308 Winchester. Barrel length is 20 inches. Turning from bolt guns to lever actions, the Puma is a copy of the Winchester 92 and it has been around for a very long time. It is now available with 16-, 18- or 20-inch barrel in 357 Magnum, 44 Magnum, 45 Colt, 454 Casull and 480 Ruger. In addition to stainless steel, you can get old-fashioned bluing or a case-colored receiver with a blued barrel.

Les Baer Custom

I never cease to be amazed at the accuracy of match-grade AR15 rifles and Lex Bauer continues to amaze me with the accuracy produced by those built in his shop. The barrel of the first Super Varmint I worked with several years ago had a 1:12 twist and it consistently delivered five-shot groups of less than ½-inch at 100 yards with handloads and bullets weighing up to the Berger 64-grain hollowpoint. The rifle I shot more recently was basically the same except for the quicker 1:8 inch twist rate of its barrel. With LBC precision EDM scope mounting rings holding a brilliantly clear Weaver 6-20X Grand Slam scope atop its flattop receiver, it weighed two ounces beyond 12 pounds on my postal scale and that, along with its incredible accuracy potential, made shooting tiny little groups falling-off-the-log easy. The group I am most proud of was fired with the Sierra 77-grain MatchKing seated atop 24.0 grains of RL-15. I wanted to shoot that load through the magazine so I used the Sierra-recommended cartridge overall length of 2.260 inches. Fired from a benchrest at 600 yards on a windless day, the group is a 10-shooter and it measures an incredible 2.842 inches (or roughly 0.474 minute-of-angle). Can I repeat that performance on demand? Absolutely not. Is the rifle capable of doing it all the time? I'd say it is.

One of the reasons I was able to shoot the Super Varmint so accurately is its two-stage Jewell trigger. The trigger finger first takes up the initial stage with 34 ounces of pull and then suddenly at the 42-ounce mark it breaks cleanly. AR triggers don't get any better than this. The barrel is benchrest-grade 416R stainless and its size accounts for a good bit of the overall weight; the 24-inch barrel has·a muzzle diameter of 0.925-inch. The Super Varmint is also available with 18- and 22-inch and rifling twist rate options are 1:7, 1:8, 1:9 and 1:12 inches. Upper and lower receivers are precision-machined from forgings and the former is available with or without forward assist. These and all other parts such as the chromed bolt and carrier, extractor, aluminum gas block with Picatinny top rail and the free-floating tubular handguard are manufactured in-house by LBC. Accessories included in the package are quick-detach Versa Pod, 20-round magazine, padded rifle case (with side pockets big enough to hold lots of stuff). Like several other AR15 variants offered by LBC, the Super Varmint comes with a half-minute-of-angle guarantee––believe me when I say it is no brag. Les Bauer's incredibly accurate rifles are available in 204 Ruger, 223 Remington and 6.5 Grendel.

Magnum Research

All versions of the custom Ruger 10/22 rifles from Magnum Research have barrels consisting of thin steel tubes encased in graphite/carbon fibers. The various models differ by their stocks: laminated wood on some, synthetic on others. Chambering options are 22 LR, 17 Mach 2, 17 HMR and 22 HMR. Also available is the Ruger Model 77/17 Graphite in 17 HMR only.

Marlin

The Winchester Model 71 with its curved grip, short magazine tube and 24-inch barrel has long been one of my favorite rifles and this probably explains why I like the looks of the latest Marlin Model 336 variants. For now, all have stainless steel barreled actions and laminated wood stocks and perhaps someday the decision-makers at Marlin will make me even happier by offering them in walnut and blued steel. You can choose among five different cartridges: 444 Marlin, 45-70, 30-30, 35 Remington or the new 308 Marlin. In performance, the latter cartridge treads closely on the heels of the 308 Winchester and that––along with the accuracy capability of Marlin

With its laminated wood stock, 24-inch stainless steel barrel, excellent accuracy and 308 Marlin chambering, this lever action can be an honest 300-yard deer rifle.

With its synthetic stock, TriNyte-coated stainless steel barreled action and chambering options ranging from 243 Winchester to 300 WSM, the new Model Seven XCR is a new addition to the Remington stable.

rifles——makes the Model 308MXLR not only a mouthful but honest 300-yard deer medicine as well. The 308 Marlin chambering is also available in the Model 308MX, which is blued steel and walnut but with a 22-inch barrel. Marlin is also offering several rifles with a factory-mounted 3-9X scope: Model 336A in 30-30, Model 60SN autoloader in 22 LR and Model 917VR bolt-gun in the same caliber. And don't forget to check out the new *faux* carbon fiber pattern on the synthetic stocks of some Marlin rifles.

McMillan Tactical

The incredibly accurate, totally reliable and extremely durable McMillan tactical rifle is now available with turn-bolt actions in three lengths that will handle cartridges such as the 308 Winchester, 300 Winchester Magnum, 338 Lapua and 50 BMG. It is available with Mauser-style internal magazine with hinged floorplate or detachable box magazine. Among its many other features are match-grade stainless steel barrel, EDM-machined bolt raceway in the receiver, three-pound trigger, Fail-Safe ejector, claw extractor, detachable muzzle brake and height-adjustable comb on the synthetic stock. The stock comes in five colors and is available in a folding version.

NoslerCustom

Each production run of the limited edition bolt-action rifle from NoslerCustom is available in only one caliber and the latest is 280 Ackley Improved. To set the record straight, P.O. Ackley never got around to improving the 280 Remington cartridge but since the improving of a cartridge by decreasing its body taper and increasing its shoulder angle for an increase in powder capacity is synonymous with his name, he gets credit for it anyhow (as he should). At

any rate, the NoslerCustom rifle is now chambered for the 280 Improved and match-grade unprimed cases and loaded ammunition are also available from Nosler. As can be expected, the latter is loaded with Nosler bullets in Partition, Ballistic Tip and AccuBond form. A less expensive version of the same rifle wears a black synthetic stock rather than fancy walnut and since John Nosler started the company in 1948 it is called the Model 48 Sporter. It is available in three WSM chamberings: 270, 300 and 325 WSM. On page four of the 2007 Nosler catalog is a photo of J.R. Nosler and a nice Yukon grizzly taken by him with a Model 48 in 323 WSM and the 200-grain AccuBond bullet.

During the 2006 season I spent two weeks hunting grizzly, caribou and moose in the Yukon with Bob Nosler and his son J.R. Bob and I did it the way his father John did it back in the 1940s. We wore Filson wool rather than modern synthetics and we carried Model 70 rifles in 300 H&H Magnum, which is what John Nosler hunted with. Bob's rifle even wore a Lyman Alaskan scope. To cap it all off, I used 180-grain Partition bullets that were made by John Nosler back in the 1940s. Believe it or not, my handload with that bullet and IMR-4350 powder averaged less than an inch for three shots at 100 yards when fired in the Model 70. Not bad for a rifle and a batch of bullets made before many who will read this report were born.

Remington

Biggest news from Remington for 2007 is the development for a new fire-control system for the Model 700/Seven family of rifles. Called the X-Mark Pro Trigger it blocks both the sear and the fingerpiece when engaged and it comes with a long list of improvements such as smoother component parts engagement surfaces, up to 45 percent lighter pull from the factory, greater resistance to

rust and corrosion and fully adjustable for pre-travel, sear engagement and pull weight. From this point on all Model 700 and Model Seven rifles will leave the factory with the new trigger.

A new chambering for 2007 is the 17 Fireball which can be described as the 221 Fireball Case necked down or a commercial version of the 17 Mach IV. Word I get from Pat Ryan at Redding is the body of the 17 Fireball is a few thousandths smaller at the shoulder and headspace is slightly shorter so the 17 Mach IV full-length resizing die many of us already have probably won't work. On the positive side, a 17 Mach IV bullet seating die should work fine with the Remington cartridge. The 17-221, by the way, was created by P.O. Ackley and he, along with Las Vegas gunsmith Vern O'Brien, were first to build custom rifles for it. O'Brien gave it the 17 Mach IV name but called it the 17 Mach III in custom XP-100 pistols he also built. I once owned one of his rifles in this chambering on the Sako L46 action but eventually sold it to a collector. At any rate, the 17 Fireball as Remington chooses to call it will be loaded with a 20-grain AccuTip-V bullet at 4000 fps. It is slated for availability in several rifles on the Model 700 and Model Seven actions.

And speaking of the Model Seven, the new XCR variant has a stainless steel barreled action replete with TriNyte finish, a synthetic stock with Realtree AP camo skin and fluted barrels, 20-inch in 243 Winchester, 7mm-08 and 308 and 22 inches in 270 WSM and 300 WSM. Nominal weights are seven pounds for standard cartridges and two ounces more for the magnums.

The incredibly affordable Model 710 rifle has now been replaced by an improved version called Model 770. The new synthetic stock has molded-in sling swivel posts and the rifle comes from the factory with a Bushnell 3-9X scope already mounted. Bolt travel of the 770 is smoother and it has a more durable magazine latch. With the magazine full and a cartridge in the chamber it holds four 308s and three 300 WSMs. Other available chamberings are 243 Winchester, 7mm-08, 270 Winchester, 30-06 and 300 Winchester Magnum. A youth version with shorter stock is also available, but only in 243 Winchester.

Everyone has their favorite Model 700 variation and my pick for hunting in bluebird weather is the Model 700 CDL with its trim, classical-style stock. Switch the blued steel barreled action to one made of stainless steel (and flute the barrel) and you have the Model 700 CDL SF in both short and long actions and in a variety of chamberings from 7mm-08 and 308 to 30-06 and 300 WSM. A limited-production version of that rifle sold during 2006 in 30-06 celebrated the 100th anniversary of that cartridge and for 2007 its chamber is 17 Fireball. Among other nice things it has a 24-inch barrel and special engraving on its floorplate announces the introduction of the 17 Fireball.

If the Model 700 CDL is my fair weather rifle then the Model 700 XCR with its synthetic stock and TriNyte protected stainless steel barreled action has to be my favorite for hunting during bad weather. Mine is in 7mm Remington Magnum but you can also get it in 25-06, 270 Winchester, 270 WSM, 7mm-08, 7mm Ultra Mag, 30-06, 300 Ultra Mag, 300 WSM, 300 Winchester Magnum, 338 Ultra Mag, 338 Winchester Magnum and 375 H&H Magnum. Only a few weeks before writing this I equipped my rifle with one of the first Burris LaserScopes to come off the assembly line and used it on a successful hunt for whitetail deer in northern Wyoming.

Rossi

This company is seriously into economy-grade, break-action, single-shot rifles that come in multiple-barrel packages capable of covering lots of hunting and shooting territory. A good example is the Model S202250YM with three interchangeable barrels, 50-caliber muzzleloader, 20-gauge shotgun and 22 Long Rifle pot filler. Another model teams up a 50-caliber muzzleloader barrel with barrels in 243 Winchester and 12 gauge. Latest addition is the Trifecta with a black synthetic stock (with removable cheekpiece) and barrels in 22 LR, 243 Winchester and 20 gauge.

Ruger

The new Hawkeye version of the Model 77 rifle has one of the slimmest, trimmest, most handsome stocks ever worn by a Ruger bolt-action rifle. It is also available in a rough-weather version with synthetic stock and stainless steel barreled action. Both rifles have Ruger's new LC6 trigger and a variety of interesting chamberings including 223 Remington, 257 Roberts, 270 Winchester, 338 Federal and 358 Winchester. The African version has iron sights on its 23-inch barrel, is available only in 375 Ruger and wears a walnut stock. Switch the stock to synthetic, shorten the barrel to 20 inches and you have, in addition to plenty of muzzle blast, the Alaskan version in the same caliber. In case you are questioning the existence of the 375 Ruger, keep in mind that except for the more expensive Mark II Magnum, the company

From this day forward all Models 700 and Seven rifles built by Remington will have the new X-Mark Pro trigger.

had no action long enough to handle cartridges longer than the 30-06 and 338 Winchester Magnum and other cartridges of similar lengths. The new cartridge pretty much duplicates the performance of the 375 H&H Magnum but is short enough to work in the Ruger standard-length action. Other news from Ruger includes the 10/22 Target with laminated wood stock and heavy blued steel barrel and the Mini-14 Target with its medium-weight barrel replete with boop tube and thumbhole-style stock. They say it will shoot more than one bullet inside an inch at 100 yards.

Sako

A lot of water has passed under the bridge since I traveled to Finland in October of 1996 for the unveiling of an improved version the Model 75 rifle and further refinements and improvements made since then have prompted Sako

The new Trifecta from Rossi comes with interchangeable barrels in 22 LR, 243 Winchester and 20 gauge.

Improvements made to the Model 75 action since its introduction in 1996 have prompted Sako to change its name to Model 85.

officials to give it the new name of Model 85. Where five action-lengths were once available there are now six ranging from X-Short for the 223 Remington to X-Long for the 416 Rigby. Bolt rotation has been reduced to 70 degrees, the receiver bridge has been slightly lengthened for a smoother bolt throw, locktime of the long action has been reduced to 1.3 milliseconds and the single-set trigger on the varmint version is the very best trigger available on a factory rifle. Latest variants of the Model 85 are the Finnlight in synthetic and stainless steel and the Laminated SS Varmint with its stock of laminated. Finnlights in 7mm-08 and 338 Federal are an especially useful pair and the varmint in 223 with its marvelous single-set trigger is one of the top three varmint rifles presently available.

Savage Arms

My old friend Gary Roberson who owns Burnham Brothers Game Calls and who I consider to be the world's greatest coyote caller came up with the idea for the new Savage Model 10 Predator Hunter. In addition to being chambered to 223 Remington which just happens to be his favorite coyote cartridge, it has other details that Gary looks for in a rifle, including 22-inch medium-heavy barrel, synthetic stock with rounded forearm for use with shooting sticks and Mossy Oak Brush camo finish. Adjustment range for its AccuTrigger is 1½ to 6 pounds.

Then we have the new Model 12 Long Range Precision Varminter, a rifle better suited for the sitting varmint shooter rather than those like Gary Roberson who walk a long ways between sits. A single-shot, it has a solid-bottom receiver for rigidity and its left-side loading port combined with a right-side bolt handle allow the rifle to be loaded with one hand and shot with the other. Measuring a full inch in diameter, the barrel is heavy enough to dampen the already mild recoil generated by the 204 Ruger, 223 Remington and 22-250 cartridges and its 30-inch length shifts muzzle blast a few inches further away from the ears than most varmint rifles. The 223 barrel is available with either a 1:9 or 1:7 inches rifling twist rate.

Also new in the Model 12 lineup is the Precision Target Rifle series. The rifle built for F Class competitive shooting has a laminated wood stock with a three-inch wide ventilated forearm and a buttstock shaped specifically for resting atop a sandbag in the prone position. Its heavy, 30-inch stainless steel barrel is chambered to 6.5-284 Norma.

Taylor's & Company

I have no idea why they would give it a strange name like "Spirit Overtop" but I do know it is a nice-looking, break-action, single-shot rifle in walnut and blued steel replete with case-colored receiver and in 243 Winchester.

Thompson/Center

The Icon is a totally new bolt-action centerfire rifle from T/C and while the preproduction version I handled was a bit on the heavy side it did have several interesting features. One was interchangeable bolt handles in two styles, spoon-handle and conventional with round knob. Then we have a safety that locks bolt rotation in one mode but allows the bolt to be rotated with the safety engaged in another mode. Of fat-bolt design, its three locking lugs are the same diameter as the body of the bolt and it has a Sako-style extractor along with a spring-loaded, plunger-

For now, the Ruger Model 77 African is available only in an equally new chambering called 375 Ruger.

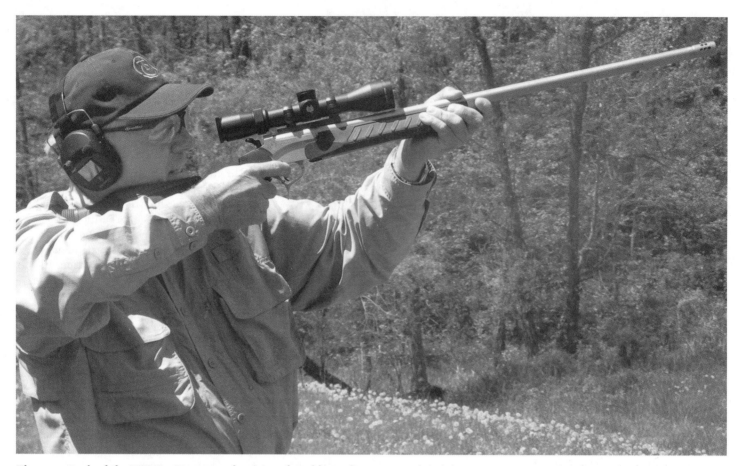

The new stock of the TCR ProHunter makes it comfortable to shoot, even when it is chambered to 416 Rigby.

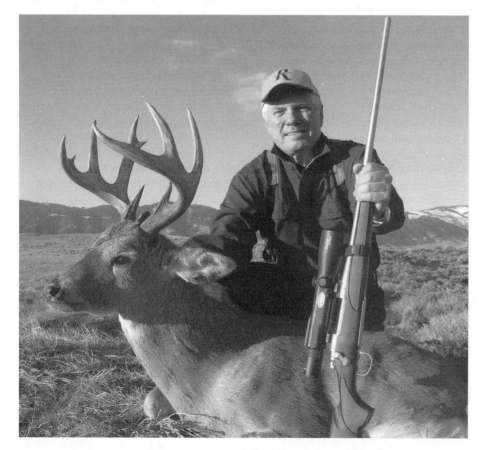

style ejector. The shape of the bolt at the rear sort of reminds me of the Mossberg 800 of the 1970s but otherwise the Icon differs greatly from that rifle. The detachable, single-stack magazine holds three cartridges with options for 2007 being 22-250, 243 Winchester, 308 Winchester and 30 TC. The 30 TC is a shortened version of the 308 Winchester case and it is loaded by Hornady with special powders that are not available to the handloader. Those propellants enable the new cartridge to exceed the velocities of standard 308 factory loads but it runs no faster than Hornady's Light Magnum loading of that cartridge. According to the latest Hornady catalog, respective velocities for the 30 TC with 150- and 165-grain bullets are 3000 and 2850 fps versus 3000 and

I used a Remington Model 700 XCR in 7mm Magnum and wearing a Burris LaserScope to take this nice whitetail in northern Wyoming.

The new short-action ICON is the first bolt-action rifle from Thompson/Center and is available in short cartridges such as 243 Winchester and 308 Winchester.

2880 fps for the 308 Light Magnum.

Latest version of the Encore rifle is the Pro Hunter with its recoil-absorbing FlexTech stock. The one I tried was in 416 Rigby and I found it quite comfortable to shoot from the offhand position, which is how most Cape buffalo are shot. Also new for 2007 are Encore barrels in 22 LR and 17 HMR.

Winchester Firearms

Imported from Russia, a bolt-action rifle called the Wildcat is chambered to 22 Long Rifle and is available in two versions, standard-weight with a thin stock combined with a lightweight barrel and varmint-weight with heavier barrel, no open sights and beavertail-style stock. Regardless of which you choose, you should also find four detachable magazines in the box, one five-rounder and three ten-rounders.

Weatherby

Back in 1961 Weatherby introduced a classy autoloading rifle in 22 Long Rifle called the Mark XXII and during its production life it was manufactured by several different companies including Beretta. The original Mark XXII (pronounced "Mark 22") was discontinued in 1988 but the name comes back to life in 2007 with the introduction of another rifle. This time around it is a bolt action, the barreled action built by Anschutz to Weatherby's specifications and stocked with American walnut in America by Americans who work for

Weatherby. Built around the Anschutz Model 64 action, it is available in 22 Long Rifle or 17 HMR and it comes with a target that certifies its sub-minute-of-angle accuracy capability. The three I shot lived up to that accuracy claim with room to spare.

The Vanguard family of centerfire rifles continues to grow and one of the latest additions is the Youth/Compact that comes with two stocks: one with a length-of-pull for short arms, the other with a standard length-of-pull for those same arms when they grow up. A Texas friend of mine bought one of these in 22-250 for his daughter and she has taken two pronghorn antelope and several whitetails with his handloads using the Nosler 60-grain Partition bullet. Other caliber options are 243 Winchester, 7mm-08 and 308 Winchester. The Vanguard Synthetic Package comes in a hard case and with a Bushnell 3-9X scope already mounted and it too has proven to be quite successful for Weatherby. I used one in 257 Magnum on several hunts and it averaged less than an inch at 100 yards with Weatherby ammo loaded with the 110-grain AccuBond and 120-grain Partition bullets. New Vanguard chamberings for 2007 are 204 Ruger and 25-06 Remington.

Answers To Questions At Beginning Of Report

1. When the fifth and final working model of his new action was completed in 1957, Roy Weatherby had not come up with a name for the rifle

that would be built around when he showed it to his friend Elgin Gates. In addition to being a world-traveled big-game hunter, Gates was the West Coast representative of Mercury outboard motors, a company that called its various models "Mark" this or "Mark" that. Gates suggested "Mark V" as a name for the new Weatherby rifle and it stuck.

2. When the bullet he was using opened up too quickly and failed to penetrate to the vitals of a Canadian moose, John Nosler went home and designed his Partition bullet.

3. All use bullets of the same .224-inch diameter.

4. Winchester Model 70: the African in 458 Magnum, the Alaskan in 338 Magnum and the Westerner in 264 Magnum.

5. Incorrect; James Howe developed the cartridge and named it in honor of Whelen.

6. The Model 700 and its new cartridge, the 7mm Remington Magnum were introduced in 1962.

7. The Winchester Model 88.

8. Weatherby.

9. Hot air. Remington's 20-grain loading of the 17 Remington and Federal's 40-grain loading of the 220 Swift are loaded to 4250 fps which is presently faster than any 204 Ruger load.

10. Invented by J.D. Pederson, the Pederson Device was officially designated "Automatic Pistol, 30 caliber, Model of 1918" as a way to preserve secrecy during its development.

Unlike the Weatherby Mark XXII autoloader of yesteryear, the new Mark XXII is a bolt action in 17 HMR and 22 LR, its barreled action built by Anschutz and stocked in walnut by Weatherby.

Benelli's Super Black Eagle II; their first
autoloader to tame the recoil of a 3 1/2"
12 gauge.

SHOTGUN REVIEW

by John Haviland

Shotguns are a durable product. To maintain demand, manufacturers must constantly promote innovations such as embellishments, and easier handling and shooting. Those trimmings and improvements certainly catch shooters' eyes because Americans bought approximately half a million imported shotguns and nearly 600,000 domestically produced shotguns in 2005. Let's see what shotguns manufacturers have come up with this year to tempt us.

Benelli

The ComforTech system, which consists of shock-absorbing material in recoil pad and bands in the stock, has been added to the Cordoba, Super Sport, Sport II, Super Black Eagle II, M2 Field and new M4 Tactical. The M4 Tactical uses Benelli's inertia drive operating system and has an adjustable-aperture ghost ring rear sight, fixed blade front sight and a pistol grip stock in desert camouflage or matte black. The Montefeltro Silver has nickel-plating on its aluminum receiver with scroll engraving and game birds in gold.

Beretta

The Beretta family of AL391 semi-automatics has two enhanced versions and a recoil reducer in its down-in-the-mud gun.

The Urika Premium has a high-grade finish on its wood and polished appearance on its exposed metal to match the deep black of the barrel bluing. Teknys Stonecoat, in 20- and 12-gauge standard and slug guns, feature a multi-layered finish of nickel and chrome and a final protective layer of titanium and zirconium to their receiver, bolt, bolt handle, follower and trigger.

The Xtrema2 has the option of the Kick Off recoil reduction system that features two hydraulic dampers incorporated into the stock. On a sea duck hunt on the Maine coast last season I shot Federal's 12-gauge 3- and 3½-inch shells through an Xtrema2 with the Kick Off. The recoil was almost gentle with 3-inch shells and bearable with 3½s.

The SO10 over-and-under 20-gauge is a sidelock with side plates that can be removed by hand with two hidden keys. With no pins or screws on the surface of the plates, six engraving patterns are available on the SO10. The ejectors on the gun have been increased in area to catch more of the shell rim for improved extraction and ejection. The top lever is also long and closer to the breech for more leverage to break the action. The gun has 26-, 28- or 30-inch barrels.

The Silver Pigeon and DT10 Trident L Trap and Double Trap have been

A Beretta Xtrema2 is posed with a common eider.

This hunter is shooting a Beretta Xtrema2 with the Kick Off recoil reduction system. His quarry is sea ducks off the coast of Maine.

This greenhead mallard was taken with a Beretta 3901 Statesman 12-gauge firing Federal's new Black Cloud steel shot. The steel pellets have a cutting band around their outside that make nasty wounds in waterfowl.

dressed up. The Silver Pigeon V has color case-hardened sideplates, trigger guard, trigger plate, top lever and hinge pins. Its side plates wear game scenes of gold ducks and pheasants in the 12-gauge and quail and partridge in the 20- and 28-gauge and .410. The DT10s have English and floral engraving.

Browning

The Cynergy over and under has lots of new models. The Cynergy Feather 12-gauge weighs only six pounds, losing nearly 1½ pounds with its alloy receiver.

Other lightweight Cynergys are the 20- and 28-gauge and .410-bore in the Classic Field and Classic Sporting series. The Cynergy Grade III features full receiver high-relief engraving. The 12-gauge depicts pheasants on the left side and mallards on the right, the 20-gauge teal on the left side of the receiver and partridge on the right. The Grade VI 12-gauge is embellished with gold-enhanced engraving of pheasants on the left side of the receiver and mallards on the right. The Cynergy Euro Sporting has a European-style rib and is available in Sporting, Sporting

Adjustable with an adjustable comb, and Sporting Composite with a composite stock. The Cynergy Field Composite 12-gauge is now available with 3½-inch chambers. Its composite buttstock and forearm are finished in Mossy Oak Duck Blind camo and have Dura-Touch rubber over moldings in the grip areas. Its comb is adjustable for drop, and features the recoil-reducing Inflex recoil pad system. The Field includes Full, Modified and Improved Cylinder choke tubes. The Cynergy Nickel Tin has a steel receiver with a matte gray nickel tin finish, gold-enhanced engraving and matte blue barrels with a ventilated rib. Its black composite stock has rubber overmolding in grip areas. The Cynergy Sporting Red, White, Blue has a blue marble gloss finish on its receiver that, to say the least, contrasts with the chopped-up American flag pattern on its composite stock. This 12-gauge has 2¾-inch chambers and ported barrels with ventilated top and side ribs. The Cynergy Classic Trap has a Monte Carlo or adjustable comb.

The Citori 525 Field Grade VI has a nitride finish with gold-enhanced engraving complimented with an oil-finished walnut stock. The 12-gauge gun has 3-inch chambers, lightweight profile barrels with a ventilated rib and Improved Cylinder, Modified and Full screw-in choke tubes. The Citori Lightning and 525 Sporting 12-gauges comes with the option of a gray laminated hardwood stock and forend with a satin finish. A gray nickel finish on the receivers and barrels

H&R's new Excell Walnut Auto comes standard with 3-inch chambers, 5-shot magazines and, in this version, a walnut stock.

H&R's Excell Waterfowl Auto is fitted with a camouflage-pattern synthetic stock.

match the laminate. The Lightning is also covered with Mossy Oak Duck Blind camo. A Dura-Touch coating also covers the stock and forearm. The gun is chambered for 12-gauge 3½-inch shells, just in case someone is brave enough to fire such a big shell in the fixed-action gun. The Lightning Pheasants Forever 25th Anniversary has a blued steel receiver with silver pheasants and a glossy walnut stock. The 12-gauge has 3-inch chambers and interchangeable choke tubes at the muzzle of its 28-inch barrels and weighs 8 pounds, 2 ounces. The Citori 525 Feather has an alloy receiver with steel breech face and hinge pin, engraving and oil-finished high-grade wood. The Citori 525 Field Grade III has a steel/nitride receiver, high-relief engraving and high-grade oil-finished wood.

The BT-99 now has a more utilitarian laminate hardwood gray Monte Carlo comb stock and forearm. Its receiver and barrel match with a gray nickel finish. A matte black ventilated rib stands in contrast.

The Browning Pump Shotgun High Capacity holds seven rounds in an extended magazine tube. The 12-gauge has a 20-inch barrel with a 3-inch chamber and a fixed Cylinder choke. Its handles are composite.

After having great success shooting deer with today's 20-gauge slugs, like the Remington BuckHammer, I'm not going back to the brutal recoil of 12-gauge slugs. Browning is chambering its BPS 20-gauge with a rifled barrel and calling it the Rifled

Deer Shotgun. The gun comes with a satin finished wood stock and forend and synthetic with Mossy Oak Break-Up camo finish with Dura-Touch armor coating. A cantilever scope base is included to mount optic sights.

The Silver Hunter autoloader has been dressed up to honor Pheasants Forever's 25th anniversary. Its blued receiver has silver-enhanced engraving. The blued barrel has a ventilated rib and the Invector Plus choke tube system. The Silver Lightning has a semi-humpback receiver with a silver finish and a slim profile barrel with ventilated rib and a gloss finish and cut checkering on its wood.

Marlin

Marlin has added the 28-gauge and .410-bore to the Italian side-by-side they import and call the L.C. Smith. Both guns feature fleur-de-lis checkering patterns on their walnut stocks and forearms, single selective trigger, selective automatic ejectors and Improved Cylinder, Modified and Full screw-in choke tubes. The 26-inch chrome-lined barrels carry a solid rib and a bead front sight. The receiver is case-colored with a gold pheasant embossed on the side and bottom. The 28 has a 2¾-inch chamber and the .410 a 3-inch chamber. Both guns weigh 6½ pounds.

Marlin's H&R is importing a line of autoloading 12-gauges called the Excell Auto with 3-inch chambers and 5-shot magazines. The Excell

Synthetic has a black synthetic stock, the Waterfowl a synthetic stock with a camouflage pattern and the Walnut, a walnut stock. All three guns weigh seven pounds with a 28-inch barrel and a ventilated rib. Four screw-in choke tubes include Improved Cylinder, Modified, Improved Modified and Full. The Turkey has a camo synthetic stock with a 22-inch barrel and a ventilated rib with a fiber optic front and rear sight. It comes with Improved Cylinder, Modified, Full, Extra Full and TURKEY screw-in chokes. The Combo has a black synthetic stock with a 28-inch ventilated rib barrel and a 24-inch rifled barrel. The smoothbore barrel has a bead front sight and Improved Cylinder, Modified, Improved Modified and Full screw-in chokes. The slug barrel wears fiber optic front and rear sights.

The H&R Tamer, in 20-gauge or .410, is just right for potting grouse and rabbits. It uses the Topper break-action single-shot receiver with a nickel matte-finish and matching 20-inch barrel with a Full choke. The polymer stock has a thumbhole grip and stores four .410 or three 20-gauge shells in the right side of the stock. The receiver includes automatic spent shell ejection, transfer bar to prevent accidental firing and a locking system. The Tamer weighs six pounds.

Remington

The Premier over-under shotguns have three new models. The Premier STS Competition that was introduced

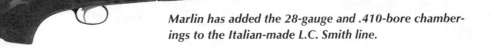

Marlin has added the 28-gauge and .410-bore chamberings to the Italian-made L.C. Smith line.

in 2006 with 28- or 30-inch barrels, is now available with 32-inch barrels. The Premier Adjustable Comb has 30- or 32-inch barrels and its comb can be altered for height and cast. The Premier Field Over & Under Ruffed Grouse Society is chambered in 20-gauge. The gun has a straight grip walnut stock with a Schnabel forend and cut checkering. The 26-inch barrels have a white front bead and five ProBore choke tubes. The receiver is finished in black and offsets the gold Ruffed Grouse Society logo on both sides of the receiver and the Remington "R" on the frame bottom. The gun weighs 6-½ pounds and comes in a lockable hard case.

The Model SP-10 Magnum Waterfowl is fully coated with Mossy Oak Duck Blind camo. Its 26-inch barrel accepts Briley Waterfowl Chokes that include Decoying, Intermediate and Ported Pass Shooting extended tubes. The front sight is a HiViz fiber optic bead. To tame the recoil of 10-gauge 3½-inch shells, the gun weighs 10 pounds 14 ounces and wears an R3 recoil pad.

A turkey-hunting version of the SP-10 Magnum features a thumbhole laminated wood stock that allows the palm of the hand to absorb some of the recoil from 10-gauge magnum loads. Further recoil reduction comes from an R3 recoil pad and a ported Briley choke tube. The SP-10 Thumbhole Camo has a 23-inch barrel with Williams FireSights which include a fiber-optic front bead and fully adjustable rear sight. A supplied sling will make it easier to carry the nearly 11-pound gun.

Mossy Oak Break-Up camo now completely covers the Model 11-87 Sportsman 12- and 20-gauge guns. The Camo 12-gauge has a 28-inch barrel, while the 20-gauge version has a 26-inch barrel.

The Model 11-87 SPS Super Magnum is now available in a Waterfowl style with the Mossy Oak Duck Blind pattern. A SpeedFeed shell holder in each side of the synthetic stock holds a total of four extra shells for quick reloading. A HiViz fiber-optic sight, with interchangeable light pipes, comes on its 30-inch barrel.

The Model 870 pump Xtreme Conditions Shotgun Marine Magnum's metal is coated with Remington's TriNyte Corrosion Control System. Its trigger group parts are plated with nickel. A SpeedFeed shell holder in each side of the synthetic stock holds a total of four extra 12-gauge shells for quick reloading of its 7-round magazine. The barrel is 18 inches and has a fixed Cylinder choke.

The 870 SPS Super Magnum now has a MAX Gobbler edition. It is covered with Realtree All-Purpose Green HD camouflage and a 23-inch barrel with a super Full Turkey choke tube. Sights include Williams FireSights, which include a front and adjustable rear fiber-optic sights. The top of the receiver is also drilled and tapped to accept a Weaver-style base to mount optic sights. The synthetic stock has a pistol grip and a length of pull that is instantly adjustable from 12 to 16 inches.

The Model 870 Express has three new additions for hunting. The Super Magnum Waterfowl is offered with Mossy Oak's Duck Blind camo. The 870 Express Combo includes a 12-gauge, 3-inch chambering with a 21-inch barrel with a Turkey Extra Full choke tube for turkeys. A 23-inch barrel can be installed come deer season. It is fully rifled and has a cantilever mount for adding a scope. An 870 Express now holds 7, 20-gauge shells.

The 870 line has also been expanded to include black gun models. The Tac-2 SpecOps Stock has an 18-inch barrel with a 2-shot extension. Its synthetic stock has a Knoxx SpecOps stock with a pistol grip and a length of pull adjustable from 12 to 16 inches. The Tac-3 has a 20-inch barrel with a 3-round magazine extension and a pistol grip stock. Both models are also available with Knoxx SpecOps Folder stocks. The stocks have a wire frame over-molded with soft rubber. A push of a release unlocks the stock so it can fold over the top of the receiver.

The Model 1100 line has been expanded to include the Tac-2 and Tac-4 models, both dressed in black. The Tac-2 SpeedFeed IV version has a 2-shot magazine tube extension under its 18-inch barrel with a fixed improved cylinder choke. An extended carrier release and an oversized bolt handle make reloading quick. Accessories include a Weaver-type base for mounting a scope and front and rear swivel studs. The Tac-4 has a 4-shell magazine extension under its 22-inch barrel with three screw-in choke tubes.

Rossi

The Rossi Slug Gun is based on Rossi's break-action single shot and features a fully rifled barrel in 12- or 20-gauge. The barrel is ported at the muzzle to help reduce the kick of slug loads. Fiber optic

Remington's 870 SPS Super Magnum's new MAX Gobbler edition is covered with Realtree All-Purpose Green HD camouflage.

Remington's Model 870 pump XCS Marine Magnum's metal is coated with Remington's TriNyte Corrosion Control System.

Weatherby's Semi-Automatic Shotgun is now covered with Skyline's Fall flight pattern for waterfowl hunters.

sights are mounted on the barrel. The barrel is also drilled and tapped to mount a provided Weaver-type rail to mount a scope or other optic sights. The Slug Guns have blued steel, and wood stocks and forends.

Smith & Wesson

Smith & Wesson is importing a line of break-action and autoloading shotguns from Turkey.

The Elite Gold is a side-by-side 20 gauge with 26- or 28-inch barrels and fixed Improved Cylinder and Modified chokes. It features a trigger plate action with selective automatic ejectors and a rounded and sculpted receiver with bone charcoal case-hardening, 24 lines-per-inch hand-cut checkering on the Turkish walnut forend and straight-grip stock.

The Elite Silver is an over/under 12-gauge with many of the same cosmetic features of the Gold. The Silver, though, has 26-, 28- or 30-inch barrels with five choices of interchangeable choke tubes.

Smith & Wesson states each Elite gun comes with a lifetime warranty for the original buyer, as well as the buyer's chosen heir.

The 1000 Series of semi-automatic shotguns include the 1012, 12-gauge 3-inch, Super 12-gauge 3½-inch and 1020 20-gauge 3-inch. These gas-operated guns are made with aluminum receivers and the 12-gauge guns include two different gas rings, one for loads up to 1¼ ounces and the other for 1½ ounce and heavier loads. The barrels are chrome-lined with ventilated ribs and TRUGLO fiber optic front beads and plain beads at mid-rib. Five screw-in choke tubes of various constrictions are provided. Shim kits allow altering the cast, cant and drop of the stock. Stocks and forends are either Turkish walnut with point patterns or synthetic of black or Realtree Max-4 or APG camouflage. All in all, Smith & Wesson states there will be 29 variations of the 1000, from turkey and duck guns to youth guns.

Winchester

The Winchester Super X3 has had a makeover with flowing lines to add, as Winchester states, "a modern flair." Its stock, grip and forearm have been slimmed for a better fit in the hands. A Pachmayr Decelerator pad helps absorb recoil. Length of pull and comb drop and cast are easy to alter with provided shims. Its magazine tube and recoil spring system have also been lightened to remove half a pound of weight. A gunmetal gray Perma-Cote Ultra Tough finish on the metal is the "toughest finish ever applied to a shotgun," according to Winchester.

The Super X3 Waterfowl 3½-inch is covered with Mossy Oak Duck Blind or Brush camo. Its composite stock and forearm are covered with Dura-Touch Armor Coating finish for a sure grip. The bolt is plated with electroless nickel for corrosion resistance and the barrel incorporates the Invector-Plus choke tube system with three provided tubes. With a 28-inch barrel, the gun weighs 7 pounds, 4 ounces. Extra barrels are also available. The Super X3 Cantilever Deer Extra Barrels are 22 inches long. Spare barrels are also available in 26- or 28-inch lengths and 3- or 3½-inch chambers.

A few brief mentions

* Bill Hanus Birdguns continues to promote the 16-gauge. Browning made a small run of 16s in its Citori over/under and Hanus is trying to get his hands on all of them he can. Hopefully he will have a few Lightning Classics, Superlights and 525s in various grades for sale in 2007. "These guns are built on 16-gauge frames, so they usually weigh about seven ounces more than a comparable 20-gauge model and a pound less than the 12-gauge," Hanus says. "These guns appear to have about one-eighth inch of cast-off and a 14¼-inch length of pull and the field guns do not have pads."

* Mossberg's Just In Case (JIC) package includes about everything required to endure a wilderness emergency situation. Inside a plastic carrying tube, Mossberg includes one of its Model 800 pump-action shotguns in a blued Cruiser model or coated Mariner model with an 18½-inch barrel and a pistol grip. Included with the Cruiser shotgun is a survival kit complete with matches, fishing hooks and other survival items. The Mariner version includes a multi-tool and a serrated folding knife.

* Weatherby's Semi-Automatic Shotgun is now covered with Skyline Excel camouflage for turkey hunters and Fall flight pattern for waterfowl hunters.

* Birchwood Casey's Barrel Boss is a complete 12- or 20-gauge barrel cleaning kit stored in a plastic tube. The kit contains an aluminum rod for conventional cleaning and a fluffy rod to wipe the gunk out of a barrel. The hollow handle has enough room to store a provided bore brush and cleaning patches.

S&W's 1000 Series of semi-automatic shotguns include the Model 1012 12-gauge 3-inch (shown), Super 12-gauge 3½-inch and Model 1020 20-gauge 3-inch.

S&W's Elite Gold is a side-by-side 20 gauge with 26- or 28-inch barrels and fixed Improved Cylinder and Modified chokes.

A typical American Fowler, a plain gun with clean crisp lines, by David Dodds. Robert Weil photo.

BLACKPOWDER REVIEW

by Doc Carlson

Probably no other area of firearms offers as much diversification as the muzzleloading field. On the one hand, we have the very primitive firearm, such as the matchlock; on the other, we have today's sophisticated muzzleloaders that incorporate the very latest in modern materials and design. Both ends of the spectrum have their adherents and champions, and discussions go on and on about which is better or more "right." There are definitely more of the hunting-oriented shooters that embrace the latest in muzzleloading development, mostly due to the proliferation of special muzzleloading seasons in nearly all states. While the traditional sidehammer shooter is in the minority today, there are still large numbers of folks who want to "do it like our forefathers did." Between custom gunsmiths and the muzzleloading industry, both groups are supplied with a wide variety of firearms and accessories that cater to whatever interest those hunters and shooters may have.

The Holy Grail for the traditional shooter is a custom hand-built gun by one of the top gunmakers. These guns are often works of art, and rank up there with fine paintings and sculpture. They quickly become heirlooms that are passed down in families from one generation to the next. While they are collectible art, they have the advantage of being completely useable

and, in fact, are intended for use in the hunting field and on the target range. Guns by known makers appreciate in value, the same as paintings by known artists. Lucky is the fellow that gets a nice rifle made by a relatively unknown maker who later becomes a noted gunbuilder. His investment in the rifle will continue to grow as the reputation of the builder grows.

Mark Silver

One of the very best of the custom builders working today is Mark Silver, a Michigan gunmaker. Silver has been a full-time gunbuilder since 1976, is very well known and recognized as one of the premier builders working today. Early in his carrer, he worked as a journeyman for a couple of years with the late John Bivins. Bivins was considered by many to be the leading authority on early golden age rifle-building. Silver is a past president of both the Contemporary Longrifle Association and the American Custom Gunmakers Guild, which shows the regard that other custom gunmakers have for him. He regularly teaches courses related to gun-building at the gunmakers' seminars sponsored each year at Western Kentucky University by the National Muzzle Loading Rifle Association.

Silver will build most any style gun that the customer wants, but

specializes in the Kentucky rifle of the Golden Age, as well as fine Continental rifles and fowlers. He builds guns using the same hand tools that the gunsmiths of the 1700s used: hand saws, planes, chisels, gouges and scrapers. The finishes he uses are the traditional nitric acid stains, spirit varnishes, oils and waxes that were available to the 18th century gunsmith.

The first rifle we'll look at is an American flintlock long rifle done in the style of the Moravian gunmakers of Christians Spring, Pennsylvania and Bethabara (now Salem), North

Lock detail of the London rifle. Mark Silver photo.

Above: A mid-1700s London type rifle by Mark Silver. Clean, balanced lines mark this as a shooter's rifle. Mark Silver photo.

Right: A Moravian-style rifle made by gunmaker Mark Silver. Mark Silver photo.

Carolina during the 1770-80 period. The 54-caliber rifle has a 44-inch barrel and weighs in at 9¼ pounds. The curly maple stock is stained with nitric acid stain and finished with a red-tinted varnish. The gun is brass-mounted with hand-wrought buttplate, sideplate, ramrod pipes and forend tip. The barrel is blued to duplicate the charcoal bluing that was common on these rifles. The finely tuned flintlock is custom shaped and detailed, engraved in the Moravian style and finished with color case-hardening that is worn to enhance the relief borders and engraving. The attention to detail is fantastic, making this a serious work of art.

The second gun we'll examine is a rifle of the type that would have been made by top London gunsmiths in the 1735-55 period. This 7-pound rifle has a 28-inch 54-caliber rifled barrel and is, of course, a flintlock. The gun is steel-mounted and charcoal blued with hand-chiseled relief sideplate and hammer. There is a relief border on the lockplate with the color case-hardening selectively removed to highlight the relief work. The lock features a hand-pierced pan, 24k gold-lined, typical on finer English rifles of the period. The rifle is stocked in figured English walnut, and is carved with a shell behind the barrel tang and scrolls along the wrist. The fore-stock has a relief molding along the ramrod channel that transitions into simple relief and incised decoration behind the rear ramrod pipe. Overall, a typical high-quality rifle that would have been made by a London gunmaker for landed aristocracy.

David L. Dodds

Another custom maker who does fine work is David L. Dodds, a full-time gunmaker who has been building since 1969. He says he got his start and early training by studying a series of articles on gunbuilding written by John Bivins for *Rifle* magazine. He was also helped with advice from close neighbor and well-known gunmaker Ron Ehlert,

A very nice French Fusil by David Dodds. Robert Weil photo.

and another master craftsman, Jim Chambers. The above, combined with a great deal of natural talent, put him on the road to becoming a fine gunbuilder.

Dodds' major interest lies in duplicating original guns. This is a difficult task as we all tend to bring some of our own personality into whatever we are doing. Duplicating an original firearm in the style of the original gunmaker is much akin to copying someone's handwriting – some folks can do it well, but they are rare. Dodds appears to be one of those rare individuals as well as being a fine gunmaker in his own right. Presently, he is interested in the Reading school of design. These guns tend to be rather plain, with little or no carving and engraving, but they show an eye-pleasing architectural line that is very functional. Ordering a rifle from any of the better gunmakers is akin to having a tailored suit of clothes made. Measurements are taken so the finished gun will fit your physical build. You can specify style, type of wood (within limits – it has to match the gun you are ordering), barrel, caliber, lock and a myriad of other details. Be prepared for a long wait as most of these folks are several months behind on orders. You get in line and wait your turn. The wait is very much worth it, however.

Taylor's & Company

Taylor's & Company is well known for supplying high-quality reproductions of early firearms, both muzzleloading and cartridge models, to traditional shooters that have interests in the various eras of blackpowder

Taylor's & Co. reproduction of the rifle carried by the John C. Fremont expedition in the mid-1800s.

use from the pre-Revolutionary War period through the Civil War, and on into the taming of the American West. They have a new rifle that will tempt those with an interest in early exploration of the West, as well as those who just like large-caliber rifles.

The new rifle is a faithful copy of a Short Model 1842 rifle musket that was made up especially for the Fremont Expedition in 1847 at the Springfield Armory. These rifles were the same pattern as the regulation 1842 with the exception of being shortened to 48½ inches overall.

The 69-caliber rifled barrel is 33 inches long with a bayonet lug at the muzzle. An elevating rear sight is combined with a blade front, per the 1842 Model. All furniture is iron and the gun has sling swivels of standard loop size for military rifles and muskets of the time. The stock is walnut with an oil-type finish. A steel ramrod with a trumpet-shaped end is supplied and is held in place under the barrel with a spoon-type spring located in the bottom part of the ramrod channel in the stock.

The percussion lock is marked with the typical eagle head and the date 1847. The nipple takes

Musket caps. The rear sling swivel is attached to the iron trigger guard.

This rifle is a very nice copy of the Fremont gun, with excellent fit and finish. The 69-caliber bore should handle either the patched roundball or the hollow-base Minie very well. I look forward to getting one of these military big bores in my hands for a shooting session.

Thompson/Center

Thompson/Center is a name well known to muzzleloaders for their line of both muzzleloading and cartridge firearms. They were one of the very first to put a mass-produced muzzleloader on the market many years ago and they continue to expand and improve their front-stuffer line to this day.

The newest addition is called the Triumph. This is a 50-caliber break-open type of modern muzzleloader. The T/C folks have added some really innovative design components that make this top-break stand out of the crowd. The gun shows a streamlined shape with a center-hung visible hammer and only 4 moving parts, including the locking system for

the tip-up barrel. The hammer is a rebounding type that locks in a safety position so that an accidental blow to the hammer will not fire the rifle; the trigger must be pulled for the hammer to contact the firing mechanism. The trigger pull is crisp and factory set at 3 to 3½ pounds, just about right for hunting or target shooting. The composite stock is capped with a SIMS Limbsaver recoil pad that effectively cuts felt recoil approximaely 25 percent. A solid aluminum ramrod is supplied and the barrel is available in either the standard blue, or with the Weather Shield finish in either black or stainless. The Weather Shield finish is an advanced metal coating that protects the metal and wears very well, being much tougher than standard bluing.

The most unique design feature of the Triumph, however, is the new Speed Breech. This #209 primer breech plug can be removed by hand for greater ease of cleaning, or for clearing a loading mistake in the field, by rotating it 90 degrees and pulling it out of the barrel; potentially a real hunt-saving feature.

There are three gas-seal

*Above: **The very streamlined look of the new Thompson/Center Triumph rifle.***

*Right: **The new T/C breech plug. Rotate it 90 degrees and it comes out for easy cleaning of the bore.***

The gas-seal rings on the T/C Triumph keep powder gasses out of the breech threads and action of the rifle.

rings on the front of the breech plug to stop gasses from coming back into the threads of the plug, or into the action itself. These are very similar to the piston rings in the cylinders of your car. The interrupted thread on the breech that allows easy removal is very similar to that used on the breeches of large cannon for many years, so strength is certainly not a concern. The breech plug is knurled at the rear for easy grasping during removal. There's really nothing new here; several good designs were brought together to create this innovative breech plug.

This type of breech plug is also available on the Encore series of guns. This breech is partnered with a #209 extractor that rotates to the side with finger pressure to allow the Speed Breech to be easily removed. This eliminates the need to remove the extractor before breech plug removal as was necessary in the past. These T/C innovations will make the care and feeding of their muzzleloaders easier.

Knight Rifles

Another name that is associated with firsts in the muzzleloading field is Knight Rifles. The MK85 Knight rifle was the first really practical and widely distributed rifle featuring the now-familiar inline design. It seems that every year this company comes out with something new and different, often leading the pack with innovative products. Their newest offering is new thinking on a familiar style – the top-break type of muzzleloader.

Called the KPI, this rifle seems a typical center-hung, exposed hammer top-break design but it is engineered to be taken down to its component parts in less than 30 seconds – without tools. The forearm is removed by pulling down on a lever, the action is opened by the push of a button, the hinge pin is removed, which releases the barrel from the receiver, and the trigger group, with the hammer attached, is removed from the receiver by pushing a small lever in front of the trigger. It takes less time to do it than to tell about it. The ease of removing the barrel is important for another reason besides ease of cleaning, but more on that later.

The gun is available in blue or stainless with a composite stock in either black or camo. High-visibility sights are standard and the barrel is drilled and tapped for scope mounting. What makes this rifle unique, besides the quick take-down, is that extra barrels can be interchanged in the following chamberings: (centerfire) 223, 243, 270, 30/06 and 300 Win. Mag.; (rimfire) 17 HMR and 22 LR, as well as the 50-caliber muzzle-loading barrel. This makes the KPI about as close to an all-around gun as one can get. The multicaliber range of barrels available will allow hunting a wide variety of game over various seasons. The change from centerfire to rimfire is easily accomplished with a screwdriver and Allen wrench. With an overall length of 39½ inches (centerfire/rimfire) and 43½ inches in the muzzleloader configuration and a weight of around 8 pounds, this is a trim and versatile little rifle.

Traditions Performance Firearms

Traditions has added a recoil-reducing system to their Pursuit XLT Extreme. The system, which utilizes a cam, roller and spring contained in the buttstock, is reportedly reduces felt recoil by 75 percent – a very significant amount. Given hunters' proclivity for the heavy magnum charges these days, this is good news for those of us who are recoil-sensitive.

Ballard Rifle and Cartridge Co.

Ballard, based in Cody, Wyoming, has recently undergone a change of ownership and reorganization. The company is expanding the line of fine blackpowder cartridge rifles that they are known for. They, of course, build a beautiful reproduction of the venerable Ballard rifle. They are also doing a very nice copy of the Winchester High Wall and Low Wall rifles in various calibers. With high grade walnut and literally breath-taking authentic bone and charcoal color case-hardening, all three models are fine examples of the gunmaker's art. Dimensions are exactly the same as the original guns. In fact, part of the Ballard business is doing restorations of original guns. Their parts will interchange with originals and a "clunker" can be brought back to "as new" in the Ballard shop.

The Ballard model rifles are being seen more and more on the firing lines at various black powder cartridge silhouette competitions, including the Nationals at Raton, NM as well as Schuetzen competitions throughout the country. The Ballard action is a popular basis for fine target rifles. The record for blackpowder and lead bullets was fired in 1902 from a Ballard rifle, a 10-round group measuring 0.722-inch at 200 yards. That record still stands.

Ballard rifles can be had in most of the blackpowder-era cartridges, as well as appropriate modern

The Knight KPI muzzleloader has the ability to change into a centerfire or rimfire cartridge rifle with the simple switch of the barrel.

The Ballard Pacific rifle is very popular with hunters and target shooters alike.

Based upon the venerable Winchester High Wall action, the African Express can be ordered in a variety of blackpowder or smokeless chamberings.

smokeless calibers. Their target chamberings are done on a custom basis to extremely close tolerances; so close, in fact, that chambers are cut to match the make of brass used. No wonder the darn things shoot!

The High Wall action is well-liked by blackpowder cartridge shooters in the silhouette game and there is a high percentage of this action type seen on those firing lines. and often in the winners' circle. The very strong High Wall action lends itself not only to most any blackpowder cartridge, but it can also be chambered for some modern cartridges in the magnum family.

Ballard's attention to quality and range of models make these guns popular with shooters of all interests, be it target shooting with

The MDM "cartridge" combines powder and bullet in one handy package.

blackpowder cartridges or hunting with the latest smokeless calibers. One would be hard-pressed to find better quality reproduction rifles from the late blackpowder era.

Millennium Designed Muzzleloaders

From the time of the earliest muzzleloaders, packaged loads have been used. The military, especially, used various "cartridges" to enclose powder and projectile in one package that was easy and quick for the soldier to handle when reloading. Most of these were paper-type cartridges that the soldier tore open with his teeth, then dumped the powder down the muzzle, followed by the bullet and, usually, the paper that wrapped the unit.

The latest upgrade of the packaged reload is one from Millennium Designed Muzzleloaders. MDM has teamed up with Magkor, the producer of Black Mag 3, a blackpowder substitute, to produce the "ThunderCharge," a consumable cartridge for muzzleloaders. Using MDM's Dyno-Core bullets of from 225 to 325 grains, the optimum charge of Black Mag 3 is compressed and attached to the bullet base. To load, the complete package is pushed down the barrel at one time, eliminating the need to handle the bullet and powder separately. As stated, the powder charge is matched to each bullet weight to deliver

not only the best accuracy, but the best terminal ballistics as well.

Presently available only in 50-caliber, the consumable cartridges will come in packages of either 6 or 8. Next thing you know, someone will figure out how to wrap the whole thing in a brass case with the primer attached.

Connecticut Valley Arms

Along with self-contained cartridges, a new ignition system is coming to muzzleloading. Connecticut Valley Arms (CVA) is introducing a muzzleloading rifle with electronic ignition. Due to be on dealers' shelves by mid-year, the Electra looks like a typical inline rifle, but with a projection in front of the trigger guard that resembles the magazine of a cartridge rifle. The projection contains the electronics that fire the rifle. A thumb-operated safety disconnects the system for safe carry or loading. A pull of the trigger initiates an arc in the breech plug that ignites the powder charge. There is no primer explosion and no displacement of the powder charge from the force of a primer ignition. Trigger pull is very smooth with no release felt – the trigger is merely a switch that activates the electric arc in the breech plug. The system is supplied with a standard 9-volt battery that will fire the rifle at least 500 times and will last around 600 hours if left turned on. This is definitely something entirely new to the sport of muzzleloading. ✺

HANDLOADING UPDATE

by Larry S. Sterett

The big news for handloaders in 2007 was the introduction by **Hornady Manufacturing** of so many new cartridges, or loads for previously difficult-to-obtain cartridges, ultimately resulting in more reloading die sets and components – which Hornady is also producing. Among the new loads available now are the 30 T/C (Thompson/Center), 308 Marlin Express, 9.3x74R, 375 Ruger, 450/400 Nitro Express, and the 450 Bushmaster, with the 338 Lapua Magnum on the shelves by the time you read this. That's just for a start. There's a baker's dozen new bullets, plus the 7th edition of the Hornady *Handbook of Cartridge Reloading*, and a Joyce Hornady DVD on reloading and bullet accuracy. Loading dies and components are available for some of these new cartridges already, and the others are on the way.

One of the most unusual new products this shooter has seen for handloaders is Season Shot, a non-toxic, biodegradable, seasoned, dissolving shot. Initial offerings will be garlic and herb-flavored, with lemon pepper, Cajun, Terriyaki, mesquite and Mexican (hot?) flavors to be added. Invented by Brett Holm and his partner, Dave Feig, this new shot should on the market by the time you read this. The hardened pellets are said to be comparable in range and patterning to regular steel shot, with "knock-down" power out

to 45 yards on upland birds, and 25 yards on turkeys. It will take ducks and geese if they are settling in to a decoy spread, but larger size shot is being developed for use on waterfowl.

Holm stated the shot was developed after he chipped a tooth while eating a bird bagged using steel shot. "I just knew there had to be a better way." While hard enough to penetrate birds, the Season Shot pellets in the dressed birds melt from the oven heat, dissolving and providing flavor to the meat from the inside out. Bag your bird using

Season Shot, clean and dress it, bake or roast, and enjoy eating garlic- and herb-flavored meat.

Lyman Products Corporation

Lyman has introduced four new loading die sets, a three-die set for the 5.7x28mm FN cartridge, plus similar sets for three 'cowboy action' shooter cartridges, the 40-60, 45-60, and 45-75 Winchester rounds of yesteryear. (The new production '76 Winchester lever-action rifles are now available

A couple of sets of Hornady's Custom Grade New Dimension loading dies for two of Hornady's new loads, along with the correct shellholder.

Some of the new cartridges being loaded by Hornady, and for which handloading dies and components will be available: L/R: 30 T/C, 308 Marlin Express, 9.3x74mmR, 375 Ruger, 450/400 Nitro Express and 450 Bushmaster.

in these original chamberings.) Neck-sizing dies are also available for these cartridges. For those shooters wanting to take a step back further in time, the Lyman or Ideal 310 Tong Tool and dies are available for the 40-65 Winchester cartridge, in addition to some other old calibers, such as the 45-70 Government. (The 310 Tong may be slow, but having used one in his younger days, this shooter can vouch for the fact it does load shootable cartridges.)

For those handloaders who cast their own bullets, Lyman has brought back Ideal mould #403168. This mould will cast a 200-grain flat-nose bullet with two lube grooves and a plain base.

Shotshell reloaders will appreciate the new 5th edition of Lyman's *Shotshell Reloading Handbook*. This latest edition features more than 230 pages of data for reloading shotshells from the .410-bore to 10-gauge, using the most popular powders. Discussion of non-toxic shot, including the development and history, plus case identification featuring full color drawings, tips for producing better handloads and data for loading buckshot and slug are also included.

Forster Precision Products

Forster has added several calibers to their Bench Rest die sets. Some feature full-length sizing dies, some neck-sizing and seating dies, of course. New to the Forster line are dies for the 6mm Dasher (6mm BR Improved), 6mm XC, 6.8mm Remington SPC, and the 325 WSM. Also new are the Precision Plus Bushing Bump Sizing dies. The Bump dies are matched to the caliber of a specific rifle, and a set consists of three pre-selected or 'you choose' smooth-as-silk bushings, which are available in thousandth of an inch (.001) increments. This permits the case neck to be sized for a specific chamber, and reduces the possibility of overworking the case neck.

Currently, the Bushing Bump Die, with three pre-selected bushings, is available for a baker's dozen cartridges, from the 204 Ruger to the 30-06 Springfield. By the time you read this, dies and bushings should be available for the 6.5mm/284, 7mm Remington Magnum, and 30 BR cartridges, with others possibly later. The bushings and the Bushing Bump Die can be purchased separately.

Handloaders who don't like to change a die setting once it's established, but have to in order to return the die to its box, will like the new Forster Deluxe Die Box. With an overall length of 8½ inches, and a thickness of 2½ inches, the new double-walled boxes will handle dies for the extra-long Ultra Mag calibers, in addition to the Ultra Micrometer Bench Rest dies.

Handloaders who salvage bullets from surplus ammunition, or replace full metal jacket bullets with a soft- or hollow-point design of equal or lesser weight, should appreciate Forster's new 8mm (.323") Superfast Bullet Puller. The Puller will work in most presses taking ⅞x14-thread dies. While it will leave scratches on the pulled bullet jacket, it will pull even the tough, lacquered bullets from military rounds.

Not new – but a must for sizing cases – is a high-pressure lubricant which adheres to the case. Under the Bonanza label Forster has a lubricant that allows case resizing with a minimum of effort.

J & J Products

J&J has been in the thermoplastic injection-molding business for over three and one-half decades. Their various transparent ammunition boxes carry a lifetime guarantee against latch or hinge failure, and are designed to interlock to permit stacking of boxes for storage. Available in a variety of colors from smoke through red to camouflage, the boxes have capacities of 20, 50 or 100 rounds, depending on the model. The newest boxes in a 50-round hinge-top design will hold the 500 S&W and similar big-bore handgun cartridges – plus some of the shorter rifle cartridges of a similar size.

Redding Reloading Equipment

Redding has a host of new products available for handloaders; among which are ten new die sets. These include the 17 Remington Fireball, 6x47mm Lapua, 6.5x47mm Lapua, 6.5mm Grendel, 30 T/C, 308 Marlin Express, 9.3mmx74R, 375 Ruger, 45-60 Winchester and 470 Nitro Express. New also are the Universal Decapping Dies in two sizes, Small for calibers 22 through 50 and lengths up to 2.625 inches, and the Large, which will handle cases up to

The Redding Big Boss II 'O'-frame press features a one-inch diameter ram, with 3.8 inches of usable stroke. Another feature is the spent primer collection system, which funnels ejected spent primers through the ram and down a tube to a collection point below.

three inches in length, but with a neck diameter no smaller than 25-caliber. An optional 17-caliber decapping rod is available to fit the small die, and accommodate the small (0.060-inch) flash hole PPC and BR cases.

If ten new die sets aren't news, then the introduction of the Big Boss II Reloading Press definitely is 'big news.' Featuring a one-inch diameter ram with 3.8 inches of usable stroke, this large 'O'-frame press has the largest window opening of any press in its class, making it capable of reloading most of the larger cartridges. The Boss II features the "Spent Primer Collection System" in which spent primers automatically drop through the large-diameter ram into a flexible plastic tube that can be easily routed into a collection container for later emptying. The "Smart Primer Arm" on the Boss II automatically swings into position during the ram stroke and moves out of position when not in use. Priming is done at the end of the ram stroke to ensure maximum sensitivity while at the lowest possible leverage. (An optional bushing to handle 1"x14 threaded dies is available For the Boss II, as is an extra Slide Bar Primer Assembly for the T-7 Turret Reloading Press.)

Handloaders who are also competition shooters have found the uniformity of neck wall thickness to be a contributing factor to consistently accurate loads. Any large variation (over 0.0015-inch) in neck wall thickness can decrease accuracy. Redding has a new Case Neck Gauge that permits easy and rapid sorting of cases by neck wall thickness and uniformity. Two mandrel sizes are supplied with the Gauge to allow measurement of all cases from 17- to 338-caliber, including cases with small (0.060-inch) flash holes. The Gauge mounts directly to the reloading bench, and comes with a large dial indicator accurate to 0.001-inch. Pilot stops are required for each caliber, and two stops, 22-caliber (#06121)

Redding loading dies are available for some cartridges, such as the 17 Remington Fireball, which weren't in the pipeline when this photo was taken.

A few of the new Redding loading die sets available. Some are for old cartridges in which new interest is being shown, and many are for new, recently introduced cartridges.

indenter into a bullet. The relative hardness of the bullet is read off a Vernier scale calibrated in arbitrary units from 0 (pure lead) to 10 (approx. 22 Brinell). Magnum handgun and gas check rifle bullets work best if cast from an alloy with a SAECO hardness reading of 8 or over.

Cowboy Action Shooters use rather large quantities of cast lead bullets. Redding has a score of moulds to cast an assortment of classic design bullets from a 140-grain 30-caliber (#630) to a 525-grain 45-caliber (#745). All the designs feature rounded lube grooves, and a front band near bore diameter, tapering up to slightly larger than groove diameter. This type of bullet was preferred by the famed barrel-maker Harry Pope a century ago, and was frequently used by Schuetzen shooters.

RCBS/ATK

RCBS has a number of new products for handloaders, beginning with an economical new AmmoMaster Chronograph. The AmmoMaster is self-contained and has its own carrying case, operates on a 9V DC battery and features a detachable

and 30-caliber (#06130) are provided with the Gauge. These stainless steel pilot stops, which also can be used with the flash hole deburring Tools, are currently available in fourteen sizes from 17-caliber to 338-caliber.

It may seem a small thing, but flash holes and primer pocket uniformity are more important than many handloaders realize. Redding has both primer pocket uniformers and flash hole deburring tools for small and large primer pockets and small (0.060-inch) and large (0.080-inch) flash holes. The primer pocket uniformers are designed for Large

Rifle primers, but not for Large Pistol primers, while the tools for the Small Rifle primers are dimensionally correct for the Small Pistol primers. The tools come with handles and the deburrers are supplied with one pilot stop.

Redding has an easy to use SAECO Lead Hardness Tester that allows the user to check bullet metal up to approximately 22 Brinell. This is accomplished by the depth of penetration of a hardened steel

Redding's new Case Neck Gauge will handle cases from 17- to 338-caliber, and is accurate to 0.001-inch.

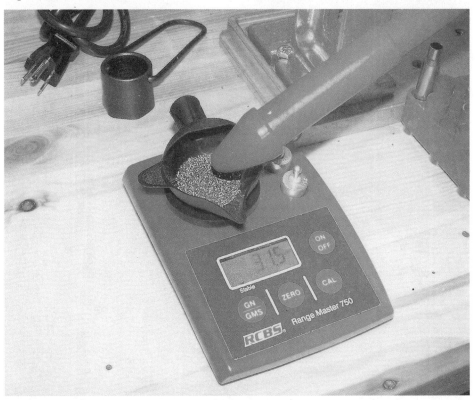

The spout of the RCBS Powder Trickler System trickles the powder charge from the measure directly onto the pan of the Model 750 Range Master scale.

keyboard display with a 100-shot memory. Velocity range is 50 to 7,000 feet/second, and the chronograph mounts on any standard camera tripod. The detachable keypad has a twenty-foot cord to permit editing a string right at the bench. (The edit function allows the deleting of a particular shot, and will display high, low, and average velocities – plus extreme spread and standard deviation.)

Case tumblers aren't new items, but RCBS does have a new large capacity vibratory Mega Tumbler. The Mega holds up to six pounds of corncob or walnut hull media, and can clean and polish up to 1,000 38 Special cases at a time. Both 120- and 240-volt units are available, with the latter ideal for handloaders in Europe.

Ever wish trickling power onto a scale pan for weighing was easier? RCBS has a new Powder Trickler System that allows you to dispense and trickle a powder charge directly onto a scale pan without having to remove the scale pan for the initial filling. The dispensing chute adjusts to allow you to drop the powder charge directly onto the scale pan, and the unit can be adjusted for left- or right-hand use. (The Trickler system attaches to any Uniflow, Quick Change or Little Dandy powder measure, and is used in conjunction with the Advanced Powder Measure Stand.)

The Advanced Powder Measure Stand, which can be purchased separately, will accept any power measure having a ⅞-14 thread. It can be easily bolted to a reloading bench or table, and leaves plenty of space for positioning a loading block filled with cases, or a powder scale pan. RCBS has a new Black Powder Measure having a charging capacity of 120 grains. The metering cylinder is constructed of brass, with the one-pound capacity powder hopper and cap being aluminum. (The cap features a non-sparking powder level indicator to show how much powder is left in the hopper.) A 24-inch aluminum drop tube is available as an option.

New powder baffles are available for the Quick Change and Quick Change High Capacity (two pounds of powder) Powder Measures. Extra metering assemblies can be purchased to have them preset for favorite smokeless powder charges, and Quick Change Accessories can be purchased to upgrade Uniflow Measures to the QC system.

RCBS has an extensive line of reloading dies (over 3,300, sizing and seating) available to take care of handloading almost any modern cartridge, in addition to many obsolete calibers. These range from 17-caliber, with possibly a few 10-, 12- and 14-caliber reamers still back in the stacks, to the 50 BMG round, and include the Precisioneered, Gold Medal Match Series, Competition, Legacy Series, Cowboy, X-Dies and Custom die series. The newest RCBS dies are for the 325 Winchester Short Mag (WSM),

In the foreground the new RCBS Black Powder Measure with non-sparking brass metering cylinder and aluminum powder hopper. To the right the new RCBS Shotshell Die in use, with a brass 12-gauge shell about to be de-primed and sized. An empty brass 12-gauge shell is shown in the far left foreground.

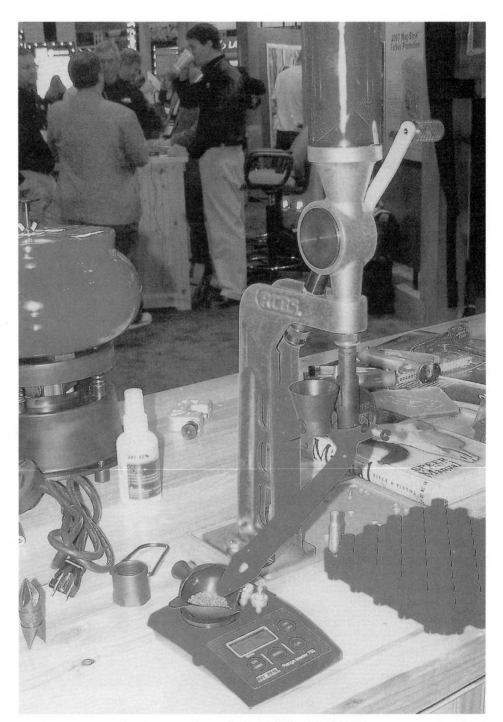

The new RCBS Advanced Powder Measure Stand, with measure and attached new Powder Trickler System placing the powder directly into the pan on the scale.

plus the Cowboy Shotshell Die.

The Shotshell Die is designed to size, decap and crimp 12-gauge brass shotshells in any single-stage RCBS press with a removable bushing. In the single stage, size the shell hull and decap it. Repriming is done using the standard priming device on this press. The sized, decapped and reprimed shell is then transferred to a regular shotshell loading press for charging with powder, seating of wads and spacers and charging with shot. The charged but uncrimped shell is placed back on the single-stage press, the resizing ring removed from the shotshell die, an overshot wad placed on top the shot charge and the shell run up into the die to crimp the case mouth. Result: a newly-handloaded 12-gauge brass shotshell. It may sound like a lot of work, but if done in batches of fifty shells at a time in a loading block, it's not difficult. Size, decap and reprime fifty shells, move and charge fifty shells, move back to the single-stage press and crimp fifty shells. You now have fifty newly-reloaded brass shotshells.

Shellholders have a tendency to become misplaced – not lost – just misplaced. RCBS has a new Shell Holder Rack that will hold two dozen shellholders, two on each of a dozen posts, plus six Trim Pro shell holders as well. The top of the plastic rack is clear, allowing a view of the shell holder number. The rack can be used on the bench, or mounted on the wall and additional racks can be snapped together if more storage space is needed.

Handloaders of shotshells will appreciate the new RCBS *Handbook of Shotshell Reloading*. This 284-page manual contains new information, cut-a-way and mechanical drawings, color photographs and more than 2,000 shotshell loads for various gauge shotshells. It features the use of RCBS reloading presses, contains a wealth of essential data not available elsewhere, and is destined to be a definitive

handbook on the reloading of shotshells.

New cartridges require loading dies, and Teppo Jutsu LLC, home of the 458 SOCOM cartridge, has a couple of new ones. The big boy is the 470 Rhino, the largest of a possible line of Rhino cartridges, and the 30 HRT. The 470 is based on a shortened and necked-down 500 Jeffery case, while the 30 HRT is based on a neck-expanded 6.8x43mm SPC case. The 470 can push a 500-grain A-Frame bullet out the muzzle at about 2,150 fps and was designed to used in an compatible receiver fitted

to the AR-10 lower unit, as was the 500 Phantom. The 30 HRT can do anything the rimmed 30 Herrett can do, and can be chambered and fitted to a regular AR-15 receiver. (Current Savage, Remington, etc., rifles could be rebarreled for these cartridges.)

C&H/Lee Precision

Loading dies for the Rhino and HRT cartridges are available from C&H Tool & Die 4-D and Lee Precision Inc. C&H was one of the early firms turning out top quality loading dies and H-presses for handloaders some fifty years ago. (The Swage-o-Matic was a beauty.) With the death of founder, Charles Heckman, in an automobile accident, the firm disappeared for awhile. However, like the phoenix, the firm returned. Now in Ohio, C&H has the ability to provide die sets for some 1,420 different cartridges, including at least one 12-caliber, ten 14-caliber and right on up to the 50 BMG – and larger. There are also dies for forming belts on your favorite wildcat, if needed.

The C&H loading presses include the non-progressive No. 444, 4-station H-press, and the 444-X Pistol Champ. Both presses use standard 7/8x14 dies, and are capable of loading up to 200 rounds per hour.

For handloaders of the 'Big Fifty,' C&H has regular dies, a bullet puller, and a micrometer straight-line seater. All require a press capable of handling die bodies with 11/2x12 threading. The regular loading dies consist of a full-length sizer and a crimp seater. The Puller die uses R-8 collets of the type used in Bridgeport milling machines, and replacement collets are available in several size increments up to one-inch, or from 4mm to 25mm. If you need to pull bullets from surplus military 50 BMG ammunition the C&H die, which has a roller thrust washer and spring ejector to ensure easy operation without

marring the bullet, will do the job.

If you shoot the Big Fifty at 1,000 yards, using Barnes or Hornady bullets, you need to take a bit more care than loading with surplus 50-caliber bullets. The C&H Micrometer Die incorporates a micrometer spindle graduated in 0.001-inch with a Vernier scale to 0.0001-inch. It takes good equipment to turn out accurate loads, and if you need a precise setting when seating the 750-grain bullets, this is the die needed.

If you happen to have one of the old Herter 'C' or Lachmiller presses that used a non-standard shellholder (The shellholder on some such presses was held in position with one or two set screws.), C&H's adapter can help you. This adapter allows the use of regular snap-in shellholders used by all modern loading press manufacturers. Herter's also produced a few presses using a threaded shell holder and C&H has an adapter for this as well.

Magma Engineering Company

Magma, home of the Bullet Master and Magma Bullet Moulds, has moulds for ten new gas-check bullets, a Digital Temperature Controller for the Master Caster, Cast Master and Master Pot machines, and is now the home for the Littleton Shotmaker. The Controller, which can be located off the machines for ease and convenience of the operator,

will maintain pot temperature to plus or minus 2 degrees Fahrenheit.

The Littleton Shotmaker is available with a choice of 120 or 220 VAC power unit, and is capable of producing thirty-five to forty pounds of high antimony, perfectly round shot per hour, using seven drippers. The unit measures a foot square by six inches high, and drippers are available in shot sizes 5, 6, 7, 7½, 8, 8½ and 9.

The new Magma gas-check bullet moulds are all flat-tip designs, and include a 115-grain for the 32-20 Winchester, three 38-caliber designs, including a 260-grain for the 38-55 Winchester, a 260-grain for the 40-65 Winchester, two designs – 300 and 340 grains – for the 45-70 Government, a 265-grain for the 454 Casull and two 50-calibers: 300 and 440 grains.

Wolfe Publishing Company

Anyone in the handloading game for long should know the name of Ken Waters. Wolfe has a new book, *Ken Waters' Notebook*, available. Featuring previously unpublished personal correspondence, with many personal insights on various subjects, this new volume also contains considerable reloading information.

Corbin Mfg. & Supply

Every handloader who loads for more than one caliber has found, at one time or another, the cannelure groove on the bullet being loaded wasn't where the crimp was being made. No problem. The Oregon firm of Corbin Mfg. & Supply has a hand-operated tool, the HCT-1 Hand Cannelure Tool, which will place the cannelure where you need it, on any bullet from 17- to 72-caliber. Just set the exact depth you want the cannelure, position the bullet and turn the crank. It's handy, fast, easy to use and produces a perfect cannelure where you need it.

UniqueTek, Inc.

Users of the Fillon 550 and 650 reloading presses may have noticed a bit of looseness in the toolhead fit to the frame. UniqueTek, Inc. has a kit to tighten the fit. It eliminates looseness, reduces any overall case length variation and stabilizes the

The Frankford Arsenal Micro Reloading Scale. The cartridge on the pan is a 5.7x28mm FNH, and a quarter is shown to the right, above a pair of tweezers, and a powder dipper. This scale comes with a soft case, and will fit into a shirt pocket. Accurate to 0.1 grain, it's ideal for taking to the range, along with a small press, if any reloading of handgun cartridges, etc., needs doing.

shellplate alignment. It does not require any modification to the press frame, so standard toolheads can still be used. It comes with instructions.

Ayers Arsenal

Some four or so decades back when most shotshells used paper hulls, the case mouths sometimes became frayed before the pinholes began to appear above the case head. Slipping the cases mouth over a heated 'shell former' for a couple of seconds usually straightened the mouth, especially on Winchester-Western hulls which contained a bit of wax impregnation. The Minnesota firm of Herter's had an electrically-heated plug die which could be hand-held with an oven glove, or mounted on a single-stage press to re-form the case mouth in the step after decapping. (Leaving a plastic hull on the former for any length of time would usually ruin the case, as the plastic had a tendency to shrink.) Unfortunately, the original Herter firm is long gone.

Wisconsin's Ayers Arsenal has what they call a Thermagic Conditioner that will do the same job as the old Herter die. The Thermagic unit operates on a 110-115 VAC line and can be bench-mounted or clamped in a vise. It incorporates a thermostat for use with different plastic or paper cases. (A bit of trial and error use is necessary, as not all shotshell hulls are of the same formula plastic, plus there are paper hulls still available.) Slip the hull mouth down onto the forming mandrel with a rotating motion for a few seconds, and remove with a rotating motion in the opposite direction. Quickly slip the hot hull onto a separate cooling mandrel, rotate, remove and examine. If it's not near-perfect, try leaving the hull on the forming mandrel a second or two longer. (Roll crimps form best when using new, uncrimped hulls, but a The ermagic-treated previously crimped hull will also produced some good roll crimps.)

Caldwell Shooting Supplies

Loading ammunition is only part of the game. It has to be accurate ammunition to be worth the time and effort. Checking it for accuracy is required, and the best way to accomplish that is with the aid of a mechanical rest of some type. For handgun users, Caldwell Shooting Supplies, by Battenfeld Technologies, Inc., has the H.A.M.M.R. (Handgun Accurizing Mechanical Machine Rest). If used properly, this device allows a shooter to test a handgun for accuracy free from outside interference. (It does require a sturdy, non-moving shooting bench to which the HAMMR can be securely clamped or mounted.) Firing is done remotely, using a cable-operated trigger actuator bar.

Currently, stock grip inserts for the HAMMR are available to fit various Smith & Wesson and Ruger revolvers, plus Beretta, SIG-Sauer, Glock, Para-Ordnance and HK pistols, as well as the M1911 Colt and clones. There is also a Universal Grip Casting Kit available, and inserts for other models are forthcoming. The original stocks on pistols and revolvers must be removed prior to installing the HAMMR inserts, and it's possible some Ransom grip inserts can be used. If handguns with polymer frames and non-removable stocks are to be used for test work, care must be taken not to over-tighten the clamping knobs during installation.

Hyskore Power Aisle, Inc.

There are a number of mechanical rests for rifle users, including the excellent Lead Sled from Caldwell Shooting Supplies. One of the best new rests for checking accuracy is the Model 30012 Dangerous Game Machine Rest from Hyskore Power Aisle, Inc. This rest, as with the HAMMR, employs remote firing, but via a hydraulic trigger release in place of a cable. The rest should be attached to a non-moving shooting bench; a concrete bench would be ideal. The Dangerous Game Rest will handle rifles in calibers from the 223 Remington to the 416 Weatherby Magnum, using one of three compression dampers provided with the Rest. (A table listing the approximate recoil in foot-pounds of energy is provided for each of the three dampers—mild (#1), medium (#2), and heavy (#3)—when used with rifles weighing seven, eight and nine pounds. The #1 damper should be used with rifles chambered for cartridges from the 223 Remington to the 308 Winchester. Damper #2 will handle rifles chambered for cartridges from the 7mm Remington Magnum to the 375 H&H Magnum, and including 12-gauge shotguns. Damper #3 will take care of the larger cartridges, from the 338 RUM to the 416 Weatherby Magnum, including the 416 Rigby and 458 Winchester Magnum. However, the 458 is not to be used in the Rest if the rifle weighs less than eight pounds, nor should the 416 Weatherby be used in the Rest if the rifle weighs less than nine pounds. Otherwise, damage may result to the rest and/or the rifle, according to Power Aisle.

Power Aisle stresses caution in all aspects when using the Rest, following the instructions, calculating the anticipated recoil prior to beginning so the correct damper is used, and checking everything, including the Velcro security straps, after every third shot. As the instructions state: "If you do something dumb, bad things can happen."

Ballistic Technology

Handloads intended for defensive or hunting use can be checked for expansion properties using the Bullet Test Tube by Ballistic Technology. (This shooter has used a variety of mediums over the years, from actual beef – it was cheaper then – to saturated wetpack. None provided a reliable, semi-permanent wound cavity for later analysis, although the wetpack and moist clay did well after drying for a period of time.) The bullet expansion material in the Test Tube can be melted and reused, using moulds that are available. Currently, the Bullet Test Tube can be obtained in sizes to handle handgun and/or rifle calibers. There are also moulds, material solvents, etc. available. For handloaders wanting to check the effects of their load/bullet combination, the Bullet Test Tube provides the means.

There's always something new for handloaders. It may be components, loading data, new or improved presses, dies, scale, powder measure – or even an ammunition box. What's been presented in this update represents some of what's new. There is no doubt that additional products will have been introduced by the time you read this. It's all part of what makes handloading enjoyable, that and the ability to turn out the best and most accurate handloads you can possibly produce. ✳

AMMUNITION, BALLISTICS & COMPONENTS

by Holt Bodinson

The steady introduction of new calibers and high-tech loads is fueling the firearms industry. One has to look no further than Hornady to sense the pace of the ammunition market. This year Hornady is introducing four completely new cartridges – the 308 Marlin Express, 30 T/C, 375 Ruger and 460 Bushmaster. It is also bringing into production two great classics – the 450/400 N.E.-3" and the 9.3x74R. Remington, which has controlled the 17-caliber centerfire market with its swift 17 Remington for years, decided it was time to rev up the market and created the appealing 17 Remington Fireball along with five bolt-action rifles to shoot it in. The heavy end of the handgun market keeps boiling with a number of new loads for the 460 S&W and 500 S&W, including Hornady's 500-grain FP-XTP for 500 S&W shooters who like a bit of kick to their loads. Over in scattergun territory, the accent is still on the development of dense shot including Winchester's Extended Range High Density, Remington's Wingmaster HD and Federal's Black Cloud FS Steel. It's been a busy year!

A-Square Company

A-Square has aggressively tamed a number of excellent wildcats by domesticating them through the AAMI protocols. Two of the successful cartridges, the 6.5-06 A-Square and the 338-06 A-Square, will be joined this year by the 416 Taylor A-Square. Developed by Robert Chatfield Taylor in the 1970s by necking down the 458 Win. Magnum case to .416", the compact and highly efficient 416 Taylor is capable of churning up 2400 fps with a 400-grain bullet. Move over 416 Rigby and 416 Remington, the Taylor A-Square runs on less powder and doesn't require a magnum length action to equal your classic ballistics. It's good to see that the 416 Taylor has now been standardized and is available loaded with A-Square's unique "Triad" of big game bullets. www.a-squarecompany.com

Ballistic Products

Ballistic Products new "HITS" program is changing the way shotshell reloaders optimize their choice of components around a specific game species or shooting game. Standing for "Hull Integrated Technology System," the HITS program provides the reloader with a bundle of the best components, except for powder and shot, plus reloading instructions to assemble the finest pheasant, waterfowl, sporting clays and 20-gauge shotshells. There's also a new multi-purpose 16-gauge field wad available this year. Designated the "Multi-Metal 16," it can handle lead, steel and Hevi-Shot loadings. www.ballisticproducts.com

Barnes Bullets

Celebrating their 75th anniversary, Barnes is introducing no less than

Barnes' Triple-Shock X Bullet is so effective, it's being factory loaded by Federal, Black Hills and Weatherby.

Featuring a copper-tin core, Barnes' Varmint Grenade .224" bullet promises explosive performance.

41 new bullet designs this year. Noteworthy as well is that the Barnes bullets are being factory loaded today by Black Hills, Cor-Bon, Federal, Norma and Weatherby. Brand new to the Barnes family is the "Varmint Grenade" – a 36-grain HP in .224", featuring a highly frangible, copper-tin core. It's a "green" bullet, accurate and designed for explosive expansion of game and a minimum of ricochets. The line of Maximum-Range X-Bullets (MRX) introduced last year, featuring tungsten-alloy cores and polymer tips in the familiar Triple-Shock platform, has been expanded to cover every popular caliber from 270 through 338. Barnes' line of solids has been completely redesigned with multi-grooved shanks that reduce pressure, minimize fouling and enhance accuracy. The new "Banded Solid" line has been expanded to cover every popular caliber from 224 through 600, and this includes some classic big game calibers such as the 9.3mm, 450/400, 404 Jeffrey, 470 Nitro, 505 Gibbs and 500 Nitro. The 30/30 gets a new high performance bullet this year, a flat-nose, 150-grain Triple Shock. Finally, look for a variety of new XPB pistol bullets including new weights and designs for the 357, 357 Sig, 40 S&W, 44 Spl. and 45 GAP. www.barnesbullets.com

Berger Bullets

In an interesting turn of events, Berger is pitching its Match Grade Very Low Drag (VLD) line as perfectly suitable for hunting big game. Berger's tests, which are available on a free DVD from the company, show that the sharp nose of a VLD bullet penetrates at least 2 inches of initial tissue and then expands rapidly in the vital area. Added to the lineup this year are a 120-grain/6.5mm Match BT and a 130-grain/6.5mm Match VLD. www.bergerbullets.com

Bismuth

Working with Berger, Bismuth has developed and is loading a 175-grain/30-caliber VLD match grade bullet with a pure Bismuth, non-toxic core in the 308 Win., 30-'06, 300 Win. Mag. and 300 WSM. Test results show exceptionally fine accuracy and rapid fragmentation. Bismuth continues to offer a complete line of shotshells and Bismuth component shot for handloaders. Bismuth is the only non-toxic shot that is suitable for pre-steel shot shotgun barrels, be they breech or muzzleloaders. www.bismuth-notox.com

Black Hills

With S&W returning the Model 1917 to its line, a lot of shooters will be searching for 45 Auto Rim ammunition. It's hard to find, but not at Black Hills. Their new 45 Auto Rim loading features a hard-cast 255-grain SWC at an honest 750 fps. The hottest new varmint load this year is Black Hills' 223 "Varmint Grenade." Built around Barnes' new copper particle-cored 36-grain bullet, the Varmint Grenade is running at 3750 fps and is said to be "humanely devastating"

on small critters. Long known for their custom match ammunition, Black Hills is loading a 123-grain/6.5mm Sierra MatchKing in the 6.5 Grendel cartridge for Les Baer, who is reporting .5 MOA accuracy from his custom AR-15s. Similarly, they have developed a long-range tactical match load for the 260 Rem. cartridge, featuring a 139-grain Lapua Scenar bullet at 2770 fps. The tactical match 260 Rem. load will be marketed exclusively through G.A. Precision rifles. Finally, their premium line of hunting ammunition, Black Hills Gold, is being expanded with Hornady SST bullets added to the 243 Win., 270 Win. and 7mm Rem. Mag. Great people – great ammo. www.black-hills.com

Brenneke USA

The 16-gauge continues to creep up in popularity, and why not. A 16-gauge built on a 20-gauge frame is a delight to shoot and carry. Well, Brenneke

Above: If you don't handload, Black Hills' 223 ammunition line now includes Barnes' Varmint Grenade bullet.

45 Auto Rim has been in short supply, but no longer. Black Hills is bringing it back.

Brenneke's extensive slug line-up features a new 16 ga. 1 oz. slug at 1600 fps.

has upgraded their 1 oz/16-gauge slug with a new wad system that is capable of 2.5" groups at 50 yards. Velocity is right up there at 1600 fps. Over the past year, Brenneke commissioned ballistics expert Tom Burczynski to run a series of comparative tests on all brands of shotguns slugs. Interestingly, the Brenneke 12-gauge Heavy Field Short Magnum out-penetrated the competition by a long margin and ranked second in terms of accuracy and muzzle energy. See the test results at www.brennekeusa.com

DKG Trading

DKG has emerged as a great resource if you're looking for NobelSport or Centurion shotshells. Manufactured in Italy, both lines feature some interesting variations like NobelSport's 20-gauge steel trap load and 12-gauge sporting clays spreader load. Under the Centurion banner, one will find a unique 12-gauge buckshot load featuring one 0.650" round ball and six #1 buck and a .410 shell stuffed with five #00 buck. See the whole lines at www.dkgtrading.com

Extreme Shock

Extreme Shock ammunition is designed to fragment and dump all its energy within the target. With a technology based on bullets having Tungsten powder cores, the lines now cover personal defense and aircraft

Centurion packs a lethal load of one .650" ball plus six #1 buck.

safe handgun rounds, short and long range 5.56mm tactical rounds, subsonic, door-breaching and even a 675-grain 50 BMG load. See them all at www.extremeshockusa.com

Federal

Waterfowl beware! The new Black Cloud FS Steel cartridge is described as "Dropping Ducks Like Rain." Basically, a combination of Federal's proven Flitecontrol wad and a steel shot pellet that features a cutting edge around its circumference, Black Cloud FS is a new step-up in steel shot lethality. Twelve and twenty gauge slugs also have been given a facelift by the addition of a streamlined polymer spitzer tip to Federal's Barnes Expander sabot

Federal's 12 and 20-gauge sabot slug loads feature a spitzer-tipped Barnes Expander.

slug. The factory standard is 2 inches at 100 yards – no exceptions. Speaking of Barnes, the 7mm/140-grain Triple Shock X-Bullet has been added to the 7mm-08, 280 Rem. and 7mm Rem. Mag. under the Premium Vital-Shok label. Also new under the same label are a 150-grain Nosler AccuBond in the 30-'06 and a 165-grain AccuBond in the 308 Win. The popularity of the 460 S&W keeps growing so Federal has once again teamed up with Barnes to load a 275-grain Expander in that big bore handgun caliber. www.federalpremium.com

Fiocchi

Break out those Broomhandles! Fiocchi is reintroducing the 7.63 Mauser cartridge in a full-power loading sporting an 88-grain FMJ bullet at 1425 fps. www.fiocchiusa.com

Hastings

A 3½"/20-gauge slug? Famous for their slug gun barrels and sabot slug ammunition, Hastings is introducing a 3½"/20-gauge case stuffed with a 350-grain Laser Accurate Slug at 2000 fps. It's the ultimate 20-gauge magnum but suitable only for single-shot shotguns at the moment. www.hastingsammunition.com

Hodgdon

Having taken over the distribution of Winchester canister powders, Hodgdon is releasing two classic Winchester shotshell powders: WAALite – the same powder used by Winchester to create the Feather Light AA12FL shell; and Super-Handicap – useful for duplicating Winchester's clays-crushing Super-Handicap 12-gauge loading that tough competitors call the "silver bullet." There's a new short cut powder this year, IMR 4007 SSC. "SSC" stands for "Super Short Cut" and the burning rate of the new powder falls between IMR 4064 and IMR 4350. The new IMR 4007 SSC is turning in outstanding velocities and accuracy in the short magnums as well as in the 22-250, 220 Swift, 243 Win. and the classic 30-'06. Be sure to buy the new Hodgdon Reloading Manual that now includes thousands of proven recipes for IMR and

Hodgdon is releasing two classic Winchester shotshell powders: AA Lite and AA Super-Handicap.

Winchester, as well as the traditional Hodgdon powders. www.hodgdon.com

Hornady

After last year's introduction of the "LeverEvolution" family of cartridges, we expected Hornady to take a breather. Not so, this year Hornady is producing four completely new cartridges, the 375 Ruger, 308 Marlin Express, 30 T/C and 450 Bushmaster as well as bringing into production two great classics, the 450/400 Nitro Express 3" and the 9.3x74R. The 375 Ruger is based on a 30-'06-length case and loaded with a 270-grain SP and 300-grain SP or FMJ, it is capable of duplicating 375 H&H performance in a 20-inch barrel. The 308 Marlin Express features a 160-grain spitzer bullet with a high B.C. rating of .400 that leaves the muzzle of Marlin's new XLR lever action at 2600 fps. If you like Marlin lever actions, you'll like this new cartridge. The 30 T/C is a short-action case designed

specifically for T/C's forward-looking ICON bolt-action rifle. Producing 3000 fps with a 150-grain bullet and 2850 fps with a 165-grain pill, Hornady claims the new case uses less powder than the 308 or 30-'06, exceeds the factory velocities of those classic 30s in a 20-inch barrel, and produces noticeably less recoil. Designed to take your Bushmaster AR-15 big-game hunting, the 450 Bushmaster will produce over 2000 fps with a .425-caliber/250-grain SST bullet. The overall length of the new cartridge matches the 223 Rem. at 2.250 inches. Just change your uppers and go hunting. www.hornady.com

Huntington

This is the handloader's emporium for bullets, cases and RCBS tooling and parts. Buzz Huntington does an exceptional job of rounding up the hardest-to-get components and will go to any length to find them. Need lead bullets for the 310 Martini, newly drawn

cases for the 577 Snider, or samples of the 600 and 700 Nitro Express cases or bullets. Huntington keeps them in stock. I enjoy shooting the oddball and obsolete cartridges, and I haven't been able to stump Buzz yet.

Huntington's catalog is as educational a reference as you will find in the trade.www.huntingtons.com

Kent Cartridge

"Speed Kills," states their catalog, and Kent has the shotshells to prove it. New this year under their "Faststeel" waterfowl label is a 12-gauge/3½" shell packing 1¼ oz of BB, 1, 2 and 3s at 1625 fps. That's fast! Then there's a new 12-gauge/2¾" upland lead load featuring 1⅜ oz of 4, 5 and 6s at 1460 fps. Look to Kent for speed. It kills. www.kentgamebore.com

Lightfield

Famous for their exceptionally accurate and lethal shotgun slugs, Lightfield has capitalized on its experience with plastic sabots and projectile design to develop a new 50-caliber muzzleloading round. Named the "Alpha Gold 300," it consists of a pure lead 300-grain boattail hollowpoint bullet wrapped in a gold-colored sabot. The hollow point is serrated to generate controlled expansion upon impact and a bullet seater is provided in each blister pack to ensure the soft spitzer point is not deformed when loading. The plastic sabot is formulated to take both blackpowder and smokeless pressures. It's a good looking round and early reports from the field indicate it's exceptionally lethal. Also new this year are several new sabot shotgun slugs and a full range of non-lethal law enforcement and wildlife control loads. Most important may be Lightfield's well-written instructional guides on benchresting and sighting in a slug gun, and analyzing recovered muzzleloading sabots to fine-tune your load. www.lightfieldslugs.com and www.lightfieldlesslethal.com

Midway

Do you have a vintage 12-gauge side-by-side that would be pleasant and safe to shoot with a low-pressure

Hornady's puts some muscle in the AR-15 with the new 450 Bushmaster.

shell? Midway has the shell. Loaded by Federal to Midway's specifications, the 12-gauge/2¾" shell features ⅞ oz. of #7½ shot at 1200 fps. The chamber pressure is a mild 5,000 pounds and recoil is equally as light. The shell would be a great practice round in any 12-gauge gun and is ideal for recoil-sensitive shooters. Available by the case, see it at www.midway-usa.com.

Norma

Norma fields its "African PH" series of big game ammunition. Featuring FMJ and SP Woodleigh bullets, the new cartridge family includes the 375 H&H, 404 Jeffery, 416 Rigby and Rem. Mag., 450 Rigby, 458 Lott, 470 NE, 500 NE and 505 Gibbs. The "African PH" catalog, featuring stories on a number of past and present professional hunters, is a great read and well worth ordering. In another interesting development, Norma will be bringing out a new 6mm competition cartridge designed by David Tubb. Called the "6XC," the case is based on an improved 22-250 design with minimum case taper and a 30-degree shoulder. The 6XC will be factory loaded with a moly-coated 105-grain Berger bullet loaded to approximately 3000 fps. Norma is considering introducing the 6XC as a hunting cartridge as well, noting its superiority over the 243 Win. www.norma.cc

Nosler

Expanding its highly successful AccuBond line, Nosler is introducing four new bullets: a 130-grain/6.5mm, 130-grain/270, 225-grain/35 and a 250-grain/9.3mm. There's a new 32-grain/20 caliber Ballistic Tip varmint pill and a new 140-

grain/6.5mm HPBT target bullet in the line. Nosler continues to expand its brand of custom brass and is cataloguing the 260 Rem., 280 Ackley Improved, 300 H&H and 300 SAUM this year. www.nosler.com

Polywad

Always a fertile center for shotshell innovations, Polywad is introducing the "Gram Crak-R Shell," a buffered shot load, wrapped in a high-sided craft paper shot cup. The results in the 28-gauge and .410 are amazing. With the 28-gauge shell, I was taking doves out to 50 yards this past season while the .410 Crak-R performs more like a 28-gauge. The secret is in the buffer and in the environmentally friendly shotcup that holds the shot together, producing a short shot string and a tight shot pattern with a minimum of aberrant pellets. www.polywad.com

Remington

Having opened the 17-caliber door years ago with their sensational 17 Remington, Big Green has done it again. Necking down the cute-looking 221 Fireball, they're introducing the 17 Remington Fireball with a 20-grain AccuTip-V at 4000 fps in no less than four different model rifles. Another ballistic break-through this year is Wingmaster HD waterfowl, turkey and predator loads. Utilizing their proprietary tungsten-bronze-iron alloy with a pellet density of 12 gm/cc, the new shot is perfectly spherical and offers optimum pattern densities in gauges from 10 through 20. The predator loading in the 3" and 3½"/12 gauge is based on "T" shot at 1300-1350 fps –

should be deadly on coyotes at extended ranges. Working with the concept of stair-stepping loads, Remington is offering three different power level loads for the 300 Rem. Ultra Mag. Power Level 1 tames the 300 RUM to 30-'06 level performance; Level 2 to 300 Win. performance; and Level 3 brings out the full power level we buy the 300 RUM for in the first place. Remington states that the point-of-impact of all three power levels is within 2 inches at 200 yards, making scope adjustments unnecessary. In the shotshell slug department, there is a new Managed-Recoil addition featuring a 1 oz./12 ga. Copper Solid Sabot Slug at a mild 1200 fps. Look for Remington Core-Lokt Ultra Bonded component bullets this year in calibers 243 through 338. www.remington.com

Schroeder Bullets

For uncommon custom diameter bullets and brass, always check out Schroeder.

This year he is adding formed brass for the 204 Ruger Rimmed, 223 Rimmed, 222 Mag. Rimmed, 17-357 Maximum, 5.7x28mm Rimmed, 30 Herrett, and 7x61 S&H. New custom bullets include a 60-grain HP in .234" diameter and 225-grain and 250-grain spire points in .356" diameter. If you own a 5mm Rem. Mag. rifle, Schroeder offers a simple and inexpensive conversion to 5mm centerfire. (619) 423-3523

Sierra Bullets

Meeting the demand for 6.5mm match bullets, Sierra has added a 123-grain HPBT MatchKing to its existing line-up of superb 6.5mm competition projectiles. www.sierrabullets.com

SSK

JD Jones and David Frickie have teamed up to produce a series of unique bullets turned from brass or copper. There are a variety of styles in 6.5mm, 6.8mm, 338, 375, 416, 458, 500, 510, 13mm, 14.5mm, 62 and 95 caliber. If you have a self-designed bullet in mind, Jones and Frickie will get it into CNC production for a modest cost of $300. Working with Michael McCourry, SSK now offers

Remington's Wingmaster HD shot is perfectly round, 10 percent denser than lead and 16 percent softer than Premium Hevi-Shot.

a completely new line of custom 50, 416 and 458 caliber cartridges based on WSM and Rem. Ultra Mag. brass, including a 50-caliber Alaskan cartridge that is giving outstanding performance in the Win. Model 71 and Marlin 1895. Dies, bullets, brass and custom gunsmithing are available through SSK. www.sskindustries.com

Speer

Speer's continued production of "Special Purpose Rifle Bullets" is a blessing shooters should not overlook. In spite of what must be a very limited demand, the "Special Purpose" line includes properly cannelured bullets for the 218 Bee, 25-20, 7-30 Waters, 30 Carbine and 32-20. Stock up! www.speer-bullets.com

Swift

If you're a 25-caliber shooter, there's a great new bullet in the Scirocco line. It's a streamlined 100-grain boattail spitzer with a high BC of .429. www.swiftbullet.com

Weatherby

Weatherby was the first major company to integrate Nosler Partition bullets into their entire line. They continue to search out and load premium, high-tech component bullets. This year, Barnes Triple-Shock X-Bullet and Nosler's AccuBond bullet are being added across the Weatherby family of high-performance cartridges that already sport the Nosler Partition, Nosler

Weatherby's focus on premium bullets now includes the Barnes' Triple Shock.

Ballistic Tip and Hornady Interlock bullets. www.weatherby.com

Winchester

Winchester's top-of-the-line ammunition family, the Supreme Elite line, includes a number of firsts this year. The 243 Win and the 243 WSSM have been tipped off with Winchester's finest controlled expansion, bonded core bullet, the 95-grain/XP3. The popular 270 Win. and 270 WSM are also being upgraded with a 130-grain XP3 bullet. Respective velocities are 3050 fps and 3275 fps. Designed for rifled shotgun bores, there's a striking new XP3/12-gauge shotgun slug featuring a sharp polymer tip, controlled expansion jacket, and a refined sabot. The combination is said to be highly accurate and very flat shooting. As we go to print, the shell's velocity has not been announced. Predator hunters will like the Supreme Elite Xtended Range High Density Coyote 3"/12-gauge load featuring 1⅜ oz of Hi-Density B size pellets. Lots of knockdown power with minimum pelt damage. The 3"/20-gauge is getting some additional octane this year with the introduction of an Xtended Range turkey load packing 1⅛ oz of #5 shot at 1225 fps. Finally, the premium line features a 3"/12-gauge Xtended Range waterfowl load, loaded with 1⅜ oz of #6 Hi-Density shot. The old 30-30 gets a facelift with a new 150-grain, slightly pointed, Ballistic Silvertip ripping out at 2390 fps. If the full-power 500 S&W seems a bit much for extended target sessions, Winchester has a new reduced recoil load consisting of a 350-grain bullet at 1400 fps. Delivering only ⅓ the recoil of the full-power cartridge, big-bore handgunners should love it. Speaking of reduced recoil, there's a new line of WinLite Low Recoil shotgun ammunition covering target, buckshot and slug applications. Finally, honoring the late John Wayne on what would be his 100th birthday, Winchester is issuing a limited edition collector's set of ammunition in 44-40, 45 Colt and 30-30 calibers, featuring special headstamps and commemorative packaging. www.winchester.com

Woodleigh

Constructed with pure lead, bonded cores, the Woodleigh line

Celebrating the "Duke" legend, Winchester is offering a collector's edition of 44-40, 45 Colt and 30-30 ammunition.

Putting pizzazz in the 20-gauge, Winchester has added an Extended Range turkey load featuring 1⅛ oz of #5s at 1225 fps.

Even the old 30-30 gets a facelift this year with a slightly pointed Ballistic Silvertip ripping out at 2390 fps.

of premium big-game bullets is being expanded this year with an ultra heavy, 240-grain protected point, Weldcore bullet for the 30-'06, 200 and 220-grain PP bullets for the 325 Win., a 400-grain FN for the 500 S&W, and a 450-grain RN in .510" diameter for the 500 Nitro. See the whole line. www.woodleighbullets.com.au

Many manufacturers do not supply suggested retail prices. Others did not get their pricing to us before press time. All pricing can vary dependent on the exact brand and style of ammo selected and/or the retail outlet from which you make your purchase. Pricing has been rounded to the nearest dollar and represents our best estimate of average pricing. An * after the cartridge means these loads are available with Nosler Partition or Swift A-Frame bullets. Listed pricing may or may not reflect this bullet type.
** = these are packed 50 to box, all others are 20 to box. Wea. Mag.= Weatherby Magnum. Spfd. = Springfield. A-Sq.= A-Square. N.E.=Nitro Express.

Cartridge	Bullet Wgt. Grs.	VELOCITY (fps)					ENERGY (ft. lbs.)					TRAJ. (in.)				Est. Price/box
		Muzzle	100 yds.	200 yds.	300 yds.	400 yds.	Muzzle	100 yds.	200 yds.	300 yds.	400 yds.	100 yds.	200 yds.	300 yds.	400 yds.	
17, 22																
17 Remington Fireball	20	4000	3380	2840	2360	1930	710	507	358	247	165	1.6	1.5	-2.8	-13.5	NA
17 Remington	25	4040	3284	2644	2086	1606	906	599	388	242	143	+2.0	+1.7	-4.0	-17.0	$17
204 Ruger	32	4225	3632	3114	2652	2234	1268	937	689	500	355	.6	0.0	-4.2	-13.4	NA
204 Ruger	40	3900	3451	3046	2677	2336	1351	1058	824	636	485	.7	0.0	-4.5	-13.9	NA
204 Ruger	45	3625	3188	2792	2428	2093	1313	1015	778	589	438	1.00	0.0	-5.5	-16.9	NA
221 Fireball	50	2800	2137	1580	1180	988	870	507	277	155	109	+0.0	-7.0	-28.0	0.0	$14
22 Hornet	34	3050	2132	1415	1017	852	700	343	151	78	55	+0.0	-6.6	-15.5	-29.9	NA
22 Hornet	35	3100	2278	1601	1135	929	747	403	199	100	67	+2.75	0.0	-16.9	-60.4	NA
22 Hornet	45	2690	2042	1502	1128	948	723	417	225	127	90	+0.0	-7.7	-31.0	0.0	$27**
218 Bee	46	2760	2102	1550	1155	961	788	451	245	136	94	+0.0	-7.2	-29.0	0.0	$46**
222 Remington	40	3600	3117	2673	2269	1911	1151	863	634	457	324	+1.07	0.0	-6.13	-18.9	NA
222 Remington	50	3140	2602	2123	1700	1350	1094	752	500	321	202	+2.0	-0.4	-11.0	-33.0	$11
222 Remington	55	3020	2562	2147	1773	1451	1114	801	563	384	257	+2.0	-0.4	-11.0	-33.0	$12
22 PPC	52	3400	2930	2510	2130	NA	1335	990	730	525	NA	+2.0	1.4	-5.0	0.0	NA
223 Remington	40	3650	3010	2450	1950	1530	1185	805	535	340	265	+2.0	+1.0	-6.0	-22.0	$14
223 Remington	40	3800	3305	2845	2424	2044	1282	970	719	522	371	0.84	0.0	-5.34	-16.6	NA
223 Remington	50	3300	2874	2484	2130	1809	1209	917	685	504	363	1.37	0.0	-7.05	-21.8	NA
223 Remington	52/53	3330	2882	2477	2106	1770	1305	978	722	522	369	+2.0	+0.6	-6.5	-21.5	$14
223 Remington	55	3240	2748	2305	1906	1556	1282	922	649	444	296	+2.0	-0.2	-9.0	-27.0	$12
223 Remington	60	3100	2712	2355	2026	1726	1280	979	739	547	397	+2.0	+0.2	-8.0	-24.7	$16
223 Remington	64	3020	2621	2256	1920	1619	1296	977	723	524	373	+2.0	-0.2	-9.3	-23.0	$14
223 Remington	69	3000	2720	2460	2210	1980	1380	1135	925	750	600	+2.0	+1.0	-5.8	-17.5	$15
223 Remington	75	2790	2554	2330	2119	1926	1296	1086	904	747	617	2.37	0.0	-8.75	-25.1	NA
223 Remington	77	2750	2584	2354	2169	1992	1293	1110	948	804	679	1.93	0.0	-8.2	-23.8	NA
223 WSSM	55	3850	3438	3064	2721	2402	1810	1444	1147	904	704	0.7	0.0	-4.4	-13.6	NA
223 WSSM	64	3600	3144	2732	2356	2011	1841	1404	1061	789	574	1.0	0.0	-5.7	-17.7	NA
222 Rem. Mag.	55	3240	2748	2305	1906	1556	1282	922	649	444	296	+2.0	-0.2	-9.0	-27.0	$14
225 Winchester	55	3570	3066	2616	2208	1838	1556	1148	836	595	412	+2.0	+1.0	-5.0	-20.0	$19
224 Wea. Mag.	55	3650	3192	2780	2403	2057	1627	1244	943	705	516	+2.0	+1.2	-4.0	-17.0	$32
22-250 Rem.	40	4000	3320	2720	2200	1740	1420	980	660	430	265	+2.0	+1.8	-3.0	-16.0	$14
22-250 Rem.	50	3725	3264	2641	2455	2103	1540	1183	896	669	491	0.89	0.0	-5.23	-16.3	NA
22-250 Rem.	52/55	3680	3137	2656	2222	1832	1654	1201	861	603	410	+2.0	+1.3	-4.0	-17.0	$13
22-250 Rem.	60	3600	3195	2826	2485	2169	1727	1360	1064	823	627	+2.0	+2.0	-2.4	-12.3	$19
220 Swift	40	4200	3678	3190	2739	2329	1566	1201	904	666	482	+0.51	0.0	-4.0	-12.9	NA
220 Swift	50	3780	3158	2617	2135	1710	1586	1107	760	506	325	+2.0	+1.4	-4.4	-17.9	$20
220 Swift	50	3850	3396	2970	2576	2215	1645	1280	979	736	545	0.74	0.0	-4.84	-15.1	NA
220 Swift	55	3800	3370	2990	2630	2310	1765	1390	1090	850	650	0.8	0.0	-4.7	-14.4	NA
220 Swift	55	3650	3194	2772	2384	2035	1627	1246	939	694	506	+2.0	+2.0	-2.6	-13.4	$19
220 Swift	60	3600	3199	2824	2475	2156	1727	1364	1063	816	619	+2.0	+1.6	-4.1	-13.1	$19
22 Savage H.P.	71	2790	2340	1930	1570	1280	1225	860	585	390	190	+2.0	-1.0	-10.4	-35.7	NA
6mm (24)																
6mm BR Rem.	100	2550	2310	2083	1870	1671	1444	1185	963	776	620	+2.5	-0.6	-11.8	0.0	$22
6mm Norma BR	107	2822	2667	2517	2372	2229	1893	1690	1506	1337	1181	+1.73	0.0	-7.24	-20.6	NA
6mm PPC	70	3140	2750	2400	2070	NA	1535	1175	895	665	NA	+2.0	+1.4	-5.0	0.0	NA
243 Winchester	55	4025	3597	3209	2853	2525	1978	1579	1257	994	779	+0.6	0.0	-4.0	-12.2	NA
243 Winchester	60	3600	3110	2660	2260	1890	1725	1285	945	680	475	+2.0	+1.8	-3.3	-15.5	$17
243 Winchester	70	3400	3040	2700	2390	2100	1795	1435	1135	890	685	1.1	0.0	-5.9	-18.0	NA
243 Winchester	75/80	3350	2955	2593	2259	1951	1993	1551	1194	906	676	+2.0	+0.9	-5.0	-19.0	$16
243 Winchester	85	3320	3070	2830	2600	2380	2080	1770	1510	1280	1070	+2.0	+1.2	-4.0	-14.0	$18
243 Winchester	90	3120	2871	2635	2411	2199	1946	1647	1388	1162	966	1.4	0.0	-6.4	-18.8	NA
243 Winchester*	100	2960	2697	2449	2215	1993	1945	1615	1332	1089	882	+2.5	+1.2	-6.0	-20.0	$16
243 Winchester	105	2920	2689	2470	2261	2062	1988	1686	1422	1192	992	+2.5	+1.6	-5.0	-18.4	$21
243 Light Mag.	100	3100	2839	2592	2358	2138	2133	1790	1491	1235	1014	+1.5	0.0	-6.8	-19.8	NA
243 WSSM	55	4060	3628	3237	2880	2550	2013	1607	1280	1013	794	0.6	0.0	-3.9	-12.0	NA
243 WSSM	95	3250	3000	2763	2538	2325	2258	1898	1610	1359	1140	1.2	0.0	-5.7	-16.9	NA
243 WSSM	100	3110	2838	2583	2341	2112	2147	1789	1481	1217	991	1.4	0.0	-6.6	-19.7	NA
6mm Remington	80	3470	3064	2694	2352	2036	2139	1667	1289	982	736	+2.0	+1.1	-5.0	-17.0	$16
6mm Remington	100	3100	2829	2573	2332	2104	2133	1777	1470	1207	983	+2.5	+1.6	-5.0	-17.0	$16
6mm Remington	105	3060	2822	2596	2381	2177	2105	1788	1512	1270	1059	+2.5	+1.1	-3.3	-15.0	$21
6mm Rem. Light Mag.	100	3250	2997	2756	2528	2311	2345	1995	1687	1418	1186	1.59	0.0	-6.33	-18.3	NA
6.17(.243) Spitfire	100	3350	3122	2905	2698	2501	2493	2164	1874	1617	1389	2.4	3.20	0.0	-8.0	NA
240 Wea. Mag.	87	3500	3202	2924	2663	2416	2366	1980	1651	1370	1127	+2.0	+2.0	-2.0	-12.0	$32
240 Wea. Mag.	100	3395	3106	2835	2581	2339	2559	2142	1785	1478	1215	+2.5	+2.8	-2.0	-11.0	$43
25																
25-20 Win.	86	1460	1194	1030	931	858	407	272	203	165	141	0.0	-23.5	0.0	0.0	$32**
25-35 Win.	117	2230	1866	1545	1282	1097	1292	904	620	427	313	+2.5	-4.2	-26.0	0.0	$24
250 Savage	100	2820	2504	2210	1936	1684	1765	1392	1084	832	630	+2.5	+0.4	-9.0	-28.0	$17
257 Roberts	100	2980	2661	2363	2085	1827	1972	1572	1240	965	741	+2.5	-0.8	-5.2	-21.6	$20
257 Roberts+P	117	2780	2411	2071	1761	1488	2009	1511	1115	806	576	+2.5	-0.2	-10.2	-32.6	$18

Many manufacturers do not supply suggested retail prices. Others did not get their pricing to us before press time. All pricing can vary dependent on the exact brand and style of ammo selected and/or the retail outlet from which you make your purchase. Pricing has been rounded to the nearest dollar and represents our best estimate of average pricing. An * after the cartridge means these loads are available with Nosler Partition or Swift A-Frame bullets. Listed pricing may or may not reflect this bullet type. ** = these are packed 50 to box, all others are 20 to box. Wea. Mag.= Weatherby Magnum. Spfd. = Springfield. A-Sq. = A-Square. N.E.=Nitro Express.

Cartridge	Bullet Wgt. Grs.	VELOCITY (fps)					ENERGY (ft. lbs.)					TRAJ. (in.)				Est. Price/ box
		Muzzle	100 yds.	200 yds.	300 yds.	400 yds.	Muzzle	100 yds.	200 yds.	300 yds.	400 yds.	100 yds.	200 yds.	300 yds.	400 yds.	
257 Roberts+P	120	2780	2560	2360	2160	1970	2060	1750	1480	1240	1030	+2.5	+1.2	-6.4	-23.6	$22
257 Roberts	122	2600	2331	2078	1842	1625	1831	1472	1169	919	715	+2.5	0.0	-10.6	-31.4	$21
257 Light Mag.	117	2940	2694	2460	2240	2031	2245	1885	1572	1303	1071	+1.7	0.0	-7.6	-21.8	NA
25-06 Rem.	87	3440	2995	2591	2222	1884	2286	1733	1297	954	686	+2.0	+1.1	-2.5	-14.4	$17
25-06 Rem.	90	3440	3043	2680	2344	2034	2364	1850	1435	1098	827	+2.0	+1.8	-3.3	-15.6	$17
25-06 Rem.	100	3230	2893	2580	2287	2014	2316	1858	1478	1161	901	+2.0	+0.8	-5.7	-18.9	$17
25-06 Rem.	117	2990	2770	2570	2370	2190	2320	2000	1715	1465	1246	+2.5	+1.0	-7.9	-26.6	$19
25-06 Rem.*	120	2990	2730	2484	2252	2032	2382	1985	1644	1351	1100	+2.5	+1.2	-5.3	-19.6	$17
25-06 Rem.	122	2930	2706	2492	2289	2095	2325	1983	1683	1419	1189	+2.5	+1.8	-4.5	-17.5	$23
25 WSSM	85	3470	3156	2863	2589	2331	2273	1880	1548	1266	1026	1.0	0.0	-5.2	-15.7	NA
25 WSSM	115	3060	284	2639	2442	2254	2392	2066	1778	1523	1398	1.4	0.0	-6.4	-18.6	NA
25 WSSM	120	2990	2717	2459	2216	1987	2383	1967	1612	1309	1053	1.6	0.0	-7.4	-21.8	NA
257 Wea. Mag.	87	3825	3456	3118	2805	2513	2826	2308	1870	1520	1220	+2.0	+2.7	-0.3	-7.6	$32
257 Wea. Mag.	100	3555	3237	2941	2665	2404	2806	2326	1920	1576	1283	+2.5	+3.2	0.0	-8.0	$32
257 Scramjet	100	3745	3450	3173	2912	2666	3114	2643	2235	1883	1578	+2.1	+2.77	0.0	-6.93	NA
6.5																
6.5x47 Lapua	123	2887	NA	2554	NA	2244	2285	NA	1788	NA	1380	NA	4.53	0.00	-10.7	NA
6.5x50mm Jap.	139	2360	2160	1970	1790	1620	1720	1440	1195	985	810	+2.5	-1.0	-13.5	0.0	NA
6.5x50mm Jap.	156	2070	1830	1610	1430	1260	1475	1155	900	695	550	+2.5	-4.0	-23.8	0.0	NA
6.5x52mm Car.	139	2580	2360	2160	1970	1790	2045	1725	1440	1195	985	+2.5	0.0	-9.9	-29.0	NA
6.5x52mm Car.	156	2430	2170	1930	1700	1500	2045	1630	1285	1005	780	+2.5	-1.0	-13.9	0.0	NA
6.5x52mm Carcano	160	2250	1963	1700	1467	1271	1798	1369	1027	764	574	+3.8	0.0	-15.9	-48.1	NA
6.5x55mm Light Mag.	129	2750	2549	2355	2171	1994	2166	1860	1589	1350	1139	+2.0	0.0	-8.2	-23.9	NA
6.5x55mm Swe.	140	2550	NA	NA	NA	NA	2020	NA	NA	NA	NA	0.0	0.0	0.0	0.0	$18
6.5x55mm Swe.*	139/140	2850	2640	2440	2250	2070	2525	2170	1855	1575	1330	+2.5	+1.6	-5.4	-18.9	$18
6.5x55mm Swe.	156	2650	2370	2110	1870	1650	2425	1950	1550	1215	945	+2.5	0.0	-10.3	-30.6	NA
260 Remington	125	2875	2669	2473	2285	2105	2294	1977	1697	1449	1230	1.71	0.0	-7.4	-21.4	NA
260 Remington	140	2750	2544	2347	2158	1979	2351	2011	1712	1448	1217	+2.2	0.0	-8.6	-24.6	NA
6.5-284 Norma	142	3025	2890	2758	2631	2507	2886	2634	2400	2183	1982	1.13	0.0	-5.7	-16.4	NA
6.71 (264) Phantom	120	3150	2929	2718	2517	2325	2645	2286	1969	1698	1440	+1.3	0.0	-6.0	-17.5	NA
6.5 Rem. Mag.	120	3210	2905	2621	2353	2102	2745	2248	1830	1475	1177	+2.5	+1.7	-4.1	-16.3	Disc.
264 Win. Mag.	140	3030	2782	2548	2326	2114	2854	2406	2018	1682	1389	+2.5	+1.4	-5.1	-18.0	$24
6.71 (264) Blackbird	140	3480	3261	3053	2855	2665	3766	3307	2899	2534	2208	+2.4	+3.1	0.0	-7.4	NA
6.8mm Rem.	115	2775	2472	2190	1926	1683	1966	1561	1224	947	723	+2.1	0.0	-3.7	-9.4	NA
27																
270 Winchester	100	3430	3021	2649	2305	1988	2612	2027	1557	1179	877	+2.0	+1.0	-4.9	-17.5	$17
270 Win. (Rem.)	115	2710	2482	2265	2059	NA	1875	1485	1161	896	NA	0.0	4.8	-17.3	0.0	NA
270 Winchester	130	3060	2776	2510	2259	2022	2702	2225	1818	1472	1180	+2.5	+1.4	-5.3	-18.2	$17
270 Win. Supreme	130	3150	2881	2628	2388	2161	2865	2396	1993	1646	1348	1.3	0.0	-6.4	-18.9	NA
270 Winchester	135	3000	2780	2570	2369	2178	2697	2315	1979	1682	1421	+2.5	+1.4	-6.0	-17.6	$23
270 Winchester*	140	2940	2700	2480	2260	2060	2685	2270	1905	1590	1315	+2.5	+1.8	-4.6	-17.9	$20
270 Win. Light Magnum	130	3215	2998	2790	2590	2400	2983	2594	2246	1936	1662	1.21	0.0	-5.83	-17.0	NA
270 Winchester*	150	2850	2585	2336	2100	1879	2705	2226	1817	1468	1175	+2.5	+1.2	-6.5	-22.0	$17
270 Win. Supreme	150	2930	2693	2468	2254	2051	2860	2416	2030	1693	1402	1.7	0.0	-7.4	-21.6	NA
270 WSM	130	3275	3041	2820	2609	2408	3096	2669	2295	1564	1673	1.1	0.0	-5.5	-16.1	NA
270 WSM	140	3125	2865	2619	2386	2165	3035	2559	2132	1769	1457	1.4	0.0	-6.5	-19.0	NA
270 WSM	150	3120	2923	2734	2554	2380	3242	2845	2490	2172	1886	1.3	0.0	-5.9	-17.2	NA
270 Wea. Mag.	100	3760	3380	3033	2712	2412	3139	2537	2042	1633	1292	+2.0	+2.4	-1.2	-10.1	$32
270 Wea. Mag.	130	3375	3119	2878	2649	2432	3287	2808	2390	2026	1707	+2.5	-2.9	-0.9	-9.9	$32
270 Wea. Mag.*	150	3245	3036	2837	2647	2465	3507	3070	2681	2334	2023	+2.5	+2.6	-1.8	-11.4	$47
7mm																
7mm BR	140	2216	2012	1821	1643	1481	1525	1259	1031	839	681	+2.0	-3.7	-20.0	0.0	$23
7mm Mauser*	139/140	2660	2435	2221	2018	1827	2199	1843	1533	1266	1037	+2.5	0.0	-9.6	-27.7	$17
7mm Mauser	145	2690	2442	2206	1985	1777	2334	1920	1568	1268	1017	+2.5	+0.1	-9.6	-28.3	$18
7mm Mauser	154	2690	2490	2300	2120	1940	2475	2120	1810	1530	1285	+2.5	+0.8	-7.5	-23.5	$17
7mm Mauser	175	2440	2137	1857	1603	1382	2313	1774	1340	998	742	+2.5	-1.7	-16.1	0.0	$17
7x57 Light Mag.	139	2970	2730	2503	2287	2082	2722	2301	1933	1614	1337	+1.6	0.0	-7.2	-21.0	NA
7x30 Waters	120	2700	2300	1930	1600	1330	1940	1405	990	685	470	+2.5	-0.2	-12.3	0.0	$18
7mm-08 Rem.	120	3000	2725	2467	2223	1992	2398	1979	1621	1316	1058	+2.0	0.0	-7.6	-22.3	$18
7mm-08 Rem.*	140	2860	2625	2402	2189	1988	2542	2142	1793	1490	1228	+2.5	+0.8	-6.9	-21.9	$18
7mm-08 Rem.	154	2715	2510	2315	2128	1950	2520	2155	1832	1548	1300	+2.5	+1.0	-7.0	-22.7	$23
7mm-08 Light Mag.	139	3000	2790	2590	2399	2216	2777	2403	2071	1776	1515	+1.5	0.0	-6.7	-19.4	NA
7x64mm Bren.	140				Not Yet Announced											$17
7x64mm Bren.	154	2820	2610	2420	2230	2050	2720	2335	1995	1695	1430	+2.5	+1.4	-5.7	-19.9	NA
7x64mm Bren.*	160	2850	2669	2495	2327	2166	2885	2530	2211	1924	1667	+2.5	+1.6	-4.8	-17.8	$24
7x64mm Bren.	175				Not Yet Announced											$17
284 Winchester	150	2860	2595	2344	2108	1886	2724	2243	1830	1480	1185	+2.5	+0.8	-7.3	-23.2	$24
280 Remington	120	3150	2866	2599	2348	2110	2643	2188	1800	1468	1186	+2.0	+0.6	-6.0	-17.9	$17
280 Remington	140	3000	2758	2528	2309	2102	2797	2363	1986	1657	1373	+2.5	+1.4	-5.2	-18.3	$17
280 Remington*	150	2890	2624	2373	2135	1912	2781	2293	1875	1518	1217	+2.5	+0.8	-7.1	-22.6	$17

Many manufacturers do not supply suggested retail prices. Others did not get their pricing to us before press time. All pricing can vary dependent on the exact brand and style of ammo selected and/or the retail outlet from which you make your purchase. Pricing has been rounded to the nearest dollar and represents our best estimate of average pricing. An * after the cartridge means these loads are available with Nosler Partition or Swift A-Frame bullets. Listed pricing may or may not reflect this bullet type. ** = these are packed 50 to box, all others are 20 to box. Wea. Mag.= Weatherby Magnum. Spfd. = Springfield. A-Sq. = A-Square. N.E.=Nitro Express.

Cartridge	Bullet Wgt. Grs.	VELOCITY (fps)					ENERGY (ft. lbs.)					TRAJ. (in.)				Est. Price/ box
		Muzzle	100 yds.	200 yds.	300 yds.	400 yds.	Muzzle	100 yds.	200 yds.	300 yds.	400 yds.	100 yds.	200 yds.	300 yds.	400 yds.	
280 Remington	160	2840	2637	2442	2556	2078	2866	2471	2120	1809	1535	+2.5	+0.8	-6.7	-21.0	$20
280 Remington	165	2820	2510	2220	1950	1701	2913	2308	1805	1393	1060	+2.5	+0.4	-8.8	-26.5	$17
7x61mm S&H Sup.	154	3060	2720	2400	2100	1820	3200	2520	1965	1505	1135	+2.5	+1.8	-5.0	-19.8	NA
7mm Dakota	160	3200	3001	2811	2630	2455	3637	3200	2808	2456	2140	+2.1	+1.9	-2.8	-12.5	NA
7mm Rem. Mag. (Rem.)	140	2710	2482	2265	2059	NA	2283	1915	1595	1318	NA	0.0	-4.5	-1.57	0.0	NA
7mm Rem. Mag.*	139/140	3150	2930	2710	2510	2320	3085	2660	2290	1960	1670	+2.5	+2.4	-2.4	-12.7	$21
7mm Rem. Hvy Mag	139	3250	3044	2847	2657	2475	3259	2860	2501	2178	1890	1.1	0.0	-5.5	-16.2	NA
7mm Rem. Mag.	150/154	3110	2830	2568	2320	2085	3221	2667	2196	1792	1448	+2.5	+1.6	-4.6	-16.5	$21
7mm Rem. Mag.*	160/162	2950	2730	2520	2320	2120	3090	2650	2250	1910	1600	+2.5	+1.8	-4.4	-17.8	$34
7mm Rem. Mag.	165	2900	2699	2507	2324	2147	3081	2669	2303	1978	1689	+2.5	+1.2	-5.9	-19.0	$28
7mm Rem Mag.	175	2860	2645	2440	2244	2057	3178	2718	2313	1956	1644	+2.5	+1.0	-6.5	-20.7	$21
7mm Rem. SA ULTRA MAG	140	3175	2934	2707	2490	2283	3033	2676	2277	1927	1620	1.3	0.0	-6	-17.7	NA
7mm Rem. SA ULTRA MAG	150	3110	2828	2563	2313	2077	3221	2663	2188	1782	1437	2.5	2.1	-3.6	-15.8	NA
7mm Rem. SA ULTRA MAG	160	2960	2762	2572	2390	2215	3112	2709	2350	2029	1743	2.6	2.2	-3.6	-15.4	NA
7mm Rem. WSM	140	3225	3008	2801	2603	2414	3233	2812	2438	2106	1812	1.2	0.0	-5.6	-16.4	NA
7mm Rem. WSM	160	2990	2744	2512	2081	1883	3176	2675	2241	1864	1538	1.6	0.0	-7.1	-20.8	NA
7mm Wea. Mag.	140	3225	2970	2729	2501	2283	3233	2741	2315	1943	1621	+2.5	+2.0	-3.2	-14.0	$35
7mm Wea. Mag.	154	3260	3023	2799	2586	2382	3539	3044	2609	2227	1890	+2.5	+2.8	-1.5	-10.8	$32
7mm Wea. Mag.*	160	3200	3004	2816	2637	2464	3637	3205	2817	2469	2156	+2.5	+2.7	-1.5	-10.6	$47
7mm Wea. Mag.	165	2950	2747	2553	2367	2189	3188	2765	2388	2053	1756	+2.5	+1.8	-4.2	-16.4	$43
7mm Wea. Mag.	175	2910	2693	2486	2288	2098	3293	2818	2401	2033	1711	+2.5	+1.2	-5.9	-19.4	$35
7.21(.284) Tomahawk	140	3300	3118	2943	2774	2612	3386	3022	2693	2393	2122	2.3	3.20	0.0	-7.7	NA
7mm STW	140	3325	3064	2818	2585	2364	3436	2918	2468	2077	1737	+2.3	+1.8	-3.0	-13.1	NA
7mm STW Supreme	160	3150	2894	2652	2422	2204	3526	2976	2499	2085	1727	1.3	0.0	-6.3	-18.5	NA
7mm Rem. Ultra Mag.	140	3425	3184	2956	2740	2534	3646	3151	2715	2333	1995	1.7	1.60	-2.6	-11.4	NA
7mm Firehawk	140	3625	3373	3135	2909	2695	4084	3536	3054	2631	2258	+2.2	+2.9	0.0	-7.03	NA
30																
7.21(.284) Firebird	140	3750	3522	3306	3101	2905	4372	3857	3399	2990	2625	1.6	2.4	0.0	-6.0	NA
30 Carbine	110	1990	1567	1236	1035	923	977	600	373	262	208	0.0	-13.5	0.0	0.0	$28**
303 Savage	190	1890	1612	1327	1183	1055	1507	1096	794	591	469	+2.5	-7.6	0.0	0.0	$24
30 Remington	170	2120	1822	1555	1328	1153	1696	1253	913	666	502	+2.5	-4.7	-26.3	0.0	$20
7.62x39mm Rus.	123/125	2300	2030	1780	1550	1350	1445	1125	860	655	500	+2.5	-2.0	-17.5	0.0	$13
30-30 Win.	55	3400	2693	2085	1570	1187	1412	886	521	301	172	+2.0	0.0	-10.2	-35.0	$18
30-30 Win.	125	2570	2090	1660	1320	1080	1830	1210	770	480	320	-2.0	-2.6	-19.9	0.0	$13
30-30 Win.	150	2390	2040	1723	1447	1225	1902	1386	989	697	499	0.0	-7.5	-27.0	-63.0	NA
30-30 Win. Supreme	150	2480	2095	1747	1446	1209	2049	1462	1017	697	487	0.0	-6.5	-24.5	0.0	NA
30-30 Win.	160	2300	1997	1719	1473	1268	1879	1416	1050	771	571	+2.5	-2.9	-20.2	0.0	$18
30-30 Win. Lever Evolution	160	2400	2150	1916	1699	NA	2046	1643	1304	1025	NA	3.00	0.20	-12.1	NA	NA
30-30 PMC Cowboy	170	1300	1198	1121			638	474				0.0	-27.0	0.0	0.0	NA
30-30 Win.*	170	2200	1895	1619	1381	1191	1827	1355	989	720	535	+2.5	-5.8	-23.6	0.0	$13
300 Savage	150	2630	2354	2094	1853	1631	2303	1845	1462	1143	886	+2.5	-0.4	-10.1	-30.7	$17
300 Savage	180	2350	2137	1935	1754	1570	2207	1825	1496	1217	985	+2.5	-1.6	-15.2	0.0	$17
30-40 Krag	180	2430	2213	2007	1813	1632	2360	1957	1610	1314	1064	+2.5	-1.4	-13.8	0.0	$18
7.65x53mm Arg.	180	2590	2390	2200	2010	1830	2685	2280	1925	1615	1345	+2.5	0.0	-27.6	0.0	NA
7.5x53mm Argentine	150	2785	2519	2269	2032	1814	2583	2113	1714	1376	1096	+2.0	0.0	-8.8	-25.5	NA
308 Marlin Express	160	2660	2430	2226	2026	1836	2513	2111	1761	1457	1197	3.0	1.7	-6.7	-23.5	NA
307 Winchester	150	2760	2321	1924	1575	1289	2530	1795	1233	826	554	+2.5	-1.5	-13.6	0.0	Disc.
307 Winchester	180	2510	2179	1874	1599	1362	2519	1898	1404	1022	742	+2.5	-1.6	-15.6	0.0	$20
7.5x55 Swiss	180	2650	2450	2250	2060	1880	2805	2390	2020	1700	1415	+2.5	+0.6	-8.1	-24.9	NA
7.5x55mm Swiss	165	2720	2515	2319	2132	1954	2710	2317	1970	1665	1398	+2.0	0.0	-8.5	-24.6	NA
308 Winchester	55	3770	3215	2726	2286	1888	1735	1262	907	638	435	-2.0	+1.4	-3.8	-15.8	$22
308 Winchester	150	2820	2533	2263	2009	1774	2648	2137	1705	1344	1048	+2.5	+0.4	-8.5	-26.1	$17
308 Winchester	165	2700	2440	2194	1963	1748	2670	2180	1763	1411	1199	+2.5	0.0	-9.7	-28.5	$20
308 Winchester	168	2680	2493	2314	2143	1979	2678	2318	1998	1713	1460	+2.5	0.0	-8.9	-25.3	$18
308 Win. (Fed.)	170	2000	1740	1510	NA	NA	1510	1145	860	NA	NA	0.0	0.0	0.0	0.0	NA
308 Winchester	178	2620	2415	2220	2034	1857	2713	2306	1948	1635	1363	+2.5	0.0	-9.6	-27.6	$23
308 Winchester*	180	2620	2393	2178	1974	1782	2743	2288	1896	1557	1269	+2.5	-0.2	-10.2	-28.5	$17
308 Light Mag.*	150	2980	2703	2442	2195	1964	2959	2433	1986	1606	1285	+1.6	0.0	-7.5	-22.2	NA
308 Light Mag.	165	2870	2658	2456	2263	2078	3019	2589	2211	1877	1583	+1.7	0.0	-7.5	-21.8	NA
308 High Energy	165	2870	2600	2350	2120	1890	3020	2485	2030	1640	1310	+1.8	0.0	-8.2	-24.0	NA
308 Light Mag.	168	2870	2658	2456	2263	2078	3019	2589	2211	1877	1583	+1.7	0.0	-7.5	-21.8	NA
308 High Energy	180	2740	2550	2370	2200	2030	3000	2600	2245	1925	1645	+1.9	0.0	-8.2	-23.5	NA
30-06 Spfd.	55	4080	3485	2965	2502	2083	2033	1483	1074	764	530	+2.0	+1.9	-2.1	-11.7	$22
30-06 Spfd. (Rem.)	125	2660	2335	2034	1757	NA	1964	1513	1148	856	NA	0.0	-5.2	-18.9	0.0	NA
30-06 Spfd.	125	3140	2780	2447	2138	1853	2736	2145	1662	1279	953	+2.0	+1.0	-6.2	-21.0	$17
30-06 Spfd.	150	2910	2617	2342	2083	1853	2820	2281	1827	1445	1135	+2.5	+0.8	-7.2	-23.4	$17
30-06 Spfd.	152	2910	2654	2413	2184	1968	2858	2378	1965	1610	1307	+2.5	+1.0	-6.6	-21.3	$23
30-06 Spfd.*	165	2800	2534	2283	2047	1825	2872	2352	1909	1534	1220	+2.5	+0.4	-8.4	-25.5	$17
30-06 Spfd.	168	2710	2522	2346	2169	2003	2739	2372	2045	1754	1497	+2.5	+0.4	-8.0	-23.5	$18
30-06 Spfd. (Fed.)	170	2000	1740	1510	NA	NA	1510	1145	860	NA	NA	0.0	0.0	0.0	0.0	NA

Many manufacturers do not supply suggested retail prices. Others did not get their pricing to us before press time. All pricing can vary dependent on the exact brand and style of ammo selected and/or the retail outlet from which you make your purchase. Pricing has been rounded to the nearest dollar and represents our best estimate of average pricing.
An * after the cartridge means these loads are available with Nosler Partition or Swift A-Frame bullets. Listed pricing may or may not reflect this bullet type.
** = these are packed 50 to box, all others are 20 to box. Wea. Mag.= Weatherby Magnum. Spfd. = Springfield. A-Sq. = A-Square. N.E.=Nitro Express.

Cartridge	Bullet Wgt. Grs.	VELOCITY (fps)					ENERGY (ft. lbs.)					TRAJ. (in.)				Est. Price/ box
		Muzzle	100 yds.	200 yds.	300 yds.	400 yds.	Muzzle	100 yds.	200 yds.	300 yds.	400 yds.	100 yds.	200 yds.	300 yds.	400 yds.	
30 -06 Spfd.	178	2720	2511	2311	2121	1939	2924	2491	2111	1777	1486	+2.5	+0.4	-8.2	-24.6	$23
30 -06 Spfd.*	180	2700	2469	2250	2042	1846	2913	2436	2023	1666	1362	-2.5	0.0	-9.3	-27.0	$17
30 -06 Spfd.	220	2410	2130	1870	1632	1422	2837	2216	1708	1301	988	+2.5	-1.7	-18.0	0.0	$17
30 Mag.																
30-06 Light Mag.	150	3100	2815	2548	2295	2058	3200	2639	2161	1755	1410	+1.4	0.0	-6.8	-20.3	NA
30-06 Light Mag.	180	2880	2676	2480	2293	2114	3316	2862	2459	2102	1786	+1.7	0.0	-7.3	-21.3	NA
30-06 High Energy	180	2880	2690	2500	2320	2150	3315	2880	2495	2150	1845	+1.7	0.0	-7.2	-21.0	NA
30 T/C	150	3000	2772	2555	2348	2151	2997	2558	2173	1836	1540	1.5	0.0	-6.9	-20.0	NA
30 T/C	165	2850	2644	2447	2258	2078	2975	2560	2193	1868	1582	1.7	0.0	-7.6	-22.0	NA
300 REM SA ULTRA MAG	150	3200	2901	2622	2359	2112	3410	2803	2290	1854	1485	1.3	0.0	-6.4	-19.1	NA
300 REM SA ULTRA MAG	165	3075	2792	2527	2276	2040	3464	2856	2339	1898	1525	1.5	0.0	-7	-20.7	NA
300 REM SA ULTRA MAG	180	2960	2761	2571	2389	2214	3501	3047	2642	2280	1959	2.6	2.2	-3.6	-15.4	NA
7.82 (308) Patriot	150	3250	2999	2762	2537	2323	3519	2997	2542	2145	1798	+1.2	0.0	-5.8	-16.9	NA
300 WSM	150	3300	3061	2834	2619	2414	3628	3121	2676	2285	1941	1.1	0.0	-5.4	-15.9	NA
300 WSM	180	2970	2741	2524	2317	2120	3526	3005	2547	2147	1797	1.6	0.0	-7.0	-20.5	NA
300 WSM	180	3010	2923	2734	2554	2380	3242	2845	2490	2172	1886	1.3	0	-5.9	-17.2	NA
308 Norma Mag.	180	3020	2820	2630	2440	2270	3645	3175	2755	2385	2050	+2.5	+2.0	-3.5	-14.8	NA
300 Dakota	200	3000	2824	2656	2493	2336	3996	3542	3131	2760	2423	+2.2	+1.5	-4.0	-15.2	NA
300 H&H Magnum*	180	2880	2640	2412	2196	1990	3315	2785	2325	1927	1583	+2.5	+0.8	-6.8	-21.7	$24
300 H&H Magnum	220	2550	2267	2002	1757	NA	3167	2510	1958	1508	NA	-2.5	-0.4	-12.0	0.0	NA
300 Win. Mag.	150	3290	2951	2636	2342	2068	3605	2900	2314	1827	1424	+2.5	+1.9	-3.8	-15.8	$22
300 Win. Mag.	165	3100	2877	2665	2462	2269	3522	3033	2603	2221	1897	+2.5	+2.4	-3.0	-16.9	$24
300 Win. Mag.	178	2900	2760	2568	2375	2191	3509	3030	2606	2230	1897	+2.5	+1.4	-5.0	-17.6	$29
300 Win. Mag.*	180	2960	2745	2540	2344	2157	3501	3011	2578	2196	1859	+2.5	+1.2	-5.5	-18.5	$22
300 W.M. High Energy	180	3100	2830	2580	2340	2110	3840	3205	2660	2190	1790	+1.4	0.0	-6.6	-19.7	NA
300 W.M. Light Mag.	180	3100	2879	2668	2467	2275	3840	3313	2845	2431	2068	+1.39	0.0	-6.45	-18.7	NA
300 Win. Mag.	190	2885	1691	2506	2327	2156	3511	3055	2648	2285	1961	+2.5	+1.2	-5.7	-19.0	$26
300 W.M. High Energy	200	2930	2740	2550	2370	2200	3810	3325	2885	2495	2145	+1.6	0.0	-6.9	-20.1	NA
300 Win. Mag.*	200	2825	2595	2376	2167	1970	3545	2991	2508	2086	1742	-2.5	+1.6	-4.7	-17.2	$36
300 Win. Mag.	220	2680	2448	2228	2020	1823	3508	2927	2424	1993	1623	+2.5	0.0	-9.5	-27.5	$23
300 Rem. Ultra Mag.	150	3450	3208	2980	2762	2556	3964	3427	2956	2541	2175	1.7	1.5	-2.6	-11.2	NA
300 Rem. Ultra Mag.	150	2910	2686	2473	2279	2077	2820	2403	2037	1716	1436	1.7	0.0	-7.4	-21.5	NA
300 Rem. Ultra Mag.	180	3250	3037	2834	2640	2454	4221	3686	3201	2786	2407	2.4	0.0	-3.0	-12.7	NA
300 Rem. Ultra Mag.	180	2960	2774	2505	2294	2093	3501	2971	2508	2103	1751	2.7	2.2	-3.8	-16.4	NA
300 Rem. Ultra Mag.	200	3032	2791	2562	2345	2138	4083	3459	2916	2442	2030	1.5	0.0	-6.8	-19.9	NA
300 Wea. Mag.	100	3900	3441	3038	2652	2305	3714	2891	2239	1717	1297	+2.0	+2.6	-0.6	-8.7	$32
300 Wea. Mag.	150	3600	3307	3033	2776	2533	4316	3642	3064	2566	2137	+2.5	+3.2	0.0	-8.1	$32
300 Wea. Mag.	165	3450	3210	3000	2792	2593	4360	3796	3297	2855	2464	+2.5	+3.2	0.0	-7.8	NA
300 Wea. Mag.	178	3120	2902	2695	2497	2308	3847	3329	2870	2464	2104	+2.5	-1.7	-3.6	-14.7	$43
300 Wea. Mag.	180	3330	3110	2910	2710	2520	4430	3875	3375	2935	2540	+1.0	0.0	-5.2	-15.1	NA
300 Wea. Mag.	190	3030	2830	2638	2455	2279	3873	3378	2936	2542	2190	+2.5	+1.6	-4.3	-16.0	$38
300 Wea. Mag.	220	2850	2541	2283	1964	1736	3967	3155	2480	1922	1471	+2.5	+0.4	-8.5	-26.4	$35
300 Warbird	180	3400	3180	2971	2772	2582	4620	4042	3528	3071	2664	+2.59	+3.25	0.0	-7.95	NA
300 Pegasus	180	3500	3319	3145	2978	2817	4896	4401	3953	3544	3172	+2.28	+2.89	0.0	-6.79	NA
31																
32-20 Win.	100	1210	1021	913	834	769	325	231	185	154	131	0.0	-32.3	0.0	0.0	$23**
303 British	150	2685	2441	2210	1992	1787	2401	1984	1627	1321	1064	+2.5	+0.6	-8.4	-26.2	$18
303 British	180	2460	2124	1817	1542	1311	2418	1803	1319	950	687	+2.5	-1.8	-16.8	0.0	$18
303 Light Mag.	150	2830	2570	2325	2094	1884	2667	2199	1800	1461	1185	+2.0	0.0	-8.4	-24.6	NA
7.62x54mm Rus.	146	2950	2730	2520	2320	NA	2820	2415	2055	1740	NA	+2.5	+2.0	-4.4	-17.7	NA
7.62x54mm Rus.	180	2580	2370	2180	2000	1820	2650	2250	1900	1590	1100	+2.5	0.0	-9.8	-28.5	NA
7.7x58mm Jap.	150	2640	2399	2170	1954	1752	2321	1916	1568	1271	1022	+2.3	0.0	-9.7	-28.5	NA
7.7x58mm Jap.	180	2500	2300	2100	1920	1750	2490	2105	1770	1475	1225	+2.5	0.0	-10.4	-30.2	NA
8x56 R	205	2400	2188	1987	1797	1621	2621	2178	1796	1470	1196	+2.9	0.0	-11.7	-34.3	NA
8mm																
8x57mm JS Mau.	165	2850	2520	2210	1930	1670	2965	2330	1795	1360	1015	+2.5	+1.0	-7.7	0.0	NA
32 Win. Special	170	2250	1921	1626	1372	1175	1911	1393	998	710	521	+2.5	-3.5	-22.9	0.0	$14
8mm Mauser	170	2360	1969	1622	1333	1123	2102	1464	993	671	476	+2.5	-3.1	-22.2	0.0	$18
325 WSM	180	3060	2841	2632	2432	2242	3743	3226	2769	2365	2009	+1.4	0.0	-6.4	-18.7	NA
325 WSM	200	2950	2753	2565	2384	2210	3866	3367	2922	2524	2170	+1.5	0.0	-6.8	-19.8	NA
325 WSM	220	2840	2605	2382	2169	1968	3941	3316	2772	2300	1893	+1.8	0.0	-8.0	-23.3	NA
8mm Rem. Mag.	185	3080	2761	2464	2186	1927	3896	3131	2494	1963	1525	+2.5	+1.4	-5.5	-19.7	$30
8mm Rem. Mag.	220	2830	2581	2346	2123	1913	3912	3254	2688	2201	1787	+2.5	+0.6	-7.6	-23.5	Disc.
33																
338 Federal	180	2830	2590	2350	2130	1930	3200	2670	2215	1820	1480	1.80	0.00	-8.2	-23.9	NA
338 Federal	185	2750	2550	2350	2160	1980	3105	2660	2265	1920	1615	1.90	0.00	-8.3	-24.1	NA
338 Federal	210	2630	2410	2200	2010	1820	3225	2710	2265	1880	1545	2.30	0.00	-9.4	-27.3	NA
338-06	200	2750	2553	2364	2184	2011	3358	2894	2482	2118	1796	+1.9	0.0	-8.22	-23.6	NA
330 Dakota	250	2900	2719	2545	2378	2217	4668	4103	3595	3138	2727	+2.3	+1.3	-5.0	-17.5	NA

Many manufacturers do not supply suggested retail prices. Others did not get their pricing to us before press time. All pricing can vary dependent on the exact brand and style of ammo selected and/or the retail outlet from which you make your purchase. Pricing has been rounded to the nearest dollar and represents our best estimate of average pricing. An * after the cartridge means these loads are available with Nosler Partition or Swift A-Frame bullets. Listed pricing may or may not reflect this bullet type.
** = these are packed 50 to box, all others are 20 to box. Wea. Mag.= Weatherby Magnum. Spfd. = Springfield. A-Sq. = A-Square. N.E.=Nitro Express.

Cartridge	Bullet Wgt. Grs.	VELOCITY (fps)					ENERGY (ft. lbs.)					TRAJ. (in.)				Est. Price/ box
		Muzzle	100 yds.	200 yds.	300 yds.	400 yds.	Muzzle	100 yds.	200 yds.	300 yds.	400 yds.	100 yds.	200 yds.	300 yds.	400 yds.	
338 Lapua	250	2963	2795	2640	2493	NA	4842	4341	3881	3458	NA	+1.9	0.0	-7.9	0.0	NA
338 Win. Mag.	200	2960	2658	2375	2110	1862	3890	3137	2505	1977	1539	+2.5	+1.0	-6.7	-22.3	$27
338 Win. Mag.*	210	2830	2590	2370	2150	1940	3735	3130	2610	2155	1760	+2.5	+1.4	-6.0	-20.9	$33
338 Win. Mag.*	225	2785	2517	2266	2029	1808	3871	3165	2565	2057	1633	+2.5	+0.4	-8.5	-25.9	$27
338 W.M. Heavy Mag.	225	2920	2678	2449	2232	2027	4259	3583	2996	2489	2053	+1.75	0.0	-7.65	-22.0	NA
338 W.M. High Energy	225	2940	2690	2450	2230	2010	4320	3610	3000	2475	2025	+1.7	0.0	-7.5	-22.0	NA
338 Win. Mag.	230	2780	2573	2375	2186	2005	3948	3382	2881	2441	2054	+2.5	+1.2	-6.3	-21.0	$40
338 Win. Mag.*	250	2660	2456	2261	2075	1898	3927	3348	2837	2389	1999	+2.5	+0.2	-9.0	-26.2	$27
338 W.M. High Energy	250	2800	2610	2420	2250	2080	4350	3775	3260	2805	2395	+1.8	0.0	-7.8	-22.5	NA
338 Ultra Mag.	250	2860	2645	2440	2244	2057	4540	3882	3303	2794	2347	1.7	0.0	-7.6	-22.1	NA
8.59(.338) Galaxy	200	3100	2899	2707	2524	2347	4269	3734	3256	2829	2446	3	3.80	0.0	-9.3	NA
340 Wea. Mag.*	210	3250	2991	2746	2515	2295	4924	4170	3516	2948	2455	+2.5	+1.9	-1.8	-11.8	$56
340 Wea. Mag.*	250	3000	2806	2621	2443	2272	4995	4371	3812	3311	2864	+2.5	+2.0	-3.5	-14.8	$56
338 A-Square	250	3120	2799	2500	2220	1958	5403	4348	3469	2736	2128	+2.5	+2.7	-1.5	-10.5	NA
338-378 Wea. Mag.	225	3180	2974	2778	2591	2410	5052	4420	3856	3353	2902	3.1	3.80	0.0	-8.9	NA
338 Titan	225	3230	3010	2800	2600	2409	5211	4524	3916	3377	2898	+3.07	+3.80	0.0	-8.95	NA
338 Excalibur	200	3600	3361	3134	2920	2715	5755	5015	4363	3785	3274	+2.23	+2.87	0.0	-6.99	NA
338 Excalibur	250	3250	2922	2618	2333	2066	5863	4740	3804	3021	2370	+1.3	0.0	-6.35	-19.2	NA
34, 35																
348 Winchester	200	2520	2215	1931	1672	1443	2820	2178	1656	1241	925	+2.5	-1.4	-14.7	0.0	$42
357 Magnum	158	1830	1427	1138	980	883	1175	715	454	337	274	0.0	-16.2	-33.1	0.0	$25**
35 Remington	150	2300	1874	1506	1218	1039	1762	1169	755	494	359	+2.5	-4.1	-26.3	0.0	$16
35 Remington	200	2080	1698	1376	1140	1001	1921	1280	841	577	445	+2.5	-6.3	-17.1	-33.6	$16
35 Rem. Lever Evolution	200	2225	1963	1721	1503	NA	2198	1711	1315	1003	NA	3.00	-1.30	-17.5	NA	NA
356 Winchester	200	2460	2114	1797	1517	1284	2688	1985	1434	1022	732	+2.5	-1.8	-15.1	0.0	$31
356 Winchester	250	2160	1911	1682	1476	1299	2591	2028	1571	1210	937	+2.5	-3.7	-22.2	0.0	$31
358 Winchester	200	2490	2171	1876	1619	1379	2753	2093	1563	1151	844	+2.5	-1.6	-15.6	0.0	$31
358 STA	275	2850	2562	2292	2039	NA	4958	4009	3208	2539	NA	+1.9	0.0	-8.6	0.0	NA
350 Rem. Mag.	200	2710	2410	2130	1870	1631	3261	2579	2014	1553	1181	+2.5	-0.2	-10.0	-30.1	$33
35 Whelen	200	2675	2378	2100	1842	1606	3177	2510	1958	1506	1145	+2.5	-0.2	-10.3	-31.1	$20
35 Whelen	225	2500	2300	2110	1930	1770	3120	2650	2235	1870	1560	+2.6	0.0	-10.2	-29.9	NA
35 Whelen	250	2400	2197	2005	1823	1652	3197	2680	2230	1844	1515	+2.5	-1.2	-13.7	0.0	$20
358 Norma Mag.	250	2800	2510	2230	1970	1730	4350	3480	2750	2145	1655	+2.5	+1.0	-7.6	-25.2	NA
358 STA	275	2850	2562	229*2	2039	1764	4959	4009	3208	2539	1899	+1.9	0.0	-8.58	-26.1	NA
9.3mm																
9.3x57mm Mau.	286	2070	1810	1590	1390	1110	2710	2090	1600	1220	955	+2.5	-2.6	-22.5	0.0	NA
9.3x62mm Mau.	286	2360	2089	1844	1623	NA	3538	2771	2157	1670	1260	+2.5	-1.6	-21.0	0.0	NA
9.3x64mm	286	2700	2505	2318	2139	1968	4629	3984	3411	2906	2460	+2.5	+2.7	-4.5	-19.2	NA
9.3x74Rmm	286	2360	2136	1924	1727	1545	3536	2896	2351	1893	1516	0.0	-6.1	-21.7	-49.0	NA
375																
38-55 Win.	255	1320	1190	1091	1018	963	987	802	674	587	525	0.0	-23.4	0.0	0.0	$25
375 Winchester	200	2200	1841	1526	1268	1089	2150	1506	1034	714	527	+2.5	-4.0	-26.2	0.0	$27
375 Winchester	250	1900	1647	1424	1239	1103	2005	1506	1126	852	676	+2.5	-6.9	-33.3	0.0	$27
376 Steyr	225	2600	2331	2078	1842	1625	3377	2714	2157	1694	1319	2.5	0.0	-10.6	-31.4	NA
376 Steyr	270	2600	2372	2156	1951	1759	4052	3373	2787	2283	1855	2.3	0.0	-9.9	-28.9	NA
375 Dakota	300	2600	2316	2051	1804	1579	4502	3573	2800	2167	1661	+2.4	0.0	-11.0	-32.7	NA
375 N.E. 2-1/2"	270	2000	1740	1507	1310	NA	2398	1815	1362	1026	NA	+2.5	-6.0	-30.0	0.0	NA
375 Flanged	300	2450	2150	1886	1640	NA	3998	3102	2369	1790	NA	+2.5	-2.4	-17.0	0.0	NA
375 Ruger	270	2840	2600	2372	2156	1951	4835	4052	3373	2786	2283	1.8	0.0	-8.0	-23.6	NA
375 Ruger	300	2660	2344	2050	1780	1536	4713	3660	2800	2110	1572	2.4	0.0	-10.8	-32.6	NA
375 H&H Magnum	250	2670	2450	2240	2040	1850	3955	3335	2790	2315	1905	+2.5	-0.4	-10.2	-28.4	NA
375 H&H Magnum	270	2690	2420	2166	1928	1707	4337	3510	2812	2228	1747	+2.5	0.0	-10.0	-29.4	$28
375 H&H Magnum*	300	2530	2245	1979	1733	1512	4263	3357	2608	2001	1523	+2.5	-1.0	-10.5	-33.6	$28
375 H&H Hvy. Mag.	270	2870	2628	2399	2182	1976	4937	4141	3451	2150	1845	+1.7	0.0	-7.2	-21.0	NA
375 H&H Hvy. Mag.	300	2705	2386	2090	1816	1568	4873	3793	2908	2195	1637	+2.3	0.0	-10.4	-31.4	NA
375 Rem. Ultra Mag.	270	2900	2558	2241	1947	1678	5041	3922	3010	2272	1689	1.9	2.7	-8.9	-27.0	NA
375 Rem. Ultra Mag.	300	2760	2505	2263	2035	1822	5073	4178	3412	2759	2210	2.0	0.0	-8.8	-26.1	NA
375 Wea. Mag.	300	2700	2420	2157	1911	1685	4856	3901	3100	2432	1891	+2.5	-.04	-10.7	0.0	NA
378 Wea. Mag.	270	3180	2976	2781	2594	2415	6062	5308	4635	4034	3495	+2.5	+2.6	-1.8	-11.3	$71
378 Wea. Mag.	300	2929	2576	2252	1952	1680	5698	4419	3379	2538	1881	+2.5	+1.2	-7.0	-24.5	$77
375 A-Square	300	2920	2626	2351	2093	1850	5679	4594	3681	2917	2281	+2.5	+1.4	-6.0	-21.0	NA
38-40 Win.	180	1160	999	901	827	764	538	399	324	273	233	0.0	-33.9	0.0	0.0	$42**
40, 41																
400 A-Square DPM	400	2400	2146	1909	1689	NA	5116	2092	3236	2533	NA	2.98	0.00	-10.0	NA	NA
400 A-Square DPM	170	2980	2463	2001	1598	NA	3352	2289	1512	964	NA	2.16	0.00	-11.1	NA	NA
408 CheyTac	419	2850	2752	2657	2562	2470	7551	7048	6565	6108	5675	-1.02	0.00	1.9	4.2	NA
405 Win.	300	2200	1851	1545	1296		3224	2282	1589	1119		4.6	0.0	-19.5	0.0	NA
450/400-3"	400	2050	1815	1595	1402	NA	3732	2924	2259	1746	NA	0.0	NA	-33.4	NA	NA
416 Dakota	400	2450	2294	2143	1998	1859	5330	4671	4077	3544	3068	+2.5	-0.2	-10.5	-29.4	NA

Many manufacturers do not supply suggested retail prices. Others did not get their pricing to us before press time. All pricing can vary dependent on the exact brand and style of ammo selected and/or the retail outlet from which you make your purchase. Pricing has been rounded to the nearest dollar and represents our best estimate of average pricing. An * after the cartridge means these loads are available with Nosler Partition or Swift A-Frame bullets. Listed pricing may or may not reflect this bullet type.
** = these are packed 50 to box, all others are 20 to box. Wea. Mag.= Weatherby Magnum. Spfd. = Springfield. A-Sq. = A-Square. N.E.=Nitro Express.

Cartridge	Bullet Wgt. Grs.	VELOCITY (fps)					ENERGY (ft. lbs.)					TRAJ. (in.)				Est. Price/ box
		Muzzle	100 yds.	200 yds.	300 yds.	400 yds.	Muzzle	100 yds.	200 yds.	300 yds.	400 yds.	100 yds.	200 yds.	300 yds.	400 yds.	
416 Taylor	400	2350	2117	1896	1693	NA	4905	3980	3194	2547	NA	+2.5	-1.2	15.0	0.0	NA
416 Hoffman	400	2380	2145	1923	1718	1529	5031	4087	3285	2620	2077	+2.5	-1.0	-14.1	0.0	NA
416 Rigby	350	2600	2449	2303	2162	2026	5253	4661	4122	3632	3189	+2.5	-1.8	-10.2	-26.0	NA
416 Rigby	400	2370	2210	2050	1900	NA	4990	4315	3720	3185	NA	+2.5	-0.7	-12.1	0.0	NA
416 Rigby	410	2370	2110	1870	1640	NA	5115	4050	3165	2455	NA	+2.5	-2.4	-17.3	0.0	$110
416 Rem. Mag.*	350	2520	2270	2034	1814	1611	4935	4004	3216	2557	2017	+2.5	-0.8	-12.6	-35.0	$82
416 Rem. Mag.*	400	2400	2175	1962	1763	1579	5115	4201	3419	2760	2214	+2.5	-1.5	-14.6	0.0	$80
416 Wea. Mag.*	400	2700	2397	2115	1852	1613	6474	5104	3971	3047	2310	+2.5	0.0	-10.1	-30.4	$96
10.57 (416) Meteor	400	2730	2532	2342	2161	1987	6621	5695	4874	4147	3508	+1.9	0.0	-8.3	-24.0	NA
404 Jeffrey	400	2150	1924	1716	1525	NA	4105	3289	2614	2064	NA	+2.5	-4.0	-22.1	0.0	NA
425, 44																
425 Express	400	2400	2160	1934	1725	NA	5115	4145	3322	2641	NA	+2.5	-1.0	-14.0	0.0	NA
44-40 Win.	200	1190	1006	900	822	756	629	449	360	300	254	0.0	-33.3	0.0	0.0	$36**
44 Rem. Mag.	210	1920	1477	1155	982	880	1719	1017	622	450	361	0.0	-17.6	0.0	0.0	$14
44 Rem. Mag.	240	1760	1380	1114	970	878	1650	1015	661	501	411	0.0	-17.6	0.0	0.0	$13
444 Marlin	240	2350	1815	1377	1087	941	2942	1753	1001	630	472	+2.5	-15.1	-31.0	0.0	$22
444 Marlin	265	2120	1733	1405	1160	1012	2644	1768	1162	791	603	+2.5	-6.0	-32.2	0.0	Disc.
444 Marlin Light Mag	265	2335	1913	1551	1266		3208	2153	1415	943		2.0	-4.90	-26.5	0.0	NA
444 Mar. Lever Evolution	265	2325	1971	1652	1380	NA	3180	2285	1606	1120	NA	3.00	-1.40	-18.6	NA	NA
45																
45-70 Govt.	300	1810	1497	1244	1073	969	2182	1492	1031	767	625	0.0	-14.8	0.0	0.0	$21
45-70 Govt. Supreme	300	1880	1558	1292	1103	988	2355	1616	1112	811	651	0.0	-12.9	-46.0	-105.0	NA
45-70 Lever Evolution	325	2050	1729	1450	1225	NA	3032	2158	1516	1083	NA	3.00	-4.10	-27.8	NA	NA
45-70 Govt. CorBon	350	1800	1526	1296			2519	1810	1307			0.0	-14.6	0.0	0.0	NA
45-70 Govt.	405	1330	1168	1055	977	918	1590	1227	1001	858	758	0.0	-24.6	0.0	0.0	$21
45-70 Govt. PMC Cowboy	405	1550	1193				1639	1280				0.0	-23.9	0.0	0.0	NA
45-70 Govt. Garrett	415	1850					3150					3.0	-7.0	0.0	0.0	NA
45-70 Govt. Garrett	530	1550	1343	1178	1062	982	2828	2123	1633	1327	1135	0.0	-17.8	0.0	0.0	NA
450 Marlin	350	2100	1774	1488	1254	1089	3427	2446	1720	1222	922	0.0	-9.7	-35.2	0.0	NA
450 Mar. Lever Evolution	325	2225	1887	1585	1331	NA	3572	2569	1813	1278	NA	3.00	-2.20	-21.3	NA	NA
458 Win. Magnum	350	2470	1990	1570	1250	1060	4740	3065	1915	1205	870	+2.5	-2.5	-21.6	0.0	$43
458 Win. Magnum	400	2380	2170	1960	1770	NA	5030	4165	3415	2785	NA	+2.5	-0.4	-13.4	0.0	$73
458 Win. Magnum	465	2220	1999	1791	1601	NA	5088	4127	3312	2646	NA	+2.5	-2.0	-17.7	0.0	NA
458 Win. Magnum	500	2040	1823	1623	1442	1237	4620	3689	2924	2308	1839	+2.5	-3.5	-22.0	0.0	$61
458 Win. Magnum	510	2040	1770	1527	1319	1157	4712	3547	2640	1970	1516	+2.5	-4.1	-25.0	0.0	$41
450 Dakota	500	2450	2235	2030	1838	1658	6663	5544	4576	3748	3051	+2.5	-0.6	-12.0	-33.8	NA
450 N.E. 3-1/4"	465	2190	1970	1765	1577	NA	4952	4009	3216	2567	NA	+2.5	-3.0	-20.0	0.0	NA
450 N.E. 3-1/4"	500	2150	1920	1708	1514	NA	5132	4093	3238	2544	NA	+2.5	-4.0	-22.9	0.0	NA
450 No. 2	465	2190	1970	1765	1577	NA	4952	4009	3216	2567	NA	+2.5	-3.0	-20.0	0.0	NA
450 No. 2	500	2150	1920	1708	1514	NA	5132	4093	3238	2544	NA	+2.5	-4.0	-22.9	0.0	NA
458 Lott	465	2380	2150	1932	1730	NA	5848	4773	3855	3091	NA	+2.5	-1.0	-14.0	0.0	NA
458 Lott	500	2300	2062	1838	1633	NA	5873	4719	3748	2960	NA	+2.5	-1.6	-16.4	0.0	NA
450 Ackley Mag.	465	2400	2169	1950	1747	NA	5947	4857	3927	3150	NA	+2.5	-1.0	-13.7	0.0	NA
450 Ackley Mag.	500	2320	2081	1855	1649	NA	5975	4085	3820	3018	NA	+2.5	-1.2	-15.0	0.0	NA
460 Short A-Sq.	500	2420	2175	1943	1729	NA	6501	5250	4193	3319	NA	+2.5	-0.8	-12.8	0.0	NA
460 Wea. Mag.	500	2700	2404	2128	1869	1635	8092	6416	5026	3878	2969	+2.5	+0.6	-8.9	-28.0	$72
475																
500/465 N.E.	480	2150	1917	1703	1507	NA	4926	3917	3089	2419	NA	+2.5	-4.0	-22.2	0.0	NA
470 Rigby	500	2150	1940	1740	1560	NA	5130	4170	3360	2695	NA	+2.5	-2.8	-19.4	0.0	NA
470 Nitro Ex.	480	2190	1954	1735	1536	NA	5111	4070	3210	2515	NA	+2.5	-3.5	-20.8	0.0	NA
470 Nitro Ex.	500	2150	1890	1650	1440	1270	5130	3965	3040	2310	1790	+2.5	-4.3	-24.0	0.0	$177
475 No. 2	500	2200	1955	1728	1522	NA	5375	4243	3316	2573	NA	+2.5	-3.2	-20.9	0.0	NA
50, 58																
505 Gibbs	525	2300	2063	1840	1637	NA	6166	4922	3948	3122	NA	+2.5	-3.0	-18.0	0.0	NA
500 N.E.-3"	570	2150	1928	1722	1533	NA	5850	4703	3752	2975	NA	+2.5	-3.7	-22.0	0.0	NA
500 N.E.-3"	600	2150	1927	1721	1531	NA	6158	4947	3944	3124	NA	+2.5	-4.0	-22.0	0.0	NA
495 A-Square	570	2350	2117	1896	1693	NA	5850	4703	3752	2975	NA	+2.5	-1.0	-14.5	0.0	NA
495 A-Square	600	2280	2050	1833	1635	NA	6925	5598	4478	3562	NA	+2.5	-2.0	-17.0	0.0	NA
500 A-Square	600	2380	2144	1922	1766	NA	7546	6126	4920	3922	NA	+2.5	-3.0	-17.0	0.0	NA
500 A-Square	707	2250	2040	1841	1567	NA	7947	6530	5318	4311	NA	+2.5	-2.0	-17.0	0.0	NA
500 BMG PMC	660	3080	2854	2639	2444	2248	13688		500 yd. zero			+3.1	+3.9	+4.7	+2.8	NA
577 Nitro Ex.	750	2050	1793	1562	1360	NA	6990	5356	4065	3079	NA	+2.5	-5.0	-26.0	0.0	NA
577 Tyrannosaur	750	2400	2141	1898	1675	NA	9591	7633	5996	4671	NA	+3.0	0.0	-12.9	0.0	NA
600, 700																
600 N.E.	900	1950	1680	1452	NA	NA	7596	5634	4212	NA	NA	+5.6	0.0	0.0	0.0	NA
700 N.E.	1200	1900	1676	1472	NA	NA	9618	7480	5774	NA	NA	+5.7	0.0	0.0	0.0	NA

CENTERFIRE HANDGUN CARTRIDGE—BALLISTICS & PRICES

Notes: Blanks are available in 32 S&W, 38 S&W and 38 Special. "V" after barrel length indicates test barrel was vented to produce ballistics similar to a revolver with a normal barrel-to-cylinder gap. Ammo prices are per 50 rounds except when marked with an ** which signifies a 20 round box; *** signifies a 25-round box. Not all loads are available from all ammo manufacturers. Listed loads are those made by Remington, Winchester, Federal, and others. DISC. is a discontinued load.
Prices are rounded to the nearest whole dollar and will vary with brand and retail outlet. † = new bullet weight this year; "c" indicates a change in data.

Cartridge	Bullet Wgt. Grs.	VELOCITY (fps)			ENERGY (ft. lbs.)			Mid-Range Traj. (in.)		Bbl. Lgth. (in).	Est. Price/ box
		Muzzle	50 yds.	100 yds.	Muzzle	50 yds.	100 yds.	50 yds.	100 yds.		
22, 25											
221 Rem. Fireball	50	2650	2380	2130	780	630	505	0.2	0.8	10.5"	$15
25 Automatic	35	900	813	742	63	51	43	NA	NA	2"	$18
25 Automatic	45	815	730	655	65	55	40	1.8	7.7	2"	$21
25 Automatic	50	760	705	660	65	55	50	2.0	8.7	2"	$17
30											
7.5mm Swiss	107	1010	NA	NA	240	NA	NA	NA	NA	NA	NEW
7.62mmTokarev	87	1390	NA	NA	365	NA	NA	0.6	NA	4.5"	NA
7.62 Nagant	97	790	NA	NA	134	NA	NA	NA	NA	NA	NEW
7.63 Mauser	88	1440	NA	NA	405	NA	NA	NA	NA	NA	NEW
30 Luger	93†	1220	1110	1040	305	255	225	0.9	3.5	4.5"	$34
30 Carbine	110	1790	1600	1430	785	625	500	0.4	1.7	10"	$28
30-357 AeT	123	1992	NA	NA	1084	NA	NA	NA	NA	10"	NA
32											
32 S&W	88	680	645	610	90	80	75	2.5	10.5	3"	$17
32 S&W Long	98	705	670	635	115	100	90	2.3	10.5	4"	$17
32 Short Colt	80	745	665	590	100	80	60	2.2	9.9	4"	$19
32 H&R Magnum	85	1100	1020	930	230	195	165	1.0	4.3	4.5"	$21
32 H&R Magnum	95	1030	940	900	225	190	170	1.1	4.7	4.5"	$19
32 Automatic	60	970	895	835	125	105	95	1.3	5.4	4"	$22
32 Automatic	60	1000	917	849	133	112	96			4"	NA
32 Automatic	65	950	890	830	130	115	100	1.3	5.6	NA	NA
32 Automatic	71	905	855	810	130	115	95	1.4	5.8	4"	$19
8mm Lebel Pistol	111	850	NA	NA	180	NA	NA	NA	NA	NA	NEW
8mm Steyr	112	1080	NA	NA	290	NA	NA	NA	NA	NA	NEW
8mm Gasser	126	850	NA	NA	200	NA	NA	NA	NA	NA	NEW
9mm, 38											
380 Automatic	60	1130	960	NA	170	120	NA	1.0	NA	NA	NA
380 Automatic	85/88	990	920	870	190	165	145	1.2	5.1	4"	$20
380 Automatic	90	1000	890	800	200	160	130	1.2	5.5	3.75"	$10
380 Automatic	95/100	955	865	785	190	160	130	1.4	5.9	4"	$20
38 Super Auto +P	115	1300	1145	1040	430	335	275	0.7	3.3	5"	$26
38 Super Auto +P	125/130	1215	1100	1015	425	350	300	0.8	3.6	5"	$26
38 Super Auto +P	147	1100	1050	1000	395	355	325	0.9	4.0	5"	NA
9x18mm Makarov	95	1000	NA	NA	NA	NA	NA	NA	NA	NA	NEW
9x18mm Ultra	100	1050	NA	NA	240	NA	NA	NA	NA	NA	NEW
9x23mm Largo	124	1190	1055	966	390	306	257	0.7	3.7	4"	NA
9x23mm Win.	125	1450	1249	1103	583	433	338	0.6	2.8	NA	NA
9mm Steyr	115	1180	NA	NA	350	NA	NA	NA	NA	NA	NEW
9mm Luger	88	1500	1190	1010	440	275	200	0.6	3.1	4"	$24
9mm Luger	90	1360	1112	978	370	247	191	NA	NA	4"	$26
9mm Luger	95	1300	1140	1010	350	275	215	0.8	3.4	4"	NA
9mm Luger	100	1180	1080	NA	305	255	NA	0.9	NA	4"	NA
9mm Luger	115	1155	1045	970	340	280	240	0.9	3.9	4"	$21
9mm Luger	123/125	1110	1030	970	340	290	260	1.0	4.0	4"	$23
9mm Luger	140	935	890	850	270	245	225	1.3	5.5	4"	$23
9mm Luger	147	990	940	900	320	290	265	1.1	4.9	4"	$26
9mm Luger +P	90	1475	NA	NA	437	NA	NA	NA	NA	NA	NA
9mm Luger +P	115	1250	1113	1019	399	316	265	0.8	3.5	4"	$27
9mm Federal	115	1280	1130	1040	420	330	280	0.7	3.3	4"V	$24
9mm Luger Vector	115	1155	1047	971	341	280	241	NA	NA	4"	NA
9mm Luger +P	124	1180	1089	1021	384	327	287	0.8	3.8	4"	NA
38											
38 S&W	146	685	650	620	150	135	125	2.4	10.0	4"	$19
38 Short Colt	125	730	685	645	150	130	115	2.2	9.4	6"	$19
39 Special	100	950	900	NA	200	180	NA	1.3	NA	4"V	NA
38 Special	110	945	895	850	220	195	175	1.3	5.4	4"V	$23
38 Special	110	945	895	850	220	195	175	1.3	5.4	4"V	$23
38 Special	130	775	745	710	175	160	120	1.9	7.9	4"V	$22

Notes: Blanks are available in 32 S&W, 38 S&W and 38 Special. "V" after barrel length indicates test barrel was vented to produce ballistics similar to a revolver with a normal barrel-to-cylinder gap. Ammo prices are per 50 rounds except when marked with an ** which signifies a 20 round box; *** signifies a 25-round box. Not all loads are available from all ammo manufacturers. Listed loads are those made by Remington, Winchester, Federal, and others. DISC. is a discontinued load.
Prices are rounded to the nearest whole dollar and will vary with brand and retail outlet. † = new bullet weight this year; "c" indicates a change in data.

Cartridge	Bullet Wgt. Grs.	VELOCITY (fps)			ENERGY (ft. lbs.)			Mid-Range Traj. (in.)		Bbl. Lgth. (in.)	Est. Price/box
		Muzzle	50 yds.	100 yds.	Muzzle	50 yds.	100 yds.	50 yds.	100 yds.		
38 Special Cowboy	140	800	767	735	199	183	168			7.5" V	NA
38 (Multi-Ball)	140	830	730	505	215	130	80	2.0	10.6	4"V	$10**
38 Special	148	710	635	565	165	130	105	2.4	10.6	4"V	$17
38 Special	158	755	725	690	200	185	170	2.0	8.3	4"V	$18
38 Special +P	95	1175	1045	960	290	230	195	0.9	3.9	4"V	$23
38 Special +P	110	995	925	870	240	210	185	1.2	5.1	4"V	$23
38 Special +P	125	975	929	885	264	238	218	1	5.2	4"	NA
38 Special +P	125	945	900	860	250	225	205	1.3	5.4	4"V	#23
38 Special +P	129	945	910	870	255	235	215	1.3	5.3	4"V	$11
38 Special +P	130	925	887	852	247	227	210	1.3	5.50	4"V	NA
38 Special +P	147/150(c)	884	NA	NA	264	NA	NA	NA	NA	4"V	$27
38 Special +P	158	890	855	825	280	255	240	1.4	6.0	4"V	$20
357											
357 SIG	115	1520	NA	NA	593	NA	NA	NA	NA	NA	NA
357 SIG	124	1450	NA	NA	578	NA	NA	NA	NA	NA	NA
357 SIG	125	1350	1190	1080	510	395	325	0.7	3.1	4"	NA
357 SIG	150	1130	1030	970	420	355	310	0.9	4.0	NA	NA
356 TSW	115	1520	NA	NA	593	NA	NA	NA	NA	NA	NA
356 TSW	124	1450	NA	NA	578	NA	NA	NA	NA	NA	NA
356 TSW	135	1280	1120	1010	490	375	310	0.8	3.5	NA	NA
356 TSW	147	1220	1120	1040	485	410	355	0.8	3.5	5"	NA
357 Mag., Super Clean	105	1650									NA
357 Magnum	110	1295	1095	975	410	290	230	0.8	3.5	4"V	$25
357 (Med.Vel.)	125	1220	1075	985	415	315	270	0.8	3.7	4"V	$25
357 Magnum	125	1450	1240	1090	585	425	330	0.6	2.8	4"V	$25
357 (Multi-Ball)	140	1155	830	665	420	215	135	1.2	6.4	4"V	$11**
357 Magnum	140	1360	1195	1075	575	445	360	0.7	3.0	4"V	$25
357 Magnum	145	1290	1155	1060	535	430	360	0.8	3.5	4"V	$26
357 Magnum	150/158	1235	1105	1015	535	430	360	0.8	3.5	4"V	$25
357 Mag. Cowboy	158	800	761	725	225	203	185				NA
357 Magnum	165	1290	1189	1108	610	518	450	0.7	3.1	8-3/8"	NA
357 Magnum	180	1145	1055	985	525	445	390	0.9	3.9	4"V	$25
357 Magnum	180	1180	1088	1020	557	473	416	0.8	3.6	8"V	NA
357 Mag. CorBon F.A.	180	1650	1512	1386	1088	913	767	1.66	0.0		NA
357 Mag. CorBon	200	1200	1123	1061	640	560	500	3.19	0.0		NA
357 Rem. Maximum	158	1825	1590	1380	1170	885	670	0.4	1.7	10.5"	$14**
40, 10mm											
40 S&W	135	1140	1070	NA	390	345	NA	0.9	NA	4"	NA
40 S&W	155	1140	1026	958	447	362	309	0.9	4.1	4"	$14***
40 S&W	165	1150	NA	NA	485	NA	NA	NA	NA	4"	$18***
40 S&W	180	985	936	893	388	350	319	1.4	5.0	4"	$14***
40 S&W	180	1015	960	914	412	368	334	1.3	4.5	4"	NA
400 Cor-Bon	135	1450	NA	NA	630	NA	NA	NA	NA	5"	NA
10mm Automatic	155	1125	1046	986	436	377	335	0.9	3.9	5"	$26
10mm Automatic	170	1340	1165	1145	680	510	415	0.7	3.2	5"	$31
10mm Automatic	175	1290	1140	1035	650	505	420	0.7	3.3	5.5"	$11**
10mm Auto. (FBI)	180	950	905	865	361	327	299	1.5	5.4	4"	$16**
10mm Automatic	180	1030	970	920	425	375	340	1.1	4.7	5"	$16**
10mm Auto H.V.	180†	1240	1124	1037	618	504	430	0.8	3.4	5"	$27
10mm Automatic	200	1160	1070	1010	495	510	430	0.9	3.8	5"	$14**
10.4mm Italian	177	950	NA	NA	360	NA	NA	NA	NA	NA	NEW
41 Action Exp.	180	1000	947	903	400	359	326	0.5	4.2	5"	$13**
41 Rem. Magnum	170	1420	1165	1015	760	515	390	0.7	3.2	4"V	$33
41 Rem. Magnum	175	1250	1120	1030	605	490	410	0.8	3.4	4"V	$14**
41 (Med. Vel.)	210	965	900	840	435	375	330	1.3	5.4	4"V	$30
41 Rem. Magnum	210	1300	1160	1060	790	630	535	0.7	3.2	4"V	$33
41 Rem. Magnum	240	1250	1151	1075	833	706	616	0.8	3.3	6.5V	NA
44											
44 S&W Russian	247	780	NA	NA	335	NA	NA	NA	NA	NA	NA
44 S&W Special	180	980	NA	NA	383	NA	NA	NA	NA	6.5"	NA

Notes: Blanks are available in 32 S&W, 38 S&W and 38 Special. "V" after barrel length indicates test barrel was vented to produce
ballistics similar to a revolver with a normal barrel-to-cylinder gap. Ammo prices are per 50 rounds except when marked with an **
which signifies a 20 round box; *** signifies a 25-round box. Not all loads are available from all ammo manufacturers.
Listed loads are those made by Remington, Winchester, Federal, and others. DISC. is a discontinued load.
Prices are rounded to the nearest whole dollar and will vary with brand and retail outlet. † = new bullet weight this year; "c" indicates a change in data.

Cartridge	Bullet Wgt. Grs.	VELOCITY (fps)			ENERGY (ft. lbs.)			Mid-Range Traj. (in.)		Bbl. Lgth. (in).	Est. Price/ box
		Muzzle	50 yds.	100 yds.	Muzzle	50 yds.	100 yds.	50 yds.	100 yds.		
44 S&W Special	180	1000	935	882	400	350	311	NA	NA	7.5"V	NA
44 S&W Special	200†	875	825	780	340	302	270	1.2	6.0	6"	$13**
44 S&W Special	200	1035	940	865	475	390	335	1.1	4.9	6.5"	$13**
44 S&W Special	240/246	755	725	695	310	285	265	2.0	8.3	6.5"	$26
44-40 Win. Cowboy	225	750	723	695	281	261	242				NA
44 Rem. Magnum	180	1610	1365	1175	1035	745	550	0.5	2.3	4"V	$18**
44 Rem. Magnum	200	1400	1192	1053	870	630	492	0.6	NA	6.5"	$20
44 Rem. Magnum	210	1495	1310	1165	1040	805	635	0.6	2.5	6.5"	$18**
44 (Med. Vel.)	240	1000	945	900	535	475	435	1.1	4.8	6.5"	$17
44 R.M. (Jacketed)	240	1180	1080	1010	740	625	545	0.9	3.7	4"V	$18**
44 R.M. (Lead)	240	1350	1185	1070	970	750	610	0.7	3.1	4"V	$29
44 Rem. Magnum	250	1180	1100	1040	775	670	600	0.8	3.6	6.5"V	$21
44 Rem. Magnum	250	1250	1148	1070	867	732	635	0.8	3.3	6.5"V	NA
44 Rem. Magnum	275	1235	1142	1070	931	797	699	0.8	3.3	6.5"	NA
44 Rem. Magnum	300	1200	1100	1026	959	806	702	NA	NA	7.5"	$17
44 Rem. Magnum	330	1385	1297	1220	1406	1234	1090	1.83	0.00	NA	NA
440 CorBon	260	1700	1544	1403	1669	1377	1136	1.58	NA	10"	NA
45, 50											
450 Short Colt/450 Revolver	226	830	NA	NA	350	NA	NA	NA	NA	NA	NEW
45 S&W Schofield	180	730	NA	NA	213	NA	NA	NA	NA	NA	NA
45 S&W Schofield	230	730	NA	NA	272	NA	NA	NA	NA	NA	NA
45 G.A.P.	185	1090	970	890	490	385	320	1.0	4.7	5"	NA
45 G.A.P.	230	880	842	NA	396	363	NA	NA	NA	NA	NA
45 Automatic	165	1030	930	NA	385	315	NA	1.2	NA	5"	NA
45 Automatic	185	1000	940	890	410	360	325	1.1	4.9	5"	$28
45 Auto. (Match)	185	770	705	650	245	204	175	2.0	8.7	5"	$28
45 Auto. (Match)	200	940	890	840	392	352	312	2.0	8.6	5"	$20
45 Automatic	200	975	917	860	421	372	328	1.4	5.0	5"	$18
45 Automatic	230	830	800	675	355	325	300	1.6	6.8	5"	$27
45 Automatic	230	880	846	816	396	366	340	1.5	6.1	5"	NA
45 Automatic +P	165	1250	NA	NA	573	NA	NA	NA	NA	NA	NA
45 Automatic +P	185	1140	1040	970	535	445	385	0.9	4.0	5"	$31
45 Automatic +P	200	1055	982	925	494	428	380	NA	NA	5"	NA
45 Super	185	1300	1190	1108	694	582	504	NA	NA	5"	NA
45 Win. Magnum	230	1400	1230	1105	1000	775	635	0.6	2.8	5"	$14**
45 Win. Magnum	260	1250	1137	1053	902	746	640	0.8	3.3	5"	$16**
45 Win. Mag. CorBon	320	1150	1080	1025	940	830	747	3.47			NA
455 Webley MKII	262	850	NA	NA	420	NA	NA	NA	NA	NA	NA
45 Colt	200	1000	938	889	444	391	351	1.3	4.8	5.5"	$21
45 Colt	225	960	890	830	460	395	345	1.3	5.5	5.5"	$22
45 Colt + P CorBon	265	1350	1225	1126	1073	884	746	2.65	0.0		NA
45 Colt + P CorBon	300	1300	1197	1114	1126	956	827	2.78	0.0		NA
45 Colt	250/255	860	820	780	410	375	340	1.6	6.6	5.5"	$27
454 Casull	250	1300	1151	1047	938	735	608	0.7	3.2	7.5"V	NA
454 Casull	260	1800	1577	1381	1871	1436	1101	0.4	1.8	7.5"V	NA
454 Casull	300	1625	1451	1308	1759	1413	1141	0.5	2.0	7.5"V	NA
454 Casull CorBon	360	1500	1387	1286	1800	1640	1323	2.01	0.0		NA
460 S&W	200	2300	2042	1801	2350	1851	1441	0	-1.60	NA	NA
460 S&W	260	2000	1788	1592	2309	1845	1464	NA	NA	7.5"V	NA
460 S&W	250	1900	1640	1412	2004	1494	1106	0	-2.75	NA	NA
460 S&W	395	1550	1389	1249	2108	1691	1369	0	-4.00	NA	NA
475 Linebaugh	400	1350	1217	1119	1618	1315	1112	NA	NA	NA	NA
480 Ruger	325	1350	1191	1076	1315	1023	835	2.6	0.0	7.5	NA
50 Action Exp.	325	1400	1209	1075	1414	1055	835	0.2	2.3	6"	$24**
500 S&W	275	1665	1392	1183	1693	1184	854	1.5	NA	8.375	NA
500 S&W	350	1400	1231	1106	1523	1178	951	NA	NA	10"	NA
500 S&W	400	1675	1472	1299	2493	1926	1499	1.3	NA	8.375	NA
500 S&W	440	1625	1367	1169	2581	1825	1337	1.6	NA	8.375	NA
500 S&W	500	1425	1281	1164	2254	1823	1505	NA	NA	10"	NA

RIMFIRE AMMUNITION—BALLISTICS & PRICES

Note: The actual ballistics obtained with your firearm can vary considerably from the advertised ballistics.
Also, ballistics can vary from lot to lot with the same brand and type load.

Cartridge	Bullet Wt. Grs.	Velocity (fps) 22-1/2" Bbl.		Energy (ft. lbs.) 22-1/2" Bbl.		Mid-Range Traj. (in.)	Muzzle Velocity
		Muzzle	100 yds.	Muzzle	100 yds.	100 yds.	6" Bbl.
17 Aguila	20	1850	1267	NA	NA	NA	NA
17 Hornady Mach 2	17	2100	1530	166	88	0.7	NA
17 HMR	17	2550	1902	245	136	NA	NA
17 HMR	20	2375	1776	250	140	NA	NA
22 Short Blank	—	—	—	—	—	—	—
22 Short CB	29	727	610	33	24	NA	706
22 Short Target	29	830	695	44	31	6.8	786
22 Short HP	27	1164	920	81	50	4.3	1077
22 Colibri	20	375	183	6	1	NA	NA
22 Super Colibri	20	500	441	11	9	NA	NA
22 Long CB	29	727	610	33	24	NA	706
22 Long HV	29	1180	946	90	57	4.1	1031
22 LR Pistol Match	40	1070	890	100	70	4.6	940
22 LR Sub Sonic HP	38	1050	901	93	69	4.7	NA
22 LR Standard Velocity	40	1070	890	100	70	4.6	940
22 LR AutoMatch	40	1200	990	130	85	NA	NA
22 LR HV	40	1255	1016	140	92	3.6	1060
22 LR Silhoutte	42	1220	1003	139	94	3.6	1025
22 SSS	60	950	802	120	86	NA	NA
22 LR HV HP	40	1280	1001	146	89	3.5	1085
22 Velocitor GDHP	40	1435	0	0	0	NA	NA
22 LR Hyper HP	32/33/34	1500	1075	165	85	2.8	NA
22 LR Stinger HP	32	1640	1132	191	91	2.6	1395
22 LR Hyper Vel	30	1750	1191	204	93	NA	NA
22 LR Shot #12	31	950	NA	NA	NA	NA	NA
22 WRF LFN	45	1300	1015	169	103	3	NA
22 Win. Mag.	30	2200	1373	322	127	1.4	1610
22 Win. Mag. V-Max BT	33	2000	1495	293	164	0.60	NA
22 Win. Mag. JHP	34	2120	1435	338	155	1.4	NA
22 Win. Mag. JHP	40	1910	1326	324	156	1.7	1480
22 Win. Mag. FMJ	40	1910	1326	324	156	1.7	1480
22 Win. Mag. Dyna Point	45	1550	1147	240	131	2.60	NA
22 Win. Mag. JHP	50	1650	1280	300	180	1.3	NA
22 Win. Mag. Shot #11	52	1000	—	NA	—	—	NA

NOTES: * = 10 rounds per box. ** = 5 rounds per box. Pricing variations and number of rounds per box can occur with type and brand of ammunition. Listed pricing is the average nominal cost for load style and box quantity shown. Not every brand is available in all shot size variations. Some manufacturers do not provide suggested list prices. All prices rounded to nearest whole dollar. The price you pay will vary dependent upon outlet of purchase. # = new load spec this year; "C" indicates a change in data.

Dram Equiv.	Shot Ozs.	Load Style	Shot Sizes	Brands	Avg. Price/ box	Velocity (fps)
10 Gauge 3-1/2" Magnum						
4-1/2	2-1/4	premium	BB, 2, 4, 5, 6	Win., Fed., Rem.	$33	1205
Max	2	premium	4, 5, 6	Fed., Win.	NA	1300
4-1/4	2	high velocity	BB, 2, 4	Rem.	$22	1210
Max	18 pellets	premium	00 buck	Fed., Win.	$7**	1100
Max	1-7/8	Bismuth	BB, 2, 4	Bis.	NA	1225
Max	1-3/4	high density	BB, 2	Rem.	NA	1300
4-1/4	1-3/4	steel	TT, T, BBB, BB, 1, 2, 3	Win., Rem.	$27	1260
Mag	1-5/8	steel	T, BBB, BB, 2	Win.	$27	1285
Max	1-5/8	Bismuth	BB, 2, 4	Bismuth	NA	1375
Max	1-1/2	steel	T, BBB, BB, 1, 2, 3	Fed.	NA	1450
Max	1-3/8	steel	T, BBB, BB, 1, 2, 3	Fed., Rem.	NA	1500
Max	1-3/8	steel	T, BBB, BB, 2	Fed., Win.	NA	1450
Max	1-3/4	slug, rifled	slug	Fed.	NA	1280
Max	24 pellets	Buckshot	1 Buck	Fed.	NA	1100
Max	54 pellets	Super-X	4 Buck	Win.	NA	1150
12 Gauge 3-1/2" Magnum						
Max	2-1/4	premium	4, 5, 6	Fed., Rem., Win.	$13*	1150
Max	2	Lead	4, 5, 6	Fed.	NA	1300
Max	2	Copper plated turkey	4, 5	Rem.	NA	1300
Max	18 pellets	premium	00 buck	Fed., Win., Rem.	$7**	1100
Max	1-7/8	Wingmaster HD	4, 6	Rem.	NA	1225
Max	1-7/8	heavyweight	5, 6	Fed.	NA	1300
Max	1-3/4	high density	BB, 2, 4, 6	Rem.		1300
Max	1-7/8	Bismuth	BB, 2, 4	Bis.	NA	1225
Max	1-5/8	Hevi-shot	T	Hevi-shot	NA	1350
Max	1-5/8	Wingmaster HD	T	Rem.	NA	1350
Max	1-5/8	high density	BB, 2	Fed.	NA	1450
Max	1-3/8	Heavyweight	2, 4, 6	Fed.	NA	1450
Max	1-3/8	steel	T, BBB, BB, 2, 4	Fed., Win., Rem.	NA	1450
Max	1-1/2	FS steel	BBB, BB, 2	Fed.	NA	1500
Max	1-1/2	Supreme H-V	BBB, BB, 2, 3	Win.	NA	1475
Max	1-3/8	H-speed steel	BB, 2	Rem.	NA	1550
Max	1-1/4	Steel	BB, 2	Win.	NA	1625
Max	24 pellets	Premium	1 Buck	Fed.	NA	1100
Max	54 pellets	Super-X	4 Buck	Win.	NA	1050
12 Gauge 3" Magnum						
4	2	premium	BB, 2, 4, 5, 6	Win., Fed., Rem.	$9*	1175
4	1-7/8	premium	BB, 2, 4x6	Win., Fed., Rem.	$19	1210
4	1-7/8	duplex	4x6	Rem.	$9*	1210
Max	1-3/4	turkey	4, 5, 6	Fed., Fio., Win., Rem.	NA	1300
Max	1-3/4	high density	BB, 2, 4	Rem.	NA	1450
Max	1-5/8	high density	BB, 2	Fed.	NA	1450
Max	1-5/8	Wingmaster HD	4, 6	Rem.	NA	1227
Max	1-5/8	high velocity	4, 5, 6	Fed.	NA	1350
4	1-5/8	premium	2, 4, 5, 6	Win., Fed., Rem.	$18	1290
Max	1-1/2	Wingmaster HD	T	Rem.	NA	1300
Max	1-1/2	Hevi-shot	T	Hevi-shot	NA	1300
Max	1-1/2	high density	BB, 2, 4	Rem.	NA	1300
Max	1-5/8	Bismuth	BB, 2, 4, 5, 6	Bis.	NA	1250
4	24 pellets	buffered	1 Buck	Win., Fed., Rem.	$5**	1040
4	15 pellets	buffered	00 buck	Win., Fed., Rem.	$6**	1210
4	10 pellets	buffered	000 buck	Win., Fed., Rem.	$6**	1225
4	41 pellets	buffered	4 buck	Win., Fed., Rem.	$6**	1210
Max	1-3/8	heavyweight	5, 6	Fed.	NA	1300
Max	1-3/8	high density	B, 2, 4, 6	Rem. Win.	NA	1450
Max	1-3/8	slug	slug	Bren.	NA	1476
Max	1-1/4	slug, rifled	slug	Fed.	NA	1600
Max	1-3/16	saboted slug	copper slug	Rem.	NA	1500
Max	7/8	slug, rifled	slug	Rem.	NA	1875

Dram Equiv.	Shot Ozs.	Load Style	Shot Sizes	Brands	Avg. Price/ box	Velocity (fps)
12 Gauge 3" Magnum (cont.)						
Max	1-1/8	low recoil	BB	Fed.	NA	850
Max	1-1/8	steel	BB, 2, 3, 4	Fed., Win., Rem.	NA	1550
Max	1-1/16	high density	2, 4	Win.	NA	1400
Max	1	steel	4, 6	Fed.	NA	1330
Max	1-3/8	buckhammer	slug	Rem.	NA	1500
Max	1	slug, rifled	slug, magnum	Win., Rem.	$5**	1760
Max	1	saboted slug	slug	Rem., Win., Fed.	$10**	1550
Max	385 grs.	partition gold	slug	Win.	NA	2000
3-5/8	1-3/8	steel	BBB, BB, 1, 2, 3, 4	Win., Fed., Rem.	$19	1275
Max	1-1/8	steel	BB, 2, 4	Rem.	NA	1500
Max	1-1/8	steel	T, BBB, BB, 2, 4, 5, 6	Fed., Win.	NA	1450
Max	1-1/8	steel	BB, 2	Fed.	NA	1400
4	1-1/4	steel	T, BBB, BB, 1, 2, 3, 4, 6	Win., Fed., Rem.	$18	1400
Max	1-1/4	FS steel	BBB, BB, 2	Fed.	NA	1450
12 Gauge 2-3/4"						
Max	1-5/8	magnum	4, 5, 6	Win., Fed.	$8*	1250
Max	1-3/8	lead	4, 5, 6	Fiocchi	NA	1485
Max	1-3/8	turkey	4, 5, 6	Fio.	NA	1250
Max	1-3/8	steel	4, 5, 6	Fed.	NA	1400
Max	1-3/8	Bismuth	BB, 2, 4, 5, 6	Bis.	NA	1300
3-3/4	1-1/2	magnum	BB, 2, 4, 5, 6	Win., Fed., Rem.	$16	1260
Max	1-1/4	Supreme H-V	4, 5, 6, 7-1/2	Win. Rem.	NA	1400
3-3/4	1-1/4	high velocity	BB, 2, 4, 5, 6, 7-1/2, 8, 9	Win., Fed., Rem., Fio.	$13	1330
Max	1-1/4	high density	B, 2, 4	Win.	NA	1450
Max	1-1/4	high density	4, 6	Rem.	NA	1325
3-1/4	1-1/4	standard velocity	6, 7-1/2, 8, 9	Win., Fed., Rem., Fio.	$11	1220
Max	1-1/8	Hevi-shot	5	Hevi-shot	NA	1350
3-1/4	1-1/8	standard velocity	4, 6, 7-1/2, 8, 9	Win., Fed., Rem., Fio.	$9	1255
Max	1-1/8	steel	2, 4	Rem.	NA	1390
Max	1	steel	BB, 2	Fed.	NA	1450
3-1/4	1	standard velocity	6, 7-1/2, 8	Rem., Fed., Fio., Win.	$6	1290
3-1/4	1-1/4	target	7-1/2, 8, 9	Win., Fed., Rem.	$10	1220
3	1-1/8	spreader	7-1/2, 8, 8-1/2, 9	Fio.	NA	1200
3	1-1/8	target	7-1/2, 8, 9, 7-1/2x8	Win., Fed., Rem., Fio.	$7	1200
2-3/4	1-1/8	target	7-1/2, 8, 8-1/2, 9, 7-1/2x8	Win., Fed., Rem., Fio.	$7	1145
2-3/4	1-1/8	low recoil	7-1/2, 8	Rem.	NA	1145
2-1/2	26 grams	low recoil	8	Win.	NA	980
2-1/4	1-1/8	target	7-1/2, 8, 8-1/2, 9	Rem., Fed.	$7	1080
Max	1-1/8	spreader	7-1/2, 8, 8-1/2, 9	Fio.	NA	1300
3-1/4	28 grams (1 oz)	target	7-1/2, 8, 9	Win., Fed., Rem., Fio.	$8	1290
3	1	target	7-1/2, 8, 8-1/2, 9	Win., Fio.	NA	1235
2-3/4	1	target	7-1/2, 8, 8-1/2, 9	Fed., Rem., Fio.	NA	1180
3-1/4	24 grams	target	7-1/2, 8, 9	Fed., Win., Fio.	NA	1325
3	7/8	light	8	Fio.	NA	1200
3-3/4	8 pellets	buffered	000 buck	Win., Fed., Rem.	$4**	1325
4	12 pellets	premium	00 buck	Win., Fed., Rem.	$5**	1290
3-3/4	9 pellets	buffered	00 buck	Win., Fed., Rem., Fio.	$19	1325
3-3/4	12 pellets	buffered	0 buck	Win., Fed., Rem.	$4**	1275
4	20 pellets	buffered	1 buck	Win., Fed., Rem.	$4**	1075
3-3/4	16 pellets	buffered	1 buck	Win., Fed., Rem.	$4**	1250
4	34 pellets	premium	4 buck	Fed., Rem.	$5**	1250
3-3/4	27 pellets	buffered	4 buck	Win., Fed., Rem., Fio.	$4**	1325
Max	1	saboted slug	slug	Win., Fed., Rem.	$10**	1450

NOTES: * = 10 rounds per box. ** = 5 rounds per box. Pricing variations and number of rounds per box can occur with type and brand of ammunition. Listed pricing is the average nominal cost for load style and box quantity shown. Not every brand is available in all shot size variations. Some manufacturers do not provide suggested list prices. All prices rounded to nearest whole dollar. The price you pay will vary dependent upon outlet of purchase. # = new load spec this year; "C" indicates a change in data.

Dram Equiv.	Shot Ozs.	Load Style	Shot Sizes	Brands	Avg. Price/ box	Velocity (fps)
12 Gauge 2-3/4" (cont.)						
Max	1-1/4	slug, rifled	slug	Fed.	NA	1520
Max	1-1/4	slug	slug	Lightfield		1440
Max	1-1/4	saboted slug	attached sabot	Rem.	NA	1550
Max	1	slug, rifled	slug, magnum	Rem., Fio.	$5**	1680
Max	1	slug, rifled	slug	Win., Fed., Rem.	$4**	1610
Max	1	sabot slug	slug	Sauvestre		1640
Max	7/8	slug, rifled	slug	Rem.	NA	1800
Max	400	plat. tip	sabot slug	Win.	NA	1700
Max	385 grains	Partition Gold Slug	slug	Win.	NA	1900
Max	385 grains	Core-Lokt bonded	sabot slug	Rem.	NA	1900
Max	325 grains	Barnes Sabot	slug	Fed.	NA	1900
Max	300 grains	SST Slug	sabot slug	Hornady	NA	2050
3	1-1/8	steel target	6-1/2, 7	Rem.	NA	1200
2-3/4	1-1/8	steel target	7	Rem.	NA	1145
3	1#	steel	7	Win.	$11	1235
3-1/2	1-1/4	steel	T, BBB, BB, 1, 2, 3, 4, 5, 6	Win., Fed., Rem.	$18	1275
3-3/4	1-1/8	steel	BB, 1, 2, 3, 4, 5, 6	Win., Fed., Rem., Fio.	$16	1365
3-3/4	1	steel	2, 3, 4, 5, 6, 7	Win., Fed., Rem., Fio.	$13	1390
Max	7/8	steel	7	Fio.	NA	1440
16 Gauge 2-3/4"						
3-1/4	1-1/4	magnum	2, 4, 6	Fed., Rem.	$16	1260
3-1/4	1-1/8	high velocity	4, 6, 7-1/2	Win., Fed., Rem., Fio.	$12	1295
Max	1-1/8	Bismuth	4, 5	Bis.	NA	1200
2-3/4	1-1/8	standard velocity	6, 7-1/2, 8	Fed., Rem., Fio.	$9	1185
2-1/2	1	dove	6, 7-1/2, 8, 9	Fio., Win.	NA	1165
2-3/4	1		6, 7-1/2, 8	Fio.	NA	1200
Max	15/16	steel	2, 4	Fed., Rem.	NA	1300
Max	7/8	steel	2, 4	Win.	$16	1300
3	12 pellets	buffered	1 buck	Win., Fed., Rem.	$4**	1225
Max	4/5	slug, rifled	slug	Win., Fed., Rem.	$4**	1570
Max	.92	sabot slug	slug	Sauvestre	NA	1560
20 Gauge 3" Magnum						
3	1-1/4	premium	2, 4, 5, 6, 7-1/2	Win., Fed., Rem.	$15	1185
Max	1-1/4	Wingmaster HD	4, 6	Rem.	NA	1185
3	1-1/4	turkey	4, 6	Fio.	NA	1200
Max	1-1/4	Hevi-shot	2, 4, 6	Hevi-shot	NA	1250
Max	1-1/8	high density	4, 6	Rem.	NA	1300
Max	18 pellets	buck shot	2 buck	Fed.	NA	1200
Max	24 pellets	buffered	3 buck	Win.	$5**	1150
2-3/4	20 pellets	buck	3 buck	Rem.	$4**	1200
3-1/4	1	steel	1, 2, 3, 4, 5, 6	Win., Fed., Rem.	$15	1330
Max	7/8	steel	2, 4	Win.	NA	1300
Max	1-1/16	high density	2, 4	Win.	NA	1400
Max	1-1/16	Bismuth	2, 4, 5, 6	Bismuth	NA	1250
Mag	5/8	saboted slug	275 gr.	Fed.	NA	1900

Dram Equiv.	Shot Ozs.	Load Style	Shot Sizes	Brands	Avg. Price/ box	Velocity (fps)
20 Gauge 2-3/4"						
2-3/4	1-1/8	magnum	4, 6, 7-1/2	Win., Fed., Rem.	$14	1175
2-3/4	1	high velocity	4, 5, 6, 7-1/2, 8, 9	Win., Fed., Rem., Fio.	$12	1220
Max	1	Bismuth	4, 6	Bis.	NA	1200
Max	1	Hevi-shot	5	Hevi-shot	NA	1250
Max	1	Supreme H-V	4, 6, 7-1/2	Win. Rem.	NA	1300
Max	7/8	Steel	2, 3, 4	Fio.	NA	1500
2-1/2	1	standard velocity	6, 7-1/2, 8	Win., Rem., Fed., Fio.	$6	1165
2-1/2	7/8	clays	8	Rem.	NA	1200
2-1/2	7/8	promotional	6, 7-1/2, 8	Win., Rem., Fio.	$6	1210
2-1/2	1	target	8, 9	Win., Rem.	$8	1165
Max	7/8	clays	7-1/2, 8	Win.	NA	1275
2-1/2	7/8	target	8, 9	Win., Rem., Fed.	$8	1200
Max	3/4	steel	2, 4	Rem.	NA	1425
2-1/2	7/8	steel - target	7	Rem.	NA	1200
Max	1	buckhammer	slug	Rem.	NA	1500
Max	5/8	Saboted Slug	Copper Slug	Rem.	NA	1500
Max	20 pellets	buffered	3 buck	Win., Fed.	$4	1200
Max	5/8	slug, saboted	slug	Win.	$9**	1400
2-3/4	5/8	slug, rifled	slug	Rem.	$4**	1580
Max	3/4	saboted slug	copper slug	Fed., Rem.	NA	1450
Max	3/4	slug, rifled	slug	Win., Fed., Rem., Fio.	$4**	1570
Max	.9	sabot slug	slug	Sauvestre		1480
Max	260 grains	Partition Gold Slug	slug	Win.	NA	1900
Max	260 grains	Core-Lokt Ultra	slug	Rem.	NA	1900
Max	260 grains	saboted slug	platinum tip	Win.	NA	1700
Max	3/4	steel	2, 3, 4, 6	Win., Fed., Rem.	$14	1425
Max	250 grains	SST slug	slug	Hornady	NA	1800
Max	1/2	rifled, slug	slug	Rem.	NA	1800
28 Gauge 2-3/4"						
2	1	high velocity	6, 7-1/2, 8	Win.	$12	1125
2-1/4	3/4	high velocity	6, 7-1/2, 8, 9	Win., Fed., Rem., Fio.	$11	1295
2	3/4	target	8, 9	Win., Fed., Rem.	$9	1200
Max	3/4	sporting clays	7-1/2, 8-1/2	Win.	NA	1300
Max	5/8	Bismuth	4, 6	Bis.	NA	1250
410 Bore 3"						
Max	11/16	high velocity	4, 5, 6, 7-1/2, 8, 9	Win., Fed., Rem., Fio.	$10	1135
Max	9/16	Bismuth	4	Bis.	NA	1175
410 Bore 2-1/2"						
Max	1/2	high velocity	4, 6, 7-1/2	Win., Fed., Rem.	$9	1245
Max	1/5	slug, rifled	slug	Win., Fed., Rem.	$4**	1815
1-1/2	1/2	target	8, 8-1/2, 9	Win., Fed., Rem., Fio.	$8	1200
Max	1/2	sporting clays	7-1/2, 8, 8-1/2	Win.	NA	1300
Max		Buckshot	5-000 Buck	Win.	NA	1135

2008 GUNS ILLUSTRATED Complete Compact CATALOG

GUNDEX

GUNDEX

GUNDEX

SEMI-CUSTOM

HANDGUNS

RIFLES

SHOTGUNS

BLACKPOWDER

AIRGUNS

COMPENDIUM

MANUFACTURER'S
DIRECTORY

GUNDEX

GUNDEX

GUNDEX

GUNDEX

Browning Luxus
Grade B2

Browning Luxus
Renaissance Argent

Ed Brown Classic Custom

Ed Brown EC-BB

Ed Brown Executive Target

Ed Brown Kobra Carry

Ed Brown Executive

Ed Brown Kobra

Kase Reeder
1 Asterisk

BRILEY 1911-STYLE AUTO PISTOLS

Caliber: 9mm Para., 38 Super, 40 S&W, 10-shot magazine; 45 ACP, 8-shot magazine. **Barrel:** 3.6" or 5". **Weight:** NA. **Length:** NA. **Grips:** Rosewood or rubber. **Sights:** Bo-Mar adjustable rear, Briley dovetail blade front. **Features:** Modular or Caspian alloy, carbon steel or stainless steel frame; match barrel and trigger group; lowered and flared ejection port; front and rear serrations on slide; beavertail grip safety; hot blue, hard chrome or stainless steel finish. Introduced 2000. Made in U.S. From Briley Manufacturing Inc.

Price: Fantom (3.6" bbl., fixed low-mount rear sight, armor
coated lower receiver), from **$1,900.00**
Price: Fantom with two-port compensator, from **$2,245.00**
Price: Advantage (5" bbl., adj. low-mount rear sight, checkered
mainspring housing), from **$1,650.00**
Price: Versatility Plus (5" bbl., adj. low-mount rear sight, modular
or Caspian frame), from **$1,850.00**
Price: Signature Series (5" bbl., adj. low-mount rear sight,
40 S&W only), from **$2,250.00**
Price: Plate Master (5" bbl. with compensator, lightened slide,
Briley scope mount), from **$1,895.00**
Price: El Presidente (5" bbl. with Briley quad compensator,
Briley scope mount), from **$2,550.00**

BROWNING HI-POWER LUXUS

The legendary Browning Hi-Power pistol still produced in Belgium is available in four grades in the Luxus series: Grade II, Renaissance Argent, Grade B2 and the gold-finished Renaissance OR. Other specifications NA.
Price: From **$4,391.00**

ED BROWN CLASSIC CUSTOM AND CLASS A LIMITED 1911-STYLE AUTO PISTOLS

Caliber: 45 ACP. **Barrel:** 4.25", 5". **Weight:** NA. **Length:** NA. **Grips:** Cocobolo exotic checkered wood. **Sights:** Bo-Mar or Novak rear, blade front. **Features:** Blued or stainless steel frame; ambidextrous safety; beavertail grip safety; checkered forestrap and mainspring housing; match-grade barrel; slotted hammer; long lightweight or steel trigger. Many options offered. Made in U.S. by Ed Brown Products, Inc.

Price: Classic Custom (45 ACP, 5" barrel), from **$2,895.00**
Price: Executive Elite (45 ACP, 5" barrel), from **$2,195.00**
Price: Executive Carry (4.25" bbl., has "bobtail™" modification
to reduce overall length), from **$2,295.00**
Price: Kobra (45 ACP only, 5" bbl., completely hand-fitted with
heavy dehorning), from **$1,995.00**
Price: Kobra Carry (45 ACP only, 4.25" bbl., has exclusive snakeskin pattern
on frame, top portion of mainspring housing and slide),
from **$2,195.00**
Price: Executive Target, (45 ACP, 5" government model, features exclusive
25 lpi checkering and Bo-Mar adjustable sights), from **$2,370.00**

KASE REEDER 1 ASTERISK

Caliber: Full custom M1911. **Barrel:** Varies by model. **Weight:** Varies by model. **Length:** Varies by model. **Grips:** NA. **Sights:** NA. **Features:** Full combat features including see-thru Lexan grip panel. Jeweled hammer and trigger, tuned action, model name engraved on barrel. Made in U.S. by Kase Reeder Custom Guns.
Price: From **$995.00**

Kimber Custom Royal II

Kimber Custom Target II

Kimber Ultra CDP

Les Baer Thunder Ranch Special

Les Baer Premier II LW1

KIMBER CUSTOM II 1911-STYLE AUTO PISTOLS

Caliber: 9mm Para., 38 Super, 9-shot magazines; 40 S&W, 8-shot magazine; 45 ACP, 7-shot magazine. **Barrel:** 5". **Weight:** 38 oz. **Length:** 8.7" overall. **Grips:** Black synthetic, smooth or double-diamond checkered rosewood, or double-diamond checkered walnut. **Sights:** McCormick low profile or Kimber adjustable rear, blade front. **Features:** Machined steel slide, frame and barrel; front and rear beveled slide serrations; cut and button-rifled, match-grade barrel; adjustable aluminum trigger; full-length guide rod; Commander-style hammer; high-ride beavertail safety; beveled magazine well. Other models available. Made in U.S. by Kimber Mfg. Inc.
Price: Custom II (black matte finish) **$730.00**
Price: Custom Royal II (polished blue finish, checkered
rosewood grips) **$886.00**
Price: Custom Stainless II (satin-finished stainless steel frame
and slide) **$832.00**
Price: Custom Target II (matte black or stainless finish, Kimber
adj. sight) **$945.00**
Price: Custom Compact CDP II (4" bbl., alum. frame, tritium
three-dot sights, 28 oz.) **$1,141.00**
Price: Custom Pro CDP II (4" bbl., alum. frame, tritium sights,
full-length grip, 28 oz.) **$1,141.00**
Price: Ultra CDP II (3" bbl., aluminum frame, tritium sights,
25 oz.) **$1,141.00**
Price: Gold Match II (polished blue finish, hand-fitted barrel,
ambid. safety), from **$1,168.00**
Price: Stainless Gold Match II (stainless steel frame and slide,
hand-fitted bbl., amb. safety) . . . . **$1,315.00 to $1,345.00**

KORTH REVOLVERS

Caliber: 22 LR, 22 WMR, 32 S&W Long, 38 Sp., 357 Mag., 9mm Para. **Barrel:** 3", 4", 5.25", 6". **Weight:** 32-52 oz. **Grips:** Walnut, palisander, amboinia, ivory (Combat, Sport), German walnut. Matte with oil finish, adjustable ergonomic competition style (Target). **Sights:** Adjustable Patridge (Sport) or Baughman (Combat), interchangeable and adjustable rear w/Patridge front (Target) in blue and matte. **Features:** DA/SA, 3 models, over 50 configurations, externally adjustable trigger stop and weight, interchangeable cylinder, removable wide milled trigger shoe on Target model. Deluxe models are highly engraved, high polish blue finish, plasma coated in high polish or matted silver, gold, blue or charcoal. Many deluxe options available. 6-shot. Made in Germany. Imported by Korth USA.
Price: . . . . **$5000.00 to $8000.00**
Price: Deluxe . . . . **$9000.00 to $12000.00**

KORTH AUTO PISTOLS

Caliber: 9mm Para, 9x21 (10-shot). **Barrel:** 4", 4.5". **Weight:** 39.9 oz. **Grips:** Walnut, palisander, amboinia, ivory. **Sights:** Fully adjustable. **Features:** Recoil-operated, locking block system, forged steel, fully machine and ground to final tolerances. DA/SA, 2 models available with either rounded or combat-style trigger guard. Available finishes: high polish blue plasma, high polish or matted silver plasma, or high polish standard blue. Schalldampfer Modell has special threaded 4.5-inch barrel and thread protector, many deluxe options available. Made in Germany. Imported by Korth USA.
Price: . . . . **$7,000.00 to $12,000.00**

LES BAER CUSTOM 1911-STYLE AUTO PISTOLS

Caliber: 9mm Para., 38 Super, 40 S&W, 45 ACP, 400 Cor-Bon; 7- or 8-shot magazine. **Barrel:** 4-1/4", 5", 6". **Weight:** 28 to 40 oz. **Length:** NA. **Grips:** Checkered cocobolo. **Sights:** Low-mount combat fixed, combat fixed with tritium inserts or low-mount adjustable rear, dovetail front. **Features:** Forged steel or aluminum frame; slide serrated front and rear; lowered and flared ejection port; beveled magazine well; speed trigger with 4-pound pull; beavertail grip safety; ambidextrous safety. Other models available. Made in U.S. by Les Baer Custom.
Price: Baer 1911 Premier II 5" Model (5" bbl., optional stainless steel
frame and slide), from **$1,498.00**
Price: Premier II 6" Model (6" barrel), from **$1,675.00**
Price: Premier II LW1 (forged aluminum frame, steel slide and barrel),
from **$1,835.00**
Price: Custom Carry (4" or 5" barrel, steel frame), from **$1,728.00**
Price: Custom Carry (4" barrel, aluminum frame), from **$2,039.00**
Price: Swift Response Pistol (fixed tritium sights, Bear Coat finish),
from **$2,339.00**
Price: Monolith (5" barrel and slide with extra-long dust cover),
from **$1,660.00**
Price: Stinger (4-1/4" barrel, steel or aluminum frame), from **$1,552.00**
Price: Thunder Ranch Special (tritium fixed combat sight,
Thunder Ranch logo), from **$1,685.00**
Price: National Match Hardball (low-mount adj. sight; meets
DCM rules), from **$1,425.00**
Price: Bullseye Wadcutter Pistol (Bo-Mar rib w/ adj. sight,
guar. 2-1/2" groups), from **$1,560.00**
Price: Ultimate Master Combat (5" or 6" bbl., adj. sights,
checkered front strap), from **$2,530.00**
Price: Ultimate Master Combat Compensated
(four-port compensator, adj. sights), from **$2,558.00**

Les Baer Stinger

Les Baer Ultimate Master Combat

Les Baer Bulseye Wadcutter

Rock River Arms Ultimate Match Achiever

Rock River Arms Limited Match

Volquartsen Stingray

ROCK RIVER ARMS 1911-STYLE AUTO PISTOLS
Caliber: 9mm Para., 38 Super, 40 S&W, 45 ACP. **Barrel:** 4" or 5". **Weight:** NA. **Length:** NA. **Grips:** Double-diamond, checkered cocobolo or black synthetic. **Sights:** Bo-Mar low-mount adjustable, Novak fixed with tritium inserts, Heine fixed or Rock River scope mount; dovetail front blade. **Features:** Chrome-moly, machined steel frame and slide; slide serrated front and rear; aluminum speed trigger with 3.5-4 lb. pull; national match KART barrel; lowered and flared ejection port; tuned and polished extractor; beavertail grip safety; beveled mag. well. Other frames offered. Made in U.S. by Rock River Arms Inc.

Price: Elite Commando (4" barrel, Novak tritium sights) **$1,395.00**
Price: Standard Match (5" barrel, Heine fixed sights) **$1,150.00**
Price: National Match Hardball (5" barrel, Bo-Mar adj. sights), from **$1,275.00**
Price: Bullseye Wadcutter (5" barrel, Rock River slide scope mount), from **$1,380.00**
Price: Basic Limited Match (5" barrel, Bo-Mar adj. sights), from . **$1,395.00**
Price: Limited Match (5" barrel, guaranteed 1-1/2" groups at 50 yards), from **$1,795.00**
Price: Hi-Cap Basic Limited (5" barrel, four frame choices), from **$1,895.00**
Price: Ultimate Match Achiever (5" bbl. with compensator, mount and Aimpoint), from **$2,255.00**
Price: Match Master Steel (5" bbl. with compensator, mount and Aimpoint) **$5,000.00**

STI COMPACT AUTO PISTOLS
Caliber: 9mm, 40 S&W. **Barrel:** 3.4". **Weight:** 28 oz. **Length:** 7" overall. **Grips:** Checkered double-diamond rosewood. **Sights:** Heine Low Mount fixed rear, slide integral front. **Features:** Similar to STI 2011 models except has compact frame, 7-shot magazine in 9mm (6-shot in 40 cal.), single-sided thumb safety, linkless barrel lockup system, matte blue finish. From STI International.
Price: (9mm or 40 S&W), from **$746.50**

VOLQUARTSEN CUSTOM 22 CALIBER AUTO PISTOLS
Caliber: 22 LR; 10-shot magazine. **Barrel:** 3.5" to 10"; stainless steel air gauge. **Weight:** 2-1/2 to 3 lbs. 10 oz. **Length:** NA. **Grips:** Finger-grooved plastic or walnut. **Sights:** Adjustable rear and blade front or Weaver-style scope mount. **Features:** Conversions of Ruger Mk. II Auto pistol. Variety of configurations featuring compensators, underlug barrels, etc. Stainless steel finish; black Teflon finish available for additional $85; target hammer, trigger. Made in U.S. by Volquartsen Custom.
Price: 3.5 Compact (3.5" barrel, T/L adjustable rear sight, scope base optional) **$640.00**
Price: Deluxe (barrel to 10", T/L adjustable rear sight) **$675.00**
Price: Deluxe with compensator **$745.00**
Price: Masters (6.5" barrel, finned underlug, T/L adjustable rear sight, compensator) **$950.00**
Price: Olympic (7" barrel, recoil-reducing gas chamber, T/L adjustable rear sight) **$870.00**
Price: Stingray (7.5" ribbed, ported barrel; red-dot sight) **$995.00**
Price: Terminator (7.5" ported barrel, grooved receiver, scope rings) **$730.00**
Price: Ultra-Light Match (6" tensioned barrel, Weaver mount, weighs 2-1/2 lbs.) **$885.00**
Price: V-6 (6", triangular, ventilated barrel with underlug, T/L adj. sight) **$1,030.00**
Price: V-2000 (6" barrel with finned underlug, T/L adj. sight) **$1,095.00**
Price: V-Magic II (7.5" barrel, red-dot sight) **$1,055.00**

Gary Reeder Bandit

Gary Reeder Belle Star

Gary Reeder Black Widow

Gary Reeder Classic Hunter

Gary Reeder Coyote Classic

Gary Reeder Doc Holiday Classic

Gary Reeder Improved #5

GARY REEDER CUSTOM GUNS REVOLVERS

Caliber: 22 WMR, 22 Hornet, 218 Bee, 356 GMR, 41 GNR, 410 GNR, 510 GNR, 357 Magnum, 45 Colt, 44-40, 41 Magnum, 44 Magnum, 454 Casull, 475 Linebaugh, 500 Linebaugh. **Barrel:** 2-1/2" to 12". **Weight:** Varies by model. **Length:** Varies by model. **Grips:** Black Cape buffalo horn, laminated walnut, simulated pearl, black and ivory micarta, others. **Sights:** Notch fixed or adjustable rear, blade or ramp front. **Features:** Custom conversions of Ruger Vaquero, Blackhawk Bisley and Super Blackhawk frames. Jeweled hammer and trigger, tuned action, model name engraved on barrel, additional engraving on frame and cylinder, integral muzzle brake, finish available in high-polish or satin stainless steel or black Chromex. Also available on customer's gun at reduced cost. Other models available. Made in U.S. by Gary Reeder Custom Guns.

Price: 45 Backpacker (weighs 28 oz., comes in 45 Long Colt, all stainless except for lightweight aircraft aluminum gripframe, black Micarta grips, not recommended for Plus P ammo), from **$995.00**

Price: 510 Hunter (octagonal bbl., set back trigger, adjustable sights, 510 GNR 5-shot, built on customer-furnished Ruger frame), from . . **$1,295.00**

Price: African Hunter (6" bbl., with or without muzzle brake, 475 or 500 Linebaugh. Built on customer's gun), from **$1,295.00**

Price: Alaskan Hunter (4-1/2" bbl., 5-shot unfluted freewheeling cylinder, black Micarta grips, soft satin vapor honed finish. Built on customer's gun), from **$1,295.00**

Price: Alaskan Survivalist (3" bbl., Redhawk frame, engraved bear, 45 Colt or 44 Magnum. Built on customer's gun), from **$995.00**

Price: American Hunter (475 Linebaugh or 500 Linebaugh, built to customers specs on furnished Ruger frame), from **$1,395.00**

Price: Arizona Ranger (choice of calibers and barrel lengths, stainless or Black Chromex finish, engraved with original Arizona Ranger badge), from **$850.00**

Price: Badlands Classic (all stainless, 4-1/2" bbl., high polished, fully engraved, Gunfighter grip and cowboy pearl grips), from **$950.00**

Price: Bandit (3-1/2" bbl., special Lightning style grip frame built on a Ruger Vaquero frame, engraved, set back trigger, Colt-style hammer), from **$1,095.00**

Price: Belle Starr Classic (engraved with gunfighter grip, 32 H&R. Built on customer's gun), from **$950.00**

Price: Black Widow (4-5/8" bbl., black Chromex finish, black widow spider engraving), from **$950.00**

Price: BMF (500 Maximum or 500 Linebaugh, 4" barrel, round butt), from **$2,395.00**

Price: Border Classic (Built on customer furnished Schofield; 3" bbl., full scroll engraving, solid silver Mexican coin front sight, custom grips), from **$1,095.00**

Price: Classic 475 (Built on customer furnished base gun, 475 Linebaugh, 5 shot; satin black finish, gunfighter grip, set-back trigger, from **$1,295.00**

Price: Cowtown Classic (stainless finish, engraved with imaged symbolizing the old west, from **$950.00**

Price: Coyote Classic (chambered in 22 Hornet, 22 K-Hornet, 218 Bee, 218 Mashburn Bee, 17 Ackley Bee, 17 Ackley Hornet, 256 Winchester, 25-20, 6-shot unfluted cylinder, heavy 8" barrel, Super Blackhawk gripframe, finish of satin stainless, satin Black Chromex or high polished, comes with laminated cherry grips and Gunfighter grip. Built on customer's gun), from **$1,295.00**

Price: Doc Holliday Classic (3-1/2" bbl., engraved cards and dice, white pearl grips), from **$950.00**

Price: Double Deuce (8" heavy bbl., adjustable sights, laminated grips, 22 WMR 8-shot), from **$995.00**

Price: Gamblers Classic (2-1/2" bbl., engraved cards and dice, no ejector rod housing), from **$950.00**

Price: Improved #5 (field grade or deluxe grade, many options to choose from **$1,495.00**

Gary Reeder Night Hawk

Gary Reeder Rio Grande

Gary Reeder Sidewinder

Gary Reeder Southern Comfort

500 Linebaugh

Gary Reeder Ultimate Black Widow

Price: Kodiak Magnum (heavy 8-1/2" bbl. with deep crown and tight barrel/cylinder gap, satin vapor honed finish), from **$1,095.00**

Price: Lawman Classic (Full custom Vaquero, two-tone finish, Lawman-style engraving, special Lawman gripframe with lanyard ring), from **$950.00**

Price: Lonestar Classic (7-1/2" bbl., highly polished, to a mirror finish, engraved with items relevant to the state of Texas), from **$950.00**

Price: Long Rider Classic (45 long Colt, choice of barrel lengths, midnight black trigger and hammer, gold rings), from **$1,095.00**

Price: Montana Hunter Series (45 long Colt, 4-5/8" bbl., all stainless steel, 5-shot, soft satin finish, walnut grips. Built on customer's gun), from **$1,295.00**

Price: Night Hawk (4" bbl., dual purpose as conceal carry or hunting revolver), from **$1,095.00**

Price: Night Rider (7-1/2" bbl., fully engraved with contrasting light colored stag grips), from **$1,095.00**

Price: O.K. Corral Classic (12-1/2" bbl., engraved with western trappings, Black Chromex finish), from **$1,095.00**

Price: Professional Hunter (stretch frame stainless 5-shot available in calibers including 475 Maximum and 500 Maximum), from **$2,395.00**

Price: Rio Grande Classic (built on any caliber Vaquero in barrel length of choice, Gunfighter grip, engraving is old southwest type with a few western features, specially designed base pin, long tapered hammer, from **$1,095.00**

Price: Sidewinder (3-1/2" bbl., snake scales over entire frame and barrel, black micarta grips), from **$950.00**

Price: Southern Comfort (5-shot cylinder, heavy duty base pin, tear drop hammer, special set back trigger, interchangeable blade system, special gripframe, satin Vapor Honed finish. Built on customer's gun), from **$1,295.00**

Price: Texas Ranger Classic (45 long Colt, 5-1/2" bbl. with other calibers and barrel lengths available, engraved with Texas Ranger badge, gunfighter grip, simulated pearl handles, Black Chromex finish), from **$1,095.00**

Price: Tombstone Classic (3-1/2" bbl. with gold bands, notch sight, birdshead grips), from **$1,095.00**

Price: Trail Rider Classic (7-1/2" bbl., more lengths available, fully engraved with western trappings, pearl grips), from **$1,095.00**

Price: Ultimate 41 (410 GNR 5-shot, built on customer furnished Ruger frame), from **$1,195.00**

Price: Ultimate 44 (ported, special recoil-taming grip frame, sling swivels, 44 Mag. 5-shot, built on customer furnished Ruger Hunter), from . . **$1,395.00**

Price: Ultimate 410 GNR (5-shot 410 GNR freewheeling cylinder), from **$1,295.00**

Price: Ultimate 480 (choice of barrel lengths in any caliber, full vapor honed stainless steel, satin finish Black Chromex or two-toned finish, 5-shot cylinder, heavy barrel, Gunfighter grip, full action job, custom laminated grips, freewheeling cylinder, Belt Mountain base pin), from **$1,195.00**

Price: Ultimate 500 (built on stretch frame in 500 S&W, 5-shot. Choice of bbl. lengths, gunfigher grip, set-back trigger, from **$2,495.00**

Price: Ultimate Back Up (3-1/2" bbl., fixed sights, choice of animal engraving, 475 Linebaugh, 500 Linebaugh built on customer's gun), from **$1,395.00**

Price: Ultimate Black Widow (475 Linebaugh or 500 Linebaugh, heavy duty 5 shot cylinder, heavy high grade barrel, Gunfighter Grip with black Micarta grips, Belt Mountain base pin), from **$1,395.00**

Price: Ultimate Vaquero (engraved barrel, frame and cylinder, made to customer specs), from **$950.00**

Price: Western Classic (standard fieid grade and deluxe grade, many options to choose from) **$1,295.00**

Price: Wichita Classic (41 and 45 Special, stainless steel pins and screws) **$1,095.00**

LINEBAUGH CUSTOM SIXGUNS REVOLVERS

Caliber: 45 Colt, 44 Linebaugh Long, 458 Linebaugh, 475 Linebaugh, 500 Linebaugh, 500 Linebaugh Long, 445 Super Mag. **Barrel:** 4-3/4", 5-1/2", 6", 7-1/2"; other lengths available. **Weight:** NA. **Length:** NA. **Grips:** Dustin Linebaugh Custom made to customer's specs. **Sights:** Bowen steel rear or factory Ruger; blade front. **Features:** Conversions using customer's Ruger Blackhawk Bisley and Vaquero Bisley frames. Made in U.S. by Linebaugh Custom Sixguns.

Price: Small 45 Colt conversion (rechambered cyl., new barrel), from **$1,200.00**

Price: Large 45 Colt conversion (oversized cyl., new barrel, 5- or 6-shot), from **$1,800.00**

Price: 475 Linebaugh, 500 Linebaugh conversions, from **$1,800.00**

Price: Linebaugh and 445 Super Mag calibers on 357 Maximum frame, from **$3,000.00**

SEMI-CUSTOM HANDGUNS — Revolvers

500 Linebaugh Long

**Uberti World Class Top Break
1875 2nd Model Top Break Nickel**

**Uberti World Class Top Break
1875 2nd Model Top Break**

UBERTI WORLD CLASS REVOLVERS
Caliber: 45 Colt, 45-70. **Barrel:** 7". **Weight:** 2.6 lbs. **Length:** 12.8". **Grips:** AA-Grade walnut or pearl-style synthetic. **Sights:** Notch fixed, blade front. **Features:** Engraved versions of 1875 2nd Model Top Break and 1875 2nd Model Top Break Nickel. Made in Italy by Uberti, imported by Benelli USA.
Price: **$2900.00**

SEMI-CUSTOM HANDGUNS — Single Shot

Gary Reeder Ultimate Encore

**Gary Reeder Kodiak
Hunter Dall Sheep**

GARY REEDER CUSTOM GUNS G-2 AND ENCORE PISTOLS
Caliber: 22 Cheetah, 218 Bee, 22 K-Hornet, 22 Hornet, 218 Mashburn Bee, 22-250 Improved, 6mm/284, 7mm STW, 7mm GNR, 30 GNR, 338 GNR, 300 Win. Magnum, 338 Win. Magnum, 350 Rem. Magnum, 358 STA, 375 H&H, 378 GNR, 416 Remington, 416 GNR, 450 GNR, 475 Linebaugh, 500 Linebaugh, 50 Alaskan, 50 AE, 454 Casull; others available. **Barrel:** 8" to 15" (others available). **Weight:** NA. **Length:** Varies with barrel length. **Grips:** Walnut fingergroove. **Sights:** Express-style adjustable rear and barrel band front (Kodiak Hunter); none furnished most models. **Features:** Offers complete guns and barrels in the T/C Contender and Encore. Integral muzzle brake, engraved animals and model name, tuned action, high-polish or satin stainless steel or black Chromex finish. Made in U.S. by Gary Reeder Custom Guns.
Price: Kodiak Hunter (50 AE, 475 Linebaugh, 500 Linebaugh,
510 GNR, or 454 Casull, from **$1,295.00**
Price: Ultimate Encore (15" bbl. with muzzle brake, custom
engraving), from **$1,295.00**

SSK INDUSTRIES CONTENDER AND ENCORE PISTOLS
Caliber: More than 400, including most standard pistol and rifle calibers, as well as 226 JDJ, 6mm JDJ, 257 JDJ, 6.5mm JDJ, 7mm JDJ, 6.5mm Mini-Dreadnaught, 30-06 JDJ, 280 JDJ, 375 JDJ, 6mm Whisper, 300 Whisper and 338 Whisper. **Barrel:** 10" to 26"; blued or stainless; variety of configurations. **Weight:** Varies with barrel length and features. **Length:** Varies with barrel length. **Grips:** Pachmayr, wood models available.

SSK Industries Contender

Features: Offers frames, barrels and complete guns in the T/C Contender and Encore. Fluted, diamond, octagon and round barrels; chrome-plating; muzzle brakes; trigger jobs; variety of stocks and forends; sights and optics. Made in U.S. by SSK Industries.
Price: Blued Contender frame, from **$390.00**
Price: Stainless Contender frame, from **$390.00**
Price: Blued Encore frame, from **$290.00**
Price: Stainless Encore frame, from **$318.00**
Price: Contender barrels, from **$315.00**
Price: Encore barrels, from **$340.00**

Ed Brown Tactical

Ed Brown Marine Sniper

ED BROWN CUSTOM 704 BOLT-ACTION RIFLES

Caliber: 222, 223, 22-250, 220 Swift, 243, 243 Ackley Imp., 25-06, 270 Win., 280 Rem., 280 Ackley Imp., 6mm, 6.5/284, 7mm/08, 7mm Rem. Mag., 7STW, 30/06, 308, 300 Win. Mag., 338 Win. Mag., 375 H&H, 404 Jeffery, 416 Rem. Mag., 416 Rigby, 458 Win. Mag. **Barrel:** 21", 24", 26". **Weight:** NA. **Length:** NA. **Stock:** Fiberglass syn- thetic; swivel studs; recoil pad. **Sights:** Optional; Talley scope rings and base furnished; scope mounting included in price (scope extra). **Features:** Machined receiver; hand-fitted bolt with welded handle; M16-type extractor; three-position safety; trigger adjustable for pull and overtravel; match-quality, hand-lapped barrel with deep countersunk crowning. Made in U.S. by Ed Brown Custom, Inc.

    Price: Model 702 Savanna short- or long-action repeater (lightweight 24" or medium-weight 26" barrel), from . **$3,195.00**
    Price: Model 704 Tactical long-action repeater (heavy contour 26" barrel), from **$2,995.00**
    Price: Model 704 Compact Varmint short-action repeater (med. 21" barrel), from **$3,195.00**
    Price: Model 704 Bushveld dangerous game rifle (24" med. or heavy barrel), from **$2,995.00**
    Price: Model 704 Tactical sniper rifle (26" heavy bbl.), from **$2,995.00**
    Price: Model 704 Marine Sniper (24" heavy bbl.), from **$2,995.00**

Dakota 76 Classic

Dakota 76 Safari

Dakota 97 Hunter

DAKOTA 76 RIFLE

    Caliber: All calibers from 22-250 through 458 Win. Mag. **Barrel:** 23". **Weight:** 6-1/2 lbs. **Length:** NA. **Stock:** Choice of X-grade oil-finished English, Bastogne or Claro walnut. **Features:** Short, standard short magnum or long magnum actions, hand checkered stock with 1" black recoil pad, steel grip cap and single screw stud sling swivels. Many options and upgrades available.

    Price: Dakota 76 Classic, from **$4,995.00**
    Price: Dakota 76 Safari (23" bbl., calibers from 257 Roberts through 458 Win. Mag. drop belly magazine
        with straddle floorplate), from **$5,995.00**
    Price: Dakota 76 African (24" bbl., 450 Dakota, 416 Dakota, 416 Rigby, 404 Jeffrey, four-round magazine),
        from **$6,795.00**
    Price: Dakota 97 Hunter (24" bbl., calibers from 25-06 to 375 Dakota, synthetic stock), from **$2,195.00**
    Price: Longbow Tactical Engagement Rifle (28" bbl., 338 Lapua Mag., 330 Dakota, 300 Dakota,
        McMillan fiberglass stock with full-length action bedding), from **$4,500.00**

SEMI-CUSTOM RIFLES — Bolt-Action

Remington Model 700 ABG

Remington Model 700 Custom KS Safari

Remington Model 700 APR

REMINGTON MODEL 700 CUSTOM SHOP RIFLES

Caliber: 270 Win., 280 Rem., 30-06, 7mm Rem. Mag., 7mm STW, 300 Win. Mag., 300 Wea. Mag., 338 Win. Mag., 8mm Rem. Mag., 35 Whelen, 375 H&H Mag., 416 Rem. Mag., 458 Win. Mag., 7mm RUM, 300 RUM, 338 RUM, 375 RUM. **Barrel:** 22", 24", 26". **Weight:** 6 lbs. 6 oz. to 9 lbs. **Length:** 44-1/4" to 46-1/2" overall. **Stock:** Laminated hardwood, walnut or Kevlar-reinforced fiberglass. **Sights:** Adjustable rear (Safari models); all receivers drilled and tapped for scope mounts. **Features:** Black matte, satin blue or uncolored stainless steel finish; hand-fitted action is epoxy-bedded to stock; tuned trigger; bolt-supported extractor for sure extraction; fancy wood and other options available. Made in U.S. by Remington Arms Co.

Price: Custom KS Mountain Rifle (24" barrel, synthetic stock, 6-3/4 lbs. in mag. cals.), from $1,314.00
Price: Custom KS Safari Stainless (22" barrel, synthetic stock, 9 lbs.), from $2,532.00
Price: Model ABG (African Big Game: 26" bbl., laminated stock, satin blue finish), from $2,865.00
Price: APR (African Plains Rifle: 26" barrel, laminated stock, satin blue finish), from $2,532.00
Price: AWR (Alaskan Wilderness Rifle: 24" barrel, syn. stock, black matte finish), from $2,665.00
Price: Model 700 Custom C Grade, from $2,332.00
Price: Model 700 Custom KS Mountain Rifle, from. $2,265.00

Remington 40-XC KS

Remington 40-XRBR KS

Remington 40-XB Rangemaster

REMINGTON MODEL 40-X CUSTOM SHOP TARGET RIFLES

Caliber: 22 BR, 220 Swift, 22 WMR, 222 Rem., 223 Rem., 22-250, 243 Win., 6mm BR Rem., 6mm Rem., 25-06, 260 Rem., 7mm BR Rem., 7mm Rem. Mag., 7mm STW, 7mm Rem. Ultra Mag., 7.62mm NATO (308 Win.), 30-06, 300 Win. Mag., 300 Rem. Ultra Mag. **Barrel:** 24", 27-1/4"; various twist rates offered. **Weight:** 9-3/4 to 11 lbs. **Length:** 40" to 47" overall. **Stock:** Walnut, laminated wood or Kevlar-reinforced fiberglass. **Sights:** None; receiver drilled and tapped for scope mounts. **Features:** Single shot or 5-shot repeater; carbon steel or stainless steel receiver; externally adjustable trigger (1-1/2 to 3-1/2 lbs.); rubber butt pad. From Remington Arms Co.

Price: 40-XB Rangemaster (27-1/4" bbl., walnut stock, forend rail with hand stop), from $2,265.00
Price: 40-XB (with thumbhole stock), from $2,532.00
Price: 40-XB KS (27-1/4" bbl., black synthetic stock), from $2,532.00
Price: 40-XRBR KS (24" bbl., Remington green synthetic stock with straight comb), from $2,665.00
Price: 40-XC KS (24" bbl., gray synthetic stock with adj. comb), from $2,732.00
Price: 40-XB Tactical (27-1/4" bbl., synthetic stock, matte finish), from $2,665.00

SEMI-CUSTOM RIFLES — Bolt-Action

Remington Model Seven Custom MS

Remington Model Seven AWR

Remington Model Seven Custom KS

REMINGTON MODEL SEVEN CUSTOM SHOP RIFLES

Caliber: 222 Rem., 223 Rem., 22-250 Rem., 243 Win., 6mm Rem., 250 Savage, 257 Roberts, 260 Rem., 308 Win., 7mm-08 Rem., 35 Rem., 350 Rem. Mag. **Barrel:** 20". **Weight:** 5-3/4 to 6-1/2 lbs. **Length:** 39-1/2" overall. **Stock:** Laminated hardwood or Kevlar-reinforced fiberglass. **Sights:** Adjustable ramp rear, hooded blade front. **Features:** Hand-fitted action; epoxy bedded; deep blue or non-reflective black matte finish; drilled and tapped for scope mounts. From Remington Arms Co.
    Price: Model Seven Custom MS (20" bbl., Mannlicher stock, deep blue finish), from **$2,665.00**
    Price: Model Seven Custom KS (20" bbl., synthetic stock, matte finish), from **$2,265.00**
    Price: Model Seven AWR Alaskan Wilderness Rifle, 22" bbl., synthetic stock, from **$2,665.00**

Remington No. 1 Rolling Block Sporter

Remington No. 1 Rolling Block Silhouette

REMINGTON NO. 1 ROLLING BLOCK RIFLES

Caliber: 45-70 Gov't. Barrel: 30". Polished, blued finish, 1:18" twist. Two versions, Sporter and Silhouette. Silhouette has 1.125" diameter, heavy round barrel. Weight: 8.75 lbs. Length: 46.5" overall. Stock: On Sporter, pistol-grip American walnut, sharp-cut checkering on forend and buttstock. Silhouette is shotgun-style buttstock with pistol grip. Sights: Sights: Adjustable, center-notch buckhorn rear sight, front blade sight on Sporter. On Silhouette, front sight dovetail, no sights. Tang-mounted vernier sight and front globe sight with spirit level optional. Features: Single set trigger, meets NRA blackpowder cartridge rifle (BPCR) silhouette requirements. Button-rifled barrel .004" deep, suitable for cast bullets. From Remington Arms Co.
    Price: Mid-Range Sporter **$2,665.00**
    Price: Silhouette **$3,065.00**

SEMI-CUSTOM RIFLES — Bolt-Action

John Rigby African Express Rifle

JOHN RIGBY CUSTOM AFRICAN EXPRESS RIFLE

Caliber: 375 H&H Magnum, 416 Rigby, 458 Winchester. **Barrel:** To customer specs. **Weight:** NA. **Length:** To customer specs. **Stock:** Customer's choice. **Sights:** Express-type rear, hooded ramp front; scope mounts offered. **Features:** Handcrafted bolt-action rifle built to customer specifications. Variety of engraving and stock wood options available.

    Price: African Express Rifle,
       from **$28,500.00**

John Rigby African Express Rifle engraving

JOHN RIGBY BOLT-ACTION RIFLES

Caliber: 300 H&H, 375 H&H, 416 Rigby, 458 Win., 500 Jeffrey (other calibers upon request) **Barrel:** NA. **Weight:** NA. **Length:** NA. **Stock:** Exhibition grade English walnut. **Sights:** Quarter rib with Express sights containing flip up night sight. **Features:** Stock custom-fitted to buyer specifications, detachable scope mounts included, Pac Nor Match Grade barrel.
    Price: John Rigby Bolt Action Rifle, from **$28,500.00**

TIME PRECISION BOLT-ACTION RIFLES

Caliber: 22 LR, 222, 223, 308, 378, 300 Win. Mag., 416 Rigby, others. **Barrel:** NA. **Weight:** 10 lbs. and up. **Length:** NA. **Stock:** Fiberglass. **Sights:** None; receiver drilled and tapped for scope mount. **Features:** Thirty different action types offered, including single shots and repeaters for bench rest, varmint and big-game hunting. Machined chrome-moly action; three-position safety; Shilen match trigger (other triggers available); twin cocking cams; dual firing pin. Built to customer specifications. From Time Precision.
    Price: 22 LR Bench Rest Rifle (Shilen match-grade stainless steel bbl., fiberglass stock), from **$2,202.00**
    Price: 22 LR Target Rifle, from **$2,220.00**
    Price: 22 LR Sporter, from **$1,980.00**
    Price: 22 LR Benchrest Rifle, from **$2,202.00**
    Price: Hunting Rifle (calibers to 30-06), from **$2,202.00**
    Price: Benchrest Rifle (most calibers), from **$2,202.00**
    Price: Hunting Rifle (7mm Rem. Mag., 300 Win. Mag., 338 Win. Mag.), from **$2,322.00**

Weatherby Safari Grade

Weatherby Crown Custom

Weatherby Custom close-up

WEATHERBY CUSTOM SHOP BOLT-ACTION RIFLES

Caliber: 257 Wby. Mag., 270 Wby. Mag., 7mm Wby. Mag., 300 Wby. Mag., 340 Wby. Mag., 375 H&H Mag., 378 Wby. Mag., 416 Wby. Mag., 460 Wby. Mag. **Barrel:** 24", 26", 28". **Weight:** NA. **Length:** NA. **Stock:** Monte Carlo, modified Monte Carlo or Classic design in Exhibition- or Exhibition Special Select grades of claro or French wal- nut; injection-molded synthetic in Snow Camo, Alpine Camo or Dark Timber colors. **Sights:** Quarter-rib rear with one standing and one folding leaf, hooded ramp front (Safari Grade); drilled and tapped for scope mount. Features: Rosewood or ebony pistol-grip caps with inlaid diamonds in rosewood, walnut or maple; three grades of engraving patterns for receiver, bolt and handle; gold inlays; wooden inlaid buttstock, forearm and magazine box; three grades of engraved and gold inlaid rings and bases; canvas/leather, solid leather or leather with oak trim case. From the Weatherby Custom Shop.

Price: Safari Grade (engr. floorplate, oil-finished French wal. stock w/fleur-de-lis checkering.) **$6.050.00**
Price: Crown (engr., inlaid floorplate, engr. bbl. and receiver, hand-carved walnut stock) **$7,757.00**
Price: Crown Custom (engraved barrel, receiver and triggerguard, hand-carved walnut stock, damascened bolt and follower with checkered knob), from **$7,757.00**
Price: Outfitter Krieger (Krieger stainless steel bbl.) **$3,639.00**
Price: Outfitter Custom (standard barrel, Bell and Carlson syn. camo stock), from **$2,583.00**
Price: Dangerous Game Rifle (chrome moly Criterion barrel by Krieger Monte Carlo-style composite stock, Mark V action), from **$3,095.00**

Winchester African Express

WINCHESTER MODEL 70 CLASSIC CUSTOM RIFLES

Caliber: 375 H&H Mag., 416 Rem. Mag., 458 Win. Mag., 458 Lott, 470 Capstick, 257 Roberts, 260 Rem., 7mm- 08 Rem., 300 WSM, 270 WSM, 7mm WSM, 308 Win., 358 Win., 450 Marlin, 270 Win., 7mm Win., 30-06 Spfld., 25-06 Rem., 6.5x55 Swe., 264 Win. Mag., 280 Rem., 35 Whelen, 7mm Rem. Mag., 7mm Ultra Mag., 7mm STW, 300 Win. Mag., 300 Wea. Mag., 300 Ultra. Mag., 338 Ultra Mag., 375 H&H (Lwt). **Barrel:** 22", 24", 26". **Weight:** 6.5 to 9.5 lbs. **Length:** NA. **Stock:** Various grades of walnut and synthetic stocks available. **Sights:** Three-leaf express rear, adjustable front, (Express models); none furnished on other models. **Features:** Match-grade cut rifled barrels with squared, hand-honed actions. Most are available in stainless or blued, and right- or left-handed, hand-fitted actions. All utilize the pre-'64 type action with controlled round feed, receiver-mounted blade ejector and specially-tuned trigger systems. All are shipped in a hard case. Made in U.S.A. by Winchester/U.S. Repeating Arms Co.

Price: Model 70 Classic Custom African Express (22" or 24" barrel, 9.25 to 9.5 lbs), from **$4,572.00**
Price: Safari Express (24" barrel, 9 to 9.25 lbs.), from **$3,043.00**
Price: Short Action (24" barrel, 7.5 to 8.25 lbs.), from **$2,708.00**
Price: Featherweight (22" barrel, 7.25 lbs., 270 Win., 7mm Win., 30-06 Spfld.), from **$2,708.00**
Price: Carbon (24" or 26" barrel, 6.5 to 7 lbs.), from **$3,233.00**
Price: Ultimate Classic (24" or 26" barrel, 7.5 to 7.75 lbs.), from **$2,941.00**
Price: Extreme Weather (22", 24" or 26" barrel, 7.25 to 7.5 lbs.), from **$2,525.00**

Bushmaster DCM Competition Rifle

Volquartsen Grey Ghost

BROWNING SEMI-AUTO 22 LUXE

Caliber: 22 LR. **Barrel:** 19-1/4". **Weight:** 5 lbs. 3 oz. **Length:** 37". **Stock:** Polished walnut. **Sights:** Adjustable folding leaf rear, gold bead front. **Features:** The traditional John Browning-designed .22 takedown autoloader with bottom eject. Grooved receiver will accept most groove or tip-off type mounts or receiver sights. Custom shop ver- sions are available in two grades: SA 22 Grade II and SA 22 Grade III.
    Price: From **$2,920.00**

BROWNING BAR MARK I

The original Browning BAR Mark I from the Browning Custom Shop in Belgium available in Grade IV and Grade D.
    Price: From **$7,216.00**

BUSHMASTER SEMI-AUTO RIFLES

Caliber: 223. **Barrel:** 16" regular or fluted, 20" regular, heavy or fluted, 24" heavy or fluted. **Weight:** 6.9 to 8.37 lbs. **Length:** 34.5" to 38.25" overall. **Stock:** Polymer. **Sights:** Fully adjustable dual flip-up aperture rear, blade front or Picatinny rail for scope mount. **Features:** Versions of the AR-15 style rifle. Aircraft-quality aluminum receiver; chrome-lined barrel and chamber; chrome-moly-vanadium steel barrel with 1:9" twist; manganese phosphate matte finish; forged front sight; receiver takes down without tools; serrated, finger groove pistol grip. Made in U.S.A. by Bushmaster Firearms/Quality Parts Co.
    Price: DCM Competition Rifle **$1,495.00**

LES BAER AR 223 AUTO RIFLES

Caliber: 223. **Barrel:** 16-1/4", 20", 22" or 24"; cryo-treated, stainless steel bench-rest grade. **Weight:** NA. **Length:** NA. **Stock:** Polymer. **Sights:** None; Picatinny rail for scope mount. **Features:** Forged and machined upper and lower receiver; single- or double-stage adjustable trigger; free-float handguard; Bear Coat protective finish. Made in U.S.A. by Les Baer Custom.
    Price: Ultimate Super Varmint (Jewell two-stage trigger, guar. to shoot 1/2 MOA groups), from **$1,989.00**
    Price: Ultimate M4 Flattop (16-1/4" bbl., Ultra single-stage trigger), from **$2,195.00**
    Price: Ultimate IPSC Action (20" bbl., Jewell two-stage trigger), from **$2,230.00**

SSK INDUSTRIES AR-15 RIFLES

Caliber: 223, 6mm PPC, 6.5mm PPC, 6.5 Grendel, 300 Whisper and other wildcats. **Barrel:** 16-1/2" and longer (to order). **Weight:** NA. **Length:** NA. **Stock:** Black plastic. **Sights:** Blade front, adjustable rear (scopes and red- dot sights available). **Features:** Variety of designs to full match-grade guns offered. Customer's gun can be rebarreled or accurized. From SSK Industries.
    Price: Complete AR-15, from **$1,800.00**
    Price: A2 upper unit (front sight, short handguard **$1,100.00**
    Price: Match Grade upper unit (bull barrel, tubular handguard, scope mount) **$1,100.00**

VOLQUARTSEN CUSTOM 22 CALIBER AUTO RIFLES

Caliber: 22 LR, 22 Magnum. **Barrel:** 16-1/2" to 20"; stainless steel air gauge. **Weight:** 4-3/4 to 5-3/4 lbs. **Length:** NA. **Stock:** Synthetic or laminated. **Sights:** Not furnished; Weaver base provided. **Features:** Conversions of the Ruger 10/22 rifle. Tuned trigger with 2-1/2 to 3-1/2 lb. pull. Variety of configurations and features. From Volquartsen Custom.
    Price: Ultra-Light (22 LR, 16-1/2" tensioned barrel, synthetic stock, from **$670.00**
    Price: Grey Ghost (22 LR, 18-1/2" barrel, laminated wood stock), from **$690.00**
    Price: Deluxe (22 LR, 20" barrel, laminated wood or fiberglass stock), from **$850.00**
    Price: Mossad (22 LR, 20" fluted and ported barrel, fiberglass thumbhole stock), from **$970.00**
    Price: VX-2500 (22 LR, 20" fluted and ported barrel, aluminum/fiberglass stock), from **$1,044.00**
    Price: Volquartsen 22 LR (stainless steel receiver), from **$920.00**
    Price: Volquartsen 22 Mag (22 WMR, stainless steel receiver), from **$950.00**

John Rigby Boxlock

John Rigby Sidelock close-up

BERETTA EXPRESS DOUBLE RIFLES

Caliber: 9.3x74R, 375 H&H Mag., 416 Rigby, 458 Win. Mag., 470 Nitro Express, 500 Nitro Express. **Barrel:** 23" to 25". **Weight:** 11 lbs. **Length:** NA. **Stock:** Hand-finished, hand-checkered walnut with cheek rest. **Sights:** Folding-leaf, Express-type rear, blade front. **Features:** High-strength steel action with reinforced receiver sides; top tang extends to stock comb for strength; double triggers (articulated front trigger and automatic blocking device eliminate chance of simultaneous discharge); hand-cut, stepped rib; engraved receiver; trapdoor compartment in stock for extra cartridges; spare front sights stored in pistol-grip cap. Imported from Italy by Beretta USA.

Price: SSO6 o/u (optional claw mounts for scope), from **$21,000.00**
Price: SSO6 EELL o/u (engraved game scenes or color case-hardened with gold inlays), from **$23,500.00**
Price: 455 s/s (color case-hardened action), from **$36,000.00**
Price: 455 EELL s/s (receiver engraved with big-game animals), from **$47,000.00**

BROWNING EXPRESS RIFLES

Still made in Belgium in the traditional manner, two models are available, Herstal and CCS 375. Produced in five different grades of embellishment. Other specifications NA.
Price: From **$11,733.00**

JOHN RIGBY DOUBLE RIFLES

Caliber: 375 H&H, 500/416, 450 Nitro Express, 470 Nitro Express, 500 Nitro Express, 577 Nitro Express. **Barrel:** To customer specs. **Weight:** NA. **Length:** To customer specs. **Stock:** To customer specs. **Sights:** Dovetail, express-type sights; claw-foot scope mount available. **Features:** Handcrafted to customer specifications. Boxlock or sidelock action, hand-fitted; variety of engraving and other options offered.

Price: Rigby Boxlock, from **$28,500.00**
Price: Rigby Sidelock, from **$45,500.00**

Ballard No. 5 Pacific

BALLARD RIFLE, LLC

Caliber: 22 LR, 32-40, 38-55, 40-65 Win., 40-70 SS, 40-90, 45-70 Gov't., 45-90, 45-110, 50-70 Gov't., 50-90.
Barrel: 24", 26", 30", 32", 34". **Weight:** 7-1/2 to 11-1/2 lbs. **Stock:** American black walnut. **Sights:** Blade front, Rocky Mountain rear, others. **Features:** Authentic reproductions faithful to the original patent. Receivers and internal parts machined from solid 8620 steel stock, not castings. Hand finished. Many options.

Price: No. 1-1/2 Hunter's Rifle (30" round bbl., single trigger, S lever), from $2,050.00
Price: No. 1-3/4 Far West (30" round regular or heavyweight bbl., S lever), from $2,250.00
Price: No. 3 Gallery Rifle (24", 26" or 30" lightweight octagon bbl., rifle bottsrock with
      steel crescent buttplate, S lever), from $2,050.00
Price: No. 3F Fine Gallery Rifle (26", 28" or 30" octagon bbl., pistol grip,
      single or double set triggers), from $2,500.00
Price: No. 4 Perfection (30" or 32" octagon bbl. single or double set trigger), from $2,250.00
Price: No. 4-1/2 Mid Range (30" or 32" standard or heavyweight half octagon bbl.,
      single or double set triggers, pistol grip shotgun buttstock), from $2,250.00
Price: No. 5 Pacific (30" or 32" standard or heavyweight octagon bbl., standard stocks in
      rifle or shotgun configuration), from $2,575.00
Price: No. 5-1/2 Montana Model (30" or 32" heavyweight octagon bbl., under-barrel wiping
      rod, set triggers, ring lever), from $2,725.00
Price: No. 6 Off Hand Rifle (30", 32" or 34" half octagon bbl., blade front sight,
      pistol grip receiver, double set triggers), from $2,550.00
Price: No. 7 Long Range (32" or 34" standard or heavyweight half octagon bbl.,
      pistol grip shotgun buttstock, single or double set trigger), from $2,250.00
Price: No. 8 Union Hill Model (30" half octagon standard or heavyweight bbl., double set triggers,
      pistol grip stock with cheekpiece, full loop lever) from $2,500.00
Price: Standard Sporting Model 1885 High Wall (30" or 32" octagonal bbl., single trigger, small S lever), from . $2,050.00
Price: Special Sporting Model 1885 High Wall (32" bbl., shotgun buttstock with cheekpiece,
      shotgun buttplate, double set triggers), from $2,200.00

C. Sharps Model 1885 Highwall Classic Sporting

C. Sharps Model 1877 Custom LR Target

C. SHARPS ARMS RIFLES

Caliber: 22 RF to 50-140-3 1/4 Sharps. **Barrel:** Octagon 18" to 34". **Weight:** 9-18 lbs. **Stock:** American English walnut (premium straight grain to presentation). **Sights:** Short range to long range target. **Features:** Authentic replicas of Sharps rifles. Models 1874, 1877 & 1885 machined from solid steel. Made in U.S. by C. Sharps Arms Co. Inc.

Price: Model 1874 Hartford, from $1,775.00
Price: Model 1874 Bridgeport, from $1,495.00
Price: Model 1875 Sporting, from $1,095.00
Price: Model 1875 Classic, from $1,385.00
Price: Model 1875 Target, from $1,136.63
Price: Model 1877 Custom LR Target, from $5,500.00
Price: Model 1885 Highwall Sporting, from $1,350.00
Price: Model 1885 Highwall Classic Sporting, from $1,550.00

SEMI-CUSTOM RIFLES — Single Shot

Dakota Model 10

DAKOTA MODEL 10

Caliber: Most from 22 LR through 404 Dakota. **Barrel:** 23". **Length:** NA. **Weight:** 5-1/2 lbs. **Stock:** Walnut.
Sights: NA. **Features:** Falling block action machined from prehardened 4140 bar stock. Many options.
Price: Dakota Model 10, from $3,795.00

Lone Star Silhouette

LONE STAR ROLLING BLOCK RIFLES

Caliber: 30-40 Krag, 30-30, 32-40, 38-55, 40-50 SS, 40-50 BN, 40-65, 40-70 SS, 40-70 BN, 40-82, 40-90 SBN, 40-90 SS, 44-90 Rem. Sp., 45 Colt, 45-120 (3-1/4"), 45-110 (2-7/8"), 45-100, 45-90, 45- 70, 50-70, 50-90. **Barrel:** 26" to 34". **Weight:** 6 to 11 lbs. **Length:** NA. **Stock:** American walnut. **Sights:** Buckhorn rear, blade or Beech front. **Features:** Authentic replicas of Remington rolling block rifles. Octagon barrel; bone-pack, color case-hardened action; drilled and tapped for Vernier sight; single, single-set or double-set trigger; variety of sight, finish and engraving options. Fires blackpowder or factory ammo. Made in U.S. by Lone Star Rifle Co. Inc.
    Price: No. 5 Classic Sporting Rifle (30-30, 25-35, .33 WCF octagon, 30-40 Krag,
       26" barrel, buckhorn rear sight) $2,500.00
    Price: Cowboy Action Rifle (28" octagonal barrel, buckhorn rear sight) $1,995.00
    Price: Silhouette Rifle (32" or 34" octagonal barrel, drilled and tapped for Vernier sight) $1,995.00
    Price: Sporting Rifle (straight grip, semi-crescent butt, octagonal bbl.), from $1,995.00
    Price: Creedmoor (34" bbl. identical to original rifle) $1,995.00
    Price: Buffalo Rifle (12 or 16 lbs., octagonal bbl.) $3,500.00
    Price: Custer Commemorative (50-70 only, octagonal bbl.) exact replica of General George Armstrong
       Custer's Remington Sporting Rifle $3,500.00

Meacham Low-Wall

MEACHAM HIGH-WALL SILHOUETTE RIFLE

Caliber: Any rimmed cartridge. **Barrel:** 30", 34" octagon. **Weight:** 8 to 15 lbs. **Length:** NA. **Stock:** Fancy eastern black walnut with cheekpiece and shadow line. **Sights:** Tang drilled for Win. base, 3/8" front dovetail. **Features:** Parts interchangeable copy of '85 Winchester. Numerous options include single trigger, single set trigger, or Schuetzen double set triggers, thick side or thin side bone charcoal color case-hardened action.
    Price: Meacham High-Wall Silhouette, from $3,999.00
    Price: Meacham Low-Wall Rifle (Calibers: 22 RF Match or 17 HMR,
       rimfire and centerfire pistol cartridges, .22 Hornet or Bee), from $3,999.00

Remington No. 1 Mid-Range Sporter

REMINGTON CUSTOM SHOP ROLLING BLOCK RIFLES

Caliber: 45-70. **Barrel:** 30". **Weight:** NA. **Length:** NA. **Stock:** American walnut. **Sights:** Buckhorn rear and blade front (optional tang-mounted Vernier rear, globe with spirit level front). **Features:** Satin blue finish with case-colored receiver; single set trigger; steel Schnabel fore end tip; steel buttplate. From Remington Arms Co. Custom Gun Shop.
    Price: No. 1 Mid-Range Sporter (round or half-octagon barrel) $1,450.00
    Price: No. 1 Silhouette (heavy barrel with 1:18" twist; no sights) $1,560.00

Benelli Executive I

Benelli Executive II

Benelli Executive III

Close-up of Benelli Executive I engraving

Close-up of Benelli Executive II engraving

Close-up of Benelli Executive III engraving

BENELLI WORLD CLASS SHOTGUNS

Gauge: 12 or 20, 3" chamber; **Barrel:** 26". **Weight:** 6 to 7.4 lbs. **Length:** 47.6" **Stock:** AA or AAA Select Grade oil-finished walnut.
Features: Giovanelli-engraved stainless steel lowever receiver, high-polish blue upper receiver and barrel. Sterling silver grip cap medallion for initials. Walnut buttplates, cut-checkered and attached with brass escutcheons. From Benelli USA.

Price: Executive I	**$6,900.00**
Price: Executive II	**$7,800.00**
Price: Executive III	**$8,800.00**
Price: Elite Set, 12/20 ga.	**$4,300.00**

SEMI-CUSTOM SHOTGUNS

Beretta Jubilee II 12-gauge

Beretta ASE Deluxe

Close-up of Beretta Jubilee II engraving

Close-up of Beretta ASE Deluxe engraving

BERETTA PREMIUM GRADE SHOTGUNS

Gauge: 12, 20, 410, 3" chamber; 28, 2-3/4" chamber. **Barrel:** 26", 28", 30", 32". **Weight:** 5 to 7-1/2 lbs. **Length:** NA. **Stock:** Highly figured English or American walnut; straight or pistol grip; hand-checkered. **Features:** Machined nickel-chrome-moly action, hand-fitted; cross-bolt breech lock; Boehler Antinit steel barrels with fixed chokes or Mobilchoke tubes; single selective or non-selective or double trigger; numerous stock and engraving options. From Beretta USA.

Price: Giubileo (Jubilee) o/u (engraved sideplates, trigger guard, safety and top lever), from **$12,900.00**
Price: Giubileo II (Jubilee II) s/s (English-style stock, engraved sideplates and fixtures), from **$12,900.00**
Price: ASE Deluxe o/u (engraved receiver and forend cap), from **$24,000.00**
Price: SO5 Trap (single, non-selective trigger, heavy beavertail forend, fixed chokes), from **$17,490.00**
Price: SO5 Skeet (26" or 28" bbl., heavy beavertail forend, fixed chokes), from **$17,490.00**
Price: SO5 Sporting (single, selective trigger, Mobilchoke tubes), from **$17,490.00**
Price: SO6 EELL o/u (engraved receiver with gold inlays, custom-fit stock), from **$34,900.00**
Price: SO6 EL o/u (light English scroll engravings on receiver), from **$23,900.00**
Price: SO6 EESS o/u (enamel-colored receiver in green, red or blue, arabesque engravings), from **$34,900.00**
Price: SO9 o/u (single, non-selective trigger, engraved receiver and fixtures), from **$44,500.00**

Beretta SO6 EELL 12-gauge

Beretta SO6 EELL engraving

Beretta SO6 EL engraving

SEMI-CUSTOM SHOTGUNS

Browning LC1

Browning LC2

BROWNING SUPERPOSED & BSL SHOTGUNS

Gauge: 20, Both the BSL side-by-side and the Superposed over-and under are still made in Belgium in the traditional, time-honored manner. The BSL is available in two grades, LC1 (blued receiver) and LC2 (silver-colored receiver). The Superposed is available in 18 grades. Custom options include: engraving of name or initials, second set of barrels, special finish or checkering, special stock dimensions, personalized engraving scenes and upgraded wood. Other specifications NA.
    Price: From **$18,566.00**

DAKOTA LEGEND/PREMIER SHOTGUNS

Available in all standard gauges, features include exhibition English walnut stock, French grey finish, 50 percent coverage engraving, straight grip, splinter forend, double trigger, 27" barrels, game rib with gold bead, selective ejectors, choice of chokes. Various options available.
    Price: Dakota Premier Grade, from **$13,950.00**
    Price: Dakota Legend Shotgun (27" bbls., special selection English walnut stock,
        straight grip, splinter forend), from **$18,000.00**

Franchi Fenice

Franchi Veloce

FRANCHI FENICE SEMIAUTO, VELOCE SP O/U SHOTGUNS

Gauge: 20, 28, 2-3/4" chamber. **Barrel:** 26", 28". **Weight:** 5.4-5.7 lbs. **Length:** 48". **Stock:** AAA-Grade walnut, hand-rubbed oil finish.
Features: Fenice based on AL48 semiauto shotgun. Aluminum alloy receiver, nickel plated, engraved , includes gold inlays, gold-plated trigger. Veloce has monobloc receiver, jewel finished, wooden buttplate, gold-plated trigger
    Price: Fenice. **$1,199.00**
    Price: Veloce. **$2.499.00**

JOHN RIGBY SHOTGUNS

*John Rigby Side-by-Side
12-gauge engraving*

Gauge: 12, 16, 20, 28 and 410 bore. **Barrel:** To customer specs. **Weight:** NA. **Length:** To customer specs. **Stock:** Customer's choice. **Features:** True sidelock side-by-side and over-under shotguns made to customer's specifications. Hand-fitted actions and stocks; engraved receivers embellished with game scenes; over-under includes removable choke tubes.
Price: Sidelock over-under (single selective,
    non-selective or double triggers), from **$47,500.00**
Price: Sidelock side-by-side (engraved receiver,
    choice of stock wood), from **$39,950.00**
Price: Hammer shotguns (manual-cocking hammers,
    rebounding firing pins and hammers;
    extractors only), from **$30,000.00**

SEMI-CUSTOM SHOTGUNS

Merkel 47E **Merkel 47SL** **Merkel 280EL** **Merkel 303EL** **Merkel 2001EL**

MERKEL EXHIBITION, VINTAGERS EXPO AND CUSTOM ENGRAVED SHOTGUNS

Gauge: 12, 16, 20, 28, 410. **Barrel:** 26-3/4", 28"; others optional. **Weight:** NA. **Length:** NA. **Stock:** Highly figured walnut; English (straight) or pistol grip. **Features:** Highly engraved versions of Merkel over-under and side-by-side shotguns. Imported from Germany by GSI Inc.
Price: .... **Call**

PERAZZI SCO, SCO GOLD, EXTRA AND EXTRA GOLD SHOTGUNS

Gauge: 12, 20, 28, 410. **Barrel:** 23-5/8" to 34". **Weight:** 6 lbs. 3 oz. to 8 lb. 13 oz. **Length:** NA. **Stock:** To customer specs. **Features:** Enhanced, engraved models of game and competition over-under shotguns. Customer may choose from many engraved hunting and wildlife scenes. Imported from Italy by Perazzi USA Inc.
Price: SCO Grade in competition and game o/u guns (fully engraved receiver), from **$31,275.00**
Price: SCO Gold Grade in comp. and game o/u guns (engraved w/gold inlays), from **$35,336.00**
Price: Extra Grade in competition and game o/u guns (highly detailed engraving), from **$85,140.00**
Price: Extra Gold Grade in comp. and game o/u guns (detailed engraving w/gold inlays), from **$91,684.00**
Price: SCO Grade with engraved sideplates (extends engraved area), from **$47,968.00**
Price: SCO Gold Grade with engraved sideplates, from **$54,137.00**

Perazzi MX-8

Perazzi MX-10

Perazzi SCO Grade engraving   *Perazzi SCO Gold engraving*   *Perazzi Extra engraving*

SEMI-CUSTOM SHOTGUNS

Remington 11-87 "F" Grade

REMINGTON CUSTOM SHOP AUTO SHOTGUNS

Gauge: 10, 12, 20, 28. **Barrel:** 21" to 30". **Weight:** NA. **Length:** NA. **Stock:** Two grades of American walnut. **Features:** Engraved versions of the Model 11-87 and Model 1100 shotgun. "D" or "F" grade fancy walnut, hand-checkered stock; choice of ebony, rosewood, skeleton steel or solid steel grip cap; choice of solid steel, standard, Old English or ventilated recoil pad; optional inletted gold oval with three initials on bottom of stock. From Remington Arms. Co. Custom Gun Shop.
   Price: 11-87 and 1100 "D" Grade (English scroll engraving on receiver, breech and trig. guard) $3,723.00
   Price: 11-87 and 1100 "F" Grade (engraved game scene, "F" Grade walnut stock) $7,245.00
   Price: 11-87 and 1100 "F" Grade with gold inlay (inlaid three-panel engraved game scene) $10,663.00

REMINGTON CUSTOM SHOP PUMP SHOTGUNS

Gauge: 10, 12, 20, 28, 410. **Barrel:** 20" to 30". **Weight:** NA. **Length:** NA. **Stock:** Two grades of American walnut. **Features:** Engraved versions of the Model 870 shotgun. "D" or "F" grade fancy walnut hand-checkered stock; choice of ebony, rosewood, skeleton steel or solid steel grip cap; choice of solid steel, standard, Old English or ventilated recoil pad; optional inletted gold oval with three initials on bottom of stock. From Remington Arms Co. Custom Gun Shop.
   Price: 870 "D" Grade (English scroll engraving on receiver, breech and trig. guard) $3,723.00
   Price: 870 "F" Grade (engraved game scene, "F" grade walnut stock) $7,245.00
   Price: 870 "F" Grade with gold inlay (inlaid three-panel engraved game scene) $10,663.00

REMINGTON CUSTOM SHOP OVER/UNDER SHOTGUNS

Gauge: 12. **Barrel:** 26", 28", 30". **Weight:** 7-1/2 to 8 lbs. **Length:** 42-1/2" to 47-1/4". **Stock:** American walnut. **Features:** Barrels made of chrome-moly steel with 3" chambers, finger grooved forend, fully brazed barrel side ribs, hardened trunions, automatic ejectors. Made in U.S. by Remington Arms Co. Custom Gun Shop.
   Price: Remington Model 332 D Grade, from $4,184.00
   Price: Model 332 F Grade, from $7,706.00
   Price: Model 332 F Grade w/gold inlay, from $11,122.00

Tar-Hunt DSG

TAR-HUNT DSG (DESIGNATED SLUG GUN)

Gauge: 12, 16. **Barrel:** 23". **Weight:** NA. **Length:** NA. **Stock:** NA. **Features:** Tar-Hunt converts the basic Remington 870 shotgun into a configuration for shooting slugs only by installation of a non-removable custom fit Shaw rifled slug barrel with muzzle brake. The 870 Wingmaster is fitted with a barrel with 2-3/4" chamber, the 870 Express Mag. and Wingmaster Mag. have a 3-inch chamber and the 870 Express Super Mag. will have a 3-1/2" chamber. Included are Leupold two-piece windage bases which will accept any standard type turn in rings.
   Price: Tar-Hunt DSG (with customer furnished Remington 870) $450.00
   Price: Tar-Hunt Express (complete gun with black synthetic stock) $695.00
   Price: Tar-Hunt Wingmaster $950.00

UBERTI WORLD CLASS SHARPS SPORTING

Caliber: 45-70. **Barrel:** 32". **Weight:** NA. **Length:** 9.5 lbs. **Stock:** AAA-Grade walnut for both buttstock and forend. **Features:** Engraved receiver with bison and bison's head.
   Price $3,500.00

Includes models suitable for several forms of competition and other sporting purposes.

Accu-Tek AT-380 II 380 ACP

Auto-Ordnance
1911A1 Standard

Auto-Ordnance Deluxe

Baer Custom Carry

Auto-Ordnance
1911PKZSEW

Baer Premium II

Baer Premium II Super-Tac

ACCU-TEK AT-380 II 380 ACP PISTOL
Caliber: 380 ACP, 6-shot magazine. **Barrel:** 2.8". **Weight:** 23.5 oz. **Length:** 6.125" overall. **Grips:** Textured black composition. **Sights:** Blade front, rear adjustable for windage. **Features:** Made from 17-4 stainless steel, has an exposed hammer, manual firing-pin safety block and trigger disconnect. Magazine release located on the bottom of the grip. American made, lifetime warranty. Comes with two 6-round stainless steel magazines and a California-approved cable lock. Introduced 2006. Made in U.S.A. by Accu-Tek.
Price: Satin stainless **$249.00**

AUTO-ORDNANCE 1911A1 AUTOMATIC PISTOL
Caliber: 45 ACP, 7-shot magazine. **Barrel:** 5". **Weight:** 39 oz. **Length:** 8.5" overall. **Grips:** Brown checkered plastic with medallion. **Sights:** Blade front, rear drift-adjustable for windage. **Features:** Same specs as 1911A1 military guns-parts interchangeable. Frame and slide blued; each radius has non-glare finish. Made in U.S.A. by Kahr Arms.
Price: 1911SE Standard, blued **$609.00**
Price: 1911WGSE Deluxe, black textured wraparound grips **$615.00**
Price: 1911PKZSEW Parkerized, intr. 2007 . . . . **$662.00**

BAER 1911 CUSTOM CARRY AUTO PISTOL
Caliber: 45 ACP, 7- or 10-shot magazine. **Barrel:** 5". **Weight:** 37 oz. **Length:** 8.5" overall. **Grips:** Checkered walnut. **Sights:** Baer improved ramp-style dovetailed front, Novak low-mount rear. **Features:** Baer forged NM frame, slide and barrel with stainless bushing. Baer speed trigger with 4-lb. pull. Partial listing shown. Made in U.S.A. by Les Baer Custom, Inc.
Price: Standard size, blued **$1,640.00**
Price: Standard size, stainless **$1,690.00**
Price: Comanche size, blued **$1,640.00**
Price: Comanche size, stainless **$1,690.00**
Price: Comanche size, aluminum frame, blued slide **$1,923.00**
Price: Comanche size, aluminum frame, stainless slide **$1,995.00**

BAER 1911 ULTIMATE RECON PISTOL
Caliber: 45 ACP, 7- or 10-shot magazine. **Barrel:** 5". **Weight:** 37 oz. **Length:** 8.5" overall. **Grips:** Checkered cocobolo. **Sights:** Baer improved

ramp-style dovetailed front, Novak low-mount rear. **Features:** NM Caspian frame, slide and barrel with stainless bushing. Baer speed trigger with 4-lb. pull. Includes integral Picatinny rail and Sure-Fire X-200 light. Made in U.S.A. by Les Baer Custom, Inc. Introduced 2006.
Price: Bead blast blued **$2,988.00**
Price: Bead blast chrome **$3,230.00**

BAER 1911 PREMIER II AUTO PISTOL
Caliber: 38 Super, 400 Cor-Bon, 45 ACP, 7- or 10-shot magazine. **Barrel:** 5". **Weight:** 37 oz. **Length:** 8.5" overall. **Grips:** Checkered rosewood, double diamond pattern. **Sights:** Baer dovetailed front, low-mount Bo-Mar rear with hidden leaf. **Features:** Baer NM forged steel frame and barrel with stainless bushing, deluxe Commander hammer and sear, beavertail grip safety with pad, extended ambidextrous safety; flat mainspring housing; 30 lpi checkered front strap. Made in U.S.A. by Les Baer Custom, Inc.
Price: 5" 45 ACP **$1,598.00**
Price: 5" 400 Cor-Bon **$1,645.00**
Price: 5" 38 Super **$1,789.00**
Price: 6" 45 ACP (400 Cor-Bon and 38 Super available) **$1,755.00**
Price: Super-Tac 45 ACP (400 Cor-Bon and
38 Super available) **$2,098.00**

Baer 1911 S.R.P.

Baer 1911 Stinger

Beretta 92FS

Beretta 84 Cheetah

Beretta Bobcat

Beretta Tomcat

Beretta U22 Neos

BAER 1911 S.R.P. PISTOL
Caliber: 45 ACP. **Barrel:** 5". **Weight:** 37 oz. **Length:** 8.5" overall. **Grips:** Checkered walnut. **Sights:** Trijicon night sights. **Features:** Similar to the F.B.I. contract gun except uses Baer forged steel frame. Has Baer match barrel with supported chamber, Complete tactical action. Has Baer Ultra Coat finish. Introduced 1996. Made in U.S.A. by Les Baer Custom, Inc.
Price: Government or Comanche length $2,339.00

BAER 1911 STINGER PISTOL
Caliber: 45 ACP, 7-round magazine. **Barrel:** 5". **Weight:** 34 oz. **Length:** 8.5" overall. **Grips:** Checkered cocobolo. **Sights:** Baer dovetailed front, low-mount Bo-Mar rear with hidden leaf. **Features:** Baer NM frame. Baer Commanche slide, Officer's style grip frame, beveled mag well. Made in U.S.A. by Les Baer Custom, Inc.
Price: Blued $1,666.00
Price: Stainless $1,675.00

BAER 1911 PROWLER III PISTOL
Caliber: 45 ACP, 8-round magazine. **Barrel:** 5". **Weight:** 34 oz. **Length:** 8.5" overall. **Grips:** Checkered cocobolo. **Sights:** Baer dovetailed front, low-mount Bo-Mar rear with hidden leaf. **Features:** Similar to Premier II with tapered cone stub weight, rounded corners. Made in U.S.A. by Les Baer Custom, Inc.
Price: Blued $2,215.00

BERETTA MODEL 92FS PISTOL
Caliber: 9mm Para., 10-shot magazine. **Barrel:** 4.9". **Weight:** 34 oz. **Length:** 8.5" overall. **Grips:** Checkered black plastic. **Sights:** Blade front,

rear adjustable for windage. Tritium night sights available. **Features:** Double action. Extractor acts as chamber loaded indicator, squared trigger guard, grooved front and backstraps, inertia firing pin. Matte or blued finish. Introduced 1977. Made in U.S.A.
Price: With plastic grips $650.00

BERETTA MODEL 80 CHEETAH SERIES DA PISTOLS
Caliber: 380 ACP, 10-shot magazine (M84); 8-shot (M85); 22 LR, 7-shot (M87). **Barrel:** 3.82". **Weight:** About 23 oz. (M84/85); 20.8 oz. (M87). **Length:** 6.8" overall. **Grips:** Glossy black plastic (wood optional at extra cost). **Sights:** Fixed front, drift-adjustable rear. **Features:** Double action, quick takedown, convenient magazine release. Introduced 1977. Made in U.S.A.
Price: Model 84 Cheetah, plastic grips $675.00

BERETTA MODEL 21 BOBCAT PISTOL
Caliber: 22 LR or 25 ACP. Both double action. **Barrel:** 2.4". **Weight:** 11.5 oz.; 11.8 oz. **Length:** 4.9" overall. **Grips:** Plastic. **Features:** Available in nickel, matte, engraved or blue finish. Introduced in 1985.
Price: Bobcat, 22 or 25, blue $275.00
Price: Bobcat, 22, stainless $325.00
Price: Bobcat, 22 or 25, matte $250.00

BERETTA MODEL 3032 TOMCAT PISTOL
Caliber: 32 ACP, 7-shot magazine. **Barrel:** 2.45". **Weight:** 14.5 oz. **Length:** 5" overall. **Grips:** Checkered black plastic. **Sights:** Blade front, drift-adjustable rear. **Features:** Double action with exposed hammer; tip-up barrel for direct loading/unloading; thumb safety; polished or matte blue finish. Made in U.S.A. Introduced 1996.
Price: Blue $375.00
Price: Matte $350.00
Price: Stainless $450.00
Price: With Tritium sights $425.00

BERETTA MODEL U22 NEOS
Caliber: 22 LR, 10-shot magazine. **Barrel:** 4.5"; 6". **Weight:** 32 oz.; 36 oz. **Length:** 8.8"; 10.3". **Sights:** Target. **Features:** Integral rail for standard scope mounts, light, perfectly weighted, 100% American made by Beretta.
Price: $250.00
Price: Inox $325.00
Price: DLX $350.00
Price: Inox $375.00

Beretta PX4 Storm

Beretta PX4 Sub-Compact with laser

Beretta Model M9

Beretta Model M9A1

Bersa Thunder 380

Browning Hi-Power 9mm

Browning Buck Mark Hunter

BERETTA MODEL PX4 STORM
Caliber: 9mm, 40 S&W. **Capacity:** 17 (9mm); 14 (40 S&W). **Barrel:** 4".
Weight: 27.5 oz. **Grips:** Black checkered w/3 interchangeable backstraps. **Sights:** 3-dot ystems coated in Superluminova; removable front and rear sights. **Features:** DA/SA, manual safety/hammer decocking lever (ambi) and automatic firing pin block safety. Picatinny rail. Comes with two magazines (17/10 in 9mm and 14/10 in 40 S&W). Removable hammer unit. American made by Beretta. Introduced 2005.
Price: **$598.00**
Price: Subcompact, intr. 2007 . . . . **$575.00**

BERETTA MODEL M9
Caliber: 9mm. **Capacity:** 15. **Barrel:** 4.9". **Weight:** 32.2-35.3 oz. **Grips:** Plastic. **Sights:** Dot and post, low profile, windage adjustable rear. **Features:** DA/SA, forged aluminum alloy frame, delayed locking-bolt system, manual safety doubles as decocking lever, combat-style trigger guard, loaded chamber indicator. Comes with two magazines (15/10). American made by Beretta. Introduced 2005.
Price: **$750.00**

BERETTA MODEL M9A1
Caliber: 9mm. **Capacity:** 15. **Barrel:** 4.9". **Weight:** 32.2-35.3 oz. **Grips:** Plastic. **Sights:** Dot and post, low profile, windage adjustable rear. **Features:** Same as M9, but also includes integral Mil-Std-1913 Picatinny rail, has checkered frontstrap and backstrap. Comes with two magazines (15/10). American made by Beretta. Introduced 2005.
Price: **$750.00**

BERSA THUNDER 45 ULTRA COMPACT PISTOL
Caliber: 45 ACP. **Barrel:** 3.6". **Weight:** 27 oz. **Length:** 6.7" overall. **Grips:** Anatomicaly designed polymer. **Sights:** White outline rear. **Features:** Double action; firing pin safeties, integral locking system. Available in matte, satin nickel, gold, or duo-tone. Introduced 2003. Imported from Argentina by Eagle Imports, Inc.
Price: Thunder 45, matte blue **$441.95**
Price: Thunder 45, duo-tone **$499.95**
Price: Thunder 45, satin nickel **$466.95**

BERSA THUNDER 380 SERIES PISTOLS
Caliber: 380 Auto, 7 rounds **Barrel:** 3.5". **Weight:** 23 oz. **Length:** 6.6" overall. **Features:** Otherwise similar to Thunder 45 Ultra Compact. 380 DLX has 9-round capacity. 380 Concealed Carry has 8 round capacity. Imported from Argentina by Eagle Imports, Inc.
Price: Thunder 380 matte **$274.95**
Price: Thunder 380 satin nickel **$299.95**
Price: Thunder 380 blue DLX **$308.95**
Price: Thunder 380 matte CC (2006) **$291.95**

BERSA THUNDER 9 ULTRA COMPACT/40 SERIES PISTOLS
Caliber: 9mm, 40 S&W. **Barrel:** 3.5". **Weight:** 24.5 oz. **Length:** 6.6" overall. **Features:** Otherwise similar to Thunder 45 Ultra Compact. 9mm High Capacity model has 17-round capacity. 40 High Capacity model has 13-round capacity. Imported from Argentina by Eagle Imports, Inc.
Price: Thunder 9mm matte **$441.95**
Price: Thunder 40 high capacity satin nickel **$484.95**

BROWNING HI-POWER 9MM AUTOMATIC PISTOL
Caliber: 9mm Para., 13-round magazine; 40 S&W, 10-round magazine. **Barrel:** 4-5/8". **Weight:** 32 to 39 oz. Overall length: 7-3/4". Metal Finishes: Blued (Standard); black-epoxy/silver-chrome (Practical); black-epoxy (Mark III). **Grips:** Molded (Mark III); wraparound Pachmayr (Practical); or walnut grips (Standard). **Sights:** Fixed (Practical, Mark III, Standard); low-mount adjustable rear (Standard). Cable lock supplied. **Features:** External hammer with half-cock and thumb safeties. Fixed rear sight model available. Commander-style (Practical) or spur-type hammer, single action. Includes gun lock. Imported from Belgium by Browning.
Price: Mark III **$813.00**
Price: Standard, fixed sights **$836.00**
Price: Standard, adjustable sights **$896.00**

Browning Buck Mark Challenge

Browning Buck Mark Bulleye Target Stainless

Browning Buck Mark Contour 5.5

Browning Buck Mark Lite Splash 5.5

Browning Buck Mark Standard

Browning Buck Mark Camper

Browning FLD Plus Rosewood UDX

Browning Buckmark Stainless Plus UDX

BROWNING BUCK MARK PISTOLS

Common Features: Caliber: 22 LR, 10-shot magazine. **Action:** Blowback semi-auto. Trigger: Wide grooved style. **Sights:** Ramp front, Browning Pro-Target rear adjustable for windage and elevation. **Features:** Machined aluminum frame. Includes gun lock. Introduced 1985. Hunter, Camper Stainless, STD Stainless, 5.5 Target, 5.5 Field all introduced 2005. 18 variations, as noted below. **Grips:** Cocobolo, target-style (Hunter, 5.5 Target, 5.5 Field); polymer (Camper, Camper Stainless, Micro Nickel, Standard URX, Standard Stainless URX); checkered walnut (Challenge); laminated (Plus and Plus Nickel); laminated rosewood (Bullseye Target, FLD Plus); rubber (Bullseye Target URX). **Metal finishes:** Matte blue (Hunter, Camper, Challenge, Plus, Bullseye Target URX, 5.5 Target, 5.5 Field, Field Plus); matte stainless (Camper Stainless, Standard Stainless URX, Micro Standard URX); nickel-plated (Micro Nickel, Plus Nickel, and Nickel). Made in U.S.A. From Browning.

Price: Hunter, 7.25" heavy barrel, 38 oz., Truglo sight **$389.00**
Price: Camper, 5.5" heavy barrel, 34 oz. **$300.00**
Price: Camper Stainless, 5.5" tapered bull barrel, 34 oz. **$329.00**
Price: Standard URX, 5.5" flat-side bull barrel, 34 oz. **$319.00**
Price: Standard Stainless URX, 5.5" flat-side bull barrel, 34 oz. . . **$362.00**
Price: Micro Standard URX, 4" flat-side bull barrel, 32 oz. **$362.00**
Price: Micro Standard Stainless URX, 4" flat-side bull barrel,
  32 oz. **$399.00**

Price: Challenge, 5.5" lightweight taper barrel, 25 oz. **$363.00**
Price: Bullseye Target URX, 7.25" fluted bull barrel, 39 oz. **$497.00**
Price: Bullseye Target Stainless URX,
  7.25" fluted bull barrel, 39 oz. **$656.00**
Price: Contour 5.5 URX, 5.5" matte blued finished barrel,
  full-length scope base, 36 oz. **$421.00**
Price: Contour 7.25 URX, 7.25" matte blued finished barrel,
  full-length scope base, 39 oz. **$436.00**
Price: Lite Splash 5.5 URX, 5.5" matte blued finished barrel
  with gold splash anodizing, 30 oz., Truglo sight **$447.00**
Price: Lite Splash 7.25 URX, 7.25" matte blued finished barrel
  with gold splash anodizing, 30 oz., Truglo sight **$463.00**
Price: 5.5 Target, 5.5" round bull barrel, target sights, 35.5 oz. . . **$511.00**
Price: 5.5 Field, 5.5" round bull barrel, 35 oz. **$511.00**
Price: Plus Stainless UDX, intr. 2007 . . . . **$461.00**
Price: Plus UDX, intr. 2007 . . . . **$425.00**
Price: FLD Plus Rosewood UDX, intr. 2007 . . . . **$425.00**

Browning Pro-9

Charles Daly Empire EFS

Charles Daly
M-5 Government

Cobra Patriot 380

Cobra Patriot 45

BROWNING PRO-9, PRO-40 PISTOLS
Caliber: 9mm Luger, 16-round magazine; 40 S&W, 14-round magazine. **Barrel:** 4". **Weight:** 30-33 oz. **Overall length:** 7.25". **Features:** Polymer frame, stainless-steel frames and barrels, double-action, ambidextrous decocker and safety. Fixed, 3-dot-style sights, 6" sight radius. Molded composite grips with interchangeable backstrap inserts. Cable lock supplied.
Price: **$628.00**

CHARLES DALY ENHANCED 1911 PISTOLS
Caliber: 45 ACP. **Barrel:** 5". **Weight:** 38 oz. **Length:** 8-3/4" overall. **Grips:** Checkered double diamond hardwood. **Sights:** Dovetailed front and dovetailed snag-free low profile rear sights, 3-dot system. **Features:** Extended high-rise beavertail grip safety, combat trigger, combat hammer, beveled magazine well, flared and lowered ejection port. Field Grade models are satin-finished blued steel. EMS series includes an ambidextrous safety, 4" barrel, 8-shot magazine. ECS series has a contoured left hand safety, 3.5" barrel, 6-shot magazine Two magazines, lockable carrying case. Introduced 1998. Empire series are stainless versions. Imported from the Philippines by K.B.I., Inc.
Price: EFS, blued, 39.5 oz., 5" barrel **$529.00**
Price: EMS, blued, 37 oz., 4" barrel **$529.00**
Price: ECS, blued, 34.5 oz., 3.5" barrel **$529.00**
Price: EFS Empire, stainless, 38.5 oz., 5" barrel **$629.00**
Price: EMS Empire, matte stainless, 36.5 oz., 4" barrel **$619.00**
Price: ECS Empire, matte stainless, 33.5 oz., 3.5" barrel **$619.00**

CHARLES DALY ENHANCED TARGET 1911 PISTOLS
Caliber: 45 ACP. **Barrel:** 5". **Weight:** 38.5 oz. **Length:** 8-3/4" overall. **Features:** Similar to Daly Field and Empire models but with dovetailed front and fully adjustable rear target sights. Imported from the Philippines by K.B.I., Inc.
Price: EFS Target, stainless, 38.5 oz., 5" barrel **$724.00**
Price: EFS Custom Match Target, high-polish stainless **$799.00**

CHARLES DALY HP 9MM SINGLE-ACTION PISTOL
Caliber: 9mm, 10 round magazine. **Barrel:** 4.6". **Weight:** 34.5 oz. **Length:** 7-3/8" overall. **Grips:** Uncle Mike's padded rubber grip panels. **Sights:** XS Express Sight system set into front and rear dovetails. **Features:** John Browning design. Matte-blued steel frame and slide, thumb safety. Made in the U.S. by K.B.I., Inc.
Price: Hi-Power w/XS Sights **$549.00**

CHARLES DALY M-5 POLYMER-FRAMED HI-CAP 1911 PISTOL
Caliber: 9mm, 12-round magazine; 40 S&W 17-round magazine; 45 ACP, 13-round magazine. **Barrel:** 5". **Weight:** 33.5 oz. **Length:** 8.5" overall. **Grips:** Checkered polymer. **Sights:** Blade front, adjustable low-profile rear. **Features:** Stainless steel beaver-tail grip safety, rounded trigger-guard, tapered bull barrel, full-length guide rod, matte blue finish on frame and slide. 40 S&W models in M-5 Govt. 1911, M-5 Commander, and M-5 IPSC introduced 2006; M-5 Ultra X Compact in 9mm and 45 ACP introduced 2006; M-5 IPSC .45 ACP introduced 2006. Made in Israel by BUL, imported by K.B.I., Inc.
Price: M-5 Govt. 1911, 40 S&W/45 ACP, matte blue **$719.00**
Price: M-5 Commander, 40 S&W/45 ACP, matte blue **$719.00**
Price: M-5 Ultra X Compact, 9mm, 3.1" barrel, 7" OAL, 28 oz. . . . **$719.00**
Price: M-5 Ultra X Compact, 45 ACP, 3.1" barrel, 7" OAL, 28 oz. **$719.00**
Price: M-5 IPSC, 40 S&W/45 ACP, 5" barrel, 8.5" OAL,
33.5 oz. **$1,499.00**

COBRA ENTERPRISES FS380 AUTO PISTOL
Caliber: 380 ACP, 7-shot magazine. **Barrel:** 3.5". **Weight:** 2.1 lbs. **Length:** 6-3/8" overall. **Grips:** Black composition. **Sights:** Fixed. **Features:** Choice of bright chrome, satin nickel or black finish. Introduced 2002. Made in U.S.A. by Cobra Enterprises of Utah, Inc.
Price: **$130.00**

COBRA ENTERPRISES FS32 AUTO PISTOL
Caliber: 32 ACP, 8-shot magazine. **Barrel:** 3.5". **Weight:** 2.1 lbs. **Length:** 6-3/8" overall. **Grips:** Black composition. **Sights:** Fixed. **Features:** Choice of black, satin nickel or bright chrome finish. Introduced 2002. Made in U.S.A. by Cobra Enterprises of Utah, Inc.
Price: **$158.00**

COBRA ENTERPRISES PATRIOT PISTOL
Caliber: 380 ACP, 9mm Luger, 10-shot magazine. **Barrel:** 3.3". **Weight:** 20 oz. **Length:** 6" overall. **Grips:** Checkered polymer. **Sights:** Fixed. **Features:** Stainless steel or black slide with load indicator; double-action-only trigger system. Introduced 2002. Made in U.S.A. by Cobra Enterprises of Utah, Inc.
Price: **$315.00**

COBRA ENTERPRISES CA32, CA380
Caliber: 32 ACP, 380 ACP. **Barrel:** 2.8" **Weight:** 22 oz. **Length:** 5.4". **Grips:** Black molded synthetic . **Sights:** Fixed. **Features:** Choice of black, satin nickle, or chorme finish. Made in U.S.A. by Cobra Enterprises of Utah, Inc.
Price: **$152.00**

COLT MODEL 1991 MODEL O AUTO PISTOL
Caliber: 45 ACP, 7-shot magazine. **Barrel:** 5". **Weight:** 38 oz. **Length:** 8.5" overall. **Grips:** Checkered black composition. **Sights:** Ramped blade front, fixed square notch rear, high profile. **Features:** Matte finish. Continuation of serial number range used on original G.I. 1911A1 guns. Comes with one magazine and molded carrying case. Introduced 1991.
Price: Blue **$786.00**
Price: Stainless **$839.00**

Colt XSE Government

Colt XSE Lightweight Commander

Colt Defender

Colt 38 Super Bright

Colt 38 Super

Colt Series 70

Colt 1911 WWI Replica

CZ 75B 9mm

COLT XSE SERIES MODEL O AUTO PISTOLS

Caliber: 45 ACP, 8-shot magazine. **Barrel:** 4.25", 5". **Grips:** Checkered, double diamond rosewood. **Sights:** Drift-adjustable 3-dot combat. **Features:** Brushed stainless finish; adjustable, two-cut aluminum trigger; extended ambidextrous thumb safety; upswept beavertail with palm swell; elongated slot hammer. Introduced 1999. From Colt's Mfg. Co., Inc.
Price: XSE Government (5" bbl.) $944.00
Price: XSE Government (4.25" bbl.) $944.00

COLT XSE LIGHTWEIGHT COMMANDER AUTO PISTOL

Caliber: 45 ACP, 8-shot. **Barrel:** 4-1/4". **Weight:** 26 oz. **Length:** 7-3/4" overall. **Grips:** Double diamond checkered rosewood. **Sights:** Fixed, glare-proofed blade front, square notch rear. **Features:** Brushed stainless slide, nickeled aluminum frame; McCormick elongated slot enhanced hammer, McCormick two-cut adjustable aluminum hammer. Made in U.S.A. by Colt's Mfg. Co., Inc.
Price: Stainless $944.00

COLT DEFENDER

Caliber: 45 ACP, 7-shot magazine. **Barrel:** 3". **Weight:** 22-1/2 oz. **Length:** 6-3/4" overall. **Grips:** Pebble-finish rubber wraparound with finger grooves. **Sights:** White dot front, snag-free Colt competition rear. **Features:** Stainless finish; aluminum frame; combat-style hammer; Hi Ride grip safety, extended manual safety, disconnect safety. Introduced 1998. Made in U.S.A. by Colt's Mfg. Co., Inc.
Price: $885.00

COLT SERIES 70

Caliber: 45 ACP. **Barrel:** 5". **Weight:** NA. **Length:** NA. **Grips:** Rosewood with double diamond checkering pattern. **Sights:** Fixed. **Features:** Custom replica of the Original Series 70 pistol with a Series 70 firing system, original rollmarks. Introduced 2002. Made in U.S.A. by Colt's Mfg. Co., Inc.
Price: Blued $919.00
Price: Stainless $950.00

COLT 38 SUPER

Caliber: 38 Super. **Barrel:** 5". **Weight:** NA. **Length:** 8-1/2" **Grips:** Checkered rubber (stainless and blue models); wood with double diamond checkering pattern (bright stainless model). **Sights:** 3-dot. **Features:** Beveled magazine well, standard thumb safety and service-style grip safety. Introduced 2003. Made in U.S.A. by Colt's Mfg. Co., Inc.
Price: Blued $837.00
Price: Stainless $866.00
Price: Bright Stainless $1,090.00

COLT 1911 WWI REPLICA

Caliber: 45 ACP, 2 7-round magazines. **Barrel:** 5". **Weight:** 38 oz. **Length:** 8.5". **Grips:** Checkered walnut with double diamond checkering pattern. **Sights:** Tapered blade front sight, U-shaped rear notch. **Features:** Reproduction based on original 1911 blueprints. Original rollmarks and inspector marks. Smooth mainspring housing with lanyard loop, WWI-style manual thumb and grip safety, Carbonia blued finish. Introduced 2005. Made in U.S.A. by Colt's Mfg. Co., Inc.
Price: Blued $990.00

CZ 75B AUTO PISTOL

Caliber: 9mm Para., 40 S&W, 10-shot magazine. **Barrel:** 4.7". **Weight:** 34.3 oz. **Length:** 8.1" overall. **Grips:** High impact checkered plastic. **Sights:** Square post front, rear adjustable for windage; 3-dot system. **Features:** Single action/double action design; firing pin block safety; choice of black polymer, matte or high-polish blue finishes. All-steel frame. B-SA is a single action with a drop-free magazine. Imported from the Czech Republic by CZ-USA.
Price: 75B, black polymer, 16-shot magazine $509.00
Price: 75B, glossy blue, dual-tone or satin nickel $525.00
Price: 40 S&W, black polymer, 12-shot magazine $525.00
Price: 75B SA, 9mm/40 S&W, single action . . . . $518.00/$535.00
Price: 75 Stainless 9mm (2006), 16-shot magazine $565.00

CZ 75B Decocker

CZ 97B

CZ 75/85 Kadet

CZ 85

CZ 100

CZ 75B Decocker
Similar to the CZ 75B except has a decocking lever in place of the safety lever. All other specifications are the same. Introduced 1999. Imported from the Czech Republic by CZ-USA.
Price: 9mm, black polymer **$518.00**

CZ 75B Compact Auto Pistol
Similar to the CZ 75 except has 14-shot magazine in 9mm, 3.9" barrel and weighs 32 oz. Has removable front sight, non-glare ribbed slide top. Trigger guard is squared and serrated; combat hammer. Introduced 1993. Imported from the Czech Republic by CZ-USA.
Price: 9mm, black polymer **$539.00**
Price: 9mm, dual tone or satin nickel **$554.00**
Price: 9mm D PCR Compact, alloy frame **$554.00**
Price: 40 S&W, black polymer, 10+1, 37.8 oz. (2006) **$594.00**

CZ 75 Champion Pistol
Similar to the CZ 75B except has a longer frame and slide, rubber grip to accommodate new heavy-duty magazine. Ambidextrous thumb safety, extended magazine release; three-port compensator. Blued slide and stain nickel frame finish. Introduced 2005. Imported from the Czech Republic by CZ USA.
Price: 9mm, 16-shot mag. **$1,646.00**

CZ 75 Tactical Sport
Similar to the CZ 75B except the CZ 75 TS is a competition ready pistol designed for IPSC standard division (USPSA limited division). Fixed target sights, tuned single-action operation, lightweight polymer match trigger with adjustments for take-up and overtravel, competition hammer, extended magazine catch, ambidextrous manual safety, checkered walnut grips, polymer magazine well, two tone finish. Introduced 2005. Imported from the Czech Republic by CZ USA.
Price: 9mm, 20-shot mag. **$1,152.00**
Price: 40 S&W, 16-shot mag. **$1,152.00**

CZ 75 SP-01 Pistol
Similar to NATO-approved CZ 75 Compact P-01 model. Features an integral 1913 accessory rail on the dust cover, rubber grip panels, black polycoat finish, extended beavertail, new grip geometry with checkering on front and back straps, and double or single action operation. Introduced 2005. The Shadow variant designed as an IPSC "production" division competition firearm. Includes competition hammer, competition rear sight and fiber-optic front sight, modified slide release, lighter recoil and main spring for use with "minor power factor" competition ammunition. Includes polycoat finish and slim walnut grips. Finished by CZ Custom Shop. Imported from the Czech Republic by CZ-USA.

Price: SP-01 9mm, black polymer, 19+1 . . . . **$595.00**
Price: SP-01 Shadow **$615.00**

CZ 85B/85 Combat Auto Pistol
Same gun as the CZ 75 except has ambidextrous slide release and safety levers; non-glare, ribbed slide top; squared, serrated trigger guard; trigger stop to prevent overtravel. Introduced 1986. The CZ 85 Combat features a fully adjustable rear sight, extended magazine release, ambidextrous slide stop and safety catch, drop free magazine and overtravel adjustment. Imported from the Czech Republic by CZ-USA.
Price: 9mm, Black polymer **$536.00**
Price: Combat, black polymer **$599.00**
Price: Combat, dual-tone, glossy blue, satin nickel **$623.00**

CZ 83B DOUBLE-ACTION PISTOL
Caliber: 32 ACP, 380 ACP, 12-shot magazine. **Barrel:** 3.8". **Weight:** 26.2 oz. **Length:** 6.8" overall. **Grips:** High impact checkered plastic. **Sights:** Removable square post front, rear adjustable for windage; 3-dot system. **Features:** Single action/double action; ambidextrous magazine release and safety. Blue finish; non-glare ribbed slide top. Imported from the Czech Republic by CZ-USA.
Price: Glossy blue, 32 ACP or 380 ACP **$420.00**
Price: Satin Nickel **$420.00**

CZ 97B AUTO PISTOL
Caliber: 45 ACP, 10-shot magazine. **Barrel:** 4.85". **Weight:** 40 oz. **Length:** 8.34" overall. **Grips:** Checkered walnut. **Sights:** Fixed. **Features:** Single action/double action; full-length slide rails; screw-in barrel bushing; linkless barrel; all-steel construction; chamber loaded indicator; dual transfer bars. Introduced 1999. Imported from the Czech Republic by CZ-USA.
Price: Black polymer **$663.00**
Price: Glossy blue **$680.00**

CZ 75 KADET AUTO PISTOL
Caliber: 22 LR, 10-shot magazine. **Barrel:** 4.88". **Weight:** 36 oz. **Grips:** High impact checkered plastic. **Sights:** Blade front, fully adjustable rear. **Features:** Single action/double action mechanism; all-steel construction. Introduced 1999. Kadet conversion kit consists of barrel, slide, adjustable sights, and magazine to convert the centerfire 75 to rimfire. Imported from the Czech Republic by CZ-USA.
Price: Black polymer **$510.00**
Price: Kadet conversion kit **$299.00**

CZ 100 B AUTO PISTOL
Caliber: 9mm Para., 40 S&W. **Barrel:** 3.7". **Weight:** 24 oz. **Length:** 6.9" overall. **Grips:** Grooved polymer. **Sights:** Blade front with dot, white outline rear drift adjustable for windage. **Features:** Double action only with firing pin block; polymer frame, steel slide; has laser sight mount. Introduced 1996. Imported from the Czech Republic by CZ-USA.
Price: 9mm Para, 12-shot magazine **$449.00**
Price: 40 S&W, 10-shot magazine **$449.00**

CZ 2075 RAMI AUTO PISTOL
Caliber: 9mm Para., 40 S&W. **Barrel:** 3". **Weight:** 25 oz. **Length:** 6.5" overall. **Grips:** Rubber. **Sights:** Blade front with dot, white outline rear drift adjustable for windage. **Features:** Single-action/double-action; alloy or polymer frame, steel slide; has laser sight mount. Imported from the Czech Republic by CZ-USA.
Price: 9mm Para, alloy frame, 10 and 14-shot magazines **$576.00**
Price: 40 S&W, alloy frame, 8-shot magazine **$576.00**
Price: 9mm Para, polymer frame, 10 and 14-shot magazines . . . **$510.00**
Price: 40 S&W, alloy frame, 8-shot magazine **$510.00**

Dan Wesson Pointman

Dan Wesson DW RZ-10

Desert Baby Eagle

Desert Eagle Mark XIX

EAA Witness

CZ P-01 AUTO PISTOL
Caliber: 9mm Para. **Barrel:** 3.85". **Weight:** 27 oz. **Length:** 7.2" overall. **Grips:** Checkered rubber. **Sights:** Blade front with dot, white outline rear drift adjustable for windage. **Features:** Based on the CZ 75, except with forged aircraft-grade aluminum alloy frame. Hammer forged barrel, decocker, firing-pin block, M3 rail, dual slide serrations, squared triggerguard, re-contoured trigger, lanyard loop on butt. Serrated front and back strap. Introduced 2006. Imported from the Czech Republic by CZ-USA.
Price: 9mm Para,14-shot magazines **$586.00**

DAN WESSON FIREARMS POINTMAN SEVEN AUTO PISTOL
Caliber: 10mm, 45 ACP. **Barrel:** 5". **Grips:** Diamond checkered cocobolo. **Sights:** Bo-Mar style adjustable target sight. **Weight:** 38 oz. **Features:** Stainless-steel frame and serrated slide. Series 70-style 1911, stainless-steel frame, forged stainless-steel slide. One-piece match-grade barrel and bushing. 20-LPI checkered mainspring housing, front and rear slide cocking serrations, beveled magwell, dehorned by hand. Lowered and flared ejection port, Ed Brown slide stop and memory groove grip safety, tactical extended thumb safety. Commander-style match hammer, match grade sear, aluminum trigger with stainless bow, Wolff springs. Introduced 2000. Made in U.S.A. by Dan Wesson Firearms, distributed by CZ-USA.
Price: 45 ACP, 7+1 .... **$1,079.00**
Price: 10mm, 8+1 .... **$1,079.00**

Dan Wesson Commander Classic Bobtail Auto Pistols
Similar to Pointman Seven, a Commander-sized frame with 4.25" barrel. Available with stainless finish, fixed night sights. Introduced 2005. Made in U.S.A. by Dan Wesson Firearms, distributed by CZ-USA.
Price: 45 ACP, 7+1, 34 oz. **$1,169.00**
Price: 10mm, 8+1, 34 oz. **$1,179.00**

DAN WESSON DW RZ-10 AUTO PISTOL
Caliber: 10mm. **Barrel:** 5". **Grips:** Diamond checkered cocobolo. **Sights:** Bo-Mar style adjustable target sight. **Weight:** 38.3 oz. **Features:** Stainless-steel frame and serrated slide. Series 70-style 1911, stainless-steel frame, forged stainless-steel slide. Commander-style match hammer. Reintroduced 2005. Made in U.S.A. by Dan Wesson Firearms, distributed by CZ-USA.
Price: 10mm, 8+1 .... **$1,089.00**

DESERT EAGLE MARK XIX PISTOL
Caliber: 357 Mag., 9-shot; 44 Mag., 8-shot; 50 AE, 7-shot. **Barrel:** 6", 10", interchangeable. **Weight:** 357 Mag.-62 oz.; 44 Mag.-69 oz.; 50 AE-72 oz.

Length: 10-1/4" overall (6" bbl.). **Grips:** Polymer; rubber available. **Sights:** Blade on ramp front, combat-style rear. Adjustable available. **Features:** Interchangeable barrels; rotating three-lug bolt; ambidextrous safety; adjustable trigger. Military epoxy finish. Satin, bright nickel, chrome, brushed, matte or black finishes available. 10" barrel extra. Imported from Israel by Magnum Research, Inc.
Price: 357, 6" bbl., standard pistol **$1,369.00**
Price: 44 Mag., 6", standard pistol **$1,369.00**
Price: 50 Magnum, 6" bbl., standard pistol **$1,369.00**

DESERT BABY EAGLE PISTOLS
Caliber: 9mm Para., 40 S&W, 45 ACP, 10-round magazine. **Barrel:** 3.5", 3.7", 4.72". **Weight:** 26.8-39.8 oz. **Length:** 7.25" to 8.25" overall. **Grips:** Polymer. **Sights:** Drift-adjustable rear, blade front. **Features:** Steel frame and slide; slide safety; decocker. Reintroduced in 1999. Imported from Israel by Magnum Research, Inc.
Price: Standard (9mm or 40 cal.; 4.72" barrel, 8.25" overall) **$549.00**
Price: Semi-Compact (9mm, 40 or 45 cal.; 3.7" barrel, 7.75" overall) **$549.00**
Price: Compact (9mm or 40 cal.; 3.5" barrel, 7.25" overall) **$549.00**
Price: Polymer (9mm or 40 cal; polymer frame; 3.25" barrel, 7.25" overall) **$549.00**

EAA WITNESS FULL SIZE AUTO PISTOL
Caliber: 9mm Para., 38 Super, 18-shot magazine; 40 S&W, 10mm, 15-shot magazine; 45 ACP, 10-shot magazine. **Barrel:** 4.50". **Weight:** 35.33 oz. **Length:** 8.10" overall. **Grips:** Checkered rubber. **Sights:** Undercut blade front, open rear adjustable for windage. **Features:** Double-action/single-action trigger system; round trigger guard; frame-mounted safety. Introduced 1991. Polymer frame introducted 2005. Imported from Italy by European American Armory.
Price: 9mm, 38 Super, 10mm, 40 S&W, 45 ACP, full-size steel frame, Wonder finish **$459.00**
Price: 45/22 22 LR, full-size steel frame, blued **$429.00**
Price: 9mm, 40 S&W, 45 ACP, full-size polymer frame **$429.00**

EAA WITNESS COMPACT AUTO PISTOL
Caliber: 9mm Para., 40 S&W, 10mm, 12-shot magazine; 45 ACP, 8-shot magazine. **Barrel:** 3.6". **Weight:** 30 oz. **Length:** 7.3" overall. Otherwise similar to Full Size Witness. Polymer frame introducted 2005. Imported from Italy by European American Armory.
Price: 9mm, 10mm, 40 S&W, 45 ACP, steel frame, Wonder finish **$459.00**
Price: 9mm, 40 S&W, 45 ACP, polymer frame **$429.00**

EAA WITNESS-P CARRY AUTO PISTOL
Caliber: 10mm, 15-shot magazine; 45 ACP, 10-shot magazine. **Barrel:** 3.6". **Weight:** 27 oz. **Length:** 7.5" overall. Otherwise similar to Full Size Witness. Polymer frame introducted 2005. Imported from Italy by European American Armory.
Price: 10mm, 45 ACP, polymer frame, from **$469.00**

Ed Brown Classic Custom

Ed Brown Kobra K-SB

Ed Brown Kobra Carry

Ed Brown Kobra

Ed Brown Executive

Ed Brown Special Forces

Excel Arms Accelerator MP-22

Firestorm 45 Gov't

Firestorm Mini

ED BROWN CLASSIC CUSTOM
Caliber: 45 ACP, 7 shot. **Barrel:** 5". **Weight:** 40 oz. Stocks: Cocobolo wood. **Sights:** Bo-Mar adjustable rear, dovetail front. **Features:** Single-action, M1911 style, custom made to order, stainless frame and slide available. Special mirror-finished slide.
Price: Model CC-BB, blued $2,895.00
Price: Model CC-SB, blued and stainless $2,995.00
Price: Model CC-SS, stainless $3,095.00

ED BROWN KOBRA AND KOBRA CARRY
Caliber: 45 ACP, 7-shot magazine. **Barrel:** 5" (Kobra); 4.25" (Kobra Carry). **Weight:** 39 oz. (Kobra); 34 oz. (Kobra Carry). **Grips:** Hogue exotic wood. **Sights:** Ramp, front; fixed Novak low-mount night sights, rear. **Features:** Has snakeskin pattern serrations on forestrap and mainspring housing, dehorned edges, beavertail grip safety.
Price: Kobra K-BB, blued $1,995.00
Price: Kobra K-SB, stainless and blued $2,095.00
Price: Kobra K-SS, stainless $2,195.00
Price: Kobra Carry KC-BB, blued $2,095.00

Ed Brown Executive Pistols
Similar to other Ed Brown products, but with 25-lpi checkered frame and mainspring housing.
Price: Elite blued, blued/stainless, or stainless, from $2,195.00
Price: Carry blued, blued/stainless, or stainless, from $2,295.00
Price: Target blued, blued/stainless, or stainless, intr. 2006,
          from $2,470.00

Ed Brown Special Forces Pistol
Similar to other Ed Brown products, but with ChainLink treatment on forestrap and mainspring housing. Slide coated with Gen III finish. "Square cut" serrations on rear of slide only. Dehorned. Introduced 2006.
Price: SF-BB blued $1,995.00

EXCEL ARMS ACCELERATOR MP-17/MP-22 PISTOLS
Caliber: 17HMR, 22WMR, 9-shot magazine. **Barrel:** 8.5" bull barrel. **Weight:** 54 oz. **Length:** 12.875" overall. **Grips:** Textured black composition. **Sights:** Fully adjustable target sights. **Features:** Made from 17-4 stainless steel, comes with aluminum rib, integral Weaver base, internal hammer, firing-pin block. American made, lifetime warranty. Comes with two 9-round stainless steel magazines and a California-approved cable lock. 22 WMR Introduced 2006. Made in U.S.A. by Excel Arms.
Price: $412.00
Price: SP-17 17 Mach 2 . . . . $412.00
Price: SP-22 22LR $412.00

FIRESTORM AUTO PISTOLS
Caliber: 22LR, 32 ACP, 10-shot magazine; 380 ACP, 7-shot magazine; 9mm, 40 S&W, 10-shot magazine; 45 ACP, 7-shot magazine. **Barrel:** 3.5". **Weight:** From 23 oz. **Length:** From 6.6" overall. **Grips:** Rubber. **Sights:** 3-dot. **Features:** Double action. Distributed by SGS Importers International.
Price: 22LR, matte or duotone, from $241.95
Price: 380, matte or duotone, from $241.95
Price: Mini Firestorm 32 ACP, intr. 2006 . . . . $358.95
Price: Mini Firestorm 9mm, matte, duotone, nickel, from $358.95
Price: Mini Firestorm 40 S&W, matte, duotone, nickel, from $358.95
Price: Mini Firestorm 45 ACP, matte, duotone, chrome, from . . . $308.95

Glock 17C   Glock 26   Glock 34

Glock 22   Glock 35

GLOCK 17/17C AUTO PISTOL
Caliber: 9mm Para., 17/19/33-shot magazines. **Barrel:** 4.49". **Weight:** 22.04 oz. (without magazine). **Length:** 7.32" overall. **Grips:** Black polymer. **Sights:** Dot on front blade, white outline rear adjustable for windage. **Features:** Polymer frame, steel slide; double-action trigger with "Safe Action" system; mechanical firing pin safety, drop safety; simple takedown without tools; locked breech, recoil operated action. ILS designation refers to Internal Locking System. Adopted by Austrian armed forces 1983. NATO approved 1984. Imported from Austria by Glock, Inc.
Price: Fixed sight $599.00
Price: Fixed sight w/ILS $624.00
Price: Adjustable sight $617.00
Price: Adjustable sight w/ILS $642.00
Price: Night sight $646.00
Price: Night sight w/ILS $671.00
Price: 17C Compensated (fixed sight) $621.00
Price: 17C Compensated (fixed sight) w/ILS $646.00

GLOCK 19/19C AUTO PISTOL
Caliber: 9mm Para., 15/17/19/33-shot magazines. **Barrel:** 4.02". **Weight:** 20.99 oz. (without magazine). **Length:** 6.85" overall. Compact version of Glock 17. Pricing the same as Model 17. Imported from Austria by Glock, Inc.
Price: Fixed sight $599.00
Price: 19C Compensated (fixed sight) $621.00

GLOCK 26 AUTO PISTOL
Caliber: 9mm Para. 10/12/15/17/19/33-shot magazines. **Barrel:** 3.46". **Weight:** 19.75 oz. **Length:** 6.29" overall. Subcompact version of Glock 17. Pricing the same as Model 17. Imported from Austria by Glock, Inc.
Price: Fixed sight $599.00

GLOCK 34 AUTO PISTOL
Caliber: 9mm Para. 17/19/33-shot magazines. **Barrel:** 5.32". **Weight:** 22.9 oz. **Length:** 8.15" overall. Competition version of Glock 17 with extended barrel, slide, and sight radius dimensions. Imported from Austria by Glock, Inc.
Price: Adjustable sight $679.00
Price: Adjustable sight w/ILS $704.00

GLOCK 22/22C AUTO PISTOL
Caliber: 40 S&W, 15/17-shot magazines. **Barrel:** 4.49". **Weight:** 22.92 oz. (without magazine). **Length:** 7.32" overall. **Features:** Otherwise similar to Model 17, including pricing. Imported from Austria by Glock, Inc. Introduced 1990.
Price: Fixed sight $599.00
Price: Fixed sight w/ILS $624.00
Price: Adjustable sight $617.00
Price: Adjustable sight w/**ILS** $642.00

Price: Night sight $646.00
Price: Night sight w/ILS $671.00
Price: 22C Compensated (fixed sight) $621.00
Price: 22C Compensated (fixed sight) w/ILS $646.00

GLOCK 23/23C AUTO PISTOL
Caliber: 40 S&W, 13/15/17-shot magazines. **Barrel:** 4.02". **Weight:** 21.16 oz. (without magazine). **Length:** 6.85" overall. **Features:** Otherwise similar to Model 22, including pricing. Compact version of Glock 22. Imported from Austria by Glock, Inc. Introduced 1990.
Price: Fixed sight $599.00
Price: 23C Compensated (fixed sight) $621.00

GLOCK 27 AUTO PISTOL
Caliber: 40 S&W, 9/11/13/15/17-shot magazines. **Barrel:** 3.46". **Weight:** 19.75 oz. (without magazine). **Length:** 6.29" overall. **Features:** Otherwise similar to Model 22, including pricing. Subcompact version of Glock 22. Imported from Austria by Glock, Inc. Introduced 1996.
Price: Fixed sight $599.00

GLOCK 35 AUTO PISTOL
Caliber: 40 S&W, 15/17-shot magazines. **Barrel:** 5.32". **Weight:** 24.52 oz. (w/o magazine). **Length:** 8.15" overall. **Features:** Otherwise similar to Model 22. Competition version of Glock 22 with extended barrel, slide, and sight radius dimensions. Imported from Austria by Glock, Inc. Introduced 1996.
Price: Fixed sight $679.00
Price: Adjustable sight w/ILS $704.00

GLOCK 20/20C 10MM AUTO PISTOL
Caliber: 10mm, 15-shot magazines. **Barrel:** 4.6". **Weight:** 27.68 oz. (without magazine). **Length:** 7.59" overall. **Features:** Otherwise similar to Model 17. Imported from Austria by Glock, Inc. Introduced 1990.
Price: Fixed sight $637.00
Price: Fixed sight w/ILS $662.00
Price: Adjustable sight $655.00
Price: Adjustable sight w/ILS $680.00
Price: Night sight $684.00
Price: Night sight w/ILS $709.00
Price: 20C Compensated (fixed sight) $676.00
Price: 20C Compensated (fixed sight) w/ILS $701.00

GLOCK 29 AUTO PISTOL
Caliber: 10mm, 10/15-shot magazines. **Barrel:** 3.78". **Weight:** 24.69 oz. (without magazine). **Length:** 6.77" overall. **Features:** Otherwise similar to Model 20, including pricing. Subcompact version of Glock 20. Imported from Austria by Glock, Inc. Introduced 1997.
Price: Fixed sight $637.00

Glock 30

Glock 36

Glock 31

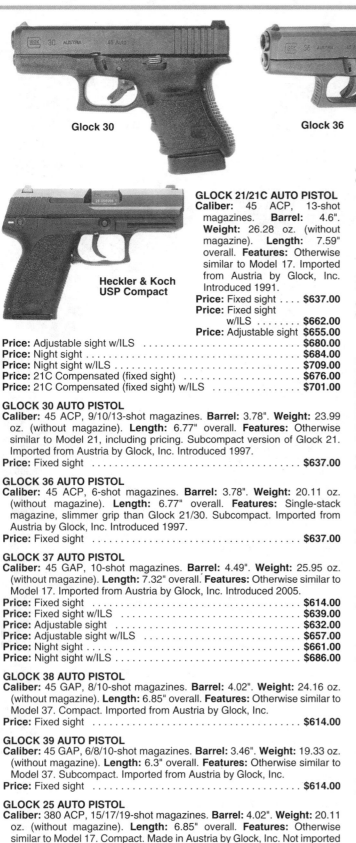

Heckler & Koch
USP Compact

Heckler & Koch
USP45

GLOCK 21/21C AUTO PISTOL
Caliber: 45 ACP, 13-shot magazines. **Barrel:** 4.6". **Weight:** 26.28 oz. (without magazine). **Length:** 7.59" overall. **Features:** Otherwise similar to Model 17. Imported from Austria by Glock, Inc. Introduced 1991.
Price: Fixed sight $637.00
Price: Fixed sight
w/ILS $662.00
Price: Adjustable sight $655.00
Price: Adjustable sight w/ILS $680.00
Price: Night sight $684.00
Price: Night sight w/ILS $709.00
Price: 21C Compensated (fixed sight) $676.00
Price: 21C Compensated (fixed sight) w/ILS $701.00

GLOCK 30 AUTO PISTOL
Caliber: 45 ACP, 9/10/13-shot magazines. **Barrel:** 3.78". **Weight:** 23.99 oz. (without magazine). **Length:** 6.77" overall. **Features:** Otherwise similar to Model 21, including pricing. Subcompact version of Glock 21. Imported from Austria by Glock, Inc. Introduced 1997.
Price: Fixed sight $637.00

GLOCK 36 AUTO PISTOL
Caliber: 45 ACP, 6-shot magazines. **Barrel:** 3.78". **Weight:** 20.11 oz. (without magazine). **Length:** 6.77" overall. **Features:** Single-stack magazine, slimmer grip than Glock 21/30. Subcompact. Imported from Austria by Glock, Inc. Introduced 1997.
Price: Fixed sight $637.00

GLOCK 37 AUTO PISTOL
Caliber: 45 GAP, 10-shot magazines. **Barrel:** 4.49". **Weight:** 25.95 oz. (without magazine). **Length:** 7.32" overall. **Features:** Otherwise similar to Model 17. Imported from Austria by Glock, Inc. Introduced 2005.
Price: Fixed sight $614.00
Price: Fixed sight w/ILS $639.00
Price: Adjustable sight $632.00
Price: Adjustable sight w/ILS $657.00
Price: Night sight $661.00
Price: Night sight w/ILS $686.00

GLOCK 38 AUTO PISTOL
Caliber: 45 GAP, 8/10-shot magazines. **Barrel:** 4.02". **Weight:** 24.16 oz. (without magazine). **Length:** 6.85" overall. **Features:** Otherwise similar to Model 37. Compact. Imported from Austria by Glock, Inc.
Price: Fixed sight $614.00

GLOCK 39 AUTO PISTOL
Caliber: 45 GAP, 6/8/10-shot magazines. **Barrel:** 3.46". **Weight:** 19.33 oz. (without magazine). **Length:** 6.3" overall. **Features:** Otherwise similar to Model 37. Subcompact. Imported from Austria by Glock, Inc.
Price: Fixed sight $614.00

GLOCK 25 AUTO PISTOL
Caliber: 380 ACP, 15/17/19-shot magazines. **Barrel:** 4.02". **Weight:** 20.11 oz. (without magazine). **Length:** 6.85" overall. **Features:** Otherwise similar to Model 17. Compact. Made in Austria by Glock, Inc. Not imported to U.S.
Price: . . . . NA

GLOCK 28 AUTO PISTOL
Caliber: 380 ACP, 10/12/15/17/19-shot magazines. **Barrel:** 3.46". **Weight:** 18.66 oz. (without magazine). **Length:** 6.29" overall. **Features:** Otherwise similar to Model 25. Subcompact. Made in Austria by Glock, Inc. Not imported to U.S.
Price: . . . . NA

GLOCK 31/31C AUTO PISTOL
Caliber: 357 Auto, 15/17-shot magazines. **Barrel:** 4.49". **Weight:** 23.28 oz. (without magazine). **Length:** 7.32" overall. **Features:** Otherwise similar to Model 17. Imported from Austria by Glock, Inc.
Price: Fixed sight $599.00
Price: Fixed sight w/ILS $624.00
Price: Adjustable sight $617.00
Price: Adjustable sight w/ILS $642.00
Price: Night sight $646.00
Price: Night sight w/ILS $671.00
Price: 31C Compensated (fixed sight) $621.00
Price: 31C Compensated (fixed sight) w/ILS $646.00

GLOCK 32/32C AUTO PISTOL
Caliber: 357 Auto, 13/15/17-shot magazines. **Barrel:** 4.02". **Weight:** 21.52 oz. (without magazine). **Length:** 6.85" overall. **Features:** Otherwise similar to Model 31. Compact. Imported from Austria by Glock, Inc.
Price: Fixed sight $599.00
Price: 32C Compensated (fixed sight) $621.00

GLOCK 33 AUTO PISTOL
Caliber: 357 Auto, 9/11/13/15/17-shot magazines. **Barrel:** 3.46". **Weight:** 19.75 oz. (without magazine). **Length:** 6.29" overall. **Features:** Otherwise similar to Model 31. Subcompact. Imported from Austria by Glock, Inc.
Price: Fixed sight $599.00

HAMMERLI "TRAILSIDE" TARGET PISTOL
Caliber: 22 LR. **Barrel:** 4.5", 6". **Weight:** 28 oz. **Grips:** Synthetic. **Sights:** Fixed. **Features:** 10-shot magazine. Imported from by Larry's Guns of Maine.
Price: $579.00

HECKLER & KOCH USP AUTO PISTOL
Caliber: 9mm Para., 15-shot magazine; 40 S&W, 13-shot magazine; 45 ACP, 12-shot magazine. **Barrel:** 4.25-4.41". **Weight:** 1.65 lbs. **Length:** 7.64-7.87" overall. **Grips:** Non-slip stippled black polymer. **Sights:** Blade front, rear adjustable for windage. **Features:** New HK design with polymer frame, modified Browning action with recoil reduction system, single control lever. Special "hostile environment" finish on all metal parts. Available in SA/DA, DAO, left- and right-hand versions. Introduced 1993. 45 ACP Introduced 1995. Imported from Germany by Heckler & Koch, Inc.
Price: USP 45 . . . . $839.00
Price: USP 40 and USP 9mm $769.00

Heckler & Koch USP Compact Auto Pistol
Caliber: 9mm Para., 13-shot magazine; 40 S&W and .357 SIG, 12-shot magazine; 45 ACP, 8-shot magazine. **Barrel:** Similar to the 9mm Para., 357 SIG, and 40 S&W have 3.58" barrels, measure 6.81" overall, and weigh 1.47 lbs. (9mm). Introduced 1996. 45 ACP measures 7.09" overall. Introduced 1998. Imported from Germany by Heckler & Koch, Inc.
Price: USP Compact 45 . . . . $874.00
Price: USP Compact 9mm Para., 357 SIG, and 40 S&W $799.00

**Heckler & Koch
USP45 Tactical**

**Heckler & Koch
Mark 23 Special Operations**

**Heckler & Koch
USP45 Compact**

Hi-Point 9MM Comp

Hi-Point C-9

HECKLER & KOCH USP45 TACTICAL PISTOL
Caliber: 40 S&W, 13-shot magazine; 45 ACP, 12-shot magazine. **Barrel:** 4.90-5.09". **Weight:** 1.9 lbs. **Length:** 8.64" overall. **Grips:** Non-slip stippled polymer. **Sights:** Blade front, fully adjustable target rear. **Features:** Has extended threaded barrel with rubber O-ring; adjustable trigger; extended magazine floorplate; adjustable trigger stop; polymer frame. Introduced 1998. Imported from Germany by Heckler & Koch, Inc.
Price: USP Tactical 45 .... **$1,115.00**
Price: USP Tactical 40 .... **$1,019.00**

Heckler & Koch USP Compact Tactical Pistol
Caliber: 45 ACP, 8-shot magazine. Similar to the USP Tactical except measures 7.72" overall, weighs 1.72 lbs. Introduced 2006. Imported from Germany by Heckler & Koch, Inc.
Price: USP Compact Tactical **$1,115.00**

HECKLER & KOCH MARK 23 SPECIAL OPERATIONS PISTOL
Caliber: 45 ACP, 12-shot magazine. **Barrel:** 5.87". **Weight:** 2.42 lbs. **Length:** 9.65" overall. **Grips:** Integral with frame; black polymer. **Sights:** Blade front, rear drift adjustable for windage; 3-dot. **Features:** Civilian version of the SOCOM pistol. Polymer frame; double action; exposed hammer; short recoil, modified Browning action. Introduced 1996. Imported from Germany by Heckler & Koch, Inc.
Price: **$2,412.00**

HECKLER & KOCH P2000 AUTO PISTOL
Caliber: 9mm Para., 13-shot magazine; 40 S&W and .357 SIG, 12-shot magazine. **Barrel:** 3.62". **Weight:** 1.5 lbs. **Length:** 7" overall. **Grips:** Interchangeable panels. **Sights:** Fixed Patridge style, drift adjustable for windage, standard 3-dot. Incorporates features of HK USP Compact pistol, including Law Enforcement Modification (LEM) trigger, double-action hammer system, ambidextrous magazine release, dual slide-release levers, accessory mounting rails, recurved, hook trigger guard, fiber-reinforced polymer frame, modular grip with exchangeable back straps, nitro-carburized finish, lock-out safety device. Introduced 2003. Imported from Germany by Heckler & Koch, Inc.
Price: **$887.00**
Price: P2000 LEM DAO, 357 SIG, intr. 2006 .... **$887.00**
Price: P2000 SA/DA, 357 SIG, intr. 2006 .... **$887.00**

HECKLER & KOCH P2000 SK AUTO PISTOL
Caliber: 9mm Para., 10-shot magazine; 40 S&W and .357 SIG, 9-shot magazine. **Barrel:** 3.27". **Weight:** 1.3 lbs. **Length:** 6.42" overall. **Sights:** Fixed Patridge style, drift adjustable. **Features:** Standard accessory rails, ambidextrous slide release, polymer frame, polygonal bore profile. Smaller version of P2000. Introduced 2005. Imported from Germany by Heckler & Koch, Inc.
Price: **$929.00**

HI-POINT FIREARMS MODEL 9MM COMPACT PISTOL
Caliber: 9mm Para., 8-shot magazine. **Barrel:** 3.5". **Weight:** 25 oz. **Length:** 6.75" overall. **Grips:** Textured plastic. **Sights:** Combat-style adjustable 3-dot system; low profile. **Features:** Single-action design; frame-mounted magazine release; polymer frame. Scratch-resistant matte finish. Introduced 1993. Comps are similar except they have a 4" barrel with muzzle brake/compensator. Compensator is slotted for laser or flashlight mounting. Introduced 1998. Made in U.S.A. by MKS Supply, Inc.
Price: C-9 9mm **$140.00**
Price: C-9 Comp **$169.00**
Price: C-9 Comp-L w/laser sight **$219.00**

Hi-Point Firearms Model 380 Polymer Pistol
Similar to the 9mm Compact model except chambered for 380 ACP, 8-shot magazine, adjustable 3-dot sights. Weighs 25 oz. Polymer frame. Action locks open after last shot. Includes 10-shot and 8-shot magazine; trigger lock. Introduced 1998. Comps are similar except they have a 4" barrel with muzzle compensator. Introduced 2001. Made in U.S.A. by MKS Supply, Inc.
Price: CF-380 .... **$120.00**
Price: 380 Comp **$120.00**
Price: 380 Comp-L w/laser sight **$190.00**

HI-POINT FIREARMS 40SW/POLY AND 45 AUTO PISTOLS
Caliber: 40 S&W, 8-shot magazine; 45 ACP (9-shot). **Barrel:** 4.5". **Weight:** 32 oz. **Length:** 7.72" overall. **Sights:** Adjustable 3-dot. **Features:** Polymer frames, last round lock-open, grip mounted magazine release, magazine disconnect safety, integrated accessory rail, trigger lock. Introduced 2002. Made in U.S.A. by MKS Supply, Inc.
Price: 40SW Poly **$179.00**
Price: 40SW Poly w/laser **$239.00**
Price: 45 ACP **$179.00**
Price: 45 ACP w/laser **$239.00**

Kahr K9

Kahr PM45

Kahr TP45

Kahr TP9093-Novak

KAHR K SERIES AUTO PISTOLS
Caliber: K9: 9mm Para., 7-shot; K40: 40 S&W, 6-shot magazine. **Barrel:** 3.5". **Weight:** 25 oz. **Length:** 6" overall. **Grips:** Wraparound textured soft polymer. **Sights:** Blade front, rear drift adjustable for windage; bar-dot combat style. **Features:** Trigger-cocking double-action mechanism with passive firing pin block. Made of 4140 ordnance steel with matte black finish. Contact maker for complete price list. Introduced 1994. Made in U.S.A. by Kahr Arms.
Price: K9093C K9, matte stainless steel **$741.00**
Price: K9093NC K9, matte stainless steel w/tritium night sights . . **$853.00**
Price: K9094C K9 matte blackened stainless stee **$772.00**
Price: K9098 K9 Elite 2003, stainless steel **$806.00**
Price: K4043 K40, matte stainless steel **$741.00**
Price: K4043N K40, matte stainless steel w/tritium night sights . . **$853.00**
Price: K4044 K40, matte blackened stainless steel **$772.00**
Price: K4048 K40 Elite 2003, stainless steel **$806.00**

Kahr MK Series Micro Pistols
Similar to the K9/K40 except is 5.35" overall, 4" high, with a 3.08" barrel. Weighs 23.1 oz. Has snag-free bar-dot sights, polished feed ramp, dual recoil spring system, DA-only trigger. Comes with 5-round flush baseplate and 6-shot grip extension magazine. Introduced 1998. Made in U.S.A. by Kahr Arms.
Price: M9093 MK9, matte stainless steel **$741.00**
Price: M9093N MK9, matte stainless steel, tritium night sights . . **$853.00**
Price: M9093-BOX MK9, matte stainless steel frame,
matte black slide **$475.00**
Price: M9098 MK9 Elite 2003, stainless steel **$806.00**
Price: M4043 MK40, matte stainless steel **$741.00**
Price: M4043N MK40, matte stainless steel, tritium night sights . **$853.00**
Price: M4048 MK40 Elite 2003, stainless steel **$806.00**

Kahr P Series Pistols
Caliber: 9x19, 40 S&W. Similar to K9/K40 steel frame pistol except has polymer frame, matte stainless steel slide. Barrel length 3.5"; overall length 5.8"; weighs 17 oz. Includes two 7-shot magazines, hard polymer case, trigger lock. Introduced 2000. Made in U.S.A. by Kahr Arms.
Price: KP9093 P9 . . . . **$697.00**
Price: KP9093N P9, tritium night sight **$808.00**
Price: KPS9093 P9 Covert, shortened grip, 15 oz., 6+1 . . . . **$697.00**
Price: KP4043 P40 . . . . **$697.00**
Price: KPS4043N P40 Covert, shortened grip, tritium night sights **$697.00**

Kahr PM Series Pistols
Caliber: 9x19, 40 S&W. Similar to P-Series pistols except has smaller polymer frame (Polymer Micro). Barrel length 3.08"; overall length 5.35";

weighs 17 oz. Includes two 7-shot magazines, hard polymer case, trigger lock. Introduced 2000. Made in U.S.A. by Kahr Arms.
Price: PM9093 PM9 . . . . **$728.00**
Price: PM9093N PM9, tritium night sight **$839.00**
Price: PM4043 PM40 . . . . **$728.00**
Price: PM45 (2007) **$814.00**

KAHR T SERIES PISTOLS
Caliber: T9: 9mm Para., 8-shot magazine; T40: 40 S&W, 7-shot magazine. **Barrel:** 4". **Weight:** 28.1-29.1 oz. **Length:** 6.5" overall. **Grips:** Checkered Hogue Pau Ferro wood grips. **Sights:** Rear: Novak low profile 2-dot tritium night sight, front tritium night sight. **Features:** Similar to other Kahr makes, but with longer slide and barrel upper, longer butt. Trigger cocking DAO; lock breech; "Browning-type" recoil lug; passive striker block; no magazine disconnect. Comes with two magazines. Introduced 2004. Made in U.S.A. by Kahr Arms.
Price: KT9093 T9 matte stainless steel **$792.00**
Price: KT9093-NOVAK T9, "Tactical 9," Novak night sight **$921.00**

KAHR TP SERIES PISTOLS
Caliber: TP9: 9mm Para., 7-shot magazine; TP40: 40 S&W, 6-shot magazine. **Barrel:** 4". **Weight:** 19.1-20.1 oz. **Length:** 6.5-6.7" overall. **Grips:** Textured polymer. Similar to T-series guns, but with polymer frame, matte stainless slide. Comes with two magazines. TP40s introduced 2006. Made in U.S.A. by Kahr Arms.
Price: TP9093 TP9 . . . . **$697.00**
Price: TP9093-Novak TP9 . . . . **$839.00**
Price: TP4043 TP40 . . . . **$697.00**
Price: TP45 (2007) **$697.00**

KAHR CW SERIES PISTOL
Caliber: 9mm Para., 7-shot magazine; 40 S&W, 6-shot magazine. **Barrel:** 3.5-3.6". **Weight:** 17.7-18.7 oz. **Length:** 5.9-6.36" overall. **Grips:** Textured polymer. Similar to P-Series, but CW Series have conventional rifling, metal-injection-molded slide stop lever, no front dovetail cut, one magazine. CW40 introduced 2006. Made in U.S.A. by Kahr Arms.
Price: CW9093 CW9 . . . . **$533.00**
Price: CW4043 CW40 . . . . **$533.00**

KEL-TEC P-11 AUTO PISTOL
Caliber: 9mm Para., 10-shot magazine. **Barrel:** 3.1". **Weight:** 14 oz. **Length:** 5.6" overall. **Grips:** Checkered black polymer. **Sights:** Blade front, rear adjustable for windage. **Features:** Ordnance steel slide, aluminum frame. Double-action-only trigger mechanism. Introduced 1995. Made in U.S.A. by Kel-Tec CNC Industries, Inc.
Price: Blue/Hard Chrome/Parkerized . . . . **$320.00/$375.00/$362.00**

KEL-TEC PF-9 PISTOL
Caliber: 9mm Luger; 7 rounds. **Weight:** 12.7 oz. **Sights:** Rear sight adjustable for windage and elevation. Barrel **Length:** 3.1". **Length:** 5.85". **Features:** Barrel, locking system, slide stop, assembly pin, front sight, recoil springs and guide rod adapted from P-11. Trigger system with integral hammer block and the extraction system adapted from P-3AT. MIL-STD-1913 Picatinny rail. Made in U.S.A. by Kel-Tec CNC Industries, Inc.
Price: Blue/Parkerized/Hard Chrome . . . . **$314.00/$355.00/$368.00**

Kel-Tec P-3AT

Kel-Tec P-32

Kimber Pro Carry II

Kimber CDP II

Kimber Ten II
High Capacity Polymer

Kimber
Ultra Carry II

Kimber Gold Match II

KEL-TEC P-32 AUTO PISTOL
Caliber: 32 ACP, 7-shot magazine. **Barrel:** 2.68". **Weight:** 6.6 oz. **Length:** 5.07" overall. **Grips:** Checkered composite. **Sights:** Fixed. **Features:** Double-action-only mechanism with 6-lb. pull; internal slide stop. Textured composite grip/frame. Now available in 380 ACP. Made in U.S.A. by Kel-Tec CNC Industries, Inc.
Price: Blue/Hard Chrome/Parkerized .... **$300.00/$355.00/$340.00**

KEL-TEC P-3AT PISTOL
Caliber: 380 Auto; 7-rounds. **Weight:** 7.2 oz. **Length:** 5.2". **Features:** Lightest 380 auto made; aluminum frame, steel barrel.
Price: Blue/Hard Chrome/Parkerized .... **$300.00/$355.00/$340.00**

KEL-TEC PLR-16 PISTOL
Caliber: 5.56mm NATO; 10-round magazine. **Weight:** 51 oz. **Sights:** Rear sight adjustable for windage, front sight is M-16 blade. Barrel **Length:** 9.2". **Length:** 18.5". **Features:** Muzzle is threaded 1/2"-28 to accept standard attachments such as a muzzle brake. Except for the barrel, bolt, sights, and mechanism, the PLR-16 pistol is made of high-impact glass fiber reinforced polymer. Gas-operated semi-auto. Conventional gas-piston operation with M-16 breech locking system. MIL-STD-1913 Picatinny rail. Made in U.S.A. by Kel-Tec CNC Industries, Inc.
Price: Blued **$640.00**

KIMBER CUSTOM II AUTO PISTOL
Caliber: 45 ACP, 40 S&W, 38 Super, 9mm, 10mm. **Barrel:** 5", match grade; 9mm, 10mm, 40 S&W, 38 Super barrels ramped. **Weight:** 38 oz. **Length:** 8.7" overall. **Grips:** Checkered black rubber, walnut, rosewood. **Sights:** Dovetailed front and rear, Kimber low profile adj. or fixed sights. **Features:** Slide, frame and barrel machined from steel or stainless steel. Match grade barrel, chamber and trigger group. Extended thumb safety, beveled magazine well, beveled front and rear slide serrations, high ride beavertail grip safety, checkered flat mainspring housing, kidney cut under trigger guard, high cut grip, match grade stainless steel barrel bushing, polished breech face, Commander-style hammer, lowered and flared ejection port, Wolff springs, bead blasted black oxide or matte stainless finish. Introduced in 1996. Made in U.S.A. by Kimber Mfg., Inc.
Price: Custom II **$768.00**
Price: Custom II Walnut (double-diamond walnut grips) **$775.00**
Price: Stainless II **$865.00**
Price: Stainless II 40 S&W **$884.00**
Price: Stainless II Target 45 ACP (stainless, adj. sight) **$983.00**
Price: Stainless II Target 38 Super **$1,014.00**

Kimber Compact Stainless II Auto Pistol
Similar to Pro Carry II except has stainless steel frame, 4-inch bbl., grip is .400" shorter than standard, no front serrations. Weighs 34 oz. 45 ACP only. Introduced in 1998. Made in U.S.A. by Kimber Mfg., Inc.
Price: **$907.00**

Kimber Pro Carry II Auto Pistol
Similar to Custom II, has aluminum frame, 4" bull barrel fitted directly to the slide without bushing. HD with stainless steel frame. Introduced 1998. Made in U.S.A. by Kimber Mfg., Inc.
Price: Pro Carry II **$779.00**
Price: Pro Carry II w/night sights **$902.00**
Price: Pro Carry II Stainless w/night sights **$985.00**
Price: Pro Carry HD II **$906.00**

Kimber Ultra Carry II Auto Pistol
Lightweight aluminum frame, 3" match grade bull barrel fitted to slide without bushing. Grips .4" shorter. Low effort recoil. Weighs 25 oz. Introduced in 1999. Made in U.S.A. by Kimber Mfg., Inc.
Price: **$791.00**
Price: Ultra Carry II Stainless **$875.00**
Price: Ultra Carry II Stainless 40 S&W **$921.00**

Kimber Ten II High Capacity Polymer Pistol
Similar to Custom II, Pro Carry II and Ultra Carry II depending on barrel length. Thirteen-round magazine capacity (double stack and flush fitting). Polymer grip frame molded over stainless steel or aluminum (BP Ten pistols only) frame insert. Checkered front strap and belly of trigger guard. All models have fixed sights except Gold Match Ten II, which has adjustable sight. Frame grip dimensions approximately that of the standard 1911. **Weight:** 24 to 34 oz. Improved version of the Kimber Polymer series. Made in U.S.A. by Kimber Mfg., Inc.
Price: Pro Carry Ten II **$794.00**
Price: Stainless Ten II **$786.00**

Kimber Gold Match II Auto Pistol
Similar to Custom II models. Includes stainless steel barrel with match grade chamber and barrel bushing, ambidextrous thumb safety, adjustable sight, premium aluminum trigger, hand-checkered double diamond rosewood grips. Barrel hand-fitted for target accuracy. Made in U.S.A. by Kimber Mfg., Inc.
Price: Gold Match II **$1,204.00**
Price: Gold Match Stainless II 45 ACP **$1,369.00**
Price: Gold Match Stainless II 40 S&W **$1,400.00**

Kimber Eclipse II

Kimber Eclipse Pro II

Kimber LTP II

Korth Auto Pistol

North American Arms Guardian

Olympic Arms Matchmaster 5

Kimber Gold Match Ten II Polymer Auto Pistol

Similar to Stainless Gold Match II. High capacity polymer frame with 13-round magazine. Thumb safety. Introduced 1999. Made in U.S.A. by Kimber Mfg., Inc.

Price: **$1,072.00**

Kimber Gold Combat II Auto Pistol

Similar to Gold Match II except designed for concealed carry. Extended and beveled magazine well, Meprolight Tritium night sights; premium aluminum trigger; 30 lpi front strap checkering; extended magazine well. Introduced 1999. Made in U.S.A. by Kimber Mfg., Inc.

Price: Gold Combat II **$1,733.00**
Price: Gold Combat Stainless II **$1,674.00**

Kimber CDP II Series Auto Pistol

Similar to Custom II, but designed for concealed carry. Aluminum frame. Standard features include stainless steel slide, fixed Meprolight tritium 3-dot (green) dovetail-mounted night sights, match grade barrel and chamber, 30 LPI front strap checkering, two-tone finish, ambidextrous thumb safety, hand-checkered double diamond rosewood grips. Introduced in 2000. Made in U.S.A. by Kimber Mfg., Inc.

Price: Ultra CDP II 40 S&W **$1,215.00**
Price: Ultra CDP II (3" barrel, short grip) **$1,177.00**
Price: Compact CDP II (4" barrel, short grip) **$1,177.00**
Price: Pro CDP II (4" barrel, full length grip) **$1,177.00**
Price: Custom CDP II (5" barrel, full length grip) **$1,177.00**

Kimber Eclipse II Series Auto Pistol

Similar to Custom II and other stainless Kimber pistols. Stainless slide and frame, black oxide, two-tone finish. Gray/black laminated grips. 30 lpi front strap checkering. All models have night sights; Target versions have Meprolight adjustable Bar/Dot version. Made in U.S.A. by Kimber Mfg., Inc.

Price: Eclipse Ultra II (3" barrel, short grip) **$1,085.00**
Price: Eclipse Pro II (4" barrel, full length grip) **$1,085.00**
Price: Eclipse Pro Target II (4" barrel, full length grip,
adjustable sight) **$1,189.00**
Price: Eclipse Custom II (5" barrel, full length grip) **$1,105.00**
Price: Eclipse Target II (5" barrel, full length grip,
adjustable sight) **$1,189.00**
Price: Eclipse Custom II (10mm) **$1,220.00**

Kimber LTP II Auto Pistol

Similar to Gold Match II. Built for Limited Ten competition. First Kimber pistol with new, innovative Kimber external extractor. KimPro premium finish. Stainless steel match grade barrel. Extended and beveled magazine well.

Checkered front strap and trigger guard belly. Tungsten full length guide rod. Premium aluminum trigger. Ten-round single stack magazine. Wide ambidextrous thumb safety. Made in U.S.A. by Kimber Mfg., Inc.

Price: **$2,099.00**

Kimber Super Match II Auto Pistol

Similar to Gold Match II. Built for target and action shooting competition. Tested for accuracy, target included. Stainless steel barrel and chamber. KimPro finish on stainless steel slide. Stainless steel frame. 30 lpi checkered front strap, premium aluminum trigger, Kimber adjustable sight. Introduced in 1999.

Price: **$1,986.00**

KORTH AUTO PISTOLS

Caliber: 9mm Para, 9x21 (10-shot). **Barrel:** 4", 4.5". **Weight:** 39.9 oz. **Grips:** Walnut, palisander, amboinia, ivory. **Sights:** Fully adjustable. **Features:** Recoil-operated, locking block system, forged steel, fully machine and ground to final tolerances. DA/SA, 2 models available with either rounded or combat-style trigger guard. Available finishes: high polish blue plasma, high polish or matted silver plasma, or high polish standard blue. Schalldampfer Modell has special threaded 4.5-inch barrel and thread protector, many deluxe options available. Made in Germany. Imported by Korth USA.

Price: . . . . **$7,000.00 to $12,000.00**

NORTH AMERICAN ARMS GUARDIAN DAO PISTOL

Caliber: 25 NAA, 32 ACP, 380 ACP, 32NAA, 6-shot magazine. **Barrel:** 2.49". **Weight:** 20.8 oz. **Length:** 4.75" overall. **Grips:** Black polymer. **Sights:** Low profile fixed. **Features:** Double-action only mechanism. All stainless steel construction. Introduced 1998. Made in U.S.A. by North American Arms.

Price: . . . . **$402.00 to $479.00**

OLYMPIC ARMS MATCHMASTER 5 1911 PISTOL

Caliber: 45 ACP, 7-shot magazine. **Barrel:** 5" stainless steel. **Weight:** 40 oz. **Length:** 8.75" overall. **Grips:** Smooth walnut with laser-etched scorpion icon. **Sights:** Ramped blade, LPA adjustable rear. **Features:** Matched frame and slide, fitted and head-spaced barrel, complete ramp and throat jobs, lowered and widened ejection port, beveled mag well, hand-stoned-to-match hammer and sear, lightweight long-shoe over-travel adjusted trigger, shaped and tensioned extractor, extended thumb safety, wide beavertail grip safety and full-length guide rod. Made in U.S.A. by Olympic Arms, Inc.

Price: **$714.00**

Olympic Arms Matchmaster 6

Olympic Arms Enforcer

Olympic Arms Cohort

Olympic Arms Big Deuce

Olympic Arms Westerner

Olympic Arms Trail Boss

Olympic Arms Constable

OLYMPIC ARMS MATCHMASTER 6 1911 PISTOL
Caliber: 45 ACP, 7-shot magazine. **Barrel:** 6" stainless steel. **Weight:** 44 oz. **Length:** 9.75" overall. **Grips:** Smooth walnut with laser-etched scorpion icon. **Sights:** Ramped blade, LPA adjustable rear. **Features:** Matched frame and slide, fitted and head-spaced barrel, complete ramp and throat jobs, lowered and widened ejection port, beveled mag well, hand-stoned-to-match hammer and sear, lightweight long-shoe over-travel adjusted trigger, shaped and tensioned extractor, extended thumb safety, wide beavertail grip safety and full length guide rod. Made in U.S.A. by Olympic Arms, Inc.
Price: **$774.00**

OLYMPIC ARMS ENFORCER 1911 PISTOL
Caliber: 45 ACP, 6-shot magazine. **Barrel:** 4" bull stainless steel. **Weight:** 35 oz. **Length:** 7.75" overall. **Grips:** Smooth walnut with etched black widow spider icon. **Sights:** Ramped blade front, LPA adjustable rear. **Features:** Compact Enforcer frame. Busingless bull barrel with triplex counter-wound self-contained recoil system. Matched frame and slide, fitted and head-spaced barrel, complete ramp and throat jobs, lowered and widened ejection port, beveled mag well, hand-stoned-to-match hammer and sear, lightweight longshoe over-travel adjusted trigger, shaped and tensioned extractor, extended thumb safety, wide beavertail grip safety and full length guide rod. Made in U.S.A. by Olympic Arms.
Price: **$750.00**

OLYMPIC ARMS COHORT PISTOL
Caliber: 45 ACP, 7-shot magazine. **Barrel:** 4" bull stainless steel. **Weight:** 36 oz. **Length:** 7.75" overall. **Grips:** Fully checkered walnut. **Sights:** Ramped blade front, LPA adjustable rear. **Features:** Full size 1911 frame. Bushingless bull barrel with triplex counter-wound self-contained recoil system. Matched frame and slide, fitted and head-spaced barrel, complete ramp and throat jobs, lowered and widened ejection port, beveled mag well, hand-stoned-to-match hammer and sear, lightweight long-shoe over-travel adjusted trigger, shaped and tensioned extractor, extended thumb safety, wide beavertail grip safety and full length guide rod. Made in U.S.A. by Olympic Arms.
Price: **$779.00**

OLYMPIC ARMS BIG DEUCE PISTOL
Caliber: 45 ACP, 7-shot magazine. **Barrel:** 6"stainless steel. **Weight:** 44 oz. **Length:** 9.75" overall. **Grips:** Double diamond checkered exotic cocobolo wood. **Sights:** Ramped blade front, LPA adjustable rear. **Features:** Carbon steel parkerized slide with satin bead blast finish full size frame. Matched frame and slide, fitted and head-spaced barrel, complete ramp and throat jobs, lowered and widened ejection port, beveld mag well, hand-stoned-to-match hammer and sear, lightweight long-shoe over-travel adjusted trigger, shaped and tensioned extractor, extended thumb safety, wide beavertail grip safety and full length guide rod. Made in U.S.A. by Olympic Arms.
Price: **$834.00**

OLYMPIC ARMS WESTERNER SERIES 1911 PISTOLS
Caliber: 45 ACP, 7-shot magazine. **Barrel:** 4", 5", 6" stainless steel. **Weight:** 35-43 oz. **Length:** 7.75-9.75" overall. **Grips:** Smooth ivory laser-etched Westerner icon. **Sights:** Ramped blade, LPA adjustable rear. **Features:** Matched frame and slide, fitted and head-spaced barrel, complete ramp and throat jobs, lowered and widened ejection port, beveld mag well, hand-stoned-to-match hammer and sear, lightweight long-shoe over-travel adjusted trigger, shaped and tensioned extractor, extended thumb safety, wide beavertail grip safety and full length guide rod. Entire pistol is fitted and assembled, then disassembled and subjected to the color case hardening process. Made in U.S.A. by Olympic Arms, Inc.
Price: Constable, 4" barrel, 35 oz. **$935.00**
Price: Westerner, 5" barrel, 39 oz. **$834.00**
Price: Trail Boss, 6" barrel, 43 oz. **$959.00**

OLYMPIC ARMS SCHUETZEN PISTOL WORKS 1911 PISTOLS
Caliber: 45 ACP, 7-shot magazine.**Barrel:** 4", 5.2", bull stainless steel. **Weight:** 35-38 oz. **Length:** 7.75-8.75" overall. **Grips:** Double diamond checkered exotic cocobolo wood. **Sights:** Ramped blade, LPA adjustable rear. **Features:** Carbon steel parkerized slide with satin bead blast finish full size frame. Matched frame and slide, fitted and head-spaced barrel, complete ramp and throat jobs, lowered and widened ejection port, beveld mag well, hand-stoned-to-match hammer and sear, lightweight long-shoe over-travel adjusted trigger, shaped and tensioned extractor, extended thumb safety, wide beavertail grip safety and full length guide rod. Custom made by Olympic Arms Schuetzen Pistol Works. Parts are hand selected and fitted by expert pistolsmiths. Several no-cost options to choose from. Made in U.S.A. by Olympic Arms Schuetzen Pistol Works.
Price: Journeyman, 4" bull barrel, 35 oz. **$1,299.00**
Price: Street Deuce, 5.2" bull barrel, 38 oz. **$1,299.00**

Olympic Arms
Journeyman

Olympic Arms
Street Deuce

Olympic Arms
OA-98

Olympic Arms
OA-93

Olympic Arms
Whitney Wolverine

Para-Ordnance SSP-SE1

OLYMPIC ARMS OA-93 AR PISTOL
Caliber: 5.56 NATO. **Barrel:** 6.5" button-rifled stainless steel. **Weight:** 4.46 lbs. **Length:** 17" overall. **Sights:** None. **Features:** Olympic Arms integrated recoil system on the upper receiver eliminates the buttstock, flat top upper, free floating tubular match handguard, threaded muzzle with flash suppressor. Made in U.S.A. by Olympic Arms, Inc.
Price: **$1,080.00**

Olympic Arms OA-98 AR Pistol
Caliber: 5.56 NATO. **Barrel:** 6.5" button-rifled stainless steel. **Length:** 15.25" overall. **Weight:** 49 oz. **Sights:** None. **Features:** Olympic Arms integrated recoil system on the upper receiver eliminates the buttstock, skeletonized receivers and grip for weight, flat top upper, protective barrel shroud, crowned muzzle. Conforms to AWB, legal in post-ban restricted states, except CA. Made in U.S.A. by Olympic Arms, Inc.
Price: **$1,080.00**

OLYMPIC ARMS K23PAR PISTOL
Caliber: 5.56 NATO. **Barrel:** 6.5" button-rifled chrome-moly steel. **Length:** 22.25" overall. **Weight:** 5.12 lbs. **Sights:** Adjustable A2 rear, elevation adjustable front post. **Features:** A2 upper with rear sight, free floating tubular match handguard, threaded muzzle with flash suppressor, receiver extension tube with foam cover, no bayonet lug. Made in U.S.A. by Olympic Arms, Inc. Introduced 2007.
Price: **$839.00**

OLYMPIC ARMS K23P-A3-TC AR PISTOL
Caliber: 5.56 NATO. **Barrel:** 6.5" button-rifled chrome-moly steel. **Length:** 22.25" overall. **Weight:** 5.12 lbs. **Sights:** Adjustable A2 rear, elevation adjustable front post. **Features:** Flat-top upper with detachable carry handle, free floating FIRSH rail handguard, threaded muzzle with flash suppressor, receiver extension tube with foam cover, no bayonet lug. Made in U.S.A. by Olympic Arms, Inc. Introduced 2007.
Price: **$938.00**

OLYMPIC ARMS WHITNEY WOLVERINE PISTOL
Caliber: 22 LR, 10-shot magazine. **Barrel:** 4.625" stainless steel. **Weight:** 19.2 oz. **Length:** 9" overall. **Grips:** Black checkered with fire/safe markings. **Sights:** Ramped blade front, dovetail rear. **Features:** Polymer frame with natural ergonomics and ventilated rib. Barrel with 6-groove 1x16 trwist rate. All metal magazine shell. Made in U.S.A. by Olympic Arms.
Price: **$279.50**

PARA-ORDNANCE PXT 1911 SINGLE-ACTION SINGLE-STACK AUTO PISTOLS
Caliber: 38 Super, 45 ACP. **Barrel:** 3.5", 4.25", 5". **Weight:** 28-40 oz. **Length:** 7.1-8.5" overall. **Grips:** Checkered cocobolo, textured composition, Mother of Pearl synthetic. **Sights:** Blade front, low-profile Novak Extreme Duty adjustable rear. High visibility 3-dot system. **Features:** Available with alloy, steel or stainless steel frames. Skeletonized trigger, spurred hammer. Manual thumb, grip and firing pin lock safeties. Full-length guide rod. PXT designates new Para Power Extractor throughout the line. Introduced 2004. Made in Canada by Para-Ordnance.
Price: SSP-SE1 (2006), midnight blue, 7+1, 5" barrel **$1,094.00**
Price: OPS, stainless, Griptor grooves front strap (2006) **$1,043.00**
Price: LTC, blued or stainless, 7+1, 4.25" barrel . . . **$884.00 to 1,043.00**
Price: SSP, blued or stainless, 7+1, 4.25" barrel . . . **$884.00 to 1,043.00**

PARA-ORDNANCE PXT 1911 SINGLE-ACTION HIGH-CAPACITY AUTO PISTOLS
Caliber: 9mm, 45 ACP, 10//14/18-shot magazines. **Barrel:** 3", 5". **Weight:** 34-40 oz. **Length:** 7.1-8.5" overall. **Grips:** Textured composition. **Sights:** Blade front, low-profile Novak Extreme Duty adjustable rear or fixed sights. High visibility 3-dot system. **Features:** Available with alloy, steel or stainless steel frames. Skeletonized match trigger, spurred hammer, flared ejection port. Manual thumb, grip and firing pin lock safeties. Full-length guide rod. Introduced 2004. Made in Canada by Para-Ordnance.
Price: P14-45MB (2006), midnight blue, 14+1, 5" barrel **$899.00**
Price: P14-45 stainless, 14+1, 5" barrel **$998.00**
Price: P18-9 stainless,18+1 9mm, 5" barrel **$1,049.00**

Para-Ordnance Todd Jarrett

Para-Ordnance LDA

Para-Ordnance Carry

Para-Ordnance CCO

Para-Ordnance Tac-Four

Para-Ordnance Tac-S

Para-Ordnance Colonel

Para-Ordnance Nite-Trac

Para-Ordnance Warthog

Para-Ordnance PXT Limited Pistols
Similar to the PXT-Series pistols except with full-length recoil guide system; fully adjustable rear sight; tuned trigger with over-travel stop; beavertail grip safety; competition hammer; front and rear slide serrations; ambidextrous safety; lowered ejection port; ramped match-grade barrel; dove-tailed front sight. Introduced 2004. Made in Canada by Para-Ordnance.
Price: S12-45 LTD, 45 ACP, 12+1, stainless, Novak sights . . . **$1,163.00**
Price: Todd Jarrett 40 S&W, 16+1, stainless **$1,163.00**

Para-Ordnance LDA Single-Stack Carry Auto Pistols
Similar to PXT-series except has double-action trigger mechanism, flush hammers, brushed stainless finish, checkered composition grips. Available in 45 ACP. Introduced 1999. Made in Canada by Para-Ordnance.
Price: Carry, 6+1, 3" barrel, stainless **$1,049.00**
Price: Carry, 6+1, 3" barrel, covert black **$1,133.00**
Price: CCO, 7+1, 3.5" barrel **$1,049.00**
Price: CCW, 7+1, 4.5" barrel **$1,049.00**

Para-Ordnance LDA High-Cap Carry Auto Pistols
Similar to LDA-series with double-action trigger mechanism. Also, bobbed beavertail, high-cap mags. Available in 9mm Para., 45 ACP. Introduced 1999. Made in Canada by Para-Ordnance.
Price: Carry 12, 12+1, 3.5" barrel, stainless **$1,133.00**
Price: Tac-Four, 13+1, 4.5" barrel, stainless **$1,028.00**
Price: C TX189B, 18+1, 5" barrel, covert black, Novak sights . **$1,163.00**

Para-Ordnance LDA Single-Stack Auto Pistols
Similar to LDA-series with double-action trigger mechanism. Cocobolo and polymer grips. Available in 45 ACP. Introduced 1999. Made in Canada by Para-Ordnance.
Price: Black Watch Companion, 7+1, 3.5" barrel **$1,133.00**

Price: Tac-S, 7+1, 4.5" barrel, Spec Ops matte finish **$944.00**
Price: Tac-S, 7+1, 4.5" barrel, stainless **$1,028.00**
Price: Limited, 7+1, 5" barrel, stainless **$1,193.00**

Para-Ordnance LDA Hi-Capacity Auto Pistols
Similar to LDA-series with double-action trigger mechanism. Polymer grips. Available in 9mm, 40 S&W, 45 ACP. Introduced 1999. Made in Canada by Para-Ordnance.
Price: Colonel, 14+1, 4.25" barrel **$944.00**
Price: Hi-Cap 45, 14+1, 5" barrel, stainless **$1,028.00**
Price: Hi-Cap 9, 18+1, 5" barrel, covert black finish **$944.00**
Price: Hi-Cap LTD 45 45 ACP, 14+1, 5" barrel, stainless **$1,193.00**
Price: Hi-Cap LTD 40 40 S&W, 15+1, 5" barrel, stainless . . . **$1,193.00**
Price: Hi-Cap LTD 9 9mm, 18+1, 5" barrel, stainless **$1,193.00**

Para-Ordnance LDA Light Rail Pistols
Similar to PXT and LDA-series above, with built-in light rail. Polymer grips. Available in 9mm, 40 S&W, 45 ACP. Made in Canada by Para-Ordnance.
Price: Nite-Tac 45, 14+1 45 ACP, 5" barrel, covert black **$1,034.00**
Price: Nite-Tac 40, 16+1 40 S&W, 5" barrel, stainless (2006) . **$1,103.00**
Price: Nite-Tac 9, 16+1 9mm, 5" barrel, stainless (2006) **$1,103.00**

PARA-ORDNANCE WARTHOG
Caliber: 9mm, 45 ACP, 6, 10, or 12-shot magazines. **Barrel:** 3". **Weight:** 24 to 31.5 oz. **Length:** 6.5". **Grips:** Varies by model. **Features:** Single action. Made in Canada by Para-Ordnance.
Price: Slim Hawg (2006) single stack .45 ACP, stainless, 6+1 . **$1,043.00**
Price: Nite Hawg .45 ACP, black finish, 10+1 . . . . **$1,013.00**
Price: Warthog .45 ACP, Regal finish, 10+1 . . . . **$884.00**
Price: Stainless Warthog .45 ACP (2006), brushed finish, 10+1 . **$989.00**
Price: Hawg 9 9mm Regal finish, alloy frame, 12+1 . . . . **$884.00**
Price: Lite Hawg 9 9mm (2006) black finish, alloy frame, 12+1 **$1,049.00**

Para-Ordnance Nite Hawg

Para-Ordnance Slim Hawg

Para-Ordnance Lite Hawg

Phoenix Arms HP22

Ruger P89

Ruger P90

Ruger KP944D

Ruger KP9515

PHOENIX ARMS HP22, HP25 AUTO PISTOLS
Caliber: 22 LR, 10-shot (HP22), 25 ACP, 10-shot (HP25). **Barrel:** 3". **Weight:** 20 oz. **Length:** 5-1/2" overall. **Grips:** Checkered composition. **Sights:** Blade front, adjustable rear. **Features:** Single action, exposed hammer; manual hold-open; button magazine release. Available in satin nickel, matte blue finish. Introduced 1993. Made in U.S.A. by Phoenix Arms.
Price: With gun lock **$130.00**
Price: HP Range kit with 5" bbl.,
locking case and assessories
(1 Mag) **$171.00**
Price: HP Deluxe Range kit with 3" and
5" bbls., 2 mags., case **$210.00**

ROCK RIVER ARMS BASIC CARRY AUTO PISTOL
Caliber: 45 ACP. **Barrel:** NA. **Weight:** NA. **Length:** NA. **Grips:** Rosewood, checkered. **Sights:** dovetail front sight, Heinie rear sight. **Features:** NM frame with 20-, 25- or 30-LPI checkered front strap, 5-inch slide with double serrations, lowered and flared ejection port, throated NM Kart barrel with NM bushing, match Commander hammer and match sear, aluminum speed trigger, dehorned, Parkerized finish, one magazine, accuracy guarantee. 3.5 lb. Trigger pull. Introduced 2006. Made in U.S.A. From Rock River Arms.
Price: PS2700 . . . . **$1,540.00**

RUGER P89 AUTOLOADING PISTOL
Caliber: 9mm Para., 15-shot magazine. **Barrel:** 4.50". **Weight:** 32 oz. **Length:** 7.75" overall. **Grips:** Grooved black synthetic composition. **Sights:** Square post front, square notch rear adjustable for windage, both with white dot inserts. **Features:** Double action, ambidextrous slide-mounted safety-levers. Slide 4140 chrome-moly steel or 400-series stainless steel, frame lightweight aluminum alloy. Ambidextrous magazine release. Blue, stainless steel. Introduced 1986; stainless 1990.
Price: P89, blue, extra mag and mag loader, plastic case locks . . **$475.00**
Price: KP89, stainless, extra mag and mag loader,
plastic case locks **$525.00**

Ruger P89D Decocker Autoloading Pistol
Similar to standard P89 except has ambidextrous decocking levers in place of regular slide-mounted safety. Decocking levers move firing pin inside slide where hammer cannot reach. Blue, stainless steel. Introduced 1990.
Price: P89D, blue, extra mag and mag loader, plastic case locks **$475.00**
Price: KP89D, stainless, extra mag and mag loader,
plastic case locks **$525.00**

RUGER P90 MANUAL SAFETY MODEL AUTOLOADING PISTOL
Caliber: 45 ACP, 8-shot magazine. **Barrel:** 4.50". **Weight:** 33.5 oz. **Length:** 7.75" overall. **Grips:** Grooved black synthetic composition. **Sights:** Square post front, square notch rear adjustable for windage, both with white dot. **Features:** Double action; ambidextrous slide-mounted safety-levers. Stainless steel only. Introduced 1991.
Price: KP90 with extra mag, loader, case and gunlock **$565.00**
Price: P90 (blue) **$525.00**

Ruger KP94 Autoloading Pistol
Sized midway between full-size P-Series and compact KP94. 4.25" barrel, 7.5" overall length, weighs about 34 oz. KP94 manual safety model. Slide gripping grooves roll over top of slide. KP94 has ambidextrous safety-levers; Matte finish stainless slide, barrel, alloy frame. Also blue. Includes hard case and lock. Introduced 1994. Made in U.S.A. by Sturm, Ruger & Co.
Price: P944, blue (manual safety) **$495.00**
Price: KP944 (40-caliber) (manual safety-stainless) **$575.00**
Price: KP944D **$575.00**

RUGER P95 AUTOLOADING PISTOL
Caliber: 9mm Para., 15-shot magazine. **Barrel:** 3.9". **Weight:** 27 oz. **Length:** 7.25" overall. **Grips:** Grooved; integral with frame. **Sights:** Blade front, rear drift adjustable for windage; 3-dot system. **Features:** Molded polymer grip frame, stainless steel or chrome-moly slide. Suitable for +P+ ammunition. Safety model, decocker. Introduced 1996. Made in U.S.A. by Sturm, Ruger & Co. Comes with lockable plastic case, spare magazine, loader and lock, Picatinny rails.
Price: P95DPR15 decocker only **$445.00**
Price: P95PR15 stainless steel decocker only **$480.00**
Price: KP95PR15 safety model, stainless steel **$480.00**
Price: P95PR15 safety model, blued finish **$445.00**

Ruger KP512 MKIII

Ruger Mark III Hunter

Ruger KP45HMKIII

Sabre Defence 45 ACP

Sabre Defence 9mm

Sigarms Revolution

RUGER MARK III STANDARD AUTOLOADING PISTOL

Caliber: 22 LR, 10-shot magazine. **Barrel:** 4-3/4", 5-1/2", 6", or 6-7/8". **Weight:** 35 oz. (4-3/4" bbl.). **Length:** 9" (4-3/4" bbl.). **Grips:** Checkered composition grip panels. **Sights:** Fixed, wide blade front, fixed rear. **Features:** Updated design of original Standard Auto and Mark II series. Standard models have lighter barrels. Target models have cocobolo grips; bull, target, competition, and hunter barrels; and adjustable sights. Introduced 2005.

Price: MKIII4, MKIII6 (blued)	$322.00
Price: MKIII512 (blued)	$382.00
Price: KMKIII512 (stainless)	$483.00
Price: MKIII678 (blued)	$382.00
Price: KMKIII678GC (stainless slabside barrel)	$555.00
Price: KMKIII678GH (stainless fluted barrel)	$567.00

Ruger 22/45 Mark III Pistol

Similar to other 22 Mark III autos except has Zytel grip frame that matches angle and magazine latch of Model 1911 45 ACP pistol. Available in 4" standard, 4-1/2" and 5-1/2" bull barrels. Comes with extra magazine, plastic case, lock. Introduced 1992. Hunter introduced 2006.

Price: P4MKIII, 4" bull barrel, adjustable sights	$307.00
Price: P45GCMKIII, 4.5" bull barrel, fixed sights	$305.00
Price: P512MKIII (5-1/2" bull blued barrel, adj. sights)	$307.00
Price: KP512MKIII (5-1/2" stainless bull barrel, adj. sights)	$398.00
Price: Hunter KP45HMKIII 4.5" barrel (2007), KP678HMKIII, 6-7/8" stainless fluted bull barrel, adj. sights	$487.00

SABRE DEFENCE SPHINX 3000 PISTOLS

Caliber: 9mm, 45 ACP., 10-shot magazine. **Barrel:** 4.43". **Weight:** 39.15 oz. **Length:** 8.27" overall. **Grips:** Textured polymer. **Sights:** Fixed Trijicon Night Sights. **Features:** CNC engineered from stainless steel billet; grip frame in stainless steel, titanium or high-strength aluminum. Integrated accessory rail, high-cut beavertail, decocking lever. Made in Switzerland. Imported by Sabre Defence Industries.

Price: 45 ACP (2007)	$2,990.00
Price: 9mm Standard, titanium w/decocker	$2,700.00
Price: 9mm Tactical, 3.74" barrel	$2,425.00

SEECAMP LWS 32 STAINLESS DA AUTO

Caliber: 32 ACP Win. Silvertip, 6-shot magazine. **Barrel:** 2", integral with frame. **Weight:** 10.5 oz. **Length:** 4-1/8" overall. **Grips:** Glass-filled nylon. **Sights:** Smooth, no-snag, contoured slide and barrel top. **Features:** Aircraft quality 17-4 PH stainless steel. Inertia-operated firing pin. Hammer fired double-action-only. Hammer automatically follows slide down to safety rest position after each shot, no manual safety needed. Magazine safety disconnector. Polished stainless. Introduced 1985. From L.W. Seecamp.

Price:	$425.00

SIGARMS REVOLUTION PISTOLS

Caliber: 45 ACP, 8-shot magazine. **Barrel:** 5". **Weight:** 40.3 oz. **Length:** 8.65" overall. **Grips:** Checkered wood grips. **Sights:** Novak night sights. Blade front, drift adjustable rear for windage. **Features:** Single-action 1911. Hand-fitted dehorned stainless-steel frame and slide; match-grade barrel, hammer/sear set and trigger; 25-lpi front strap checkering, 20-lpi mainspring housing checkering. Beavertail grip safety with speed bump, extended thumb safety, firing pin safety and hammer intercept notch. Introduced 2005. XO series has contrast sights, Ergo Grip XT textured polymer grips. Target line features adjustable target night sights, match barrel, custom wood grips, non-railed frame in stainless or Nitron finishes. TTT series is two-tone 1911 with Nitron slide and black controls on stainless frame. Includes burled maple grips, adjustable combat night sights. STX line available from SIGARMS Custom Shop; two-tone 1911, non-railed, Nitron slide, stainless frame, burled maple grips. Polished cocking serrations, flat-top slide, magwell. Carry line has Novak night sights, lanyard attachment point, gray diamondwood or rosewood grips, 8+1 capacity. Compact series has 6+1 capacity, 7.7" OAL, 4.25" barrel, slim-profile wood grips, weighs 30.3 oz. RCS line (Revolution Compact SAS) is Customs Shop version with anti-snag dehorning. Stainless or Nitron finish, Novak night sights, slim-profile gray diamondwood or rosewood grips. 6+1 capacity. Imported from Germany by SIGARMS, Inc.

Price: Revolution Nitron finish, w/ or w/o Picatinny rail	$1,069.00
Price: Revolution Stainless, w/ or w/o Picatinny rail	$1,050.00
Price: Revolution XO Black	$890.00
Price: Revolution XO Stainless, intr. 2006	$860.00
Price: Revolution Target Nitron, intr. 2006	$1,100.00
Price: Revolution TTT, intr. 2006	$1,070.00
Price: Revolution STX, intr. 2006	$1,300.00
Price: Revolution Carry Nitron, 4.25" barrel, intr. 2006	$1,070.00
Price: Revolution Compact, Nitron finish	$1,080.00
Price: Revolution RCS, Nitron finish	$1,150.00

SIGARMS P220

SIG-Sauer P245 Compact

SIG-Sauer Pro 2009

SIG-Sauer P232

SIG-Sauer P226 X-Five

SIG-Sauer Mosquito

SIGARMS P220 AUTO PISTOLS

Caliber: 45 ACP, (7- or 8-shot magazine). **Barrel:** 4.4". **Weight:** 27.8 oz. **Length:** 7.8" overall.
Grips: Checkered black plastic. **Sights:** Blade front, drift adjustable rear for windage. Optional Siglite night sights. **Features:** Double action. Stainless-steel slide, Nitron finish, alloy frame, M1913 Picatinny rail; safety system of decocking lever, automatic firing pin safety block, safety intercept notch, and trigger bar disconnector. Squared combat-type trigger guard. Slide stays open after last shot. Introduced 1976. P220 SAS Anti-Snag has dehorned stainless steel slide, front Siglite Night Sight, rounded trigger guard, dust cover, Custom Shop wood grips. Equinox line is Custom Shop product with Nitron stainless-steel slide with a black hard-anodized alloy frame, brush-polished flats and nickel accents. Truglo tritium fiber-optic front sight, rear Siglite night sight, gray laminated wood grips with checkering and stippling. Imported from Germany by SIGARMS, Inc.
Price: P220R **$840.00**
Price: P220R Two-Tone, matte-stainless slide, black alloy frame **$840.00**
Price: P220 Stainless **$935.00**
Price: P220 Crimson Trace, w/lasergrips **$1,150.00**
Price: P220 SAS Anti-Snag **$1,000.00**
Price: P220 Two-Tone SAO, single action, intr. 2006, from **$929.00**
Price: P220R DAK (intr. 2006) **$840.00**
Price: P220R Equinox (intr. 2006) **$1,070.00**

SIGARMS P220 CARRY AUTO PISTOLS

Caliber: 45 ACP, 8-shot magazine. **Barrel:** 3.9". **Weight:** NA. **Length:** 7.1" overall. **Grips:** Checkered black plastic. **Sights:** Blade front, drift adjustable rear for windage. Optional Siglite night sights. **Features:** Similar to full-size P220, except is "Commander" size. Single stack, DA/SA operation, Nitron finish, Picatinny rail, and either post and dot contrast or 3-dot Siglite night sights. Introduced 2005. Imported from Germany by SIGARMS, Inc.
Price: P220 Carry, from **$840.00**
Price: P220 Carry Two-Tone, from **$915.00**
Price: P220 Carry Equinox, wood grips, two tone, from **$1,070.00**

SIG-Sauer P229 DA Auto Pistol

Similar to the P228 except chambered for 9mm Para. (10- or 15-round magazines), 40 S&W, 357 SIG (10- or 12-round magazines). Has 3.86" barrel, 7.1" overall length and 3.35" height. Weight is 32.4 oz. Introduced 1991. Frame made in Germany, stainless steel slide assembly made in U.S.; pistol assembled in U.S. From SIGARMS, Inc.
Price: P229R, from **$840.00**
Price: P229R Crimson Trace, w/lasergrips, from **$1,150.00**

SIG-SAUER SP2022 PISTOLS

Caliber: 9mm Para., 357 SIG, 40 S&W, 10-, 12-, or 15-shot magazines. **Barrel:** 3.9". **Weight:** 30.2 oz. **Length:** 7.4" overall. **Grips:** Composite and rubberized one-piece. **Sights:** Blade front, rear adjustable for windage. Optional Siglite night sights. **Features:** Polymer frame, stainless steel slide; integral frame accessory rail; replaceable steel frame rails; left- or right-handed magazine release, two interchangeable grips. From SIGARMS, Inc.
Price: SP2009, Nitron finish, from **$640.00**

SIG-Sauer P226 Pistols

Similar to the P220 pistol except has 4.4" barrel, measures 7.7" overall, weighs 34 oz. Chambered in 9mm, 357 SIG, or 40 S&W. X-Five series has factory tuned single-action trigger, 5" slide and barrel, ergonomic wood Nill grips with beavertail, ambidextrous thumb safety and stainless slide and frame with magwell, low-profile adjustable target sights, front cocking serrations and a 25-meter factory test target. Imported from Germany by SIGARMS, Inc.
Price: P226R, Nitron finish, night sights **$915.00**
Price: P226R Two Tone, Nitron/stainless finish **$969.00**
Price: P226 Stainless, from **$935.00**
Price: P226 X-Five **$2,500.00**
Price: P226 X-Five Tactical, Ilaflon finish, high cap, from **$1,500.00**

SIG-SAUER P232 PERSONAL SIZE PISTOL

Caliber: 380 ACP, 7-shot. **Barrel:** 3.6". **Weight:** 17.6-22.4 oz. **Length:** 6.6" overall. **Grips:** Checkered black composite. **Sights:** Blade front, rear adjustable for windage. **Features:** Double action/single action or DAO. Blowback operation, stationary barrel. Introduced 1997. Imported from Germany by SIGARMS, Inc.
Price: P232, blued **$519.00**
Price: P232 Stainless **$709.00**
Price: P232 Two-Tone **$539.00**

SIG-SAUER P239 PISTOL

Caliber: 9mm Para., 8-shot, 357 SIG 40 S&W, 7-shot magazine. **Barrel:** 3.6". **Weight:** 25.2 oz. **Length:** 6.6" overall. **Grips:** Checkered black composite. **Sights:** Blade front, rear adjustable for windage. Optional Siglite night sights. **Features:** SA/DA or DAO; blackened stainless steel slide, aluminum alloy frame. Introduced 1996. Made in U.S.A. by SIGARMS, Inc.
Price: P239 . . . . **$739.00**
Price: P239 Two-Tone, w/night sights **$895.00**
Price: P239 DAK, double action **$739.00**

SIG-SAUER MOSQUITO PISTOL

Caliber: 22LR, 10-shot magazine. **Barrel:** 3.9". **Weight:** 24.6 oz. **Length:** 7.2" overall. **Grips:** Checkered black composite. **Sights:** Blade front, rear adjustable for windage. **Features:** Blowback operated, fixed barrel, polymer frame, slide-mounted ambidextrous safety. Introduced 2005. Made in U.S.A. by SIGARMS, Inc.
Price: Mosquito, blued **$390.00**
Price: Mosquito w/threaded barrel, intr. 2006 . . . . **$500.00**
Price: Mosquito Combat Green **$460.00**

Smith & Wesson M&P

Smith & Wesson
M&P Compact

Smith & Wesson
M&P 45 Bi-Tone

Smith & Wesson
457 TDA

Smith &
Wesson 908

Smith & Wesson
4013 TSW

Smith & Wesson
410 DA

Smith & Wesson
910 DA

SMITH & WESSON M&P AUTO PISTOLS

Caliber: 9mm, 40 S&W, 357 SIG. **Barrel:** 4.25". **Weight:** 24.25 oz. **Length:** 7.5" overall. **Grips:** One-piece Xenoy, wraparound with straight backstrap. **Sights:** Ramp dovetail mount front; tritium sights optional; Novak Lo-mount Carry rear. **Features:** Zytel polymer frame, embedded stainless steel chassis; stainless steel slide and barrel, stainless steel structural components, black Melonite finish, reversible magazine catch, 3 interchangeable palmswell grip sizes, universal rail, sear deactivation lever, internal lock system, magazine disconnect. Ships with 2 magazines. Internal lock models available. Overall height: 5.5"; width: 1.2"; sight radius: 6.4". Introduced November 2005. 45 ACP version introduced 2007, 10+1 or 14+1 capacity. **Barrel:** 4.5". **Length:** 8.05". **Weight:** 29.6 ounces. **Features:** Picatinny-style equipment rail; black or bi-tone, dark-earth-brown frame. Bi-tone M&P45 includes ambidextrous, frame-mounted thumb safety, take down tool with lanyard attachment. Compact 9mm/357 SIG/40 S&W versions introduced 2007. Compacts have 3.5" barrel, OAL 6.7". 10+1 or 12+1 capacity. **Weight:** 21.7 ounces. **Features:** Picatinny-style equipment rail. Made in U.S.A. by Smith & Wesson.
Price: **$624.00**
Price: M&P 45 Bi-tone (2007) **$678.00**
Price: M&P Compacts (2007) **$624.00**

SMITH & WESSON MODEL 457 TDA AUTO PISTOL

Caliber: 45 ACP, 7-shot magazine. **Barrel:** 3-3/4". **Weight:** 29 oz. **Length:** 7-1/4" overall. **Grips:** One-piece Xenoy, wraparound with straight backstrap. **Sights:** Post front, fixed rear, 3-dot system. **Features:** Aluminum alloy frame, matte blue carbon steel slide; bobbed hammer; smooth trigger. Introduced 1996. Made in U.S.A. by Smith & Wesson.
Price: Model 457, black matte finish **$711.00**
Price: Model 457S, matte finish stainless **$711.00**

SMITH & WESSON MODEL 908 AUTO PISTOL

Caliber: 9mm Para., 8-shot magazine. **Barrel:** 3-1/2". **Weight:** 24 oz. **Length:** 6-13/16". **Grips:** One-piece Xenoy, wraparound with straight backstrap. **Sights:** Post front, fixed rear, 3-dot system. **Features:** Aluminum alloy frame, matte blue carbon steel slide; bobbed hammer; smooth trigger. Introduced 1996. Made in U.S.A. by Smith & Wesson.

Price: Model 908, black matte finish **$648.00**
Price: Model 908S, stainless matte finish **$648.00**
Price: Model 908S Carry Combo, with holster **$672.00**

SMITH & WESSON MODEL 4013 TSW AUTO

Caliber: 40 S&W, 9-shot magazine. **Barrel:** 3-1/2". **Weight:** 26.8 oz. **Length:** 6 3/4" overall. **Grips:** Xenoy one-piece wraparound. **Sights:** Novak 3-dot system. **Features:** Traditional double-action system; stainless slide, alloy frame; fixed barrel bushing; ambidextrous decocker; reversible magazine catch, equipment rail. Introduced 1997. Made in U.S.A. by Smith & Wesson.
Price: Model 4013 TSW **$1,027.00**

SMITH & WESSON MODEL 410 DA AUTO PISTOL

Caliber: 40 S&W, 10-shot magazine. **Barrel:** 4". **Weight:** 28.5 oz. **Length:** 7.5". **Grips:** One-piece Xenoy, wraparound with straight backstrap. **Sights:** Post front, fixed rear; 3-dot system. **Features:** Aluminum alloy frame; blued carbon steel slide; traditional double action with left-side slide-mounted decocking lever. Introduced 1996. Made in U.S.A. by Smith & Wesson.
Price: From **$687.00**

SMITH & WESSON MODEL 910 DA AUTO PISTOL

Caliber: 9mm Para., 10-shot magazine. **Barrel:** 4". **Weight:** 28 oz. **Length:** 7-3/8" overall. **Grips:** One-piece Xenoy, wraparound with straight backstrap. **Sights:** Post front with white dot, fixed 2-dot rear. **Features:** Alloy frame, blue carbon steel slide. Slide-mounted decocking lever. Introduced 1995.
Price: From **$616.00**

Smith & Wesson
3913 LadySmith

Smith & Wesson SW1911

Springfield Armory
Service Bi-Tone

Springfield Armory
Service Bi-Tone

Springfield Armory
XD 45 ACP Extended

Springfield Armory
XD 45 ACP

SMITH & WESSON MODEL 3913 TRADITIONAL DOUBLE ACTIONS

Caliber: 9mm Para., 8-shot magazine. **Barrel:** 3-1/2". **Weight:** 24.8 oz. **Length:** 6-3/4" overall. **Grips:** One-piece Delrin wraparound, textured surface. **Sights:** Post front with white dot, Novak LoMount Carry with two dots. **Features:** TSW has aluminum alloy frame, stainless slide. Bobbed hammer with no half-cock notch; smooth .304" trigger with rounded edges. Straight backstrap. Equipment rail. Extra magazine included. Introduced 1989. The 3913-LS Ladysmith has frame that is upswept at the front, rounded trigger guard. Comes in frosted stainless steel with matching gray grips. Grips are ergonomically correct for a woman's hand. Novak LoMount Carry rear sight adjustable for windage. Extra magazine included. Introduced 1990.
Price: 3913TSW **$924.00**
Price: 3913-LS **$909.00**

SMITH & WESSON MODEL SW1911 PISTOLS

Caliber: 45 ACP, 8 rounds. **Barrel:** 5". **Weight:** 39 oz. **Length:** 8.7". **Grips:** Wood or rubber. **Sights:** Novak Lo-Mount Carry, white dot front. **Features:** Large stainless frame and slide with matte finish, single-side external safety. No. 108284 has adjustable target rear sight, ambidextrous safety levers, 20-lpi checkered front strap, comes with two 8-round magazines. DK model (Doug Koenig) also has oversized magazine well, Doug Koenig speed hammer, flat competition speed trigger with overtravel stop, rosewood grips with Smith & Wesson silver medallions, oversized magazine well, special serial number run. No. 108295 has olive drab Crimson Trace lasergrips. No. 108299 has carbon-steel frame and slide with polished flats on slide, standard GI recoil guide, laminated double-diamond walnut grips with silver Smith & Wesson medallions, adjustable target sights. Tactical Rail No. 108293 has a Picatinny rail, black Melonite finish, Novak Lo-Mount Carry Sights, scandium alloy frame. Tactical Rail Stainless introduced 2006. SW1911PD gun is Commander size, scandium-alloy frame, 4.25" barrel, 8" OAL, 28.0 oz., non-reflective black matte finish. Gunsite edition has scandium alloy frame, beveled edges, solid match aluminum trigger, Herrett's logoed tactical oval walnut stocks, special serial number run, brass bead Novak front sight. SC model has 4.25" barrel, scandium alloy frame, stainless-steel slide, non-reflective matte finish.
Price: From **$1,011.00**

SMITH & WESSON ENHANCED SIGMA SERIES DAO PISTOLS

Caliber: 9mm Para., 40 S&W; 10-, 16-shot magazine. **Barrel:** 4". **Weight:** 24.7 oz. **Length:** 7-1/4" overall. **Grips:** Integral. **Sights:** White dot front, fixed rear; 3-dot system. Tritium night sights available. **Features:** Ergonomic polymer frame; low barrel centerline; internal striker firing system; corrosion-resistant slide; Teflon-filled, electroless-nickel coated magazine, equipment rail. Introduced 1994. Made in U.S.A. by Smith & Wesson.
Price: From **$419.00**

SMITH & WESSON MODEL CS9 CHIEF'S SPECIAL AUTO

Caliber: 9mm Para., 7-shot magazine. **Barrel:** 3". **Weight:** 20.8 oz. **Length:** 6-1/4" overall. **Grips:** Hogue wraparound rubber. **Sights:** White dot front, fixed 2-dot rear. **Features:** Traditional double-action trigger mechanism. Alloy frame, stainless slide. Ambidextrous safety. Introduced 1999. Made in U.S.A. by Smith & Wesson.
Price: Stainless **$782.00**

SMITH & WESSON MODEL CS45 CHIEF'S SPECIAL AUTO

Caliber: 45 ACP, 6-shot magazine. **Weight:** 23.9 oz. **Features:** Introduced 1999. Made in U.S.A. by Smith & Wesson.
Price: Stainless **$830.00**

SPRINGFIELD ARMORY XD POLYMER AUTO PISTOLS

Caliber: 9mm Para., 357 SIG, 40 S&W, 45 ACP, 45 GAP. **Barrel:** 3", 4", 5". **Weight:** 20.5-31 oz. **Length:** 6.26-8" overall. **Grips:** Textured polymer. **Sights:** Varies by model; Fixed sights are dovetail front and rear steel 3-dot units. **Features:** Three sizes in X-Treme Duty (XD) line: Sub-Compact (3" barrel), Service (4" barrel), Tactical (5" barrel). Three ported models available. Ergonomic polymer frame, hammer-forged barrel, no-tool disassembly, ambidextrous magazine release, visual/tactile loaded chamber indicator, visual/tactile striker status indicator, grip safety, XD gear system included. Introduced 2004. XD 45 introduced 2006. Compact line introduced 2007. Compacts ship with one extended magazine (13) and one compact magazine (10). From Springfield Armory.
Price: Sub-Compact Black 9mm, fixed sights **$536.00**
Price: Sub-Compact Black 9mm/40 S&W, Heinie night sights . . . **$633.00**
Price: Sub-Compact Bi-Tone 9mm/40 S&W, fixed sights **$566.00**
Price: Sub-Compact OD Green 9mm/40 S&W, fixed sights **$536.00**
Price: Service Black 9mm/40 S&W/357 SIG, fixed sights **$536.00**
Price: Service Black 45 ACP, fixed sights **$559.00**
Price: Service Black 45 GAP, fixed sights **$536.00**
Price: Service Black 9mm/40 S&W, Heinie night sights **$626.00**
Price: Service Bi-Tone 9mm/40 S&W/357 SIG/45 GAP,
    fixed sights **$566.00**
Price: Service Bi-Tone 45 ACP, fixed sights **$595.00**
Price: Service OD Green 9mm/40 S&W/357 SIG/45 GAP,
    fixed sights **$536.00**
Price: V-10 Ported Black 9mm/40 S&W/357 SIG **$566.00**
Price: Tactical Black 45 ACP, fixed sights **$595.00**
Price: Tactical Black 9mm/40 S&W/357 SIG, fixed sights **$566.00**
Price: Tactical Bi-Tone 45 ACP/45 GAP, fixed sights . . . **$626.00/$595.00**
Price: Tactical OD Green 9mm/40 S&W/357 SIG/45 GAP,
    fixed sights **$566.00**
Price: Tactical OD Green 45 ACP, fixed sights **$595.00**
Price: Compact, 4" barrel (2007) **$589.00**
Price: Compact, 5" barrel (2007) **$619.00**
Price: Compact, 5" barrel, Trijicon night sights (2007) **$709.00**

Springfield Armory
1911A1 Standard

Springfield Armory
Full-Size 1911A1

Springfield Armory
Micro-Compact

Springfield Armory EMP

Springfield Armory TRP

SPRINGFIELD ARMORY CUSTOM LOADED FULL-SIZE 1911A1 AUTO PISTOL

Caliber: 9mm Para., 9-shot; 45 ACP, 7-shot. **Barrel:** 5". **Weight:** 30-42 oz. **Length:** 8.5" overall. **Grips:** Cocobolo, polymer. **Sights:** Fixed 3-dot system or adjustable. **Features:** Beveled magazine well; lowered and flared ejection port. All forged parts, including frame, barrel, slide. All new production. Introduced 1990. From Springfield Armory.

Price: Tactical Combat Black Stainless Steel, fixed sights **$904.00**
Price: Stainless Steel, fixed sights **$902.00**
Price: Service Model 5" Lightweight, bi-tone finish **$934.00**
Price: Stainless Steel, adjustable target sights **$966.00**
Price: Black Stainless, adjustable Bo-Mar rear, 3-dot tritium . . **$1,124.00**
Price: Stainless Steel 9mm, fixed combat sights **$976.00**

SPRINGFIELD ARMORY GI 45 1911A1 AUTO PISTOLS

Caliber: 45 ACP; 6-, 7-, 13-shot magazines. **Barrel:** 3", 4", 5". **Weight:** 28-36 oz. **Length:** 5.5-8.5" overall. **Grips:** Checkered double-diamond walnut, "U.S" logo. **Sights:** Fixed GI style. **Features:** Similar to WWII GI-issue 45s at hammer, beavertail, mainspring housing. From Springfield Armory. Enhanced Micro Pistol (EMP) introduced 2007.

Price: GI .45 4" Lightweight Champion, 7+1, 28 oz. **$564.00**
Price: GI .45 5" High Capacity, 13+1, 36 oz. **$617.00**
Price: GI .45 5" OD Green, 7+1, 36 oz. **$564.00**
Price: GI .45 3" Micro Compact, 6+1, 32 oz. **$608.00**
Price: EMP 9mm 3", (2007) **$940.00**

SPRINGFIELD ARMORY MIL-SPEC 1911A1 AUTO PISTOLS

Caliber: 38 Super, 9-shot magazines; 45 ACP, 7-shot magazines. **Barrel:** 5". **Weight:** 35.6-39 oz. **Length:** 8.5-8.625" overall. **Features:** Similar to GI 45s. From Springfield Armory.

Price: Mil-Spec Parkerized, 7+1, 35.6 oz. **$660.00**
Price: Mil-Spec Stainless Steel, 7+1, 36 oz. **$724.00**
Price: Mil-Spec 38 Super, Nickel finish, 9+1, 39 oz. **$1,254.00**

Springfield Armory Custom Loaded Champion 1911A1 Pistol

Similar to standard 1911A1, slide and barrel are 4". 7.5" OAL. Available in 45 ACP only. Novak Night Sights. Delta hammer and cocobolo grips. Parkerized or stainless. Introduced 1989.

Price: Stainless, 34 oz. **$952.00**
Price: Lightweight, 28 oz. **$913.00**

Springfield Armory Custom Loaded Ultra Compact Pistol

Similar to 1911A1 Compact, shorter slide, 3.5" barrel, 6+1, 7" OAL. Beavertail grip safety, beveled magazine well, fixed sights. Videki speed trigger, flared ejection port, stainless steel frame, blued slide, match grade barrel, rubber grips. Introduced 1996. From Springfield Armory.

Price: Stainless Steel **$952.00**

SPRINGFIELD ARMORY CUSTOM LOADED MICRO-COMPACT 1911A1 PISTOL

Caliber: 45 ACP, 6+1 capacity. **Barrel:** 3" 1:16 LH. **Weight:** 24-32 oz. **Length:** 4.7". **Grips:** Slimline cocobolo. **Sights:** Novak LoMount tritium. Dovetail front. **Features:** Aluminum hard-coat anodized alloy frame, forged steel slide, forged barrel, ambi-thumb safety, Extreme Carry Bevel dehorning. Lockable plastic case, 2 magazines.

Price: Bi-Tone Operator w/light rail **$1,284.00**
Price: Lightweight Bi-Tone **$1,220.00**

SPRINGFIELD ARMORY CUSTOM LOADED LONG SLIDE 1911A1 PISTOL

Caliber: 45 ACP, 7+1 capacity. **Barrel:** 6" 1:16 LH. **Weight:** 41 oz. **Length:** 9.5". **Grips:** Slimline cocobolo. **Sights:** Dovetail front; fully adjustable target rear. **Features:** Longer sight radius, 7.9".

Price: Bi-Tone Operator w/light rail **$1,097.00**

Springfield Armory TRP Pistols

Similar to 1911A1 except 45 ACP only, checkered front strap and main-spring housing, Novak Night Sight combat rear sight and matching dove-tailed front sight, tuned, polished extractor, oversize barrel link; lightweight speed trigger and combat action job, match barrel and bushing, extended ambidextrous thumb safety and fitted beavertail grip safety. Checkered cocobolo wood grips, comes with two Wilson 7-shot magazines. Frame is engraved "Tactical," both sides of frame with "TRP." Introduced 1998. TRP-Pro Model meets FBI specifications for SWAT Hostage Rescue Team. From Springfield Armory.

Price: Standard with Armory Kote finish **$1,606.00**
Price: Standard, stainless steel **$1,606.00**
Price: Standard with Operator Light Rail Armory Kote **$1,689.00**
Price: TRP-Pro, Armory Kote finish **$2,395.00**

Springfield Armory Loaded Operator 1911A1 Pistol

Similar to Full-Size 1911A1, except light-mounting rail is forged into frame. From Springfield Armory.

Price: Loaded Full-Size MC Operator, 42 oz., 8.5" OAL **$1,254.00**
Price: TRP Light Rail Armory Kote, 42 oz. **$1,689.00**
Price: Micro Compact LW, w/XML Mini Light, 32 oz., 6.7 OAL . **$1,284.00**

Springfield Armory Trophy Match 1911A1 Pistol

Similar to Full Size model, 5" match barrel and slide, fully adjustable sights. From Springfield Armory.

Price: Trophy Match 45 ACP, stainless **$1,452.00**

Taurus 22

Taurus 1911B-1

Stoeger Cougar 8000

Taurus 92

Taurus 24-7 OSS

Taurus 24

Taurus 99SS

STOEGER COUGAR
Caliber: 9mm, 40 S&W. **Capacity:** 15 (9mm); 11 (40 S&W). **Barrel:** 3.6".
Length: 7.0". **Weight:** 32.5 oz. **Grips:** Black checkered w/3 interchangeable backstraps. **Sights:** 3-dot . **Features:** Aluminum frame, DA/SA, ambisafety. Comes with two magazines. Same design as Beretta-made version. Rotating barrel, hard-chromed bores, removable front sight, combat trigger, Made in Turkey, imported by Benelli USA. Introduced 2007.
Price: $370.00

TAURUS MODEL 800 Series
Caliber: 9mm, 40 S&W, 45 ACP. **Barrel:** 4". **Weight:** 32 oz. **Length:** 8.25".
Grips: Checkered. **Sights:** Novak. **Features:** DA/SA. Blue and Stainless Steel finish. Introduced in 2007. Imported from Brazil by Taurus International.
Price: 809B, 9mm, Blue, 17+1 .... NA
Price: 809SS, 9mm, Stainless Steel, 17+1 .... NA
Price: 840B, .40 cal., Blue, 15+1 .... NA
Price: 840SS, .40 cal., Stainless Steel, 15+1 .... NA
Price: 845B, .45 ACP, Blue, 12+1 .... NA
Price: 845SS, .45ACP, Stainless Steel, 12+1 .... NA

TAURUS MODEL 1911
Caliber: 45 ACP, 8+1 capacity. **Barrel:** 5". **Weight:** 33 oz. **Length:** 8.5".
Grips: Checkered Black. **Sights:** Heinie Straight 8. **Features:** SA. Blue, Stainless Steel, Duotone Blue, and Blue/Gray finish. Standard/Picatinny Rail, Standard Frame, Alloy Frame, and Alloy/Picatinny Rail. Introduced in 2007. Imported from Brazil by Taurus International.
Price: 1911B-1, Blue .... NA
Price: 1911SS, Stainless Steel .... NA
Price: 1911SS-1, Stainless Steel .... NA
Price: 1911 DT, Duotone Blue .... NA
Price: 1911 AL, Blue/Gray .... NA
Price: 1911 ALR, Blue/Gray .... NA

TAURUS MODEL 917
Caliber: 9mm, 19+1 capacity. **Barrel:** 4.3". **Weight:** 32.2 oz. **Length:** 8.5".
Grips: Checkered Rubber. **Sights:** Fixed. **Features:** SA/DA. Blue and Stainless Steel finish. Medium Frame. Introduced in 2007. Imported from Brazil by Taurus International.
Price: 917B-20, Blue .... NA
Price: 917SS-20, Stainless Steel .... NA

TAURUS MODEL 22/25 AUTO PISTOLS
Caliber: 22 LR, 8-shot (PT 22); 25 ACP, 9-shot (PT 25). **Barrel:** 2.75".
Weight: 12.3 oz. **Length:** 5.25" overall. **Grips:** Smooth rosewood or mother-of-pearl. **Sights:** Fixed. **Features:** Double action. Tip-up barrel for loading, cleaning. Blue, nickel, duo-tone or blue with gold accents.

Introduced 1992. Made in U.S.A. by Taurus International.
Price: 22B or 25B, checkered wood grips,
  blued finish $236.00
Price: 22BR or 25BR, rosewood grips,
  blued finish $236.00
Price: 22N or 25N, nickel finish, checkered
  wood grips $236.00
Price: 22NBR or 25NBR, two-tone,
  rosewood grips $236.00

TAURUS MODEL 24/7
Caliber: 9mm, 40 S&W, 45 ACP. **Barrel:** 4". **Weight:** 27.2 oz. **Length:** 7-1/8". **Grips:** "Ribber" rubber-finned overlay on polymer. **Sights:** Adjustable. **Features:** SA/DA; accessory rail, four safeties, blue or stainless finish. One-piece guide rod, flush-fit magazine, flared bushingless barrel, Picatinny accessory rail, manual safety, user changeable sights, loaded chamber indicator, tuned ejector and lowered port, one piece guide rod and flat wound captive spring. Introduced 2003. Long Slide models have 5" barrels, measure 8-1/8" overall, weigh 27.2 oz. Imported from Brazil by Taurus International.
Price: 40BP, 40 S&W, blued, 10+1 or 15+1 .... $503.00
Price: 40SSP, 40 S&W, stainless slide, 10+1 or 15+1 .... $520.00
Price: 45BP, 45 ACP, blued, 10+1 or 12+1 .... $503.00
Price: Long Slide OSS-D45, 45 ACP, blued, 10+1 or 12+1, intr. 2007 . NA

TAURUS MODEL 92 AUTO PISTOL
Caliber: 9mm Para., 10- or 17-shot mags. **Barrel:** 5". **Weight:** 34 oz. **Length:** 8.5" overall. **Grips:** Checkered rubber, rosewood, mother-of-pearl. **Sights:** Fixed notch rear. 3-dot sight system. Also offered with micrometer-click adjustable night sights. **Features:** Double action, ambidextrous 3-way hammer drop safety, allows cocked & locked carry. Blue, stainless steel, blue with gold highlights, stainless steel with gold highlights, forged aluminum frame, integral key-lock. .22 LR conversion kit available. Imported from Brazil by Taurus International.
Price: Blued or Stainless .... $602.00 to $664.00

Taurus Model 99 Auto Pistol
Similar to 92, fully adjustable rear sight.
Price: Blue .... $617.00 to $633.00
Price: 22 Conversion kit for PT 92 and PT99
  (includes barrel and slide) $266.00

Taurus 100

**Taurus 132
Millennium Pro**

**Taurus 138
Millennium Pro**

**Taurus 140
Millennium Pro**

**Taurus 745
Millennium Pro**

Taurus 940

Taurus 38SS

TAURUS MODEL 100/101 AUTO PISTOL
Caliber: 40 S&W, 10- or 11-shot mags. **Barrel:** 5".
Weight: 34 oz. **Length:** 8-1/2". **Grips:** Checkered
rubber, rosewood, mother-of-pearl. **Sights:** 3-dot fixed or adjustable;
night sights available. **Features:** Single/double action with three-position
safety/decocker. Reintroduced in 2001. Imported by Taurus International.
Price: PT100 . . . . **$602.00 to $664.00**
Price: PT101, adjustable rear sight . . . . **$617.00 to $633.00**

TAURUS MODEL 111 MILLENNIUM PRO AUTO PISTOL
Caliber: 9mm Para., 10- or 12-shot mags. **Barrel:** 3.25". **Weight:** 18.7 oz.
Length: 6-1/8" overall. **Grips:** Checkered polymer. **Sights:** 3-dot fixed;
night sights available. Low profile, 3-dot combat. **Features:** Double action
only, polymer frame, matte stainless or blue steel slide, manual safety,
integral key-lock. Deluxe models with wood grip inserts.
Price: . . . . **$406.00 to $422.00**
Price: Titanium Slide **$520.00**

TAURUS 132 MILLENNIUM PRO AUTO PISTOL
Caliber: 32 ACP, 10-shot mag. **Barrel:** 3.25". **Weight:** 18.7 oz. **Grips:**
Polymer. **Sights:** 3-dot fixed; night sights available. **Features:** Double-
action-only, polymer frame, matte stainless or blue steel slide, manual
safety, integral key-lock action. Introduced 2001.
Price: . . . . **$406.00 to $422.00**

TAURUS 138 MILLENNIUM PRO SERIES
Caliber: 380 ACP, 10- or 12-shot mags. **Barrel:** 3.25". **Weight:** 18.7 oz.
Grips: Polymer. **Sights:** Fixed 3-dot fixed. **Features:** Double-action-only,
polymer frame, matte stainless or blue steel slide, manual safety, integral
key-lock.
Price: . . . . **$406.00 to $422.00**

TAURUS 140 MILLENNIUM PRO AUTO PISTOL
Caliber: 40 S&W, 10-shot mag. **Barrel:** 3.25". **Weight:** 18.7 oz. **Grips:**
Checkered polymer. **Sights:** 3-dot fixed; night sights available. **Features:**
Double action only; matte stainless or blue steel slide, black polymer
frame, manual safety, integral key-lock action. From Taurus International.
Price: . . . . **$422.00 to $439.00**

TAURUS 145 MILLENNIUM AUTO PISTOL
Caliber: 45 ACP, 10-shot mag. **Barrel:** 3.27". **Weight:** 23 oz. Stock:
Checkered polymer. **Sights:** 3-dot fixed; night sights available. **Features:**
Double-action only, matte stainless or blue steel slide, black polymer
frame, manual safety, integral key-lock. Compact model is 6+1 with a
3.25" barrel, weighs 20.8 oz. From Taurus International.
Price: 145, blued or stainless . . . . **$422.00 to $439.00**
Price: 745 Compact, blued or stainless, intr. 2005 . . **$410.00 to $425.00**

TAURUS MODEL 911 AUTO PISTOL
Caliber: 9mm Para., 10-shot mag. **Barrel:** 4". **Weight:** 28.2 oz. **Length:** 7"
overall. **Grips:** Checkered rubber, rosewood, mother-of-pearl. **Sights:**

Fixed, 3-dot blue or stainless; night sights optional. **Features:** Double
action, semi-auto ambidextrous 3-way hammer drop safety, allows cocked
& locked carry. Blue, stainless steel, blue with gold highlights, or stainless
steel with gold highlights, forged aluminum frame, integral key-lock.
Price: **$569.00**

TAURUS MODEL 940 AUTO PISTOL
Caliber: 40 S&W, 10-shot mag. **Barrel:** 3-5/8". **Weight:** 28.2 oz. **Length:**
7" overall. **Grips:** Checkered rubber, rosewood or mother-of-pearl.
Sights: Fixed, 3-dot blue or stainless; night sights optional. **Features:**
Double action, semi-auto ambidextrous 3-way hammer drop safety,
allows cocked & locked carry. Blue, stainless steel, blue with gold
highlights, or stainless steel with gold hightlights, forged aluminum frame,
integral key-lock.
Price: From **$569.00**

TAURUS MODEL 945/38S SERIES
Caliber: 45 ACP, 8-shot mag. **Barrel:** 4.25". **Weight:** 28.2/29.5 oz. **Length:**
7.48" overall. **Grips:** Checkered rubber, rosewood or mother-of-pearl.
Sights: Fixed, 3-dot; night sights optional. **Features:** Double-action with
ambidextrous 3-way hammer drop safety allows cocked & locked carry.
Forged aluminum frame, 945C has ported barrel/slide. Blue, stainless,
blue with gold highlights, stainless with gold highlights, integral key-lock.
Introduced 1995. 38 Super line based on 945 frame introduced 2005. 38S
series is 10+1, 30 oz., 7.5" overall. Imported by Taurus International.
Price: From **$609.00**

THOMPSON CUSTOM 1911A1 AUTOMATIC PISTOL
Caliber: 45 ACP, 7-shot magazine. **Barrel:** 4.3". **Weight:** 34 oz. **Length:** 8"
overall. **Grips:** Checkered laminate grips with a Thompson bullet logo inlay.
Sights: Front and rear sights are black with serrations and are dovetailed
into the slide. **Features:** Machined from 420 stainless steel, matte finish.
Thompson bullet logo on slide. Flared ejection port, angled front and rear
serrations on slide, 20-lpi checkered mainspring housing and frontstrap.
Adjustable trigger, combat hammer, stainless steel full-length recoil guide
rod, extended beavertail grip safety; extended magazine release;
checkered slide-stop lever.Made in U.S.A. by Kahr Arms.
Price: 1911CC (2006), stainless frame **$775.00**
Price: 1911TC, 5", 39 oz., 8.5" overall, stainless frame **$775.00**
Price: 1911CCF (2006), 27 oz., aluminum frame **$775.00**
Price: 1911CAF, 5", 31.5 oz., 8.5" overall, aluminum frame **$775.00**

Thompson
1911A1 CAF

U.S. Fire Arms 1911 Military

Walther PPK/S

U.S. Fire Arms Super 38

Walther PPK

Walther P99

Walther P22

U.S. FIRE ARMS 1910 COMMERCIAL MODEL AUTOMATIC PISTOL
Caliber: 45 ACP, 7-shot magazine. **Barrel:** 5". **Weight:** NA. **Length:** NA. **Grips:** Browning original wide design, full checkered diamond walnut grips. **Sights:** Fixed. **Features:** High polish Armory Blue, fire blue appointments, 1905 patent dates, grip safety, small contoured checkered thumb safety and round 1905 fire blue hammer with hand cut checkering. Introduced 2006. Made in U.S.A. by United States Fire Arms Mfg. Co.
Price: **$1,895.00**

U.S. FIRE ARMS 1911 MILITARY MODEL AUTOMATIC PISTOL
Caliber: 45 ACP, 7-shot magazine. **Barrel:** 5". **Weight:** NA. **Length:** NA. **Grips:** Browning original wide design, full checkered diamond walnut grips. **Sights:** Fixed. **Features:** Military polish Armory Blue, fire blue appointments, 1905 patent dates, grip safety, small contoured checkered thumb safety and round 1905 fire blue hammer with hand cut checkering. Introduced 2006. Made in U.S.A. by United States Fire Arms Mfg. Co.
Price: **$1,895.00**

U.S. FIRE ARMS SUPER 38 AUTOMATIC PISTOL
Caliber: 38 Auto, 9-shot magazine. **Barrel:** 5". **Weight:** NA. **Length:** NA. **Grips:** Browning original wide design, full checkered diamond walnut grips. **Sights:** Fixed. **Features:** Armory blue, fire blue appointments, 1913 patent date, grip safety, small contoured checkered thumb safety and spur 1911 hammer with hand cut checkering. Supplied with two Super 38 Auto. mags. Super .38 roll mark on base. Introduced 2006. Made in U.S.A. by United States Fire Arms Mfg. Co.
Price: **$1,995.00**

U.S. FIRE ARMS ACE .22 LONG RIFLE AUTOMATIC PISTOL
Caliber: 22 LR, 10-shot magazine. **Barrel:** 5". **Weight:** NA. **Length:** NA. **Grips:** Browning original wide design, full checkered diamond walnut grips. **Sights:** Fixed. **Features:** Armory blue commercial finish, fire blue appointments, 1913 patent date, grip safety, small contoured checkered thumb safety and spur 1911 hammer with hand cut checkering. Supplied with two magazines. Ace roll mark on base. Introduced 2006. Made in U.S.A. by United States Fire Arms Mfg. Co.
Price: **$1,995.00**

WALTHER PPK/S AMERICAN AUTO PISTOL
Caliber: 380 ACP, 7-shot magazine. **Barrel:** 3.27". **Weight:** 23-1/2 oz. **Length:** 6.1" overall. **Stocks:** Checkered plastic. **Sights:** Fixed, white markings. **Features:** Double action; manual safety blocks firing pin and drops hammer; chamber loaded indicator on 32 and 380; extra finger rest magazine provided. Made in the United States. Introduced 1980.
Price: 380 ACP only, blue **$563.00**
Price: As above, 32 ACP or 380 ACP, stainless **$543.00**

Walther PPK American Auto Pistol
Similar to Walther PPK/S except weighs 21 oz., has 6-shot capacity. Made in the U.S. Introduced 1986.
Price: Stainless, 32 ACP or 380 ACP **$543.00**
Price: Blue, 380 ACP only **$543.00**

WALTHER P99 AUTO PISTOL
Caliber: 9mm Para., 9x21, 40 S&W,10-shot magazine. **Barrel:** 4". **Weight:** 25 oz. **Length:** 7" overall. **Grips:** Textured polymer. **Sights:** Blade front (comes with three interchangeable blades for elevation adjustment), micrometer rear adjustable for windage. **Features:** Double-action mechanism with trigger safety, decock safety, internal striker safety; chamber loaded indicator; ambidextrous magazine release levers; polymer frame with interchangeable backstrap inserts. Comes with two magazines. Introduced 1997. Imported from Germany by Smith & Wesson U.S.A.
Price: **$665.00**

WALTHER P22 PISTOL
Caliber: 22 LR. **Barrel:** 3.4", 5". **Weight:** 19.6 oz. (3.4"), 20.3 oz. (5"). **Length:** 6.26", 7.83". **Grips:** NA. **Sights:** Interchangeable white dot, front, 2-dot adjustable, rear. **Features:** A rimfire version of the Walther P99 pistol, available in nickel slide with black frame, or green frame with black slide versions. Made in Germany and distributed in the U.S. by Smith & Wesson.
Price: From **$295.00**

Includes models suitable for several forms of competition and other sporting purposes.

Baer 1911 Ultimate Master

Colt Gold Cup Model O

Baer 1911 Ultimate Master 5"

Baer 1911 Bullseye Wadcutter

Colt Special Combat Government

BAER 1911 ULTIMATE MASTER COMBAT PISTOL
Caliber: 38 Super, 400 Cor-Bon 45 ACP (others available), 10-shot magazine. **Barrel:** 5", 6"; Baer NM. **Weight:** 37 oz. **Length:** 8.5" overall. **Grips:** Checkered cocobolo. **Sights:** Baer dovetail front, low-mount Bo-Mar rear with hidden leaf. **Features:** Full-house competition gun. Baer forged NM blued steel frame and double serrated slide; Baer triple port, tapered cone compensator; fitted slide to frame; lowered, flared ejection port; Baer reverse recoil plug; full-length guide rod; recoil buff; beveled magazine well; Baer Commander hammer, sear; Baer extended ambidextrous safety, extended ejector, checkered slide stop, beavertail grip safety with pad, extended magazine release button; Baer speed trigger. Made in U.S.A. by Les Baer Custom, Inc.
Price: 45 ACP Compensated $2,599.00
Price: 38 Super Compensated $2,789.00
Price: 6" 45 ACP $2,586.00
Price: 6" 38 Super $2,780.00
Price: 6" 400 Cor-Bon $2,668.00
Price: 5" 45 ACP $2,540.00
Price: 5" 38 Super $2,699.00
Price: 5" 400 Cor-Bon $2,589.00

BAER 1911 NATIONAL MATCH HARDBALL PISTOL
Caliber: 45 ACP, 7-shot magazine. **Barrel:** 5". **Weight:** 37 oz. **Length:** 8.5" overall. **Grips:** Checkered walnut. **Sights:** Baer dovetail front with undercut post, low-mount Bo-Mar rear with hidden leaf. **Features:** Baer NM forged steel frame, double serrated slide and barrel with stainless bushing; slide fitted to frame; Baer match trigger with 4-lb. pull; polished feed ramp, throated barrel; checkered front strap, arched mainspring housing; Baer beveled magazine well; lowered, flared ejection port; tuned extractor; Baer extended ejector, checkered slide stop; recoil buff. Made in U.S.A. by Les Baer Custom, Inc.
Price: $1,689.00

Baer 1911 Bullseye Wadcutter Pistol
Similar to National Match Hardball except designed for wadcutter loads only. Polished feed ramp and barrel throat; Bo-Mar rib on slide; full length recoil rod; Baer speed trigger with 3-1/2-lb. pull; Baer deluxe hammer and sear; Baer beavertail grip safety with pad; flat mainspring housing checkered 20 lpi. Blue finish; checkered walnut grips. Made in U.S.A. by Les Baer Custom, Inc.
Price: From $1,710.00
Price: With 6" barrel, from $1,865.00

BF CLASSIC PISTOL
Caliber: Customer orders chamberings. **Barrel:** 8-15" Heavy Match Grade with 11-degree target crown. **Weight:** Approx 3.9 lbs. **Length:** From 16" overall. **Grips:** Thumbrest target style. **Sights:** Bo-Mar/Bond ScopeRib I Combo with hooded post front adjustable for height and width, rear notch available in .032", .062", .080" and .100" widths; 1/2-MOA clicks. **Features:** Hand fitted and headspaced, drilled and tapped for scope mount. Etched receiver; gold-colored trigger. Introduced 1988. Made in U.S.A. by E. Arthur Brown Co. Inc.
Price: $789.00

COLT GOLD CUP MODEL O PISTOL
Caliber: 45 ACP, 8-shot magazine. **Barrel:** 5", with new design bushing. **Weight:** 39 oz. **Length:** 8-1/2". **Grips:** Checkered rubber composite with silver-plated medallion. **Sights:** Patridge-style front, Bo-Mar-style rear adjustable for windage and elevation, sight radius 6-3/4". **Features:** Arched or flat housing; wide, grooved trigger with adjustable stop; ribbed-top slide, hand fitted, with improved ejection port.
Price: Blue $1,022.00
Price: Stainless $1,077.00

COLT SPECIAL COMBAT GOVERNMENT
Caliber: 45 ACP, 38 Super. **Barrel:** 5". **Weight:** 39 oz. **Length:** 8-1/2". **Grips:** Rosewood w/double diamond checkering pattern. **Sights:** Clark dovetail, front; Bo-Mar adjustable, rear. **Features:** A competition-ready pistol with enhancements such as skeletonized trigger, upswept grip safety, custom tuned action, polished feed ramp. Blue or satin nickel finish. Introduced 2003. Made in U.S.A. by Colt's Mfg. Co.
Price: $1,543.00

Competitor Single Shot

CZ 75 Champion

EAA Witness Gold Team

Freedom Arms 83 22 Silhouette Class

Hammerli SP 20

COMPETITOR SINGLE-SHOT PISTOL
Caliber: 22 LR through 50 Action Express, including belted magnums. **Barrel:** 14" standard; 10.5" silhouette; 16" optional. **Weight:** About 59 oz. (14" bbl.). **Length:** 15.12" overall. **Grips:** Ambidextrous; synthetic (standard) or laminated or natural wood. **Sights:** Ramp front, adjustable rear. **Features:** Rotary cannon-type action cocks on opening; cammed ejector; interchangeable barrels, ejectors. Adjustable single stage trigger, sliding thumb safety and trigger safety. Matte blue finish. Introduced 1988. From Competitor Corp., Inc.
Price: 14", standard calibers, synthetic grip **$480.00**

CZ 75 CHAMPION COMPETITION PISTOL
Caliber: 9mm Para., 40 S&W, 16-shot mag. **Barrel:** 4.4". **Weight:** 2.5 lbs. **Length:** 9.4" overall. **Grips:** Black rubber. **Sights:** Blade front, fully adjustable rear. **Features:** Single-action trigger mechanism; three-port compensator (40 S&W, 9mm have two port) full-length guide rod; extended magazine release; ambidextrous safety; flared magazine well; fully adjustable match trigger. Introduced 1999. Imported from the Czech Republic by CZ-USA.
Price: Dual-tone finish **$1,646.00**

EAA WITNESS GOLD TEAM AUTO
Caliber: 9mm Para., 9x21, 38 Super, 40 S&W, 45 ACP. **Barrel:** 5.1". **Weight:** 44 oz. **Length:** 10.5" overall. **Grips:** Checkered walnut, competition-style. **Sights:** Square post front, fully adjustable rear. **Features:** Triple-chamber cone compensator; competition SA trigger; extended safety and magazine release; competition hammer; beveled magazine well; beavertail grip. Hand-fitted major components. Hard chrome finish. Match-grade barrel. From E.A.A. Custom Shop. Introduced 1992. From European American Armory.
Price: **$1,699.00**

FREEDOM ARMS MODEL 83 22 FIELD GRADE SILHOUETTE CLASS
Caliber: 22 LR, 5-shot cylinder. **Barrel:** 10". **Weight:** 63 oz. **Length:** 15.5" overall. **Grips:** Black Micarta. **Sights:** Removable Patridge front blade; Iron Sight Gun Works silhouette rear, click adjustable for windage and elevation (optional adj. front sight and hood). **Features:** Stainless steel, matte finish, manual sliding-bar safety system; dual firing pins, lightened

hammer for fast lock time, pre-set trigger stop. Introduced 1991. Made in U.S.A. by Freedom Arms.
Price: Silhouette Class **$1,913.95**

FREEDOM ARMS MODEL 83 CENTERFIRE SILHOUETTE MODELS
Caliber: 357 Mag., 41 Mag., 44 Mag.; 5-shot cylinder. **Barrel:** 10", 9" (357 Mag. only). **Weight:** 63 oz. (41 Mag.). **Length:** 15.5", 14-1/2" (357 only). **Grips:** Pachmayr Presentation. **Sights:** Iron Sight Gun Works silhouette rear sight, replaceable adjustable front sight blade with hood. **Features:** Stainless steel, matte finish, manual sliding-bar safety system. Made in U.S.A. by Freedom Arms.
Price: Silhouette Models **$1,683.95**

HAMMERLI SP 20 TARGET PISTOL
Caliber: 22 LR, 32 S&W. **Barrel:** 4.6". **Weight:** 34.6-41.8 oz. **Length:** 11.8" overall. **Grips:** Anatomically shaped synthetic Hi-Grip available in five sizes. **Sights:** Integral front in three widths, adjustable rear with changeable notch widths. **Features:** Extremely low-level sight line; anatomically shaped trigger; adjustable JPS buffer system for different recoil characteristics. Receiver available in red, blue, gold, violet or black. Introduced 1998. Imported from Switzerland by Larry's Guns of Maine.
Price: Hammerli 22 LR **$1,450.00**
Price: Hammerli 32 S&W **$1,560.00**

HAMMERLI X-ESSE SPORT PISTOL
An all-steel .22 LR target pistol with a Hi-Grip in a new anatomical shape and an adjustable hand rest. Made in Switzerland. Introduced 2003.
Price: **$750.00**

High Standard Trophy

High Standard Victor

Kimber Super Match II

Ruger MKIII512

Smith & Wesson Model 41

HIGH STANDARD SUPERMATIC TROPHY TARGET PISTOL
Caliber: 22 LR, 9-shot mag. **Barrel:** 5.5" bull or 7.25" fluted. **Weight:** 44-46 oz. **Length:** 9.5-11.25" overall. Stock: Checkered hardwood with thumbrest. **Sights:** Undercut ramp front, frame-mounted micro-click rear adjustable for windage and elevation; drilled and tapped for scope mounting. **Features:** Gold-plated trigger, slide lock, safety-lever and magazine release; stippled front grip and backstrap; adjustable trigger and sear. Barrel weights optional. From High Standard Manufacturing Co., Inc.
Price: 5.5" barrel, adjustable sights **$795.00**
Price: 7.25", adjustable sights **$845.00**

HIGH STANDARD VICTOR TARGET PISTOL
Caliber: 22 LR, 10-shot magazine. **Barrel:** 4-1/2" or 5-1/2"; push-button takedown. **Weight:** 46 oz. **Length:** 9.5" overall. **Stock:** Checkered hardwood with thumbrest. **Sights:** Undercut ramp front, micro-click rear adjustable for windage and elevation. Also available with scope mount, rings, no sights. **Features:** Stainless steel construction. Full-length vent rib. Gold-plated trigger, slide lock, safety-lever and magazine release; stippled front grip and backstrap; polished slide; adjustable trigger and sear. Comes with barrel weight. From High Standard Manufacturing Co., Inc.
Price: 4.5" or 5.5" barrel, universal scope base **$745.00**

KIMBER SUPER MATCH II
Caliber: 45 ACP, 8-shot magazine. **Barrel:** 5". **Weight:** 38 oz. **Length:** 8.7" overall. **Grips:** Rosewood double diamond. **Sights:** Blade front, Kimber fully adjustable rear. **Features:** Guaranteed shoot 1" group at 25 yards. Stainless steel frame, black KimPro slide; two-piece magazine well; premium aluminum match-grade trigger; 30 lpi front strap checkering;

stainless match-grade barrel; ambidextrous safety; special Custom Shop markings. Introduced 1999. Made in U.S.A. by Kimber Mfg., Inc.
Price: **$1,994.00**

RUGER MARK III TARGET MODEL AUTOLOADING PISTOL
Caliber: 22 LR, 10-shot magazine. **Barrel:** 5-1/2" to 6-7/8". **Weight:** 41 to 45 oz. **Length:** 9.75" to 11-1/8" overall. **Grips:** Checkered cocobolo. **Sights:** .125" blade front, micro-click rear, adjustable for windage and elevation, loaded chamber indicator; integral lock, magazine disconnect. Plastic case with lock included. Mark II series introduced 1982, discontinued 2004. Mark III introduced 2005.
Price: MKIII512 (bull barrel, blued) **$382.00**
Price: KMKIII512 (bull barrel, stainless) **$483.00**
Price: MKIII678 (blued Target barrel, 6-7/8") **$382.00**
Price: KMKIII678GC (stainless slabside barrel) **$555.00**
Price: KMKIII678GH (stainless fluted barrel) **$567.00**

SMITH & WESSON MODEL 41 TARGET
Caliber: 22 LR, 10-shot clip. **Barrel:** 5.5", 7". **Weight:** 41 oz. (5-1/2" barrel). **Length:** 10-1/2" overall (5-1/2" barrel). **Grips:** Checkered walnut with modified thumbrest, usable with either hand. **Sights:** 1/8" Patridge on ramp base; micro-click rear adjustable for windage and elevation. **Features:** 3/8" wide, grooved trigger; adjustable trigger stop drilled and tapped.
Price: S&W Bright Blue, either barrel **$1,153.00**

SMITH & WESSON MODEL 22A PISTOLS
Caliber: 22 LR, 10-shot magazine. **Barrel:** 4", 5.5" bull. **Weight:** 28-39 oz. **Length:** 9-1/2" overall. **Grips:** Dymondwood® with ambidextrous thumbrests and flared bottom or rubber soft touch with thumbrest. **Sights:** Patridge front, fully adjustable rear. **Features:** Sight bridge with Weaver-style integral optics mount; alloy frame, stainless barrel and slide; blue/black finish. Introduced 1997. The 22S is similar to the Model 22A except has stainless steel frame. Introduced 1997. Made in U.S.A. by Smith & Wesson.
Price: From **$261.00**

Smith & Wesson Model 22S

Smith & Wesson Model 22A

Springfield Armory 1911A1 Trophy Match

STI Executive

STI Eagle 5.0

STI Trojan 6-inch

SPRINGFIELD ARMORY LEATHAM LEGEND TGO SERIES PISTOLS
Three models of 5" barrel, 45 ACP 1911 pistols built for serious competition. TGO 1 has deluxe low mount Bo-Mar rear sight, Dawson fiber optics front sight, 3.5 lb. trigger pull.
Price: TGO 1 . . . . **$2,999.00**

Springfield Armory Trophy Match Pistol
Similar to Springfield Armory's Full Size model, but designed for bullseye and action shooting competition. Available with a Service Model 5" frame with matching slide and barrel in 5" and 6" lengths. Fully adjustable sights, checkered frame front strap, match barrel and bushing. In 45 ACP only. From Springfield Inc.
Price: **$1,248.00**

STI EAGLE 5.0, 6.0 PISTOL
Caliber: 9mm, 9x21, 38 & 40 Super, 40 S&W, 10mm, 45 ACP, 10-shot magazine. **Barrel:** 5", 6" bull. **Weight:** 34.5 oz. **Length:** 8.62" overall. **Grips:** Checkered polymer. **Sights:** STI front, Novak or Heine rear. **Features:** Standard frames plus 7 others; adjustable match trigger;

skeletonized hammer; extended grip safety with locator pad. Introduced 1994. Made in U.S.A. by STI International.
Price: . . . . (5.0 Eagle) $1,794.00, (6.0 Eagle) $1,894.00

STI EXECUTIVE PISTOL
Caliber: 40 S&W. **Barrel:** 5" bull. **Weight:** 39 oz. **Length:** 8-5/8". **Grips:** Gray polymer. **Sights:** Dawson fiber optic, front; STI adjustable rear. **Features:** Stainless mag. well, front and rear serrations on slide. Made in U.S.A. by STI.
Price: **$2,389.00**

STI TROJAN
Caliber: 9mm, 38 Super, 40S&W, 45 ACP. **Barrel:** 5", 6". **Weight:** 36 oz. **Length:** 8.5". **Grips:** Rosewood. **Sights:** STI front with STI adjustable rear. **Features:** Stippled front strap, flat top slide, one-piece steel guide rod.
Price: (Trojan 5") **$1,024.00**
Price: (Trojan 6", not available in 38 Super) **$1,344.00**

Includes models suitable for hunting and competitive courses of fire, both police and international.

Charter Arms Bulldog

Charter Arms Off Duty

Charter Arms Undercover

Charter Arms Mag Pug

Comanche I

Comanche II

Comanche III

Dan Wesson Firearms Alaskan Guide Special

ARMSPORT MODEL 4540 REVOLVER
Caliber: 38 Special. **Barrel:** 4". **Weight:** 32 oz. **Length:** 9" overall. **Sights:** Fixed rear, blade front. **Features:** Ventilated rib; blued finish. Imported from Argentina by Armsport Inc.
Price: $140.00

CHARTER ARMS BULLDOG REVOLVER
Caliber: 44 Special. **Barrel:** 2.5". **Weight:** NA. **Sights:** Blade front, notch rear. **Features:** 6-round cylinder, soft-rubber pancake-style grips, shrouded ejector rod, wide trigger and hammer spur. American made by Charter Arms, distributed by MKS Supply.
Price: Blued **$324.00**
Price: Stainless **$347.00**
Price: Police Bulldog, .38 Special, 4" barrel, 24 oz. **$299.00**

CHARTER ARMS OFF DUTY REVOLVER
Caliber: 38 Special. **Barrel:** 2". **Weight:** 12.5 oz. **Sights:** Blade front, notch rear. **Features:** 5-round cylinder, aluminum casting, DAO. American made by Charter Arms, distributed by MKS Supply.
Price: Aluminum **$353.00**

CHARTER ARMS UNDERCOVER REVOLVER
Caliber: 38 Special. **Barrel:** 2". **Weight:** 16 oz. **Sights:** Blade front, notch rear. **Features:** 6-round cylinder. American made by Charter Arms, distributed by MKS Supply.
Price: Blued **$359.00**

CHARTER ARMS UNDERCOVER SOUTHPAW REVOLVER
Caliber: 38 Special +P. **Barrel:** 2". **Weight:** 12 oz. **Sights:** NA. **Features:** Cylinder release is on the right side and the cylinder opens to the right side. Exposed hammer for both single and double-action firiing. 5-round cylinder. American made by Charter Arms, distributed by MKS Supply.
Price: Blued **$375.00**

CHARTER ARMS MAG PUG REVOLVER
Caliber: 357 Magnum. **Barrel:** 2.2". **Weight:** 23 oz. **Sights:** Blade front, notch rear. **Features:** 5-round cylinder. American made by Charter Arms, distributed by MKS Supply.
Price: Blued **$325.00**
Price: Stainless **$335.00**

COLT SINGLE-ACTION ARMY
Caliber: 32-20, 38 Special, 357 Magnum, 38-40, 44-4-, 44 Special, 45 Long Colt. **Barrel:** 4.7 5", 5.5", 7.5". **Weight:** 40-44 oz. **Sights:** Blade front,

notch rear. **Features:** Available in black powder and sheriff's models; nickel, blued or case-hardened frame; 6-round cylinder.
Price: . . . . (Blued) **$1,290.00**; (Nickel) **$1,490.00**

COMANCHE I, II, III DA REVOLVERS
Features: Adjustable sights. Blue or stainless finish. Distributed by SGS Importers.
Price: I 22 LR, 6" bbl., 9-shot, blue **$249.95**
Price: I 22LR, 6" bbl., 9-shot, stainless **$274.95**
Price: II 38 Special, 2" bbl., 6-shot, blue, intr. 2006 . . . . **$258.95**
Price: II 38 Special, 4" bbl., 6-shot, stainless **$249.95**
Price: III 357 Mag, 3" bbl., 6-shot, blue **$266.95**
Price: III 357 Mag, 2" bbl., 6-shot, blue **$274.95**
Price: II 38 Special, 3" bbl., 6-shot, stainless steel **$266.95**

DAN WESSON FIREARMS ALASKAN GUIDE SPECIAL
Caliber: 445 SuperMag; also chambers and fires 44 Magnum, 44 Special, 6 shots. **Sights:** Blade front, adjustable rear. **Barrel:** Compensated 4" vent heavy barrel assembly. **Weight:** 54.4 oz. **Length:** 11.7". **Features:** Stainless steel with baked on, non-glare, matte black coating, special laser engraving. Made in U.S.A. by Dan Wesson Firearms, distributed by CZ-USA.
Price: **$1,295.00**

DAN WESSON FIREARMS VH8 445 SUPERMAG
Caliber: 445 SuperMag; also chambers and fires 44 Magnum, 44 Special, 6 shots. **Sights:** Blade front, adjustable rear. **Barrel:** 8" full-length underlug. **Weight:** 54.4 oz. **Length:** 14.6". **Features:** Stainless-steel frame and barrel. Interchangeable barrels. Made in U.S.A. by Dan Wesson Firearms, distributed by CZ-USA.
Price: **$1,070.00**

EAA Windicator

Korth Combat

Rossi Model 971

Rossi Model 972

Rossi Model R351

Rossi Model 851

Ruger GP-100

Ruger KGP-141

Ruger GP-161

EAA WINDICATOR REVOLVERS
Caliber: 38 Spec., 6-shot; 357 magnum, 6-shot. **Barrel:** 2", 4". **Weight:** 30 oz. (4"). **Length:** 8.5" overall (4" bbl.). **Grips:** Rubber with finger grooves. **Sights:** Blade front, fixed or adjustable on rimfires; fixed only on 32, 38. **Features:** Swing-out cylinder; hammer block safety; blue finish. Introduced 1991. Imported from Germany by European American Armory.
Price: 38 Special 2" barrel, alloy frame **$249.00**
Price: 38 Special 4" barrel, alloy frame **$259.00**
Price: 357 Mag, 2" barrel, steel frame **$259.00**
Price: 357 Mag, 4" barrel, steel frame **$279.00**

KORTH REVOLVERS
Caliber: 22 LR, 22 WMR, 32 S&W Long, 38 Sp., 357 Mag., 9mm Para. **Barrel:** 3", 4", 5.25", 6". **Weight:** 32-52 oz. **Grips:** Walnut, palisander, amboinia, ivory (Combat, Sport), German walnut. Matte with oil finish, adjustable ergonomic competition style (Target). **Sights:** Adjustable Patridge (Sport) or Baughman (Combat), interchangeable and adjustable rear w/Patridge front (Target) in blue and matte. **Features:** DA/SA, 3 models, over 50 configurations, externally adjustable trigger stop and weight, interchangeable cylinder, removable wide milled trigger shoe on Target model. Deluxe models are highly engraved, high polish blue finish, plasma coated in high polish or matted silver, gold, blue or charcoal. Many deluxe options available. 6-shot. Made in Germany. Imported by Korth USA.
Price: . . . . **$5,000.00 to $8,000.00**
Price: Deluxe . . . . **$9,000.00 to $12,000.00**

ROSSI MODEL R351/R352/R851 REVOLVERS
Caliber: .38 Sp. **Barrel:** 2" (R35), 4" (R85). **Weight:** 24-32 oz. **Grips:** Rubber. **Sights:** Fixed (R35), Fully Adjustable (R85). **Features:** DA/SA, 3 models available, +P rated frame, blue carbon or high polish stainless steel, patented Taurus Security System, 5-shot (R35) 6-shot (R85).
Price: . . . . **$343.00 to 398.00**

ROSSI R461/R462/R971/R972
Caliber: .357Mag. **Barrel:** 2" (R46), 4" (R971), 6" (R972). **Weight:** 26-35 oz. **Grips:** Rubber. **Sights:** Fixed (R46), Fully Adjustable (R97). **Features:** DA/SA, 4 models available, +P rated frame, blue carbon or high polish stainless steel, patented Taurus Security System, 6-shot.
Price: . . . . **$343.00 to $432.00**

ROSSI MODEL 971/972 REVOLVERS
Caliber: 357 Magnum +P, 6-shot. **Barrel:** 4", 6". **Weight:** 32 oz. **Length:** 8.5" or 10.5" overall. **Grips:** Rubber. **Sights:** Blade front, adjustable rear. **Features:** Single/double action. Patented key-lock Taurus Security System; forged steel frame. Introduced 2001. Made in Brazil by Amadeo Rossi. Imported by BrazTech/Taurus.
Price: Model 971 (blued finish, 4" bbl.) **$362.00**
Price: Model 972 (stainless steel finish, 6" bbl.) **$410.00**

Rossi Model 851
Similar to Model 971/972, chambered for 38 Special +P. Blued finish, 4" barrel. Introduced 2001. Made in Brazil by Amadeo Rossi. From BrazTech/Taurus.
Price: **$313.00**

RUGER GP-100 REVOLVERS
Caliber: 38 Spec. +P, 357 Mag., 6-shot. **Barrel:** 3" full shroud, 4" full shroud, 6" full shroud. **Weight:** 3" full shroud-36 oz., 4" full shroud-38 oz. **Sights:** Fixed; adjustable on 4" full shroud, all 6" barrels. **Grips:** Ruger Santoprene Cushioned Grip with Goncalo Alves inserts. **Features:** Uses action, frame features of both the Security-Six and Redhawk revolvers. Full length, short ejector shroud. Satin blue and stainless steel.
Price: GPF-141 (357, 4" full shroud, adj. sights, blue) **$575.00**
Price: GP-161 (357, 6" full shroud, adj. sights, blue), 46 oz. **$575.00**
Price: KGP-141 (357, 4" full shroud, adj. sights, stainless) **$635.00**
Price: KGP-161 (357, 6" full shroud, adj. sights, stainless) 46 oz. **$635.00**
Price: KGPF-331 (357, 3" full shroud, stainless) **$615.00**

Ruger SP101

Ruger Redhawk

Ruger Redhawk KRH-444

Ruger Super Redhawk

Smith & Wesson Model 36LS

Smith & Wesson Model 442

Smith & Wesson Model 638

RUGER SP101 REVOLVERS
Caliber: 32 H&R Mag., 6-shot; 38 Spec. +P, 357 Mag., 5-shot. **Barrel:** 2-1/4", 3-1/16". **Weight:** (38 & 357 mag models) 2-1/4"-25 oz.; 3-1/16"-27 oz. **Sights:** Adjustable on 32, fixed on others. **Grips:** Ruger Cushioned Grip with inserts. **Features:** Compact, small frame, double-action revolver. Full-length ejector shroud. Stainless steel only. Introduced 1988.
Price: KSP-321X (2-1/4", 357 Mag.) **$550.00**
Price: KSP-3231X (3-1/16", 32 H&R), 30 oz. **$550.00**
Price: KSP-331X (3-1/16", 357 Mag.) **$550.00**
Price: KSP-821X (2-1/4", 38 Spec.) **$550.00**

Ruger SP101 Double-Action-Only Revolver
Similar to standard SP101 except double-action-only with no single-action sear notch. Spurless hammer, floating firing pin and transfer bar safety system. Available with 2-1/4" barrel in 357 Magnum. Weighs 25 oz., overall length 7.06". Natural brushed satin, high-polish stainless steel. Introduced 1993.
Price: KSP321XL (357 Mag.) **$550.00**

RUGER REDHAWK
Caliber: 44 Rem. Mag., 6-shot. **Barrel:** 5-1/2", 7-1/2". **Weight:** About 54 oz. (7-1/2" bbl.). **Length:** 13" overall (7-1/2" barrel). **Grips:** Square butt cushioned grip panels. **Sights:** Interchangeable Patridge-type front, rear adjustable for windage and elevation. **Features:** Stainless steel, brushed satin finish, blued ordnance steel. 9-1/2" sight radius. Introduced 1979.
Price: KRH-44, stainless, 7-1/2" barrel **$780.00**
Price: KRH-44R, stainless 7.5" barrel w/scope mount **$829.00**
Price: KRH-445, stainless 5.5" barrel **$780.00**
Price: RH-445, blued 5.5" barrel **$715.00**
Price: KRH-444, stainless 4" barrel (2007) **$780.00**

RUGER SUPER REDHAWK REVOLVER
Caliber: 44 Rem. Mag., 45 Colt, 454 Casull, 480 Ruger 6-shot. **Barrel:** 2.5", 5.5", 7.5", 9.5". **Weight:** About 54 oz. (7.5" bbl.). **Length:** 13" overall (7.5" barrel). **Grips:** Square butt cushioned grip panels, Hogue Tamer Monogrip. **Features:** Similar to standard Redhawk except has heavy extended frame with Ruger Integral Scope Mounting System on wide topstrap. Wide hammer spur lowered for better scope clearance. Incorporates mechanical design features and improvements of GP-100. Ramp front sight base has Redhawk-style Interchangeable Insert sight

blades, adjustable rear sight. Satin stainless steel and low-glare stainless finishes. Introduced 1987.
Price: KSRH-2454, 2.5" 454 Casull/45 Colt, Hogue Tamer
        Monogrip **$899.00**
Price: KSRH-2480, 2.5" 480 Ruger, Hogue Tamer Monogrip **$899.00**
Price: KSRH-7, 7.5" 44 Mag, Ruger grip **$829.00**
Price: KSRH-7454, 7.5" 45 Colt/454 Casull, low glare stainless . . . **$899.00**
Price: KSRH-7480, 7.5" 480 Ruger, low glare stainless **$899.00**
Price: KSRH-9, 9" 44 Mag, Ruger grip **$829.00**

SMITH & WESSON J-FRAME REVOLVERS
The smallest S&W wheelguns come in a variety of chamberings, barrel lengths, and materials, as noted in the individual model listings below.

SMITH & WESSON 36LS/60LS/642LS LADYSMITH REVOLVERS
Caliber: .38 Special +P, 357 Mag., 5-shot. **Barrel:** 1-7/8" (36LS, 642LS); 2-1/8" (60LS) **Weight:** 14.5 oz. (642LS); 20 oz. (36LS); 21.5 oz. (60LS); **Length:** 6.25" overall (36LS); 6.6" overall (60LS); . **Grips:** Wood. **Sights:** Black blade, serrated ramp front, fixed notch rear. **Features:** 36/60LS models have a Chiefs Special-style frame. 642LS has Centennial-style frame, frosted matte finish, smooth combat wood grips. Introduced 1996. Comes in a fitted carry/storage case. Introduced 1989. Made in U.S.A. by Smith & Wesson.
Price: From **$672.00**

SMITH & WESSON MODEL 442/637/638/642 AIRWEIGHT REVOLVERS
Caliber: 38 Special +P, 5-shot. **Barrel:** 1-7/8". **Weight:** 15 oz. (37, 442); 20 oz. (3); 21.5 oz. (); **Length:** 6-3/8" overall. **Grips:** Soft rubber. **Sights:** Fixed, serrated ramp front, square notch rear. **Features:** Aluminum-alloy frames. Models 37, 637; Chiefs Special-style frame with exposed hammer. Introduced 1996. Models 442, 642; Centennial-style frame, enclosed hammer. Model 638, Bodyguard style, shrouded hammer. Comes in a fitted carry/storage case. Introduced 1989. Made in U.S.A. by Smith & Wesson.
Price: From **$498.00**

SMITH & WESSON MODEL 60 CHIEF'S SPECIAL
Caliber: 357 Magnum, 38 Special +P, 5-shot. **Barrel:** 2-1/8", 3" or 5". **Weight:** 22.5 oz. (2-1/8" barrel). **Length:** 6-5/8 overall (2-1/8" barrel). **Grips:** Rounded butt synthetic grips. **Sights:** Fixed, serrated ramp front, square notch rear. **Features:** Stainless steel construction, satin finish, internal lock. Introduced 1965. The 5-inch-barrel model has target semi-lug barrel, rosewood grip, red ramp front sight, adjustable rear sight. Made in U.S.A. by Smith & Wesson.
Price: 2-1/8" barrel, intr. 2005 . . . . **$672.00**
Price: 3" barrel, 7.5" OAL, 24 oz. **$695.00**
Price: 5" semi-lug barrel, 9-3/8" OAL, 30.5 oz. **$735.00**

Smith & Wesson
Model 60 Chief's Special

Smith & Wesson
Model 317 AirLite

Smith & Wesson Model 340

Smith & Wesson Model 360 PD
Airlite SC Chief's Special

Smith & Wesson
Model 649 Bodyguard

Smith & Wesson
Model 10

Smith & Wesson Model 386

SMITH & WESSON MODEL 317 AIRLITE REVOLVERS
Caliber: 22 LR, 8-shot. **Barrel:** 1-7/8", 3". **Weight:** 10.5 oz. **Length:** 6.25" overall (1-7/8" barrel). **Grips:** Rubber. **Sights:** Serrated ramp front, fixed notch rear. **Features:** Aluminum alloy, carbon and stainless steels, Chiefs Special-style frame with exposed hammer. Smooth combat trigger. Clear Cote finish. Introduced 1997. Made in U.S.A. by Smith & Wesson.
Price: Model 317, 1-7/8" barrel **$632.00**
Price: Model 317 w/HiViz front sight, 3" barrel, 7.25 OAL **$695.00**

SMITH & WESSON MODEL 340/340PD AIRLITE SC CENTENNIAL
Caliber: 357 Magnum, 38 Spec. +P, 5-shot. **Barrel:** 1-7/8". **Weight:** 12 oz. **Length:** 6-3/8" overall (1-7/8" barrel). **Grips:** Rounded butt rubber. **Sights:** Black blade front, rear notch **Features:** Centennial-style frame, enclosed hammer. Internal lock. Matte silver finish. Scandium alloy frame, titanium cylinder, stainless steel barrel liner. Made in U.S.A. by Smith & Wesson.
Price: From **$940.00**

SMITH & WESSON MODEL 351PD REVOLVER
Caliber: 22 Mag., 7-shot. **Barrel:** 1-7/8". **Weight:** 10.6 oz. **Length:** 6.25" overall (1-7/8" barrel). **Sights:** HiViz front sight, rear notch. **Grips:** Wood. **Features:** Seven-shot, aluminum-alloy frame. Chiefs Special-style frame with exposed hammer. Nonreflective matte-black finish. Internal lock. Made in U.S.A. by Smith & Wesson.
Price: **$695.00**

SMITH & WESSON MODEL 360/360PD AIRLITE CHIEF'S SPECIAL
Caliber: 357 Magnum, 38 Spec. +P, 5-shot. **Barrel:** 1-7/8". **Weight:** 12 oz. **Length:** 6-3/8" overall (1-7/8" barrel). **Grips:** Rounded butt rubber. **Sights:** Black blade front, fixed rear notch. **Features:** Chiefs Special-style frame with exposed hammer. Internal lock. Scandium alloy frame, titanium cylinder, stainless steel barrel. Made in U.S.A. by Smith & Wesson.
Price: From **$940.00**

SMITH & WESSON MODEL 640 CENTENNIAL DA ONLY
Caliber: 357 Mag., 38 Spec. +P, 5-shot. **Barrel:** 2-1/8". **Weight:** 23 oz. **Length:** 6-3/4" overall. **Grips:** Uncle Mike's Boot grip. **Sights:** Serrated ramp front, fixed notch rear. **Features:** Stainless steel. Fully concealed hammer, snag-proof smooth edges. Internal lock. Introduced 1995 in 357 Magnum.
Price: **$672.00**

SMITH & WESSON MODEL 649 BODYGUARD REVOLVER
Caliber: 357 Mag., 38 Spec. +P, 5-shot. **Barrel:** 2-1/8". **Weight:** 23 oz. **Length:** 6-5/8" overall. **Grips:** Uncle Mike's Combat. **Sights:** Black pinned ramp front, fixed notch rear. **Features:** Stainless steel construction, satin finish. Internal lock. Bodyguard style, shrouded hammer. Made in U.S.A. by Smith & Wesson.
Price: **$672.00**

SMITH & WESSON K-FRAME/L-FRAME REVOLVERS
These mid-size S&W wheelguns come in a variety of chamberings, barrel lengths, and materials, as noted in the individual model listings below. 17 variations for 2006.

SMITH & WESSON MODEL 10 REVOLVER
Caliber: 38 Spec.+P, 6-shot. **Barrel:** 4". **Weight:** 36 oz. **Length:** 8-7/8" overall. **Grips:** Soft rubber; square butt. **Sights:** Fixed; black blade front, square notch rear. Blued carbon steel frame.
Price: Blue **$632.00**

SMITH & WESSON MODEL 64/67 REVOLVERS
Caliber: 38 Spec. +P, 6-shot. **Barrel:** 3". **Weight:** 33 oz. **Length:** 8-7/8" overall. **Grips:** Soft rubber. **Sights:** Fixed, 1/8" serrated ramp front, square notch rear. Model 67 (**Weight:** 36 oz. **Length:** 8-7/8") similar to Model 64 except for adjustable sights. **Features:** Satin finished stainless steel, square butt.
Price: From **$632.00**

SMITH & WESSON MODEL 386 SC/S
Caliber: 357 Magnum, 38 Spec. +P, 7-shot. **Barrel:** 3-1/8". **Weight:** 18.5 oz. **Length:** 8-1/8" overall. **Grips:** Rubber. **Sights:** Adjustable, HiViz front. **Features:** Scandium alloy frame, titanium cylinder, stainless steel barrel liner. Internal lock. Made in U.S.A. by Smith & Wesson.
Price: Matte silver finish **$869.00**

SMITH & WESSON MODEL 617 REVOLVERS
Caliber: 22 LR, 6- or 10-shot. **Barrel:** 4". **Weight:** 41 oz. (4" barrel). **Length:** 9-1/8" (4" barrel). **Grips:** Soft rubber. **Sights:** Patridge front, adjustable rear. Drilled and tapped for scope mount. **Features:** Stainless steel with satin finish; 4" has .312" smooth trigger, .375" semi-target hammer; 6" has either .312" combat or .400" serrated trigger, .375" semi-target or .500" target hammer; 8-3/8" with .400" serrated trigger, .500" target hammer. Introduced 1990.
Price: From **$774.00**

Smith & Wesson
Model 686

Smith & Wesson
Model 686 SSR

Smith & Wesson Model 21

Smith & Wesson
Model 325PD

Smith & Wesson
Model 625

Smith & Wesson Model 657

SMITH & WESSON MODELS 619/620 REVOLVERS
Caliber: 38 Special +P; 357 Mag., 7 rounds. **Barrel:** 4". **Weight:** 37.5 oz. **Length:** 9-1/2". **Grips:** Rubber. **Sights:** Integral front blade, fixed rear notch on the 619; adjustable white-outline target style rear, red ramp front on 620. **Features:** Replaces Models 65 and 66. Two-piece semi-lug barrel. Satin stainless frame and cylinder. Made in U.S.A. by Smith & Wesson.
Price: **$711.00**

SMITH & WESSON MODEL 686/686 PLUS REVOLVERS
Caliber: 357 Mag., 38 S&W Special; 6 rounds. **Barrel:** 2.5", 4", 6". **Weight:** 35 oz. (2.5" barrel). **Length:** 7-1/2", (2.5" barrel). **Grips:** Rubber. **Sights:** White outline adjustable rear, red ramp front. **Features:** Satin stainless frame and cylinder. Plus series guns have 7-shot cylinders. Introduced 1996. Powerport (PP) has Patridge front, adjustable rear sight. Introduced early 1980s. Stock Service Revolver (SSR) intr. 2007. Capacity: 6. **Barrel:** 4". Sight: Interchangeable front, adjustable rear. Grip: Wood Finish: Satin stainless frame and cylinder. **Weight:** 38.3 oz. **Features:** Chamfered charge holes, custom barrel w/recessed crown, bossed mainspring. High-hold ergonomic grip. Made in U.S.A. by Smith & Wesson.
Price: 686 .... **$766.00**
Price: Plus, 7 rounds **$790.00**
Price: PP, 6" barrel, 6 rounds, 11-3/8" OAL **$790.00**
Price: SSR .... **NA**

SMITH & WESSON N-FRAME REVOLVERS
These large-frame S&W wheelguns come in a variety of chamberings, barrel lengths, and materials, as noted in the individual model listings below. 18 major variations for 2006.

SMITH & WESSON MODEL 21
Caliber: 44 Special, 6-round. **Barrel:** 4" tapered. **Weight:** NA. **Length:** NA. **Grips:** Smooth wood. **Sights:** Pinned half-moon service front; service rear. **Features:** Carbon steel frame, blued finish.
Price: **$855.00**

SMITH & WESSON MODEL 29 50TH ANNIVERSARY REVOLVER
Caliber: 44 Mag, 6-round. **Barrel:** 6.5". **Weight:** 48.5 oz. **Length:** 12". **Grips:** Cocobolo. **Sights:** Adjustable white-outline rear, red ramp front. **Features:** Carbon steel frame, polished-blued finish. Introduced 2005. Includes 24 carat gold-plated anniversary logo on frame, cleaning kit with screwdriver, mahogany presentation case, square-butt frame, serrated trigger. Original Model 29 made famous by "Dirty Harry" character created in 1971 by Clint Eastwood.
Price: Dealer pricing, no MSRP .... **NA**

SMITH & WESSON MODEL 325PD/329PD/357PD AIRLITE REVOLVERS
Caliber: 41 Mag. (357PD); 44 Spec., 44 Mag. (329PD); 45 ACP (325PD); 6-round. **Barrel:** 2-3/4" (325PD). **Weight:** 21.5 oz. (325PD, 2-3/4" barrel). **Length:** 7-1/4" (325PD, 2-3/4" barrel). **Grips:** Wood. **Sights:** Adj. rear, HiViz orange-dot front. **Features:** Scandium alloy frame, titanium cylinder. 4" model has HiViz green front sight and Ahrends finger-groove wood grips. Weighs 26.5 oz.
Price: From **$1,067.00**

SMITH & WESSON MODEL 625 REVOLVERS
Caliber: 45 ACP, 6-shot. **Barrel:** 4", 5". **Weight:** 43 oz. (4" barrel). **Length:** 9-3/8" overall (4" barrel). **Grips:** Soft rubber; wood optional. **Sights:** Patridge front on ramp, S&W micrometer click rear adjustable for windage and elevation. **Features:** Stainless steel construction with .400" semi-target hammer, .312" smooth combat trigger; full lug barrel. Glass beaded finish. Introduced 1989. "Jerry Miculek" Professional (JMP) Series has .265"-wide grooved trigger, special wooden Miculek Grip, five full moon clips, gold bead Patridge front sight on interchangeable front sight base, bead blast finish. Unique serial number run. Mountain Gun has 4" tapered barrel, drilled and tapped, Hogue Rubber Monogrip, pinned black ramp front sight, micrometer click-adjustable rear sight, satin stainless frame and barrel, weighs 39.5 oz.
Price: From **$869.00**

SMITH & WESSON MODEL 629 REVOLVERS
Caliber: 44 Magnum, 44 S&W Special, 6-shot. **Barrel:** 4", 5", 6-1/2". **Weight:** 41.5 oz. (4" bbl.). **Length:** 9-5/8" overall (4" bbl.). **Grips:** Soft rubber; wood optional. **Sights:** 1/8" red ramp front, white outline rear, internal lock, adjustable for windage and elevation. Classic similar to standard Model 629, except Classic has full-lug 5" barrel, chamfered front of cylinder, interchangeable red ramp front sight with adjustable white outline rear, Hogue grips with S&W monogram, drilled and tapped for scope mounting. Factory accurizing and endurance packages. Introduced 1990. Classic Power Port has Patridge front sight and adjustable rear sight. Model 629CT has 5" barrel, Crimson Trace Hoghunter Lasergrips, 10.5" OAL, 45.5 oz. weight. Introduced 2006.
Price: From **$869.00**

SMITH & WESSON MODEL 657 REVOLVER
Caliber: 41 Mag., 6-shot. **Barrel:** 7-1/2" full lug. **Weight:** 52 oz. **Grips:** Soft rubber. **Sights:** Pinned 1/8" red ramp front, micro-click rear adjustable for windage and elevation. Target hammer, drilled and tapped, unfluted cylinder. **Features:** Stainless steel construction.
Price: **$869.00**

Smith & Wesson
Model 460V

Smith & Wesson Model 500

Taurus Judge

Taurus Model 85

Taurus Model 17 Tracker

Taurus Model 44

SMITH & WESSON X-FRAME REVOLVERS
These extra-large X-frame S&W wheelguns come in a variety of chamberings, barrel lengths, and materials, as noted in the individual model listings below. 7 variations for 2006.

SMITH & WESSON MODEL 460V REVOLVERS
Caliber: 460 S&W Mag., 5-shot. Also chambers 454 Casull, 45 Colt. **Barrel:** 8-3/8" gain-twist rifling. **Weight:** 62.5 oz. **Length:** 11.25". **Grips:** Rubber. **Sights:** Adj. rear, red ramp front. **Features:** Satin stainless steel frame and cylinder, interchangeable compensator. 460XVR (X-treme Velocity Revolver) has black blade front sight with interchangeable green Hi-Viz tubes, adjustable rear sight. 7.5"-barrel version has Lothar-Walther barrel, 360-degree recoil compensator, tuned Performance Center action, pinned sear, integral Weaver base, non-glare surfaces, scope mount accessory kit for mounting full-size scopes, flashed-chromed hammer and trigger, Performance Center gun rug and shoulder sling. Interchangeable Hi-Viz green dot front sight, adjustable black rear sight, Hogue Dual Density Monogrip, matte-black frame and shroud finish with glass-bead cylinder finish, 72 oz. Compensated Hunter has tear drop chrome hammer, .312 chrome trigger, Hogue Dual Density Monogrip, satin/matte stainless finish, HiViz interchangeable front sight, adjustable black rear sight. XVR introduced 2006.
Price: 460V **$1,256.00**
Price: 460XVR, from **$1,401.00**

SMITH & WESSON MODEL 500 REVOLVERS
Caliber: 500 S&W Mag., 5 rounds. **Barrel:** 4", 8-3/8". **Weight:** 72.5 oz. **Length:** 15" (8-3/8" barrel). **Grips:** Hogue Sorbothane Rubber. **Sights:** Interchangeable blade, front, adjustable rear. **Features:** Recoil compensator, ball detent cylinder latch, internal lock. 6-1/2"-barrel model has orange-ramp dovetail Millett front sight, adjustable black rear sight, Hogue Dual Density Monogrip, .312" chrome trigger with over-travel stop, chrome tear-drop hammer, glassbead finish. 10-1/2"-barrel model has red ramp front sight, adjustable rear sight, .312 chrome trigger with overtravel stop, chrome tear drop hammer with pinned sear, hunting sling. Compensated Hunter has .400 orange ramp dovetail front sight, adjustable black blade rear sight, Hogue Dual Density Monogrip, glassbead finish w/black passivate clear coat. Made in U.S.A. by Smith & Wesson.
Price: From **$1,256.00**

TAURUS MODEL JUDGE
Caliber: 3" mag 410ga./.45LC, 2-1/2" 410ga./.45LC. **Barrel:** 3". **Weight:** 35.2 oz., 22.4 oz. **Length:** 7.5". **Grips:** Ribber. **Sights:** Fiber Optic. **Features:** DA/SA. Matte Stainless and Ultra-Lite Stainless finish. Introduced in 2007. Imported from Brazil by Taurus International.
Price: 4510TKR-3MAG, Matte Stainless . . . . **NA**
Price: 4510TKR-3UL, Ultra-Lite Stainless . . . . **NA**

TAURUS MODEL 85
Caliber: .38 Special +P. **Barrel:** 2". **Weight:** 12.4 oz. **Length:** 6.5". **Grips:** Rubber. **Sights:** Fixed, Fiber Optic. **Features:** DA/SA. Hy-Lite Magnesium and Ultra-Lite Gray finish. Introduced in 2007. Imported from Brazil by Taurus International.
Price: 85HL2MG, Hy-Lite Magnesium . . . . **NA**
Price: 85ULGRYFO, Ultra-Lite Gray . . . . **NA**
Price: 85ULGRY, Ultra-Lite Gray . . . . **NA**
Price: 85SS2CHUL **$398.00**

TAURUS MODEL 850
Caliber: .38 Special +P. **Barrel:** 2". **Weight:** 15.6 oz. **Length:** 6.5". **Grips:** Rubber. **Sights:** Fixed. **Features:** DAO. Small Frame. Ultra-Lite Blue and Ultra-Lite Stainless. Incredibly Strong, Lightweight Forged Alloy Frame. Introduced in 2007. Imported from Brazil by Taurus International.
Price: 850B2UL, Ultra-Lite Blue . . . . **NA**
Price: 850SS2UL, Ultra-Lite Stainless . . . . **NA**

TAURUS MODEL 17 "TRACKER"
Caliber: 17 HMR, 7-shot. **Barrel:** 6-1/2". **Weight:** 45.8 oz. **Grips:** Rubber. **Sights:** Adjustable. **Features:** Double action, matte stainless, integral key-lock.
Price: From **$390.00**

TAURUS MODEL 44 REVOLVER
Caliber: 44 Mag., 6-shot. **Barrel:** 4", 6-1/2", 8-3/8". **Weight:** 44-3/4 oz. **Grips:** Rubber. **Sights:** Adjustable. **Features:** Double-action. Integral key-lock. Introduced 1994. New Model 44S12 has 12" vent rib barrel. Imported from Brazil by Taurus International Manufacturing, Inc.
Price: Blue or stainless steel . . . . **$445.00 to $602.00**

Taurus Model 44 Series Revolver
Similar to Taurus Model 60 series, but in .44 Rem. Mag. With six-shot cylinder, blue and matte stainless finishes.
Price: From **$602.00**

TAURUS MODEL 65 REVOLVER
Caliber: 357 Mag., 6-shot. **Barrel:** 4". **Weight:** 38 oz. **Length:** 10-1/2" overall. **Grips:** Soft rubber. **Sights:** Fixed. **Features:** Double action, integral key-lock. Seven models for 2006 Imported by Taurus International.
Price: From **$406.00**

Taurus Model 65

Taurus Model 66

Taurus Model 82

Taurus Model 85

Taurus Model 94

Taurus Model 416 Raging Bull

Taurus Model 425

Taurus Model 444 Raging Bull

Taurus Model 605

Taurus Model 731

Taurus Model 66 Revolver
Similar to Model 65, 4" or 6" barrel, 7-shot cylinder, adjustable rear sight. Integral key-lock action. Imported by Taurus International.
Price: From $455.00

TAURUS MODEL 82 HEAVY BARREL REVOLVER
Caliber: 38 Spec., 6-shot. **Barrel:** 4", heavy. **Weight:** 36.5 oz. **Length:** 9-1/4" overall (4" bbl.). **Grips:** Soft black rubber. **Sights:** Serrated ramp front, square notch rear. **Features:** Double action, solid rib, integral key-lock. Imported by Taurus International.
Price: From $391.00

TAURUS MODEL 85 REVOLVER
Caliber: 38 Spec., 5-shot. **Barrel:** 2". **Weight:** 17-24.5 oz., titanium 13.5-15.4 oz. **Grips:** Rubber, rosewood or mother-of-pearl. **Sights:** Ramp front, square notch rear. **Features:** Blue, matte stainless, blue with gold accents, stainless with gold accents; rated for +P ammo. Integral keylock. Some models have titantium frame. Introduced 1980. Imported by Taurus International.
Price: From $391.00

TAURUS MODEL 94 REVOLVER
Caliber: 22 LR, 9-shot cylinder; 22 Mag, 8-shot cylinder **Barrel:** 2", 4", 5". **Weight:** 18.5-27.5 oz. **Grips:** Soft black rubber. **Sights:** Serrated ramp front, click-adjustable rear. **Features:** Double action, integral key-lock. Introduced 1989. Imported by Taurus International.
Price: From $358.00

TAURUS RAGING BULL MODEL 416
Caliber: 41 Magnum, 6-shot. **Barrel:** 6-1/2". **Weight:** 61.9 oz. **Grips:** Rubber. **Sights:** Adjustable. **Features:** Double-action, ported, ventilated rib, matte stainless, integral key-lock.
Price: $691.00

TAURUS MODEL 425/627 TRACKER REVOLVERS
Caliber: 357 Mag., 7-shot; 41 Mag., 5-shot. **Barrel:** 4" and 6". **Weight:** 28.8-40 oz. (titanium) 24.3-28. (6"). **Grips:** Rubber. **Sights:** Fixed front, adjustable rear. **Features:** Double-action stainless steel, Shadow Gray or

Total Titanium; vent rib (steel models only); integral key-lock action. Imported by Taurus International.
Price: .... $531.00 to $766.00
Price: Total Titanium $766.00

TAURUS MODEL 444 ULTRALIGHT
Caliber: 44 Mag, 5-shot. **Barrel:** 4". **Weight:** 28.3 oz. **Length:** 9.8" overall. **Grips:** Cushioned inset rubber. **Sights:** Fixed red-fiber optic front, adjustable rear. **Features:** UltraLite titanium blue finish, titanium/alloy frame built on Raging Bull design. Smooth trigger shoe, 1.760" wide, 6.280" tall. Barrel rate of twist 1:16", 6 grooves. Introduced 2005. Imported by Taurus International.
Price: $650.00

TAURUS MODEL 444/454/480 RAGING BULL REVOLVERS
Caliber: 44 Mag., 45 LC, 454 Casull, 480 Ruger, 5-shot. **Barrel:** 5", 6-1/2", 8-3/8". **Weight:** 53-63 oz. **Length:** 12" overall (6-1/2" barrel). **Grips:** Soft black rubber. **Sights:** Patridge front, adjustable rear. **Features:** Double-action, ventilated rib, ported, integral key-lock. Introduced 1997. Imported by Taurus International.
Price: From $619.00

TAURUS MODEL 605 REVOLVER
Caliber: 357 Mag., 5-shot. **Barrel:** 2". **Weight:** 24 oz. **Grips:** Rubber. **Sights:** Fixed. **Features:** Double-action, blue or stainless or titanium, concealed hammer models DAO, porting optional, integral key-lock. Introduced 1995. Imported by Taurus International.
Price: From $391.00

Taurus Model 731 Revolver
Similar to the Taurus Model 605, except in .32 Magnum.
Price: $455.00

Taurus Model 608

Taurus Model 617

Taurus Model 650

Taurus Model 651

Taurus Model 817

Taurus Model 850

Taurus Model 941

Taurus Model 970 Tracker

TAURUS MODEL 608 REVOLVER
Caliber: 357 Mag. 38 Spec., 8-shot. **Barrel:** 4", 6-1/2", 8-3/8". **Weight:** 44-57 oz. **Length:** 9-3/8" overall. **Grips:** Soft black rubber. **Sights:** Adjustable. **Features:** Double-action, integral key-lock action. Available in blue or stainless. Introduced 1995. Imported by Taurus International.
Price: $569.00

TAURUS MODEL 617 REVOLVER
Caliber: 357 Magnum, 7-shot. **Barrel:** 2". **Weight:** 28.3 oz. **Length:** 6-3/4" overall. **Grips:** Soft black rubber. **Sights:** Fixed. **Features:** Double-action, blue, Shadow Gray, bright spectrum blue or matte stainless steel, integral key-lock. Available with porting, concealed hammer. Introduced 1998. Imported by Taurus International.
Price: .... $391.00 to $453.00
Price: Total Titanium, 19.9 oz. $602.00

TAURUS MODEL 650CIA REVOLVER
Caliber: 357 Magnum, 5-shot. **Barrel:** 2". **Weight:** 24.5 oz. **Grips:** Rubber. **Sights:** Ramp front, square notch rear. **Features:** Double-action only, blue or matte stainless steel, integral key-lock, internal hammer. Introduced 2001. From Taurus International.
Price: From $398.00

TAURUS MODEL 651 PROTECTOR REVOLVER
Caliber: 357 Magnum, 5-shot. **Barrel:** 2". **Weight:** 17-24.5 oz. **Grips:** Rubber. **Sights:** Fixed. **Features:** Concealed single-action/double-action design. Shrouded cockable hammer, blue, matte stainless, Shadow Gray, Total Titanium, integral key-lock. Made in Brazil. Imported by Taurus International Manufacturing, Inc.
Price: From $398.00

TAURUS MODEL 817 ULTRA-LITE REVOLVER
Caliber: 38 Spec., 7-shot. **Barrel:** 2". **Weight:** 21 oz. **Length:** 6-1/2" overall. **Grips:** Soft rubber. **Sights:** Fixed. **Features:** Double-action, integral key-lock. Rated for +P ammo. Introduced 1999. Imported from Brazil by Taurus International.
Price: From $422.00

TAURUS MODEL 850CIA REVOLVER
Caliber: 38 Special, 5-shot. **Barrel:** 2". **Weight:** 17-24.5 oz. **Grips:** Rubber, mother-of-pearl. **Sights:** Ramp front, square notch rear. **Features:** Double-action only, blue or matte stainless steel, rated for +P ammo, integral key-lock, internal hammer. Introduced 2001. From Taurus International.
Price: From $398.00

TAURUS MODEL 941 REVOLVER
Caliber: 22 LR (Mod. 94), 22 WMR (Mod. 941), 8-shot. **Barrel:** 2", 4", 5". **Weight:** 27.5 oz. (4" barrel). **Grips:** Soft black rubber. **Sights:** Serrated ramp front, rear adjustable. **Features:** Double-action, integral key-lock. Introduced 1992. Imported by Taurus International.
Price: From $373.00

TAURUS MODEL 970/971 TRACKER REVOLVERS
Caliber: 22 LR (Model 970), 22 Magnum (Model 971); 7-shot. **Barrel:** 6". **Weight:** 53.6 oz. **Grips:** Rubber. **Sights:** Adjustable. **Features:** Double barrel, heavy barrel with ventilated rib; matte stainless finish, integral key-lock. Introduced 2001. From Taurus International.
Price: From $439.00

Both classic six-shooters and modern adaptations for hunting and sport.

Cimarron Lightning

Cimarron Model P
New Sheriff

Cimarron Bisley

Cimarron Model P Jr.

Cimarron USV

Cimarron Open Top

CHARLES DALY 1873 SINGLE-ACTION REVOLVER
Caliber: 357 Mag., 45 Colt, 6-shot. **Barrel:** 4.75", 5.5", 7.5". **Weight:** 36 oz. (4.75" barrel). **Length:** 10" overall (4.75" barrel). **Grips:** Hardwood with company logo near tang. **Sights:** Blade front, notch rear. **Features:** Stainless steel and color case hardened finishes. From K.B.I., Inc.
Price: 1873 Steel, 45 Colt, 4.75", 5.5", 7.5" barrel, brass frame . . **$449.00**
Price: 1873 Steel, 357 Mag, 4.75", 5.5", 7.5" barrel, brass frame . **$479.00**
Price: 1873 Steel, 45 Colt, 4.75", 5.5", 7.5" barrel, steel frame . **$449.00**
Price: 1873 Stainless Steel, 357 Mag, 4.75", 5.5", 7.5" barrel . . . **$659.00**
Price: 1873 Stainless Steel, 45 Colt, 4.75", 5.5", 7.5" barrel **$659.00**

CIMARRON LIGHTNING SA
Caliber: 32-20, 32 H&R, 38 Colt, 38 Special. **Barrel:** 3-1/2", 4-3/4", 5-1/2". **Grips:** Smooth or checkered walnut. **Sights:** Blade front. **Features:** Replica of the Colt 1877 Lightning DA. Similar to Cimarron Thunderer™, except smaller grip frame to fit smaller hands. Standard blue, charcoal blue or nickel finish with forged, old model, or color case hardened frame. Introduced 2001. From Cimarron F.A. Co.
Price: . . . . **$499.00 to $559.00**

CIMARRON MODEL P
Caliber: 32 WCF, 38 WCF, 357 Mag., 44 WCF, 44 Spec., 45 Colt, 45 LC and 45 ACP. **Barrel:** 4-3/4", 5-1/2", 7-1/2". **Weight:** 39 oz. **Length:** 10" overall (4" barrel). **Grips:** Walnut. **Sights:** Blade front, fixed or adjustable rear. **Features:** Uses "old model" black powder frame with "Bullseye" ejector or New Model frame. Imported by Cimarron F.A. Co.
Price: . . . . **$499.00 to $559.00**
Price: Laser Engraved **$843.70**
Price: New Sheriff . . . . **$499.00 to $559.00**

Cimarron Bisley Model Single-Action Revolvers
Similar to 1873 Model P, special grip frame and trigger guard, knurled wide-spur hammer, curved trigger. Available in 357 Mag., 44 WCF, 44 Spl., 45 Colt. Introduced 1999. Imported by Cimarron F.A. Co.
Price: **$525.00**

CIMARRON MODEL "P" JR.
Caliber: 32-20, 32 H&R, 38 Special. **Barrel:** 3-1/2", 4-3/4", 5-1/2". **Grips:** Checkered walnut. **Sights:** Blade front. **Features:** Styled after 1873 Colt Peacemaker, except 20 percent smaller. Blue finish with color case-hardened frame; Cowboy Comp® action. Introduced 2001. From Cimarron F.A. Co.
Price: . . . . **$489.00 to $529.00**

CIMARRON U. S. VOLUNTEER ARTILLERY MODEL SINGLE-ACTION
Caliber: 45 Colt. **Barrel:** 5-1/2". **Weight:** 39 oz. **Length:** 11-1/2" overall. **Grips:** Walnut. **Sights:** Fixed. **Features:** U.S. markings and cartouche, case-hardened frame and hammer; 45 Colt only. Imported by Cimarron F.A. Co.
Price: . . . . **$549.00 to $599.00**

CIMARRON 1872 OPEN TOP REVOLVER
Caliber: 38, 44 Special, 44 Colt, 44 Russian, 45LC, 45 S&W Schofield. **Barrel:** 5-1/2" and 7-1/2". **Grips:** Walnut. **Sights:** Blade front, fixed rear. **Features:** Replica of first cartridge-firing revolver. Blue, charcoal blue, nickel or Original® finish; Navy-style brass or steel Army-style frame. Introduced 2001 by Cimarron F.A. Co.
Price: . . . . **$529.00 to $599.00**

Cimarron Thunderer

Colt Single-Action Army

EAA Bounty Hunter

EMF Hartford

EMF 1894 Bisley

EMF Hartford Pinkerton

CIMARRON THUNDERER REVOLVER
Caliber: 357 Mag., 44 WCF, 44 Spl, 45 Colt, 6-shot. **Barrel:** 3-1/2", 4-3/4", 5-1/2", 7-1/2", with ejector. **Weight:** 38 oz. (3-1/2" barrel). **Grips:** Smooth or checkered walnut. **Sights:** Blade front, notch rear. **Features:** Thunderer grip; color case-hardened frame with balance blued. Introduced 1993. Imported by Cimarron F.A. Co.

Price: 3-1/2", 4-3/4", smooth grips	$519.00 to $549.00
Price: As above, checkered grips	$564.00 to $584.00
Price: 5-1/2", 7-1/2", smooth grips	$519.00 to $549.00
Price: As above, checkered grips	$564.00 to $584.00

COLT SINGLE-ACTION ARMY REVOLVER
Caliber: 357 Mag., 38 Special, .32/20, 44-40, 45 Colt, 6-shot. **Barrel:** 4-3/4", 5-1/2", 7-1/2". **Weight:** 40 oz. (4-3/4" barrel). **Length:** 10-1/4" overall (4-3/4" barrel). **Grips:** Black Eagle composite. **Sights:** Blade front, notch rear. **Features:** Available in full nickel finish with nickel grip medallions, or Royal Blue with color case-hardened frame. Reintroduced 1992.

Price: . . . . $1,290.00 to $1,490.00

EAA BOUNTY HUNTER SA REVOLVERS
Caliber: 22 LR/22 WMR, 357 Mag., 44 Mag., 45 Colt, 6-shot. **Barrel:** 4-1/2", 7-1/2". **Weight:** 2.5 lbs. **Length:** 11" overall (4-5/8" barrel). **Grips:** Smooth walnut. **Sights:** Blade front, grooved topstrap rear. **Features:** Transfer bar safety; 3-position hammer; hammer forged barrel. Introduced 1992. Imported by European American Armory.

Price: Blue or case-hardened	$369.00
Price: Nickel	$399.00
Price: 22LR/22WMR, blue	$269.00
Price: As above, nickel	$299.00

EMF MODEL 1873 FRONTIER MARSHAL
Caliber: 357 Mag., 45 Colt. **Barrel:** 4-3/4", 5-1/2, 7-1/2". **Weight:** 39 oz. **Length:** 10-1/2" overall. **Grips:** One-piece walnut. **Sights:** Blade front, notch rear. **Features:** Bright brass trigger guard and backstrap, color case-hardened frame, blued barrel and cylinder. Introduced 1998. Imported from Italy.

Price: $390.00

EMF HARTFORD SINGLE-ACTION REVOLVERS
Caliber: 357 Mag., 32-20, 38-40, 44-40, 44 Spec., 45 Colt. **Barrel:** 4-3/4", 5-1/2", 7-1/2". **Weight:** 45 oz. **Length:** 13" overall (7-1/2" barrel). **Grips:** Smooth walnut. **Sights:** Blade front, fixed rear. **Features:** Identical to the original Colts. All major parts serial numbered using original Colt-style lettering, numbering. Bullseye ejector head and color case-hardening on old model frame and hammer. Introduced 1990. Imported by E.M.F.

Price: Old Model	$450.00
Price: Cavalry or Artillery	$475.00
Price: Nickel plated, add	$200.00
Price: Case-hardened New Model frame	$450.00

EMF 1894 Bisley Revolver
Similar to the Hartford single-action revolver except has special grip frame and trigger guard, wide spur hammer; available in 45 Colt, 4-3/4", 5-1/2" or 7-1/2" barrel. Introduced 1995. Imported by E.M.F.

Price: Case-hardened/blue	$490.00
Price: Nickel, add	$200.00

EMF Hartford Pinkerton Single-Action Revolver
Same as the regular Hartford except has 4" barrel with ejector tube and bird's-head grip. Calibers: 357 Mag., 45 Colt. Introduced 1997. Imported by E.M.F.

Price: $450.00

EMF GWII Express Single-Action Revolver
Same as the regular model except uses grip of the Colt Lightning revolver. Barrel lengths of 4-3/4". Introduced 2006. Imported by E.M.F.

Price: Standard	$490.00
Price: Custom	$665.00

EMF 1875 Outlaw

EMF 1890 Police

Freedom Arms Model 83 Premier Grade

Freedom Arms Model 83 475 Linebaugh

Freedom Arms Model 83 Field Grade

Freedom Arms Model 97 Premier Grade

EMF 1875 OUTLAW REVOLVER
Caliber: 357 Mag., 44-40, 45 Colt. **Barrel:** 7-1/2", 9-1/2". **Weight:** 46 oz. **Length:** 13-1/2" overall. **Grips:** Smooth walnut. **Sights:** Blade front, fixed groove rear. **Features:** Authentic copy of 1875 Remington with firing pin in hammer; color case-hardened frame, blue cylinder, barrel, steel backstrap and trigger guard. Also available in nickel, factory engraved. Imported by E.M.F.
Price: All calibers **$450.00**
Price: Nickel **$650.00**
Price: Laser Engraved **$660.00**

EMF 1890 Police Revolver
Similar to the 1875 Outlaw except has 5-1/2" barrel, weighs 40 oz., with 12-1/2" overall length. Has lanyard ring in butt. No web under barrel. Calibers: 45 Colt. Imported by E.M.F.
Price: **$450.00**
Price: Nickel **$650.00**

EMF 1873 GREAT WESTERN II
Caliber: .357, 45LC, 44/40. **Barrel:** 4 3/4", 5-1/2", 7-1/2". **Weight:** 36 oz.. **Length:** 11" (5-1/2"). **Grips:** Walnut. **Sights:** Blade front, notch rear.
Features: Authentic reproduction of the original 2nd generation Colt single-action revolver. Standard and bone case hardening. Coil hammer spring. Hammer-forged barrel.
Price: 1873 Californian **$460.00**
Price: 1873 Custom series, bone or nickel, ivory-like grips **$650.00**
Price: 1873 Stainless steel, ivory-like grips **$640.00**

FREEDOM ARMS MODEL 83 PREMIER GRADE REVOLVER
Caliber: 357 Mag., 41 Mag., 44 Mag., 454 Casull, 475 Linebaugh, 500 Wyo. Exp., 5-shot. **Barrel:** 4-3/4", 6", 7-1/2", 9" (357 Mag. only), 10" (except 357 Mag. and 500 Wyo. Exp. **Weight:** 53 oz. (7-1/2" bbl. In 454 Casull). **Length:** 13" (7-1/2" bbl.). **Grips:** Impregnated hardwood. **Sights:** Adjustable rear with replaceable front sight. Fixed rear notch and front blade. **Features:** Stainless steel construction with brushed finish; manual sliding safety bar. Micarta grips optional. 500 Wyo. Exp. Introduced 2006. Lifetime warranty. Made in U.S.A. by Freedom Arms, Inc.
Price: 500 WE, 454 Casull, 475 Linebaugh, 454 Casull **$2,120.00**
Price: 454 Casull, fixed sight **$2,038.00**
Price: 357 Mag., 41 Mag., 44 Mag. **$2,035.00**

FREEDOM ARMS MODEL 83 FIELD GRADE REVOLVER
Caliber: 22 LR, 357 Mag., 41 Mag., 44 Mag., 454 Casull, 475 Linebaugh, 500 Wyo. Exp., 5-shot. **Barrel:** 4-3/4", 6", 7-1/2", 9" (357 Mag. only), 10"

(except 357 Mag. and 500 Wyo. Exp.) **Weight:** 56 oz. (7-1/2" bbl. In 454 Casull). **Length:** 13.1" (7-1/2" bbl.). **Grips:** Pachmayr standard, impregnated hardwood or Micarta optional. **Sights:** Adjustable rear with replaceable front sight. Model 83 frame. All stainless steel. Introduced 1988. Made in U.S.A. by Freedom Arms Inc.
Price: 454 Casull, 475 Linebaugh, 500 WE adj. sights **$1,639.00**
Price: 357 Mag., 41 Mag., 44 Mag. **$1,573.00**
Price: 22 LR with match chambers and 10" barrel **$1,803.00**

FREEDOM ARMS MODEL 97 PREMIER GRADE REVOLVER
Caliber: 17HMR, 22 LR, 32 H&R, 357 Mag., 6-shot; 41 Mag., 44 Special, 45 Colt, 5-shot. **Barrel:** 4-1/4", 5-1/2", 7-1/2", 10" (17 HMR, 22LR & 32 H&R). **Weight:** 40 oz. (5-1/2" 357 Mag.). **Length:** 10-3/4" (5-1/2" bbl.). **Grips:** Impregnated hardwood; Micarta optional. **Sights:** Adjustable rear, replaceable blade front. Fixed rear notch and front blade. **Features:** Stainless steel construction, brushed finish, automatic transfer bar safety system. Introduced in 1997. Lifetime warranty. Made in U.S.A. by Freedom Arms.
Price: Centerfire cartridges, adjustable sights **$1,718.00**
Price: Rimfire cartridges **$1,784.00**
Price: 32 H&R, 357 Mag., 6-shot; 45 Colt, fixed sights **$1,624.00**
Price: Extra fitted cylinders, centerfire, 22 WMR, 17 Mach II **$272.00**
Price: Extra fitted 22 LR match grade cylinder **$404.00**
Price: 22 LR match cylinder in place of 22 LR sporting cylinde . . **$132.00**
Price: 357 Mag., 45 Colt, fixed sight **$1,576.00**
Price: Extra fitted cylinders 38 Special, 45 ACP **$264.00**
Price: 22 LR with sporting chambers **$1,732.00**
Price: Extra fitted 22 WMR cylinder **$264.00**
Price: Extra fitted 22 LR match grade cylinder **$476.00**
Price: 22 match grade chamber instead of 22 LR sport chamber . **$214.00**

Heritage Rough Rider

Navy Arms Bisley

Magnum Research Long Cylinder BFR

Navy Arms 1873

Navy Arms 1873 Gunfighter SA

Navy Arms 1875 Schofield

HERITAGE ROUGH RIDER REVOLVER
Caliber: 17HMR, 17LR, 32 H&R, 32 S&W, 32 S&W Long, 357 Mag, 44-40, 45 LC, 22 LR, 22 LR/22 WMR combo, 6-shot. **Barrel:** 2-3/4", 3-1/2", 4-3/4", 5-1/2", 6-1/2", 7-1/2", 9". **Weight:** 31 to 38 oz. **Length:** NA. **Grips:** Exotic cocobolo laminated wood or mother-of-pearl; bird's-head models offered. **Sights:** Blade front, fixed rear. Adjustable sight on 4", 6" and 9" models. **Features:** Hammer block safety. Transfer bar with Big Bores. High polish blue, black satin, silver satin, case-hardened and stainless finish. Introduced 1993. Made in U.S.A. by Heritage Mfg., Inc.
Price: . . . . **$159.95 to $499.95**

MAGNUM RESEARCH BFR SINGLE-ACTION REVOLVER
(Long cylinder) Caliber: 30/30, 45/70 Government, 444 Marlin, 460 S&W, 45 LC/410, 450 Marlin, .500 S&W. **Barrel:** 7.5", 10". **Weight:** 4 lbs., 4.36 lbs. **Length:** 15", 17.5".
(Short cylinder) Caliber: 50AE, 454 Casull, 22 Hornet, BFR 480/475. **Barrel:** 6.5", 7.5", 10". **Weight:** 3.2 lbs, 3.5 lbs., 4.36 lbs. (10"). **Length:** 12.75 (6"), 13.75", 16.25".
Sights: All have fully adjustable rear, black blade ramp front. **Features:** Stainless steel construction, rubber grips, all 5-shot capacity. Barrels are stress-relieved and cut rifled. Made in U.S.A. From Magnum Research, Inc.
Price: **$899.00**

NAVY ARMS BISLEY MODEL SINGLE-ACTION REVOLVER
Caliber: 44-40 or 45 Colt, 6-shot cylinder. **Barrel:** 4-3/4", 5-1/2", 7-1/2". **Weight:** 40 oz. **Length:** 12-1/2" overall (7-1/2" barrel). **Grips:** Smooth walnut. **Sights:** Blade front, notch rear. **Features:** Replica of Colt's Bisley

Model. Polished blue finish, color case-hardened frame. Introduced 1997. Imported by Navy Arms.
Price: **$511.00**

NAVY ARMS 1873 GUNFIGHTER SINGLE-ACTION REVOLVER
Caliber: 357 Mag., 44-40, 45 Colt, 6-shot cylinder. **Barrel:** 4-3/4", 5-1/2", 7-1/2". **Weight:** 37 oz. **Length:** 10-1/4" overall (4-3/4" barrel). **Grips:** Checkered black polymer. **Sights:** Blade front, notch rear. **Features:** Blued with color case-hardened receiver, trigger and hammer; German Silver backstrap and triggerguard. American made Wolff trigger and mainsprings installed. Introduced 2005. Imported by Navy Arms.
Price: **$511.00**
Price: Stainless steel **$608.00**

NAVY ARMS 1875 SCHOFIELD REVOLVER
Caliber: 44-40, 45 Colt, 6-shot cylinder. **Barrel:** 3-1/2", 5", 7". **Weight:** 39 oz. **Length:** 10-3/4" overall (5" barrel). **Grips:** Smooth walnut. **Sights:** Blade front, notch rear. **Features:** Replica of Smith & Wesson Model 3 Schofield. Single-action, top-break with automatic ejection. Polished blue finish. Introduced 1994. Imported by Navy Arms.
Price: Hideout Model, 3-1/2" barrel **$849.00**
Price: Wells Fargo, 5" barrel **$849.00**
Price: U.S. Cavalry model, 7" barrel, military markings **$849.00**

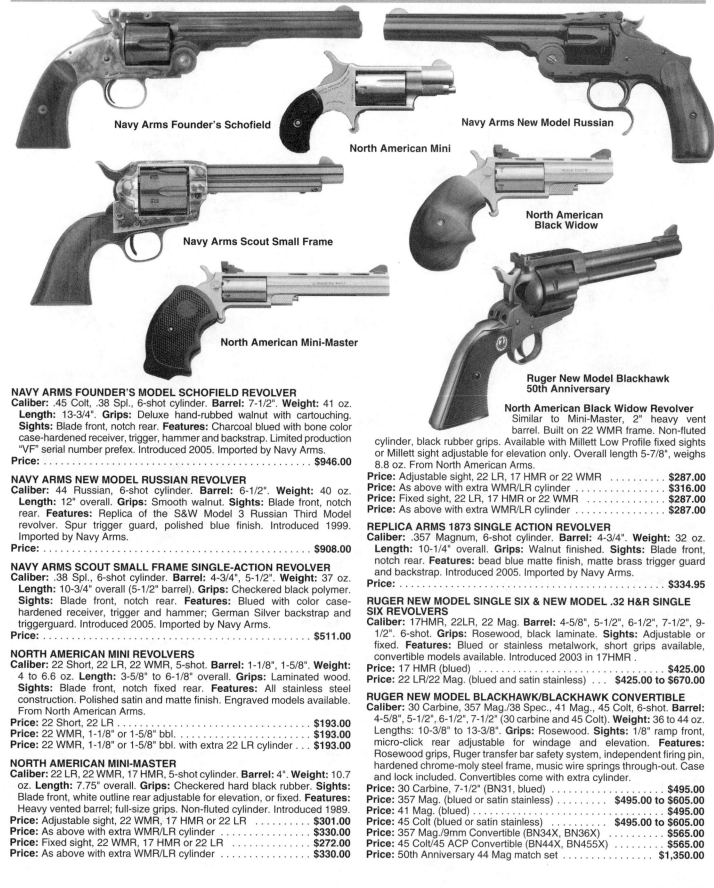

Navy Arms Founder's Schofield

North American Mini

Navy Arms New Model Russian

Navy Arms Scout Small Frame

North American Black Widow

North American Mini-Master

Ruger New Model Blackhawk 50th Anniversary

NAVY ARMS FOUNDER'S MODEL SCHOFIELD REVOLVER
Caliber: .45 Colt, .38 Spl., 6-shot cylinder. **Barrel:** 7-1/2". **Weight:** 41 oz. **Length:** 13-3/4". **Grips:** Deluxe hand-rubbed walnut with cartouching. **Sights:** Blade front, notch rear. **Features:** Charcoal blued with bone color case-hardened receiver, trigger, hammer and backstrap. Limited production "VF" serial number prefex. Introduced 2005. Imported by Navy Arms.
Price: **$946.00**

NAVY ARMS NEW MODEL RUSSIAN REVOLVER
Caliber: 44 Russian, 6-shot cylinder. **Barrel:** 6-1/2". **Weight:** 40 oz. **Length:** 12" overall. **Grips:** Smooth walnut. **Sights:** Blade front, notch rear. **Features:** Replica of the S&W Model 3 Russian Third Model revolver. Spur trigger guard, polished blue finish. Introduced 1999. Imported by Navy Arms.
Price: . . . . — **$908.00**

NAVY ARMS SCOUT SMALL FRAME SINGLE-ACTION REVOLVER
Caliber: .38 Spl., 6-shot cylinder. **Barrel:** 4-3/4", 5-1/2". **Weight:** 37 oz. **Length:** 10-3/4" overall (5-1/2" barrel). **Grips:** Checkered black polymer. **Sights:** Blade front, notch rear. **Features:** Blued with color case-hardened receiver, trigger and hammer; German Silver backstrap and triggerguard. Introduced 2005. Imported by Navy Arms.
Price: **$511.00**

NORTH AMERICAN MINI REVOLVERS
Caliber: 22 Short, 22 LR, 22 WMR, 5-shot. **Barrel:** 1-1/8", 1-5/8". **Weight:** 4 to 6.6 oz. **Length:** 3-5/8" to 6-1/8" overall. **Grips:** Laminated wood. **Sights:** Blade front, notch fixed rear. **Features:** All stainless steel construction. Polished satin and matte finish. Engraved models available. From North American Arms.
Price: 22 Short, 22 LR **$193.00**
Price: 22 WMR, 1-1/8" or 1-5/8" bbl. **$193.00**
Price: 22 WMR, 1-1/8" or 1-5/8" bbl. with extra 22 LR cylinder . . . **$193.00**

NORTH AMERICAN MINI-MASTER
Caliber: 22 LR, 22 WMR, 17 HMR, 5-shot cylinder. **Barrel:** 4". **Weight:** 10.7 oz. **Length:** 7.75" overall. **Grips:** Checkered hard black rubber. **Sights:** Blade front, white outline rear adjustable for elevation, or fixed. **Features:** Heavy vented barrel; full-size grips. Non-fluted cylinder. Introduced 1989.
Price: Adjustable sight, 22 WMR, 17 HMR or 22 LR **$301.00**
Price: As above with extra WMR/LR cylinder **$330.00**
Price: Fixed sight, 22 WMR, 17 HMR or 22 LR **$272.00**
Price: As above with extra WMR/LR cylinder **$330.00**

North American Black Widow Revolver
Similar to Mini-Master, 2" heavy vent barrel. Built on 22 WMR frame. Non-fluted cylinder, black rubber grips. Available with Millett Low Profile fixed sights or Millett sight adjustable for elevation only. Overall length 5-7/8", weighs 8.8 oz. From North American Arms.
Price: Adjustable sight, 22 LR, 17 HMR or 22 WMR **$287.00**
Price: As above with extra WMR/LR cylinder **$316.00**
Price: Fixed sight, 22 LR, 17 HMR or 22 WMR **$287.00**
Price: As above with extra WMR/LR cylinder **$287.00**

REPLICA ARMS 1873 SINGLE ACTION REVOLVER
Caliber: .357 Magnum, 6-shot cylinder. **Barrel:** 4-3/4". **Weight:** 32 oz. **Length:** 10-1/4" overall. **Grips:** Walnut finished. **Sights:** Blade front, notch rear. **Features:** bead blue matte finish, matte brass trigger guard and backstrap. Introduced 2005. Imported by Navy Arms.
Price: **$334.95**

RUGER NEW MODEL SINGLE SIX & NEW MODEL .32 H&R SINGLE SIX REVOLVERS
Caliber: 17HMR, 22LR, 22 Mag. **Barrel:** 4-5/8", 5-1/2", 6-1/2", 7-1/2", 9-1/2". 6-shot. **Grips:** Rosewood, black laminate. **Sights:** Adjustable or fixed. **Features:** Blued or stainless metalwork, short grips available, convertible models available. Introduced 2003 in 17HMR .
Price: 17 HMR (blued) **$425.00**
Price: 22 LR/22 Mag. (blued and satin stainless) . . . **$425.00 to $670.00**

RUGER NEW MODEL BLACKHAWK/BLACKHAWK CONVERTIBLE
Caliber: 30 Carbine, 357 Mag./38 Spec., 41 Mag., 45 Colt, 6-shot. **Barrel:** 4-5/8", 5-1/2", 6-1/2", 7-1/2" (30 carbine and 45 Colt). **Weight:** 36 to 44 oz. Lengths: 10-3/8" to 13-3/8". **Grips:** Rosewood. **Sights:** 1/8" ramp front, micro-click rear adjustable for windage and elevation. **Features:** Rosewood grips, Ruger transfer bar safety system, independent firing pin, hardened chrome-moly steel frame, music wire springs through-out. Case and lock included. Convertibles come with extra cylinder.
Price: 30 Carbine, 7-1/2" (BN31, blued) **$495.00**
Price: 357 Mag. (blued or satin stainless) . . . . **$495.00 to $605.00**
Price: 41 Mag. (blued) **$495.00**
Price: 45 Colt (blued or satin stainless) . . . . **$495.00 to $605.00**
Price: 357 Mag./9mm Convertible (BN34X, BN36X) **$565.00**
Price: 45 Colt/45 ACP Convertible (BN44X, BN455X) **$565.00**
Price: 50th Anniversary 44 Mag match set **$1,350.00**

Ruger Bisley Single-Action

Ruger New Model Blackhawk

Ruger Super Blackhawk Hunter

Ruger New Vaquero

Ruger New Bearcat

Taurus Gaucho 357

Taurus Gaucho 45

Ruger Bisley Single-Action Revolver

Similar to standard Blackhawk, hammer is lower with smoothly curved, deeply checkered wide spur. The trigger is strongly curved with wide smooth surface. Longer grip frame. Adjustable rear sight, ramp-style front. Unfluted cylinder and roll engraving, adjustable sights. Chambered for 44 Mag. and 45 Colt; 7-1/2" barrel; overall length 13-1/2"; weighs 48-51 oz. Plastic lockable case. Orig. fluted cylinder introduced 1985; discontinued 1991. Unfluted cylinder introduced 1986.
Price: RB-44W (44 Mag), RB45W (45 Colt) **$625.00**

RUGER NEW MODEL SUPER BLACKHAWK

Caliber: 44 Mag., 6-shot. Also fires 44 Spec. **Barrel:** 4-5/8", 5-1/2", 7-1/2", 10-1/2" bull. **Weight:** 45-55 oz. **Length:** 10.5" to 16.5" overall. **Grips:** Rosewood. **Sights:** 1/8" ramp front, micro-click rear adjustable for windage and elevation. **Features:** Ruger transfer bar safety system, fluted or unfluted cylinder, steel grip and cylinder frame, round or square back trigger guard, wide serrated trigger, wide spur hammer. With case and lock.
Price: Blue, 4-5/8", 5-1/2", 7-1/2" (S458N, S45N, S47N) **$595.00**
Price: Blue, 10-1/2" bull barrel (S411N) **$605.00**
Price: Stainless, 4-5/8", 5-1/2", 7-1/2" (KS458N, KS45N, KS47N) **$610.00**
Price: Stainless, 10-1/2" bull barrel (KS411N) **$635.00**

RUGER NEW MODEL SUPER BLACKHAWK HUNTER

Caliber: 44 Mag., 6-shot. **Barrel:** 7-1/2", full-length solid rib, unfluted cylinder. **Weight:** 52 oz. **Length:** 13-5/8". **Grips:** Black laminated wood. **Sights:** Adjustable rear, replaceable front blade. **Features:** Reintroduced Ultimate SA revolver. Includes instruction manual, high-impact case, set 1" medium scope rings, gun lock, ejector rod as standard.
Price: **$715.00**
Price: Hunter model, satin stainless, 7-1/2" (KS47NHNN) **$715.00**
Price: Hunter model, Bisley frame, satin stainless 7-1/2"
(KS47NHB) **$715.00**

RUGER NEW VAQUERO SINGLE-ACTION REVOLVER

Caliber: 357 Mag., 45 Colt, 6-shot. **Barrel:** 4-5/8", 5-1/2", 7-1/2". **Weight:** 39-45 oz. **Length:** 10-1/2" overall (4-5/8" barrel). **Grips:** Rubber with

Ruger medallion. **Sights:** Blade front, fixed notch rear. **Features:** Transfer bar safety system and loading gate interlock. Blued model color case-hardened finish on frame, rest polished and blued. Engraved model available. Gloss stainless. Introduced 2005.
Price: 357 Mag., blued or stainless **$609.00**
Price: 45 Colt, blued or stainless **$609.00**

RUGER NEW BEARCAT SINGLE-ACTION

Caliber: 22 LR, 6-shot. **Barrel:** 4". **Weight:** 24 oz. **Length:** 9" overall. **Grips:** Smooth rosewood with Ruger medallion. **Sights:** Blade front, fixed notch rear. **Features:** Reintroduction of the Ruger Bearcat with slightly lengthened frame, Ruger transfer bar safety system. Available in blue only. Rosewood grips. Introduced 1996 (blued), 2003 (stainless). With case and lock.
Price: SBC4, blued **$425.00**
Price: KSBC-4, satin stainless **$480.00**

TAURUS SINGLE-ACTION GAUCHO REVOLVERS

Caliber: 38 Spl, 357 Mag, 44-40, 45 Colt, 6-shot. **Barrel:** 4.75", 5.5", 7.5", 12". **Weight:** 36.7-37.7 oz. **Length:** 13". **Grips:** Checkered black polymer. **Sights:** Blade front, fixed notch rear. Integral transfer bar; blue, blue with case hardened frame, matte stainless and the hand polished "Sundance" stainless finish. Removable cylinder, half-cock notch. Introduced 2005. Imported from Brazil by Taurus International.
Price: S/A-357-B, 357 Mag., Sundance blue finish, 5.5" barrel . . **$520.00**
Price: S/A-357-S/S7, 357 Mag., polished stainless, 7.5" barrel . . **$536.00**
Price: S/A-45-B **$52.00**

Tristar Regulator

Uberti 1873 Cattleman

Uberti 1870 Schofield

Uberti Bisley

Uberti 1875 Outlaw

TRISTAR/UBERTI REGULATOR REVOLVER
Caliber: 45 Colt. **Barrel:** 4-3/4", 5.5". **Weight:** 32-38 oz. **Length:** 8-1/4" overall (4-3/4" bbl.) **Grips:** One-piece walnut. **Sights:** Blade front, notch rear. **Features:** Uberti replica of 1873 Colt Model "P" revolver. Color-case hardened steel frame, brass backstrap and trigger guard, hammer-block safety. Imported from Italy by Tristar Sporting Arms.
Price: Regulator **$455.00**
Price: Regulator Deluxe (blued backstrap, trigger guard) **$489.00**
Price: Stallion (.17 HMR and .17 M2 Cylinders) **$459.00**

UBERTI 1858 NEW ARMY CONVERSION REVOLVER
Caliber: 45 Colt, 6-shot engraved cylinlder. **Barrel:** 8" **Weight:** 2.6 lbs. **Length:** 13.8". **Grips:** One-piece walnut. **Sights:** Blade front, groove rear. **Features:** Brass backstrap, trigger guard; color case-hardened frame, blued barrel, cylinder. Introduced 2007. Imported from Italy by Uberti U.S.A.
Price: **$450.00**

UBERTI 1851-1860 CONVERSION REVOLVERS
Caliber: 38 Sp., 45 Colt, 6-shot engraved cylinlder. **Barrel:** 4-3/4", 5-1/2", 7-1/2", 8" **Weight:** 2.6 lbs. (5-1/2" bbl.). **Length:** 13" overall (5-1/2" bbl.). **Grips:** Walnut. **Features:** Brass backstrap, trigger guard; color case-hardened frame, blued barrel, cylinder. Introduced 2007. Imported from Italy by Uberti U.S.A.
Price: 1851 Navy, 38 Special **$435.00**
Price:1860 Army, 45 Colt **$485.00**

UBERTI 1871-1872 OPEN TOP REVOLVERS
Caliber: 38 Sp., 45 Colt, 6-shot engraved cylinlder. **Barrel:** 4-3/4", 5-1/2", 7-1/2". **Weight:** 2.6 lbs. (5-1/2" bbl.). **Length:** 13" overall (5-1/2" bbl.). **Grips:** Walnut. **Features:** Blued backstrap, trigger guard; color case-hardened frame, blued barrel, cylinder. Introduced 2007. Imported from Italy by Uberti U.S.A.
Price: 1872 Open Top **$445.00**
Price: 1871 Open Top **$415.00**

UBERTI 1873 CATTLEMAN SINGLE-ACTION
Caliber: 45 Colt; 6-shot fluted cylinder **Barrel:** 4-3/4", 5-1/2", 7-1/2". **Weight:** 2.3 lbs. (5-1/2" bbl.). **Length:** 11" overall (5-1/2" bbl.). **Grips:** Styles: Frisco (pearl styled); Desperado (buffalo horn styled); Chisholm (checkered walnut); Gunfighter (black checkered), Cody (ivory styled), one-piece walnut. **Sights:** Blade front, groove rear. **Features:** Steel or brass backstrap, trigger guard; color case-hardened frame, blued barrel, cylinder. NM designates New Model plunger style frame; OM designates Old Model screw cylinder pin retainer. Imported from Italy by Uberti U.S.A.
Price: 1873 Cattleman Frisco **$650.00**

Price: 1873 Cattleman Desperado (2006) **$650.00**
Price: 1873 Cattleman Chisholm (2006) **$390.00**
Price: 1873 Cattleman NM, blued 4-3/4" barrel **$400.00**
Price: 1873 Cattleman NM, stainless steel 7-1/2" barrel **$535.00**
Price: 1873 Cattleman OM, Old West finish, 5-1/2" barrel **$535.00**
Price: 1873 Cattleman NM, Nickel finish, 7-1/2" barrel **$555.00**

UBERTI 1873 CATTLEMAN BIRD'S HEAD SINGLE ACTION
Caliber: 357 Mag., 45 Colt; 6-shot fluted cylinder **Barrel:** 3-1/2", 4", 4-3/4", 5-1/2". **Weight:** 2.3 lbs. (5-1/2" bbl.). **Length:** 10.9" overall (5-1/2" bbl.). **Grips:** One-piece walnut. **Sights:** Blade front, groove rear. **Features:** Steel or brass backstrap, trigger guard; color case-hardened frame, blued barrel, cylinder. Imported from Italy by Uberti U.S.A.
Price: 1873 Cattleman Bird's Head OM 3-1/2" barrel **$500.00**

UBERTI 1873 BUNTLINE AND REVOLVER CARBINE SINGLE ACTION
Caliber: 357 Mag., 44-40, 45 Colt; 6-shot fluted cylinder **Barrel:** 18". **Length:** 22.9" to 34". **Grips:** Walnut pistol grip or rifle stock. **Sights:** Fixed or adjustable. **Features:** Imported from Italy by Uberti U.S.A.
Price: 1873 Revolver Carbine, 18" barrel, 34" OAL **$585.00**
Price: 1873 Catttleman Buntline Target, 18" barrel, 22.9" OAL . . **$520.00**

UBERTI OUTLAW, FRONTIER, AND POLICE REVOLVERS
Caliber: 45 Colt, 6-shot fluted cylinder. **Barrel:** 5-1/2", 7-1/2". **Weight:** 2.5 to 2.8 lbs. **Length:** 10.8" to 13.6" overall. **Grips:** Two-piece smooth walnut. **Sights:** Blade front, notch rear. **Features:** Cartridge version of 1858 Remington percussion revolver. Nickel and blued finishes. Imported by Uberti U.S.A.
Price: 1875 Outlaw nickel finish **$515.00**
Price: 1875 Frontier, blued finish **$435.00**
Price: 1890 Police, blued finish **$440.00**

U.S. Fire Arms Single Action Army Revolver

U.S. Fire Arms Single Action Flattop Target

U.S. Fire Arms Single Action Omni-Potent

U.S. Fire Arms Single Action Bisley

U.S. Fire Arms Rodeo Cowboy Action

U.S. Firearms United States Pre-War

UBERTI 1870 SCHOFIELD-STYLE BREAK-TOP REVOLVER
Caliber: 38, 44 Russian, 44-40, 45 Colt, 6-shot cylinder. **Barrel:** 3-1/2", 5", 7". **Weight:** 2.4 lbs. (5" barrel) **Length:** 10.8" overall (5" barrel). **Grips:** Two-piece smooth walnut or pearl. **Sights:** Blade front, notch rear. **Features:** Replica of Smith & Wesson Model 3 Schofield. Single-action, top-break with automatic ejection. Polished blue finish (first model). Introduced 1994. Imported by Uberti U.S.A.
Price: No. 3-2nd Model, nickel finish $975.00

UBERTI BISLEY AND STALLION MODELS SINGLE-ACTION REVOLVERS
Caliber: 357 Mag., 45 Colt (Bisley); 22LR and 38 Special (Stallion), both with 6-shot fluted cylinder. **Barrel:** 4-3/4", 5-1/2", 7-1/2". **Weight:** 2 to 2.5 lbs. **Length:** 12.7" overall (7-1/2" barrel). **Grips:** Two-piece walnut. **Sights:** Blade front, notch rear. **Features:** Replica of Colt's Bisley Model. Polished blue finish, color case-hardened frame. Introduced 1997. Imported by Uberti U.S.A.
Price: 1873 Stallion, 5-1/2" barrel $425.00
Price: 1873 Bisley, 7-1/2" barrel $500.00

U.S. FIRE ARMS SINGLE-ACTION REVOLVER
Caliber: 45 Colt (standard); 32 WCF, 38 WCF, 38 Special, 44 WCF, 44 Special, 6-shot cylinder. **Barrel:** 4-3/4", 5-1/2", 7-1/2". **Weight:** 37 oz. **Length:** NA. **Grips:** Hard rubber. **Sights:** Blade front, notch rear. **Features:** Recreation of original guns; 3" and 4" have no ejector. Available with all-blue, blue with color case-hardening, or full nickel-plate finish. Other models include Government Inspector Series ($1,485, walnut grips), Custer Battlefield Gun ($1,485, 7-1/2" barrel), Patriot Series ($1,280, lanyard loop in 30 Carbine), Flattop Target ($1,495), Sheriff's Model ($1,085, with barrel lengths starting at 2"), Snubnose ($1,295, barrel lengths 2", 3", 4"), Omni-Potent Six-Shooter and Omni-Target Six-Shooter (from $1,485), Bisley and Bisley Target (from $1,485, introduced 2006). Made in U.S.A. by United States Fire Arms Mfg. Co.
Price: Blue/cased-colors $1,085.00
Price: Nickel $1,485.00

U.S. FIRE ARMS RODEO COWBOY ACTION REVOLVER
Caliber: 45 Colt, 38 Special. **Barrel:** 4-3/4", 5-1/2". **Grips:** Rubber. **Features:** Historically correct Armory bone case hammer, blue satin finish, transfer bar safety system, correct solid firing pin. Entry level basic cowboy SASS gun. Other models include Cowboy ($945) and Gunslinger ($1,045). 2006 version includes brown-rubber stocks.
Price: $649.00

U.S. FIRE ARMS U.S. PRE-WAR
Caliber: 45 Colt (standard); 32 WCF, 38 WCF, 38 Special, 44 WCF, 44 Special. **Barrel:** 4-3/4", 5-1/2", 7-1/2". **Grips:** Hard rubber. **Features:** Armory bone case/Armory blue finish standard, cross-pin or black powder frame. Introduced 2002. Made in U.S.A. by United States Firearms Mfg. Co.
Price: $1,345.00

Specially adapted single-shot and multi-barrel arms.

Bond Arms Texas Defender

Bond Arms Century 2000 Defender

Bond Arms Cowboy Defender

Bond Arms Snake Slayer IV

Cobra Big Bore

Cobra Standard Derringer

Charter Arms Dixie Derringer

ANSCHUTZ MODEL 64P SPORT/TARGET PISTOL
Caliber: 22 LR, 22 WMR, 5-shot magazine. **Barrel:** 10". **Weight:** 3 lbs. 8 oz. **Length:** 18-1/2" overall. Stock: Choate Rynite. **Sights:** None furnished; grooved for scope mounting. **Features:** Right-hand bolt; polished blue finish. Introduced 1998. Imported from Germany by AcuSport.
Price: 22 LR **$455.95**
Price: 22 WMR **$479.95**

BOND ARMS TEXAS DEFENDER DERRINGER
Caliber: From 22 LR to 45 LC/410 shotshells. **Barrel:** 3". **Weight:** 20 oz. **Length:** 5". **Grips:** Rosewood. **Sights:** Blade front, fixed rear. **Features:** Interchangeable barrels, stainless steel firing pins, cross-bolt safety, automatic extractor for rimmed calibers. Stainless steel construction, brushed finish. Right or left hand.
Price: **$389.00**
Price: Interchangeable barrels, 22 LR thru 45 LC, 3" **$139.00**
Price: Interchangeable barrels, 45 LC, 3.5" **$159.00**

BOND ARMS CENTURY 2000 DEFENDER
Caliber: 45LC/410 shotshells. **Barrel:** 3.5". **Weight:** 21 oz. **Length:** 5.5". **Features:** Similar to Defender series.
Price: **$404.00**

BOND ARMS COWBOY DEFENDER
Caliber: From 22 LR to 45 LC/410 shotshells. **Barrel:** 3". **Weight:** 19 oz. **Length:** 5.5". **Features:** Similar to Defender series. No trigger guard.
Price: **$389.00**

BOND ARMS SNAKE SLAYER
Caliber: 45 LC/410 shotshell (2-1/2" or 3"). **Barrel:** 3.5". **Weight:** 21 oz. **Length:** 5.5". **Grips:** Extended rosewood. **Sights:** Blade front, fixed rear. **Features:** Single-action; interchangeable barrels; stainless steel firing pin. Introduced 2005.
Price: **$455.00**

BOND ARMS SNAKE SLAYER IV
Caliber: 45 LC/410 shotshell (2-1/2" or 3"). **Barrel:** 4.25". **Weight:** 22 oz. **Length:** 6.25". **Grips:** Extended rosewood. **Sights:** Blade front, fixed rear. **Features:** Single-action; interchangeable barrels; stainless steel firing pin. Introduced 2006.
Price: **$485.00**

BROWN CLASSIC SINGLE-SHOT PISTOL
Caliber: 17 Ackley Hornet through 375x444. **Barrel:** 15" air-gauged match grade. **Weight:** About 3 lbs. 7 oz. **Grips:** Walnut; thumb rest target-style. **Sights:** None furnished; drilled and tapped for scope mounting. **Features:**

Falling block action gives rigid barrel-receiver mating; hand fitted and headspaced. Introduced 1998. Made in U.S.A. by E.A. Brown Mfg.
Price: **$589.00**

CHARTER ARMS DIXIE DERRINGERS
Caliber: 22 LR, 22 WMR. **Barrel:** 1.125". **Weight:** 5-6 oz. **Length:** 4" overall. **Grips:** Black polymer **Sights:** Blade front, fixed notch rear. **Features:** Stainless finish. Introduced 2006. Made in U.S.A. by Charter Arms, distributed by MKS Supply.
Price: **$112.00**

COBRA BIG BORE DERRINGERS
Caliber: 22 WMR, 32 H&R Mag., 38 Spec., 9mm, 380 ACP. **Barrel:** 2.75". **Weight:** 14 oz. **Length:** 4.65" overall. **Grips:** Textured black synthetic or laminated rosewood. **Sights:** Blade front, fixed notch rear. **Features:** Alloy frame, steel-lined barrels, steel breech block. Plunger-type safety with integral hammer block. Black, chrome or satin finish. Introduced 2002. Made in U.S.A. by Cobra Enterprises of Utah, Inc.
Price: **$160.00**

COBRA LONG-BORE DERRINGERS
Caliber: 22 WMR, 38 Spec., 9mm. **Barrel:** 3.5". **Weight:** 16 oz. **Length:** 5.4" overall. **Grips:** Black synthetic or rosewood. **Sights:** Fixed. **Features:** Chrome, satin nickel, or black Teflon finish. Introduced 2002. Made in U.S.A. by Cobra Enterprises of Utah, Inc.
Price: **$160.00**

COBRA STANDARD SERIES DERRINGERS
Caliber: 22 LR, 22 WMR, 25 ACP, 32 ACP. **Barrel:** 2.4". **Weight:** 9.5 oz. **Length:** 4" overall. **Grips:** Laminated wood or pearl. **Sights:** Blade front, fixed notch rear. **Features:** Choice of black powder coat, satin nickel or chrome finish. Introduced 2002. Made in U.S.A. by Cobra Enterprises of Utah, Inc.
Price: **$140.00**

COMANCHE SUPER SINGLE-SHOT PISTOL
Caliber: 45 LC, 410 ga. **Barrel:** 10". **Sights:** Adjustable. **Features:** Blue finish, not available for sale in CA, MA. Distributed by SGS Importers International, Inc.
Price: **$183.95**
Price: Satin nickel **$199.95**
Price: Camo, intr. 2006 . . . . **$216.95**

DOWNSIZER WSP SINGLE-SHOT PISTOL
Caliber: 357 Magnum, 45 ACP, 38 Special. **Barrel:** 2.10". **Weight:** 11 oz. **Length:** 3.25" overall. **Grips:** Black polymer. **Sights:** None. **Features:** Single shot, tip-up barrel. Double action only. Stainless steel construction. Measures .900" thick. Introduced 1997. From Downsizer Corp.
Price: **$499.00**

Downsizer WSP Single Shot

Comanche Super Single Shot

Maximum Single Shot

RPM XL Pistol

Thompson/Center Encore

Thompson/Center G2 Contender

GAUCHER GN1 SILHOUETTE PISTOL
Caliber: 22 LR, single shot. **Barrel:** 10". **Weight:** 2.4 lbs.
Length: 15.5" overall. **Grips:** European hardwood.
Sights: Blade front, open adjustable rear. **Features:** Bolt
action, adjustable trigger. Introduced 1990. Imported
from France by Mandall Shooting Supplies.
Price: About $525.00
Price: Model GP Silhouette $425.00

MAXIMUM SINGLE-SHOT PISTOL
Caliber: 22 LR, 22 Hornet, 22 BR, 22 PPC, 223 Rem., 22-250, 6mm BR,
6mm PPC, 243, 250 Savage, 6.5mm-35M, 270 MAX, 270 Win., 7mm
TCU, 7mm BR, 7mm-35, 7mm INT-R, 7mm-08, 7mm Rocket, 7mm Super-
Mag., 30 Herrett, 30 Carbine, 30-30, 308 Win., 30x39, 32-20, 350 Rem.
Mag., 357 Mag., 357 Maximum, 358 Win., 375 H&H, 44 Mag., 454 Casull.
Barrel: 8-3/4", 10-1/2", 14". **Weight:** 61 oz. (10-1/2" bbl.); 78 oz. (14" bbl.).
Length: 15", 18-1/2" overall (with 10-1/2" and 14" bbl., respectively).
Grips: Smooth walnut stocks and forend. Also available with 17" finger
groove grip. **Sights:** Ramp front, fully adjustable open rear. **Features:**
Falling block action; drilled and tapped for M.O.A. scope mounts; integral
grip frame/receiver; adjustable trigger; Douglas barrel (interchangeable).
Introduced 1983. Made in U.S.A. by M.O.A. Corp.
Price: Stainless receiver, blue barrel $799.00
Price: Stainless receiver, stainless barrel $883.00
Price: Extra blued barrel $254.00
Price: Extra stainless barrel $317.00
Price: Scope mount $60.00

RPM XL SINGLE SHOT PISTOL
Caliber: 22 LR through 45-70. **Barrel:** 8", 10-3/4", 12", 14". **Weight:** About
60 oz. **Grips:** Smooth Goncalo Alves with thumb and heel rests.
Features: Barrel drilled and tapped for scope mount. Visible cocking
indicator. Spring-loaded barrel lock, positive hammer-block safety. Trigger
adjustable for weight of pull and over-travel. Contact maker for complete
price list. Made in U.S.A. by RPM.

Price: XL Hunter model (action only) **$1,045.00**
Price: Extra barrel .... **$250.00 to $300.00**

THOMPSON/CENTER ENCORE PISTOL
Caliber: 22-250, 223, 204 Ruger, 6.8 Rem., 260 Rem., 7mm-08, 243, 308,
270, 30-06, 375 JDJ, 204 Ruger, 44 Mag., 454 Casull, 480 Ruger, 444
Marlin single shot, 450 Marlin with muzzle tamer, no sights. **Barrel:** 12",
15", tapered round. **Weight:** NA. **Length:** 21" overall with 12" barrel.
Grips: American walnut with finger grooves, walnut forend. **Sights:** Blade
on ramp front, adjustable rear, or none. **Features:** Interchangeable
barrels; action opens by squeezing the trigger guard; drilled and tapped
for scope mounting; blue finish. Announced 1996. Made in U.S.A. by
Thompson/Center Arms.
Price: .... **$589.00 to $592.00**
Price: Extra 12" barrels **$262.00**
Price: Extra 15" barrels **$270.00**
Price: 45 Colt/410 barrel, 12" **$292.00**
Price: 45 Colt/410 barrel, 15" **$299.00**

Thompson/Center Stainless Encore Pistol
Similar to blued Encore, made of stainless steel, available with 15" barrel
in 223, 22-250, 243 Win., 7mm-08, 308, 30/06 Sprgfld., 45/70 Gov't.,
45/410 VR. With black rubber grip and forend. Made in U.S.A. by
Thompson/Center Arms.
Price: .... **$636.00 to $644.00**

Thompson/Center G2 Contender Pistol
A second generation Contender pistol maintaining the same barrel
interchangeability with older Contender barrels and their corresponding
forends (except Herrett forend). The G2 frame will not accept old-style
grips due to the change in grip angle. Incorporates an automatic hammer
block safety with built-in interlock. Features include trigger adjustable for
overtravel, adjustable rear sight; ramp front sight blade, blued steel finish.
Price: **$570.00**

Both classic arms and recent designs in American-style repeaters for sport and field shooting.

Armalite M15A2

Armalite AR-10A2

Armalite AR-10(T)

ARMALITE M15A2 CARBINE
Caliber: 223, 30-round magazine. **Barrel:** 16" heavy chrome lined; 1:9" twist. **Weight:** 7 lbs. **Length:** 35-11/16" overall. **Stock:** Green or black composition. **Sights:** Standard A2. **Features:** Upper and lower receivers have push-type pivot pin; hard coat anodized; A2-style forward assist; M16A2-type raised fence around magazine release button. Made in U.S.A. by ArmaLite, Inc.
Price: Green **$1,100.00**
Price: Black **$1,100.00**

ARMALITE AR-10A4 SPECIAL PURPOSE RIFLE
Caliber: 308 Win., 10- and 20-round magazine. **Barrel:** 20" chrome-lined, 1:11.25" twist. **Weight:** 9.6 lbs. **Length:** 41" overall. **Stock:** Green or black composition. **Sights:** Detachable handle, front sight, or scope mount available; comes with international style flattop receiver with Picatinny rail. **Features:** Forged upper receiver with case deflector. Receivers are hard-coat anodized. Introduced 1995. Made in U.S.A. by ArmaLite, Inc.
Price: Green **$1,506.00**
Price: Black **$1,506.00**

ArmaLite AR-10(T)
Similar to the ArmaLite AR-10A4 but with stainless steel, barrel, machined tool steel, two-stage National Match trigger group and other features.
Price: AR-10(T) rifle **$2,126.00**

ArmaLite AR-10A2
Utilizing the same 20" double-lapped, heavy barrel as the ArmaLite AR-10A4 Special Purpose Rifle. Offered in 308 caliber only. Made in U.S.A. by ArmaLite, Inc.
Price: AR-10A2 rifle or carbine **$1,506.00**

ARMALITE AR-180B RIFLE
Caliber: 223, 10-shot magazine. **Barrel:** 19.8". **Weight:** 6 lbs. **Length:** 38". **Stock:** Synthetic. **Sights:** Rear sight adjustable for windage, small and large apertures. **Features:** Lower receiver made of polymer, upper formed of sheet metal. Uses standard AR-15 magazines. Made in U.S.A. by Armalite.
Price: **$750.00**

ARSENAL USA SSR-56
Caliber: 7.62x39mm. **Barrel:** 16.25". **Weight:** 7.4 lbs. **Length:** 35.5" **Stock:** Black polymer. **Sights:** Adjustable rear. **Features:** An AK-47-style rifle built on a hardened Hungarian FEG receiver with the required six U.S.-made parts to make it legal for use with all extra-capacity magazines. From Arsenal I, LLC.
Price: **$565.00**

ARSENAL USA SSR-74-2
Caliber: 5.45x39mm **Barrel:** 16.25" **Weight:** 7 lbs. **Length:** 36.75" **Stock:** Polymer or wood. **Sights:** Adjustable. **Features:** Built with parts from an unissued Bulgarian AK-47 rifle, it has a Buffer Technologies recoil buffer, enough U.S.-made parts to allow pistol grip stock and use with all extra-capacity magazines. Assembled in U.S.A. From Arsenal I, LLC.
Price: **$499.00**

ARSENAL USA SSR-85C-2
Caliber: 7.62x39mm. **Barrel:** 16.25". **Weight:** 7.1 lbs. **Length:** 35.5". **Stock:** Polymer or wood. **Sights:** Adjustable rear calibrated to 800 meters. **Features:** Built from parts obtained from unissued Polish AK-47 rifles, the gas tube is vented and the receiver cover is plain. Rifle contains enough U.S.-sourced parts to allow pistol grip stock and use with all extra-capacity magazines. Assembled in U.S.A. by Arsenal I, LLC.
Price: **$499.00**

AUTO-ORDNANCE 1927 A-1 THOMPSON
Caliber: 45 ACP. **Barrel:** 16-1/2". **Weight:** 13 lbs. **Length:** About 41" overall (Deluxe). **Stock:** Walnut stock and vertical forend. **Sights:** Blade front, open rear adjustable for windage. **Features:** Recreation of Thompson Model 1927. Semi-auto only. Deluxe model has finned barrel, adjustable rear sight and compensator; Standard model has plain barrel and military sight. From Auto-Ordnance Corp.
Price: Deluxe **$950.00**
Price: 1927A1C lightweight model (9-1/2 lbs.) **$950.00**

Auto-Ordnance 1927 A-1 Thompson

Barrett Model 82A-1

Benelli R1

Benelli R1 APG Camo

Auto-Ordnance Thompson M1/M1-C
Similar to the 1927 A-1 except is in the M-1 configuration with side cocking knob, horizontal forend, smooth unfinned barrel, sling swivels on butt and forend. Matte black finish. Introduced 1985.
Price: M1 semi-auto carbin **$950.00**
Price: M1-C lightweight semi-auto **$925.00**

Auto-Ordnance 1927 A-1 Commando
Similar to the 1927 A-1 except has Parkerized finish, black-finish wood butt, pistol grip, horizontal forend. Comes with black nylon sling. Introduced 1998. Made in U.S.A. by Auto-Ordnance Corp.
Price: **$950.00**

BARRETT MODEL 82A-1 SEMI-AUTOMATIC RIFLE
Caliber: 50 BMG, 10-shot detachable box magazine. **Barrel:** 29". **Weight:** 28.5 lbs. **Length:** 57" overall. **Stock:** Composition with energy-absorbing recoil pad. **Sights:** Scope optional. **Features:** Semi-automatic, recoil operated with recoiling barrel. Three-lug locking bolt; muzzle brake. Adjustable bipod. Introduced 1985. Made in U.S.A. by Barrett Firearms.
Price: From **$7,200.00**

BENELLI R1 RIFLE
Caliber: 300 Win. Mag., 300 WSM, 270 WSM (24" barrel); 30-06, 308 (22" barrel); 300 Win. Mag., 30-06, (20" barrel). **Weight:** 7.1 lbs. **Length:** 43.75" to 45.75" **Stock:** Select satin walnut or synthetic. **Sights:** None. **Features:** Auto-regulating gas-operated system, three-lug rotary bolt, interchangeable barrels, optional recoil pads. Introduced 2003. Imported from Italy by Benelli USA.
Price: Synthetic with ComforTech gel recoil pad **$1,435.00**
Price: Satin walnut **$1,265.00**
Price: Black synthetic , Grip Tight, ComforTech, .270 WSM or
    .300 WSM (2007) **$1,435.00**

BERETTA CX4/PX4 STORM CARBINE
Caliber: 9mm Para, 40 S&W, 45 ACP. **Weight:** 5.75 lbs. **Barrel Length:** 16.6", chrome lined, rate of twist 1:16 (40 S&W) or 1:10 (9mm). **Length:** NA. **Stock:** Black synthetic. **Sights:** NA. **Features:** Introduced 2005. Imported from Italy by Beretta USA.
Price: Cx4 Carbine, 40 S&W, 10+1 . . . . **$800.00**
Price: Cx4 Carbine, 8000 Series, 9mm, 10+1 . . . . **$775.00**
Price: Cx4 Carbine, 8045 Series,45 ACP, 8+1 . . . . **$800.00**
Price: Cx4 Px4 Carbine, 40 S&W, 14+1 . . . . **$850.00**
Price: Cx4 Px4 Carbine, 9mm, 17+1 . . . . **$850.00**

Beretta CX4 Carbine

Browning Mark II Safari

Browning Lightweight Stalker

Browning BAR ShortTrac Left-Hand

Browning Lightweight Stalker

Bushmaster M17S Bullpup

BROWNING BAR SAFARI AND SAFARI W/BOSS SEMI-AUTO RIFLES

Caliber: Safari: 243, 25-06, 270, 7mm Rem Mag., 30-06, 308, 300 Win. Mag., 338 Win Mag. Safari w/BOSS: 270, 7mm Rem Mag., 30-06, 300 Win. Mag., 338 Win Mag., plus 270 WSM, 7mm WSM, 300 WSM. **Barrel:** 22-24" round tapered. **Weight:** 7.4-8.2 lbs. **Length:** 43-45" overall. **Stock:** French walnut pistol grip stock and forend, hand checkered. **Sights:** No sights. **Features:** Has new bolt release lever; removable trigger assembly with larger trigger guard; redesigned gas and buffer systems. Detachable 4-round box magazine. Scroll-engraved receiver is tapped for scope mounting. BOSS barrel vibration modulator and muzzle brake system available. Mark II Safari introduced 1993. Imported from Belgium by Browning.

Price: BAR MK II Safari, from $934.00
Price: BAR Safari w/BOSS, from $1,038.00

BROWNING BAR SHORTTRAC/LONGTRAC AUTO RIFLES

Caliber: (ShortTrac models) 270 WSM, 7mm WSM, 300 WSM, 243 Win., 308 Win.; (Long Trac models) 270 Win., 30-06 Sprfld., 7mm Rem. Mag., 300 Win. Mag. **Barrel:** 23". **Weight:** 6 lbs. 10 oz. to 7 lbs. 4 oz. **Length:** 41-1/2" to 44". **Stock:** Satin-finish walnut, pistol-grip, fluted forend. **Sights:** Adj. rear, bead front standard, no sights on BOSS models (optional). **Features:** Designed to handle new WSM chamberings. Gas-operated, blued finish, rotary bolt design (Long Trac models).

Price: BAR ShortTrac, 243 Win., 308 Win. from $930.00
Price: BAR ShortTrac Left-Hand, intr. 2007, from $967.00
Price: BAR ShortTrac WSM, 270 WSM, 7mm WSM, 300 WSM . . . $965.00
Price: BAR LongTrac, 270 Win., 30-06 Sprfld. $885.00
Price: BAR LongTrac, 7mm Rem. Mag., 300 Win. Mag. $965.00

Price: BAR LongTrac Mossy Oak Break Up, intr. 2007, from **$1,055.00**
Price: BAR LongTrac Left-Hand, intr. 2007, from **$967.00**

BROWNING BAR LIGHTWEIGHT STALKER AUTO RIFLE

Caliber: 243, 308, 270, 30-06, 270 WSM, 7mm WSM, 300 WSM, 300 Win. Mag., 338 Win. Mag. **Barrel:** 20-24". **Weight:** 7.1-7.75 LBS. **Length:** 41-45" overall. **Stock:** Black composite stock and forearm. **Sights:** Hooded front and adjustable rear. **Features:** Gas-operated action with seven-lug rotary bolt; dual action bars; 2-, 3- or 4-shot magazine (depending on cartridge). Introduced 2001. Imported by Browning.

Price: BAR Lightweight Stalker, from **$927.00**
Price: BAR Lightweight Stalker, WSM and magnums **$964.00**

BUSHMASTER M17S BULLPUP RIFLE

Caliber: 223, 10-shot magazine. **Barrel:** 21.5", chrome lined; 1:9" twist. **Weight:** 8.2 lbs. **Length:** 30" overall. **Stock:** Fiberglass-filled nylon. **Sights:** Designed for optics-carrying handle incorporates scope mount rail for Weaver-type rings; also includes 25-meter open iron sights. **Features:** Gas-operated, short-stroke piston system; ambidextrous magazine release. Introduced 1993. Made in U.S.A. by Bushmaster Firearms, Inc./Quality Parts Co.

Price: **$765.00**

Bushmaster XM15 E2S Carbine

Bushmaster M4/M4A3 Post-Ban Carbine

Century International AES-10 Hi-Cap with bipod

Century International WASR-10 Hi-Cap

BUSHMASTER SHORTY XM15 E2S CARBINE
Caliber: 223,10-shot magazine. **Barrel:** 16", heavy; 1:9" twist. **Weight:** 7.2 lbs. **Length:** 34.75" overall. **Stock:** A2 type; fixed black composition. **Sights:** Fully adjustable M16A2 sight system. **Features:** Patterned after Colt M-16A2. Chrome-lined barrel with manganese phosphate finish. "Shorty" handguards. Has forged aluminum receivers with pushpin. Made in U.S.A. by Bushmaster Firearms, Inc.
Price: (A2) **$985.00**
Price: (A3) **$1,085.00**

Bushmaster XM15 E2S Dissipator Carbine
Similar to the XM15 E2S Shorty carbine except has full-length "Dissipator" handguards. Weighs 7.6 lbs.; 34.75" overall; forged aluminum receivers with push-pin style takedown. Made in U.S.A. by Bushmaster Firearms, Inc.
Price: (A2 type) **$995.00**
Price: (A3 type) **$1,095.00**

Bushmaster XM15 E25 AK Shorty Carbine
Similar to the XM15 E2S Shorty except has 14.5" barrel with an AK muzzle brake permanently attached giving 16" barrel length. Weighs 7.3 lbs. Introduced 1999. Made in U.S.A. by Bushmaster Firearms, Inc.
Price: (A2 type) **$1,005.00**
Price: (A3 type) **$1,105.00**

Bushmaster M4/M4A3 Post-Ban Carbine
Similar to the XM15 E2S except has 14.5" barrel with Mini Y compensator, and fixed telestock. MR configuration has fixed carry handle; M4A3 has removeable carry handle.

Price: (M4) **$1,065.00**
Price: (M4A3) **$1,165.00**

BUSHMASTER VARMINTER RIFLE
Caliber: 223 Rem., 5-shot. **Barrel:** 24", 1:9" twist, fluted, heavy, stainless. **Weight:** 8-3/4 lbs. **Length:** 42-1/4". **Stock:** Rubberized pistol grip. **Sights:** 1/2" scope risers. **Features:** Gas-operated, semi-auto, two-stage trigger, slotted free floater forend, lockable hard case.
Price: **$1,245.00**

CENTURY INTERNATIONAL AES-10 HI-CAP RIFLE
Caliber: 7.62x39mm. 30-shot magazine. **Barrel:** 23.2". **Weight:** NA. **Length:** 41.5" overall. **Stock:** Wood grip, forend. **Sights:** Fixed-notch rear, windage-adjustable post front. **Features:** RPK-style, accepts standard double-stack AK-type mags. Side-mounted scope mount, integral carry handle, bipod. Imported by Century Arms Int'l.
Price: AES-10, from **$450.00**

CENTURY INTERNATIONAL GP WASR-10 HI-CAP RIFLE
Caliber: 7.62x39mm. 30-shot magazine. **Barrel:** 16.25", 1:10 rh twist. **Weight:** 7.2 lbs. **Length:** 34.25" overall. **Stock:** Wood laminate or composite, grip, forend. **Sights:** Fixed-notch rear, windage-adjustable post front. **Features:** Two 30-rd. detachable box magazines, cleaning kit, bayonet. Version of AKM rifle; U.S.-parts added for BATFE compliance. Threaded muzzle, folding stock, bayonet lug, compensator, Dragunov stock available. Made in Romania by Cugir Arsenal. Imported by Century Arms Int'l.
Price: GP WASR-10, from **$350.00**

Century Arms M70AB2 Sporter

Colt Match Target Lightweight

CENTURY INTERNATIONAL WASR-2 HI-CAP RIFLE
Caliber: 5.45x39mm. 30-shot magazine. **Barrel:** 16.25". **Weight:** 7.5 lbs. **Length:** 34.25" overall. **Stocks:** Wood laminate. **Sights:** Fixed-notch rear, windage-adjustable post front. **Features:** 1 30-rd. detachable box magazine, cleaning kit, sling. WASR-3 HI-CAP chambered in 223 Rem. Imported by Century Arms Int'l.
Price: GP WASR-2/3, from **$250.00**

CENTURY INTERNATIONAL M70AB2 SPORTER RIFLE
Caliber: 7.62x39mm. 30-shot magazine. **Barrel:** 16.25". **Weight:** 7.5 lbs. **Length:** 34.25" overall. **Stocks:** Metal grip, wood forend. **Sights:** Fixed-notch rear, windage-adjustable post front. **Features:** 2 30-rd. double-stack magazine, cleaning kit, compensator, bayonet lug and bayonet. Paratrooper-style Kalashnikov with under-folding stock. Imported by Century Arms Int'l.
Price: M70AB2, from **$480.00**

COLT MATCH TARGET MODEL RIFLE
Caliber: 223 Rem., 5-shot magazine. **Barrel:** 16.1" or 20". **Weight:** 7.1 to 8-1/2 lbs. **Length:** 34-1/2" to 39" overall. **Stock:** Composition stock, grip, forend. **Sights:** Post front, rear adjustable for windage and elevation. **Features:** 5-round detachable box magazine, flash suppressor, sling swivels. Forward bolt assist included. Introduced 1991. Made in U.S.A. by Colt's Mfg. Co., Inc.
Price: Match Target HBAR, from **$1,172.00**

DPMS PANTHER ARMS AR-15 RIFLES
Caliber: 223 Rem., 7.62x39. **Barrel:** 16" to 24". **Weight:** 7-3/4 to 11-3/4 lbs. **Length:** 34-1/2" to 42-1/4" overall. **Stock:** Black Zytel® composite. **Sights:** Square front post, adjustable A2 rear. **Features:** Steel or stainless steel heavy or bull barrel; hardcoat anodized receiver; aluminum free-float tube handguard; many options. From DPMS Panther Arms.
Price: Panther Bull A-15 (20" stainless bull bbl.) **$915.00**
Price: Panther Bull Twenty-Four (24" stainless bull bbl.) **$945.00**
Price: Bulldog (20" stainless fluted bbl., flattop receiver) **$1,219.00**
Price: Panther Bull Sweet Sixteen (16" stainless bull bbl.) **$885.00**
Price: DCM Panther (20" stainless heavy bbl., n.m. sights) **$1,099.00**
Price: Panther 7.62x39 (20" steel heavy bbl.) **$849.00**

DSA Z4 GTC CARBINE WITH C.R.O.S.
Caliber: 5.56 NATO **Barrel:** 16" 1:9 twist M4 profile fluted chrome lined heavy barrel with threaded Vortec flash hider. **Weight:** 7.6 lbs. **Stock:** 6 position collapsible M4 stock, Predator P4X free float tactical rail. **Sights:** Chrome lined Picatinny gas block w/removable front sight. **Features:** The Corrosion Resistant Operating System incorporates the new P.O.F. Gas Trap System with removable gas plug eliminates problematic features of standard AR gas system, Forged 7075T6 DSA lower receiver. Introduced 2006. Made in U.S.A. by DSA, Inc.
Price: **$1,700.00**

DSA CQB MRP, STANDARD MRP
Caliber: 5.56 NATO **Barrel:** 16" or 18" 1:7 twist chrome-lined or stainless steel barrel with A2 flash hider **Stock:** 6 position collapsible M4 stock. **Features:** LMT_1/2" MRP upper receiver with 20-1/2" Standard quad rail or 16-1/2" CQB quad rail, LMT_enhanced bolt with dual extractor springs, free float barrel, quick change barrel system, forged 7075T6 DSA lower receiver. EOTech and vertical grip additional. Introduced 2006. Made in U.S.A. by DSA, Inc.
Price: CQB MRP w/16" chrome lined barrel **$2,420.00**
Price: CQB MRP w/16" stainless steel barrel **$2,540.00**
Price: Standard MRP w/16" chrome lined barrel **$2,620.00**
Price: Standard MRP w/16" or 18" stainless steel barrel **$2,720.00**

DSA STD CARBINE
Caliber: 5.56 NATO. **Barrel:** 16" 1:9 twist D4 w/A2 flash hider. **Weight:** 6.25 lbs. **Length:** 31". **Stock:** A2 buttstock, D4 handguard w/heatshield. **Sights:** Forged A2 front sight with lug. **Features:** Forged 7075T6 DSA lower receiver, forged A2 or flattop upper receiver. Introduced 2006. Made in U.S.A. by DSA, Inc.
Price: A2 or Flattop STD Carbine......................... **$1,025.00**
Price: With LMT SOPMOD stock **$1,267.00**

DSA 1R CARBINE
Caliber: 5.56 NATO. **Barrel:** 16" 1:9 twist D4 w/A2 flash hider. **Weight:** 6.25 lbs. **Length:** Variable. **Stock:** 6 position collapsible M4 stock, D4 handguard w/heatshield. **Sights:** Forged A2 front sight with lug. **Features:** Forged 7075T6 DSA lower receiver, forged A2 or flattop upper receiver. Introduced 2006. Made in U.S.A. by DSA, Inc.
Price: A2 or Flattop 1R Carbine **$1,055.00**
Price: With VLTOR ModStock **$1,175.00**

DSA XM CARBINE
Caliber: 5.56 NATO. **Barrel:** 11-1/2" 1:9 twist D4 with 5-1/2" permanently attached flash hider. **Weight:** 6.25 lbs. **Length:** Variable. **Stock:** Collapsible, Handguard w/heatshield. **Sights:** Forged A2 front sight with lug. **Features:** Forged 7075T6 DSA lower receiver, forged A2 upper receiver. Introduced 2006. Made in U.S.A. by DSA, Inc.
Price: **$1,055.00**

DSA STANDARD
Caliber: 5.56 NATO. **Barrel:** 20" 1:9 twist heavy barrel w/A2 flash hider. **Weight:** 6.25 lbs. **Length:** 38-7/16". **Stock:** A2 buttstock, A2 handguard w/heatshield. **Sights:** Forged A2 front sight with lug. **Features:** Forged 7075T6 DSA lower receiver, forged A2 or flattop upper receiver. Introduced 2006. Made in U.S.A. by DSA, Inc.
Price: A2 or Flattop Standard **$1,025.00**

DSA DCM Rifle
Caliber: .223 Wylde Chamber. **Barrel:** 20" 1:8 twist chrome moly match grade Badger Barrel. **Weight:** 10 lbs. **Length:** 39.5". **Stock:** DCM freefloat handguard system, A2 buttstock. **Sights:** Forged A2 front sight with lug. **Features:** NM two stage trigger, NM rear sight, forged 7075T6 DSA lower receiver, forged A2 upper receiver. Introduced 2006. Made in U.S.A. by DSA, Inc.
Price: **$1,520.00**

DSA SA58 Congo

DSA SA58 Gray Wolf

DSA SA58 G1

DSA SA58
Standard

DSA S1
Caliber: .223 Match Chamber. **Barrel:** 16", 20" or 24" 1:8 twist stainless steel bull barrel. **Weight:** 8.0, 9.5 and 10 lbs. **Length:** 34.25", 38.25" and 42.25". **Stock:** A2 buttstock with free float aluminum handguard. **Sights:** Picatinny gas block sight base. **Features:** Forged 7075T6 DSA lower receiver, Match two stage trigger, forged flattop upper receiver, fluted barrel optional. Introduced 2006. Made in U.S.A. by DSA, Inc.
Price: **$1,155.00**

DSA SA58 CONGO, PARA CONGO
Caliber: 308 Win. **Barrel:** 18" w/short Belgian short flash hider. **Weight:** 8.6 lbs. (Congo); 9.85 lbs. (Para Congo). **Length:** 39.75" **Stock:** Synthetic w/military grade furniture (Congo); Synthetic with non-folding steel para stock (Para Congo). **Sights:** Elevation adjustable protected post front sight, windage adjustable rear peep (Congo); Belgian type Para Flip Rear (Para Congo). **Features:** Fully-adjustable gas system, high-grade steel upper receiver with carry handle. Made in U.S.A. by DSA, Inc.
Price: Congo **$1,695.00**
Price: Para Congo **$1,995.00**

DSA SA58 GRAY WOLF
Caliber: 308 Win. **Barrel:** 21" match-grade bull w/target crown. **Weight:** 13 lbs. **Length:** 41.75". **Stock:** Synthetic. **Sights:** Elevation-adjustable post front sight, windage-adjustable match rear peep. **Features:** Fully-adjustable gas system, high-grade steel upper receiver, Picatinny scope mount, DuraCoat finish. Made in U.S.A. by DSA, Inc.
Price: **$2,120.00**

DSA SA58 PREDATOR
Caliber: 243 Win., 260 Rem., 308 Win. **Barrel:** 16" and 19" w/target crown. **Weight:** 9 to 9.3 lbs. **Length:** 36.25" to 39.25". **Stock:** Green synthetic. **Sights:** Elevation-adjustable post front; windage-adjustable match rear peep. **Features:** Fully-adjustable gas system, high-grade steel upper receiver, Picatinny scope mount, DuraCoat solid and camo finishes. Made in U.S.A. by DSA, Inc.

Price: 243 Win., 260 Rem. **$1,695.00**
Price: 308 Win. **$1,640.00**

DSA SA58 T48
Caliber: 308 Win. **Barrel:** 21" with Browning long flash hider. **Weight:** 9.3 lbs. **Length:** 44.5". **Stock:** European walnut. **Sights:** Elevation-adjustable post front, windage adjustable rear peep. **Features:** Gas-operated semi-auto with fully adjustable gas system, high grade steel upper receiver with carry handle. DuraCoat finishes. Made in U.S.A. by DSA, Inc.
Price: **$1,995.00**

DSA SA58 G1
Caliber: 308 Win. **Barrel:** 21" with quick-detach flash hider. **Weight:** 10.65 lbs. **Length:** 44". **Stock:** Steel bipod cut handguard with hardwood stock and synthetic pistol grip. **Sights:** Elevation-adjustable post front, windage adjustable rear peep. **Features:** Gas-operated semi-auto with fully adjustable gas system, high grade steel upper receiver with carry handle, original GI steel lower receiver with GI bipod. DuraCoat finishes. Made in U.S.A. by DSA, Inc.
Price: **$1,850.00**

DSA SA58 STANDARD
Caliber: 308 Win. **Barrel:** 21" bipod cut w/threaded flash hider. **Weight:** 8.75 lbs. **Length:** 43". **Stock:** Synthetic, X-Series or optional folding para stock. **Sights:** Elevation-adjustable post front, windage-adjustable rear peep. **Features:** Fully adjustable short gas system, high grade steel or 416 stainless upper receiver. Made in U.S.A. by DSA, Inc.
Price: High-grade steel **$1,595.00**
Price: Folding para stock **$1,845.00**

DSA SA58 Carbine

DSA SA58 Medium Contour Tactical

DSA SA58 Bull

EAA/Saiga 308

DSA SA58 CARBINE
Caliber: 308 Win. **Barrel:** 16.25" bipod cut w/threaded flash hider. **Weight:** 8.35 lbs. **Length:** 37.5". **Stock:** Synthetic, X-Series or optional folding para stock. **Sights:** Elevation-adjustable post front, windage-adjustable rear peep. **Features:** Fully adjustable short gas system, high grade steel or 416 stainless upper receiver. Made in U.S.A. by DSA, Inc.
Price: High-grade steel **$1,595.00**
Price: Stainless steel **$1,850.00**

DSA SA58 TACTICAL CARBINE
Caliber: 308 Win. **Barrel:** 16.25" fluted with A2 flash hider. **Weight:** 8.25 lbs. **Length:** 36.5". **Stock:** Synthetic, X-Series or optional folding para stock. **Sights:** Elevation-adjustable post front, windage-adjustable match rear peep. **Features:** Shortened fully adjustable short gas system, high grade steel or 416 stainless upper receiver. Made in U.S.A. by DSA, Inc.
Price: High-grade steel **$1,595.00**
Price: Stainless steel **$1,850.00**

DSA SA58 MEDIUM CONTOUR
Caliber: 308 Win. **Barrel:** 21" w/threaded flash hider. **Weight:** 9.75 lbs. **Length:** 43". **Stock:** Synthetic military grade. **Sights:** Elevation-adjustable post front, windage-adjustable match rear peep. **Features:** Gas-operated semi-auto with fully adjustable gas system, high grade steel receiver. Made in U.S.A. by DSA, Inc.
Price: **$1,595.00**

DSA SA58 BULL BARREL RIFLE
Caliber: 308 Win. **Barrel:** 21". **Weight:** 11.1 lbs. **Length:** 41.5". **Stock:** Synthetic, free floating handguard. **Sights:** Elevation-adjustable windage-adjustable post front, match rear peep. **Features:** Gas-operated semi-auto with fully adjustable gas system, high grade steel or stainless upper receiver. Made in U.S.A. by DSA, Inc.

Price: **$1,745.00**
Price: Stainless steel **$1,995.00**

DSA SA58 MINI OSW
Caliber: 308 Win. **Barrel:** 11" or 13" w/A2 flash hider. **Weight:** 9 to 9.35 lbs. **Length:** 32.75" to 35". **Stock:** Fiberglass reinforced short synthetic handguard, para folding stock and synthetic pistol grip. **Sights:** Adjustable post front, para rear sight. **Features:** Semi-auto or select fire with fully adjustable short gas system, optional FAL rail handguard, SureFire Vertical Foregrip System, EOTech HOLOgraphic Sight and ITC cheekrest. Made in U.S.A. by DSA, Inc.
Price: **$1,845.00**

EAA/SAIGA SEMI-AUTO RIFLE
Caliber: 7.62x39, 308, 223. **Barrel:** 20.5", 22", 16.3". **Weight:** 7 to 8-1/2 lbs. **Length:** 43". **Stock:** Synthetic or wood. **Sights:** Adjustable, sight base. **Features:** Based on AK Combat rifle by Kalashnikov. Imported from Russia by EAA Corp.
Price: 7.62x39 (syn.). **$239.00**
Price: 308 (syn. or wood) **$429.00**
Price: 223 (syn.) **$389.00**

EXCEL ARMS ACCELERATOR RIFLES
Caliber: 17HMR, 22WMR, 17M2, 22LR, 9-shot magazine. **Barrel:** 18" fluted stainless steel bull barrel. **Weight:** 8 lbs. **Length:** 32.5" overall. **Grips:** Textured black polymer. **Sights:** Fully adjustable target sights. **Features:** Made from 17-4 stainless steel, aluminum shroud w/Weaver rail, manual safety, firing-pin block, last-round bolt-hold-open feature. Four packages with various equipment available. American made, lifetime warranty. Comes with one 9-round stainless steel magazine and a California-approved cable lock. Introduced 2006. Made in U.S.A. by Excel Arms.
Price: MR-17 17HMR **$498.00**
Price: MR-22 22WMR **$498.00**
Price: SR-17 17 Mach 2 . . . . **$498.00**
Price: SR-22 22LR **$498.00**

Excel Arms Accelerator

Heckler & Koch USC

Hi-Point Carbine

Les Baer Flattop

HECKLER & KOCH USC CARBINE
Caliber: 45 ACP, 10-shot magazine. **Barrel:** 16". **Weight:** 8.6 lb. **Length:** 35.4" overall. **Stock:** Skeletonized polymer thumbhole. **Sights:** Blade front with integral hood, fully adjustable diopter. **Features:** Based on German UMP submachine gun. Blowback operation; almost entirely constructed of carbon fiber-reinforced polymer. Free-floating heavy target barrel. Introduced 2000. From H&K.
Price: **$1,249.00**

HI-POINT 9MM CARBINE
Caliber: 9mm Para., 40 S&W, 10-shot magazine. **Barrel:** 16-1/2" (17-1/2" for 40 S&W). **Weight:** 4-1/2 lbs. **Length:** 31-1/2" overall. **Stock:** Black polymer, camouflage. **Sights:** Protected post front, aperture rear. Integral scope mount. **Features:** Grip-mounted magazine release. Black or chrome finish. Sling swivels. Available with laser or red dot sights. Introduced 1996. Made in U.S.A. by MKS Supply, Inc.
Price: Black or chrome, 9mm **$199.00**
Price: 40 S&W **$225.00**
Price: Camo stock **$210.00**

IAI M-333 M1 GARAND
Caliber: 30-06, 8-shot clip. **Barrel:** 24". **Weight:** 9-1/2 lbs. **Length:** 43.6" overall. **Stock:** Hardwood. **Sights:** Blade front, aperture adjustable rear. **Features:** Parkerized finish; gas-operated semi-automatic; remanufactured to military specifications. From Intrac Arms International, Inc.
Price: **$971.75**

IAI M-888 M1 CARBINE SEMI-AUTOMATIC RIFLE
Caliber: 22, 30 carbine. **Barrel:** 18"-20". **Weight:** 5-1/2 lbs. **Length:** 35"-37" overall. **Stock:** Laminate, walnut or birch. **Sights:** Blade front, adjustable rear. **Features:** Gas-operated, air cooled, manufactured to military specifications. 10/15/30 rnd. mag. scope available. From Intrac Arms International, Inc.
Price: 30 cal. .... **$556.00 to $604.00**
Price: 22 cal. .... **$567.00 to $654.00**

IAI-65 Rifle
A civilian-legal version of the original HKM rifle manufactured in Hungary. Manufactured by Gordon Technologies using an original AMD-65 matching parts kit built on an AKM receiver. The original wire stock is present, but it is welded in the open position as per BATF regulations. Furnished with a 12.6" barrel with large weld-in-place muzzle brake to bring its length over the 16" federal minimum. This rifle accepts all 7.62x39mm magazines and drums. Introduced 2002. From Intrac Arms International, Inc.
Price: **$799.00**

LES BAER CUSTOM ULTIMATE AR 223 RIFLES
Caliber: 223. **Barrel:** 18", 20", 22", 24". **Weight:** 7-3/4 to 9-3/4 lb. **Length:** NA. **Stock:** Black synthetic. **Sights:** None furnished; Picatinny-style flattop rail for scope mounting. **Features:** Forged receiver; Ultra single-stage trigger (Jewell two-stage trigger optional); titanium firing pin; Versa-Pod bipod; chromed National Match carrier; stainless steel, hand-lapped and cryo-treated barrel; guaranteed to shoot 1/2 or 3/4 MOA, depending on model. Made in U.S.A. by Les Baer Custom Inc.
Price: Super Varmint Model **$1,989.00**
Price: Super Match Model (introduced 2006) **$2,144.00**
Price: M4 flattop model **$2,195.00**
Price: IPSC action model **$2,310.00**

CENTERFIRE RIFLES — Autoloaders

Les Baer IPSC

Olympic Arms K9 Carbine

Olympic Arms Plinker Plus 20

LR 300 SR LIGHT SPORT RIFLE
Caliber: 223. **Barrel:** 16-1/4"; 1:9" twist. **Weight:** 7.2 lbs. **Length:** 36" overall (extended stock), 26-1/4" (stock folded). **Stock:** Folding, tubular steel, with thumbhole-type grip. **Sights:** Trijicon post front, Trijicon rear. **Features:** Uses AR-15 type upper and lower receivers; flattop receiver with weaver base. Accepts all AR-15/M-16 magazines. Introduced 1996. Made in U.S.A. from Z-M Weapons.
Price: **$2,550.00**

OLYMPIC ARMS K9, K10, K40, K45 PISTOL-CALIBER AR15 CARBINES
Caliber: 9mm, 10mm, 40 S&W, 45 ACP; 32/10-shot modified magazines. **Barrel:** 16" button rifled stainless steel, 1x16 twist rate. **Weight:** 6.73 lbs. **Length:** 31.625" overall. **Stock:** A2 grip, M4 6-point collapsible stock. **Features:** A2 upper with adjustable rear sight, elevation adjustable front post, bayonet lug, sling swivel, threaded muzzle, flash suppressor, carbine length handguards. Made in U.S.A. by Olympic Arms, Inc.
Price: K9, 9mm, modified 32-round Sten magazine. **$834.00**
Price: K10, 10mm, modified 10-round Uzi magazine **$834.00**
Price: K40, 40 S&W, modified 10-round Uzi magazine **$834.00**
Price: K45, 45 ACP, modified 10-round Uzi magazine **$834.00**

OLYMPIC ARMS K3B SERIES AR15 CARBINES
Caliber: 5.56 NATO, 30-shot magazines. **Barrel:** 16" button rifled chromemoly steel, 1x9 twist rate. **Weight:** 5-7 lbs. **Length:** 31.75" overall. **Stock:** A2 grip, M4 6-point collapsible buttstock. **Features:** A2 upper with adjustable rear sight, elevation adjustable front post, bayonet lug, sling swivel, threaded muzzle, flash suppressor, carbine length handguards. Made in U.S.A. by Olympic Arms, Inc.
Price: K3B base model, A2 upper. **$780.00**

Price: K3B-A3 flat-top upper, detachable carry handle **$875.00**
Price: K3B-M4 M4 contoured barrel & handguards. **$839.00**
Price: K3B-M4-A3-TC A3 upper, M4 barrel, FIRSH rail
handguard **$1,012.00**
Price: K3B-CAR 11.5" barrel with 5.5" permanent flash suppressor **$810.00**
Price: K3B-FAR 16" featherweight contoured barrel **$822.00**

OLYMPIC ARMS PLINKER PLUS AR15 MODELS
Caliber: 5.56 NATO, 30-shot magazine. Barrel 16" or 20" button-rifled chrome-moly steel, 1x9 twist. **Weight:** 7.5-8.5 lbs. **Length:** 35.5"-39.5" overall. **Stock:** A2 grip, A2 buttstock. **Sights:** A1 windage rear, elevation-adjustable front post. **Features:** A1 upper, fiberite handguards, bayonet lug, threaded muzzle and flash suppressor. Made in U.S.A. by Olympic Arms, Inc.
Price: Plinker Plus. **$595.00**
Price: Plinker Plus 20 . . . . **$749.00**

PANTHER ARMS CLASSIC AUTO RIFLE
Caliber: 5.56x45mm. **Barrel:** Heavy 16" to 20" w/flash hider. **Weight:** 7 to 9 lbs. **Length:** 34-11/16" to 38-7/16". **Sights:** Adj. rear and front. **Stock:** Black Zytel w/trap door assembly. **Features:** Gas operated rotating bolt, mil spec or Teflon black finish.
Price:. **$809.00**
Price: Stainless, match sights **$1,099.00**
Price: Southpaw **$875.00**
Price: 16" bbl. **$799.00**
Price: Panther Lite, 16" bbl. **$720.00**
Price: Panther carbine . . . . **$799.00 to $989.00**
Price: Panther bull bbl . . . . **$885.00 to $1,199.00**

Remington Model 750 Woodsmaster synthetic stock

Ruger Ranch Mini 14/5R

Sabre Defence Ayoob Professional

REMINGTON MODEL 750 WOODSMASTER
Caliber: 243 Win., 270 Win., 308 Win., 30-06, 35 Whelen. 4-shot magazine. **Barrel:** 22" round tapered. **Weight:** 7.5 lbs. **Length:** 42.6" overall. **Stock:** Restyled American walnut forend and stock with machine-cut checkering. Satin finish. **Sights:** Gold bead front sight on ramp; step rear sight with windage adjustable. **Features:** Replaces wood-stocked Model 7400 line introduced 1981. Gas action, R3 recoil pad. Positive cross-bolt safety. Carbine chambered in 308, 30-06, 35 Whelen. Receiver tapped for scope mount. Introduced 2006. Made in U.S.A. by Remington Arms Co.
Price: 750 Woodsmaster **$831.00**
Price: 750 Woodsmaster Carbine (18.5" bbl.) **$831.00**
Price: 750 synthetic stock (2007) **$732.00**

ROCK RIVER ARMS STANDARD A2 RIFLE
Caliber: 45 ACP. **Barrel:** NA. **Weight:** 8.2 lbs. **Length:** NA. **Stock:** Thermoplastic. **Sights:** Standard AR-15 style sights. **Features:** Two-stage, national match trigger; optional muzzle brake. Made in U.S.A. From Rock River Arms.
Price: **$925.00**

RUGER RANCH RIFLE AUTOLOADING RIFLE
Caliber: 223 Rem., 5-shot detachable box magazine. **Barrel:** 18-1/2". Rifling twist 1:9". **Weight:** 6.4 lbs. **Length:** 37-1/4" overall. **Stock:** American hardwood, steel reinforced. **Sights:** Protected blade front, fully adjustable Ghost Ring rear. **Features:** Fixed piston gas-operated, positive primary extraction. New buffer system, redesigned ejector system. Ruger S100RM scope rings included on Ranch Rifle.
Price: Mini-14/5, Ranch Rifle, blued, scope rings **$775.00**
Price: K-Mini-14/5, Ranch Rifle, stainless, scope rings **$835.00**
Price: K-Mini-14/5P, Ranch Rifle, stainless, synthetic stock **$835.00**
Price: K-Mini-14/5T, laminate stock, adj. harmonic
    barrel weight (2007) **$995.00**

Ruger Mini Thirty Rifle
Similar to the Mini-14 Ranch Rifle except modified to chamber the 7.62x39 Russian service round. Weight is about 6-7/8 lbs. Has 6-groove barrel with 1:10" twist, Ruger Integral Scope Mount bases and protected blade front, fully adjustable Ghost Ring rear. Detachable 5-shot staggered box magazine. Stainless w/synthetic stock. Introduced 1987.
Price: Stainless, scope rings **$809.00**

SABRE DEFENCE XR15A3 SPR
Caliber: 5.56 NATO, 6.5 Grendel, 30-shot magazines. **Barrel:** 20" 410 stainless steel, 1x8 twist rate; or 18" vanadium alloy, chrome lined barrel

with Sabre Gill-Brake.**Weight:** 6.77 lbs. **Length:** 31.75" overall. **Stock:** SOCOM 3-position stock with Samson M-EX handguards. **Sights:** Flip-up front and rear sights. **Features:** Fluted barrel, Harris bipod, and two-stage match trigger, Ergo Grips; upper and matched lower CNC machined from 7075-T6 forgings. SOCOM adjustable stock, Samson tactical handguards, M4 contour barrels available in 14.5" and 16" are made of MIL-B-11595 vanadium alloy and chrome lined. Introduced 2002. From Sabre Defence Industries.
Price: 6.5 Grendel (2007) **$2,699.00**
Price: XR15A3 Competition Deluxe, 6.5 Grendel, 20" barrel. **$2,499.00**
Price: XR15A3 Competition Standard, 5.56mm, 18" barrel. **$1,899.00**
Price: Massad Ayoob Professional. **$1,999.00**
Price: SPR Carbine **$2,499.00**
Price: M4 Carbine, 14.5" barrel **$1,429.00**
Price: M4 Flat-top Carbine, 16" barrel **$1,349.00**

SIG 556 AUTOLOADING RIFLE
Caliber: 223 Rem., 30-shot detachable box magazine. **Barrel:** 16". Rifling twist 1:9". **Weight:** 6.8 lbs. **Length:** 36.5" overall. **Stock:** Polymer, folding style. **Sights:** Flip-up front combat sight, adjustable for windage and elevation. **Features:** Based on SG 550 series rifle. Two-position adjustable gas piston operating rod system, accepts standard AR magazines. Polymer forearm, three integrated Picatinny rails, forward mount for right- or left-side sling attachment. Aircraft-grade aluminum alloy trigger housing, hard-coat anodized finish; two-stage trigger, ambidextrous safety, 30-round polymer magazine, battery compartments, pistol-grip rubber-padded watertight adjustable butt stock with sling-attachment points. SIG 556 SWAT model has flat-top Picatinny railed receiver, tactical quad rail. Imported by SIGARMS, Inc.
Price: SIG 556 . . . . **$1,300.00**

SMITH & WESSON M&P15 RIFLES
Caliber: 5.56mm NATO/223, 30-shot steel magazine. **Barrel:** 16", 1:9 **Weight:** 6.74 lbs., w/o magazine. **Length:** 32-35" overall. **Stock:** Black synthetic. **Sights:** Adjustable post front sight, adjustable dual aperture rear sight. **Features:** 6-position telescopic stock, thermo-set M4 handguard. 14.75" sight radius. 7-lbs. (approx.) trigger pull. 7075 T6 aluminum upper, 4140 steel barrel. Chromed barrel bore, gas key, bolt carrier. Hard-coat black-anodized receiver and barrel finish. Introduced 2006. Made in U.S.A. by Smith & Wesson.
Price: M&P15 No. 811000 . . . . **$1,200.00**
Price: M&P15T No. 811001, free float modular rail forend **$1,700.00**
Price: M&P15A No. 811002, folding battle rear sight **$1,300.00**

Smith & Wesson M&P15T

Springfield M1A

Stoner SR-25

Winchester Super X

SPRINGFIELD ARMORY M1A RIFLE
Caliber: 7.62mm NATO (308), 5- or 10-shot box magazine. **Barrel:** 25-1/16" with flash suppressor, 22" without suppressor. **Weight:** 9-3/4 lbs. **Length:** 44-1/4" overall. **Stock:** American walnut with walnut-colored heat-resistant fiberglass handguard. Matching walnut handguard available. Also available with fiberglass stock. **Sights:** Military, square blade front, full click-adjustable aperture rear. **Features:** Commercial equivalent of the U.S. M-14 service rifle with no provision for automatic firing. From Springfield Armory

Price: Standard M1A, black fiberglass stock. **$1,498.00**
Price: Standard M1A, black fiberglass stock, stainless **$1,727.00**
Price: Standard M1A, black stock, carbon barrel **$1,379.00**
Price: Standard M1A, Mossy Oak stock, carbon barrel **$1,507.00**
Price: Scout Squad M1A . . . . **$1,653.00 to $1,727.00**
Price: National Match . . . . **$2,049.00 to $2,098.00**
Price: Super Match (heavy premium barrel) about **$3,149.00**
Price: M1A SOCOM II rifle **$1,948.00**
Price: M25 White Feather Tactical rifle **$4,648.00**

SPRINGFIELD M1 GARAND RIFLE
Caliber: 308, 30-06. **Barrel:** 24". **Weight:** 9.5 lbs. **Length:** 43-3/5". **Stock:** Walnut. **Sights:** Military aperture with MOA adjustments for both windage and elevation, rear; military square post, front. **Features:** Original U.S. government-issue parts on a new walnut stock.
Price: . . . . **$1,348.00 to $1,378.00**

STONER SR-15 M-5 RIFLE
Caliber: 223. **Barrel:** 20". **Weight:** 7.6 lbs. **Length:** 38" overall. **Stock:** Black synthetic. **Sights:** Post front, fully adjustable rear (300-meter sight). **Features:** Modular weapon system; two-stage trigger. Black finish. Introduced 1998. Made in U.S.A. by Knight's Mfg.
Price: **$1,650.00**
Price: M-4 Carbine (16" barrel, 6.8 lbs) **$1,555.00**

STONER SR-25 CARBINE
Caliber: 7.62 NATO, 10-shot steel magazine. **Barrel:** 16" free-floating **Weight:** 7-3/4 lbs. **Length:** 35.75" overall. **Stock:** Black synthetic. **Sights:** Integral Weaver-style rail. Scope rings, iron sights optional. **Features:** Shortened, non-slip handguard; removable carrying handle. Matte black finish. Introduced 1995. Made in U.S.A. by Knight's Mfg. Co.
Price: **$3,345.00**

WINCHESTER SUPER X RIFLE
Caliber: 270 WSM, 30-06, 300 Win. Mag., 300 WSM, 4-shot steel magazine. **Barrel:** 22", 1:10", blued. **Weight:** 7.25 lbs. **Length:** 41-3/8". **Stock:** Walnut, 14-1/8"x 7/8"x 1-1/4". **Sights:** None. **Features:** Gas operated, removable trigger assembly, detachable box magazine, drilled and tapped, alloy receiver, enlarged trigger guard, crossbolt safety.Introduced 2007. Made in U.S.A. by Winchester Repeating Arms.
Price: Super X Rifle, from. **$811.00**

Both classic arms and recent designs in American-style repeaters for sport and field shooting.

Browning BLR Lightweight with pistol grip

Cimarron 1866 Winchester Replica

Cimarron 1873 Long Range

Dixie 1873

BROWNING BLR RIFLES

Action: Lever action with rotating bolt head, multiple-lug breech bolt with recessed bolt face, side ejection. Rack-and-pinion lever. Flush-mounted detachable magazines, with 4+1 capacity for magnum cartridges, 5+1 for standard rounds. **Barrel:** Button-rifled chrome-moly steel with crowned muzzle. **Stock:** Buttstocks and forends are American walnut with grip and forend checkering. Recoil pad installed. **Trigger:** Wide-groove design, trigger travels with lever. Half-cock hammer safety; fold-down hammer. **Sights:** Gold bead on ramp front; low-profile square-notch adjustable rear. **Features:** Blued barrel and receiver, high-gloss wood finish. Receivers are drilled and tapped for scope mounts, swivel studs included. Action lock provided. Introduced 1996. Four model name variations for 2006, as noted below. Imported from Japan by Browning.

BROWNING BLR LIGHTWEIGHT W/PISTOL GRIP, SHORT AND LONG ACTION; LIGHTWEIGHT '81, SHORT AND LONG ACTION
Calibers, Short Action, 20" barrel: 22-250, 243, 7mm-08, 308, 358, 450 Marlin. **Calibers, Short Action, 22" barrel:** 270 WSM, 7mm WSM, 300 WSM, 325 WSM. **Calibers, Long Action 22" barrel:** 270, 30-06. **Calibers, Long Action 24" barrel:** 7mm Rem. Mag., 300 Win. Mag. **Weight:** 6.5-7.75 lbs. **Length:** 40-45" overall. **Stock:** New checkered pistol grip and Schnabel forearm. Lightweight '81 differs from Pistol Grip models with a Western-style straight grip stock and banded forearm. Lightweight w/Pistol Grip Short Action and Long Action introduced 2005. Model '81 Lightning Long Action introduced 1996.

Price: Lightweight w/Pistol Grip Short Action, from $796.00
Price: Lightweight w/Pistol Grip Long Action $842.00
Price: Lightweight '81 Short Action $878.00
Price: Lightweight '81 Long Action $807.00
Price: Lightweight Takedown, intr. 2007, from $867.00
Price: Lightweight '81 Takedown, intr. 2007, from $832.00

CIMARRON 1860 HENRY REPLICA
Caliber: 44 WCF, 45LC; 13-shot magazine. **Barrel:** 24-1/4" (rifle), 22" (carbine). **Weight:** 9-1/2 lbs. **Length:** 43" overall (rifle). **Stock:** European walnut. **Sights:** Bead front, open adjustable rear. **Features:** Brass receiver and buttplate. Uses original Henry loading system. Copy of the original rifle. Introduced 1991. Imported by Cimarron F.A. Co.
Price: $1,199.00

CIMARRON 1866 WINCHESTER REPLICAS
Caliber: 38 Spec., 357, 45LC, 32 WCF, 38 WCF, 44 WCF. **Barrel:** 24-1/4" (rifle), 19" (carbine). **Weight:** 9 lbs. **Length:** 43" overall (rifle). **Stock:** European walnut. **Sights:** Bead front, open adjustable rear. **Features:** Solid brass receiver, buttplate, forend cap. Octagonal barrel. Copy of the original Winchester '66 rifle. Introduced 1991. Imported by Cimarron F.A. Co.
Price: Rifle $965.00
Price: Carbine $950.00

CIMARRON 1873 SHORT RIFLE
Caliber: 357 Mag., 38 Spec., 32 WCF, 38 WCF, 44 Spec., 44 WCF, 45 Colt. **Barrel:** 20" tapered octagon. **Weight:** 7.5 lbs. **Length:** 39" overall. **Stock:** Walnut. **Sights:** Bead front, adjustable semi-buckhorn rear. **Features:** Has half "button" magazine. Original-type markings, including caliber, on barrel and elevator and "Kings" patent. From Cimarron F.A. Co.
Price: $1,149.00

Cimarron 1873 Sporting Rifle
Similar to the 1873 Short Rifle except has 24" barrel with half-magazine.
Price: $1,149.00

CIMARRON 1873 LONG RANGE RIFLE
Caliber: 44 WCF, 45 Colt. **Barrel:** 30", octagonal. **Weight:** 8-1/2 lbs. **Length:** 48" overall. **Stock:** Walnut. **Sights:** Blade front, semi-buckhorn ramp rear. Tang sight optional. **Features:** Color case-hardened frame; choice of modern blue-black or charcoal blue for other parts. Barrel marked "Kings Improvement." From Cimarron F.A. Co.
Price: $1,199.00

DIXIE ENGRAVED 1873 RIFLE
Caliber: 44-40, 11-shot magazine. **Barrel:** 20", round. **Weight:** 7-3/4 lbs. **Length:** 39" overall. **Stock:** Walnut. **Sights:** Blade front, adjustable rear. **Features:** Engraved and case-hardened frame. Replica of Winchester 1873. Made in Italy. From 21 Gun Works.
Price: CR204A $1,425.00
Price: Plain, blued carbine, CR201 . . . . $1,015.00

Marlin 336C

E.M.F. 1876 SPORTING RIFLE
Caliber: 40/60, 45/75. **Barrel:** 28". **Weight:** 10 lbs. **Length:** NA. **Stock:** Walnut. **Sight:** Bead front. **Features:** Case-hardened frame, blue barrel, first repeater in heavier loads. Imported by E.M.F.
Price: (2007) **$1,265.00**

E.M.F. 1860 HENRY RIFLE
Caliber: 44-40 or 45 Colt. **Barrel:** 24.25". **Weight:** About 9 lbs. **Length:** About 43.75" overall. **Stock:** Oil-stained American walnut. **Sights:** Blade front, rear adjustable for elevation. **Features:** Reproduction of the original Henry rifle with brass frame and buttplate, rest blued. Imported by E.M.F.
Price: Brass frame. **$1,050.00**
Price: Steel frame **$1,140.00**

E.M.F. 1866 YELLOWBOY LEVER ACTIONS
Caliber: 38 Spec., 44-40, 45 LC. **Barrel:** 19" (carbine), 24" (rifle). **Weight:** 9 lbs. **Length:** 43" overall (rifle). **Stock:** European walnut. **Sights:** Bead front, open adjustable rear. **Features:** Solid brass frame, blued barrel, lever, hammer, buttplate. Imported from Italy by E.M.F.
Price: Rifle. **$920.00**
Price: Carbine **$870.00**
Price: Border Rifle. **$970.00**

E.M.F. HARTFORD MODEL 1892 LEVER-ACTION RIFLE
Caliber: .357, .44Mag., 44/40, 45LC. **Barrel:** 20", 24" **Weight:** 7 lbs. **Length:** 42" overall. **Stock:** Smooth hardwood. **Sights:** Bead front, rear adjustable for windage and evaluation. **Features:** Color case-hardened frame, blue frame, brass frame or stainless steel frame. Crescent shaped butt plate. Imported by E.M.F.
Price: Blued carbine, round 20" barrel, saddle ring **$430.00**
Price: Brass or stainless frame, carbine **$475.00**
Price: Case-hardened rifle, octagonal 20" or 24" barrel **$510.00**
Price: Stainless-steel rifle, octagonal 20" or 24" barrel. **$550.00**

E.M.F. MODEL 1873 LEVER-ACTION RIFLE
Caliber: 32/20, 357 Mag., 38/40, 44-40, 45 Colt. **Barrel:** 18", 20", 24", 30". **Weight:** 8 lbs. **Length:** 43-1/4" overall. **Stock:** European walnut. **Sights:** Bead front, rear adjustable for windage and elevation. **Features:** Color case-hardened frame (blue on carbine). Imported by E.M.F.
Price: Rifle. **$1,050.00**
Price: Carbine, 19" barrel **$1,040.00**
Price: Deluxe Cowboy **$1,100.00**

E.M.F. MODEL 1873 REVOLVER CARBINE
Caliber: 357 Mag., 45 Colt. **Barrel:** 18". **Weight:** 4 lbs., 8 oz. **Length:** 34" overall. **Stock:** One-piece walnut. **Sights:** Blade front, notch rear. **Features:** Color case-hardened frame, blue barrel, backstrap and trigger guard. Introduced 1998. Imported from Italy by EMF, Inc.
Price: Standard **$580.00**

E.M.F. LIGHTNING PUMP-ACTION RIFLES
Caliber: 44/40, 45LC. **Barrel:** 20", 24", 26". **Weight:** NA. **Length:** NA. **Stock:** Walnut. **Sight:** Bead front. **Features:** Blued or deluxe case-hardened frames. Imported from Pedersoli by E.M.F.
Price: Carbine **$1,300.00**
Price: Regular **$1,425.00**
Price: Deluxe case-hardened fram **$1,600.00**

MARLIN MODEL 336C LEVER-ACTION CARBINE
Caliber: 30-30 or 35 Rem., 6-shot tubular magazine. **Barrel:** 20" Micro-Groove®. **Weight:** 7 lbs. **Length:** 38-1/2" overall. **Stock:** Checkered American black walnut, capped pistol grip. Mar-Shield® finish; rubber buttpad; swivel studs. **Sights:** Ramp front with Wide-Scan hood, semi-buckhorn folding rear adjustable for windage and elevation. **Features:** Hammer-block safety. Receiver tapped for scope mount, offset hammer spur; top of receiver sandblasted to prevent glare. Includes safety lock.
Price: **$570.00**

Marlin Model 336A Lever-Action Carbine
Same as the Marlin 336C except has cut-checkered, walnut-finished hardwood pistol grip stock with swivel studs, 30-30 only, 6-shot. Hammer-block safety. Adjustable rear sight, brass bead front. Includes safety lock.
Price: **$477.00**
Price: With 4x scope and mount **$527.00**

Marlin Model 336SS Lever-Action Carbine
Same as the 336C except receiver, barrel and other major parts are machined from stainless steel. 30-30 only, 6-shot; receiver tapped for scope. Includes safety lock.
Price: **$692.00**

Marlin Model 336W Lever-Action Rifle
Similar to the Model 336C except has walnut-finished, cut-checkered Maine birch stock; blued steel barrel band has integral sling swivel; no front sight hood; comes with padded nylon sling; hard rubber buttplate. Introduced 1998. Includes safety lock. Made in U.S.A. by Marlin.
Price: **$482.00**
Price: With 4x scope and mount **$535.00**

Marlin Model 336XLR Lever-Action Rifle
Similar to Model 336C except has an 24" stainless barrel with Ballard-type cut rifling, stainless steel receiver and other parts, laminated hardwood stock with pistol grip, nickel-plated swivel studs. Chambered for 30-30 Win. with Hornady Evolution spire-pointed Flex-Tip cartridges. Includes safety lock. Introduced 2006.
Price: (Model 336XLR) **$874.00**

MARLIN MODEL 444 LEVER-ACTION SPORTER
Caliber: 444 Marlin, 5-shot tubular magazine. **Barrel:** 22" deep cut Ballard rifling. **Weight:** 7-1/2 lbs. **Length:** 40-1/2" overall. **Stock:** Checkered American black walnut, capped pistol grip, rubber rifle buttpad. Mar-Shield® finish; swivel studs. **Sights:** Hooded ramp front, folding semi-buckhorn rear adjustable for windage and elevation. **Features:** Hammer-block safety. Receiver tapped for scope mount; offset hammer spur. Includes safety lock.
Price: **$665.00**

Marlin Model 444XLR Lever-Action Rifle
Similar to Model 444 except has an 24" stainless barrel with Ballard-type cut rifling, stainless steel receiver and other parts, laminated hardwood stock with pistol grip, nickel-plated swivel studs. Chambered for 444 Marlin with Hornady Evolution spire-pointed Flex-Tip cartridges. Includes safety lock. Introduced 2006.
Price: (Model 444XLR) **$874.00**

MARLIN MODEL 1894 LEVER-ACTION CARBINE
Caliber: 44 Spec./44 Mag., 10-shot tubular magazine. **Barrel:** 20" Ballard-type rifling. **Weight:** 6 lbs. **Length:** 37-1/2" overall. **Stock:** Checkered American black walnut, straight grip and forend. Mar-Shield® finish. Rubber rifle buttpad; swivel studs. **Sights:** Wide-Scan hooded ramp front, semi-buckhorn folding rear adjustable for windage and elevation. **Features:** Hammer-block safety. Receiver tapped for scope mount, offset hammer spur, solid top receiver sand blasted to prevent glare. Includes safety lock.
Price: **$614.00**

Marlin Model 1894C Carbine
Similar to the standard Model 1894 except chambered for 38 Spec./357 Mag. with full-length 9-shot magazine, 18-1/2" barrel, hammer-block safety, hooded front sight. Introduced 1983. Includes safety lock.
Price: **$614.00**

Marlin 1894 Cowboy

Marlin 1895

Marlin 1895M

Navy Arms Iron Frame Henry

MARLIN MODEL 1894 COWBOY

Caliber: 357 Mag., 44 Mag., 45 Colt, 10-shot magazine. **Barrel:** 20" tapered octagon, deep cut rifling. **Weight:** 7-1/2 lbs. **Length:** 41-1/2" overall. **Stock:** Straight grip American black walnut, hard rubber buttplate, Mar-Shield® finish. **Sights:** Marble carbine front, adjustable Marble semi-buckhorn rear. **Features:** Squared finger lever; straight grip stock; blued steel forend tip. Designed for Cowboy Shooting events. Introduced 1996. Includes safety lock. Made in U.S.A. by Marlin.
Price: **$889.00**

Marlin Model 1894SS

Similar to Model 1894 except has stainless steel barrel, receiver, lever, guard plate, magazine tube and loading plate. Nickel-plated swivel studs.
Price: **$752.00**

MARLIN MODEL 1895 LEVER-ACTION RIFLE

Caliber: 45-70, 4-shot tubular magazine. **Barrel:** 22" round. **Weight:** 7-1/2 lbs. **Length:** 40-1/2" overall. **Stock:** Checkered American black walnut, full pistol grip. Mar-Shield® finish; rubber buttpad; quick detachable swivel studs. **Sights:** Bead front with Wide-Scan hood, semi-buckhorn folding rear adjustable for windage and elevation. **Features:** Hammer-block safety. Solid receiver tapped for scope mounts or receiver sights; offset hammer spur. Includes safety lock.
Price: **$665.00**

Marlin Model 1895G Guide Gun Lever-Action Rifle

Similar to Model 1895 with deep-cut Ballard-type rifling; straight-grip walnut stock. Overall length is 37", weighs 7 lbs. Introduced 1998. Includes safety lock. Made in U.S.A. by Marlin.
Price: **$681.00**

Marlin Model 1895GS Guide Gun

Similar to Model 1895G except receiver, barrel and most metal parts are machined from stainless steel. Chambered for 45-70, 4-shot, 18-1/2" barrel. Overall length is 37", weighs 7 lbs. Introduced 2001. Includes safety lock. Made in U.S.A. by Marlin.
Price: **$805.00**

Marlin Model 1895 Cowboy Lever-Action Rifle

Similar to Model 1895 except has 26" tapered octagon barrel with Ballard-type rifling, Marble carbine front sight and Marble adjustable semi-buckhorn rear sight. Receiver tapped for scope or receiver sight. Overall length is 44-1/2", weighs about 8 lbs. Introduced 2001. Includes safety lock. Made in U.S.A. by Marlin.
Price: **$849.00**

Marlin Model 1895XLR Lever-Action Rifle

Similar to Model 1895 except has an 24" stainless barrel with Ballard-type cut rifling, stainless steel receiver and other parts, laminated hardwood stock with pistol grip, nickel-plated swivel studs. Chambered for 45-70 Government with Hornady Evolution spire-pointed Flex-Tip cartridges. Includes safety lock. Introduced 2006.
Price: (Model 1895MXLR) **$874.00**

Marlin Model 1895M Lever-Action Rifle

Similar to Model 1895G except has an 18-1/2" barrel with Ballard-type cut rifling. Chambered for 450 Marlin. Includes safety lock.
Price: (Model 1895M) **$733.00**

Marlin Model 1895MXLR Lever-Action Rifle

Similar to Model 1895M except has an 24" stainless barrel with Ballard-type cut rifling, stainless steel receiver and other parts, laminated hardwood stock with pistol grip, nickel-plated swivel studs. Chambered for 450 Marlin with Hornady Evolution spire-pointed Flex-Tip cartridges. Includes safety lock. Introduced 2006.
Price: (Model 1895MXLR) **$874.00**

NAVY ARMS MILITARY HENRY RIFLE

Caliber: 44-40 or 45 Colt, 12-shot magazine. **Barrel:** 24-1/4". **Weight:** 9 lbs., 4 oz. **Stock:** European walnut. **Sights:** Blade front, adjustable ladder-type rear. **Features:** Brass frame, buttplate, rest blued. Replica of the model used by cavalry units in the Civil War. Has full-length magazine tube, sling swivels; no forend. Imported from Italy by Navy Arms.
Price: **$1,199.00**

Navy Arms Iron Frame Henry

Similar to the Military Henry Rifle except receiver is blued or color case-hardened steel. Imported by Navy Arms.
Price: . . . . **$1,258.00 to $1,275.00**

Navy Arms 1866 Yellow Boy

Navy Arms 1892 Rifle

Puma Model 92

Remington 7600 Rifle

NAVY ARMS 1866 YELLOW BOY RIFLE
Caliber: 38 Spec., 44-40, 45 Colt, 12-shot magazine. **Barrel:** 20" or 24", full octagon. **Weight:** 8-1/2 lbs. **Length:** 42-1/2" overall. **Stock:** Walnut. **Sights:** Blade front, adjustable ladder-type rear. **Features:** Brass frame, forend tip, buttplate, blued barrel, lever, hammer. Introduced 1991. Imported from Italy by Navy Arms.
Price: **$942.00**
Price: Carbine, 19" barrel **$908.00**

NAVY ARMS 1866 SPORTING YELLOW BOY RIFLES
Caliber: 45 Colt. **Barrel:** 24-1/4" octagonal; 1:16" twist. **Weight:** 8.16 lbs. **Length:** 43-3/4" overall. **Stock:** Walnut. **Sights:** Blade front, adjustable folding rear. **Features:** Brass receiver; blued or white barrel; 13-shot magazine. Introduced 2001. Imported from Uberti by Navy Arms.
Price: (blued barrel)................................ **$942.00**

NAVY ARMS 1873 WINCHESTER-STYLE RIFLE
Caliber: 357 Mag., 44-40, 45 Colt, 12-shot magazine. **Barrel:** 24-1/4". **Weight:** 8-1/4 lbs. **Length:** 43" overall. **Stock:** European walnut. **Sights:** Blade front, buckhorn rear. **Features:** Color case-hardened frame, rest blued. Full-octagon barrel. Imported by Navy Arms.
Price: **$1,079.00**
Price: 1873 Carbine, 19" barrel **$1,054.00**
Price: 1873 Sporting Rifle (full oct. bbl., checkered walnut stock
    and forend) **$1,218.00**
Price: 1873 Border Model, 20" octagon barrel **$1,079.00**
Price: 1873 Deluxe Border Model **$1,218.00**

NAVY ARMS 1892 RIFLE
Caliber: 357 Mag., 44-40, 45 Colt. **Barrel:** 24-1/4" octagonal. **Weight:** 7 lbs. **Length:** 42" overall. **Stock:** American walnut. **Sights:** Blade front, semi-buckhorn rear. **Features:** Replica of Winchester's early Model 1892 with octagonal barrel, forend cap and crescent buttplate. Blued or color case-hardened receiver. Introduced 1998. Imported by Navy Arms.
Price: **$355.00**

Navy Arms 1892 Stainless Carbine
Similar to the 1892 Rifle except stainless steel, has 20" round barrel, weighs 5-3/4 lbs., and is 37-1/2" overall. Introduced 1998. Imported by Navy Arms.
Price: **$345.00**

Navy Arms 1892 Short Rifle
Similar to the 1892 Rifle except has 20" octagonal barrel, weighs 6-1/4 lbs., and is 37-3/4" overall. Replica of the rare, special order 1892 Winchester nicknamed the "Texas Special." Blued or color case-hardened receiver and furniture. Introduced 1998. Imported by Navy Arms.
Price: **$355.00**

PUMA MODEL 92 RIFLES & CARBINES
Caliber: 38 Spec./357 Mag., 44 Mag., 45 Colt, 454 Casull, 480 Ruger. **Barrel:** 16". 18", 20" round, 24" octagonal; porting and large lever loop available. **Weight:** 6.1 to 7.7 lbs. **Stock:** Walnut-stained hardwood. **Sights:** Open, buckhorn front & rear; HiViz also available. **Features:** Blue, case-hardened, stainless steel and brass receivers, matching buttplates. Blued, stainless steel barrels, full-length magazines. Thumb safety. 45 Colt and 454 Casull carbine introduced in 2002. The 480 Ruger version introduced in 2003. Imported from Brazil by Legacy Sports International.
Price: .... **$450.00 to $617.00**

REMINGTON MODEL 7600/7615 PUMP ACTION
Caliber: 243, 270, 30-06, 308. **Barrel:** 22" round tapered. **Weight:** 7.5 lbs. **Length:** 42.6" overall. **Stock:** Cut-checkered walnut pistol grip and forend, Monte Carlo with full cheekpiece. Satin or high-gloss finish. Also, black synthetic. **Sights:** Gold bead front sight on matted ramp, open step adjustable sporting rear. **Features:** Redesigned and improved version of the Model 760. Detachable 4-shot clip. Cross-bolt safety. Receiver tapped for scope mount. Introduced 1981. Model 7615 Tactical chambered in 223 Rem. **Features:** Knoxx SpecOps NRS (Non Recoil Suppressing) adjustable stock, parkerized finish, 10-round detachable magazine box, sling swivel studs. Introduced 2007.
Price: **$749.00**
Price: Carbine (18-1/2" bbl., 30-06 only) **$749.00**
Price: Model 7615 (2007) **$932.00**

CENTERFIRE RIFLES — Lever & Slide

Remington Model 7615 Carbine

Ruger Model 96/44

Tristar 1873 Sporting Rifle

Tristar 1866 Yellowboy Carbine

Tristar 1860 Henry

Uberti 1873 Sport

RUGER MODEL 96/44 LEVER-ACTION RIFLE
Caliber: 44 Mag., 4-shot rotary magazine. **Barrel:** 18-1/2". **Weight:** 6 lbs. **Length:** 37.75" overall. **Stock:** American hardwood. **Sights:** Gold bead front, folding leaf rear. **Features:** Solid chrome-moly steel receiver. Manual cross-bolt safety, visible cocking indicator; short-throw lever action; integral scope mount; blued finish; color case-hardened lever. Introduced 1996. Made In U.S. by Sturm, Ruger & Co.
Price: 96/44M, 44 Mag $599.00

TRISTAR/SHARPS 1874 SPORTING RIFLE
Caliber: 45-70. **Barrel:** 28", 32", 34" octagonal. **Weight:** 9.75 lbs. **Length:** 44.5" overall. **Stock:** Walnut. **Sights:** Dovetail front, adjustable rear. **Features:** Cut checkering, case colored frame finish.
Price: $839.00
Price: Bridgeport Sharps $899.00

TRISTAR/UBERTI 1866 SPORTING RIFLE, CARBINE
Caliber: 45 Colt. **Barrel:** 24-1/4", octagonal. **Weight:** 8.1 lbs. **Length:** 43-1/4" overall. **Stock:** Walnut. **Sights:** Blade front adjustable for windage, rear adjustable for elevation. **Features:** Frame, buttplate, forend cap of polished brass, balance charcoal blued. Imported by Tristar Sporting Arms Ltd.
Price: $1,109.00
Price: Yellowboy carbine (19" round bbl.) $999.00

TRISTAR/UBERTI 1860 HENRY RIFLE
Caliber: 45 Colt. **Barrel:** 24-1/4", half-octagon. **Weight:** 9.2 lbs. **Length:** 43-3/4" overall. **Stock:** American walnut. **Sights:** Blade front, rear adjustable for elevation. **Features:** Frame, elevator, magazine follower, buttplate are brass, balance blue. Imported by Tristar Sporting Arms Ltd. Arms, Inc.
Price: $1,359.00

TRISTAR/UBERTI 1873 SPORTING RIFLE
Caliber: 45 Colt. **Barrel:** 24-1/4", 30", octagonal. **Weight:** 8.1 lbs. **Length:** 43-1/4" overall. **Stock:** Walnut. **Sights:** Blade front adjustable for windage, open rear adjustable for elevation. **Features:** Color case-hardened frame, blued barrel, hammer, lever, buttplate, brass elevator. Imported from Italy by Tristar Sporting Arms Ltd.
Price: 24-1/4" barrel $1,259.00

Uberti 1866 Yellowboy

Uberti 1860 Henry

U.S. Fire Arms Lightning Premium Carbine

U.S. Fire Arms Standard Lightning

UBERTI 1873 SPORTING RIFLE
Caliber: 357 Mag., 44-40, 45 Colt. **Barrel:** 19", to 24-1/4". **Weight:** Up to 8.2 lbs. **Length:** Up to 43.3" overall. **Stock:** Walnut, straight grip and pistol grip. **Sights:** Blade front adjustable for windage, open rear adjustable for elevation. **Features:** Color case-hardened frame, blued barrel, hammer, lever, buttplate, brass elevator. Imported by Benelli USA.
Price: 1873 Carbine, 19" round barrel **$945.00**
Price: 1873 Short Rifle, 20" octagonal barrel **$985.00**
Price: 1873 Special Sporting Rifle, 24.25" octagonal barrel **$1,100.00**

UBERTI 1866 YELLOWBOY CARBINE, SHORT RIFLE, RIFLE
Caliber: 38 Spec., 44-40, 45 Colt. **Barrel:** 24-1/4", octagonal. **Weight:** 8.2 lbs. **Length:** 43-1/4" overall. **Stock:** Walnut. **Sights:** Blade front adjustable for windage, rear adjustable for elevation. **Features:** Frame, buttplate, forend cap of polished brass, balance charcoal blued. Imported by Benelli USA.
Price: 1866 Yellowboy Carbine, 19" round barrel **$895.00**
Price: 1866 Yellowboy Short Rifle, 20" octagonal barrel **$925.00**
Price: 1866 Yellowboy Rifle, 24.25" octagonal barrel **$925.00**

UBERTI 1860 HENRY RIFLE
Caliber: 44-40, 45 Colt. **Barrel:** 24-1/4", half-octagon. **Weight:** 9.2 lbs. **Length:** 43-3/4" overall. **Stock:** American walnut. **Sights:** Blade front, rear adjustable for elevation. **Features:** Imported by Benelli USA.
Price: 1860 Henry Trapper, 18.5" barrel, brass frame **$1,050.00**
Price: 1860 Henry Rifle, 24.25" barrel, brass frame **$1,050.00**
Price: 1860 Henry Rifle steel, 24.25" barrel, case-hardened frame **$1,150.00**
Price: 1860 Henry Rifle Iron Frame, 24.25" barrel **$1,050.00**

Uberti 1860 Henry Trapper Carbine
Similar to the 1860 Henry Rifle except has 18-1/2" barrel, measures 37-3/4" overall, and weighs 8 lbs. Introduced 1999. Imported by Benelli USA.
Price: Brass frame, blued barrel **$1,050.00**

UBERTI LIGHTNING RIFLE
Caliber: 357 Mag., 45 Colt, 10+1. **Barrel:** 20" to 24.25". **Stock:** Walnut. **Finish:** Blue or case-hardened. Introduced 2006. Imported by Benelli USA.
Price: 1875 Lightning Rifle, 24.25" barrel **$1,199.00**
Price: 1875 Lightning Short Rifle, 20" barrel **$1,199.00**
Price: 1875 Lightning Carbine, 20" barrel **$1,049.00**

UBERTI SPRINGFIELD TRAPDOOR RIFLE
Caliber: 4-70, single shot. **Barrel:** 22" or 32.5". **Stock:** Walnut. **Finish:** Blue and case-hardened. Introduced 2006. Imported by Benelli USA.
Price: Springfield Trapdoor Carbine, 22" barrel **$1,100.00**
Price: Springfield Trapdoor Army, 32.5" barrel **$1,295.00**

U.S. FIRE ARMS STANDARD LIGHTNING MAGAZINE RIFLE
Caliber: 45 Colt, 44 WCF, 44 Spl., 38 WCF, 15-shot. **Barrel:** 26". **Stock:** Oiled walnut. **Finish:** High polish blue. Nickel finish also available. Introduced 2002. Made in U.S.A. by United States Fire-Arms Manufacturing Co.
Price: Round barrel. **$1,480.00**
Price: Octagonal barrel, checkered forend **$1,750.00**
Price: Half-round barrel, checkered forend **$1,999.00**
Price: Premium Carbine, 20" round barrel **$1,480.00**
Price: Baby Carbine, 20" special taper barrel **$1,999.00**
Price: Trapper, 16" special taper barrel **$2,155.00**
Price: Cowboy Action Lightning **$1,345.00**
Price: Cowboy Action Lightning Carbine, 20" round barrel **$1,345.00**

Includes models for a wide variety of sporting and competitive purposes and uses.

Anschutz 1733D

Barrett Model 95

Blaser R93 Classic

ANSCHUTZ 1743D BOLT-ACTION RIFLE
Caliber: 222 Rem., 3-shot magazine. **Barrel:** 19.7". **Weight:** 6.4 lbs. **Length:** 39" overall. **Stock:** European walnut. **Sights:** Hooded blade front, folding leaf rear. **Features:** Receiver grooved for scope mounting; single stage trigger; claw extractor; sling safety; sling swivels. Imported from Germany by AcuSport Corp.
Price: $1,588.95

ANSCHUTZ 1740 MONTE CARLO RIFLE
Caliber: 22 Hornet, 5-shot clip; 222 Rem., 3-shot clip. **Barrel:** 24". **Weight:** 6-1/2 lbs. **Length:** 43.25" overall. **Stock:** Select European walnut. **Sights:** Hooded ramp front, folding leaf rear; drilled and tapped for scope mounting. **Features:** Uses Match 54 action. Adjustable single stage trigger. Stock has roll-over Monte Carlo cheekpiece, slim forend with Schnabel tip, Wundhammer palm swell on grip, rosewood gripcap with white diamond insert. Skip-line checkering on grip and forend. Introduced 1997. Imported from Germany by AcuSport Corp.
Price: From $1,439.00
Price: Model 1730 Monte Carlo, as above except in
    22 Hornet $1,439.00

Anschutz 1733D Rifle
Similar to the 1740 Monte Carlo except has full-length, walnut, Mannlicher-style stock with skip-line checkering, rosewood Schnabel tip, and is chambered for 22 Hornet. Weighs 6.4 lbs., overall length 39", barrel length 19.7". Imported from Germany by AcuSport Corp.
Price: $1,588.95

BARRETT MODEL 95 BOLT-ACTION RIFLE
Caliber: 50 BMG, 5-shot magazine. **Barrel:** 29". **Weight:** 22 lbs. **Length:** 45" overall. **Stock:** Energy-absorbing recoil pad. **Sights:** Scope optional. **Features:** Bolt-action, bullpup design. Disassembles without tools; extendable bipod legs; match-grade barrel; muzzle brake. Introduced 1995. Made in U.S.A. by Barrett Firearms Mfg., Inc.
Price: From $4,950.00

BLASER R93 BOLT-ACTION RIFLE
Caliber: 22-250, 243, 6.5x55, 270, 7x57, 7mm-08, 308, 30-06, 257 Wby. Mag., 7mm Rem. Mag., 300 Win. Mag., 300 Wby. Mag., 338 Win Mag., 375 H&H, 416 Rem. Mag. **Barrel:** 22" (standard calibers), 26" (magnum). **Weight:** 7 lbs. **Length:** 40" overall (22" barrel). **Stock:** Two-piece European walnut. **Sights:** None furnished; drilled and tapped for scope mounting. **Features:** Straight pull-back bolt action with thumb-activated safety slide/cocking mechanism; interchangeable barrels and bolt heads. Introduced 1994. Imported from Germany by SIGARMS.
Price: R93 Classic $3,680.00
Price: R93 LX $1,895.00
Price: R93 Synthetic (black synthetic stock) $1,595.00
Price: R93 Safari Synthetic (416 Rem. Mag. only) $1,855.00
Price: R93 Grand Lux $4,915.00
Price: R93 Attaché $5,390.00

BROWNING A-BOLT RIFLES
Common Features: Short-throw (60") fluted bolt, three locking lugs, plunger-type ejector; adjustable trigger is grooved. Chrome-plated trigger sear. Hinged floorplate, detachable box magazine. Receivers are drilled and tapped for scope mounts, swivel studs included. Barrel is free-floating and glass-bedded, recessed muzzle. Safety is top-tang sliding button. Engraving available for bolt sleeve or rifle body. Introduced 1985. 30 model name variations, as noted below. Imported from Japan by Browning.

BROWNING A-BOLT HUNTER
Calibers, 22" barrel: 223, 22-250, 243, 270 Win., 30-06, 7mm-08, 308. **Calibers, 23" barrel:** 270 WSM, 7mm WSM, 300 WSM, 325 WSM (intr. 2005). **Calibers, 24" barrel:** 25-06. **Calibers, 26" barrel:** 7mm Rem. Mag., 300 Win. Mag., 338 Win. Mag. **Weight:** 6.25-7.2 lbs. **Length:** 41.25-46.5" overall. **Stock:** Sporter-style walnut; checkered grip and forend. **Metal Finish:** Low-luster blueing.
Price: Hunter, from $719.00
Price: Hunter, Left-hand, from $750.00

Browning A-Bolt Hunter

Browning A-Bolt Medallion

Browning A-Bolt White Gold Medallion

Browning A-Bolt RMEF

BROWNING A-BOLT HUNTER FLD
Caliber, 23" barrel: 270 WSM, 7mm WSM, 300 WSM, 325 WSM (intr. 2005). **Weight:** 6.6 lbs. **Length:** 42.75" overall. **Features:** FLD has low-luster blueing and select Monte Carlo stock with right-hand palm swell, double-border checkering. Otherwise similar to A-Bolt Hunter.
Price: FLD **$808.00**

BROWNING A-BOLT HUNTER WSSM, FLD WSSM
Calibers, 22" barrel: 223 WSSM, 243 WSSM, 25 WSSM. **Weight:** 6.3 lbs. **Length:** 41.25" overall. **Features:** WSSM has classic walnut stock. FLD has low-luster blueing and select Monte Carlo stock with right-hand palm swell, double-border checkering. Otherwise similar to A-Bolt Hunter.
Price: WSSM **$755.00**
Price: FLD WSSM **$829.00**

BROWNING A-BOLT MOUNTAIN TI
Caliber: 223 WSSM, 243 WSSM, 25 WSSM (all added 2005); 270 WSM, 7mm WSM, 300 WSM. **Barrel:** 22" or 23". **Weight:** 5.25-5.5 lbs. **Length:** 41.25-42.75" overall. **Stock:** Lightweight fiberglass Bell & Carlson model in Mossy-Oak New Break Up camo. **Metal Finish:** Stainless barrel, titanium receiver. **Features:** Pachmayr Decelerator recoil pad. Introduced 1999.
Price: From **$1,673.00**

Browning A-Bolt Micro Hunter and Micro Hunter Left-Hand
Calibers, 20" barrel: 22-250, 243, 308, 7mm-08. **Calibers, 22" barrel:** 22 Hornet, 270 WSM, 7mm WSM, 300 WSM, 325 WSM (2005). **Weight:** 6.25-6.4 lbs. **Length:** 39.5-41.5" overall. **Features:** Classic walnut stock with 13.3" LOP. Otherwise similar to A-Bolt Hunter.
Price: Micro Hunter, from **$698.00**
Price: Micro Hunter Left-hand, from **$728.00**

BROWNING A-BOLT MEDALLION
Calibers, 22" barrel: 223, 22-250, 243, 308, 270 Win., 280, 30-06. **Calibers, 23" barrel:** 270 WSM, 7mm WSM, 300 WSM, 325 WSM (intr. 2005). **Calibers, 24" barrel:** 25-06. **Calibers, 26" barrel:** 7mm Rem. Mag., 300 Win. Mag., 338 Win. Mag., 375 H&H. **Weight:** 6.25-7.1 lbs. **Length:** 41.25-46.5" overall. **Stock:** Select walnut stock, glossy finish, rosewood grip and forend caps, checkered grip and forend. **Metal Finish:** Engraved high-polish blued receiver.
Price: Medallion, from. **$821.00**
Price: Medallion WSSM in 223/243/25 WSSM **$872.00**
Price: Medallion w/BOSS, intr. 1987, from **$901.00**
Price: Medallion w/Boss, left-hand, from **$854.00**

BROWNING A-BOLT WHITE GOLD MEDALLION, RMEF WHITE GOLD, WHITE GOLD MEDALLION W/BOSS
Calibers, 22" barrel: 270 Win., 30-06. **Calibers, 23" barrel:** 270 WSM, 7mm WSM, 300 WSM, 325 WSM (intr. 2005). **Calibers, 26" barrel:** 7mm Rem. Mag., 300 Win. Mag. **Weight:** 6.4-7.7 lbs. **Length:** 42.75-46.5" overall. **Stock:** select walnut stock with brass spacers between rubber recoil pad and between the rosewood gripcap and forend tip; gold-filled barrel inscription; palm-swell pistol grip, Monte Carlo comb, 22 lpi checkering with double borders. **Metal Finish:** Engraved high-polish stainless receiver and barrel. BOSS version chambered in 270 Win. and 30-06 (22" barrel) and 7mm Rem. Mag. and 300 Win. Mag. (26" barrel) Introduced 1988. RMEF version has engraved gripcap, continental cheekpiece; gold engraved, stainless receiver and bbl. Introduced 2004.
Price: White Gold Medallion, from **$1,178.00**
Price: Rocky Mt. Elk Foundation White Gold, 325 WSM, intr. 2007 . **$1,286.00**
Price: White Gold Medallion w/BOSS . . . . **$1,235.00 to $1,263.00**

BROWNING A-BOLT STAINLESS STALKER, STAINLESS STALKER LEFT-HAND
Calibers, 22" barrel: 223, 243, 270, 280, 7mm-08, 30-06, 308. **Calibers, 23" barrel:** 270 WSM, 7mm WSM, 300 WSM, 325 WSM (intr. 2005). **Calibers, 24" barrel:** 25-06. **Calibers, 26" barrel:** 7mm Rem. Mag., 300 Win. Mag., 338 Win. Mag., 375 H&H. **Weight:** 6.1-7.2 lbs. **Length:** 40.9-46.5" overall. **Features:** Similar to the A-Bolt Hunter model except receiver and barrel are made of stainless steel; other exposed metal surfaces are finished silver-gray matte. Graphite-fiberglass composite textured stock. No sights are furnished, except on 375 H&H, which comes with open sights. Introduced 1987.
Price: Stainless Stalker, from **$915.00**
Price: Stainless Stalker left-hand, from **$944.00**
Price: Stainless Stalker WSSM, 223/243/25 WSSM **$808.00**

Browning A-Bolt Stainless Stalker

Browning A-Bolt Varmint Stalker

Browning A-Bolt Composite Stalker

Browning A-Bolt Eclipse Hunter

Browning A-Bolt Eclipse M-1000

Browning A-Bolt Stainless Stalker, Stainless Stalker Left-Hand, w/BOSS
Calibers, 22" barrel: 223 WSSM, 243 WSSM, 25 WSSM, 270, 30-06. **Calibers, 23" barrel:** 270 WSM, 7mm WSM, 300 WSM, 325 WSM (intr. 2005). **Calibers, 24" barrel:** 375 H&H. **Calibers, 26" barrel:** 7mm Rem. Mag., 300 Win. Mag., 338 Win. Mag. **Features:** Similar to the A-Bolt Stainless Stalker, except includes BOSS.
Price: Stainless Stalker w/BOSS, from **$995.00**
Price: Stainless Stalker left-hand w/BOSS, from **$1,024.00**

BROWNING A-BOLT VARMINT STALKER, VARMINT STALKER WSSM
Calibers, 24" barrel: 223 Rem., 223 WSSM, 243 WSSM, 25 WSSM. **Calibers, 26" barrel:** 22-250. **Weight:** 7.8-8.2 lbs. **Length:** 42.75-45.75" overall. **Features:** Similar to the A-Bolt Stainless Stalker except has black graphite-fiberglass stock with textured finish and matte blue-finish on all exposed metal surfaces. Medium-heavy varmint barrel. No sights are furnished. Introduced 1987.
Price: Varmint Stalker **$877.00**
Price: Varmint Stalker WSSM **$928.00**

BROWNING A-BOLT COMPOSITE STALKER
Calibers, 22" barrel: 223, 22-250, 243, 270, 280, 7mm-08, 30-06, 308. **Calibers, 23" barrel:** 270 WSM, 7mm WSM, 300 WSM, 325 WSM (intr. 2005). **Calibers, 24" barrel:** 25-06. **Calibers, 26" barrel:** 7mm Rem. Mag., 300 Win. Mag., 338 Win. Mag. **Weight:** 6.1-7.2 lbs. **Length:** 40.75-46.5" overall. **Features:** Similar to the A-Bolt Stainless Stalker except has black composite stock with textured finish and matte-blued finish on all exposed metal surfaces except bolt sleeve. No sights are furnished.
Price: Composite Stalker, from............................ **$719.00**
Price: Composite Stalker, w/BOSS, from.................... **$799.00**

BROWNING A-BOLT ECLIPSE HUNTER W/BOSS, M-1000 ECLIPSE W/BOSS, M-1000 ECLIPSE WSM, STAINLESS M-1000 ECLIPSE WSM
Calibers, 22" barrel: 270, 30-06. **Calibers, 26" barrel:** 7mm Rem. Mag., 300 Win. Mag., 270 WSM, 7mm WSM, 300 WSM. **Weight:** 7.5-9.9 lbs. **Length:** 42.75-46.5" overall. **Features:** All models have gray/black laminated thumbhole stock. Introduced 1996. Two versions have BOSS barrel vibration modulator and muzzle brake. Hunter has sporter-weight barrel. M-1000 Eclipses have long actions and heavy target barrels, adjustable triggers, bench-style forends, 3-shot magazines. Introduced 1997.
Price: Eclipse Hunter w/BOSS, from **$1,157.00**
Price: M-1000 Eclipse, from **$1,078.00**
Price: M-1000 Eclipse w/BOSS, from **$1,188.00**
Price: Stainless M-1000 Eclipse WSM, from **$1,288.00**

CARBON ONE BOLT-ACTION RIFLE
Caliber: 22-250 to 375 H&H. **Barrel:** Up to 28". **Weight:** 5-1/2 to 7-1/4 lbs. **Length:** Varies. **Stock:** Synthetic or wood. **Sights:** None furnished. **Features:** Choice of Remington, Browning or Winchester action with free-floated Christensen graphite/epoxy/steel barrel, trigger pull tuned to 3 to 3-1/2 lbs. Made in U.S.A. by Christensen Arms.
Price: Carbon One Hunter Rifle, 6-1/2 to 7 lbs. **$1,499.00**
Price: Carbon One Custom, 5-1/2 to 6-1/2 lbs., Shilen trigger ... **$2,750.00**
Price: Carbon Ranger, 50 BMG, 5-shot repeater **$4,750.00**
Price: Carbon Ranger, 50 BMG, single shot **$3,950.00**

Charles Daly Field Mauser

Cooper Model 21 Bolt

CZ 527 Lux

CENTURY INTERNATIONAL M70 SPORTER DOUBLE-TRIGGER BOLT-ACTION RIFLE
Caliber: 22-250, 270, 300 Win. Mag, 308 Win., 24" barrel. **Weight:** 7.95 lbs. **Length:** 44.5" **Sights:** Flip-up U-notch rear sight, hooded blade front sight. **Features:** Mauser M98-type action; 5-rd fixed box magazine. 22-250 has hinged floorplate. Monte Carlo stock, oil finish. Adjustable trigger on double-trigger models. 300 Win. Mag. Has 3-rd. fixed box magazine. 308 holds 5 rds. 300 and 308 have buttpads. Manufactured by Zastava in Yugoslavia, imported by Century International.
Price: M70 Sporter Double-Trigger **$500.00**
Price: M70 Sporter Double-Trigger 22-250 . . . . **$475.00**
Price: M70 Sporter Single-Trigger .300 Win. Mag. **$475.00**
Price: M70 Sporter Single/Double Trigger .308 Win. **$500.00**

CHARLES DALY FIELD MAUSER RIFLE
Caliber: 22-250, 243, 25-06, 270, 308, 30-06 (in 22" barrels); 7mm Rem. Mag. and 300 Win. Mag. in 24" barrels. **Weight:** NA. **Sights:** None; drilled and tapped for scope mounts. **Features:** Mauser Model 98-type action; carbon or stainless steel barrels; slide safety; polymer stock; fully adjustable trigger.
Price: Field Grade Mauser **$459.00**
Price: Mauser SS **$549.00**
Price: Magnum calibers **$579.00**

CHEYTAC M-200
Caliber: 408 CheyTac, 7-round mag. **Barrel:** 30". **Length:** 55", stock extended. **Weight:** 27 lbs. (steel barrel); 24 lbs. (carbon fiber barrel). **Stock:** Retractable. **Sights:** None, scope rail provided. **Features:** CNC-machined receiver, attachable Picatinny rail M-1913, detachable barrel, integral bipod, 3.5-lb. trigger pull, muzzle brake. Made in U.S. by CheyTac, LLC.
Price: **$13,795.00**

COOPER MODEL 16 BOLT-ACTION RIFLE
Caliber: .223 WSSM, .243 WSSM, .25 WSSM, .22BR, 6mmBR, .22 PPC, 6mm PPC. **Barrel:** 26" stainless steel match barrel. **Weight:** 6.5-7.5 lbs. **Stock:** AA-AAA select claro walnut, 20 lpi checkering. **Sights:** None furnished. **Features:** Three front locking-lug bolt-action.
Price: Varminter. **$1.550.00**
Price: Montana Varminter **$1,520.00**
Price: Varmint Extreme **$1,995.00**

COOPER MODEL 21 BOLT-ACTION RIFLE
Caliber: .17 Rem., 19-.223, Tactical 20, .204 Ruger, .20 VarTarg, .222 Rem., .222 Rem Mag, .223 Rem, .223 Rem A.I., .22 PPC, 6mm PPC, 6x45, 6x47. **Barrel:** 22" or 24" in Classic configurations, 24"-26" in

Varminter configurations. **Weight:** 6.5-8.0 lbs., depending on type. **Stock:** AA-AAA select claro walnut, 20 lpi checkering. **Sights:** None furnished. **Features:** Three front locking-lug bolt-action single shot. **Action:** 7.75" long, Sako extractor. Button ejector. Fully adjustable single-stage trigger. Options include wood upgrades, case-color metalwork, barrel fluting, custom LOP, and many others.
Price: Phoenix. **$1,298.00**
Price: Varminter **$1,298.00**
Price: Montana Varminter **$1,520.00**
Price: Varmint Extreme **$1,995.00**
Price: Classic (blued barrel) **$1,450.00**
Price: Custom Classic (blued barrel) **$2,100.00**
Price: Western Classic (blued barrel) **$2,800.00**

COOPER MODEL 22 BOLT-ACTION RIFLE
Caliber: 22-250 Rem., 22-250 Rem. AI, 25-06 Rem., 25-06 Rem. AI, 243 Win., 243 Win. AI, 220 Swift, 250/3000 AI, 257 Roberts, 257 Roberts AI, 7mm-08, 6mm Rem., 260 Rem., 6 x 284, 6.5 x 284, 22 BR, 6mm BR, 308 Win. **Barrel:** 24" or 26" stainless match in Classic configurations. 24" or 26" in Varminter configurations. **Weight:** 7.5 to 8.0 lbs. depending on type. **Stock:** AA-AAA select claro walnut, 20 lpi checkering. **Sights:** None furnished. **Features:** Three front locking-lug bolt-action single shot. **Action:** 8.25" long, Sako style extractor. Button ejector. Fully adjustable single-stage trigger. Options include wood upgrades, case-color metalwork, barrel fluting, custom LOP, and many others.
Price: Phoenix. **$1,398.00**
Price: Varminter **$1,398.00**
Price: Montana Varminter **$1,600.00**
Price: Varmint Extreme **$2,100.00**
Price: Classic (blued barrel) **$1,498.00**
Price: Custom Classic (blued barrel) **$2,195.00**
Price: Western Classic (blued barrel) **$2,895.00**

COOPER MODEL 38 BOLT-ACTION RIFLE
Caliber: 17 Squirrel, 17 He Bee, 17 Ackley Hornet, 17 Mach IV, 19 Calhoon, 20 VarTarg, 221 Fireball, 22 Hornet, 22 K-Hornet, 22 Squirrel, 218 Bee, 218 Mashburn Bee. **Barrel:** 22" or 24" in Classic configurations, 24" or 26" in Varminter configurations. **Weight:** 6.5-8.0 lbs. depending on type. **Stock:** AA-AAA select claro walnut, 20 lpi checkering. **Sights:** None furnished. **Features:** Three front locking-lug bolt-action single shot. **Action:** 7" long, Sako style extractor. Button ejector. Fully adjustable single-stage trigger. Options include wood upgrades, case-color metalwork, barrel fluting, custom LOP, and many others.
Price: Varminter **$1,298.00**
Price: Montana Varminter **$1,520.00**
Price: Varmint Extreme **$1,995.00**
Price: Classic (blued barrel) **$1,450.00**
Price: Custom Classic (blued barrel) **$2,100.00**
Price: Western Classic (blued barrel) **$2,800.00**

CZ 527 FS

CZ 527 American

CZ 550 Lux

CZ 550 Medium Magnum

CZ 550 Magnum

CZ 527 LUX BOLT-ACTION RIFLE
Caliber: 22 Hornet, 222 Rem., 223 Rem., detachable 5-shot magazine. **Barrel:** 23-1/2"; standard or heavy barrel. **Weight:** 6 lbs., 1 oz. **Length:** 42-1/2" overall. **Stock:** European walnut with Monte Carlo. **Sights:** Hooded front, open adjustable rear. **Features:** Improved mini-Mauser action with non-rotating claw extractor; single set trigger; grooved receiver. Imported from the Czech Republic by CZ-USA.
Price: $566.00
Price: Model FS, full-length stock, cheekpiece $658.00

CZ 527 American Classic Bolt-Action Rifle
Similar to the CZ 527 Lux except has classic-style stock with 18 lpi checkering; free-floating barrel; recessed target crown on barrel. No sights furnished. Introduced 1999. Imported from the Czech Republic by CZ-USA.
Price: 22 Hornet, 222 Rem., 223 Rem.. .... **$586.00 to $609.00**

CZ 550 LUX BOLT-ACTION RIFLE
Caliber: 22-250, 243, 6.5x55, 7x57, 7x64, 308 Win., 9.3x62, 270 Win., 30-06. **Barrel:** 20.47". **Weight:** 7.5 lbs. **Length:** 44.68" overall. **Stock:** Turkish walnut in Bavarian style or FS (Mannlicher). **Sights:** Hooded front, adjustable rear. **Features:** Improved Mauser-style action with claw extractor, fixed ejector, square bridge dovetailed receiver; single set trigger. Imported from the Czech Republic by CZ-USA.
Price: Lux.. .... **$566.00 to $609.00**
Price: FS (full stock) $706.00

CZ 550 American Classic Bolt-Action Rifle
Similar to CZ 550 Lux except has American classic-style stock with 18 lpi checkering; free-floating barrel; recessed target crown. Has 25.6" barrel; weighs 7.48 lbs. No sights furnished. Introduced 1999. Imported from the Czech Republic by CZ-USA.
Price: .... **$586.00 to $609.00**

CZ 550 Medium Magnum Bolt-Action Rifle
Similar to the CZ 550 Lux except chambered for the 300 Win. Mag. and 7mm Rem. Mag.; 5-shot magazine. Adjustable iron sights, hammer-forged barrel, single-set trigger, Turkish walnut stock. Weighs 7.5 lbs. Introduced 2001. Imported from the Czech Republic by CZ-USA.
Price: $621.00

CZ 550 Magnum Bolt-Action Rifle
Similar to CZ 550 Lux except has long action for 300 Win. Mag., 375 H&H, 416 Rigby, 458 Win. Mag. Overall length is 46.45"; barrel length 25"; weighs 9.24 lbs. Hooded front sight, express rear with one standing, two folding leaves. Imported from the Czech Republic by CZ-USA.
Price: 300 Win. Mag.. .... $717.00
Price: 375 H&H $756.00
Price: 416 Rigby $809.00
Price: 458 Win. Mag. $744.00

CZ 700 M1 SNIPER RIFLE
Caliber: 308 Winchester, 10-shot magazine. **Barrel:** 25.6". **Weight:** 11.9 lbs. **Length:** 45" overall. **Stock:** Laminated wood thumbhole with adjustable buttplate and cheekpiece. **Sights:** None furnished; permanently attached Weaver rail for scope mounting. **Features:** 60-degree bolt throw; oversized trigger guard and bolt handle for use with gloves; full-length equipment rail on forend; fully adjustable trigger. Introduced 2001. Imported from the Czech Republic by CZ-USA.
Price: $2,097.00

Dakota 76 Traveler

Dakota 76 Classic

Dakota 76 Safari

Dakota Longbow

DAKOTA 76 TRAVELER TAKEDOWN RIFLE

Caliber: 257 Roberts, 25-06, 7x57, 270, 280, 30-06, 338-06, 35 Whelen (standard length); 7mm Rem. Mag., 300 Win. Mag., 338 Win. Mag., 416 Taylor, 458 Win. Mag. (short magnums); 7mm, 300, 330, 375 Dakota Magnums. **Barrel:** 23". **Weight:** 7-1/2 lbs. **Length:** 43-1/2" overall. **Stock:** Medium fancy-grade walnut in classic style. Checkered grip and forend; solid buttpad. **Sights:** None furnished; drilled and tapped for scope mounts. **Features:** Threadless disassembly. Uses modified Model 76 design with many features of the Model 70 Winchester. Left-hand model also available. Introduced 1989. African chambered for 338 Lapua Mag., 404 Jeffery, 416 Rigby, 416 Dakota, 450 Dakota, 4-round magazine, select wood, two stock cross-bolts. 24" barrel, weighs 9-10 lbs. Ramp front sight, standing leaf rear. Introduced 1989.Made in U.S.A. by Dakota Arms, Inc.
Price: Classic. $6,095.00
Price: Safari $6,995.00
Price: African $7,995.00

DAKOTA 76 CLASSIC BOLT-ACTION RIFLE

Caliber: 257 Roberts, 270, 280, 30-06, 7mm Rem. Mag., 338 Win. Mag., 300 Win. Mag., 375 H&H, 458 Win. Mag. **Barrel:** 23". **Weight:** 7-1/2 lbs. **Length:** 43-1/2" overall. **Stock:** Medium fancy grade walnut in classic style. Checkered pistol grip and forend; solid buttpad. **Sights:** None furnished; drilled and tapped for scope mounts. **Features:** Has many features of the original Winchester Model 70. One-piece rail trigger guard assembly; steel gripcap. Model 70-style trigger. Many options available.

Left-hand rifle available at same price. Introduced 1988. From Dakota Arms, Inc.
Price: From $4,595.00

DAKOTA 76 SAFARI BOLT-ACTION RIFLE

Caliber: 270 Win., 7x57, 280, 30-06, 7mm Dakota, 7mm Rem. Mag., 300 Dakota, 300 Win. Mag., 330 Dakota, 338 Win. Mag., 375 Dakota, 458 Win. Mag., 300 H&H, 375 H&H, 416 Rem. **Barrel:** 23". **Weight:** 8-1/2 lbs. **Length:** 43-1/2" overall. **Stock:** XXX fancy walnut with ebony forend tip; point-pattern with wraparound forend checkering. **Sights:** Ramp front, standing leaf rear. **Features:** Has many features of the original Winchester Model 70. Barrel band front swivel, inletted rear. Cheekpiece with shadow line. Steel gripcap. Introduced 1988. From Dakota Arms, Inc.
Price: Wood stock $5,595.00

DAKOTA LONGBOW TACTICAL E.R. RIFLE

Caliber: 300 Dakota Magnum, 330 Dakota Magnum, 338 Lapua Magnum. **Barrel:** 28", .950" at muzzle **Weight:** 13.7 lbs. **Length:** 50" to 52" overall. **Stock:** Ambidextrous McMillan A-2 fiberglass, black or olive green color; adjustable cheekpiece and buttplate. **Sights:** None furnished. Comes with Picatinny one-piece optical rail. **Features:** Uses the Dakota 76 action with controlled-round feed; three-position firing pin block safety, claw extractor; Model 70-style trigger. Comes with bipod, case tool kit. Introduced 1997. Made in U.S.A. by Dakota Arms, Inc.
Price: $4,250.00

DAKOTA 97 LIGHTWEIGHT HUNTER

Caliber: 22-250 to 330. **Barrel:** 22" to 24". **Weight:** 6.1 to 6.5 lbs. **Length:** 43" overall. **Stock:** Fiberglass. **Sights:** Optional. **Features:** Matte blue finish, black stock. Right-hand action only. Introduced 1998. Made in U.S.A. by Dakota Arms, Inc.
Price: $1,995.00

Dakota 97 Lightweight Hunter

Dakota Hunter

DSA DS-MP1

Ed Brown 702 Savanna

DAKOTA LONG-RANGE HUNTER RIFLE
Caliber: 25-06, 257 Roberts, 270 Win., 280 Rem., 7mm Rem. Mag., 7mm Dakota Mag., 30-06, 300 Win. Mag., 300 Dakota Mag., 338 Win. Mag., 330 Dakota Mag., 375 H&H Mag., 375 Dakota Mag. **Barrel:** 24", 26", match-quality; free-floating. **Weight:** 7.7 lbs. **Length:** 45" to 47" overall. **Stock:** H-S Precision black synthetic, with one-piece bedding block system. **Sights:** None furnished. Drilled and tapped for scope mounting. **Features:** Cylindrical machined receiver controlled round feed; Mauser-style extractor; three-position striker blocking safety; fully adjustable match trigger. Right-hand action only. Introduced 1997. Made in U.S.A. by Dakota Arms, Inc.
Price: From $2,995.00

DAKOTA PREDATOR RIFLE
Caliber: 17 VarTarg, 17 Rem., 17 Tactical , 20 VarTarg , 20 Tactical , .20 PPC, 204 Ruger, 221 Rem Fireball, 222 Remington, 22 PPC, 223 Rem., 6mm PPC, 6.5 Grendel. **Barrel:** 22" match grade stainless;. **Weight:** NA. **Length:** NA. **Stock:** Special select walnut, sporter-style stock, 23 lpi checkering on forend and grip. **Sights:** None furnished. Drilled and tapped for scope mounting. **Features:** 13-5/8" LOP, 1/2" black presentation pad, 11° recessed target crown. Serious Predator includes XXX walnut varmint style stock w/semi-beavertail forend, stainless receiver. All-Weather Predator includes varmint style composite stock w/semi-beavertail forend, stainless receiver. Introduced 2007. Made in U.S.A. by Dakota Arms, Inc.
Price: Classic. $4,295.00
Price: Serious $3,295.00
Price: All-Weather $2,595.00

DSA DS-MP1
Caliber: 308 Win. match chamber. **Barrel:** 22", 1:10 twist, hand-lapped stainless-steel match-grade Badger Barrel with recessed target crown. **Weight:** 11.5 lbs. **Length:** 41.75". **Stock:** Black McMillan A5 pillar bedded in Marine-Tex with 13.5" length of pull. **Sights:** Tactical Picatinny rail. **Features:** Action, action threads and action bolt locking shoulder completely trued, Badger Ordnance precision ground heavy recoil lug, machined steel Picatinny rail sight mount, trued action threads, action bolt locking shoulder, bolt face and lugs, 2.5-lb. trigger pull, barrel and action finished in Black DuraCoat, guaranteed to shoot 1/2 MOA at 100 yards with match-grade ammo. Introduced 2006. Made in U.S.A. by DSA, Inc.
Price: $2,800.00

ED BROWN SAVANNA RIFLE
Caliber: 30-06, 300 Win. Mag., 300 Weatherby, 338 Win. Mag. **Barrel:** 22", 23", 24". **Weight:** 8 to 8-1/2 lbs. **Stock:** Fully glass-bedded McMillan fiberglass sporter. **Sights:** None furnished. Talley scope mounts utilizing heavy duty 8-40 screws. **Features:** Custom action with machined steel trigger guard and hinged floor plate.
Price: $3,195.00

ED BROWN MODEL 704 BUSHVELD
Caliber: 338 Win. Mag., 375 H&H, 416 Rem. Mag., 458 Win. Mag., 458 Lott and all Ed Brown Savanna long action calibers. **Barrel:** 24" medium or heavy weight. **Weight:** 8.25 lbs. **Stock:** Fully bedded McMillan fiberglass with Monte Carlo style cheekpiece, Pachmayr Decelerator recoil pad. **Sights:** None furnished. Talley scope mounts utilizing heavy duty 8-40 screws. **Features:** Stainless steel barrel, additional calibers, iron sights.
Price: From . . . . $2,895.00 to $3,195.00

Howa Lightning

Howa M-1500 Hunter

Howa M-1500 Ultralight

Howa M-1500 Varmint Supreme

ED BROWN MODEL 704 EXPRESS
Caliber: 375 H&H, 416 Rem, 458 Lott, other calibers available. **Barrel:** 24" #4 Stainless barrel with black Gen III coating for superior rust protection. **Weight:** 9 lbs. **Stocks:** Hand-bedded McMillan fiberglass stock. Monte Carlo style with cheek piece and full 1" thick Pachmayr Decel recoil pad. **Sights:** Adjustable iron sights. **Features:** Ed Brown controlled feed action. A special dropped box magazine ensures feeding and allows a full four-round capacity in the magazine, plus one in the chamber. Barrel band is standard for lower profile when carrying the rifle through heavy brush.
Price: From **$3,695.00**

HOWA LIGHTNING BOLT-ACTION RIFLE
Caliber: 223, 22-250, 243, 204 Ruger, 270, 308, 30-06, 7mm Rem. Mag., 300 Win. Mag., 338 Win. Mag, 300 WSM, 7mm WSM, 270 WSM. **Barrel:** 22", 24" magnum calibers. **Weight:** 7-1/2 lbs. **Length:** 42-44" overall (22" barrel). **Stock:** Black Bell & Carlson Carbelite composite with Monte Carlo comb; checkered grip and forend; also Realtree camo available. **Sights:** None furnished. Drilled and tapped for scope mounting. **Features:** Three-position thumb safety; hinged floorplate; polished blue/black finish. Introduced 1993. From Legacy Sports International.
Price: Blue, standard calibers **$439.00**
Price: Blue, magnum calibers **$470.00**
Price: Stainless, standard calibers **$661.00**
Price: Stainless, magnum calibers **$690.00**

Howa M-1500 Hunter Bolt-Action Rifle
Similar to Lightning Model except has walnut-finished hardwood stock, three-position safety. Polished blue finish or stainless steel. Introduced 1999. From Legacy Sports International.
Price: Blue, standard calibers **$574.00**
Price: Stainless, standard calibers **$682.00**
Price: Blue, magnum calibers **$595.00**
Price: Stainless, magnum calibers **$704.00**
Price: Blued, camo stock **$545.00**

Howa M-1500 Supreme Rifles
Similar to Howa M-1500 Lightning except stocked with JRS Classic or Thumbhole Sporter laminated wood stocks in Nutmeg (brown/black) or Pepper (gray/black) colors. **Barrel:** 22"; 24" magnum calibers. Weights are JRS stock 8 lbs., THS stock 8.3 lbs. Three-position safety. Introduced 2001. Imported from Japan by Legacy Sports International.
Price: Blue, standard calibers, JRS stock **$646.00**
Price: Blue, standard calibers, THS stock **$704.00**
Price: Blue, magnum calibers, JRS stock **$675.00**
Price: Blue, magnum calibers, THS stock **$733.00**
Price: Stainless, standard calibers, JRS stock **$755.00**
Price: Stainless, standard calibers, THS stock **$813.00**
Price: Stainless, magnum calibers, JRS stock **$784.00**
Price: Stainless, magnum calibers, THS stock **$842.00**

Howa M-1500 Ultralight
Similar to Howa M-1500 Lightning except receiver milled to reduce weight; three-position safety; tapered 22" barrel; 1-10" twist. Chambered for 243 Win. Stocks are black texture-finished hardwood. Weighs 6.4 lbs. Length 40" overall.
Price: Blued **$539.00**
Price: Stainless model **$658.00**

Howa M-1500 Varmint and Varmint Supreme Rifles
Similar to M-1500 Lightning except has heavy 24" hammer-forged barrel. Chambered for 223, 22-250, 308. Weighs 9.3 lbs.; overall length 44.5". Introduced 1999. Imported from Japan by Interarms/Howa. Varminter Supreme has heavy barrel, target crown muzzle; three-position safety. Heavy 24" barrel, laminated wood with raised comb stocks, rollover cheekpiece, vented beavertail forearm; available in 223 Rem., 22-250 Rem., 204 Ruger, 308 Win. Weighs 9.9 lbs. Carbon fiber thumbhole stock option available. Introduced 2001. Imported from Japan by Legacy Sports International.
Price: Varminter, blue, polymer stock **$546.00**
Price: Varminter, stainless, polymer stock **$664.00**
Price: Varminter, blue, wood stock **$610.00**
Price: Varminter, stainless, wood stock **$719.00**
Price: Varminter Supreme, blued . . . . $711.00 to $733.00
Price: Varminter Supreme, stainless . . . . $820.00 to $842.00
Price: Varminter, blued, camo stock **$582.00**
Price: Varminter, stainless, camo stock **$704.00**

Kimber 8400

Kimber 84M Classic

L.A.R. Grizzly

Magnum Research Tactical

KENNY JARRETT BOLT-ACTION RIFLE
Caliber: 223 Rem., 243 Improved, 243 Catbird, 7mm-08 Improved, 280 Remington, .280 Ackley Improved, 7mm Rem. Mag., 284 Jarrett, 30-06 Springfield, 300 Win. Mag., .300 Jarrett, 323 Jarrett, 338 Jarrett, 375 H&H, 416 Rem., 450 Rigby, other modern cartridges. **Barrel:** NA. **Weight:** NA. **Length:** NA. **Stock:** NA. **Features:** Tri-Lock receiver. Talley rings and bases. Accuracy guarantees and custom loaded ammunition.
Price: Signature Series $6,880.00
Price: Wind Walker $6,650.00
Price: Original Beanfield (customer's receiver) $4,850.00
Price: Professional Hunter $9,390.00

KIMBER MODEL 8400 BOLT-ACTION RIFLE
Caliber: 270, 7mm, 300 or 325 WSM, 4 shot. **Barrel:** 24". **Weight:** 6 lbs. 3 oz. to 6 lbs 10 oz. **Length:** 43.25". **Stock:** Claro walnut or Kevlar-reinforced fiberglass. **Sights:** None; drilled and tapped for bases. **Features:** Mauser claw extractor, two-position wing safety, action bedded on aluminum pillars and fiberglass, free-floated barrel, match grade adjustable trigger set at 4 lbs., matte or polished blue or matte stainless finish. Introduced 2003. Made in U.S.A. by Kimber Mfg. Inc.
Price: Classic. . . . . $1,080.00 to $2,030.00

KIMBER MODEL 84M BOLT-ACTION RIFLE
Caliber: 22-250, 204 Ruger, 223, 243, 260 Rem., 7mm-08, 308, 5-shot. **Barrel:** 22", 24", 26". **Weight:** 5 lbs., 10 oz. to 10 lbs. **Length:** 41" to 45". **Stock:** Claro walnut, checkered with steel gripcap; synthetic or gray laminate. **Sights:** None; drilled and tapped for bases. **Features:** Mauser claw extractor, three-position wing safety, action bedded on aluminum pillars, free-floated barrel, match-grade trigger set at 4 lbs., matte blue finish. Includes cable lock. Introduced 2001. Made in U.S.A. by Kimber Mfg. Inc.
Price: Classic (243, 260, 7mm-08, 308) . . . . $945.00 to $1,828.00
Price: Varmint (22-250) $1,038.00

L.A.R. GRIZZLY 50 BIG BOAR RIFLE
Caliber: 50 BMG, single shot. **Barrel:** 36". **Weight:** 30.4 lbs. **Length:** 45.5" overall. **Stock:** Integral. Ventilated rubber recoil pad. **Sights:** None furnished; scope mount. **Features:** Bolt-action bullpup design, thumb and bolt stop safety. All-steel construction. Introduced 1994. Made in U.S.A. by L.A.R. Mfg., Inc.
Price: $2,350.00

MAGNUM RESEARCH MAGNUM LITE RIFLES
Caliber: 22-250, 223, 280, 7mm WSM, 30-06, 308, 300 WSM, 300 Win. Mag., 3-shot magazine. **Barrel:** 24" sport taper graphite; 26" bull barrel graphite. **Weight:** 7.1-9.2 lbs. **Length:** 44.5-48.25" overall (adjustable on Tactical model). **Stock:** Hogue OverMolded synthetic, H-S Precision Tactical synthetic, H-S Precision Varmint synthetic. **Sights:** None. **Features:** Remington Model 700 receiver. Introduced: 2001. From Magnum Research, Inc.
Price: MLR3006B26 H-S Tactical stock $2,295.00
Price: MLR7MMBST24 Hogue stock $2,295.00
Price: MLRT22250 H-S Tactical stock, 26" bull barrel $2,400.00

Remington 700 Classic

Remington 700 Classic Boone & Crockett

Remington 700 BDL

Remington 700 SPS Buckmaster

Remington 700 SPS Varmint

REMINGTON MODEL 700 CDL CLASSIC DELUXE RIFLE
Caliber: 223, 243, 25-06, 270, 7mm-08, 7mm Rem. Mag., 7mm Rem. Ultra Mag., 30-06, 300 Rem. Mag., 35 Whelen. **Barrel:** 24" or 26" round tapered. **Weight:** 7.4 to 7.6 lbs. **Length:** 43.6" to 46.5" overall. **Stock:** Straight-comb American walnut stock, satin finish, checkering, right-handed cheek piece, black fore-end tip and grip cap, sling swivel studs. **Sights:** None. **Features:** Satin blued finish, jeweled bolt body, drilled and tapped for scope mounts. Hinged-floorplate magazine capacity: 4, standard calibers; 3, magnum calibers. R3 gel recoil pad, cylindrical receiver, integral extractor. Introduced 2004. CDL SF (stainless fluted) introduced 2007. SF chambered for 17 Rem Fireball, 270, 270 WSM, 7mm-08, 7mm Rem. Mag., 30-06, 300 WSM. Made in U.S. by Remington Arms Co., Inc.

Price: Standard calibers, 24" barrel **$907.00**
Price: Magnum calibers, 26" barrel **$933.00**
Price: SF (2007), from **$1,039.00**
Price: Boone & Crockett (2007), from **$750.00**

REMINGTON MODEL 700 BDL RIFLE
Caliber: 243, 270, 7mm Rem. Mag. 30-06, 300 Rem Ultra Mag. **Barrel:** 22, 24, 26" round tapered. **Weight:** 7.25-7.4 lbs. **Length:** 41.6-46.5" overall. **Stock:** Walnut. Gloss-finish pistol grip stock with skip-line checkering, black forend tip and gripcap with white line spacers. Quick-release floorplate. **Sights:** Gold bead ramp front; hooded ramp, removable step-adjustable rear with windage screw. **Features:** Side safety, receiver tapped for scope mounts, matte receiver top, quick detachable swivels.

Price: 243, 270, 30-06 . . . . **$877.00**
Price: 7mm Rem. Mag. 300 Rem Ultra Mag **$904.00**

REMINGTON MODEL 700 SPS RIFLES
Caliber: 6.8 Rem SPC, 223 Rem., 243 Win., 270 Win. 270 WSM, 7mm-08 Rem., 7mm Rem. Mag., 30-06, 308 Win., 300 WSM, 300 Win. Mag., 300 Rem. Ultra Mag. **Barrel:** 20", 24" or 26" carbon steel. **Weight:** 7 to 7.6 lbs. **Length:** 39.6" to 46.5" overall. **Stock:** Black synthetic, sling swivel studs, R3 recoil pad. **Sights:** None. Introduced 2005. SPS Stainless replaces Model 700 BDL Stainless Synthetic. **Barrel:** Bead-blasted 416 stainless steel. **Features:** Plated internal fire control components; additional calibers: 204 Ruger, 22-250 Rem., 25-06 Rem. SPS DM features detachable box magazine. Buckmaster Edition versions feature Realtree Hardwoods HD camouflage and Buckmasters logo engraved on floorplate. SPS Varmint includes X-Mark Pro trigger, 26" heavy contour barrel, vented beavertail forend, dual front sling swivel studs. Made in U.S. by Remington Arms Co., Inc.

Price: SPS 17 Rem. Fireball (2007) **$604.00**
Price: SPS Youth, 20" barrel (2007) **$604.00**
Price: SPS Buckmasters (2007) **$665.00**
Price: SPS Varmint (2007) **$647.00**
Price: SPS Stainless, (2005) **$604.00**
Price: SPS DM (2005) **$633.00**

REMINGTON MODEL 700 MOUNTAIN LSS RIFLES
Caliber: 270 Win., 280 Rem., 7mm-08 Rem., 30-06. **Barrel:** 22" satin stainless steel. **Weight:** 6.6 lbs. **Length:** 41.6" to 42.5" overall. **Stock:** Brown laminated, sling swivel studs, R3 recoil pad, black forend tip. **Sights:** None. **Barrel:** Bead-blasted 416 stainless steel, lightweight contour. Made in U.S. by Remington Arms Co., Inc.

Price: 280 Rem. (2007) **$1,015.00**

CENTERFIRE RIFLES — Bolt-Action

Remington Model 700 LSS

Remington 700 Alaskan Ti

Remington 700 VLS

Remington 700 VLSS TH

Remington 700 VS SF II

REMINGTON MODEL 700 ALASKAN TI
Caliber: 25-06, 270 Win., 270 WSM, 280 Rem., 7mm-08 Rem., 7mm Rem. Mag., 30-06, 300 WSM, 300 Win. Mag. **Barrel:** 24" round tapered. **Weight:** 6 lbs. **Length:** 43.6" to 44.5" overall. **Stock:** Bell & Carlson carbon-fiber synthetic, sling swivel studs, R3 gel recoil pad. **Sights:** None. **Features:** Formerly Model 700 Titanium, introduced 2001. Titanium receiver, spiral-cut fluted bolt, skeletonized bolt handle, X-Mark Pro trigger, satin stainless finish. Drilled and tapped for scope mounts. Hinged-floorplate magazine capacity: 4, standard calibers; 3, magnum calibers. Introduced 2007. Made in U.S. by Remington Arms Co., Inc.
Price: From **$2,105.00**

REMINGTON MODEL 700 VLS/VLSS RIFLES
Caliber: 204 Ruger, 223 Rem., 22-250, 6mm, 243, 308. **Barrel:** 26" heavy contour barrel (0.820" muzzle O.D.), concave target-style barrel crown. **Weight:** 9.4 lbs. **Length:** 45.75" overall. **Stock:** Brown laminated stock, satin finish, with beavertail forend, gripcap, rubber buttpad. **Sights:** None. **Features:** Introduced 1995. VLSS (varmint laminate stock stainless) thumbhole model introduced 2007. Made in U.S. by Remington Arms Co., Inc.
Price: VLS **$928.00**
Price: VLSS TH (2007) **$1,028.00**

REMINGTON MODEL 700 VSF/VS SF II/SENDERO SF II RIFLES
Caliber: 17 Rem. Mag., 223 Rem., 22-250 Rem., 308 Win. **Barrel:** satin blued 26" heavy contour (0.820" muzzle O.D.), concave target-style barrel crown on VSF. VS SF has satin-finish stainless barreled action with 26" fluted barrel. **Weight:** 8.5 lbs. **Length:** 45.75" overall. **Stock:** H.S. Precision composite reinforced with aramid fibers, desert tan (VSF) with black webbing; black (VS SF II) Contoured beavertail fore-end with ambidextrous finger grooves, palm swell, and twin front tactical-style swivel studs. **Sights:** None. **Features:** Aluminum bedding block, right- and left-hand models. Both drilled and tapped for scope mounts, hinged floorplate magazines. VSF Introduced 1992. VS SF additionally chambered for 204 Ruger, 220 Swift. Introduced 1994. Sendero model is similar to VS SF II except chambered for 264 Win. Mag., 7mm Rem. Mag., 7mm Rem. Ultra Mag., 300 Win. Mag., 300 Rem. Ultra Mag. Polished stainless barrel. Introduced 1996. Made in U.S. by Remington Arms Co., Inc.
Price: VSF, 17 Rem. Fireball (2007) **$1,159.00**
Price: VS SF II **$1,252.00**
Price: Sendero SF II **$1,279.00**

REMINGTON MODEL 700 LV SF
Caliber: 17 Rem., 204 Ruger, 221 Rem. Fireball, 223 Rem., 22-250 Rem. **Barrel:** 22" satin stainless steel medium contour (0.657" muzzle O.D.), fluted. **Weight:** 6.75 lbs. **Length:** 41.6" overall. **Stock:** Black Bell & Carlson composite, semi-beavertail forend, swivel studs, R3 recoil pad. **Features:** Short action, pillar-bedded receiver, blind box magazine, jeweled bolt.
Price: **$1,040.00**

Remington 700 XCR

Remington 770

Remington Seven XCR Camo

Remington 798 SS Laminate

REMINGTON MODEL 700 XCR RIFLE
Caliber: 25-06 Rem., 270 Win., 270 WSM, 7mm-08 Rem., 7mm Rem. Mag., 7mm Rem Ultra Mag, 30-06, 300 WSM, 300 Win. Mag., 300 Rem. Ultra Mag., 338 Rem. Ultra Mag., 338 Win. Mag., 375 H&H Mag., 375 Rem. Ultra Mag. **Barrel:** 24" standard caliber; 26" magnum. **Weight:** 7.4 to 7.6 lbs. **Length:** 43.6" to 46.5" overall. **Stock:** Black synthetic, R3 recoil pad, rubber overmolded grip and forend. **Sights:** None. **Features:** XCR (Xtreme Conditions Rifle) includes TriNyte Corrosion Control System; drilled and tapped for scope mounts. 375 H&H Mag., 375 Rem. Ultra Mag. chamberings come with iron sights. Introduced 2005. XCR Tactical model introduced 2007. **Features:** Bell & Carlson OD green tactical stock, beavertail forend, recessed thumbhook behind pistol grip, TriNyte coating over stainless steel barrel, LTR fluting. Chambered in 223 Rem., 300 Win. Mag., 308 Win. Made in U.S. by Remington Arms Co., Inc.
Price: 25-06 Rem., 24" barrel (2007) $1,029.00
Price: 270 WSM, 24" barrel $1,103.00
Price: 7mm Rem. Mag., 26" barrel $1,056.00
Price: XCR Tactical (2007) $1,332.00

REMINGTON MODEL 770 BOLT-ACTION RIFLE
Caliber: 243 Win., 270 Win., 7mm Rem. Mag., 30-06, 300 Win. Mag. **Barrel:** 22" or 24". **Weight:** 8.5 lbs. **Length:** 42.5" to 44.5" overall. **Stock:** Black synthetic. **Sights:** Bushnell Sharpshooter 3-9x scope mounted and bore-sighted. **Features:** Upgrade of Model 710 introduced 2001. Unique action locks bolt directly into barrel; 60-degree bolt throw; 4-shot dual-stack magazine; key-operated Integrated Security System locks bolt open. Introduced 2007. Made in U.S.A. by Remington Arms Co.
Price: $452.00
Price: Youth $452.00

REMINGTON MODEL SEVEN CDL/CDL MAGNUM
Caliber: 17 Rem. Mag., 204 Ruger, 22-250, 223 Rem., 243 Win., 260 Rem., 6.8 Rem. PC, 270 WSM, 7mm-08 Rem., 308 Win. 7mm Rem SA Ultra Mag., 300 WSM, 300 Rem. SA Ultra Mag., 350 Rem. Mag. **Barrel:** 20"; 22" magnum. **Weight:** 6.5 to 7.4 lbs. **Length:** 39.25" to 41.25" overall. **Stock:** American walnut, R3 recoil pad, satin finished. **Sights:** None. **Features:** Satin finished carbon steel barrel and action, 3- or 4-round magazine, hinged magazine floorplate. Furnished with iron sights and sling swivel studs, drilled and tapped for scope mounts. CDL versions introduced 2007. XCR Camo line chambered in 243 Win., 270 WSM, 7mm-08 Rem., 300 WSM, 308 Win.
Price: CDL **$907.00**
Price: CDL Magnum **$973.00**
Price: CDL XCR Camo from **$1,080.00**
Price: Youth, 6.8 Rem. PC (2007) **$684.00**

REMINGTON MODEL 798/799 BOLT-ACTION RIFLES
Caliber: 243 Win., 25-06 Rem., .270 Win., 7mm Rem. Mag., .308 Win., .30-06 Sprg., .300 Win. Mag., .375 H&H Mag., .458 Win. Mag. **Barrel:** 20" short actions, 22" standard actions; 24" long actions. **Weight:** 7.75 lbs. **Length:** 39.5" to 42.5" overall. **Stock:** Brown or green laminated, 1-inch rubber butt pad. **Sights:** None. Receiver drilled and tapped for standard Mauser 98 (long- and short-action) scope mounts. **Features:** Model 98 Mauser action (square-bridge Mauser 98). Claw extractor, sporter style 2-position safety, solid steel hinged floorplate magazine. Introduced 2006. Made in U.S.A. by Remington Arms Co.
Price: Model 798, 22" barrel, 42.5" OAL, 7 lbs., green laminate
stock (2007) 243 Win., 25-06 Rem., 270 Win.,
.308 Win., .30-06 Sprg. **$710.00**
Price: Model 798, 24" barrel, 44.5" OAL, 7 lbs., 7mm Rem. Mag,
.300 Win. Mag. **$690.00**
Price: Model 798, 26" barrel, 46.5" OAL, 7 lbs., .375 H&H Mag.,
.458 Win. Mag. **$1,032.00**
Price: Model 799, 20" barrel, 39.5" OAL, 6.75 lbs., .22 Hornet,
.222 Rem., .22-250 Rem., .223 Rem., 7.62x39mm **$648.00**

Ruger Magnum

Ruger 77/22 Hornet Varmint

Ruger M77 Mark II

Ruger M77 Hawkeye

Ruger M77 Hawkeye Alaskan

RUGER MAGNUM RIFLE
Caliber: 375 H&H, 416 Rigby, 458 Lott. **Barrel:** 23". **Weight:** 9-1/2 to 10-1/4 lbs. **Length:** 44". **Stock:** AAA Premium Grade Circassian walnut with live-rubber recoil pad, metal gripcap, and studs for mounting sling swivels. **Sights:** Blade, front; V-notch rear express sights (one stationary, two folding) drift-adjustable for windage. **Features:** Floorplate latch secures the hinged floorplate against accidental dumping of cartridges; one-piece bolt has a non-rotating Mauser-type controlled-feed extractor; fixed-blade ejector.
Price: M77RSMMKII **$2,200.00**

RUGER 77/22 HORNET BOLT-ACTION RIFLE
Caliber: 22 Hornet, 6-shot rotary magazine. **Barrel:** 20". **Weight:** About 6 lbs. **Length:** 39-3/4" overall. **Stock:** Checkered American walnut, black rubber buttpad. **Sights:** None. **Features:** Same basic features as rimfire model except slightly lengthened receiver. Uses Ruger rotary magazine. Three-position safety. Comes with 1" Ruger scope rings. Introduced 1994.
Price: 77/22RH (rings only, no sights) **$690.00**
Price: K77/22VHZ Varmint, laminated stock, no sights **$765.00**

RUGER M77 MARK II RIFLE
Caliber: 223, 22-250, 204 Ruger, 243, 257 Roberts, 25-06, 270, 308, 30-06, 7mm Rem. Mag., 7mm/08, 300 Win. Mag., 338 Win. Mag., 3-shot magazine. **Barrel:** 20", 22"; 24" (magnums). **Weight:** About 7 lbs. **Length:** 39-3/4" overall. **Stock:** Synthetic American walnut; swivel studs, rubber buttpad. **Sights:** None furnished. Receiver has Ruger integral scope mount base, Ruger 1" rings. **Features:** All with new triggers, 3-position safety. Steel trigger guard. Left-hand available. Introduced 1989.
Price: M77LRMKII (left-hand, 25/06, 270, 30-06, 7mm Rem.
Mag.,300 Win. Mag.) **$749.00**

RUGER M77 HAWKEYE RIFLES
Caliber: 204 Ruger, 223, 22-250, 243, 257 Roberts, 25-06, 270, 280 Rem., 7mm/08, 7mm Rem. Mag., 308, 30-06, 300 Win. Mag., 338 Win. Mag., 338 Federal, 358 Win. Mag.,4-shot magazine, except 3-shot magazine for magnums; 5-shot magazine for 204 Ruger and 223 Rem. **Barrel:** 22", 24". **Weight:** 7-8.25 lbs. **Length:** 42-44.4" overall. **Stock:** American walnut. **Sights:** None furnished. Receiver has Ruger integral scope mount base, Ruger 1" rings. **Features:** Includes Ruger LC6™trigger, new red rubber recoil pad, Mauser-type controlled feeding, claw extractor, 3-position safety, hammer-forged steel barrels, Ruger scope rings. Walnut stock includes wrap-around cut checkering on the forearm and, more rounded contours on stock and top of pistol grips. Matte stainless version features synthetic stock. Hawkeye Alaskan and African chambered in 375 Ruger. Alaskan features matte-black finish, 20" barrel, Hogue OverMolded synthetic stock. African has 23" blued barrel, checkered walnut stock, left-handed model. 375s have windage adjustable shallow "V" notch rear sight, white bead front sights. Introduced 2007.
Price: HM77R walnut/blued **$749.00**
Price: HKM77RFP synthetic/stainless **$749.00**
Price: Alaska synthetic/Diamondblack **$1,095.00**
Price: African walnut/blued **$1,095.00**

Ruger KM77RLFP MKII

Ruger KM77RFP MKII

Ruger M77VT Target

Ruger Frontier

Sako 85 Grey Wolf

Ruger M77RSI International Carbine
Same as standard Model 77 except 18" barrel, full-length International-style stock, steel forend cap, loop-type steel sling swivels. Integral base receiver, open sights, Ruger 1" steel rings. Improved front sight. Available in 243, 270, 308, 30-06. Weighs 7 lbs. Length overall is 38-3/8".
Price: M77RSIMKII **$876.00**

Ruger M77 Mark II All-Weather and Sporter Model Stainless Rifle
Similar to wood-stock M77 Mark II except all metal parts are stainless steel, has an injection-molded, glass-fiber-reinforced polymer stock. Laminated wood stock. Chambered for 223, 22/250, 25/06, 260 Rem., 7mm WSM, 7mm/08, 7mm SWM, 280 Rem., 300 WSM, 204 Ruger, 243, 270, 308, 30-06, 7mm Rem. Mag., 300 Win. Mag., 325 WSM, 338 Win. Mag. Fixed-blade-type ejector, three-position safety, new trigger guard with patented floorplate latch. Integral Scope Base Receiver, 1" Ruger scope rings, built-in sling swivel loops. Introduced 1990.
Price: K77RLFPMKII Ultra-Light, synthetic stock, rings, no sights . **$759.00**
Price: K77LRBBZMKII, left-hand bolt, rings, no sights,
    laminated stock **$805.00**
Price: K77RBZMKII, no sights, laminated wood stock, 223,
    22/250, 243, 270, 280 Rem., 7mm Rem. Mag., 30-06,
    308, 300 Win. Mag., 338 Win. Mag. **$805.00**
Price: KM77RFPMKII, synthetic stock, no sights **$695.00**

Ruger M77RL Ultra Light
Similar to standard M77 except weighs 6 lbs., chambered for 223, 243, 257 Roberts, 25-06, 270, 308, 30-06, barrel tapped for target scope blocks, 20" Ultra Light barrel. Overall length 40". Ruger's steel 1" scope rings supplied. Introduced 1983.
Price: M77RLMKII **$805.00**

Ruger M77 Mark II Compact Rifles
Similar to standard M77 except reduced 16-1/2" barrel, weighs 5-3/4 lbs. Chambered for 223, 243, 260 Rem., 308, and 7mm-08.
Price: M77CR MKII (blued finish, walnut stock) **$749.00**
Price: KM77CRBBZ MKII (stainless finish, black laminated stock) . **$805.00**

RUGER M77VT TARGET RIFLE
Caliber: 22-250, 223, 204 Ruger, 243, 25-06, 308. **Barrel:** 26" heavy stainless steel with target gray finish. **Weight:** 9-3/4 lbs. **Length:** Approx. 44" overall. **Stock:** Laminated American hardwood with beavertail forend, steel swivel studs; no checkering or gripcap. **Sights:** Integral scope mount bases in receiver. **Features:** Ruger diagonal bedding system. Ruger steel 1" scope rings supplied. Fully adjustable trigger. Steel floorplate and trigger guard. New version introduced 1992.
Price: K77VTMKII **$899.00**

RUGER FRONTIER RIFLE
Caliber: 243, 7mm/08, 308, 338 Fed., 358 Win. **Barrel:** 16-1/2". **Weight:** 6-1/4 lbs. **Stock:** Black laminate. **Features:** Front scope mounting rib, blued finish; overall length 35-1/2". Introduced 2005, stainless in 2006.
Price: Blued, walnut **$799.00**
Price: Stainless, laminate **$900.00**

SAKO TRG-42 BOLT-ACTION RIFLE
Caliber: 338 Lapua Mag. and 300 Win. Mag. **Barrel:** 27-1/8". **Weight:** 11-1/4 lbs. **Length:** NA. **Stock:** NA. **Sights:** NA. **Features:** 5-shot magazine, fully adjustable stock and competition trigger. Imported from Finland by Beretta USA.
Price: **$3,525.00**

SAKO MODEL 85 BOLT-ACTION RIFLES
Caliber: 22-250, 243, 25-06, 260, 6.5x55mm, 270, 270 WSM, 7mm-08, 308, 30-06; 7mm WSM, 300 WSM, 338 Federal. **Barrel:** 22.4", 22.9", 24.4". **Weight:** 7.75 lbs. **Length:** NA. **Stock:** Polymer, laminated or high-grade walnut, straight comb, shadow-line cheekpiece. **Sights:** None furnished. **Features:** Controlled-round feeding, adjustable trigger, matte stainless or nonreflective satin blue. Quad model is polymer/stainless with four interchangeable barrels in 22LR, 22 WMR 17 HMR and 17 Mach 2; 50-degree bolt-lift, ambidextrous palm-swell, adjustable butt-pad. Introduced 2006. Imported from Finland by Beretta USA.
Price: Sako 85 Hunter, walnut/blued **$1,595.00**
Price: Sako 85 Grey Wolf, laminated/stainless **$1,495.00**
Price: Sako 85 Quad, polymer/stainless **$925.00**
Price: Sako 85 Quad Combo, four barrels **$1,800.00**

Sako 75 Hunter

Sako 75 Stainless Hunter

Sako 75 Deluxe

Sako 75 Varmint

Savage 110GXP3

SAKO 75 HUNTER BOLT-ACTION RIFLE
Caliber: 223, 22-250, 243, 25-06, 260, 270, 270 WSM, 280, 300 Win. Mag., 30-06; 7mm-08, 308 Win., 270 Wby. Mag., 7mm Rem. Mag., 7mm STW, 7mm Wby. Mag., 300 Wby. Mag., 338 Win. Mag., 340 Wby. Mag., 375 H&H. **Barrel:** 22", standard calibers; 24", 26" magnum calibers. **Weight:** About 6 lbs. **Length:** NA. **Stock:** European walnut with matte lacquer finish. **Sights:** None furnished; dovetail scope mount rails. **Features:** New design with three locking lugs and a mechanical ejector, key locks firing pin and bolt, cold hammer-forged barrel is free-floating, two-position safety, hinged floorplate or detachable magazine that can be loaded from the top, short 70-degree bolt lift. Five action lengths. Introduced 1997. Imported from Finland by Beretta USA.
Price: From **$1,375.00**

Sako 75 Stainless Synthetic Rifle
Similar to 75 Hunter except all metal is stainless steel, synthetic stock has soft composite panels molded into forend and pistol grip. Available in 22-250, 243, 308 Win., 25-06, 270, 30-06 with 22" barrel, 7mm Rem. Mag., 7mm STW, 300 Win. Mag., 338 Win. Mag. and 375 H&H Mag. with 24" barrel and 300 Wby. Mag., 300 Rem. Ultra Mag. with 26" barrel. Introduced 1997. Imported from Finland by Beretta USA.
Price: from **$1,495.00**

Sako 75 Deluxe Rifle
Similar to 75 Hunter except select wood rosewood gripcap and forend tip. Available in 17 Rem., 222, 223, 25-06, 243, 7mm-08, 308, 25-06, 270, 280, 30-06; 270 Wby. Mag., 7mm Rem. Mag., 7mm STW, 7mm Wby. Mag., 300 Win. Mag., 300 Wby. Mag., 338 Win. Mag., 340 Wby. Mag., 375 H&H, 416 Rem. Mag. Introduced 1997. Imported from Finland by Beretta USA.
Price: from **$2,050.00**

Sako 75 Varmint Stainless Laminated Rifle
Similar to Sako 75 Hunter except chambered only for 222, 223, 22-250, 22 PPC USA, 6mm PPC, heavy 24" barrel with recessed crown; set trigger; all metal is stainless steel, laminated wood stock with beavertail forend. Introduced 1999. Imported from Finland by Beretta USA.
Price: **$1,959.00**

Sako 75 Varmint Rifle
Similar to Model 75 Hunter except chambered only for 17 Rem., 222 Rem., 223 Rem., 22-250 Rem., 22 PPC and 6mm PPC, 24" heavy barrel with recessed crown; set trigger; beavertail forend. Introduced 1998. Imported from Finland by Beretta USA.
Price: **$1,850.00**

SAUER 202 BOLT-ACTION RIFLE
Caliber: Standard 243, 6.5x55, 270 Win., 308 Win., 30-06; magnum 7mm Rem. Mag., 300 Win. Mag., 300 Wby. Mag., 375 H&H. **Barrel:** 23.6" (standard), 26" (magnum). **Weight:** 7.7 lbs. (standard). **Length:** 44.3" overall (23.6" barrel). **Stock:** Select American Claro walnut with high-gloss epoxy finish, rosewood grip and forend caps; 22 lpi checkering. Synthetic also available. **Sights:** None furnished; drilled and tapped for scope mounting. **Features:** Short 60" bolt throw; detachable box magazine; six-lug bolt; quick-change barrel; tapered bore; adjustable two-stage trigger; firing pin cocking indicator. Introduced 1994. Imported from Germany by SIGARMS, Inc.
Price: Standard calibers, right-hand. **$1,035.00**
Price: Magnum calibers, right-hand **$1,106.00**
Price: Standard calibers, synthetic stock **$985.00**
Price: Magnum calibers, synthetic stock **$1,056.00**

SAVAGE MODEL 10GXP3, 110GXP3 PACKAGE GUNS
Caliber: 223 Rem., 22-250 Rem., 243 Win., 7mm-08 Rem., 308 Win., 300 WSM (10GXP3). 25-06 Rem., 270 Win., 30-06 Spfld., 7mm Rem. Mag., 300 Win. Mag., 300 Rem. Ultra Mag. (110GXP3). **Barrel:** 22" 24", 26". **Weight:** 7.5 lbs. average. **Length:** 43" to 47". **Stock:** Walnut Monte Carlo with checkering. **Sights:** 3-9x40mm scope, mounted & bore sighted. **Features:** Blued, free floating and button rifled, internal box magazines, swivel studs, leather sling. Left-hand available.
Price: Accu-trigger **$539.00**

Savage Model 10FP

Savage Model 10FPLE1

Savage Model 10FPXP-LE

SAVAGE MODEL 11FXP3, 111FXP3, 111FCXP3, 11FYXP3 (Youth) PACKAGE GUNS
Caliber: 223 Rem., 22-250 Rem., 243 Win., 308 Win., 300 WSM (11FXP3). 270 Win., 30-06 Spfld., 25-06 Rem., 7mm Rem. Mag., 300 Win. Mag., 338 Win. Mag., 300 Rem. Ultra Mag. (11FCXPE & 111FXP3). **Barrel:** 22" to 26". **Weight:** 6.5 lbs. **Length:** 41" to 47". **Stock:** Synthetic checkering, dual pillar bed. **Sights:** 3-9X40mm scope, mounted & bore sighted. **Features:** Blued, free floating and button rifled, Top loading internal box mag (except 111FXCP3 has detachable box mag.). Nylon sling and swivel studs. Some left-hand available.
Price: Model 11FXP3 . . . . **$516.00**
Price: Model 111FCXP3 . . . . **$411.00**
Price: Model 11FYXP3, 243 Win., 12.5" pull (youth) **$501.00**

SAVAGE MODEL 16FXP3, 116FXP3 SS ACTION PACKAGE GUNS
Caliber: 223 Rem., 243 Win., 308 Win., 300 WSM, 270 Win., 30-06 Spfld., 7mm Rem. Mag., 300 Win. Mag., 338 Win. Mag., 375 H&H, 7mm S&W, 7mm Rem. Ultra Mag., 300 Rem. Ultra Mag. **Barrel:** 22", 24", 26". **Weight:** 6.75 lbs. average. **Length:** 41" to 46". **Stock:** Synthetic checkering, dual pillar bed. **Sights:** 3-9X40mm scope, mounted & bore sighted. **Features:** Free floating and button rifled. Internal box mag., nylon sling and swivel studs.
Price: **$601.00**

SAVAGE MODEL 10FM SIERRA ULTRA LIGHT RIFLE
Caliber: 223, 243, 308. **Barrel:** 20". **Weight:** 6 lbs. **Length:** 41-1/2". **Stock:** "Dual Pillar" bedding in black synthetic stock with silver medallion in gripcap. **Sights:** None furnished; drilled and tapped for scope mounting. **Features:** True short action. Model 10FCM has detachable box magazine. Comes with sling and quick-detachable swivels. Introduced 1998. Made in U.S.A. by Savage Arms, Inc.
Price: **$552.00**

SAVAGE MODEL 10/110FP LONG RANGE RIFLE
Caliber: 223, 25-06, 308, 30-06, 300 Win. Mag., 7mm Rem. Mag., 4-shot magazine. **Barrel:** 24", heavy; recessed target muzzle. **Weight:** 8-1/2 lbs. **Length:** 45.5" overall. **Stock:** Black graphite/fiberglass composition; positive checkering. **Sights:** None furnished. Receiver drilled and tapped for scope mounting. **Features:** Pillar-bedded stock. Black matte finish on all metal parts. Double swivel studs on the forend for sling and/or bipod mount. Right- or left-hand. Introduced 1990. From Savage Arms, Inc.
Price: Right- or left-hand. **$601.00**

Savage Model 10FP Tactical Rifle
Similar to the Model 110FP except has true short action, chambered for 223, 308; black synthetic stock with "Dual Pillar" bedding. Introduced 1998. Made in U.S.A. by Savage Arms, Inc.
Price: **$601.00**
Price: Model 10FLP (left-hand) **$601.00**
Price: Model 10FP-LE1 (20"), 10FPLE2 (26") **$601.00**
Price: Model 10FPXP-LE w/Burris 3.5-10x50 scope, Harris bipod package **$1,805.00**

Savage Model 10FP-LE1A Tactical Rifle
Similar to the Model 110FP except weighs 10.75 lbs. and has overall length of 39.75". Chambered for 223 Rem., 308 Win. Black synthetic Choate™ adjustable stock with accessory rail and swivel studs.
Price: **$729.00**

SAVAGE MODEL 111 CLASSIC HUNTER RIFLES
Caliber: 25-06 Rem., 270 Win., 30-06 Spfld., 7mm Rem. Mag, 300 Win. Mag., 7mm RUM, 300 RUM. **Barrel:** 22", 24", 26" (magnum calibers). **Weight:** 6.5 to 7.5 lbs. **Length:** 42.75" to 47.25". **Stock:** Walnut-finished hardwood (M111G, GC); graphite/fiberglass filled composite. **Sights:** Ramp front, open fully adjustable rear; drilled and tapped for scope mounting. **Features:** Three-position top tang safety, double front locking lugs, free-floated button-rifled barrel. Comes with trigger lock, target, ear puffs. Introduced 1994. Made in U.S.A. by Savage Arms, Inc.
Price: Model 111F (270 Win., 30-06 Spfld., 7mm Rem. Mag., 300 Win. Mag.) **$486.00**
Price: Model 111F (25-06 Rem., 338 Win. Mag., 7mm Rem. Ultra Mag, 300 Rem. Ultra Mag.) **$486.00**
Price: Model 111G (wood stock, top-loading magazine, right- or left-hand) **$436.00**
Price: Model 111GNS (wood stock, detachable box magazine, no sights, right-hand only) **$518.00**

Savage Model 111F

Savage Model 111F

Savage Model 11FCNS

Savage Model 11G

Savage Model 10GY

Savage Model 12FV

Savage Model 11 Classic Hunter Rifles, Short Action
Similar to the Model 111F except has true short action, chambered for 22-250, Rem., 243 Win., 7mm-08 Rem., 308 Win.; black synthetic stock with "Dual Pillar" bedding, positive checkering. Introduced 1998. Made in U.S.A. by Savage Arms, Inc.
Price: Model 11F...$486.00
Price: Model 11FL (left-hand) $486.00
Price: Model 11FCNS (right-hand, no sights) $507.00
Price: Model 11G (wood stock) $496.00
Price: Model 11GL (as above, left-hand) $496.00

Savage Model 10GY
Similar to the Model 111G except weighs 6.3 lbs., is 42-1/2" overall, and the stock is scaled for ladies, small-framed adults and youths. Chambered for 223, 243, 308. Ramp front sight, open adjustable rear; drilled and tapped for scope mounts. Made in U.S.A. by Savage Arms, Inc.
Price: Model 10GY (short action, calibers 223, 243, 308) $496.00

SAVAGE MODEL 112 LONG RANGE RIFLES
Caliber: 5-shot magazine. **Barrel:** 26" heavy. **Weight:** 8.8 lbs. **Length:** 47.5" overall. **Stock:** Black graphite/fiberglass filled composite with positive checkering. **Sights:** None furnished; drilled and tapped for scope mounting. **Features:** Pillar-bedded stock. Blued barrel with recessed target-style muzzle. Double front swivel studs for attaching bipod. Introduced 1991. Made in U.S.A. by Savage Arms, Inc.
Price: Model 112BVSS (heavy-prone laminated stock with high comb, Wundhammer swell, fluted stainless barrel, bolt handle, trigger guard) $675.00

Savage Model 12 Long Range Rifles
Similar to the Model 112 Long Range except with true short action, chambered for 223, 22-250, 308. Models 12FV, 12FVSS have black synthetic stocks with "Dual Pillar" bedding, positive checkering, swivel studs; Model 12BVSS has brown laminated stock with beavertail forend, fluted stainless barrel. Introduced 1998. Made in U.S.A. by Savage Arms, Inc.
Price: Model 12FV (223, 22-250, 243 Win., 308 Win., blue) $549.00
Price: Model 12FVSS (blue action, fluted stainless barrel) $667.00
Price: Model 12FLV (as above, left-hand) $549.00
Price: Model 12FVS (blue action, fluted stainless barrel, single shot) $667.00
Price: Model 12BVSS (laminated stock) $721.00
Price: Model 12BVSS-S (as above, single shot) $721.00

Savage Model 12VSS

Savage Model 116FSAK

Steyr Mannlicher SBS

Steyr SBS Forester

Savage Model 12VSS Varminter Rifle

Similar to other Model 12s except blue/stainless steel action, fluted stainless barrel, Choate full pistol grip, adjustable synthetic stock, Sharp Shooter trigger. Overall length 47-1/2", weighs appx. 15 lbs. No sights; drilled and tapped for scope mounts. Chambered in 223, 22-250, 308 Win. Made in U.S.A. by Savage Arms, Inc.

Price: **$934.00**

SAVAGE MODEL 116 WEATHER WARRIORS

Caliber: 375 H&H, 300 Rem. Ultra Mag., 308 Win., 300 Rem. Ultra Mag., 300 WSM, 7mm Rem. Ultra Mag., 7mm Rem. Short Ultra Mag., 7mm S&W, 7mm-08 Rem. **Barrel:** 22", 24" for 7mm Rem. Mag., 300 Win. Mag., 338 Win. Mag. (M116FSS only). **Weight:** 6.25 to 6.5 lbs. **Length:** 41" to 47". **Stock:** Graphite/fiberglass filled composite. **Sights:** None furnished; drilled and tapped for scope mounting. **Features:** Stainless steel with matte finish; free-floated barrel; quick-detachable swivel studs; laser-etched bolt; scope bases and rings. Left-hand models available in all models, calibers at same price. Model 116FSS introduced 1991; 116FSAK introduced 1994. Made in U.S.A. by Savage Arms, Inc.

Price: Model 116FSS (top-loading magazine) **$520.00**
Price: Model 116FSAK (top-loading magazine,
    Savage adjustable muzzle brake system) **$601.00**
Price: Model 116BSS (brown laminate, 24") **$668.00**
Price: Model 116BSS (brown laminate, 26") **$668.00**

Savage Model 16FCSS Rifle

Similar to Model 116FSS except true short action, chambered for 223, 243, 22" free-floated barrel; black graphite/fiberglass stock, "Dual Pillar" bedding. Also left-hand version available. Introduced 1998. Made in U.S.A. by Savage Arms, Inc.

Price: **$552.00**

SIGARMS SHR 970 SYNTHETIC RIFLE

Caliber: 270, 30-06. **Barrel:** 22". **Weight:** 7.2 lbs. **Length:** 41.9" overall. **Stock:** Textured black fiberglass or walnut. **Sights:** None furnished; drilled and tapped for scope mounting. **Features:** Quick takedown; interchangeable barrels; removable box magazine; cocking indicator; three-position safety. Introduced 1998. Imported by SIGARMS, Inc.

Price: Synthetic stock **$499.00**
Price: Walnut stock **$550.00**

STEYR CLASSIC MANNLICHER SBS RIFLE

Caliber: 243, 25-06, 308, 6.5x55, 6.5x57, 270, 7x64 Brenneke, 7mm-08, 7.5x55, 30-06, 9.3x62, 6.5x68, 7mm Rem. Mag., 300 Win. Mag., 8x68S, 4-shot magazine. **Barrel:** 23.6" standard; 26" magnum; 20" full stock standard calibers. **Weight:** 7 lbs. **Length:** 40.1" overall. **Stock:** Hand-checkered fancy European oiled walnut with standard forend. **Sights:** Ramp front adjustable for elevation, V-notch rear adjustable for windage. **Features:** Single adjustable trigger; 3-position roller safety with "safe-bolt" setting; drilled and tapped for Steyr factory scope mounts. Introduced 1997. Imported from Austria by GSI, Inc.

Price: Full-stock, standard calibers **$1,749.00**

STEYR SBS FORESTER RIFLE

Caliber: 243, 25-06, 270, 7mm-08, 308 Win., 30-06, 7mm Rem. Mag., 300 Win. Mag. Detachable 4-shot magazine. **Barrel:** 23.6", standard calibers; 25.6", magnum calibers. **Weight:** 7.5 lbs. **Length:** 44.5" overall (23.6" barrel). **Stock:** Oil-finished American walnut with Monte Carlo cheekpiece. Pachmayr 1" swivels. **Sights:** None furnished. Drilled and tapped for Browning A-Bolt mounts. **Features:** Three-position ambidextrous roller tang safety. Matte finish on barrel and receiver; adjustable trigger. Rotary cold-hammer forged barrel. Introduced 1997. Imported by GSI, Inc.

Price: Standard calibers **$799.00**
Price: Magnum calibers **$829.00**

Steyr SBS Prohunter

Steyr Scout Rifle

Thompson/Center Icon

Tikka T-3 Hunter

Steyr SBS Prohunter Rifle
Similar to the SBS Forester except has ABS synthetic stock with adjustable butt spacers, straight comb without cheekpiece, palm swell, Pachmayr 1" swivels. Special 10-round magazine conversion kit available. Introduced 1997. Imported by GSI.
Price: Standard calibers **$769.00**
Price: Magnum calibers **$799.00**

STEYR SCOUT BOLT-ACTION RIFLE
Caliber: 308 Win., 5-shot magazine. **Barrel:** 19", fluted. **Weight:** NA. **Length:** NA. **Stock:** Gray Zytel. **Sights:** Pop-up front & rear, Leupold M8 2.5x28 IER scope on Picatinny optic rail with Steyr mounts. **Features:** luggage case, scout sling, two stock spacers, two magazines. Introduced 1998. From GSI.
Price: From **$1,969.00**

STEYR SSG BOLT-ACTION RIFLE
Caliber: 308 Win., detachable 5-shot rotary magazine. **Barrel:** 26". **Weight:** 8.5 lbs. **Length:** 44.5" overall. **Stock:** Black ABS Cycolac with spacers for length of pull adjustment. **Sights:** Hooded ramp front adjustable for elevation, V-notch rear adjustable for windage. **Features:** Sliding safety; NATO rail for bipod; 1" swivels; Parkerized finish; single or double-set triggers. Imported from Austria by GSI, Inc.
Price: SSG-PI, iron sights **$1,699.00**
Price: SSG-PII, heavy barrel, no sights **$1,699.00**
Price: SSG-PIIK, 20" heavy barrel, no sights **$1,699.00**
Price: SSG-PIV, 16.75" threaded heavy barrel with flash hider . . **$2,659.00**

THOMPSON/CENTER ICON BOLT-ACTION RIFLE
Caliber: 22-250, 243, 308, 30TC, 3-round box magazine. **Barrel:** 24", button rifled. **Weight:** 7.5 lbs. **Length:** 44.5" overall. **Stock:** Walnut, 20-lpi grip and forend cut checkering with ribbon detail. **Sights:** None; integral Weaver style scope mounts. **Features:** Interchangeable bolt handle, 60-degree bolt lift, Interlok Bedding System, 3-lug bolt with T-Slot extractor, cocking indicator, adjustable trigger, preset to 3 to 3.5 lbs of pull. Introduced 2007. From Thompson/Center Arms.
Price: . . . . **NA**

TIKKA T-3 BIG BOAR SYNTHETIC BOLT-ACTION RIFLE
Caliber: 308, 30-06, 300 WSM. **Barrel:** 19". **Weight:** 6 lbs. **Length:** 39.5" overall. **Stock:** Laminated. **Sights:** None furnished. **Features:** Detachable, 3-round. Receiver dove-tailed for scope mounting. Reintroduced 1996. Imported from Finland by Beretta USA.
Price: Left-hand **$695.00**

Tikka T-3 Super Varmint Rifle
Similar to the standard T-3 rifle except has 23-3/8" heavy stainless barrel. Chambered for 22-250, 223, 308. Reintroduced 2005. Made in Finland by Sako. Imported by Beretta USA.
Price: **$1,425.00**

TIKKA T-3 HUNTER
Caliber: 223, 22-250, 243, 308, 25-06, 270, 30-06, 300 Win. Mag., 338 Win. Mag., 270 WSM, 300 WSM, 6.5x55 Swedish Mauser, 7mm Rem. Mag. **Stock:** Walnut. **Sight:** None furnished. **Barrel:** 22-7/16", 24-3/8". **Features:** Detachable magazine, aluminum scope rings. Introduced 2005. Imported from Finland by Beretta USA.
Price: **$695.00**

Tikka T-3 Stainless Synthetic
Similar to the T-3 Hunter except stainless steel, synthetic stock. Available in 243, 25-06, 270, 308, 30-06, 270 WSM, 300 WSM, 7mm Rem. Mag., 300 Win. Mag., 338 Win. Mag. Introduced 2005. Imported from Finland by Beretta USA.
Price: **$895.00**

ULTRA LIGHT ARMS BOLT-ACTION RIFLES
Caliber: 17 Rem. to 416 Rigby. **Barrel:** Douglas, length to order. **Weight:** 4-3/4 to 7-1/2 lbs. **Length:** Varies. **Stock:** Kevlar® graphite composite, variety of finishes. **Sights:** None furnished; drilled and tapped for scope mounts. **Features:** Timney trigger, hand-lapped action, button-rifled barrel, hand-bedded action, recoil pad, sling-swivel studs, optional Jewell trigger. Made in U.S.A. by New Ultra Light Arms.
Price: Model 20 (short action) **$2,800.00**
Price: Model 24 (long action) **$2,900.00**
Price: Model 28 (magnum action) **$3,200.00**
Price: Model 40 (300 Wby. Mag., 416 Rigby) **$3,200.00**
Price: Left-hand models, add **$100.00**

Weatherby Mark V Lazermark

Weatherby Mark V Sporter

Weatherby Mark V Stainless

Weatherby Mark V Synthetic

WEATHERBY MARK V DELUXE BOLT-ACTION RIFLE
Caliber: All Weatherby calibers plus 22-250, 243, 25-06, 270 Win., 280 Rem., 7mm-08, 30-06, 308 Win. **Barrel:** 24" barrel on standard calibers. **Weight:** 8-1/2 to 10-1/2 lbs. **Length:** 46-5/8" to 46-3/4" overall. **Stock:** Walnut, Monte Carlo with cheekpiece; high luster finish; checkered pistol grip and forend; recoil pad. **Sights:** None furnished. **Features:** Cocking indicator; adjustable trigger; hinged floorplate, thumb safety; quick detachable sling swivels. Made in U.S.A. From Weatherby.
Price: 257, 270, 7mm. 300, 340 Wby. Mags., 26" barrel **$1,767.00**
Price: 416 Wby. Mag. with Accubrake, 28" barrel **$2,079.00**
Price: 460 Wby. Mag. with Accubrake, 28" barrel **$2,443.00**
Price: 24" barrel **$1,715.00**

Weatherby Mark V Lazermark Rifle
Same as Mark V Deluxe except stock has extensive oak leaf pattern laser carving on pistol grip and forend. Introduced 1981.
Price: 257, 270, 7mm Wby. Mag., 300, 340, 26". **$1,923.00**
Price: 378 Wby. Mag., 28" **$2,266.00**
Price: 416 Wby. Mag., 28", Accubrake **$2,266.00**
Price: 460 Wby. Mag., 28", Accubrake **$2,661.00**

Weatherby Mark V Sporter Rifle
Same as the Mark V Deluxe without the embellishments. Metal has low-luster blue, stock is Claro walnut with matte finish, Monte Carlo comb, recoil pad. Introduced 1993. From Weatherby.
Price: 22-250, 243, 240 Wby. Mag., 25-06, 7mm-08,
270 WCF, 280, 30-06, 308; 24". **$1,091.00**

Price: 257 Wby., 270, 7 mm Wby., 7mm Rem., 300 Wby.,
300 Win., 340 Wby., 338 Win. Mag., 26" barrel for Wby. calibers;
24" for non-Wby. calibers **$1,143.00**

Weatherby Mark V Stainless Rifle
Similar to the Mark V Deluxe except made of 410-series stainless steel. Also available in 30-378 Wby. Mag. Has lightweight injection-molded synthetic stock with raised Monte Carlo comb, checkered grip and forend, custom floorplate release. Right-hand only. Introduced 1995. Made in U.S.A. From Weatherby.
Price: 22-250 Rem., 243 Win., 240 Wby. Mag., 25-06 Rem.,
270 Win., 280 Rem., 7mm-08 Rem., 30-06 Spfld., 308 Win.,
24" barrel **$1,018.00**
Price: 257, 270, 7mm, 300, 340 Wby. Mags., 26" barrel **$1,070.00**
Price: 7mm Rem. Mag., 300 Win. Mag., 338 Win. Mag.,
375 H&H Mag., 24" barrel **$1,070.00**

Weatherby Mark V Synthetic
Similar to the Mark V Stainless except made of matte finished blued steel. Injection molded synthetic stock. Weighs 6-1/2 lbs., 24" barrel. Available in 22-250, 240 Wby. Mag., 243, 25-06, 270, 7mm-08, 280, 30-06, 308. Introduced 1997. Made in U.S.A. From Weatherby.
Price: **$923.00**
Price: 257, 270, 7mm, 300, 340 Wby. Mags., 26" barrel **$975.00**
Price: 7mm STW, 7mm Rem. Mag., 300, 338 Win. Mags **$975.00**
Price: 375 H&H, 24" barrel **$975.00**
Price: 30-378 Wby. Mag., 338-378 Wby. 28" barrel **$1,151.00**

Weatherby Mark V Accumark

Weatherby Mark V SVR

Weatherby Mark V
Dangerous Game Rifle

WEATHERBY MARK V ACCUMARK RIFLE
Caliber: 257, 270, 7mm, 300, 340 Wby. Mags., 338-378 Wby. Mag., 30-378 Wby. Mag., 7mm STW, 7mm Rem. Mag., 300 Win. Mag. **Barrel:** 26", 28". **Weight:** 8-1/2 lbs. **Length:** 46-5/8" overall. **Stock:** Bell & Carlson with full length aluminum bedding block. **Sights:** None furnished. Drilled and tapped for scope mounting. **Features:** Uses Mark V action with heavy-contour stainless barrel with black oxidized flutes, muzzle diameter of .705". Introduced 1996. Made in U.S.A. From Weatherby.
Price: 26" **$1,507.00**
Price: 30-378 Wby. Mag., 338-378 Wby. Mag., 28",
Accubrake **$1,724.00**
Price: 223, 22-250, 243, 240 Wby. Mag., 25-06, 270,
280 Rem., 7mm-08, 30-06, 308; 24" **$1,455.00**
Price: Accumark left-hand 257, 270, 7mm, 300, 340 Wby.
Mag., 7mm Rem. Mag., 7mm STW, 300 Win. Mag. **$1,559.00**
Price: Accumark left-hand 30-378, 333-378 Wby. Mags. **$1,788.00**

Weatherby Mark V Accumark Ultra Lightweight Rifles
Similar to the Mark V Accumark except weighs 5-3/4 lbs., 6-3/4 lbs. in Mag. calibers.; 24", 26" fluted barrel with recessed target crown; hand-laminated stock with CNC-machined aluminum bedding plate and faint gray "spider web" finish. Available in 257, 270, 7mm, 300 Wby. Mags., (26"); 243, 240 Wby. Mag., 25-06, 270 Win., 280 Rem., 7mm-08, 7mm Rem. Mag., 30-06, 338-06 A-Square, 308, 300 Win. Mag. (24"). Introduced 1998. Made in U.S.A. by Weatherby.
Price: . . . . **$1,459.00 to $1,517.00**
Price: Left-hand models **$1,559.00**

Weatherby Mark V SVM/SPM Rifles
Similar to the Mark V Accumark except has 26" fluted (SVM) or 24" fluted Krieger barrel, spiderweb-pattern tan laminated synthetic stock. SVM has a fully adjustable trigger. Chambered for 223, 22-250, 220 Swift (SVM only), 243, 7mm-08 and 308. Made in U.S.A. by Weatherby.
Price: SVM (Super VarmintMaster), repeater or single-shot **$1,517.00**
Price: SPM (Super Predator Master) **$1,459.00**

Weatherby Mark V Special Varmint Rifle (SVR)
Similar to the Super VarmintMaster and Accumark with 22", #3 contour chrome-moly 4140 steel Krieger Criterion button-rifled barrel with one-degree target crown and hand-laminated composite stock. Available in .223 Rem. (5+1 magazine capacity) and .22-250 Rem. (4+1 magazine capacity) in right-hand models only.
Price: **$999.00**

Weatherby Mark V Fibermark Rifles
Similar to other Mark V models except has black Kevlar® and fiberglass composite stock and bead-blast blue or stainless finish. Chambered for 19 standard and magnum calibers. Introduced 1983; reintroduced 2001. Made in U.S.A. by Weatherby.
Price: Fibermark . . . . **$1,070.00 to $1,347.00**
Price: Fibermark stainless . . . . **$1,165.00 to $1,390.00**

WEATHERBY MARK V DANGEROUS GAME RIFLE
Caliber: 375 H&H, 375 Wby. Mag., 378 Wby. Mag., 416 Rem. Mag., 416 Wby. Mag., 458 Win. Mag., .458 Lott, 460 Wby. Mag. 300 Win. Mag., 300 Wby., Mag., 338 Win. Mag., 340 Wby. Mag., 24" only **Barrel:** 24" or 26". **Weight:** 8-3/4 to 9-1/2 lbs. **Length:** 44-5/8" to 46-5/8" overall. **Stock:** Kevlar® and fiberglass composite. **Sights:** Barrel-band hooded front with large gold bead, adjustable ramp/shallow "V" rear. **Features:** Designed for dangerous game hunting. Black oxide matte finish on all metalwork; Pachmayr Decelerator™ recoil pad, short-throw Mark V action. Introduced 2001. Made in U.S.A. by Weatherby.
Price: . . . . **$2,703.00 to $2,935.00**

WEATHERBY MARK V SUPER BIG GAMEMASTER DEER RIFLE
Caliber: 240 Wby. Mag., 25-06 Rem., 270 Win., 280 Rem., 30-06 Spfld., 257 Wby. Mag., 270 Wby. Mag., 7mm Rem. Mag., 7mm Wby. Mag., 338-06 A-Square, 300 Win. Mag., 300 Wby. Mag. **Barrel:** 26", target crown. **Weight:** 5-3/4 lbs., (6-3/4 lbs. Magnum). **Stock:** Raised comb Monte Carlo composite. **Features:** Fluted barrel, aluminum bedding block, Pachmayr decelerator, 54-degree bolt lift, adj. trigger.
Price: **$1,459.00**
Price: Magnum **$1,517.00**

WEATHERBY MARK V ROYAL CUSTOM RIFLE
Caliber: 257, 270, 7mm, 300, 340 all Wby. Mags. Other calibers available upon request. **Barrel:** 26". **Stock:** Monte Carlo hand-checkered Claro walnut with high gloss finish. **Features:** Bolt and follower are damascened with checkered knob. Engraved receiver, bolt sleeve and floorplate sport scroll pattern. Animal images on floorplate optional. High gloss blue, 24-karat gold and nickel-plating. Made in U.S.A. From Weatherby.
Price: **$5,831.00**

WEATHERBY THREAT RESPONSE RIFLES (TRR) SERIES
Caliber: TRR 223 Rem., 300 Win. TRR Magnum and Magnum Custom 300 Win. Mag., 300 Wby. Mag., 30-378 Wby. Mag., 328-378 Wby. Mag. **Barrel:** 22", 26", target crown. **Stock:** Hand-laminated composite. TTR & TRR Magnum have raised comb Monte Carlo style. TRR Magnum Custom adjustable ergonomic stock. **Features:** Adjustable trigger, aluminum bedding block, beavertail forearms dual tapered, flat-bottomed. "Rocker Arm" lockdown scope mounting. 54 degree bolt. Pachmayr decelerator pad. Made in U.S.A.
Price: TRR Magnum Custom 300 . . . . **$2,699.00**
Price: 30-378, 338-378 with accubrake **$2,861.00**

WILDERNESS EXPLORER MULTI-CALIBER CARBINE
Caliber: 22 Hornet, 218 Bee, 44 Magnum, 50 A.E. (interchangeable). **Barrel:** 18", match grade. **Weight:** 5.5 lbs **Length:** 38-1/2" overall. **Stock:** Synthetic or wood. **Sights:** None furnished; comes with Weaver-style mount on barrel. **Features:** Quick-change barrel and bolt face for caliber switch. Removable box magazine; adjustable trigger with side safety; detachable swivel studs. Introduced 1997. Made in U.S.A. by Phillips & Rogers, Inc.
Price: **$995.00**

Ballard No. 5 Pacific

Ballard No. 7

Browning 1885 High Wall

ARMALITE AR-50 RIFLE
Caliber: 50 BMG **Barrel:** 31". **Weight:** 33.2 lbs. **Length:** 59.5" **Stock:** Synthetic. **Sights:** None furnished. **Features:** A single-shot bolt action rifle designed for long range shooting. Available in left-hand model. Made in U.S.A. by Armalite.
Price: **$2,999.00**

ARMSPORT 1866 SHARPS RIFLE, CARBINE
Caliber: 45-70. **Barrel:** 28", round or octagonal. **Weight:** 8.10 lbs. **Length:** 46" overall. **Stock:** Walnut. **Sights:** Blade front, folding adjustable rear. Tang sight set optionally available. **Features:** Replica of the 1866 Sharps. Color case-hardened frame, rest blued. Imported by Armsport.
Price: **$865.00**
Price: With octagonal barrel **$900.00**
Price: Carbine, 22" round barrel **$850.00**

BALLARD NO. 1 3/4 FAR WEST RIFLE
Caliber: 22 LR, 32-40, 38-55, 40-65, 40-70, 45-70, 45-110, 50-70, 50-90. **Barrel:** 30" std. or heavyweight. **Weight:** 10-1/2 lbs. (std.) or 11-3/4 lbs. (heavyweight bbl.) **Length:** NA. **Stock:** Walnut. **Sights:** Blade front, Rocky Mountain rear. **Features:** Single- or double-set triggers; S-lever or ring-style lever; color case-hardened finish; hand polished and lapped Badger barrel. Made in U.S.A. by Ballard Rifle & Cartridge Co.
Price: **$2,250.00**

BALLARD NO. 4 PERFECTION RIFLE
Caliber: 22 LR, 32-40, 38-55, 40-65, 40-70, 45-70, 45-90, 45-110, 50-70, 50-90. **Barrel:** 30" or 32" octagon, standard or heavyweight. **Weight:** 10-1/2 lbs. (standard) or 11-3/4 lbs. (heavyweight bbl.). **Length:** NA. **Stock:** Smooth walnut. **Sights:** Blade front, Rocky Mountain rear. **Features:** Rifle or shotgun-style buttstock, straight grip action, single or double-set trigger, "S" or right lever, hand polished and lapped Badger barrel. Made in U.S.A. by Ballard Rifle & Cartridge Co.
Price: **$2,250.00**

BALLARD NO. 5 PACIFIC SINGLE-SHOT RIFLE
Caliber: 32-40, 38-55, 40-65, 40-90, 40-70 SS, 45-70 Gov't., 45-110 SS, 50-70 Gov't., 50-90 SS. **Barrel:** 30", or 32" octagonal. **Weight:** 10-1/2 lbs. **Length:** NA. **Stock:** High-grade walnut; rifle or shotgun style. **Sights:** Blade front, Rocky Mountain rear. **Features:** Standard or heavy barrel; double-set triggers; under-barrel wiping rod; ring lever. Introduced 1999. Made in U.S.A. by Ballard Rifle & Cartridge Co.
Price: **$2,575.00**

BALLARD NO. 7 LONG RANGE RIFLE
Caliber: 32-40, 38-55, 40-65, 40-70 SS, 45-70 Gov't., 45-90, 45-110. **Barrel:** 32", 34" half-octagon. **Weight:** 11-3/4 lbs. **Length:** NA. **Stock:** Walnut; checkered pistol grip shotgun butt, ebony forend cap. **Sights:** Globe front. **Features:** Designed for shooting up to 1000 yards. Standard or heavy barrel; single or double-set trigger; hard rubber or steel buttplate. Introduced 1999. Made in U.S.A. by Ballard Rifle & Cartridge Co.
Price: From **$2,475.00**

BALLARD NO. 8 UNION HILL RIFLE
Caliber: 22 LR, 32-40, 38-55, 40-65 Win., 40-70 SS. **Barrel:** 30" half-octagon. **Weight:** About 10-1/2 lbs. **Length:** NA. **Stock:** Walnut; pistol grip butt with cheekpiece. **Sights:** Globe front. **Features:** Designed for 200-yard offhand shooting. Standard or heavy barrel; double-set triggers; full loop lever; hook Schuetzen buttplate. Introduced 1999. Made in U.S.A. by Ballard Rifle & Cartridge Co.
Price: From **$2,500.00**

BALLARD MODEL 1885 HIGH WALL SINGLE SHOT RIFLE
Caliber: 17 Bee, 22 Hornet, 218 Bee, 219 Don Wasp, 219 Zipper, 22 Hi-Power, 225 Win., 25-20 WCF, 25-35 WCF, 25 Krag, 7mmx57R, 30-30, 30-40 Krag, 303 British, 33 WCF, 348 WCF, 35 WCF, 35-30/30, 9.3x74R, 405 WCF, 50-110 WCF, 500 Express, 577 Express. **Barrel:** Lengths to 34". **Weight:** NA. **Length:** NA. **Stock:** Straight-grain American walnut. **Sights:** buckhorn or flattop rear, blade front. **Features:** Faithful copy of original Model 1885 High Wall; parts interchange with original rifles; variety of options available. Introduced 2000. Made in U.S.A. by Ballard Rifle & Cartridge LLC.
Price: From **$2,313.00**
Price: With single set trigger from **$2,355.00**

BARRETT MODEL 99 SINGLE SHOT RIFLE
Caliber: 50 BMG. **Barrel:** 33". **Weight:** 25 lbs. **Length:** 50.4" overall. **Stock:** Anodized aluminum with energy-absorbing recoil pad. **Sights:** None furnished; integral M1913 scope rail. **Features:** Bolt action; detachable bipod; match-grade barrel with high-efficiency muzzle brake. Introduced 1999. Made in U.S.A. by Barrett Firearms.
Price: From **$3,000.00**

BROWN MODEL 97D SINGLE SHOT RIFLE
Caliber: 17 Ackley Hornet through 45-70 Gov't. **Barrel:** Up to 26", air gauged match grade. **Weight:** About 5 lbs., 11 oz. **Stock:** Sporter style with pistol grip, cheekpiece and Schnabel forend. **Sights:** None furnished; drilled and tapped for scope mounting. **Features:** Falling block action gives rigid barrel-receiver matting; polished blue/black finish. Hand-fitted action. Many options. Made in U.S.A. by E. Arthur Brown Co., Inc.
Price: From **$699.00**

C. Sharps New Model 1875 Old Reliable

C. Sharps New Model 1885

Cabela's Sharps

Cimarron Billy Dixon

BROWNING MODEL 1885 HIGH WALL SINGLE SHOT RIFLE
Caliber: 22-250, 30-06, 270, 7mm Rem. Mag., 454 Casull, 45-70. **Barrel:** 28". **Weight:** 8 lbs., 12 oz. **Length:** 43-1/2" overall. **Stock:** Walnut with straight grip, Schnabel forend. **Sights:** None furnished; drilled and tapped for scope mounting. **Features:** Replica of J.M. Browning's high-wall falling block rifle. Octagon barrel with recessed muzzle. Imported from Japan by Browning. Introduced 1985.
Price: **$1,027.00**

C. SHARPS ARMS NEW MODEL 1875 OLD RELIABLE RIFLE
Caliber: 22LR, 32-40 & 38-55 Ballard, 38-56 WCF, 40-65 WCF, 40-90 3-1/4", 40-90 2-5/8", 40-70 2-1/10", 40-70 2-1/4", 40-70 2-1/2", 40-50 1-11/16", 40-50 1-7/8", 45-90, 45-70, 45-100, 45-110, 45-120. Also available on special order only in 50-70, 50-90, 50-140. **Barrel:** 24", 26", 30" (standard), 32", 34" optional. **Weight:** 8-12 lbs. **Stock:** Walnut, straight grip, shotgun butt with checkered steel buttplate. **Sights:** Silver blade front, Rocky Mountain buckhorn rear. **Features:** Recreation of the 1875 Sharps rifle. Production guns will have case-colored receiver. Available in Custom Sporting and Target versions upon request. Announced 1986. From C. Sharps Arms Co.
Price: 1875 Sporting Rifle (30" tapered oct. bbl.) **$1,185.00**

C. Sharps Arms 1875 Classic Sharps
Similar to New Model 1875 Sporting Rifle except 26", 28" or 30" full octagon barrel, crescent buttplate with toe plate, Hartford-style forend with cast German silver nose cap. Blade front sight, Rocky Mountain buckhorn rear. Weighs 10 lbs. Introduced 1987. From C. Sharps Arms Co.
Price: **$1,470.00**

C. Sharps Arms New Model 1875 Target & Long Range
Similar to New Model 1875 in all listed calibers except 22 LR; 34" tapered octagon barrel; globe with post front sight, Long Range Vernier tang sight with windage adjustments. Pistol grip stock with cheek rest; checkered steel buttplate. Introduced 1991. From C. Sharps Arms Co.
Price: **$1,549.50**

C. SHARPS ARMS NEW MODEL 1874 OLD RELIABLE
Caliber: 40-50, 40-70, 40-90, 45-70, 45-90, 45-100, 45-110, 45-120, 50-70, 50-90, 50-140. **Barrel:** 26", 28", 30" tapered octagon. **Weight:** About 10 lbs.

Length: NA. **Stock:** American black walnut; shotgun butt with checkered steel buttplate; straight grip, heavy forend with Schnabel tip. **Sights:** Blade front, buckhorn rear. Drilled and tapped for tang sight. **Features:** Recreation of the Model 1874 Old Reliable Sharps Sporting Rifle. Double-set triggers. Reintroduced 1991. Made in U.S.A. by C. Sharps Arms.
Price: **$1,584.00**

C. SHARPS ARMS NEW MODEL 1885 HIGHWALL RIFLE
Caliber: 22 LR, 22 Hornet, 219 Zipper, 25-35 WCF, 32-40 WCF, 38-55 WCF, 40-65, 30-40 Krag, 40-50 ST or BN, 40-70 ST or BN, 40-90 ST or BN, 45-70 2-1/10" ST, 45-90 2-4/10" ST, 45-100 2-6/10" ST, 45-110 2-7/8" ST, 45-120 3-1/4" ST. **Barrel:** 26", 28", 30", tapered full octagon. **Weight:** About 9 lbs., 4 oz. **Length:** 47" overall. **Stock:** Oil-finished American walnut; Schnabel-style forend. **Sights:** Blade front, buckhorn rear. Drilled and tapped for optional tang sight. **Features:** Single trigger; octagonal receiver top; checkered steel buttplate; color case-hardened receiver and buttplate, blued barrel. Many options available. Made in U.S.A. by C. Sharps Arms Co.
Price: From **$1,439.00**

C. SHARPS ARMS CUSTOM NEW MODEL 1877 LONG RANGE TARGET RIFLE
Caliber: 44-90 Sharps/Rem., 45-70, 45-90, 45-100 Sharps. **Barrel:** 32", 34" tapered round with Rigby flat. **Weight:** Appx. 10 lbs. **Stock:** Walnut checkered. Pistol grip/forend. **Sights:** Classic long range with windage. **Features:** Custom production only.
Price: .... **$5,550.00 and up**

CABELA'S SHARPS SPORTING RIFLE
Caliber: 45-70, 45-120, 45-110. **Barrel:** 32", tapered octagon. **Weight:** 9 lbs. **Length:** 47-1/4" overall. **Stock:** Checkered walnut. **Sights:** Blade front, open adjustable rear. **Features:** Color case-hardened receiver and hammer, rest blued. Introduced 1995. Imported by Cabela's.
Price: 45-70, 45-90 .... **$1399.99**
Price: (Heavy Target Sharps, 45-70, 45-120) **$1,599.99**
Price: (Quigley Sharps, 45-70, 45-120, 45-110) **$1,899.99**

CIMARRON BILLY DIXON 1874 SHARPS SPORTING RIFLE
Caliber: 40-40, 50-90, 50-70, 45-70. **Barrel:** 32" tapered octagonal. **Weight:** NA. **Length:** NA. **Stock:** European walnut. **Sights:** Blade front, Creedmoor rear. **Features:** Color case-hardened frame, blued barrel. Hand-checkered grip and forend; hand-rubbed oil finish. Introduced 1999. Imported by Cimarron F.A. Co.
Price: **$1,670.00**

Cimarron Quigley

Cimarron 1885 High Wall

Dakota Single Shot

Dixie 1874 Sharps Silhouette

CIMARRON QUIGLEY MODEL 1874 SHARPS SPORTING RIFLE
Caliber: 45-110, 50-70, 50-40, 45-70, 45-90, 45-120. **Barrel:** 34" octagonal. **Weight:** NA. **Length:** NA. **Stock:** Checkered walnut. **Sights:** Blade front, adjustable rear. **Features:** Blued finish; double-set triggers. From Cimarron F.A. Co.
Price: **$1,805.00**

CIMARRON SILHOUETTE MODEL 1874 SHARPS SPORTING RIFLE
Caliber: 45-70, 50-70. **Barrel:** 32" octagonal. **Weight:** NA. **Length:** NA. **Stock:** Walnut. **Sights:** Blade front, adjustable rear. **Features:** Pistol-grip stock with shotgun-style buttplate; cut-rifled barrel. From Cimarron F.A. Co.
Price: **$1,620.00**

CIMARRON MODEL 1885 HIGH WALL RIFLE
Caliber: 38-55, 40-65, 45-70, 45-90, 45-120, 30-40 Krag, 348 Winchester. **Barrel:** 30" octagonal. **Weight:** NA. **Length:** NA. **Stock:** European walnut. **Sights:** Bead front, semi-buckhorn rear. **Features:** Replica of the Winchester 1885 High Wall rifle. Color case-hardened receiver and lever, blued barrel. Curved buttplate. Optional double-set triggers. Introduced 1999. Imported by Cimarron F.A. Co.
Price: **$995.00**
Price: With pistol grip **$1,175.00**

DAKOTA MODEL 10 SINGLE SHOT RIFLE
Caliber: Most rimmed and rimless commercial calibers. **Barrel:** 23". **Weight:** 6 lbs. **Length:** 39-1/2" overall. **Stock:** Medium fancy grade walnut in classic style. Checkered grip and forend. **Sights:** None furnished. Drilled and tapped for scope mounting. **Features:** Falling block action with underlever. Top tang safety. Removable trigger plate for conversion to single set trigger. Introduced 1990. Made in U.S.A. by Dakota Arms.
Price: **$3,595.00**
Price: Barreled action **$2,095.00**
Price: Action only **$1,850.00**
Price: Magnum calibers **$3,595.00**
Price: Magnum barreled action **$2,050.00**
Price: Magnum action only **$1,675.00**

DIXIE 1874 SHARPS BLACK POWDER SILHOUETTE RIFLE
Caliber: 45-70. **Barrel:** 30"; tapered octagon; blued; 1:18" twist. **Weight:** 10 lbs., 3 oz. **Length:** 47-1/2" overall. **Stock:** Oiled walnut. **Sights:** Blade front, ladder-type hunting rear. **Features:** Replica of the Sharps #1 Sporter. Shotgun-style butt with checkered metal buttplate; color case-hardened receiver, hammer, lever and buttplate. Tang is drilled and tapped for tang sight. Double-set triggers. Meets standards for NRA blackpowder cartridge matches. Introduced 1995. Imported from Italy by Dixie Gun Works.
Price: CR0145 . . . . **$1,100.00**

Dixie 1874 Sharps Lightweight Hunter/Target Rifle
Same as the Dixie 1874 Sharps Black Powder Silhouette model except has a straight-grip buttstock with military-style buttplate. Based on the 1874 military model. Introduced 1995. Imported from Italy by Dixie Gun Works.
Price: CR0212 . . . . **$1,050.00**

E.M.F. PREMIER 1874 SHARPS RIFLE
Caliber: 45/70, 45/110, 45/120. **Barrel:** 32", 34". **Weight:** 11-13 lbs. **Length:** 49", 51" overall. **Stock:** Pistol grip, European walnut. **Sights:** Blade front, adjustable rear. **Features:** Superb quality reproductions of the 1874 Sharps Sporting Rifles; casehardened locks; double-set triggers; blue barrels. Imported from Pedersoli by E.M.F.
Price: Business Rifle. **$1,130.00**
Price: "Quigley", Patchbox, heavy barrel **$1,800.00**
Price: Silhouette, pistol-grip **$1,500.00**
Price: Super Deluxe Hand Engraved **$3,150.00**

E.M.F. 1885 HIGHWALL RIFLES
Caliber: 38/55, 45/70. **Barrel:** 30". **Weight:** 10 lbs. **Length:** 47". **Stock:** Walnut, straight or pistol grip.. **Sights:** Bead front, semi-buckhorn rear. **Features:** Reproduction of the Winchester 1885 Highwall Rifle, curved butt plate. Case-hardened receiver and lever, blue barrel. Imported by E.M.F.
Price: Standard. **$900.00**
Price: Deluxe pistol grip **$1,020.00**

HARRINGTON & RICHARDSON ULTRA VARMINT/ULTRA HUNTER RIFLES
Caliber: 204 Ruger, 22 WMR, 22-250, 223, 243, 25-06, 30-06. **Barrel:** 22" to 26" heavy taper. **Weight:** About 7.5 lbs. **Stock:** Laminated birch with Monte Carlo comb or skeletonized polymer. **Sights:** None furnished. Drilled and tapped for scope mounting. **Features:** Break-open action with side-lever release, positive ejection. Scope mount. Blued receiver and barrel. Swivel studs. Introduced 1993. Ultra Hunter introduced 1995. From H&R 1871, Inc.
Price: Ultra Varmint Fluted, 24" bull barrel, polymer stock **$406.00**
Price: Ultra Hunter Rifle, 26" bull barrel in 25-06, laminated stock . **$357.00**
Price: Ultra Varmint Rifle, 22" bull barrel in 223, laminated stock . . **$357.00**

H&R Ultra Hunter

H&R Buffalo

Model 1885 High Wall

Mossberg SSi-One Varminter

HARRINGTON & RICHARDSON BUFFALO CLASSIC & TARGET RIFLES
Caliber: 45-70. **Barrel:** 32" heavy. **Weight:** 8 lbs. **Length:** 46" overall.
Stock: Cut-checkered American black walnut. **Sights:** Williams receiver
sight; Lyman target front sight with 8 aperture inserts. **Features:** Color
case-hardened Handi-Rifle action with exposed hammer; color case-
hardened crescent buttplate; 19th century checkering pattern. Introduced
1995. Target model (introduced 1998) is similar to the Buffalo Classic rifle
except chambered for 38-55 Win., has 28" barrel. The barrel, steel trigger
guard and forend spacer, are highly polished and blued. Color case-
hardened receiver and buttplate. Made in U.S.A. by H&R 1871, LLC.
Price: Buffalo Classic Rifle **$449.00**
Price: Target Model Rifle **$449.00**

HARRIS GUNWORKS ANTIETAM SHARPS RIFLE
Caliber: 40-65, 45-75. **Barrel:** 30", 32", octagon or round, hand-lapped
stainless or chrome-moly. **Weight:** 11.25 lbs. **Length:** 47" overall. **Stock:**
Choice of straight grip, pistol grip or Creedmoor with Schnabel forend;
pewter tip optional. Standard wood is A Fancy; higher grades available.
Sights: Montana Vintage Arms #111 Low Profile Spirit Level front, #108
mid-range tang rear with windage adjustments. **Features:** Recreation of
the 1874 Sharps sidehammer. Action is color case-hardened, barrel satin
black. Chrome-moly barrel optionally blued. Optional sights include #112
Spirit Level Globe front with windage, #107 Long Range rear with
windage. Introduced 1994. Made in U.S.A. by Harris Gunworks.
Price: **$2,400.00**

KRIEGHOFF HUBERTUS SINGLE-SHOT RIFLE
Caliber: 222, 243, 270, 308, 30-06, 5.6x50R Mag., 5.6x52R, 6x62R Freres,
6.5x57R, 6.5x65R, 7x57R, 7x65R, 8x57JRS, 8x75RS, 9.3x74R, 7mm
Rem. Mag., 300 Win. Mag. **Barrel:** 23-1/2". **Weight:** 6-1/2 lbs. **Length:**
40.5. **Stock:** High-grade walnut. **Sights:** Blade front, open rear.
Features: Break-open loading with manual cocking lever on top tang;
takedown; extractor; Schnabel forearm; many options. Imported from
Germany by Krieghoff International Inc.
Price: Hubertus single shot, from **$5,995.00**
Price: Hubertus, magnum calibers **$6,995.00**

MEACHAM HIGHWALL SILHOUETTE or SCHUETZEN RIFLE
Caliber: any rimmed cartridge. **Barrel:** 26-34". **Weight:** 8-15 lbs. **Sights:**
none. Tang drilled for Win. base, 3/8 dovetail slot front. **Stock:** Fancy
eastern walnut with cheekpiece; ebony insert in forearm tip. **Features:**
Exact copy of 1885 Winchester. With most Winchester factory options
available, including double set triggers. Introduced 1994. Made in U.S.A.
by Meacham T&H Inc.
Price: From **$3,899.00**

MERKEL K-1 MODEL LIGHTWEIGHT STALKING RIFLE
Caliber: 243 Win., 270 Win., 7x57R, 308 Win., 30-06, 7mm Rem. Mag., 300
Win. Mag., 9.3x74R. **Barrel:** 23.6". **Weight:** 5.6 lbs. unscoped. **Stock:**
Satin-finished walnut, fluted and checkered; sling-swivel studs. **Sights:**
None (scope base furnished). **Features:** Franz Jager single-shot break-
open action, cocking/uncocking slide-type safety, matte silver receiver,
selectable trigger pull weights, integrated, quick detach 1" or 30mm optic
mounts (optic not included). Imported from Germany by GSI.
Price: Standard, simple border engraving **$3,795.00**
Price: Premium, light arabesque scroll **$3,795.00**
Price: Jagd, fine engraved hunting scenes **$4,395.00**

MODEL 1885 HIGH WALL RIFLE
Caliber: 30-40 Krag, 32-40, 38-55, 40-65 WCF, 45-70. **Barrel:** 26" (30-40),
28" to 30" all others. Douglas Premium #3 tapered octagon. **Weight:** 9 lbs,
4 oz. **Length:** 47" overall. **Stock:** Premium American black walnut.
Sights: Marble's standard ivory bead front, #66 long blade top rear with
reversible notch and elevator. **Features:** Receiver with octagon top, thick-
wall High Wall with coil spring action. Tang drilled, tapped for High Wall
tang sight. Receiver, lever, hammer and breechblock color case-
hardened. Available from Montana Armory, Inc.
Price: **$1,350.00**

MOSSBERG SSi-ONE SINGLE SHOT RIFLE
Caliber: 223 Rem., 22-250 Rem., 243 Win., 270 Win., 308 Rem., 30-06.
Barrel: 24". **Weight:** 8 lbs. **Length:** 40". **Stock:** Satin-finished walnut,
fluted and checkered; sling-swivel studs. **Sights:** None (scope base
furnished). **Features:** Frame accepts interchangeable barrels including
12 gauge, fully rifled slug barrel and 12 ga., 3-1/2 chambered barrel with
Ulti-Full Turkey choke tube. Lever-opening, break-action design; single-
stage trigger; ambidextrous, top-tang safety; internal eject/extract
selector. Introduced 2000. From Mossberg.
Price: SSi-One Sporter (standard barrel) or 12 ga., 3-1/2" chamber **$459.00**
Price: SSi-One Varmint (bull barrel, 22-250 Rem. only;
        weighs 10 lbs.) **$480.00**
Price: SSi-One 12 gauge Slug (fully rifled barrel, no sights,
        scope base) **$480.00**

Mossberg SSi-One Sporter

Navy Arms 1874 Sharps Cavalry Carbine

Navy Arms #2 Creedmoor

Navy Arms 1885 High Wall

Navy Arms John Bodine

NAVY ARMS 1873 SHARPS "QUIGLEY" RIFLE

Caliber: 45/70. **Barrel:** 34" heavy octagonal. **Stock:** Walnut. **Features:** Case-hardened receiver and military patchbox. Exact reproduction from "Quigley Down Under."

Price: **$1,826.00**

NAVY ARMS 1873 SHARPS NO. 2 CREEDMOOR RIFLE

Caliber: 45/70. **Barrel:** 30" tapered round. **Stock:** Walnut. **Sights:** Front globe, "soule" tang rear. **Features:** Nickel receiver and action. Lightweight sporting rifle.

Price: **$1,739.00**

NAVY ARMS 1874 SHARPS CAVALRY CARBINE

Caliber: 45-70. **Barrel:** 22". **Weight:** 7 lbs., 12 oz. **Length:** 39" overall. **Stock:** Walnut. **Sights:** Blade front, military ladder-type rear. **Features:** Replica of the 1874 Sharps miltary carbine. Color case-hardened receiver and furniture. Imported by Navy Arms.

Price: **$1,245.00**

Navy Arms Sharps Sporting Rifle

Same as the Navy Arms Sharps Plains Rifle except has pistol grip stock. Introduced 1997. Imported by Navy Arms.

Price: 45-70 only **$1,739.00**
Price: #2 Sporting with case-hardened receiver **$1,739.00**
Price: #2 Silhouette with full octagonal barrel **$1,739.00**

NAVY ARMS 1885 HIGH WALL RIFLE

Caliber: 45-70; others available on special order. **Barrel:** 28" round, 30" octagonal. **Weight:** 9.5 lbs. **Length:** 45-1/2" overall (30" barrel). **Stock:** Walnut. **Sights:** Blade front, vernier tang-mounted peep rear. **Features:** Replica of Winchester's High Wall designed by Browning. Color case-hardened receiver, blued barrel. Introduced 1998. Imported by Navy Arms.

Price: 28", round barrel, target sights **$1,169.00**
Price: 30" octagonal barrel, target sights **$1,169.00**

NAVY ARMS 1873 SPRINGFIELD CAVALRY CARBINE

Caliber: 45-70. **Barrel:** 22". **Weight:** 7 lbs. **Length:** 40-1/2" overall. **Stock:** Walnut. **Sights:** Blade front, military ladder rear. **Features:** Blued lockplate and barrel; color case-hardened breechblock; saddle ring with bar. Replica of 7th Cavalry gun. Imported by Navy Arms.

Price: **$1,195.00**

NAVY ARMS "JOHN BODINE" ROLLING BLOCK RIFLE

Caliber: 45-70. **Barrel:** 30" heavy octagonal. **Stock:** Walnut. **Sights:** Globe front, "soule" tang rear. **Features:** Double-set triggers.

Price: **$1,856.00**
Price: (#2 with deluxe nickel finished receiver) **$1,856.00**

NAVY ARMS ROLLING BLOCK BUFFALO RIFLE

Caliber: 45-70. **Barrel:** 26" heavy full octagon. **Weight:** 10 lbs., 12 oz. **Length:** 43". **Stock:** European walnut. **Sights:** Rocky Mountain style front blade and open notch rear. **Features:** Color case hardened receiver, trigger guard, barrel band and buttplate.

Price: **$910.00**

CENTERFIRE RIFLES — Single Shot

Navy Arms Rolling Block Buffalo

New England Firearms Handi-Rifle

New England Firearms Superlight

New England Firearms Survivor

NAVY ARMS SHARPS NO. 3 LONG RANGE RIFLE
Caliber: 45-70, 45-90. **Barrel:** 34" octagon. **Weight:** 10 lbs., 12 oz. **Length:** 51-1/2". **Stock:** Deluxe walnut. **Sights:** Globe target front and match grade rear tang. **Features:** Shotgun buttplate, German silver forend cap, color case hardenend receiver. Imported by Navy Arms.
Price: **$2,194.00**

NEW ENGLAND FIREARMS HANDI-RIFLE
Caliber: 204 Ruger, 22 Hornet, 223, 243, 30-30, 270, 280 Rem., 7mm-08, 308, 7.62x39 Russian, 30-06, 357 Mag., 35 Whelen, 44 Mag., 45-70, 500 S&W. **Barrel:** from 20" to 26", blued or stainless. **Weight:** 5.5 to 7 lbs. **Stock:** Walnut-finished hardwood or synthetic. **Sights:** Vary by model, but most have ramp front, folding rear, or are drilled and tapped for scope mount. **Features:** Break-open action with side-lever release. Swivel studs on all models. Blue finish. Introduced 1989. From New England Firearms.
Price: Various cartridges $292.00
Price: 7.62x39 Russian, 35 Whelen, intr. 2006 . . . . $292.00
Price: Youth, 37" OAL, 11.75" LOP, 6.75 lbs. $292.00
Price: Handi-Rifle/Pardner combo, 20 ga. synthetic, intr. 2006 . . . . $325.00
Price: Handi-Rifle/Pardner Superlight, 20 ga., 5.5 lbs., intr. 2006 . . $325.00
Price: Synthetic $302.00
Price: Stainless $364.00
Price: Superlight, 20" barrel, 35.25" OAL, 5.5 lbs. $302.00

NEW ENGLAND FIREARMS SURVIVOR RIFLE
Caliber: 223, 308 Win., .410 shotgun, 45 Colt, single shot. **Barrel:** 20" to 22". **Weight:** 6 lbs. **Length:** 34.5" to 36" overall. **Stock:** Black polymer, thumbhole design. **Sights:** None furnished; scope mount provided. **Features:** Receiver drilled and tapped for scope mounting. Stock and forend have storage compartments for ammo, etc.; comes with integral swivels and black nylon sling. Introduced 1996. Made in U.S.A. by New England Firearms.
Price: Blue or nickel finish $304.00

NEW ENGLAND FIREARMS SPORTSTER/VERSA PACK RIFLE
Caliber: 17M2, 17HMR, 22LR, 22 WMR, .410 bore single shot. **Barrel:** 20" to 22". **Weight:** 5.4 to 7 lbs. **Length:** 33" to 38.25" overall. **Stock:** Black polymer. **Sights:** Adjustable rear, ramp front. **Features:** Receiver drilled and tapped for scope mounting. Made in U.S.A. by New England Firearms.
Price: Sportster 17M2, 17HMR $193.00
Price: Sportster $161.00
Price: Sportster Youth $161.00
Price: Sportster 22/410 Versa Pack $176.00

REMINGTON MODEL XR-100 RANGEMASTER
Caliber: 204 Ruger, 223 Rem., 22-250 Rem. **Barrel:** 26" varmint-contour barrel with concave target crown, satin blued. **Weight:** 9.1 lbs. **Length:** 45.4" overall. **Stock:** Black-and-gray laminated thumbhole, rollover cheekpiece, beavertail forend with lightening-vent cuts under barrel channel, swivel studs. **Sights:** None. **Features:** Single-shot target rifle, based on Remington XP-100 pistol action. Externally adjustable Model 40-X target trigger adjustable from 1.5 to 3.5 pounds. Introduced 2005. Made in U.S. by Remington Arms Co., Inc.
Price: (2007) **$1,057.00**

Remington XR-100 Rangemaster

Remington No. 1 Mid-Range

Replica Arms Sharps "Quigley"

Rossi Single Shot

Rossi Matched Pairs

REMINGTON NO. 1 ROLLING BLOCK MID-RANGE SPORTER
Caliber: 45-70. **Barrel:** 30" round. **Weight:** 8-3/4 lbs. **Length:** 46-1/2" overall. **Stock:** American walnut with checkered pistol grip and forend. **Sights:** Beaded blade front, adjustable center-notch buckhorn rear. **Features:** Recreation of the original. Polished blue metal finish. Many options available. Introduced 1998. Made in U.S.A. by Remington.
Price: **$1,450.00**
Price: Silhouette model with single-set trigger, heavy barrel **$1,560.00**

REPLICA ARMS SHARPS "QUIGLEY" RIFLE
Caliber: .45-70. **Barrel:** 28" octagon. **Weight:** 10 lbs. **Length:** 47-1/4" overall. **Grips:** Walnut checkered at wrist and forend. **Sights:** High blade front, full buckhorn rear. **Features:** Color case-hardened receiver, trigger, patchbox, hammer and lever. Double-set triggers, German silver gripcap.
Price: **$1,241.95**

REPLICA ARMS SHARPS "BIG GAME" RIFLE
Caliber: .45-70. **Barrel:** 28" Deluxe Heavy Round. **Weight:** 8.8 lbs. **Length:** 44.8" overall. **Grips:** Walnut. **Sights:** Gold bead front, full buckhorn rear. **Features:** Color case-hardened receiver, trigger, hammer and lever. Double-set triggers.
Price: **$1,014.00**

ROSSI SINGLE-SHOT RIFLES
Caliber: .17, .223, .243Win, .270Win, .30-06, .308, 7.62x39, .22-250. **Barrel:** 22" (Youth), 23". **Weight:** 6.25-7 lbs. **Stocks:** Wood, Black Synthetic (Youth). **Sights:** Adjustable sights, drilled and tapped for scope. **Features:** Single-shot break open, 13 models available, positive ejection, internal transfer bar mechanism, manual external safety, trigger block system, Taurus Security System, Matte blue finish, youth models available.
Price: . . . . **$175.00 to $258.00**

ROSSI MATCHED PAIRS
Gauge/Caliber: 12, 20, .410, .22Mag, .22LR, .17HMR, .223Rem, .243Win, .270Win, .30-06, .308Win, .50 (black powder). **Barrel:** 23", 28". **Weight:** 5-6.3 lbs. **Stocks:** Wood or black synthetic. **Sights:** Bead front on shotgun barrel, fully adjustable front and rear on rifle barrel, drilled and tapped for scope, fully adjustable fiber optic sights (black powder). **Features:** Single-shot break open, 27 models available, internal transfer bar mechanism, manual external safety, blue finish, trigger block system, Taurus Security System, youth models available.
Price: Rimfire/Shotgun . . . . **$169.00 to $253.00**
Price: Centerfire/Shotgun. **$297.00**
Price: Black Powder Matched Pair . . . . **$249.00 to $313.00**

RUGER NO. 1B SINGLE SHOT
Caliber: 23, 204 Ruger, 25-06, 270, 30-06, 7mm Rem. Mag., 300 Win. Mag., 308 Win. **Barrel:** 26" round tapered with quarter-rib; with Ruger 1" rings. **Weight:** 8.25 lbs. **Length:** 42.25" overall. **Stock:** Walnut, two-piece, checkered pistol grip and semi-beavertail forend. **Sights:** None, 1" scope rings supplied for integral mounts. **Features:** Under-lever, hammerless falling block design has auto ejector, top tang safety.
Price: 1B **$1,030.00**
Price: K1-B-BBZ stainless steel, laminated stock 25-06, 7mm mag, 270, 300 Win Mag., 243 Win., 30-06 . . . . **$1,032.00**

Ruger No. 1A Light Sporter
Caliber: 243, 270, 7x57, 30-06. **Weight:** 7.25 lbs. Similar to the No. 1B Standard Rifle except has lightweight 22" barrel, Alexander Henry-style forend, adjustable folding leaf rear sight on quarter-rib, dovetailed ramp front with gold bead.
Price: No. 1A. **$1,030.00**

Ruger K1-B-BBZ

Ruger No. 1V Varminter

Ruger No. 1 RSI

Ruger No. 1H Tropical

Shiloh 1874 Long Range Express

Ruger No. 1A Light Standard
Caliber: 204 Ruger. **Weight:** About 7.25 lbs. **Length:** 38.25" overall. Similar to the No. 1A Light Sporter but doesn't come with sights.
Price: No. 1-AB **$1,030.00**

Ruger No. 1V Varminter
Similar to the No. 1B Standard Rifle except has 24" heavy barrel. Semi-beavertail forend, barrel ribbed for target scope block, with 1" Ruger scope rings. Calibers 204 Ruger, 22-250, 223, 25-06. Weight about 9 lbs.
Price: No. 1V **$1,030.00**
Price: K1-V-BBZ stainless steel, laminated stock 204 Ruger . . . **$1,065.00**

Ruger No. 1 RSI International
Similar to the No. 1B Standard Rifle except has lightweight 20" barrel, full-length International-style forend with loop sling swivel, adjustable folding leaf rear sight on quarter-rib, ramp front with gold bead. Calibers 243, 30-06, 270 and 7x57. Weight is about 7-1/4 lbs.
Price: No. 1 RSI **$1,065.00**

Ruger No. 1H Tropical Rifle
Similar to the No. 1B Standard Rifle except has Alexander Henry forend, adjustable folding leaf rear sight on quarter-rib, ramp front with dovetail gold bead, 24" heavy barrel. Calibers 375 H&H, 416 Rigby, 458 Lott, 405 Win. (weighs about 9 lbs.).
Price: No. 1H **$1,030.00**
Price: K1-H-BBZ, S/S, 375 H&H, 458 Lott, 416 Rigby **$1,065.00**

Ruger No. 1S Medium Sporter
Similar to the No. 1B Standard Rifle except has Alexander Henry-style forend, adjustable folding leaf rear sight on quarter-rib, ramp front sight base and dovetail-type gold bead front sight. Calibers: 9.3x74R, 45-70 with 22" barrel. Weighs about 7-1/2 lbs.
Price: No. 1S **$1,030.00**
Price: K1-S-BBZ, S/S, 45-70 . . . . **$1,065.00**

SHILOH RIFLE CO. SHARPS 1874 LONG RANGE EXPRESS
Caliber: 40-50 BN, 40-70 BN, 40-90 BN, 45-70 ST, 45-90 ST, 45-110 ST, 50-70 ST, 50-90 ST, 38-55, 40-70 ST, 40-90 ST. **Barrel:** 34" tapered octagon. **Weight:** 10-1/2 lbs. **Length:** 51" overall. **Stock:** Oil-finished walnut (upgrades available) with pistol grip, shotgun-style butt, traditional cheek rest, Schnabel forend. **Sights:** Customer's choice. **Features:** Recreation of the Model 1874 Sharps rifle. Double-set triggers. Made in U.S.A. by Shiloh Rifle Mfg. Co.
Price: **$1,638.00**
Price: Sporting Rifle No. 1 (similar to above except with 30" bbl.,
blade front, buckhorn rear sight) **$1,638.00**
Price: Sporting Rifle No. 3 (similar to No. 1 except straight-grip
stock, standard wood) **$1,547.00**

SHILOH RIFLE CO. SHARPS 1874 QUIGLEY
Caliber: 45-70, 45-110. **Barrel:** 34" heavy octagon. **Stock:** Military-style with patch box, standard grade American walnut. **Sights:** Semi buckhorn, interchangeable front and midrange vernier tang sight with windage. **Features:** Gold inlay initials, pewter tip, Hartford collar, case color or antique finish. Double-set triggers.
Price: **$2,903.00**

SHILOH RIFLE CO. SHARPS 1874 SADDLE RIFLE
Caliber: 38-55, 40-50 BN, 40-65 Win., 40-70 BN, 40-70 ST, 40-90 BN, 40-90 ST, 44-77 BN, 44-90 BN, 45-70 ST, 45-90 ST, 45-100 ST, 45-110 ST, 45-120 ST, 50-70 ST, 50-90 ST. **Barrel:** 26" full or half octagon. **Stock:** Semi fancy American walnut. Shotgun style with cheekrest. **Sights:** Buckhorn and blade. **Features:** Double-set trigger, numerous custom features can be added.
Price: **$1,594.00**

Shiloh 1874 Quigley

Shiloh 1874 Montana Roughrider

Shiloh 1874 Creedmoor

Thompson/Center Encore

Thompson/Center Contender

SHILOH RIFLE CO. SHARPS 1874 MONTANA ROUGHRIDER
Caliber: 38-55, 40-50 BN, 40-65 Win., 40-70 BN, 40-70 ST, 40-90 BN, 40-90 ST, 44-77 BN, 44-90 BN, 45-70 ST, 45-90 ST, 45-100 ST, 45-110 ST, 45-120 ST, 50-70 ST, 50-90 ST. **Barrel:** 30" full or half octagon. **Stock:** American walnut in shotgun or military style. **Sights:** Buckhorn and blade. **Features:** Double-set triggers, numerous custom features can be added.
Price: **$1,638.00**

SHILOH RIFLE CO. SHARPS CREEDMOOR TARGET
Caliber: 38-55, 40-50 BN, 40-65 Win., 40-70 BN, 40-70 ST, 40-90 BN, 40-90 ST, 44-77 BN, 44-90 BN, 45-70 ST, 45-90 ST, 45-100 ST, 45-110 ST, 45-120 ST, 50-70 ST, 50-90 ST. **Barrel:** 32", half round-half octagon. **Stock:** Extra fancy American walnut. Shotgun style with pistol grip. **Sights:** Customer's choice. **Features:** Single trigger, AA finish on stock, polished barrel and screws, pewter tip.
Price: **$2,485.00**

THOMPSON/CENTER ENCORE RIFLE
Caliber: 22-250, 223, 243, 204 Ruger, 6.8 Rem. Spec., 25-06, 270, 7mm-08, 308, 30-06, 7mm Rem. Mag., 300 Win. Mag. **Barrel:** 24", 26". **Weight:** 6 lbs., 12 oz. (24" barrel). **Length:** 38-1/2" (24" barrel). **Stock:** American walnut. Monte Carlo style; Schnabel forend or black composite. **Sights:** Ramp-style white bead front, fully adjustable leaf-type rear. **Features:** Interchangeable barrels; action opens by squeezing trigger guard; drilled and tapped for T/C scope mounts; polished blue finish. Introduced 1996. Made in U.S.A. by Thompson/Center Arms.
Price: . . . . **$604.00 to $663.00**
Price: Extra barrels **$277.00**

Thompson/Center Stainless Encore Rifle
Similar to blued Encore except stainless steel with blued sights, black composite stock and forend. Available in 22-250, 223, 7mm-08, 30-06, 308. Introduced 1999. Made in U.S.A. by Thompson/Center Arms.
Price: . . . . **$680.00 to $738.00**

THOMPSON/CENTER ENCORE "KATAHDIN" CARBINE
Caliber: 45-70 Gov't., 450 Marlin. **Barrel:** 18" with muzzle tamer. **Stock:** Composite.
Price: **$619.00**

Thompson/Center G2 Contender Rifle
Similar to the G2 Contender pistol, but in a compact rifle format. Weighs 5-1/2 lbs. Features interchangeable 23" barrels, chambered for 17 HMR, 22LR, 223 Rem., 30/30 Win. and 45/70 Gov't; plus a 45 Cal. Muzzleloading barrel. All of the 16-1/4" and 21" barrels made for the old-style Contender will fit. Introduced 2003. Made in U.S.A. by Thompson/Center Arms.
Price: . . . . **$622.00 to $637.00**

Traditions 1874 Sharps Sporting Deluxe

Traditions 1874 Sharps Standard

Traditions Rolling Block

Uberti 1885 High-Wall Sporting Rifle

Uberti 1885 High-Wall Rifle

TRADITIONS 1874 SHARPS DELUXE RIFLE
Caliber: 45-70. **Barrel:** 32" octagonal; 1:18" twist. **Weight:** 11.67 lbs. **Length:** 48.8" overall. **Stock:** Checkered walnut with German silver nose cap and steel buttplate. **Sights:** Globe front, adjustable Creedmore rear with 12 inserts. **Features:** Color case-hardened receiver; double-set triggers. Introduced 2001. Imported from Pedersoli by Traditions.
Price: **$999.00**

Traditions 1874 Sharps Sporting Deluxe Rifle
Similar to Sharps Deluxe but custom silver engraved receiver, European walnut stock and forend, satin finish, set trigger, fully adjustable.
Price: **$1,999.00**

Traditions 1874 Sharps Standard Rifle
Similar to 1874 Sharps Deluxe except has blade front and adjustable buckhorn-style rear sight. Weighs 10.67 pounds. Introduced 2001. Imported from Pedersoli by Traditions.
Price: **$769.00**

TRADITIONS ROLLING BLOCK SPORTING RIFLE
Caliber: 45-70. **Barrel:** 30" octagonal; 1:18" twist. **Weight:** 11.67 lbs. **Length:** 46.7" overall. **Stock:** Walnut. **Sights:** Blade front, adjustable rear. **Features:** Antique silver, color case-hardened receiver, drilled and tapped for tang/globe sights; brass buttplate and trigger guard. Introduced 2001. Imported from Pedersoli by Traditions.
Price: **$769.00**

TRADITIONS ROLLING BLOCK SPORTING RIFLE IN 30-30 WINCHESTER
Caliber: 30-30. **Barrel:** 28" round, blued. **Weight:** 8.25 lbs. **Stock:** Walnut.

Sights: Fixed front, adjustable rear. **Features:** Steel buttplate, trigger guard, barrel band.
Price: **$769.00**

UBERTI 1874 SHARPS SPORTING RIFLE
Caliber: 45-70. **Barrel:** 30", 32", 34" octagonal. **Weight:** 10.57 lbs. with 32" barrel. **Length:** 48.9" with 32" barrel. **Stock:** Walnut. **Sights:** Dovetail front, Vernier tang rear. **Features:** Cut checkering, case-colored finish on frame, buttplate, and lever.
Price: Standard Sharps (2006), 30" barrel.................. **$1,195.00**
Price: Special Sharps (2006) 32" barrel **$1,450.00**
Price: Deluxe Sharps (2006) 34" barrel **$2,200.00**
Price: Down Under Sharps (2006) 34" barrel **$1,799.00**
Price: Adobe Walls Sharps (2006) 32" barrel **$1,750.00**
Price: Longe Range Sharps (2006) 34" barrel **$1,799.00**

UBERTI ROLLING BLOCK CARBINE AND RIFLE
Caliber: 22 LR, 22 WMR, 22 Hornet, 357 Mag., single shot. **Barrel:** 22" to 26". **Weight:** 4.9 lbs. (Carbine) **Length:** 35.5" overall. **Stock:** Walnut stock and forend. **Sights:** Blade front, fully adjustable open rear. **Features:** Resembles Remington New Model No. 4 carbine. Brass trigger guard and buttplate; color case-hardened frame, blued barrel. Imported by Uberti USA Inc.
Price: Carbine, 22" barrel.................................. **$535.00**
Price: Rifle, 26" barrel **$600.00**

UBERTI HIGH-WALL RIFLE
Caliber: 45-70, 45-90, 45-120 single shot. **Barrel:** 28" to 23". **Weight:** 9.3 to 9.9 lbs. **Length:** 44.5" to 47" overall. **Stock:** Walnut stock and forend. **Sights:** Blade front, fully adjustable open rear. **Features:** Based on Winchester High-Wall design by John Browning. Color case-hardened frame and lever, blued barrel and buttplate. Imported by Uberti USA Inc.
Price: 1885 High-Wall, 28" round barrel..................... **$850.00**
Price: 1885 High-Wall Sporting, 30" octagonal barrel **$850.00**
Price: 1885 High-Wall Special Sporting, 32" octagonal barrel ... **$1,015.00**

Designs for sporting and utility purposes worldwide.

Beretta Express SSO

Beretta Model 455 SxS

Charles Daly Superior

Charles Daly Empire Combo

CZ 584 Solo

BERETTA EXPRESS SSO O/U DOUBLE RIFLES
Caliber: 375 H&H, 458 Win. Mag., 9.3x74R. **Barrel:** 25.5". **Weight:** 11 lbs. **Stock:** European walnut with hand-checkered grip and forend. **Sights:** Blade front on ramp, open V-notch rear. **Features:** Sidelock action with color case-hardened receiver (gold inlays on SSO6 Gold). Ejectors, double triggers, recoil pad. Introduced 1990. Imported from Italy by Beretta U.S.A.
Price: SSO6. . . . . **$21,000.00**
Price: SSO6 Gold **$23,500.00**

BERETTA MODEL 455 SxS EXPRESS RIFLE
Caliber: 375 H&H, 458 Win. Mag., 470 NE, 500 NE 3", 416 Rigby. **Barrel:** 23-1/2" or 25-1/2". **Weight:** 11 lbs. **Stock:** European walnut with hand-checkered grip and forend. **Sights:** Blade front, folding leaf V-notch rear. **Features:** Sidelock action with easily removable sideplates; color case-hardened finish (455), custom big game or floral motif engraving (455EELL). Double triggers, recoil pad. Introduced 1990. Imported from Italy by Beretta U.S.A.
Price: Model 455 . . . . **$36,000.00**
Price: Model 455EELL **$47,000.00**

CHARLES DALY SUPERIOR COMBINATION GUN
Caliber/Gauge: 12 ga. over 22 Hornet, 223 Rem., 22-250, 243 Win., 270 Win., 308 Win., 30-06. **Barrel:** 23.5", shotgun choked Imp. Cyl. **Weight:** About 7.5 lbs. **Stock:** Checkered walnut pistol grip buttstock and semi-beavertail forend. **Features:** Silvered, engraved receiver; chrome-moly steel barrels; double triggers; extractors; sling swivels; gold bead front sight. Introduced 1997. Imported from Italy by K.B.I. Inc.
Price: **$1,479.00**

Charles Daly Empire Combination Gun
Same as the Superior grade except has deluxe wood with European-style comb and cheekpiece; slim forend. Introduced 1997. Imported from Italy by K.B.I., Inc.
Price: **$2,189.00**

CZ 584 SOLO COMBINATION GUN
Caliber/Gauge: 7x57R; 12, 2-3/4" chamber. **Barrel:** 24.4". **Weight:** 7.37 lbs. **Length:** 45.25" overall. **Stock:** Circassian walnut. **Sights:** Blade front, open rear adjustable for windage. **Features:** Kersten-style double lump locking system; double-trigger Blitz-type mechanism with drop safety and adjustable set trigger for the rifle barrel; auto safety, dual extractors; receiver dovetailed for scope mounting. Imported from the Czech Republic by CZ-USA.
Price: **$851.00**

CZ 589 STOPPER OVER/UNDER GUN
Caliber: 458 Win. Magnum. **Barrels:** 21.7". **Weight:** 9.3 lbs. **Length:** 37.7" overall. **Stock:** Turkish walnut with sling swivels. **Sights:** Blade front, fixed rear. **Features:** Kersten-style action; Blitz-type double trigger; hammer-forged, blued barrels; satin-nickel, engraved receiver. Introduced 2001. Imported from the Czech Republic by CZ USA.
Price: **$2,999.00**
Price: Fully engraved model **$3,999.00**

EAA IZH-94

Hoenig Rotary Round Action Double Rifle

Hoenig Rotary Round Action Combination

Krieghoff Classic Double Rifle

DAKOTA DOUBLE RIFLE
Caliber: 470 Nitro Express, 500 Nitro Express. **Barrel:** 25". **Stock:** Exhibition-grade walnut. **Sights:** Express-style. **Features:** Round action; selective ejectors; recoil pad; Americase. From Dakota Arms Inc.
Price: **$25,000.00**

EAA/BAIKAL IZH-94 COMBINATION GUN
Caliber/Gauge: 12, 3" chamber; 222 Rem., 223, 5.6x50R, 5.6x55E, 7x57R, 7x65R, 7.62x39, 7.62x51, 308, 7.62x53R, 7.62x54R, 30-06. **Barrel:** 24", 26"; imp., mod. and full choke tubes. **Weight:** 7.28 lbs. **Stock:** Walnut; rubber buttpad. **Sights:** Express-style. **Features:** Hammer-forged barrels with chrome-lined bores; machined receiver; single-selective or double triggers. Imported by European American Armory.
Price: Blued finish **$549.00**
Price: 20 ga./22 LR, 20/22 Mag, 3" **$629.00**

GARBI EXPRESS DOUBLE RIFLE
Caliber: 7x65R, 9.3x74R, 375 H&H. **Barrel:** 24-3/4". **Weight:** 7-3/4 to 8-1/2 lbs. **Length:** 41-1/2" overall. **Stock:** Turkish walnut. **Sights:** Quarter-rib with express sight. **Features:** Side-by-side double; H&H-pattern sidelock ejector with reinforced action, chopper lump barrels of Boehler steel; double triggers; fine scroll and rosette engraving, or full coverage ornamental; coin-finished action. Introduced 1997. Imported from Spain by Wm. Larkin Moore.
Price: **$19,900.00**

HOENIG ROTARY ROUND ACTION DOUBLE RIFLE
Caliber: Most popular calibers from 225 Win. to 9.3x74R. **Barrel:** 22" to 26". **Stock:** English Walnut; to customer specs. **Sights:** Swivel hood front with button release (extra bead stored in trap door gripcap), express-style rear on quarter-rib adjustable for windage and elevation; scope mount. **Features:** Round action opens by rotating barrels, pulling forward. Inertia extractor system, rotary safety blocks strikers. Single lever quick-detachable scope mount. Simple takedown without removing forend. Introduced 1997. Made in U.S.A. by George Hoenig.
Price: **$25,000.00**

HOENIG ROTARY ROUND ACTION COMBINATION
Caliber: 28 ga. **Barrel:** 26". **Weight:** 7 lbs. **Stock:** English Walnut to customer specs. **Sights:** Front ramp with button release blades. Foldable aperture tang sight windage and elevation adjustable. Quarter-rib with scope mount. **Features:** Round action opens by rotating barrels, pulling forward. Inertia extractor; rotary safety blocks strikers. Simple takedown without removing forend. Made in U.S.A. by George Hoenig.
Price: **$25,000.00**

KRIEGHOFF CLASSIC DOUBLE RIFLE
Caliber: 7x57R, 7x65R, 308 Win., 30-06, 8x57 JRS, 8x75RS, 9.3x74R, 375NE, 500/416NE, 470NE, 500NE. **Barrel:** 23.5". **Weight:** 7.3 to 8 lbs; 10-11 lbs. Big 5. **Stock:** High grade European walnut. Standard model has conventional rounded cheekpiece, Bavaria model has Bavarian-style cheekpiece. **Sights:** Bead front with removable, adjustable wedge (375 H&H and below), standing leaf rear on quarter-rib. **Features:** Boxlock action; double triggers; short opening angle for fast loading; quiet extractors; sliding, self-adjusting wedge for secure bolting; Purdey-style barrel extension; horizontal firing pin placement. Many options available. Introduced 1997. Imported from Germany by Krieghoff International.
Price: With small Arabesque engraving **$8,950.00**
Price: With engraved sideplates **$12,300.00**
Price: For extra barrels **$5,450.00**
Price: Extra 20-ga., 28" shotshell barrels **$3,950.00**

Krieghoff Classic Big Five Double Rifle
Similar to the standard Classic except available in 375 Flanged Mag. N.E., 500/416 NE, 470 NE, 500 NE. Has hinged front trigger, non-removable muzzle wedge (models larger than 375 caliber), Universal Trigger System, Combi Cocking Device, steel trigger guard, specially weighted stock bolt for weight and balance. Many options available. Introduced 1997. Imported from Germany by Krieghoff International. Imperial Model introduced 2006.
Price: **$11,450.00**
Price: With engraved sideplates **$14,800.00**

LEBEAU-COURALLY EXPRESS RIFLE SxS
Caliber: 7x65R, 8x57JRS, 9.3x74R, 375 H&H, 470 N.E. **Barrel:** 24" to 26". **Weight:** 7-3/4 to 10-1/2 lbs. **Stock:** Fancy French walnut with cheekpiece. **Sights:** Bead on ramp front, standing left express rear on quarter-rib. **Features:** Holland & Holland-type sidelock with automatic ejectors; double triggers. Built to order only. Imported from Belgium by Wm. Larkin Moore.
Price: **$41,000.00**

Merkel 96K Engraved

Merkel 140-1

Rizzini Express

Savage 24F Combination

Springfield M6 Scout

MERKEL DRILLINGS
Caliber/Gauge: 12, 20, 3" chambers, 16, 2-3/4" chambers; 22 Hornet, 5.6x50R Mag., 5.6x52R, 222 Rem., 243 Win., 6.5x55, 6.5x57R, 7x57R, 7x65R, 308, 30-06, 8x57JRS, 9.3x74R, 375 H&H. **Barrel:** 25.6". **Weight:** 7.9 to 8.4 lbs. depending upon caliber. **Stock:** Oil-finished walnut with pistol grip; cheekpiece on 12-, 16-gauge. **Sights:** Blade front, fixed rear. **Features:** Double barrel locking lug with Greener cross bolt; scroll-engraved, case-hardened receiver; automatic trigger safety; Blitz action; double triggers. Imported from Germany by GSI.
Price: Model 96K (manually cocked rifle system), from **$7,495.00**
Price: Model 96K Engraved (hunting series on receiver) **$8,595.00**

MERKEL BOXLOCK DOUBLE RIFLES
Caliber: 5.6x52R, 243 Winchester, 6.5x55, 6.5x57R, 7x57R, 7x65R, 308 Winchester, 30-06 Springfield, 8x57 IRS, 9.3x74R. **Barrel:** 23.6". **Weight:** 7.7 oz. **Length:** NA. **Stock:** Walnut, oil finished, pistol grip. **Sights:** Fixed 100 meter. **Features:** Anson & Deely boxlock action with cocking indicators, double triggers, engraved color case-hardened receiver. Introduced 1995. Imported from Germany by GSI.
Price: Model 140-1, from. **$6,695.00**
Price: Model 140-1.1 (engraved silver-gray receiver), from **$7,795.00**

RIZZINI EXPRESS 90L DOUBLE RIFLE
Caliber: 30-06, 7x65R, 9.3x74R. **Barrel:** 24". **Weight:** 7-1/2 lbs. **Length:** 40" overall. **Stock:** Select European walnut with satin oil finish; English-style cheekpiece. **Sights:** Ramp front, quarter-rib with express sight. **Features:** Color case-hardened boxlock action; automatic ejectors; single selective trigger; polished blue barrels. Extra 20 gauge shotgun barrels available. Imported for Italy by Wm. Larkin Moore.
Price: With case **$3,850.00**

SAVAGE 24F PREDATOR O/U COMBINATION GUN
Caliber/Gauge: 22 Hornet, 223, 30-30 over 12 (24F-12) or 22 LR, 22 Hornet, 223, 30-30 over 20 ga. (24F-20); 3" chambers. **Action:** Takedown, low rebounding visible hammer. Single trigger, barrel selector spur on hammer. **Barrel:** 24" separated barrels; 12 ga. has mod. choke tubes, 20 ga. has fixed Mod. choke. **Weight:** 8 lbs. **Length:** 40-1/2" overall. **Stock:** Black Rynite composition. **Sights:** Blade front, rear open adjustable for elevation. **Features:** Introduced 1989.
Price: 24F-12 . . . . **$661.00**
Price: 24F-20 . . . . **$628.00**

SPRINGFIELD ARMORY M6 SCOUT RIFLE/SHOTGUN
Caliber/Gauge: 22 LR or 22 Hornet over 410 bore. **Barrel:** 18.25". **Weight:** 4 lbs. **Length:** 32" overall. **Stock:** Folding detachable with storage for 15 22 LR, four 410 shells. **Sights:** Blade front, military aperture for 22; V-notch for 410. **Features:** All metal construction. Designed for quick disassembly and minimum maintenance. Folds for compact storage. Introduced 1982; reintroduced 1996. Imported from the Czech Republic by Springfield Armory.
Price: Parkerized **$185.00**
Price: Stainless steel **$219.00**

Designs for hunting, utility and sporting purposes, including training for competition.

Browning Buck Mark Target

Browning Semi-Auto 22

CZ 511 Auto

Henry U.S. Survival

Magnum Research MLR22WC

AR-7 EXPLORER CARBINE
Caliber: 22 LR, 8-shot magazine. **Barrel:** 16". **Weight:** 2-1/2 lbs. **Length:** 34-1/2", 16-1/2" stowed. **Stock:** Molded Cycolac; snap-on rubber buttpad. **Sights:** Square blade front, aperture rear. **Features:** Takedown design stores barrel and action in hollow stock. Light enough to float. Reintroduced 1999. From AR-7 Industries, LLC.
Price: Black matte finish **$150.00**
Price: AR-20 Sporter (tubular stock, barrel shroud) **$200.00**
Price: AR-7 camo- or walnut-finish stock **$164.95**

BROWNING BUCK MARK SEMI-AUTO RIFLES
Caliber: 22 LR, 10+1. **Action:** A rifle version of the Buck Mark Pistol; straight blowback action; machined aluminum receiver with integral rail scope mount; manual thumb safety. **Barrel:** Recessed crowns. **Stock:** Stock and forearm with full pistol grip. **Features:** Action lock provided. Introduced 2001. Four model name variations for 2006, as noted below. **Sights:** FLD Target, FLD Carbon, and Target models have integrated scope rails. Sporter has Truglo/Marble fiber optic sights. Imported from Japan by Browning.
Price: FLD Target, 5.5 lbs., bull barrel, laminated stock **$601.00**
Price: Target, 5.4 lbs., blued bull barrel, wood stock **$583.00**
Price: Sporter, 4.4 lbs., blued sporter barrel w/sights **$583.00**

BROWNING SEMI-AUTO 22 RIFLE
Caliber: 22 LR, 11+1. **Barrel:** 16.25". **Weight:** 5.2 lbs. **Length:** 37" overall. **Stock:** Checkered select walnut with pistol grip and semi-beavertail forend. **Sights:** Gold bead front, folding leaf rear. **Features:** Engraved receiver with polished blue finish; cross-bolt safety; tubular magazine in buttstock; easy takedown for carrying or storage. The Grade VI is available with either grayed or blued receiver with extensive engraving with gold-plated animals: right side pictures a fox and squirrel in a woodland scene; left side shows a beagle chasing a rabbit. On top is a portrait of the beagle. Stock and forend are of high-grade walnut with a double-bordered cut checkering design. Introduced 1987. Imported from Japan by Browning.
Price: Grade I, scroll-engraved blued receiver **$557.00**
Price: Grade VI BL, gold-plated engraved blued receiver **$1,191.00**
Price: Grade VI GR, gold-plated engraved grayed receiver **$1,191.00**

CZ 511 AUTO RIFLE
Caliber: 22 LR, 8-shot magazine. **Barrel:** 22.2". **Weight:** 5.39 lbs. **Length:** 38.6" overall. **Stock:** Walnut with checkered pistol grip. **Sights:** Hooded front, adjustable rear. **Features:** Polished blue finish; detachable magazine; sling swivel studs. Imported from the Czech Republic by CZ-USA.
Price: **$351.00**

HENRY U.S. SURVIVAL RIFLE .22
Caliber: 22 LR, 8-shot magazine. **Barrel:** 16" steel lined. **Weight:** 2.5 lbs. **Stock:** ABS plastic. **Sights:** Blade front on ramp, aperture rear. **Features:** Takedown design stores barrel and action in hollow stock. Light enough to float. Silver, black or camo finish. Comes with two magazines. Introduced 1998. From Henry Repeating Arms Co.
Price: **$205.00**

MAGNUM RESEARCH MAGNUMLITE RIFLES
Caliber: 22 WMR, 17 HMR, 22 LR 17M2, 10-shot magazine. **Barrel:** 17" graphite. **Weight:** 4.45 lbs. **Length:** 35.5" overall. **Stock:** Hogue OverMolded synthetic or walnut. **Sights:** Integral scope base. **Features:** Magnum Lite graphite barrel, French grey anodizing, match bolt, target trigger. 22LR/17M2 rifles use factory Ruger 10/22 magazines. 4-5 lbs. average trigger pull. Graphite carbon-fiber barrel weighs approx. 13.04 ounces in .22 LR, 1:16 twist. Introduced 2007. From Magnum Research, Inc.
Price: MLR22H 22 LR **$629.00**
Price: MLR22WMH 22 WMR **$719.00**
Price: MLR22WC, walnut stock **$799.00**

Marlin Model 60

Marlin Model 70PSS Papoose

Marlin 795

Remington 552 BDL Speedmaster

MARLIN MODEL 60 AUTO RIFLE
Caliber: 22 LR, 14-shot tubular magazine. **Barrel:** 19" round tapered. **Weight:** About 5-1/2 lbs. **Length:** 37-1/2" overall. **Stock:** Press-checkered, walnut-finished Maine birch with Monte Carlo, full pistol grip; Mar-Shield® finish. **Sights:** Ramp front, open adjustable rear. **Features:** Matted receiver is grooved for scope mount. Manual bolt hold-open; automatic last-shot bolt hold-open. Model 60C is similar except has hardwood Monte Carlo stock with Mossy Oak Break-Up camouflage pattern. From Marlin.
Price: $200.00
Price: With 4x scope $208.00
Price: (Model 60C camo) $236.00
Price: (Model 60DL walnut tone finish) $236.00

Marlin Model 60SS Self-Loading Rifle
Same as the Model 60 except breech bolt, barrel and outer magazine tube are made of stainless steel; most other parts are either nickel-plated or coated to match the stainless finish. Monte Carlo stock is of black/gray Maine birch laminate, and has nickel-plated swivel studs, rubber buttpad. Introduced 1993. From Marlin.
Price: $318.00
Price: Model 60SSK (black fiberglass-filled stock) $269.00
Price: Model 60SB (walnut-finished birch stock) $235.00
Price: Model 60SB with 4x scope $270.00

MARLIN 70PSS PAPOOSE STAINLESS RIFLE
Caliber: 22 LR, 7-shot magazine. **Barrel:** 16-1/4" stainless steel, Micro-Groove®. **Weight:** 3-1/4 lbs. **Length:** 35-1/4" overall. **Stock:** Black fiberglass-filled synthetic with abbreviated forend, nickel-plated swivel studs, molded-in checkering. **Sights:** Ramp front with orange post, cut-away Wide Scan™ hood; adjustable open rear. Receiver grooved for scope mounting. **Features:** Takedown barrel; cross-bolt safety; manual bolt hold-open; last shot bolt hold-open; comes with padded carrying case. Introduced 1986. Made in U.S.A. by Marlin.
Price: $318.00

MARLIN MODEL 717M2 17 MACH 2 RIFLE
Caliber: 17 Mach 2, 7-shot. **Barrel:** 22" sporter. **Weight:** 5.5 lbs. **Length:** 37". **Stock:** Walnut-finished hardwood stock. **Sights:** Adjustable open rear, ramp front, grooved for scope mount. **Features:** Swivel studs, cross-bolt safety. Similar in design to 917 series bolt guns.
Price: 717M2 .... $264.00

MARLIN MODEL 7000 AUTO RIFLE
Caliber: 22 LR, 10-shot magazine. **Barrel:** 18" heavy target with 12-groove Micro-Groove® rifling, recessed muzzle. **Weight:** 5-1/2 lbs. **Length:** 37" overall. **Stock:** Black fiberglass-filled synthetic with Monte Carlo combo, swivel studs, molded-in checkering. **Sights:** None furnished; comes with ring mounts. **Features:** Automatic last-shot bolt hold-open, manual bolt hold-open; cross-bolt safety; steel charging handle; blue finish, nickel-plated magazine. Introduced 1997. Made in U.S.A. by Marlin Firearms Co.
Price: $263.00

MARLIN MODEL 795 AUTO RIFLE
Caliber: 22. **Barrel:** 18" with 16-groove Micro-Groove® rifling. Ramp front sight, adjustable rear. Receiver grooved for scope mount. **Stock:** Black synthetic. **Features:** 10-round magazine, last shot hold-open feature. Introduced 1997. SS is similar to Model 795 except stainless steel barrel. Most other parts nickel-plated. Adjustable folding semi-buckhorn rear sights, ramp front high-visibility post and removeable cutaway wide scan hood. Made in U.S.A. by Marlin Firearms Co.
Price: 795 .... $172.00
Price: 795SS $255.00

REMINGTON MODEL 552 BDL DELUXE SPEEDMASTER RIFLE
Caliber: 22 S (20), L (17) or LR (15) tubular mag. **Barrel:** 21" round tapered. **Weight:** 5-3/4 lbs. **Length:** 40" overall. **Stock:** Walnut. Checkered grip and forend. **Sights:** Big game. **Features:** Positive cross-bolt safety, receiver grooved for tip-off mount.
Price: $536.00
Price: Smoothbore model (2007) $575.00

REMINGTON 597 AUTO RIFLE
Caliber: 22 LR, 10-shot clip. **Barrel:** 20". **Weight:** 5-1/2 lbs. **Length:** 40" overall. **Stock:** Black synthetic. **Sights:** Big game. **Features:** Matte black finish, nickel-plated bolt. Receiver is grooved and drilled and tapped for scope mounts. Introduced 1997. Made in U.S.A. by Remington.
Price: Synthetic Scope Combo (2007) $229.00
Price: Model 597 Magnum, 17 HMR, 8-shot clip $505.00
Price: Model 597 LSS (laminated stock, stainless) $348.00
Price: Model 597 SS (22 LR, stainless steel, black synthetic stock) $283.00
Price: Model 597 LS heavy barrel (22 LR, laminated stock) $265.00
Price: Model 597 Magnum LS heavy barrel
     (22 WMR, lam. stock) $569.00
Price: Model 597 LS HB, 10-shot clip $337.00

Remington 597

Ruger 10/22 Deluxe Sporter

Ruger 10/22 Target

Savage Model 64FV

RUGER 10/22 AUTOLOADING CARBINE
Caliber: 22 LR, 10-shot rotary magazine. **Barrel:** 18-1/2" round tapered. **Weight:** 5 lbs. **Length:** 37-1/4" overall. **Stock:** American hardwood with pistol grip and barrel band or synthetic. **Sights:** Brass bead front, folding leaf rear adjustable for elevation. **Features:** Detachable rotary magazine fits flush into stock, cross-bolt safety, receiver tapped and grooved for scope blocks or tip-off mount. Scope base adaptor furnished with each rifle.
Price: Model 10/22 RB (blue) **$250.00**
Price: Model 10/22CRR Compact RB (blued), intr. 2006 . . . . **$285.00**

Ruger 10/22 Deluxe Sporter
Same as 10/22 Carbine except walnut stock with hand checkered pistol grip and forend; straight buttplate, no barrel band, has sling swivels.
Price: Model 10/22 DSP **$330.00**

Ruger 10/22T Target Rifle
Similar to the 10/22 except has 20" heavy, hammer-forged barrel with tight chamber dimensions, improved trigger pull, laminated hardwood stock dimensioned for optical sights. No iron sights supplied. Introduced 1996. Made in U.S.A. by Sturm, Ruger & Co.
Price: 10/22T **$450.00**
Price: K10/22T, stainless steel **$485.00**

Ruger K10/22RPF All-Weather Rifle
Similar to the stainless K10/22/RB except has black composite stock of thermoplastic polyester resin reinforced with fiberglass; checkered grip and forend. Brushed satin, natural metal finish with clear hardcoat finish. Weighs 5 lbs., measures 36-3/4" overall. Introduced 1997. From Sturm, Ruger & Co.
Price: **$295.00**

SAVAGE MODEL 64G AUTO RIFLE
Caliber: 22 LR, 10-shot magazine. **Barrel:** 20", 21". **Weight:** 5-1/2 lbs. **Length:** 40", 41". **Stock:** Walnut-finished hardwood with Monte Carlo-type comb, checkered grip and forend. **Sights:** Bead front, open adjustable rear. Receiver grooved for scope mounting. **Features:** Thumb-operated rotating safety. Blue finish. Side ejection, bolt hold-open device. Introduced 1990. Made in Canada, from Savage Arms.
Price: **$162.00**
Price: Model 64FSS, stainless **$202.00**
Price: Model 64F, black synthetic stock **$135.00**
Price: Model 64GXP package gun includes
4x15 scope and mounts **$171.00**
Price: Model 64FXP (black stock, 4x15 scope) **$142.00**
Price: Model 64F Camo **$135.00**

Savage Model 64FV Auto Rifle
Similar to the Model 64F except has heavy 21" barrel with recessed crown; no sights provided, comes with Weaver-style bases. Introduced 1998. Imported from Canada by Savage Arms, Inc.
Price: **$135.00**
Price: Model 64FSS, stainless **$202.00**

62 63 RIFLE
Caliber: 22 LR, 10-shot tube-fed magazine. **Barrel:** 23". **Weight:** 72 oz. **Length:** 32-1/2". **Stock:** Hand-fitted walnut-finished hardwood. **Sights:** Adjustable rear, fixed front. **Features:** Manual safety, metal buttplate, can accept Taurus tang sight. Charged and cocked with operating plunger at front of forend. Available in blue or polished stainless steel.
Price: 63 . . . . **$329.00**
Price: 63SS **$349.00**

THOMPSON/CENTER 22 LR CLASSIC RIFLE
Caliber: 22 LR, 8-shot magazine. **Barrel:** 22" match-grade. **Weight:** 5-1/2 pounds. **Length:** 39-1/2" overall. **Stock:** Satin-finished American walnut with Monte Carlo-type comb and pistol gripcap, swivel studs. **Sights:** Ramp-style front and fully adjustable rear, both with fiber optics. **Features:** All-steel receiver drilled and tapped for scope mounting; barrel threaded to receiver; thumb-operated safety; trigger guard safety lock included. New .22 Classic Benchmark TGT target rifle variant has 18" heavy barrel, brown laminated target stock, blued with matte finish, 10-shot magazine and no sights; drilled and tapped.
Price: T/C 22 LR Classic (blue) **$396.00**
Price: T/C 22 LR Classic Benchmark **$505.00**

Classic and modern models for sport and utility, including training.

Browning BL-22

Henry Lever-Action 22

Henry Golden Boy 22

Henry Pump-Action 22

Marlin Model 39A

BROWNING BL-22 RIFLES
Action: Short-throw lever action, side ejection. Rack-and-pinion lever. Tubular magazines, with 15+1 capacity for 22LR. **Barrel:** Recessed muzzle. **Stock:** Walnut, two-piece straight grip Western style. **Trigger:** Half-cock hammer safety; fold-down hammer. **Sights:** Bead post front, folding-leaf rear. Steel receiver grooved for scope mount. **Weight:** 5-5.4 lbs. **Length:** 36.75-40.75" overall. **Features:** Action lock provided. Introduced 1996. FLD Grade II Octagon has octagonal 24" barrel, silver nitride receiver with scroll engraving, gold-colored trigger. FLD Grade I has satin-nickel receiver, blued trigger, no stock checkering. FLD Grade II has satin-nickel receivers with scroll engraving; gold-colored trigger, cut checkering. Both introduced 2005. Grade I has blued receiver and trigger, no stock checkering. Grade II has gold-colored trigger, cut checkering, blued receiver with scroll engraving. Imported from Japan by Browning.
Price: BL-22 Grade I/II, from **$480.00**
Price: BL-22 FLD Grade I/II, from **$514.00**
Price: BL-22 FLD, Grade II Octagon **$756.00**

HENRY LEVER-ACTION 22
Caliber: 22 Long Rifle (15-shot). **Barrel:** 18-1/4" round. **Weight:** 5-1/2 lbs. **Length:** 34" overall. **Stock:** Walnut. **Sights:** Hooded blade front, open adjustable rear. **Features:** Polished blue finish; full-length tubular magazine; side ejection; receiver grooved for scope mounting. Introduced 1997. Made in U.S.A. by Henry Repeating Arms Co.

Price: **$279.95**
Price: Youth model (33" overall, 11-round 22 LR) **$279.95**

HENRY GOLDEN BOY 22 LEVER-ACTION RIFLE
Caliber: 22 LR, 22 Magnum, 16-shot. **Barrel:** 20" octagonal. **Weight:** 6.25 lbs. **Length:** 38" overall. **Stock:** American walnut. **Sights:** Blade front, open rear. **Features:** Brasslite receiver, brass buttplate, blued barrel and lever. Introduced 1998. Made in U.S.A. from Henry Repeating Arms Co.
Price: **$409.95**
Price: Magnum **$485.00**

HENRY PUMP-ACTION 22 PUMP RIFLE
Caliber: 22 LR, 15-shot. **Barrel:** 18.25". **Weight:** 5.5 lbs. **Length:** NA. **Stock:** American walnut. **Sights:** Bead on ramp front, open adjustable rear. **Features:** Polished blue finish; receiver groved for scope mount; grooved slide handle; two barrel bands. Introduced 1998. Made in U.S.A. from Henry Repeating Arms Co.
Price: **$309.95**

MARLIN MODEL 39A GOLDEN LEVER-ACTION RIFLE
Caliber: 22, S (26), L (21), LR (19), tubular mag. **Barrel:** 24" Micro-Groove®. **Weight:** 6-1/2 lbs. **Length:** 40" overall. **Stock:** Checkered American black walnut; Mar-Shield® finish. Swivel studs; rubber buttpad. **Sights:** Bead ramp front with detachable Wide-Scan™ hood, folding rear semi-buckhorn adjustable for windage and elevation. **Features:** Hammer block safety; rebounding hammer. Takedown action, receiver tapped for scope mount (supplied), offset hammer spur, gold-colored steel trigger. From Marlin Firearms.
Price: **$552.00**

Remington Model 572 BDL Deluxe Fieldmaster

Ruger Model 96/22

Ruger Model 96/17

Taurus 62R

Taurus 72C-SS

REMINGTON 572 BDL DELUXE FIELDMASTER PUMP RIFLE
Caliber: 22 S (20), L (17) or LR (15), tubular mag. **Barrel:** 21" round tapered. **Weight:** 5-1/2 lbs. **Length:** 40" overall. **Stock:** Walnut with checkered pistol grip and slide handle. **Sights:** Big game. **Features:** Cross-bolt safety; removing inner magazine tube converts rifle to single shot; receiver grooved for tip-off scope mount.
Price: **$407.00**

RUGER MODEL 96 LEVER-ACTION RIFLE
Caliber: 22 WMR, 9 rounds; 44 Magnum, 4 rounds; 17 HMR 9 rounds. **Barrel:** 18-1/2". **Weight:** 5-1/4 lbs. **Length:** 37-1/4" overall. **Stock:** Hardwood. **Sights:** Gold bead front, folding leaf rear. **Features:** Sliding cross button safety, visible cocking indicator; short-throw lever action. Introduced 1996. Made in U.S.A. by Sturm, Ruger & Co.
Price: 96/22M (22 WMR). **$435.00**
Price: 96/22M (44 Mag.) **$599.00**
Price: 96/17M (17 HMR) **$425.00**

TAURUS MODEL 62 PUMP RIFLE
Caliber: 22 LR, 12- or 13-shot. **Barrel:** 16-1/2" or 23" round. **Weight:** 72 oz. to 80 oz. **Length:** 39" overall. **Stock:** Premium hardwood. **Sights:** Adjustable rear, bead blade front, optional tang. **Features:** Blue, case

hardened or stainless, bolt-mounted safety, pump action, manual firing pin block, integral security lock system. Imported from Brazil by Taurus International.
Price: From **$299.00**

Taurus Model 72 Pump Rifle
Same as Model 62 except chambered in 22 Magnum or .17 HMR; 16-1/2" bbl. holds 10-12 shots, 23" bbl. holds 11-13 shots. Weighs 72 oz. to 80 oz. Introduced 2001. Imported from Brazil by Taurus International.
Price: From **$329.00**

TAURUS THUNDERBOLT PUMP ACTION
Caliber: 38/.357, 45 Long Colt, 12 or 14 rounds. **Barrel:** 26" blue or polished stainless. **Weight:** 8.1 lbs. **Length:** 43" overall. **Stock:** Hardwood stock and forend. Gloss finish. **Sights:** Longhorn adjustable rear. Introduced 2004. Imported from Brazil by Taurus International.
Price: C357BC **$515.00**
Price: C45BR **$639.00**

Includes models for a variety of sports, utility and competitive shooting.

Anchutz 1710D

Browning T-Bolt

Chipmunk Standard

Chipmunk Deluxe

ANSCHUTZ 1416D/1516D CLASSIC RIFLES
Caliber: 22 LR (1416D), 5-shot clip; 22 WMR (1516D), 4-shot clip. **Barrel:** 22-1/2". **Weight:** 6 lbs. **Length:** 41" overall. **Stock:** European hardwood with walnut finish; classic style with straight comb, checkered pistol grip and forend. **Sights:** Hooded ramp front, folding leaf rear. **Features:** Uses Match 64 action. Adjustable single stage trigger. Receiver grooved for scope mounting. Imported from Germany by AcuSport Corp.
Price: 1416D, 22 LR **$755.95**
Price: 1516D, 22 WMR **$779.95**
Price: 1416D Classic left-hand **$679.95**

Anschutz 1416D/1516D Walnut Luxus Rifles
Similar to the Classic models except have European walnut stocks with Monte Carlo cheekpiece, slim forend with Schnabel tip, cut checkering on grip and forend. Introduced 1997. Imported from Germany by AcuSport Corp.
Price: 1416D (22 LR) **$755.95**
Price: 1516D (22 WMR) **$779.95**

ANSCHUTZ 1518D LUXUS BOLT-ACTION RIFLE
Caliber: 22 WMR, 4-shot magazine. **Barrel:** 19-3/4". **Weight:** 5-1/2 lbs. **Length:** 37-1/2" overall. **Stock:** European walnut. **Sights:** Blade on ramp front, folding leaf rear. **Features:** Receiver grooved for scope mounting; single stage trigger; skip-line checkering; rosewood forend tip; sling swivels. Imported from Germany by AcuSport Corp.
Price: **$1,186.95**

ANSCHUTZ 1710D CUSTOM RIFLE
Caliber: 22 LR, 5-shot clip. **Barrel:** 24-1/4". **Weight:** 7-3/8 lbs. **Length:** 42-1/2" overall. **Stock:** Select European walnut. **Sights:** Hooded ramp front, folding leaf rear; drilled and tapped for scope mounting. **Features:** Match 54 action with adjustable single-stage trigger; roll-over Monte Carlo cheekpiece, slim forend with Schnabel tip, Wundhammer palm swell on pistol grip, rosewood gripcap with white diamond insert; skip-line checkering on grip and forend. Introduced 1988. Imported from Germany by AcuSport Corp.
Price: **$1,289.95**

BROWNING T-BOLT RIMFIRE RIFLE
Caliber: 22 LR, 10-round rotary box Double Helix magazine. **Barrel:** 22", free-floating, semi-match chamber, target muzzle crown. **Weight:** 4.8 lbs. **Length:** 40.1" overall. **Stock:** Walnut, satin finish, cut checkering, synthetic buttplate. **Sights:** None. **Features:** Straight-pull bolt-action, three-lever trigger adjustable for pull weight, dual action screws, sling swivel studs. Crossbolt lockup, enlarged bolt handle, one-piece dual extractor with integral spring and red cocking indicator band, gold-tone trigger. Top-tang, thumb-operated two-position safety, drilled and tapped for scope mounts. Varmint model has raised Monte Carlo comb, heavy barrel, wide forearm. Introduced 2006. Imported from Japan by Browning.
Price: Sporter **$623.00**
Price: Target/Varmint, intr. 2007 . . . . **$647.95**

CHARLES DALY SUPERIOR II RIMFIRE RIFLE
Caliber: 22LR, 22MRF, 17HRM. **Barrel:** 22". **Weight:** 6 pounds. **Sights:** None. Drilled and tapped for scope mounts. **Features:** Manufactured by Zastava. Walnut stock, two-position safety; 5-round magazine capacity. Introduced 2005.
Price: 22LR. **$259.00**
Price: 22WMR **$299.00**
Price: 17HMR **$334.00**

CHIPMUNK SINGLE SHOT RIFLE
Caliber: 22 LR, 22 WMR, single shot. **Barrel:** 16-1/8". **Weight:** About 2-1/2 lbs. **Length:** 30" overall. **Stocks:** American walnut. **Sights:** Post on ramp front, peep rear adjustable for windage and elevation. **Features:** Drilled and tapped for scope mounting using special Chipmunk base ($13.95). Engraved model also available. Made in U.S.A. Introduced 1982. From Rogue Rifle Co., Inc.
Price: Standard. **$194.25**
Price: Standard 22 WMR **$209.95**
Price: Deluxe (better wood, checkering) **$246.95**
Price: Deluxe 22 WMR **$262.95**
Price: Laminated stock **$209.95**
Price: Laminated stock, 22 WMR **$225.95**
Price: Bull barrel models of above, add **$16.00**

Cooper Model 57 Classic

Cooper Custom Classic

CZ 452 Lux

CZ 452 Varmint

CZ 452 American Classic

CHIPMUNK TM (TARGET MODEL)
Caliber: 22 S, L, or LR. **Barrel:** 18" blue. **Weight:** 5 lbs. **Length:** 33". Stocks: Walnut with accessory rail. **Sights:** 1/4 minute micrometer adjustable. **Features:** Manually cocking single shot bolt action, blue receiver, adjustable buttplate and buttpad.
Price: $329.95

COOPER MODEL 57-M BOLT-ACTION RIFLE
Caliber: 22 LR, 22 WMR, 17 HMR, 17 Mach 2. **Barrel:** 22" or 24" stainless steel or 4140 match grade. **Weight:** 6.5-7.5 lbs. **Stock:** AA-AAA select Claro walnut, 22 lpi hand checkering. **Sights:** None furnished. **Features:** Three rear locking lug, repeating bolt-action with 5-shot mag. for 22 LR and 17M2; 4-shot mag for 22 WMR and 17 HMR. Fully adjustable trigger. Left-hand models add $150 to base rifle price. 1/4"-group rimfire accuracy guarantee at 50 yds.; 1/2"-group centerfire accuracy guarantee at 100 yds. Options include wood upgrades, case-color metalwork, barrel fluting, custom LOP, and many others.
Price: Classic. $1,349.00
Price: LVT $1,459.00
Price: Custom Classic $1,995.00
Price: Western Classic $2,698.00
Price: TRP-3 (22 LR only, benchrest style) $1,295.00
Price: Jackson Squirrel Rifle $1,498.00
Price: Jackson Hunter (synthetic) $1,298.00

CZ 452 LUX BOLT-ACTION RIFLE
Caliber: 22 LR, 22 WMR, 5-shot detachable magazine. **Barrel:** 24.8". **Weight:** 6.6 lbs. **Length:** 42.63" overall. **Stock:** Walnut with checkered pistol grip. **Sights:** Hooded front, fully adjustable tangent rear. **Features:** All-steel construction, adjustable trigger, polished blue finish. Imported from the Czech Republic by CZ-USA.
Price: 22 LR, 22 WMR $378.00

CZ 452 Varmint Rifle
Similar to the Lux model except has heavy 20.8" barrel; stock has beavertail forend; weighs 7 lbs.; no sights furnished. Available only in 22 LR. Imported from the Czech Republic by CZ-USA.
Price: $407.00

CZ 452 American Classic Bolt-Action Rifle
Similar to the CZ 452 M 2E Lux except has classic-style stock of Circassian walnut; 22.5" free-floating barrel with recessed target crown; receiver dovetail for scope mounting. No open sights furnished. Introduced 1999. Imported from the Czech Republic by CZ-USA.
Price: 22 LR, 22 WMR $420.00

HARRINGTON & RICHARDSON
ULTRA HEAVY BARREL 22 MAG RIFLE
Caliber: 22 WMR, single shot. **Barrel:** 22" bull. **Stock:** Cinnamon laminated wood with Monte Carlo cheekpiece. **Sights:** None furnished; scope mount rail included. **Features:** Hand-checkered stock and forend; deep-crown rifling; tuned trigger; trigger locking system; hammer extension. Introduced 2001. From H&R 1871 LLC.
Price: $193.00

Henry "Mini" Bolt 22

Kimber 22 Classic

Kimber 22 SuperAmerica

Kimber 22 SVT

Kimber 22 HS

Price: Classic 22 . . . . **$1,147.00**
Price: Classic Varmint (22 or17M2) **$1,055.00**
Price: Hunter (22) **$809.00**
Price: Hunter (17M2) **$846.00**

Kimber 22 SuperAmerica Bolt-Action Rifle
Similar to 22 Classic except has AAA Claro walnut stock with wraparound 22 lpi hand-cut checkering, ebony forend tip, beaded cheekpiece. Introduced 1999. Made in U.S.A. by Kimber Mfg., Inc.
Price: **$1,865.00**

Kimber 22 SVT Bolt-Action Rifle
Similar to 22 Classic except has 18" stainless steel, fluted bull barrel, gray laminated, high-comb target-style stock with deep pistol grip, high comb, beavertail forend with bipod stud. Weighs 7.5 lbs., overall length 36.5". Matte finish on action. Introduced 1999. Made in U.S.A. by Kimber Mfg., Inc.
Price: 22 model **$1,007.00**
Price: 17M2 model **$1,055.00**

Kimber 22 HS (Hunter Silhouette) Bolt-Action Rifle
Similar to 22 Classic except 24" medium sporter match-grade barrel with half-fluting; high comb, walnut, Monte Carlo target stock with 18 lpi checkering; matte blue metal finish. Introduced 1999. Made in U.S.A. by Kimber Mfg., Inc.
Price: **$915.00**

HENRY ACU-BOLT RIFLE
Caliber: 22, 22 Mag., 17HMR; single shot. **Barrel:** 20". **Weight:** 4.15 lbs. **Length:** 36". **Stock:** One-piece fiberglass synthetic. **Sights:** Scope mount and 4x scope included. **Features:** Stainless barrel and receiver, bolt-action.
Price: **$325.00**

HENRY "MINI" BOLT ACTION 22 RIFLE
Caliber: 22 LR, single shot youth gun. **Barrel:** 16" stainless, 8-groove rifling. **Weight:** 3.25 lbs. **Length:** 30", LOP 11-1/2". **Stock:** Synthetic, pistol grip, wraparound checkering and beavertail forearm. **Sights:** William Fire sights. **Features:** One-piece bolt configuration manually operated safety.
Price: **$169.95**

KIMBER 22 CLASSIC BOLT-ACTION RIFLE
Caliber: 22 LR and 17 Mach 2, 5-shot magazine. **Barrel:** 18", 22", 24" match grade; 11-degree target crown. **Weight:** 5 to 8 lbs. **Length:** 35" to 43". **Stock:** Classic Claro walnut, hand-cut checkering, steel gripcap, swivel studs. **Sights:** None, drilled and tapped. **Features:** All-new action with Mauser-style full-length claw extractor, two-position wing safety, match trigger, pillar-bedded action with recoil lug. Introduced 1999. Made in U.S.A. by Kimber Mfg., Inc.

Marlin 917V

Marlin Model 915YN "Little Buckaroo"

Marlin Model 980S

Marlin 980V

Marlin 925

Marlin 925C

MARLIN MODEL 917/717 17 HMR/17 MACH 2 BOLT-ACTION RIFLES
Caliber: 17 HMR, 17 Mach 2, 7-shot. **Barrel:** 22". **Weight:** 6 lbs., stainless 7 lbs. **Length:** 41". **Stock:** Checkered walnut Monte Carlo SS, laminated black/grey. **Sights:** No sights but receiver grooved. **Features:** Swivel studs, positive thumb safety, red cocking indicator, safety lock, SS 1" brushed aluminum scope rings.

Price: 917 (new version 17 HMR intr. 2006, black synthetic stock) . **$269.00**
Price: 917V (17 HMR, walnut-finished hardwood stock) **$292.00**
Price: 917VS (17 HMR, heavy stainless barrel) **$433.00**
Price: 917VR (17 HMR, intr. 2006, heavy barrel) **$282.00**
Price: 917VR (17 HMR, heavy stainless fluted barrel) **$459.00**
Price: 917M2 (17 Mach 2, walnut-finished hardwood stock) **$274.00**
Price: 917M2S (17 Mach 2, 22" heavy stainless barrel) **$410.00**

MARLIN MODEL 915YN "LITTLE BUCKAROO"
Caliber: 22 S, L, LR, single shot. **Barrel:** 16-1/4" Micro-Groove®. **Weight:** 4-1/4 lbs. **Length:** 33-1/4" overall. **Stock:** One-piece walnut-finished, press-checkered Maine birch with Monte Carlo; Mar-Shield® finish. **Sights:** Ramp front, adjustable open rear. **Features:** Beginner's rifle with thumb safety, easy-load feed throat, red cocking indicator. Receiver grooved for scope mounting. Introduced 1989.

Price: **$225.00**
Price: 915YS (stainless steel with fire sights) **$255.00**

MARLIN MODEL 980S BOLT-ACTION RIFLE
Caliber: 22 LR, 7-shot clip magazine. **Barrel:** 22" Micro-Groove®. **Weight:** 6 lbs. **Length:** 41" overall. **Stock:** Black fiberglass-filled synthetic with nickel-plated swivel studs and molded-in checkering. **Sights:** Ramp front with orange post and cutaway Wide-Scan™ hood, adjustable semi-buckhorn folding rear. **Features:** Stainless steel barrel, receiver, front breech bolt and striker; receiver grooved for scope mounting. Introduced 1994. Model 880SQ (Squirrel Rifle) is similar but has heavy 22" barrel. Made in U.S.A. by Marlin.

Price: 980S **$349.00**
Price: 980V, heavy target barrel, 7 lbs., no sights **$349.00**

Marlin Model 981T Bolt-Action Rifle
Same as Marlin 980S except blued steel, tubular magazine, holds 17 Long Rifle cartridges. Weighs 6 lbs.
Price: **$229.00**

Marlin Model 925 Bolt-Action Repeater
Similar to Marlin 980S, except walnut-finished hardwood stock, adjustable open rear sight, ramp front. Weighs 5.5 lbs.
Price: **$229.00**
Price: With 4x scope and mount **$239.00**

Marlin Model 925R Bolt-Action Repeater
Similar to Marlin 925, except Monte Carlo black-fiberglass synthetic stock. Weighs 5.5 lbs. OAL: 41". Introduced 2006.
Price: **$229.00**
Price: With 4x scope and mount **$239.00**

Marlin Model 925C Bolt-Action Repeater
Same as Model 980S except Mossy Oak® Break-Up camouflage stock. Made in U.S.A. by Marlin. Weighs 5.5 lbs.
Price: **$268.00**

Marlin 983T

Rossi Matched Pair

Ruger K77/22 Varmint

MARLIN MODEL 982 BOLT-ACTION RIFLE
Caliber: 22 WMR. **Barrel:** 22" Micro-Groove®. **Weight:** 6 lbs. **Length:** 41" overall. **Stock:** Walnut Monte Carlo genuine American black walnut with swivel studs; full pistol grip; classic cut checkering; rubber rifle butt pad; tough Mar-Shield® finish. **Sights:** Adjustable semi-buckhorn folding rear, ramp front sight with brass bead and Wide-Scan™ front sight hood. **Features:** 7-shot clip, thumb safety, red cocking indicator, receiver grooved for scope mount. 982S has stainless steel front breech bolt, barrel, receiver and bolt knob. All other parts are either stainless steel or nickel-plated. Has black Monte Carlo stock of fiberglass-filled polycarbonate with molded-in checkering, nickel-plated swivel studs. Introduced 2005. Model 982S has selected heavy 22" stainless steel barrel with recessed muzzle, and comes without sights; receiver is grooved for scope mount and 1" ring mounts are included. Weighs 7 lbs. Introduced 1997. Made in U.S.A. by Marlin Firearms Co.
Price: 982 . . . . $341.00
Price: 982L (laminated hardwood stock, 6.25 lbs). $361.00
Price: 982S (stainless parts, 6.25 lbs). $377.00
Price: 982VS (heavy stainless barrel, 7 lbs). $357.00

Marlin Model 925M/925MC Bolt-Action Rifles
Similar to the Model 982 except chambered for 22 WMR. Has 7-shot clip magazine, 22" Micro-Groove® barrel, checkered walnut-finished Maine birch stock. Introduced 1989.
Price: 925M $260.00
Price: 925MC (Mossy Oak Break-Up camouflage stock) $300.00

MARLIN MODEL 983 BOLT-ACTION RIFLE
Caliber: 22 WMR. **Barrel:** 22"; 1:16" twist. **Weight:** 6 lbs. **Length:** 41" overall. **Stock:** Walnut Monte Carlo with sling swivel studs, rubber buttpad. **Sights:** Ramp front with brass bead, removable hood; adjustable semi-buckhorn folding rear. **Features:** Thumb safety, red cocking indicator, receiver grooved for scope mount. 983S is same as the Model 983 except front breech bolt, striker knob, trigger stud, cartridge lifter stud and outer magazine tube are of stainless steel; other parts are nickel-plated. Introduced 1993. 983T has a black Monte Carlo fiberglass-filled synthetic stock with sling swivel studs. Introduced 2001. Made in U.S.A. by Marlin Firearms Co.
Price: 983 . . . . $356.00
Price: 983S (stainless barrel) $377.00
Price: 983T (fiberglass stock) $273.00

MEACHAM LOW-WALL RIFLE
Caliber: Any rimfire cartridge. **Barrel:** 26-34". **Weight:** 7-15 lbs. **Sights:** none. Tang drilled for Win. base, 3/8 dovetail slot front. **Stock:** Fancy eastern walnut with cheekpiece; ebony insert in forearm tip. **Features;** Exact copy of 1885 Winchester. With most Winchester factory options available including double set triggers. Introduced 1994. Made in U.S.A. by Meacham T&H Inc.
Price: From $3,899.00

NEW ENGLAND FIREARMS SPORTSTER™ SINGLE-SHOT RIFLES
Caliber: 22 LR, 22 WMR, 17 HMR, single-shot. **Barrel:** 20". **Weight:** 5-1/2 lbs. **Length:** 36-1/4" overall. **Stock:** Black polymer. **Sights:** None furnished; scope mount included. **Features:** Break open, side-lever release; automatic ejection; recoil pad; sling swivel studs; trigger locking system. Introduced 2001. Made in U.S.A. by New England Firearms.
Price: $149.00
Price: Youth model (20" bbl., 33" overall, weighs 5-1/3 lbs.) $149.00
Price: Sportster 17 HMR $180.00

NEW ULTRA LIGHT ARMS 20RF BOLT-ACTION RIFLE
Caliber: 22 LR, single shot or repeater. **Barrel:** Douglas, length to order. **Weight:** 5-1/4 lbs. **Length:** Varies. **Stock:** Kevlar®/graphite composite, variety of finishes. **Sights:** None furnished; drilled and tapped for scope mount. **Features:** Timney trigger, hand-lapped action, button-rifled barrel, hand-bedded action, recoil pad, sling-swivel studs, optional Jewell trigger. Made in U.S.A. by New Ultra Light Arms.
Price: 20 RF single shot $800.00
Price: 20 RF repeater $850.00

ROSSI MATCHED PAIR SINGLE-SHOT RIFLE/SHOTGUN
Caliber: 22 LR or 22 Mag. **Barrel:** 18-1/2" or 23". **Weight:** 6 lbs. **Stock:** Hardwood (brown or black finish). **Sights:** Fully adjustable front and rear. **Features:** Break-open breech, transfer-bar manual safety, includes matched 410-, 20 or 12 gauge shotgun barrel with bead front sight. Introduced 2001. Imported by BrazTech/Taurus.
Price: Blue $139.95
Price: Stainless steel $169.95

RUGER K77/22 VARMINT RIFLE
Caliber: 22 LR, 10-shot, 22 WMR, 9-shot detachable rotary magazine. **Barrel:** 24", heavy. **Weight:** 6-7/8 lbs. **Length:** 43.25" overall. **Stock:** Laminated hardwood with rubber buttpad, quick-detachable swivel studs. **Sights:** None furnished. Comes with Ruger 1" scope rings. **Features:** Stainless steel or blued finish. Three-position safety, dual extractors. Stock has wide, flat forend. Introduced 1993.
Price: K77/22VBZ, 22 LR $765.00
Price: K77/22VMBZ, 22 WMR $765.00

Ruger 77/22R

Ruger 77/17

Savage Mark I-G

Savage Mark II-BV

Savage Mark II-FXP

RUGER 77/22 RIMFIRE BOLT-ACTION RIFLE
Caliber: 22 LR, 10-shot rotary magazine; 22 WMR, 9-shot rotary magazine. **Barrel:** 20". **Weight:** About 6 lbs. **Length:** 39-3/4" overall. **Stock:** Checkered American walnut, laminated hardwood, or synthetic stocks, stainless sling swivels. **Sights:** Plain barrel with 1" Ruger rings. **Features:** Mauser-type action uses Ruger's rotary magazine. Three-position safety, simplified bolt stop, patented bolt locking system. Uses the dual-screw barrel attachment system of the 10/22 rifle. Integral scope mounting system with 1" Ruger rings. Blued model introduced 1983. Stainless steel and blued with synthetic stock introduced 1989.
Price: 77/22R (no sights, rings, walnut stock) **$690.00**
Price: K77/22RP (stainless, no sights, rings, synthetic stock) **$690.00**
Price: 77/22RM (22 WMR, blue, walnut stock) **$690.00**
Price: K77/22RMP (22 WMR, stainless, synthetic stock) **$690.00**

RUGER 77/17 RIMFIRE BOLT-ACTION RIFLE
Caliber: 17HMR (9-shot rotary magazine. **Barrel:** 22" to 24". **Weight:** 6.5-7.5 lbs. **Length:** 41.25-43.25" overall. **Stock:** Checkered American walnut, laminated hardwood; stainless sling swivels. **Sights:** Plain barrel with 1" Ruger rings. **Features:** Mauser-type action uses Ruger's rotary magazine. Three-position safety, simplified bolt stop, patented bolt locking system. Uses the dual-screw barrel attachment system of the 10/22 rifle. Integral scope mounting system with 1" Ruger rings. Introduced 2002.
Price: 77/17RM (no sights, rings, walnut stock) **$690.00**
Price: K77/17VMBBZ (Target grey bbl, black laminate stock) **$746.00**

SAVAGE MARK I-G BOLT-ACTION RIFLE
Caliber: 22 LR, single shot. **Barrel:** 20-3/4". **Weight:** 5-1/2 lbs. **Length:** 39-1/2" overall. **Stock:** Walnut-finished hardwood with Monte Carlo-type comb, checkered grip and forend. **Sights:** Bead front, open adjustable rear. Receiver grooved for scope mounting. **Features:** Thumb-operated rotating safety. Blue finish. Rifled or smooth bore. Introduced 1990. Made in Canada, from Savage Arms Inc.
Price: Mark IG, rifled or smooth bore, right- or left-handed **$152.00**
Price: Mark I-GY (Youth), 19" bbl., 37" overall, 5 lbs. **$152.00**
Price: Mark I-LY (Youth), 19" bbl., color laminate **$187.00**
Price: Mark I-GSB (22 LR shot cartridge) **$152.00**

SAVAGE MARK II BOLT-ACTION RIFLE
Caliber: 22 LR, 10-shot magazine. **Barrel:** 20-1/2". **Weight:** 5-1/2 lbs. **Length:** 39-1/2" overall. **Stock:** Walnut-finished hardwood with Monte Carlo-type comb, checkered grip and forend. **Sights:** Bead front, open adjustable rear. Receiver grooved for scope mounting. **Features:** Thumb-operated rotating safety. Blue finish. Introduced 1990. Made in Canada, from Savage Arms, Inc.
Price: Mark II-BV **$264.00**
Price: Mark II Camo **$184.00**
Price: Mark II-GY (youth), 19" barrel, 37" overall, 5 lbs. **$169.00**
Price: Mark II-GL, left-hand **$169.00**
Price: Mark II-GLY (youth) left-hand **$169.00**
Price: Mark II-FXP (as above with black synthetic stock) **$158.00**
Price: Mark II-F (as above, no scope) **$151.00**

Savage Mark II-FSS Stainless Rifle
Similar to the Mark II except has stainless steel barreled action and black synthetic stock with positive checkering, swivel studs, and 20.75" free-floating and button-rifled barrel with detacheable magazine. Weighs 5.5 lbs. Introduced 1997. Imported from Canada by Savage Arms, Inc.
Price: **$213.00**

RIMFIRE RIFLES — Bolt Actions & Single Shot

Savage Model 93G

Savage Model 93FSS

Savage Model 93FVSS

Savage Model 30G Stevens "Favorite"

Savage Cub G Youth

Winchester Wildcat

SAVAGE MODEL 93G MAGNUM BOLT-ACTION RIFLE
Caliber: 22 WMR, 5-shot magazine. **Barrel:** 20-3/4". **Weight:** 5-3/4 lbs. **Length:** 39-1/2" overall. **Stock:** Walnut-finished hardwood with Monte Carlo-type comb, checkered grip and forend. **Sights:** Bead front, adjustable open rear. Receiver grooved for scope mount. **Features:** Thumb-operated rotary safety. Blue finish. Introduced 1994. Made in Canada, from Savage Arms.
Price: **$195.00**
Price: Model 93F (as above with black graphite/fiberglass stock) . . **$187.00**

Savage Model 93FSS Magnum Rifle
Similar to Model 93G except stainless steel barreled action and black synthetic stock with positive checkering. Weighs 5-1/2 lbs. Introduced 1997. Imported from Canada by Savage Arms, Inc.
Price: **$236.00**

Savage Model 93FVSS Magnum Rifle
Similar to Model 93FSS Magnum except 21" heavy barrel with recessed target-style crown, satin-finished stainless barreled action, black graphite/fiberglass stock. Drilled and tapped for scope mounting; comes with Weaver-style bases. Introduced 1998. Imported from Canada by Savage Arms, Inc.
Price: **$267.00**
Price: With scope **$305.00**

SAVAGE MODEL 30G STEVENS "FAVORITE"
Caliber: 22 LR, 22WMR Model 30GM, 17 HMR Model 30R17. **Barrel:** 21". **Weight:** 4.25 lbs. **Length:** 36.75". **Stock:** Walnut, straight grip, Schnabel forend. **Sights:** Adjustable rear, bead post front. **Features:** Lever action falling block, inertia firing pin system, Model 30G half octagonal bbl. Model 30GM full octagonal bbl.
Price: Model 30G **$228.00**
Price: Model 30GM **$266.00**
Price: Model 30R17 . . . . **$292.00**

SAVAGE CUB G YOUTH
Caliber: 22 S, L, LR; 17 Mach 2. **Barrel:** 16.125" **Weight:** 3.3 lbs. **Length:** 33" **Stock:** Walnut finished hardwood. **Sights:** Bead post, front; peep, rear. **Features:** Mini single shot bolt action, free-floating button-rifled barrel, blued finish. From Savage Arms.
Price: 22 S, L, LR **$156.00**
Price: 17 Mach 2 . . . . **$165.00**

WINCHESTER WILDCAT BOLT ACTION 22
Caliber: 22 S, L, LR; one 5-round and three 10-round magazines. **Barrel:** 21" **Weight:** NA. **Length:** NA. **Stock:** Checkered hardwood stock, checkered black synthetic Winchester buttplate, Schnabel fore-end, identical grip. cap **Sights:** Bead post, front; buckhorn rear. **Features:** Steel sling swivel studs, blued finish. Wildcat Target/Varmint rifle has .866" diameter bull barrel. Receiver drilled, tapped, and grooved for bases. Adjustable trigger, dual front steel swivel studs. Introduced 2007. From Winchester Rifles.
Price: **$230.00**
Price: Wildcat/Varmint **$265.00**

**Includes models for classic American and ISU target competition
and other sporting and competitive shooting.**

Anschutz 1451 Target

Anschutz 2013

ANSCHUTZ 1451R SPORTER TARGET RIFLE
Caliber: 22 LR, 5-shot magazine. **Barrel:** 22" heavy match. **Weight:** 6.4 lbs. **Length:** 39.75" overall. **Stock:** European hardwood with walnut finish. **Sights:** None furnished. Grooved receiver for scope mounting or Anschutz micrometer rear sight. **Features:** Sliding safety, two-stage trigger. Adjustable buttplate; forend slide rail to accept Anschutz accessories. Imported from Germany by GSI.
Price: **$549.00**

ANSCHUTZ 1451 TARGET RIFLE
Caliber: 22 LR. **Barrel:** 22". **Weight:** About 6.5 lbs. **Length:** 40". **Sights:** Optional. Receiver grooved for scope mounting. **Features:** Designed for the beginning junior shooter with adjustable length of pull from 13.25" to 14.25" via removable butt spacers. Two-stage trigger factory set at 2.6 lbs. Introduced 1999. Imported from Germany by Gunsmithing, Inc.
Price: **$347.00**
Price: #6834 Match Sight Set **$227.10**

ANSCHUTZ 1808D-RT SUPER RUNNING TARGET RIFLE
Caliber: 22 LR, single shot. **Barrel:** 32-1/2". **Weight:** 9 lbs. **Length:** 50" overall. **Stock:** European walnut. Heavy beavertail forend; adjustable cheekpiece and buttplate. Stippled grip and forend. **Sights:** None furnished. Grooved for scope mounting. **Features:** Designed for Running Target competition. Nine-way adjustable single-stage trigger, slide safety. Introduced 1991. Imported from Germany by Gunsmithing, Inc.
Price: Right-hand. **$1,364.10**

ANSCHUTZ 1903 MATCH RIFLE
Caliber: 22 LR, single shot. **Barrel:** 25.5", .75" diameter. **Weight:** 10.1 lbs. **Length:** 43.75" overall. **Stock:** Walnut-finished hardwood with adjustable cheekpiece; stippled grip and forend. **Sights:** None furnished. **Features:** Uses Anschutz Match 64 action and #5098 two-stage trigger. A medium weight rifle for intermediate and advanced Junior Match competition. Introduced 1987. Imported from Germany by Gunsmithing, Inc.
Price: Right-hand. **$720.40**
Price: Left-hand **$757.90**

ANSCHUTZ 64-MS R SILHOUETTE RIFLE
Caliber: 22 LR, 5-shot magazine. **Barrel:** 21-1/2", medium heavy; 7/8" diameter. **Weight:** 8 lbs. **Length:** 39.5" overall. **Stock:** Walnut-finished hardwood, silhouette-type. **Sights:** None furnished. **Features:** Uses Match 64 action. Designed for metallic silhouette competition. Stock has stippled checkering, contoured thumb groove with Wundhammer swell. Two-stage #5098 trigger. Slide safety locks sear and bolt. Introduced 1980. Imported from Germany by AcuSport Corp., Gunsmithing, Inc.
Price: 64-MS R **$704.30**

ANSCHUTZ 2013 BENCHREST RIFLE
Caliber: 22 LR, single shot. **Barrel:** 19.6". **Weight:** About 10.3 lbs. **Length:** 37.75" to 42.5" overall. **Stock:** Benchrest style of European hardwood. Stock length adjustable via spacers and buttplate. **Sights:** None furnished. Receiver grooved for mounts. **Features:** Uses the Anschutz 2013 target action; two-stage adjustable target trigger factory set at 3.9 oz. Introduced 1994. Imported from Germany by Gunsmithing, Inc.
Price: **$1,757.20**

Anschutz 2007 Match Rifle
Uses same action as the Model 2013, but has a lighter barrel. European walnut stock in right-hand, true left-hand or extra-short models. Sights optional. Available with 19.6" barrel with extension tube, or 26", both in stainless or blue. Introduced 1998. Imported from Germany by Gunsmithing, Inc.
Price: Right-hand, blue, no sights **$1,766.60**
Price: Right-hand, blue, no sights, extra-short stock **$1,756.60**
Price: Left-hand, blue, no sights **$1,856.80**

ANSCHUTZ 1827 BIATHLON RIFLE
Caliber: 22 LR, 5-shot magazine. **Barrel:** 21-1/2". **Weight:** 8-1/2 lbs. with sights. **Length:** 42-1/2" overall. **Stock:** European walnut with cheekpiece, stippled pistol grip and forend. **Sights:** Optional globe front specially designed for Biathlon shooting, micrometer rear with hinged snow cap. **Features:** Uses Super Match 54 action and nine-way adjustable trigger; adjustable wooden buttplate, biathlon butthook, adjustable hand-stop rail. Introduced 1982. Imported from Germany by Gunsmithing, Inc.
Price: Right-hand, with sights, about . . . . **$1,500.50 to $1,555.00**

Anschutz 1827BT Fortner Biathlon Rifle
Similar to the Anschutz 1827 Biathlon rifle except uses Anschutz/Fortner system straight-pull bolt action, blued or stainless steel barrel. Introduced 1982. Imported from Germany by Gunsmithing, Inc.
Price: Right-hand, with sights. . . . . **$1,908.00 to $2,210.00**
Price: Left-hand, with sights . . . . **$2,099.20 to $2,395.00**
Price: Right-hand, sights, stainless barrel **$2,045.20**

Anschutz 54.18MS REP

Anschutz 1913 Super Match

ANSCHUTZ SUPER MATCH SPECIAL MODEL 2013 RIFLE
Caliber: 22 LR, single shot. **Barrel:** 25.9". **Weight:** 13 lbs. **Length:** 41.7" to 42.9". **Stock:** A thumbhole version made of European walnut, both the cheekpiece and buttplate are highly adjustable. **Sights:** None furnished. **Features:** Developed by Anschütz for women to shoot in the sport rifle category. Stainless or blue. Introduced in 1997.
Price: Right-hand, blue, no sights, walnut. **$2,219.30**
Price: Right-hand, stainless, no sights, walnut **$2,345.30**
Price: Left-hand, blue, no sights, walnut **$2,319.50**

ANSCHUTZ 2012 SPORT RIFLE
Caliber: 22 LR, 5-shot magazine. **Barrel:** 22.4" match; detachable muzzle tube. **Weight:** 7.9 lbs. **Length:** 40.9" overall. **Stock:** European walnut, thumbhole design. **Sights:** None furnished. **Features:** Uses Anschutz 54.18 barreled action with two-stage match trigger. Introduced 1997. Imported from Germany by AcuSport Corp.
Price: . . . . **$1,425.00 to $2,219.95**

ANSCHUTZ 1911 PRONE MATCH RIFLE
Caliber: 22 LR, single shot. **Barrel:** 27-1/4". **Weight:** 11 lbs. **Length:** 46" overall. **Stock:** Walnut-finished European hardwood; American prone-style with adjustable cheekpiece, textured pistol grip, forend with swivel rail and adjustable rubber buttplate. **Sights:** None furnished. Receiver grooved for Anschutz sights (extra). **Features:** Two-stage trigger adjustable from 2.1 to 8.6 oz. Extremely fast lock time. Stainless or blue barrel. Imported from Germany by Gunsmithing, Inc.
Price: Right-hand, no sights **$1,714.20**

ANSCHUTZ 1912 SPORT RIFLE
Caliber: 22 LR, single shot. **Barrel:** 25.9". **Weight:** About 11.4 lbs. **Length:** 41.7 to 42.9". **Stock:** European walnut or aluminum. **Sights:** None furnished. **Features:** Lightweight sport rifle version of the 1913 but weighs 1.5 pounds less. Stainless or blue barrel. Introduced 1997.
Price: Right-hand, blue, no sights, walnut. **$1,789.50**
Price: Right-hand, blue, no sights, aluminum **$2,129.80**
Price: Right-hand, stainless, no sights, walnut **$1,910.30**
Price: Left-hand, blue, no sights, walnut **$1,879.00**

Anschutz 1913 Super Match Rifle
Same as the Model 1911 except European walnut International-type stock with adjustable cheekpiece, or color laminate, both available with straight or lowered forend, adjustable aluminum hook buttplate, adjustable hand stop, weighs 15.5 lbs., 46" overall. Stainless or blue barrel. Imported from Germany by Gunsmithing, Inc.
Price: Right-hand, blue, no sights, walnut stock . . . . **$2,139.00 to $2,175.00**

Price: Right-hand, blue, no sights, color laminate stock **$2,199.40**
Price: Right-hand, blue, no sights, walnut, lowered forend **$2,181.80**
Price: Right-hand, blue, no sights, color laminate,
     lowered forend **$2,242.20**
Price: Left-hand, blue, no sights, walnut stock . . . . **$2,233.10 to $2,275.00**

Anschutz 54.18MS REP Deluxe Silhouette Rifle
Same basic action and trigger specifications as the Anschutz 1913 Super Match but with removable 5-shot clip magazine, 22.4" barrel extendable to 30" using optional extension and weight set. Weight is 8.1 lbs. Receiver drilled and tapped for scope mounting. Stock is thumbhole silhouette version or standard silhouette version, both are European walnut. Introduced 1990. Imported from Germany by Gunsmithing, Inc.
Price: Thumbhole stock **$1,461.40**
Price: Standard stock **$1,212.10**

Anschutz 1907 Standard Match Rifle
Same action as Model 1913 but with 7/8" diameter 26" barrel (stainless or blue). Length is 44.5" overall, weighs 10.5 lbs. Choice of stock configurations. Vented forend. Designed for prone and position shooting ISU requirements; suitable for NRA matches. Also available with walnut flat-forend stock for benchrest shooting. Imported from Germany by Gunsmithing, Inc.
Price: Right-hand, blue, no sights,
     hardwood stock . . . . **$1,253.40 to $1,299.00**
Price: Right-hand, blue, no sights, colored laminated
     stock . . . . **$1,316.10 to $1,375.00**
Price: Right-hand, blue, no sights, walnut stock **$1,521.10**
Price: Left-hand, blue barrel, no sights, walnut stock **$1,584.60**

ARMALITE AR-10(T) RIFLE
Caliber: 308, 10-shot magazine. **Barrel:** 24" target-weight Rock 5R custom. **Weight:** 10.4 lbs. **Length:** 43.5" overall. **Stock:** Green or black compostion; N.M. fiberglass handguard tube. **Sights:** Detachable handle, front sight, or scope mount available. Comes with international-style flattop receiver with Picatinny rail. **Features:** National Match two-stage trigger. Forged upper receiver. Receivers hard-coat anodized. Introduced 1995. Made in U.S.A. by ArmaLite, Inc.
Price: Green **$2,126.00**
Price: Black **$2,126.00**

ARMALITE M15A4(T) EAGLE EYE RIFLE
Caliber: 223, 10-round magazine. **Barrel:** 24" heavy stainless; 1:8" twist. **Weight:** 9.2 lbs. **Length:** 42-3/8" overall. **Stock:** Green or black butt, N.M. fiberglass handguard tube. **Sights:** One-piece international-style flattop receiver with Weaver-type rail, including case deflector. **Features:** Detachable carry handle, front sight and scope mount (30mm or 1") available. Upper and lower receivers have push-type pivot pin, hard coat anodized. Made in U.S.A. by ArmaLite, Inc.
Price: Green **$1,378.00**
Price: Black. **$1,504.00**

Bushmaster A2

Bushmaster DCM

Colt Match Target HBAR

Colt Accurized

BLASER R93 LONG RANGE RIFLE
Caliber: 308 Win., 10-shot detachable box magazine. **Barrel:** 24". **Weight:** 10.4 lbs. **Length:** 44" overall. **Stock:** Aluminum with synthetic lining. **Sights:** None furnished; accepts detachable scope mount. **Features:** Straight-pull bolt action with adjustable trigger; fully adjustable stock; quick takedown; corrosion resistant finish. Introduced 1998. Imported from Germany by SIGARMS.
Price: **$2,360.00**

BUSHMASTER A2 RIFLE
Caliber: 308, 5.56mm. **Barrel:** 16", 20". **Weight:** 8.3 lbs. **Length:** 38.25" overall (20" barrel). **Stock:** Black composition; A2 type. **Sights:** Adjustable post front, adjustable aperture rear. **Features:** Patterned after Colt M-16A2. Chrome-lined barrel with manganese phosphate exterior. Forged aluminum receivers with push-pin takedown. Available in stainless barrel and camo stock versions. Made in U.S.A. by Bushmaster Firearms Co.
Price: 20" match heavy barrel (A2 type) .... **$1,025.00 to $1,185.00**
Price: (A3 type) **$1,135.00**

BUSHMASTER DCM COMPETITION RIFLE
Caliber: 223. **Barrel:** 20" extra-heavy (1" diameter) barrel with 1.8" twist for heavier competition bullets. **Weight:** Appx. 12 lbs. with balance weights. **Length:** NA. **Stock:** NA. **Sights:** A2 rear sight. **Features:** Has special competition rear sight with interchangeable apertures, extra-fine 1/2- or 1/4-MOA windage and elevation adjustments; specially ground front sight post in choice of three widths. Full-length handguards over free-floater barrel tube. Introduced 1998. Made in U.S.A. by Bushmaster Firearms, Inc.
Price: **$1,395.00**

BUSHMASTER VARMINTER RIFLE
Caliber: 5.56mm. **Barrel:** 24", fluted. **Weight:** 8.4 lbs. **Length:** 42.25" overall. **Stock:** Black composition, A2 type. **Sights:** None furnished; upper receiver has integral scope mount base. **Features:** Chrome-lined .950" extra heavy barrel with counter-bored crown, manganese phosphate finish, free-floating aluminum handguard, forged aluminum receivers with push-pin takedown, hard anodized mil-spec finish. Competition trigger optional. Made in U.S.A. by Bushmaster Firearms, Inc.
Price: 20" Match heavy barrel **$1,265.00**
Price: Stainless barrel **$1,265.00**

COLT MATCH TARGET HBAR RIFLE
Caliber: 223 Rem. **Barrel:** 20". **Weight:** 8 lbs. **Length:** 39" overall. **Stock:** Synthetic. **Sights:** Front: elevation adj. post; rear: 800-meter, aperture adj. for windage and elevation. **Features:** Heavy barrel, rate of rifling twist 1:7. Introduced 1991. Made in U.S.A. by Colt.
Price: Model MT6601, MT6601C **$1,183.00**

Colt Match Target Competition HBAR Rifle
Similar to the Match Target except has removeable carry handle for scope mounting, 1:9" rifling twist, 9-round magazine. Weighs 8.5 lbs. Introduced 1991.
Price: Model MT6700, MT6700C **$1,250.00**

Colt Match Target Competition HBAR II Rifle
Similar to the Match Target Competition HBAR except has 16:1" barrel, overall length 34.5", and weighs 7.1 lbs. Introduced 1995.
Price: Model MT6731 .... **$1,172.00**

Colt Accurized Rifle
Similar to the Match Target Model except has 24" barrel. Features flat-top receiver for scope mounting, stainless steel heavy barrel, tubular handguard, and free-floating barrel. Matte black finish. Weighs 9.25 lbs. Made in U.S.A. by Colt's Mfg. Co., Inc.
Price: Model CR6724 .... **$1,334.00**

Colt Match Target HBAR II

EAA/Izhmash URAL 5.1

EAA/IZHMASH Biathlon Target

Ed Brown Tactical

Ed Brown Marine Sniper

EAA/HW 660 MATCH RIFLE
Caliber: 22 LR. **Barrel:** 26". **Weight:** 10.7 lbs. **Length:** 45.3" overall. **Stock:** Match-type walnut with adjustable cheekpiece and buttplate. **Sights:** Globe front, match aperture rear. **Features:** Adjustable match trigger; stippled pistol grip and forend; forend accessory rail. Introduced 1991. Imported from Germany by European American Armory.
Price: About. **$999.00**
Price: With laminate stock **$1,159.00**

EAA/IZHMASH URAL 5.1 TARGET RIFLE
Caliber: 22 LR. **Barrel:** 26.5". **Weight:** 11.3 lbs. **Length:** 44.5". **Stock:** Wood, international style. **Sights:** Adjustable click rear, hooded front with inserts. **Features:** Forged barrel with rifling, adjustable trigger, aluminum rail for accessories, hooked adjustable buttplate. Adjustable comb, adjustable large palm rest. Hand stippling on grip area.
Price: . . . . **NA**

EAA/Izhmash Biathlon Target Rifle
Similar to URAL with addition of snow covers for barrel and sights, stock holding extra mags, round trigger block. Unique bolt utilizes toggle action.

Designed to compete in 40 meter biathlon event. 22 LR, 19.5" bbl.
Price: **$979.00**

EAA/Izhmash Biathalon Basic Target Rifle
Same action as Biathlon but designed for plinking or fun. Beech stock, heavy barrel with Weaver rail for scope mount. 22 LR, 19.5" bbl.
Price: **$339.00**

ED BROWN MODEL 704 TACTICAL
Caliber: 308, 300 Win. Mag. **Barrel:** 26". SS with GEN III Coating. **Weight:** 11.25 lbs. **Stock:** Hand bedded McMillan A-3 fiberglass tactical stock with recoil pad. **Sights:** None furnished. Leupold Mark 4 30mm scope mounts utilizing heavy-duty screws. **Features:** Custom short or long action, steel trigger guard, hinged floor plate, additional calibers available.
Price: From **$2,995.00**

ED BROWN MODEL 704, M40A2 MARINE SNIPER
Caliber: 308 Win., 30-06 Springfield. **Barrel:** Match-grade 24". **Weight:** 9.25 lbs. **Stock:** Hand bedded McMillan GP fiberglass tactical stock with recoil pad in special Woodland Camo molded-in colors. **Sights:** None furnished. Leupold Mark 4 30mm scope mounts with heavy-duty screws. **Features:** Steel trigger guard, hinged floor plate, three position safety. Left-hand model available.
Price: From **$2,995.00**

Olympic Arms SM-1P

Olympic Arms UM-1

Remington 40-XB Rangemaster

Remington 40-XC KS

OLYMPIC ARMS SM SERVICEMATCH AR15 RIFLES
Caliber: 223 Rem. minimum SAAMI spec, 30-shot magazine. **Barrel:** 20" broach-cut Ultramatch stainless steel 1x8 twist rate. **Weight:** 10 lbs. **Length:** 39.5" overall. **Stock:** A2 grip, A2 buttstock with trapdoor. **Sights:** A2 NM rear, elevation adjustable front post. **Features:** DCM-ready AR15, free-floating handguard looks standard, A2 upper, threaded muzzle, flash suppressor. Premium model adds pneumatic recoil buffer, Bob Jones interchangeable sights, two-stage trigger and Turner Saddlery sling. Made in U.S.A. by Olympic Arms, Inc.
Price: SM-1, 20" DCM ready **$1,099.00**
Price: SM-1P, Premium 20" DCM ready **$1,493.00**

OLYMPIC ARMS UM ULTRAMATCH AR15 RIFLES
Caliber: 223 Rem. minimum SAAMI spec, 30-shot magazine. **Barrel:** 20"or 24" bull broach-cut Ultramatch stainless steel 1x10 twist rate. **Weight:** 8-10 lbs. **Length:** 38.25" overall. **Stock:** A2 grip, A2 buttstock with trapdoor. **Sights:** None, flat-top upper and gas block with rails. **Features:** Flat top upper, free floating tubular match handguard, picatinny gas block, crowned muzzle, factory trigger job and "Ultramatch" pantograph. Premium model adds pneumatic recoil buffer, Harris S-series bipod, hand selected premium receivers and William Set Trigger. Made in U.S.A. by Olympic Arms, Inc.
Price: UM-1, 20" Ultramatch **$1,074.00**
Price: UM-1P, Premium 24" Ultramatch **$1,559.00**

OLYMPIC ARMS ML-1/ML-2 MULTIMATCH AR15 CARBINES
Caliber: 223 Rem. minimum SAAMI spec, 30-shot magazine. **Barrel:** 16" broach-cut Ultramatch stainless steel 1x10 twist rate. **Weight:** 7-8 lbs. **Length:** 34-36" overall. **Stock:** A2 grip and varying buttstock. **Sights:** None. **Features:** The ML-1 includes A2 upper with adjustable rear sight, elevation adjustable front post, free floating tubular match handguard, bayonet lug, threaded muzzle, flash suppressor and M4 6-point collapsible buttstock. The ML-2 includes bull diameter barrel, flat top upper, free floating tubular match handguard, picatinny gas block, crowned muzzle and A2 buttstock with trapdoor. Made in U.S.A. by Olympic Arms, Inc.
Price: ML-1 or ML-2 . . . . **$957.00**

OLYMPIC ARMS K8 TARGETMATCH AR15 RIFLES
Caliber: 5.56 NATO, .223 WSSM, .243 WSSM, .25 WSSM 30/7-shot magazine. **Barrel:** 20", 24" bull button-rifled stainless/chrome-moly steel 1x9/1x10 twist rate. **Weight:** 8-10 lbs. **Length:** 38"-42" overall. **Stock:** A2 grip, A2 buttstock with trapdoor. **Sights:** None. **Features:** Barrel has satin bead-blast finish; flat-top upper, free-floating tubular match handguard, Picatinny gas block, crowned muzzle and "Targetmatch" pantograph on lower receiver. K8-MAG model uses Winchester Super Short Magnum cartridges. Includes 24" bull chrome-moly barrel, flat-top upper, free-floating tubular match handguard, Picatinny gas block, crowned muzzle and 7-shot magazine. Made in U.S.A. by Olympic Arms, Inc.
Price: K8 . . . . **$803.00**
Price: K8-MAG **$1,074.00**

REMINGTON 40-XB RANGEMASTER TARGET CENTERFIRE
Caliber: 15 calibers from 220 Swift to 300 Win. Mag. **Barrel:** 27-1/4". **Weight:** 11-1/4 lbs. **Length:** 47" overall. **Stock:** American walnut, laminated thumbhole or Kevlar with high comb and beavertail forend stop. Rubber non-slip buttplate. **Sights:** None. Scope blocks installed. **Features:** Adjustable trigger. Stainless barrel and action. Receiver drilled and tapped for sights.
Price: Standard single shot (right-hand) **$1,636.00**; (left-hand) . . **$1,761.00**
Price: Repeater **$1,734.00**

REMINGTON 40-XBBR KS
Caliber: Five calibers from 22 BR to 308 Win. **Barrel:** 20" (light varmint class), 24" (heavy varmint class). **Weight:** 7-1/4 lbs. (light varmint class); 12 lbs. (heavy varmint class). **Length:** 38" (20" bbl.), 42" (24" bbl.). **Stock:** Aramid fiber. **Sights:** None. Supplied with scope blocks. **Features:** Unblued benchrest with stainless steel barrel, trigger adjustable from 1-1/2 lbs. to 3-1/2 lbs. Special two-oz. trigger extra cost. Scope and mounts extra.
Price: Single shot **$1,876.00**

Sako TRG-22

Springfield Armory M1A/M-21

Springfield Armory M-1 Garand

Stoner SR-25

REMINGTON 40-XC KS TARGET RIFLE
Caliber: 7.62 NATO, 5-shot. **Barrel:** 24", stainless steel. **Weight:** 11 lbs. without sights. **Length:** 43-1/2" overall. **Stock:** Aramid fiber. **Sights:** None furnished. **Features:** Designed to meet the needs of competitive shooters. Stainless steel barrel and action.
Price: **$1,821.00**

REMINGTON 40-XR CUSTOM SPORTER
Caliber: 22 LR, 22 WM. **Features:** Model XR-40 Target rifle action. Many options available.
Price: Single shot **$3,383.00**

SAKO TRG-22/TRG-42 BOLT-ACTION RIFLE
Caliber: 308 Win., 10-shot magazine. **Barrel:** 26". **Weight:** 10-1/4 lbs. **Length:** 45-1/4" overall. **Stock:** Reinforced polyurethane with fully adjustable cheekpiece and buttplate. **Sights:** None furnished. Optional quick-detachable, one-piece scope mount base, 1" or 30mm rings. **Features:** Resistance-free bolt, free-floating heavy stainless barrel, 60-degree bolt lift. Two-stage trigger is adjustable for length, pull, horizontal or vertical pitch. Introduced 2000. Imported from Finland by Beretta USA.
Price: TRG-22 Green Folding Stock **$4,525.00**
Price: TRG-22 Green or black stock **$2,825.00**
Price: TRG-42 300 Win Mag., green stock . . . . . . **$2,825.00 to $3,525.00**
Price: TRG-42 338 Lapua Mag., green stock . . . . . **$2,825.00 to $3,525.00**

SPRINGFIELD ARMORY M1A SUPER MATCH
Caliber: 308 Win. **Barrel:** 22", heavy Douglas Premium. **Weight:** About 11 lbs. **Length:** 44.31" overall. **Stock:** Heavy walnut competition stock with longer pistol grip, contoured area behind the rear sight, thicker butt and forend, glass bedded. **Sights:** National Match front and rear. **Features:** Has figure-eight-style operating rod guide. Introduced 1987. From Springfield Armory.
Price: About. **$2,479.00**

Springfield Armory M1A/M-21 Tactical Model Rifle
Similar to M1A Super Match except special sniper stock with adjustable cheekpiece and rubber recoil pad. Weighs 11.6 lbs. From Springfield Armory.
Price: **$2,975.00**

SPRINGFIELD ARMORY M-1 GARAND AMERICAN COMBAT RIFLES
Caliber: 30-06, 308 Win., 8-shot. **Barrel:** 24". **Weight:** 9.5 lbs. **Length:** 43.6". **Stock:** American walnut. **Sights:** Military square post front, military aperture, MOA adjustable rear. **Features:** Limited production, certificate of authenticity, all new receiver, barrel and stock with remaining parts USGI mil-spec. Two-stage military trigger.
Price: About **$2,479.00**

STONER SR-15 MATCH RIFLE
Caliber: 223. **Barrel:** 20". **Weight:** 7.9 lbs. **Length:** 38" overall. **Stock:** Black synthetic. **Sights:** None furnished; flattop upper receiver for scope mounting. **Features:** Short Picatinny rail, two-stage match trigger. Introduced 1998. Made in U.S.A. by Knight's Mfg.Co.
Price: **$1,650.00**

STONER SR-25 MATCH RIFLE
Caliber: 7.62 NATO, 10-shot steel magazine, 5-shot optional. **Barrel:** 24" heavy match; 1:11.25" twist. **Weight:** 10.75 lbs. **Length:** 44" overall. **Stock:** Black synthetic AR-15A2 design. Full floating forend of mil-spec synthetic attaches to upper receiver at a single point. **Sights:** None furnished. Has integral Weaver-style rail. Rings and iron sights optional. **Features:** Improved AR-15 trigger, AR-15-style seven-lug rotating bolt. Introduced 1993. Made in U.S.A. by Knight's Mfg. Co.
Price: **$3,345.00**
Price: SR-25 Lightweight Match (20" medium match target contour barrel, 9.5 lbs., 40" overall) **$3,345.00**

Includes a wide variety of sporting guns and guns suitable for various competitions.

Benelli Legacy

Benelli M2 20 gauge Realtree APG HD

Benelli M2 20 gauge Realtree APG HD

Benelli M4

Benelli Montefeltro

BENELLI LEGACY SHOTGUN
Gauge: 12, 20, 2-3/4" and 3" chamber. **Barrel:** 24", 26", 28" (Full, Mod., Imp. Cyl., Imp. Mod., cylinder choke tubes). Mid-bead sight. **Weight:** 5.8 to 7.4 lbs. **Length:** 49-5/8" overall (28" barrel). **Stock:** Select AA European walnut with satin finish. **Features:** Uses the rotating bolt inertia recoil operating system with a two-piece steel/aluminum etched receiver (bright on lower, blue upper). Drop adjustment kit allows the stock to be custom fitted without modifying the stock. Introduced 1998. Ultralight model has gloss-blued finish receiver. Weight is 6.0 lbs., 24" barrel, 45.5 overall length. WeatherCoat walnut stock. Introduced 2006. Imported from Italy by Benelli USA, Corp.
Price: **$1,565.00**
Price: Ultralight model, Weathercoat finish, 2+1 (2007) **$1,385.00**

BENELLI M2 FIELD SHOTGUNS
Gauge: 20 ga., 12 ga., 3" chamber. **Barrel:** 21", 24", 26", 28". **Weight:** 5.4 to 7.2 lbs. **Length:** 42.5 to 49.5" overall. **Stock:** Synthetic, Advantage® Max-4 HD, Advantage® Timber HD, APG HD. **Sights:** Red bar. **Features:** Uses the Inertia Driven™ bolt mechanism. Vent rib. Comes with set of five choke tubes. Imported from Italy by Benelli USA.
Price: Synthetic ComforTech gel recoil pad **$1,215.00**
Price: Camo ComforTech gel recoil pad **$1,335.00**
Price: Satin walnut **$1,145.00**
Price: Rifled slug synthetic **$1,280.00**
Price: Camo turkey model w/SteadyGrip stock **$1,375.00**
Price: Realtree APG HD ComforTech stock (2007) **$1,335.00**

Price: Realtree APG HD ComforTech 20 ga. (2007) **$1,335.00**
Price: Realtree APG HD LH ComforTech (2007) **$1,365.00**
Price: Realtree APG HD ComforTech Slug (2007) **$1,400.00**
Price: Realtree APG HD w/SteadyGrip stock (2007) **$1,375.00**
Price: Black Synthetic Grip Tight 20 ga. (2007) **$1,215.00**
Price: Timber HD ComforTech 20 ga. (2007) **$1,335.00**
Price: Realtree APG HD ComforTech 20 ga. (2007) **$1,335.00**

BENELLI M4 TACTICAL SHOTGUN
Gauge: 12 ga., 3" chamber. **Barrel:** 18.5". **Weight:** 7.8 lbs. **Length:** 40" overall. **Stock:** Synthetic. **Sights:** Ghost Ring rear, fixed blade front. **Features:** Auto-regulating gas-operated (ARGO) action, choke tube, Picatinny rail, standard and collapsible stocks available, optional LE tactical gun case. Introduced 2006. Imported from Italy by Benelli USA.
Price: Pistol grip stock, black synthetic. **$1,600.00**
Price: Desert camo pistol grip (2007). **$1,735.00**

BENELLI MONTEFELTRO SHOTGUNS
Gauge: 12 and 20 ga. Full, Imp. Mod, Mod., Imp. Cyl., Cyl. choke tubes. **Barrel:** 24", 26", 28". **Weight:** 5.3 to 7.1 lbs. **Stock:** Checkered walnut with satin finish. **Length of Pull:** 12-1/2 to 14-3/8" overall. **Length:** 43.6 to 49.5" overall. **Features:** Uses the Inertia Driven rotating bolt system with a simple inertia recoil design. Finish is blue. Introduced 1987.
Price: 24", 26", 28" **$1,110.00**
Price: Left hand. **$1,120.00**
Price: 20 ga. **$1,110.00**
Price: 20 ga. short stock (LOP: 12.5") **$1,120.00**
Price: Silver (AA walnut; nickle-blue receiver) **$1,535.00**
Price: Silver 20 ga. **$1,535.00**

Benelli Super Black Eagle II Realtree APG HD

Benelli Super Black Eagle II Slug

Beretta 3901 Ambassador

Beretta 3901 Citizen

BENELLI SUPER BLACK EAGLE II SHOTGUNS
Gauge: 12, 3-1/2" chamber. **Barrel:** 24", 26", 28" (Cyl. Imp. Cyl., Mod., Imp. Mod., Full choke tubes). **Weight:** 7.1 to 7.3 lbs. **Length:** 45.6 to 49.6" overall. **Stock:** European walnut with satin finish, polymer, or camo. Adjustable for drop. **Sights:** Red bar front. **Features:** Uses Benelli inertia recoil bolt system. Vent rib. Advantage® Max-4 HD™, Advantage® Timber HD™ camo patterns. Features ComforTech stock. Introduced 1991. Left-hand models available. Imported from Italy by Benelli USA.

Price: Satin walnut, non-ComforTech	**$1,480.00**
Price: Camo stock, ComforTech gel recoil pad	**$1,635.00**
Price: Black Synthetic stock	**$1,415.00**
Price: Max-4 or Timber HD Camo stock	**$1,535.00**
Price: Satin walnut Rifled slug	**$1,560.00**
Price: Timber HD turkey model w/SteadyGrip stock	**$1,615.00**
Price: Realtree APG HD SteadyGrip stock (2007)	**$1,615.00**
Price: Realtree APG HD w/ComforTech stock (2007)	**$1,665.00**
Price: Realtree APG HD LH ComforTech stock (2007)	**$1,700.00**
Price: Realtree APG HD Slug Gun (2007)	**$1,735.00**

BENELLI CORDOBA SHOTGUN
Gauge: 20; 12; 3" chamber. **Barrel:** 28" and 30", ported, 10mm sporting rib. **Weight:** 7.2 to 7.3 lbs. **Length:** 49.6 to 51.6". **Features:** Designed for high-volume sporting clays and Argentina dove shooting. Inertia-driven action, Extended Sport CrioChokes, 4+1 capacity. Ported. Imported from Italy by Benelli USA.

Price: Black synthetic GripTight ComforTech stock	**$1,735.00**
Price: Black synthetic GripTight ComforTech stock, 20 ga., (2007)	**$1,735.00**
Price: Max-4 HD ComforTech stock (2007)	**$1,870.00**

BENELLI SUPERSPORT & SPORT II SHOTGUNS
Gauge: 20; 12; 3" chamber. **Barrel:** 28" and 30", ported, 10mm sporting rib. **Weight:** 7.2 to 7.3 lbs. **Length:** 49.6 to 51.6". **Stock:** Carbon fiber, ComforTech (Supersport) or walnut (Sport II). **Sights:** Red bar front, metal midbead. Sport II is similar to the Legacy model except has nonengraved dual tone blue/silver receiver, ported wide-rib barrel, adjustable buttstock, and functions with all loads. Walnut stock with satin finish. Introduced 1997. **Features:** Designed for high-volume sporting clays. Inertia-driven action, Extended CrioChokes, 4+1 capacity. Ported. Imported from Italy by Benelli USA.

Price: Carbon fiber ComforTech stock	**$1,800.00**
Price: Carbon fiber ComforTech stock, 20 ga. (2007)	**$1,800.00**
Price: Sport II 20 ga. (2007)	**$1,580.00**

BERETTA 3901 SHOTGUNS
Gauge: 12, 20 gauge; 3" chamber, semi-auto. **Barrel:** 26", 28". **Weight:** 6.55 lbs. (20 ga.), 7.2 lbs. (12 ga.). **Length:** NA. **Stock:** Wood, X-tra wood (special process wood enhancement), and polymer. **Features:** Based on A390 shotgun introduced in 1996. Mobilchokes, removable trigger group. 3901 Target RL uses gas operating system; Sporting style flat rib with steel front bead and mid-bead, walnut stock and forearm, satin matte finish, adjustable LOP from 12–13", adjustable for cast on/off, Beretta's Memory System II to adjust the parallel comb. Weighs 7.2 lbs. 3901 Citizen has polymer stock. 3901 Statesman has basic wood and checkering treatment. 3901 Ambassador has X-tra wood stock and fore end; high-polished receiver with engraving, Gel-Tek recoil pad, optional TruGlo fiber-optic front sight. 3901 Rifled Slug Shotgun has black high-impact synthetic stock and fore end, 24" barrel,1:28 twist, Picatinny cantilever rail. Introduced 2006. Made in U.S. by Beretta USA.

Price:	**$1,295.00**
Price: 3901 Target RL	**$898.00**
Price: 3901 Citizen	**$750.00**
Price: 3901 Citizen	**$898.00**
Price: 3901 Ambassador	**$998.00**
Price: 3901 Rifled Slug Shotgun	**$799.00**

Beretta UGB

Beretta AL391 Urika Sporting

Beretta AL391 Urika Optima Camo

Beretta A391 Xtrema2 3.5

BERETTA UGB25 XCEL
Gauge: 12, 2-3/4" chambers. **Barrel:** 28", 30", 32"; competition-style interchangeable vent rib; Optima choke tubes. **Weight:** 7.7-9 lbs. **Stock:** High-grade walnut with oil finish; hand-checkered grip and forend, adjustable. **Features:** Break-open semiautomatic. High-resistance fiberglass-reinforced technopolymer trigger plate, self-lubricating firing mechanism. Rounded alloy receiver, polished sides, external cartridge carrier and feeding port, bottom eject. two technopolymer recoil dampers on breech bolt, double recoil dampers located in the receiver, Beretta Recoil Reduction System, recoil-absorbing Beretta Gel Tek recoil pad. Optima-Bore barrel with a lengthened forcing cone, Optimachoke and Extended Optimachoke tubes. Steel-shot capable, interchangeable aluminum alloy top rib. Introduced 2006. Imported from Italy by Beretta USA.
Price: .... **$,3,275.00**

BERETTA AL391 TEKNYS SHOTGUNS
Gauge: 12, 20 gauge; 3" chamber, semi-auto. **Barrel:** 26", 28". **Weight:** 5.9 lbs. (20 ga.), 7.3 lbs. (12 ga.). **Length:** NA. **Stock:** X-tra wood (special process wood enhancement). **Features:** Flat 1/4 rib, TruGlo Tru-Bead sight, recoil reducer, stock spacers, overbored bbls., flush choke tubes. Comes with fitted, lined case.
Price: From **$1,425.00**

BERETTA AL391 URIKA AND URIKA OPTIMA AUTO SHOTGUNS
Gauge: 12, 20 gauge; 3" chamber. **Barrel:** 22", 24", 26", 28", 30"; five Mobilchoke choke tubes. **Weight:** 5.95 to 7.28 lbs. **Length:** Varies by model. **Stock:** Walnut, black or camo synthetic; shims, spacers and interchangeable recoil pads allow custom fit. **Features:** Self-compensating gas operation handles full range of loads; recoil reducer in receiver; enlarged trigger guard; reduced-weight receiver, barrel and forend; hard-chromed bore. Introduced 2000. Urika Gold and Gold Sporting models are similar to AL391 Urika except features deluxe wood, jewelled bolt and carrier, gold-inlaid receiver with black or silver finish. Introduced 2000. Urika Sporting models are similar to AL391 Urika except has competition sporting stock with rounded rubber recoil pad, wide vent rib with white front and mid-rib beads, satin-black receiver with silver markings. Available in 12 and 20 gauge. Introduced 2000. Urika Trap has wide vent rib with white front and mid-rib beads, Monte Carlo stock and

special trap recoil pad. Gold Trap features highly figured walnut stock and forend, gold-filled Beretta logo and signature on receiver. Optima bore and Optima choke tubes. Introduced 2000. Urika Parallel Target RL and SL models have parallel comb, Monte Carlo stock with tighter grip radius and stepped vent rib. SL model has same features but with 13.5" length of pull stock. Introduced 2000. Urika Youth has a 24" or 26" barrel with 13.5" stock for youths and smaller shooters. Introduced 2000. Imported from Italy by Beretta USA.
Price: .... **$998.00 to $1,500.00**

BERETTA A391 XTREMA2 3.5 AUTO SHOTGUNS
Gauge: 12 ga. 3.5" chamber. **Barrel:** 24", 26", 28". **Weight:** 7.8 lbs. **Stock:** Synthetic. **Features:** Semi-auto goes with two-lug rotating bolt and self-compensating gas valve, extended tang, cross bolt safety, self-cleaning, with case.
Price: From **$1,098.00**

BROWNING GOLD AUTO SHOTGUNS
Gauge: 12, 3" or 3-1/2" chamber; 20, 3" chamber. **Barrel:** 12 ga.-26", 28", 30", Invector Plus choke tubes; 20 ga.-26", 30", Invector choke tubes. **Weight:** 7 lbs., 9 oz. (12 ga.), 6 lbs., 12 oz. (20 ga.). **Length:** 46-1/4" overall (20 ga., 26" barrel). **Stock:** 14"x1-1/2"x2-1/3"; select walnut with gloss finish; palm swell grip. **Features:** Self-regulating, self-cleaning gas system shoots all loads; lightweight receiver with special non-glare deep black finish; large reversible safety button; large rounded trigger guard, gold trigger. The 20 gauge has slightly smaller dimensions; 12 gauge have back-bored barrels, Invector Plus tube system. Introduced 1994. Gold Evolve shotguns have new rib design, HiViz sights. Gold Micro has a 26" barrel, 13-7/8" pull length and smaller pistol grip for youths and other small shooters. Introduced 2001. Gold Fusion has front HiViz Pro-Comp and center bead on tapered vent rib; ported and back-bored Invector Plus barrel; 2-3/4" chamber; satin-finished stock with solid, radiused recoil pad with hard heel insert; non-glare black alloy receiver, shim-adj. stock. Imported by Browning.
Price: Gold Evolve, 12 or 20 ga., 3" chamber **$1,220.00**
Price: Gold Hunter, 12 or 20 ga., 3" or 3-1/2" chamber, from **$1,025.00**
Price: Gold FLD, 12 or 20 ga., semi-humpback receiver **$1,025.00**
Price: Gold Rifled Deer Hunter, 12 or 20 ga., scope mount **$1,131.00**
Price: Gold Upland Special, 12 or 20 ga., 24" or 26" barrel **$1,025.00**
Price: Gold Superlite Micro, 20 ga., 24" or 26" barrel, 6.6 lbs. ... **$1,105.00**
Price: Gold Fusion, 12 or 20 ga., 6.4 to 7 lbs., ... **$1,152.00**
Price: Gold Fusion High Grade, 12 or 20 ga., intr. 2005 .... **$2,137.00**

Browning Gold Stalker

Browning Gold Deer Hunter

Browning Gold Fusion

Browning Gold Superlite Micro

Browning NWTF Mossy Oak Break-Up

Browning Golden Clays Ladies

Browning Gold Stalker Auto Shotgun

Similar to the Gold Hunter except has black composite stock and forend. Chambered in 12 gauge, 3" or 3-1/2" chamber. Gold Deer Stalker has fully rifled barrel, cantilever scope mount. Introduced 1999. Imported by Browning.

Price: Gold Stalker, 3" or 3-1/2" chamber, 26" or 28" barrel,
from . . . . **$ 1,171.00**
Price: Gold FLD Stalker, 3" chamber, semi-humpback receiver . . . **$981.00**
Price: Gold Rifled Deer Stalker, 12 ga. 3" chamber, 22" barrel . . **$1,241.00**

Browning Gold NWTF Turkey Series and Mossy Oak Shotguns

Similar to the Gold Hunter except has specialized camouflage patterns, including National Wild Turkey Federation design. Includes extra-full choke tube and HiViz fiber-optic sights on some models and Dura-Touch coating. Camouflage patterns include Mossy Oak New Break-Up (NBU) or Mossy Oak New Shadow Grass (NSG). NWTF models include NWTF logo on stock. Introduced 2001. From Browning.

Price: NWFT Gold Ultimate Turkey, 24" barrel, 3-1/2" chamber . . **$1,469.00**
Price: NWFT Gold Turkey, 24" barrel, 3" chamber **$1,202.00**
Price: Gold NSG, 26" or 28" barrel, 3" or 3-1/2" chamber, from . . **$1,127.00**
Price: Gold NBU, 26" barrel, 3" or 3-1/2" chamber, from **$1,127.00**
Price: Gold Rifle Deer NBU, 22" barrel, 3" chamber, from **$1,218.00**

BROWNING GOLD "CLAYS" AUTO SHOTGUNS

Gauge: 12, 2-3/4" chamber. **Barrel:** 28", 30", Invector Plus choke tubes. **Weight:** about 7.75 lbs. **Length:** From 47.75 to 50.5". **Stock:** Select walnut with gloss finish; palm swell grip, shim adjustable. **Features:** Ported barrels, "Golden Clays" models feature gold inlays and engraving. Otherwise similar to Gold series guns. Imported by Browning.

Price: Gold "Golden Clays" Sporting Clays, intr. 2005 . . . . **$1,848.00**
Price: Gold Sporting Clays **$1,127.00**
Price: Gold "Golden Clays" Ladies Sporting Clays, intr. 2005 . . . . **$1,848.00**
Price: Gold Ladies Sporting Clays **$1,127.00**

Browning Gold Light 10 Gauge

Charles Daly Field Pump

Charles Daly Maxi-Mag Field Hunter VR-MC

Charles Daly Superior II

Escort Model AS

Franchi I-12

Browning Gold Light 10 Gauge Auto Shotgun
Similar to the Gold Hunter except has an alloy receiver that is 1 lb. lighter than standard model. Offered in 26" or 28" bbls. With Mossy Oak® Break-Up™ or Shadow Grass coverage; 5-shot magazine. Weighs 9 lbs., 10 oz. (28" bbl.). Introduced 2001. Imported by Browning.
Price: Camo model only **$1,390.00**

CHARLES DALY FIELD SEMI-AUTO SHOTGUNS
Gauge: 12, 20, 28. **Barrel:** 22", 24", 26", 28" or 30". **Stock:** Synthetic black, Realtree Hardwoods or Advantage Timber. **Features:** Interchangeable barrels handle all loads including steel shot. Slug model has adjustable sights. Maxi-Mag is 3.5" chamber.
Price: Field Hunter **$389.00**

CHARLES DALY SUPERIOR II SEMI-AUTO SHOTGUNS
Gauge: 12, 20, 28. **Barrel:** 26", 28" or 30". **Stock:** Select Turkish walnut. **Features:** Factory ported interchangeable barrels; wide vent rib on Trap and Sport models; fluorescent red sights.
Price: Superior Hunter VR-MC **$539.00**
Price: Superior Sport **$569.00**

ESCORT SEMI-AUTO SHOTGUNS
Gauge: 12, 20. **Barrel:** 22", 24", 26", 18" (AimGuard model); 3" chambers. **Weight:** 6 lbs, 4 0. to 7 lbs., 6 oz. **Stock:** Polymer, black, or camo finish; also Turkish walnut. **Features:** Black chrome finish; top of receiver dovetailed for sight mounting. Gold-plated trigger, trigger guard safety, magazine cut-off. Three choke tubes (IC, M, F — except AimGuard); 24" bbl. model comes with turkey choke tube. **Sights:** Optional HiViz Spark and TriViz fiber-optic sights. Introduced 2002. Camo model introduced 2003. Youth, Slug, Obsession Camo models introduced 2005. Three-barrel pumpset introduced 2006. Imported from Turkey by Legacy Sports International.
Price: From **$392.00**

FRANCHI INERTIA I-12 SHOTGUN
Gauge: 12, 3" chamber. **Barrel:** 24", 26", 28" (Cyl., IC, Mod., IM, F choke tubes). **Weight:** 7.5 to 7.7. lbs. **Length:** 45" to 49". **Stock:** 14-3.8" LOP, satin walnut with checkered grip and forend, synthetic, Advantage Timber HD or Max-4 camo patterns. **Features:** Inertia-Driven action. AA walnut stock. Red bar front sight, metal mid sight. Imported from Italy by Benelli USA.
Price: Synthetic **$759.00**
Price: Camo **$839.00**
Price: Satin walnut **$839.00**
Price: Limited engraved receiver, hard case **$1,399.00**

Franchi I-12 Camo

Franchi Model 720

Franchi 48AL Deluxe

H&R Excell Auto 5

Remington Model 105 CTI

FRANCHI MODEL 720 SHOTGUNS

Gauge: 20, 3" chamber. **Barrel:** 24", 26", 28" w/(IC, Mod., F choke tubes). **Weight:** 5.9 to 6.1 lbs. **Length:** 43.25" to 49". **Stock:** WeatherCoat finish walnut, Max-4 and Timber HD camo. **Sights:** Front bead. **Features:** Made in Italy and imported by Benelli USA.

Price: Walnut w/Weathercoat $889.00
Price: Camo $919.00
Price: Walnut, 12.5" LOP, 43.25" OAL $789.00
Price: Competition Weathercoat 20 ga. $999.00

FRANCHI 48AL FIELD AND DELUXE SHOTGUNS

Gauge: 20 or 28, 2-3/4" chamber. **Barrel:** 24", 26", 28" (Full, Cyl., Mod., choke tubes). **Weight:** 5.4 to 5.7 lbs. **Length:** 42.25" to 48". **Stock:** Walnut with checkered grip and forend. **Features:** Long recoil-operated action. Chrome-lined bore; cross-bolt safety. Imported from Italy by Benelli USA.

Price: 20 ga. $779.00
Price: 20 ga. Deluxe A grade walnut $979.00
Price: 28 ga. $1089.00

FRANCHI 712 COMPETITION SHOTGUN

Gauge: 12 ; 4+1. **Barrel:** 30" ported; tapered target rib and bead front sight. **Weight:** 7.1 lbs. **Stock:** Walnut with WeatherCoat (impervious to weather). **Features:** Gas-operated, satin nickel receiver.

Price: $999.00

HARRINGTON & RICHARDSON EXCELL AUTO 5 SHOTGUNS

Gauge: 12, 3" chamber. **Barrel:** 22", 24", 28", four screw-in choke tubes (IC, M, IM, F). **Weight:** About 7 lbs. **Length:** 42.5" to 48.5" overall, depending on barrel length. **Stock:** American walnut with satin finish; cut checkering; ventilated buttpad. Synthetic stock or camo-finish. **Sights:** Metal bead front or fiber-optic front and rear. **Features:** Ventilated rib on all models except slug gun. Imported by H&R 1871, Inc.

Price: Synthetic, black, 28" barrel, 48.5" OAL $415.00
Price: Walnut, checkered grip/forend, 28" barrel, 48.5" OAL $461.00
Price: Waterfowl, camo finish $521.00
Price: Turkey, camo finish, 22" barrel, fiber optic sights $521.00
Price: Combo, synthetic black stock, with slug barrel $583.00

REMINGTON MODEL 105 CTI SHOTGUN

Gauge: 12, 3" chamber, 2-shot magazine. **Barrel:** 26", 28" (IC, Mod., Full ProBore chokes). **Weight:** 7 lbs. **Length:** 46.25" overall (26" barrel). **Stock:** Walnut with satin finish. Checkered grip and forend. **Sights:** Front bead. **Features:** Aircraft-grade titanium receiver body, skeletonized receiver with carbon fiber shell. Bottom feed and eject, target grade trigger, R3 recoil pad, FAA-approved lockable hard case, .735" overbored barrel with lengthened forcing cones. TriNyte coating; carbon/aramid barrel rib. Introduced 2006.

Price: $1,511.00

REMINGTON MODEL SPR453 SHOTGUN

Gauge: 12; 3.5" chamber, 4+1 capacity. **Barrel:** 24", 26", 28" vent rib. **Weight:** 8 to 8.25 lbs. **Stock:** Black synthetic and Mossy Oak Break-Up stock and forend. **Features:** Matte finish, dual extractors, four extended screw-in SPR choke tubes (improved cylinder, modified, full and super-full turkey. Introduced 2006. From Remington Arms Co.

Price: Black synthetic $461.00

Remington Model 11-87 Sportsman Camo

Remington Model 11-87 Special Purpose Magnum

Remington Model 11-87 SPS Cantilever

Remington Model 11-87 SPS Camo

Remington Model 1100 G3

REMINGTON MODEL 11-87 SPORTSMAN SHOTGUNS
Gauge: 12, 20, 3" chamber. **Barrel:** 26", 28", RemChoke tubes. Standard contour, vent rib. **Weight:** About 7.75 to 8.25 lbs. **Length:** 46" to 48" overall. **Stock:** Black synthetic or Mossy Oak Break Up. **Sights:** Single bead front. **Features:** Matte-black metal finish, magazine cap swivel studs. Sportsman Deer gun has 21-inch fully rifled barrel, cantilever scope mount.

Price: Sportsman Camo (2007)	**$845.00**
Price: Sportsman black synthetic	**$739.00**
Price: Sportsman Deer	**$845.00**

Remington Model 11-87 Special Purpose Magnum
Similar to the 11-87 Sportsman except has dull stock finish, Parkerized exposed metal surfaces. Bolt and carrier have dull blackened coloring. Comes with 26" or 28" barrel with RemChokes, padded Cordura nylon sling and quick detachable swivels. Introduced 1987. Thumbhole model available. Cantilever model has fully rifled barrel; synthetic stock with Monte Carlo comb; cantilever scope mount deer barrel. Comes with sling and swivels. Introduced 1994. Turkey Camo model has 21" vent rib barrel with RemChoke tube. Super Magnum Synthetic Camo has 23" vent rib barrel with Turkey Super full choke tube, chambered for 12 ga., 3-1/2", TruGlo rifle sights. Version available without TruGlo sights. Introduced 2001. Special Purpose-Deer Shotgun has fully-rifled 21" barrel with rifle sights, black non-reflective, synthetic stock and forend, black carrying sling. Introduced 1993. SPS Super Magnums have 3.5" chamber. Introduced 2000. From Remington Arms Co.

Price: SP Thumbhole rifled barrel	**$1,135.00**
Price: SP-T Thumbhole, Mossy Oak Obsession camo	**$1,241.00**
Price: SPS-T, Mossy Oak Obsession camo	**$1,175.00**
Price: SPS Super Magnum	**$1,076.00**
Price: SPS Super Magnum Camo	**$1,175.00**

REMINGTON MODEL 1100 G3 SHOTGUN
Gauge: 20, 12; 3" chamber. **Barrel:** 26", 28". **Weight:** 6.75-7.6 lbs. **Stock:** Realwood semi-Fancy carbon fiber laminate stock, high gloss finish, machine cut checkering. **Features:** Gas operating system, pressure compensated barrel, solid carbon-steel engraved receiver, titanium coating. Action bars, trigger and extended carrier release, action bar sleeve, action spring, locking block, hammer, sear and magazine tube have nickel-plated, Teflon coating. R3 recoil pad, overbored (.735" dia.) vent rib barrels, ProBore choke tubes. 20-gauges have Rem Chokes. Comes with lockable hard case. Introduced 2006. Competition model (12 gauge 2.75" chamber) has overbored (0.735" bore diameter) 30" barrel. **Weight:** 8 lbs. 10mm target-style rib with twin beads. Extended ProBore choke tubes in Skeet, Improved Cylinder, Light-Modified, Modified and Full. Semi-fancy American walnut stock and forend. Classic Trap model has polished blue receiver with scroll engraving, gold accents, 30" low-profile, light-target contoured vent rib barrel with standard .727" dimensions. Comes with specialized Rem Choke trap tubes: Singles (.027"), Mid Handicap (.034"), and Long Handicap (.041"). Monte Carlo stock of semi-fancy American walnut, deep-cut checkering, high-gloss finish.

Price: G3, 12 or 20 gauge	**$1,208.00**
Price: Competition, standard stock	**$1,492.00**
Price: Competition, adjustable comb	**$1,651.00**
Price: Classic Trap	**$1,101.00**

SHOTGUNS — Autoloaders

Remington Model 1100 Sporting 28

Remington Model 1100 Classic Trap

Remington Model 1100 Sporting 12

Remington Model SP-10

Remington Model SP-10 Thumbhole

Remington Model 1100 Sporting Shotguns
Similar to 1100 G3 but in .410 bore, 28, 20, 12 gauge. **Barrel:** 27" or 28" light target contoured vent rib barrel with twin bead target sights. **Stock:** Semi-fancy American walnut stock and forend, cut checkering, high gloss finish. **Features:** Gold-plated trigger. Four extended choke tubes: Skeet, Improved Cylinder, Light Modified and Modified. 1100 Tournament Skeet (20 and 12 gauge) receiver is roll-marked with "Tournament Skeet." 26-inch light contour, vent rib barrel has twin bead sights, Extended Target Choke Tubes (Skeet and Improved Cylinder).
Price: Sporting 12, 49" OAL, 8 lbs. **$1,057.00**
Price: Sporting 20, 48.75" OAL, 7 lbs. **$1,057.00**
Price: Sporting 28, 47.75" OAL, 6.75 lbs. **$1,101.00**
Price: Sporting 410, 47.75" OAL, 6.75 lbs. **$1,101.00**
Price: Tournament Skeet 12 gauge, 47" OAL, 7.75 lbs. **$1,057.00**

REMINGTON MODEL SP-10 MAGNUM SHOTGUN
Gauge: 10, 3-1/2" chamber, 2-shot magazine. **Barrel:** 26", 30" (full and mod. RemChokes). **Weight:** 10-3/4 to 11 lbs. **Length:** 47-1/2" overall (26"

barrel). **Stock:** Walnut with satin finish or black synthetic with 26" barrel. Checkered grip and forend. **Sights:** Twin bead. **Features:** Stainless steel gas system with moving cylinder; 3/8" vent rib. Receiver and barrel have matte finish. Brown recoil pad. Comes with padded Cordura nylon sling. Introduced 1989. SP-10 Magnum Camo has buttstock, forend, receiver, barrel and magazine cap covered with Mossy Oak® Break-Up™ camo finish; bolt body and trigger guard have matte black finish. RemChoke tube, 26" vent rib barrel with mid-rib bead and Bradley-style front sight, swivel studs and quick-detachable swivels, non-slip Cordura carrying sling in same camo pattern. Introduced 1993.
Price: . . . . **$1,684.00 to $1,844.00**
Price: Thumbhole Camo, Mossy Oak Obsession (2007). **$1,952.00**

SARSILMAZ SEMI-AUTOMATIC SHOTGUN
Gauge: 12, 3" chamber. **Barrel:** 26" or 28"; fixed chokes. **Stock:** Walnut or synthetic. **Features:** Handles 2-3/4" or 3" magnum loads. Introduced 2000. Imported from Turkey by Armsport Inc.
Price: With walnut stock **$969.95**
Price: With synthetic stock **$919.95**

Smith & Wesson 1012

Smith & Wesson 1020

Stoeger Model 2000

Traditions ALS 2100

Tristar CD Diana

SMITH & WESSON 1000/1020/1012 SUPER SEMI-AUTO SHOTGUNS
Gauge: 12, 20; 3" in 1000; 3.5" chamber in Super. **Barrel:** 24", 26", 28", 30". **Stock:** Walnut. Synthetic finishes are satin, black, Realtree MAX-4, Realtree APG. **Sights:** TruGlo fiber-optic. **Features:** 29 configurations. Gas operated, dual-piston action; chrome-lined barrels, five choke tubes, shim kit for adjusting stock. 20-ga. models are Model 1020 or Model 1020SS (short stock). Lifetime warranty. Introduced 2007. Imported from Turkey by Smith & Wesson.
Price: Black synthetic stock. . . . . **NA**

STOEGER MODEL 2000 SHOTGUNS
Gauge: 12, 3" chamber, set of five choke tubes (C, IC, M, F, XFT). **Barrel:** 24", 26", 28", 30". **Stock:** Walnut, synthetic, Timber HD, Max-4. **Sights:** Red bar front. **Features:** Inertia-recoil. Minimum recommended load: 3 dram, 1-1/8 oz. Imported by Benelli USA.
Price: Walnut **$445.00**
Price: Synthetic **$435.00**
Price: Max-4, Timber HD **$495.00**
Price: Field and slug barrel combo **$725.00**
Price: Black synthetic pistol grip (2007) **$475.00**
Price: APG HD camo pistol grip (2007) **$535.00**

TRADITIONS ALS 2100 SERIES SEMI-AUTOMATIC SHOTGUNS
Gauge: 12, 3" chamber; 20, 3" chamber. **Barrel:** 24", 26", 28" (Imp. Cyl., Mod. and Full choke tubes). **Weight:** 5 lbs., 10 oz. to 6 lbs., 5 oz. **Length:** 44" to 48" overall. **Stock:** Walnut or black composite. **Features:** Gas-operated; vent rib barrel with Beretta-style threaded muzzle. Introduced 2001 by Traditions.
Price: Field Model (12 or 20 ga., 26" or 28" bbl., walnut stock) **$479.00**
Price: Youth Model (12 or 20 ga., 24" bbl., walnut stock) **$479.00**
Price: (12 or 20 ga., 26" or 28" barrel, composite stock) **$459.00**

Traditions ALS 2100 Turkey Semi-Automatic Shotgun
Similar to ALS 2100 Field Model except chambered in 12 gauge, 3" only with

26" barrel, Mossy Oak® Break Up™ camo finish. Weighs 6 lbs.; 46" overall.
Price: **$519.00**

Traditions ALS 2100 Waterfowl Semi-Automatic Shotgun
Similar to ALS 2100 Field Model except chambered in 12 gauge, 3" only with 28" barrel and Advantage® Wetlands™ camo finish. Weighs 6.25 lbs.; 48" overall. Multi chokes.
Price: **$529.00**

Traditions ALS 2100 Hunter Combo
Similar to ALS 2100 Field Model except 2 barrels, 28" vent rib and 24" fully rifled deer. Weighs 6 to 6.5 lbs.; 48" overall. Choice TruGlo adj. sights or fixed cantilever mount on rifled barrel. Multi chokes.
Price: Walnut, rifle barrel **$609.00**
Price: Walnut, cantilever **$629.00**
Price: Synthetic **$579.00**

Traditions ALS 2100 Slug Hunter Shotgun
Similar to ALS 2100 Field Model, 12 ga., 24" barrel, overall length 44"; weighs 6.25 lbs. Designed specifically for the deer hunter. Rifled barrel has 1 in 36" twist. Fully adjustable fiber-optic sights.
Price: Walnut, rifle barrel **$529.00**
Price: Synthetic, rifle barrel **$499.00**
Price: Walnut, cantilever **$549.00**
Price: Synthetic, cantilever **$529.00**

Traditions ALS 2100 Home Security Shotgun
Similar to ALS 2100 Field Model, 12 ga., 20" barrel, overall length 40", weighs 6 lbs. Can be reloaded with one hand while shouldered and on-target. Swivel studs installed in stock.
Price: **$399.00**

TRISTAR CD DIANA AUTO SHOTGUNS
Gauge: 12, shoots 2-3/4" or 3" interchangeably. **Barrel:** 24", 26", 28" (Imp. Cyl., Mod., Full choke tubes). **Stock:** European walnut or black synthetic. **Features:** Gas-operated action; blued barrel; checkered pistol grip and forend; vent rib barrel. Available with synthetic and camo stock and in slug model. First introduced 1999 under the name "Tristar Phantom." Imported by Tristar Sporting Arms Ltd.
Price: . . . . **$399.00 to $535.00**

Weatherby SAS Field

Weatherby SAS Slug

Winchester X2 NWTF Turkey

Winchester Super X2 Sporting Clays

Winchester Super X3 Waterfowl

VERONA MODEL SX400 SEMI AUTO SHOTGUNS
Gauge: 12. **Barrel:** 26", 30". **Weight:** 6-1/2 lbs. **Stock:** Walnut, black composite. **Sights:** Red dot. **Features:** Aluminum receivers, gas-operated, 2-3/4" or 3" Magnum shells without adj. or Mod., 4 screw-in chokes and wrench included. Sling swivels, gold trigger. Blued barrel. Imported from Italy by B.C. Outdoors.
Price: 401S, 12 ga. **$398.40**
Price: 405SDS, 12 ga. **$610.00**
Price: 405L, 12 ga. **$331.20**

WEATHERBY SAS (SEMI-AUTOMATIC SHOTGUNS)
Gauge: 12 ga. **Barrel:** Vent ribbed, 24" to 30". **Weight:** 7 lbs. to 7-3/4 lbs. **Stock:** SAS field and sporting clays, walnut. SAS Shadow Grass, Break-Up™, Synthetic, composite. **Sights:** SAS sporting clays, brass front and mid-point rear. SAS Shadow Grass and Break-Up™, HiViz front and brass mid. Synthetic has brass front. **Features:** Easy to shoot, load, clean; lightweight, reduced recoil, IMC system includes 3 chrome-moly screw-in choke tubes. Slug gun has 22" rifled barrel with matte blue finish and cantilever base for scope mounting.
Price: Field, Sporting Clays, Shadow Grass, Break-Up™,
     Synthetic, Slug Gun . . . . **$879.00 to $969.00**

WINCHESTER SUPER X3 SHOTGUNS
Gauge: 12, 3" and 3.5" chambers. **Barrel:** 26", 28", .742" back-bored; Invector Plus choke tubes. **Weight:** 7 to 7.25 lbs. **Stock:** Composite, 14.25"x1.75"x2". Mossy Oak New Break-Up camo with Dura-Touch Armor Coating. Pachmayr Decelerator buttpad with hard heel insert, customizable length of pull. **Features:** Alloy magazine tube, gunmetal grey Perma-Cote UT finish, self-adjusting Active Valve gas action, lightweight recoil spring system. Electroless nickel-plated bolt, three choke tubes, two length-of-pull stock spacers, drop and cast adjustment spacers, sling swivel studs. Introduced 2006. Made in Belgium, assembled in Portugal by U.S. Repeating Arms Co.
Price: from **$945.00**
Price: Cantilever Deer. **$995.00**
Price: Waterfowl w/Mossy Oak Brush camo, intr. 2007 . . . . **$1,216.00**
Price: Field model, walnut stock, intr. 2007 . . . . **$979.00**

WINCHESTER SUPER X2 AUTO SHOTGUNS
Gauge: 12, 3", 3-1/2" chamber. **Barrel:** Belgian, 24", 26", 28"; Invector Plus choke tubes. **Weight:** 7-1/4 to 7-1/2 lbs. **Stock:** 14-1/4"x1-3/4"x2". Walnut or black synthetic. **Features:** Gas-operated action shoots all loads without adjustment; vent rib barrels; 4-shot magazine. Introduced 1999. Assembled in Portugal by U.S. Repeating Arms Co.
Price: Universal Hunter T **$1,252.00**
Price: NWTF Turkey, 3-1/2", Mossy Oak Break-Up camo **$1,236.00**
Price: Universal Hunter Model **$1,252.00**

Winchester Super X2 Sporting Clays Auto Shotguns
Similar to the Super X2 except has two gas pistons (one for target loads, one for heavy 3" loads), adjustable comb system and high-post rib. Back-bored barrel with Invector Plus choke tubes. Offered in 28" and 30" barrels. Introduced 2001. From U.S. Repeating Arms Co.
Price: Super X2 sporting clays **$999.00**
Price: Signature red stock **$1,015.00**
Price: Practical MK I, composite stock, TruGlo sights **$1,116.00**

Includes a wide variety of sporting guns and guns suitable for competitive shooting.

Benelli Supernova Pump Tactical Desert Camo

Benelli Nova Pump

Benelli Nova Pump Slug

Browning BPS 10 gauge

Browning BPS 10 gauge Mossy Oak Shadow Grass

BENELLI SUPERNOVA PUMP SHOTGUNS
Gauge: 12; 3.5" chamber. **Barrel:** 24", 26", 28". **Length:** 45.5-49.5". **Stock:** Synthetic; Max-4 , Timber, APG HD (2007). **Sights:** Red bar front, metal midbead. **Features:** 2-3/ 4", 3" chamber (3-1/2" 12 ga. only). Montefeltro rotating bolt design with dual action bars, magazine cut-off, synthetic trigger assembly, adjustable combs, shim kit, choice of buttstocks. 4-shot magazine. Introduced 2006. Imported from Italy by Benelli USA.
Price: Synthetic ComforTech **$455.00**
Price: Camo ComforTech **$545.00**
Price: SteadyGrip . . . . **$465.00 to $560.00**
Price: Tactical, Ghost Ring sight . . . . **$400.00 to $545.00**
Price: Field & Slug combo (2007) **$655.00**
Price: Rifled Slug ComforTech (2007) **$645.00**
Price: Tactical desert camo pistol grip, 18" barrel (2007) **$545.00**

BENELLI NOVA PUMP SHOTGUNS
Gauge: 12, 20. **Barrel:** 24", 26", 28". **Stock:** Black synthetic, Max-4, Timber and APG HD. **Sights:** Red bar. **Features:** 2-3/ 4", 3" chamber (3-1/2" 12 ga. only). Montefeltro rotating bolt design with dual action bars, magazine cut-off, synthetic trigger assembly, 4-shot magazine. Introduced 1999. Field & Slug Combo has 24" barrel and rifled bore; open rifle sights; synthetic stock; weighs 8.1 lbs. Imported from Italy by Benelli USA.
Price: Black synthetic stock **$360.00**
Price: Timber HD or Max-4 camo stock **$455.00**
Price: H20 model, black synthetic, matte nickel finish **$535.00**
Price: APG HD stock (2007) **$455.00**

Price: Tactical, 18.5" barrel, Ghost Ring sight **$375.00**
Price: Black synthetic stock, 20 ga. **$360.00**
Price: Black synthetic youth stock, 20 ga. **$375.00**
Price: Timber HD stock or APG HD stock (2007), 20 ga. **$455.00**
Price: Field & Slug Combo, black synthetic, cantilever mount **$560.00**

BROWNING BPS PUMP SHOTGUNS
Gauge: 10, 12, 3-1/2" chamber; 12 or 20, 3" chamber (2-3/4" in target guns), 28, 2-3/4" chamber, 5-shot magazine, .410, 3" chamber. **Barrel:** 10 ga.-24" Buck Special, 28", 30", 32" Invector; 12, 20 ga.-22", 24", 26", 28", 30", 32" (Imp. Cyl., Mod. or Full), .410-26" barrel. (Imp. Cyl., Mod. and Full choke tubes.) Also available with Invector choke tubes, 12 or 20 ga.; Upland Special has 22" barrel with Invector tubes. BPS 3" and 3-1/2" have back-bored barrel. **Weight:** 7 lbs., 8 oz. (28" barrel). **Length:** 48-3/4" overall (28" barrel). **Stock:** 14-1/4"x1-1/2"x2-1/2". Select walnut, semi-beavertail forend, full pistol grip stock. **Features:** All 12 gauge 3" guns except Buck Special and game guns have back-bored barrels with Invector Plus choke tubes. Bottom feeding and ejection, receiver top safety, high post vent rib. Double action bars eliminate binding. Vent rib barrels only. All 12 and 20 gauge guns with 3" chamber available with fully engraved receiver flats at no extra cost. Each gauge has its own unique game scene. Introduced 1977. Imported from Japan by Browning.
Price: 12 ga., 3-1/2" Stalker (black syn. stock) **$608.00**
Price: 12, 20 ga., Hunter, Invector Plus **$519.00**
Price: 20 ga. Deer Hunter (22" rifled bbl., cantilever mount),
     intr. 2007 . . . . **$651.00**
Price: 28 ga., Hunter, Invector **$555.00**
Price: .410, Hunter, Invector **$555.00**
Price: Trap, intr. 2007 . . . . **$663.00**

Browning BPS 10 gauge Camo Pump

Browning BPS Trap

Charles Daly Field Tactical

Charles Daly Maxi-Mag Turkey

BROWNING BPS 10 GAUGE CAMO PUMP SHOTGUN
Similar to the standard BPS except completely covered with Mossy Oak® Shadow Grass camouflage. Available with 24", 26", 28" barrel. Introduced 1999. Imported by Browning.
Price: **$709.00**

BROWNING BPS GAME GUN DEER HUNTER
Similar to the standard BPS except has newly designed receiver/magazine tube/barrel mounting system to eliminate play, heavy 20.5" barrel with rifle-type sights with adjustable rear, solid receiver scope mount, "rifle" stock dimensions for scope or open sights, sling swivel studs. Gloss or matte finished wood with checkering, polished blue metal. Introduced 1992.
Price: **$624.00**

BROWNING BPS STALKER PUMP SHOTGUN
Same gun as the standard BPS except all exposed metal parts have a matte blued finish and the stock has a durable black finish with a black recoil pad. Available in 10 ga. (3-1/2") and 12 ga. with 3" or 3-1/2" chamber, 22", 28", 30" barrel with Invector choke system. Introduced 1987.
Price: 12 ga., 3" chamber, Invector Plus. **$492.00**
Price: 10, 12 ga., 3-1/2" chamber **$596.00**

BROWNING BPS NWTF TURKEY SERIES PUMP SHOTGUN
Similar to the BPS Stalker except has full coverage Mossy Oak® Break-Up™ camo finish on synthetic stock, forearm and exposed metal parts. Offered in 10 and 12 gauge, 3" or 3-1/2" chamber; 24" bbl. has extra-full choke tube and HiViz fiber-optic sights. Introduced 2001. From Browning.
Price: 10 ga., 3-1/2" chamber **$775.00**
Price: 12 ga., 3-1/2" chamber **$760.00**
Price: 12 ga., 3" chamber **$636.00**

BROWNING BPS MICRO PUMP SHOTGUN
Similar to the BPS Stalker except 20 ga. only, 22" Invector barrel, stock has pistol grip with recoil pad. Length of pull is 13-1/4"; weighs 6 lbs., 12 oz. Introduced 1986.
Price: **$519.00**
Price: Micro Trap, intr. 2007. . . . . **$663.00**

CHARLES DALY FIELD PUMP SHOTGUNS
Gauge: 12, 20. Barrel: Interchangeable 18-1/2", 24", 26", 28", 30" multi-choked. Weight: NA. Stock: Synthetic, various finishes, recoil pad. Receiver: Machined aluminum. Features: Field Tactical and Slug models come with adustable sights; Youth models may be upgraded to full size. Imported from Akkar, Turkey.
Price: Field Tactical **$199.00**
Price: Field Hunter **$219.00**
Price: Field Hunter, Realtree Hardwood **$219.00**
Price: Field Hunter Advantage **$219.00**

CHARLES DALY MAXI-MAG PUMP SHOTGUNS
Gauge: 12 gauge, 3-1/2". Barrel: 24", 26", 28"; multi-choke system. Weight: NA. Stock: Synthetic black, Realtree Hardwoods, or Advantage Timber receiver, aluminum alloy. Features: Handles 2-3/4", 3" and 3-1/2" loads. Interchangeable ported barrels; Turkey package includes sling, HiViz sights, XX Full choke. Imported from Akkar, Turkey.
Price: Field Hunter **$259.00**
Price: Field Hunter Advantage **$319.00**
Price: Field Hunter Hardwoods **$319.00**
Price: Field Hunter Turkey **$389.00**

DIAMOND 12 GA. PUMP SHOTGUNS
Gauge: 12, 2-3/4" and 3" chambers. Barrel: 18"-30". Weight: 7 lbs. Stock: Walnut, synthetic. Features: Aluminum one-piece receiver sculpted for lighter weight. Double locking on fixed bolt. Gold, Elite and Panther series with vented barrels and 3 chokes. All series slug guns available (Gold and Elite with sights). Imported from Istanbul by ADCO Sales.
Price: Gold, 28" vent rib w/3 chokes, walnut **$359.00**
Price: Gold, 28", synthetic **$329.00**
Price: Gold Slug, 24" w/sights, walnut or synthetic . . . . **$329.00 to $359.00**
Price: Silver Mariner 18.5" Slug, synthetic **$399.00**
Price: Silver Mariner 22" vent rib w/3 chokes **$419.00**
Price: Elite, 22" slug w/sights; 24", 28" vent rib w/3 chokes,
    walnut . . . . **$329.00 to $349.00**
Price: Panther, 28", 30" vent rib w/3 chokes, synthetic **$279.00**
Price: Panther,18.5", 22" Slug, synthetic . . . . **$209.00 to $265.00**
Price: Imperial 12 ga., 28" vent rib w/3 chokes, 3.5" chamber,
    walnut . . . . **$$399.00**

Escort AimGuard

Escort Field Hunter

Mossberg Model 835 Mossy Oak Camo

Mossberg Model 500 Sporting

Mossberg Model 500 Bantam

E.M.F. OLD WEST PUMP (SLIDE ACTION) SHOTGUN
Gauge: 12. **Barrel:** 20". **Weight:** 7 lbs. **Length:** 39 1/2" overall. **Stock:** Smooth walnut with cushioned pad. **Sights:** Front bead. **Features:** Authentic reproduction of Winchester 1897 pump shotgun; blue receiver and barrel; standard modified choke. Introduced 2006. Imported from China for E.M.F. by TTN.
Price: $474.90

ESCORT PUMP SHOTGUNS
Gauge: 12, 20; 3" chamber. **Barrel:** 18" (AimGuard model); 22" (FH Slug model), 24", 26" and 28" (Field Hunter models), choke tubes (M, IC, F); turkey choke w/24" bbl. **Weight:** 6.4 to 7 lbs. **Stock:** Polymer, black chrome or camo finish. **Features:** Alloy receiver w/ dovetail for sight mounting. Two stock adjusting spacers included. Introduced 2003. From Legacy Sports International.
Price: Field Hunter, black stock $247.00
Price: Camo, 24" bbl. $363.00
Price: AimGuard, 20" bbl., black stock $211.00
Price: MarineGuard, nickel finish $254.00
Price: Combo (2 bbls.) $270.00

MOSSBERG MODEL 835 ULTI-MAG PUMP SHOTGUNS
Gauge: 12, 3-1/2" chamber. **Barrel:** Ported 24" rifled bore, 24", 28", Accu-Mag choke tubes for steel or lead shot. **Weight:** 7-3/4 lbs. **Length:** 48-1/2" overall. **Stock:** 14"x1-1/2"x2-1/2". Dual Comb. Cut-checkered hardwood or camo synthetic; both have recoil pad. **Sights:** White bead front, brass mid-bead; fiber-optic rear. **Features:** Shoots 2-3/4", 3" or 3-1/2" shells. Back-bored and ported barrel to reduce recoil, improve patterns. Ambidextrous thumb safety, twin extractors, dual slide bars. Mossberg Cablelock included. Introduced 1988.
Price: 28" vent rib, hardwood stock........................ $394.00
Price: Combos, 24" rifled or smooth bore, rifle sights, 24" vent rib Accu-Mag Ulti-Full choke tube, Mossy Oak® camo finish .. $556.00

Price: RealTree Camo Turkey, 24" vent rib, Accu-Mag extra-full tube, synthetic stock $574.00
Price: Mossy Oak® Camo, 28" vent rib, Accu-Mag tubes, synthetic stock $574.00
Price: OFM Camo, 28" vent rib, Accu-Mag Mod. tube, synthetic stock.................................... $438.00

Mossberg Model 835 Synthetic Stock Shotgun
Similar to the Model 835, except with 28" ported barrel with Accu-Mag Mod. choke tube, Parkerized finish, black synthetic stock and forend. Introduced 1998. Made in U.S. by Mossberg.
Price:. $394.00

MOSSBERG MODEL 500 SPORTING PUMP SHOTGUNS
Gauge: 12, 20, .410, 3" chamber. **Barrel:** 18-1/2" to 28" with fixed or Accu-Choke, plain or vent rib. **Weight:** 6-1/4 lbs. (.410), 7-1/4 lbs. (12). **Length:** 48" overall (28" barrel). **Stock:** 14"x1-1/2"x2-1/2". Walnut-stained hardwood. Cut-checkered grip and forend. **Sights:** White bead front, brass mid-bead; fiber-optic. **Features:** Ambidextrous thumb safety, twin extractors, disconnecting safety, dual action bars. Quiet Carry forend. Many barrels are ported. From Mossberg.
Price: From about $316.00
Price: Sporting Combos (field barrel and Slugster barrel). From .. $381.00

Mossberg Model 500 Bantam Pump Shotgun
Same as the Model 500 Sporting Pump except 12 or 20 gauge, 22" vent rib Accu-Choke barrel with choke tube set; has 1" shorter stock, reduced length from pistol grip to trigger, reduced forend reach. Introduced 1992.
Price:. $316.00
Price: With Realtree Hardwoods camouflage finish (20 ga. only) .. $364.00

Mossberg Model 500 Camo Pump Shotgun
Same as the Model 500 Sporting Pump except 12 gauge only and entire gun is covered with Mossy Oak® Advantage camouflage finish. Receiver drilled and tapped for scope mounting. Comes with quick detachable swivel studs, swivels, camouflage sling, Mossberg Cablelock.
Price: From about $364.00

New England Pardner Pump

Remington 870 Wingmaster

Remington Model 870 Marine Magnum

Remington Model 870 XCS

Remington Model 870 Wingmaster LW

Mossberg Model 500 Persuader/Cruiser Shotguns
Similar to Mossberg Model 500 except has 18-1/2" or 20" barrel with cylinder bore choke, synthetic stock and blue or Parkerized finish. Available in 12, 20 and .410 with bead or ghost ring sights, 6- or 8-shot magazines. From Mossberg.
Price: 12 gauge, 20" barrel, 8-shot, bead sight. **$357.00**
Price: 20 gauge or .410, 18-1/2" barrel, 6-shot, bead sight **$357.00**
Price: Home Security 410 (.410, 18-1/2" barrel with
     spreader choke) **$360.00**

Mossberg Model 590 Special Purpose Shotgun
Similar to Model 500 except has Parkerized or Marinecote finish, 9-shot magazine and black synthetic stock (some models feature Speed Feed). Available in 12 gauge only with 20", cylinder bore barrel. Weighs 7-1/4 lbs. From Mossberg.
Price: Bead sight, heat shield over barrel **$525.00**

NEW ENGLAND PARDNER PUMP SHOTGUN
Gauge: 12 ga., 3". **Barrel:** 28" vent rib, screw-in Modified choke tube. **Weight:** 7-1/2 lbs. **Length:** 48-1/2". **Stock:** American walnut, grooved forend, ventilated recoil pad. **Sights:** Bead front. **Features:** Machined steel receiver, double action bars, five-shot magazine.
Price: **$200.00**

REMINGTON MODEL 870 WINGMASTER SHOTGUNS
Gauge: 12 ga., 16 ga., 3" chamber. **Barrel:** 26", 28", 30" (RemChokes). **Weight:** 7-1/4 lbs. **Length:** 46", 48". **Stock:** Walnut, hardwood, synthetic. **Sights:** Single bead (Twin bead Wingmaster). **Features:** Light contour barrel. Double action bars, cross-bolt safety, blue finish.

Price: Wingmaster, walnut, blued, 26", 28", 30" **$755.00**
Price: 870 Wingmaster Super Magnum, 3-1/2" chamber, 28" **$732.00**

Remington Model 870 Classic Trap Shotgun
Similar to Model 870 Wingmaster except has 30" vent rib, light contour barrel, singles, mid- and long-handicap choke tubes, semi-fancy American walnut stock, high-polish blued receiver with engraving. Chamber 2.75". From Remington Arms Co.
Price: **$989.00**

Remington Model 870 Marine Magnum Shotgun
Similar to 870 Wingmaster except all metal plated with electroless nickel, black synthetic stock and forend. Has 18" plain barrel (cyl.), bead front sight, 7-shot magazine. Introduced 1992. XCS version with TriNyte corrosion control introduced 2007.
Price: **$733.00**
Price: XCS (intr. 2007). **$848.00**

Remington Model 870 Wingmaster LW Shotgun
Similar to Model 870 Wingmaster except in 28 gauge and .410-bore only, 25" vent rib barrel with RemChoke tubes, high-gloss wood finish.
Price: .410-bore **$788.00**
Price: 28 gauge **$849.00**

Remington Model 870 Express Shotguns
Similar to Model 870 Wingmaster except walnut-toned hardwood stock with solid, black recoil pad and pressed checkering on grip and forend. Outside metal surfaces have black oxide finish. Comes with 26" or 28" vent rib barrel with mod. RemChoke tube.
Price: 12 ga., 20 ga., 16 ga. (28") **$373.00**
Price: Express Combo, 12 ga., 26" vent rib with mod.
     RemChoke and 20" fully rifled barrel with rifle
     sights, or RemChoke . . . . **$507.00 to $543.00**
Price: Express Synthetic, 12-ga., 26" or 28" **$373.00**
Price: Express Synthetic, 20 ga., 18" barrel (2007) **$388.00**

Remington Model 870 Express Super Magnum Waterfowl

Remington Model 870 Express Super Magnum

Remington Model 870 Express Deer Gun

Remington Model 870 Express Youth Turkey Camo

Remington Model 870 SPS-T Camo

Remington Model 870 Express Deer Shotguns
Same as Model 870 Express except 20" barrel with fixed imp. cyl. choke, open iron sights, Monte Carlo stock. Introduced 1991.
Price: **$416.00**
Price: With fully rifled barrel **$385.00**

Remington Model 870 Express Turkey Shotguns
Same as Model 870 Express except 3" chamber, 21" vent rib turkey barrel and extra-full Rem. choke turkey tube; 12 ga. only. Introduced 1991.
Price: **$359.00**
Price: Express Turkey Camo stock has Skyline Excel camo, matte black metal **$412.00**
Price: Express Turkey Youth Camo **$445.00**

Remington Model 870 Express Synthetic 18" Shotgun
Similar to Model 870 Express with 18" barrel except synthetic stock and forend; 7-shot. Introduced 1994.
Price: **$332.00**

REMINGTON MODEL 870 SPS SUPER MAGNUM CAMO SHOTGUN
Gauge: 12, 3-1/2" chamber. **Barrel:** 26", 28", vent rib, with Full, Mod., Imp. Cyl. RemChoke. **Weight:** 7-1/4 lbs. to 7-1/2 lbs. **Length:** 46" to 481/2" overall. **Stock:** Mossy Oak® Break-Up™ camo finish. **Sights:** Metal bead front. **Features:** Synthetic stock and all metal (except bolt and trigger guard) and stock covered with Mossy Oak® Break-Up™ camo finish. Comes with camo sling, swivels.
Price: **$741.00**
Price: Max Gobbler, Realtree All-Purpose Green HD (2007) **$799.00**

STOEGER MODEL P350 SHOTGUNS
Gauge: 12, 3.5" chamber, set of five choke tubes (C, IC, M, IM, XF). **Barrel:** 18.5",24", 26", 28". **Stock:** Black synthetic, Timber HD, Max-4 HD, APG HD camos. **Sights:** Red bar front. **Features:** Inertia-recoil, mercury recoil reducer, pistol grip stocks. Imported by Benelli USA.
Price: Synthetic **$290.00**
Price: Max-4, Timber HD **$350.00**
Price: Black synthetic pistol grip (2007) **$325.00**
Price: APG HD camo pistol grip (2007) **$350.00**

Remington Model 870 Express Super Magnum Shotgun
Similar to Model 870 Express except 28" vent rib barrel with 3-1/2" chamber, vented recoil pad. Introduced 1998.
Price: . . . . — **$420.00**
Price: Super Magnum synthetic, 26" **$420.00**
Price: Super Magnum turkey camo (full-coverage RealTree Advantage camo), 23" **$513.00**
Price: Super Magnum combo (26" with Mod. RemChoke and 20" fully rifled deer barrel with 3" chamber and rifle sights; wood stock) **$579.00**
Price: Super Magnum synthetic turkey, 23" (black) . . . . **$$435.00**
Price: Super Magnum Waterfowl camo, Mossy Oak Duck Blind, 30" (2007) **$559.00**

Remington Model 870 Wingmaster Super Magnum Shotgun
Similar to Model 870 Express Super Magnum except high-polish blued finish, 28" ventilated barrel with Imp. Cyl., Modified and Full choke tubes, checkered high-gloss walnut stock. Overall length 48", weighs 7-1/2 lbs. Introduced 2000.
Price: 3-1/2" chamber **$732.00**

Remington Model 870 SPS-T Super Magnum Camo Shotguns
Similar to the Model 870 Express synthetic, chambered for 12 ga., 3" shells, has Mossy Oak® Break-Up™ synthetic stock and metal treatment, TruGlo fiber-optic sights. Introduced 2001. SPS Max Gobbler introduced 2007. Knoxx SpecOps adjustable stock, Williams Fire Sights fiber-optic sights, R3 recoil pad, Realtree APG HD camo. Drilled and tapped for Weaver-style rail
Price: 20" RS, Rem. choke **$653.00**
Price: SPS Super Mag Max Gobbler (2007) **$799.00**

Includes a variety of game guns and guns for competitive shooting.

Beretta DT Trident Skeet

Beretta Series 682 Gold E Sporting

Beretta Series 682 Gold E Trap Combo

Beretta 686 Onyx

Beretta Silver Pigeon 686S

BERETTA DT10 TRIDENT SHOTGUNS
Gauge: 12, 2-3/4", 3" chambers. **Barrel:** 28", 30", 32", 34"; competition-style vent rib; fixed or Optima choke tubes. **Weight:** 7.9 to 9 lbs. **Stock:** High-grade walnut stock with oil finish; hand-checkered grip and forend, adjustable stocks available. **Features:** Detachable, adjustable trigger group, raised and thickened receiver, forend iron has adjustment nut to guarantee wood-to-metal fit. Introduced 2000. Imported from Italy by Beretta USA.
Price: DT10 Trident Trap (selective, lockable single trigger,
    adjustable stock. **$8,500.00**
Price: DT10 Trident Top Single **$10,790.00**
Price: DT10 Trident X Trap Combo
    (single and o/u barrels) **$11,040.00**
Price: DT10 Trident Skeet (skeet stock with rounded recoil
    pad, tapered rib) **$8,030.00**
Price: DT10 Trident Sporting (sporting clays stock with
    rounded recoil pad) **$7,850.00**
Price: DT10L Sporting **$8,475.00**

BERETTA SERIES 682 GOLD E SKEET, TRAP, SPORTING O/U SHOTGUNS
Gauge: 12, 2-3/4" chambers. **Barrel:** skeet-28"; trap-30" and 32", Imp. Mod. & Full and Mobilchoke; trap mono shotguns-32" and 34" Mobilchoke; trap top single guns-32" and 34" Full and Mobilchoke; trap combo sets-from 30" O/U, to 32" O/U, 34" top single. **Stock:** Close-grained walnut, hand checkered. **Sights:** White Bradley bead front sight and center bead. **Features:** Receiver has Greystone gunmetal gray finish with gold accents. Trap Monte Carlo stock has deluxe trap recoil pad. Various grades available. Imported from Italy by Beretta USA.
Price: 682 Gold E Trap with adjustable stock **$4,325.00**
Price: 682 Gold E Trap Top Combo **$5,475.00**
Price: 682 Gold E Sporting **$3,550.00**
Price: 682 Gold E skeet, adjustable stock **$4,325.00**

BERETTA 686 ONYX O/U SHOTGUNS
Gauge: 12, 20, 28; 3", 3.5" chambers. **Barrel:** 26", 28" (Mobilchoke tubes). **Weight:** 6.8-6.9 lbs. **Stock:** Checkered American walnut. **Features:** Intended for the beginning sporting clays shooter. Has wide, vented target rib, radiused recoil pad. Polished black finish on receiver and barrels. Introduced 1993. Imported from Italy by Beretta U.S.A.
Price: White Onyx **$1,875.00**
Price: Onyx Pro **$1,875.00**
Price: Onyx Pro 3.5 . . . . **$1,975.00**

BERETTA SILVER PIGEON O/U SHOTGUNS
Gauge: 12, 20, 28, 3" chambers (2-3/4" 28 ga.). .410 bore, 3" chamber. **Barrel:** 26", 28". **Weight:** 6.8 lbs. **Stock:** Checkered walnut. **Features:** Interchangeable barrels (20 and 28 ga.), single selective gold-plated trigger, boxlock action, auto safety, Schnabel forend.
Price: Silver Pigeon S. **$2,150.00**
Price: Silver Pigeon S Combo **$2,975.00**
Price: Silver Pigeon II **$2,525.00**
Price: Silver Pigeon II, 28 ga. **$3,475.00**
Price: Silver Pigeon III **$2,650.00**
Price: Silver Pigeon IV **$2,955.00**
Price: Silver Pigeon V **$3,495.00**

Beretta Silver Pigeon S Combo

Beretta Ultralight

Beretta Ultralight Deluxe

Beretta S687 Silver Pigeon II Sporting

Beretta S687 EELL Combo

Beretta SO9

BERETTA ULTRALIGHT O/U SHOTGUNS
Gauge: 12, 2-3/4" chambers. **Barrel:** 26", 28", Mobilchoke tubes. **Weight:** About 5 lbs., 13 oz. **Stock:** Select American walnut with checkered grip and forend. **Features:** Low-profile aluminum alloy receiver with titanium breech face insert. Electroless nickel receiver with game scene engraving. Single selective trigger; automatic safety. Introduced 1992. Ultralight Deluxe except has matte electroless nickel finish receiver with gold game scene engraving; matte oil-finished, select walnut stock and forend. Imported from Italy by Beretta U.S.A.

Price: **$1,975.00**
Price: Ultralight Deluxe **$2,350.00**

BERETTA COMPETITION SHOTGUNS
Gauge: 12, 20, 28, and .410 bore, 2-3/4", 3" and 3-1/2" chambers. **Barrel:** 26" and 28" (Mobilchoke tubes). **Stock:** Close-grained walnut. **Features:** Highly-figured, American walnut stocks and forends, and a unique, weather-resistant finish on barrels. Silver designates standard 686, 687 models with silver receivers; 686 Silver Pigeon has enhanced engraving pattern, Schnabel forend; Gold indicates higher grade 686EL, 687EL models with full sideplates; Diamond is for 687EELL models with highest

grade wood, engraving. Case provided with Gold and Diamond grades. Imported from Italy by Beretta U.S.A.

Price: S687 Silver Pigeon II Sporting **$2,850.00**
Price: S687 EL Gold Pigeon II (deep relief engraving) **$5,095.00**
Price: S687 EL Gold Pigeon II combo, 20/28 or 28/.410 ...... **$6,195.00**
Price: S687 EELL Gold Pigeon Sporting (D.R. engraving) **$6,495.00**
Price: Gold Sporting Pigeon **$4,971.00**
Price: 28 and 410 combo .... **NA**

BERETTA MODEL SO5, SO6, SO9 SHOTGUNS
Gauge: 12, 2-3/4" chambers. **Barrel:** To customer specs. **Stock:** To customer specs. **Features:** SO5-trap, skeet and sporting clays models SO5; SO6-SO6 and SO6 EELL are field models. SO6 has a case-hardened or silver receiver with contour hand engraving. SO6 EELL has hand-engraved receiver in a fine floral or "fine English" pattern or game scene, with bas-relief chisel work and gold inlays. SO6 and SO6 EELL are available with sidelocks removable by hand. Imported from Italy by Beretta U.S.A.

Price: SO5 Trap, skeet, Sporting **$13,000.00**
Price: SO6 Trap, skeet, Sporting **$17,500.00**
Price: SO6 EELL Field, custom specs **$28,000.00**
Price: SO9 (12, 20, 28, .410, 26", 28", 30", any choke) **$31,000.00**

Browning Cynergy Sporting

Browning Cynergy Feather

Browning Cynergy Euro Sporting Composite

Browning Citori White Lightning

Browning Lightning Feather

Browning Citori 525 Feather

BROWNING CYNERGY O/U SHOTGUNS
Gauge: 12, 20, 28. **Barrel:** 26", 28", 30", 32". **Stock:** Walnut or composite. **Sights:** White bead front most models; HiViz Pro-Comp sight on some models; mid bead. **Features:** Mono-Lock hinge, recoil-reducing interchangeable Inflex recoil pad, silver nitride receiver; striker-based trigger, ported barrel option. 12 models cataloged for 2006. Nine new models introduced 2006: Cynergy Sporting, Adjustable Comb; Cynergy Sporting Composite with TopCote; Cynergy Sporting Composite CF; Cynergy Field, Composite; Cynergy Classic Sporting; Cynergy Classic Field; Cynergy Camo Mossy Oak New Shadow Grass; Cynergy Camo Mossy Oak New Break-Up; and Cynergy Camo Mossy Oak Brush. Imported from Japan by Browning.

Price: Cynergy Field, 12 ga., Grade 1 walnut,	**$2,048.00**
Price: Cynergy Field Small Gauge, 20 /28 ga., intr. 2005	**$2,062.00**
Price: Cynergy Sporting Small Gauge, 20 /28 ga., intr. 2005	**$3,080.00**
Price: Cynergy Field Composite, 12 ga.,	**$1,890.00**
Price: Cynergy Sporting, 12 ga.; 28", 30", or 32" barrels	**$3,046.00**
Price: Cynergy Sporting Composite 12 ga.	**$2,846.00**
Price: Cynergy Sporting, adjustable comb, intr. 2006	**$3,351.00**
Price: Cynergy Sporting Composite w/TopCote, intr. 2006	**$2,979.00**
Price: Cynergy Feather, intr. 2007	**$2,359.00**
Price: Cynergy Euro Sporting Composite, intr. 2007	**$3,199.00**

BROWNING CITORI O/U SHOTGUNS
Gauge: 12, 20, 28 and .410. **Barrel:** 26", 28" in 28 and .410. Offered with Invector choke tubes. All 12 and 20 gauge models have back-bored barrels and Invector Plus choke system. **Weight:** 6 lbs., 8 oz. (26" .410) to 7 lbs., 13 oz. (30" 12 ga.). **Length:** 43" overall (26" bbl.). **Stock:** Dense walnut, hand checkered, full pistol grip, beavertail forend. Field-type recoil pad on 12 ga. field guns and trap and skeet models. **Sights:** Medium raised beads, German nickel silver. **Features:** Barrel selector integral with safety, automatic ejectors, three-piece takedown. 25 models cataloged for 2006. Two limited-run models reintroduced 2006: Citori 4-Barrel Skeet Set, Grade I; Citori 4-Barrel Skeet Set, Grade VII. Imported from Japan by Browning.

Price: Lightning, 12 and 20 ga..	**$1,645.00**
Price: Lightning, 28 ga. and .410 bore	**$1,709.00**
Price: White Lightning, 12 and 20 ga.	**$1,714.00**
Price: White Lightning, 28 ga. and .410 bore	**$1,790.00**
Price: 525 Field, 12 and 20 ga..	**$1,981.00**
Price: 525 Field, 28 ga. and .410 bore.	**$2,010.00**
Price: Superlight Feather, 12 and 20 ga. (2-3/4"), 6.25/5.7 lbs.	**$1,938.00**
Price: Lightning Feather, 12 and 20 ga.,	**$1,869.00**
Price: Citori 4-Barrel Skeet Set, Grade I, intr. 2006	**$8,412.00**
Price: 525 Feather, 12 ga. intr. 2007	**$2,212.00**

Browning Citori Grade VII Lightning

Browning Citori GTS High Grade

Browning Citori XS Special

Browning Citori 525 Sporting Clays

Browning Citori High Post Rib

Browning Citori XT Trap

Browning Citori High Grade Shotguns
Similar to standard Citori except has engraved hunting scenes and gold inlays, high-grade, hand-oiled walnut stock and forearm. Introduced 2000. From Browning.

Price: Gran Lightning, engraved receiver, from **$2,429.00**
Price: Grade IV Lightning, engraved gray receiver,
    introduced 2005, from **$2,608.00**
Price: Grade VII Lightning, engraved gray or blue receiver,
    introduced 2005, from **$4,146.00**
Price: GTS High Grade, intr. 2007 .... **$3,900.00**

Browning Citori XS Sporting O/U Shotguns
Similar to the standard Citori except available in 12, 20, 28 or .410 with 28", 30", 32" ported barrels with various screw-in choke combinations: S (Skeet), C (Cylinder), IC (Improved Cylinder), M (Modified), and IM (Improved Modified). Has pistol grip stock, rounded or Schnabel forend. Weighs 7.1 lbs. to 8.75 lbs. Introduced 2004.

Price: XS Special, 12 ga.; 30", 32" barrels **$2,727.00**
Price: XS Sporting, 12 or 20 ga. **$2,472.00**

Price: XS Skeet, 12 or 20 ga. **$2,434.00**
Price: 525 Sporting Grade I, 12 ga. intr. 2005 .... **$2,319.00**
Price: 525 Golden Clays, 12 or 20 gauge **$3,058.00**
Price: 525 Golden Clays, 28 or .410 .... **$4,653.00**
Price: High Post Rib, intr. 2007........................... **$2,865.00**

Browning Citori XT Trap O/U Shotgun
Similar to the Citori XS Special except has engraved silver nitride receiver with gold highlights, vented side barrel rib. Available in 12 gauge with 30" or 32" barrels, Invector-Plus choke tubes, adjustable comb and buttplate. Introduced 1999. Imported by Browning.

Price: XT Trap **$2,390.00**
Price: XT Trap w/adjustable comb **$2,678.00**
Price: XT Trap Gold w/adjustable comb, introduced 2005 ..... **$4,435.00**

CENTURION O/U SHOTGUN
Gauge: 12, 2-3/4 & 3" chambers, 20, 28, 410. **Barrel:** 28", 5 choke tubes. **Weight:** 7.35 lbs. (12); 6.14 lbs. (20); 5.8 lbs. (28); 5.3 lbs. (410). **Length:** 45". **Stock:** Glossy Turkish walnut. **Features:** Single selective trigger, automatic safety, extractors, ventilated recoil pad, front bead sight. Manufactured by CFS in Turkey. Imported by Century International.
Price:.. **$470.00**

Charles Daly Superior II Trap AE-MC

Charles Daly Field Hunter

Charles Daly Superior Hunter

Charles Daly Empire II Mono Trap

Charles Daly Empire II
EDL Hunter

CHARLES DALY SUPERIOR II TRAP AE-MC O/U SHOTGUN
Gauge: 12, 2-3/4" chambers. **Barrel:** 30" choke tubes. **Weight:** About 7 lbs. **Length:** 47-3/8". **Stock:** Checkered walnut; pistol grip, semi-beavertail forend. **Features:** Silver engraved receiver, chrome-moly steel barrels; gold single selective trigger; automatic safety, automatic ejectors; red bead front sight, metal bead center; recoil pad. Introduced 1997. Imported from Italy by K.B.I., Inc.
Price: **$1,699.00**

CHARLES DALY FIELD II HUNTER O/U SHOTGUN
Gauge: 12, 20, 28 and .410 bore (3" chambers, 28 ga. has 2-3/4"). **Barrel:** 28" Mod & Full, 26" Imp. Cyl. & Mod (.410 is Full & Full). **Weight:** About 7 lbs. **Length:** 42-3/4" to 44-3/4". **Stock:** Checkered walnut pistol grip and forend. **Features:** Blued engraved receiver, chrome-moly steel barrels; gold single selective trigger; automatic safety; extractors; gold bead front sight. Introduced 1997. Imported from Italy by K.B.I., Inc.
Price: 12 or 20 ga. **$1,029.00**
Price: 28 ga., .410 bore **$1,129.00**

Charles Daly Superior II Hunter AE O/U Shotgun
Similar to the Field Hunter AE except has silvered, engraved receiver. Introduced 1997. Imported from Italy by F.B.I., Inc.
Price: 28 ga., .410 bore. **$1,519.00**

Charles Daly Field Hunter AE-MC O/U Shotgun
Similar to the Field Hunter except in 12 or 20 only, 26" or 28" barrels with five multi-choke tubes; automatic ejectors. Introduced 1997. Imported from Italy by K.B.I., Inc.
Price: 12 or 20 ga. **$1,279.00**

Charles Daly Superior II Sporting O/U Shotgun
Similar to the Field Hunter AE-MC except 28" or 30" barrels; silvered, engraved receiver; five choke tubes; ported barrels; red bead front sight. Introduced 1997. Imported from Italy by K.B.I., Inc.
Price: **$1,659.00**

CHARLES DALY EMPIRE II EDL HUNTER AE, AE-MC O/U SHOTGUNS
Gauge: 12, 20, .410, 3" chambers, 28 ga., 2-3/4". **Barrel:** 26", 28" (12, 20, choke tubes), 26" (Imp. Cyl. & Mod., 28 ga.), 26" (Full & Full, .410). **Weight:** About 7 lbs. **Stocks:** Checkered walnut pistol grip buttstock, semi-beavertail forend; recoil pad. **Features:** Silvered, engraved receiver; chrome-moly barrels; gold single selective trigger; automatic safety; automatic ejectors; red bead front sight, metal bead middle sight. Introduced 1997. Imported from Italy by K.B.I., Inc.
Price: Empire II EDL AE-MC (dummy sideplates) 12 or 20 . . . . . . **$2,029.00**
Price: Empire II EDL AE, 28 . . . . **$2,019.00**
Price: Empire II EDL AE, .410 . . . . **$2,019.00**

Charles Daly Empire II Sporting AE-MC O/U Shotgun
Similar to the Empire II EDL Hunter except 12 or 20 gauge only, 28", 30" barrels with choke tubes; ported barrels; special stock dimensions. Introduced 1997. Imported from Italy by K.B.I., Inc.
Price: **$2,049.00**

CHARLES DALY EMPIRE II TRAP AE-MC O/U SHOTGUNS
Gauge: 12, 2-3/4" chambers. **Barrel:** 30" choke tubes. **Weight:** About 7 lbs. **Stock:** Checkered walnut; pistol grip, semi-beavertail forend. **Features:** Silvered, engraved, reinforced receiver; chrome-moly steel barrels; gold single selective trigger; automatic safety, automatic ejector; red bead front sight, metal bead center; recoil pad. Imported from Italy by K.B.I., Inc.
Price: **$2,099.00**
Price: Mono AE-MC, adj. comb **$2,999.00**
Price: AE-MC combo set, adj. comb **$3,919.00**

Charles Daly Empire Sporting O/U

Charles Daly Diamond Regent GTX DL

CZ Canvasback

CZ Mallard

CZ Redhead

CHARLES DALY DIAMOND REGENT GTX DL HUNTER O/U SHOTGUNS

Gauge: 12, 20, .410, 3" chambers, 28, 2-3/4" chambers. **Barrel:** 26", 28", 30" (choke tubes), 26" (Imp. Cyl. & Mod. in 28, 26" (Full & Full) in .410. **Weight:** About 7 lbs. **Stock:** Extra select fancy European walnut with 24" hand checkering, hand rubbed oil finish. **Features:** Boss-type action with internal side lumps. Deep cut hand-engraved scrollwork and game scene set in full sideplates. GTX detachable single selective trigger system with coil springs; chrome-moly steel barrels; automatic safety; automatic ejectors, white bead front sight, metal bead center sight. Introduced 1997. Imported from Italy by K.B.I., Inc.

Price: 12 or 20 . . . . **Special order only**
Price: 28 . . . . **Special order only**
Price: .410 bore . . . . **Special order only**
Price: Diamond Regent GTX EDL Hunter (as above with engraved scroll and birds, 10 gold inlays), 12 or 20 . . . . . . **Special order only**
Price: As above, 28 . . . . **Special order only**
Price: As above, .410 . . . . **Special order only**

CHARLES DALY DIAMOND GTX SPORTING O/U SHOTGUN

Gauge: 12, 20, 3" chambers. **Barrel:** 28", 30" with choke tubes. **Weight:** About 8.5 lbs. **Stock:** Checkered deluxe walnut; sporting clays dimensions. Pistol grip; semi-beavertail forend; hand rubbed oil finish. **Features:** Chromed, hand-engraved receiver; chrome-moly steel barrels; GTX detachable single selective trigger system with coil springs, automatic safety; automatic ejectors; red bead front sight; ported barrels. Introduced 1997. Imported from Italy by K.B.I., Inc.

Price: . . . . **Price on request**

CHARLES DALY DIAMOND GTX TRAP AE-MC O/U SHOTGUN

Gauge: 12, 2-3/4" chambers. **Barrel:** 30" (Full & Full). **Weight:** About 8.5 lbs. **Stock:** Checkered deluxe walnut; pistol grip; trap dimensions; semi-beavertail forend; hand-rubbed oil finish. **Features:** Silvered, hand-engraved receiver; chrome-moly steel barrels; GTX detachable single selective trigger system with coil springs, automatic safety, automatic ejectors, red bead front sight, metal bead middle; recoil pad. Imported from Italy by K.B.I., Inc.

Price: . . . . **Price on request**

CHARLES DALY DIAMOND GTX DL HUNTER O/U SHOTGUN

Gauge: 12, 20, .410, 3" chambers, 28, 2-3/4" chambers. **Barrel:** 26", 28", choke tubes in 12 and 20 ga., 26" (Imp. Cyl. & Mod.), 26" (Full & Full) in .410-bore. **Weight:** About 8.5 lbs. **Stock:** Select fancy European walnut stock, with 24 lpi hand checkering; hand-rubbed oil finish. **Features:** Boss-type action with internal side lugs, hand-engraved scrollwork and game scene. GTX detachable single selective trigger system with coil springs; chrome-moly steel barrels, automatic safety, automatic ejectors, red bead front sight, recoil pad. Introduced 1997. Imported from Italy by K.B.I., Inc.

Price: . . . . **Special order only**

CZ CANVASBACK

Gauge: 12, 20, 3" chambers. **Barrel:** 26", 28". **Weight:** 7.3 lbs. **Length:** NA. **Stock:** NA. **Features:** Single selective trigger, set of 5 screw-in chokes, black chrome finished receiver, Schnable forend. From CZ-USA.

Price: **$708.00**

CZ MALLARD

Gauge: 12, 20, 28, .410, 3" chambers. **Barrel:** 26". **Weight:** 7.7 lbs. **Length:** NA. **Stock:** NA. **Features:** Double triggers and extractors, coin finished receiver, Schnable forend, multi chokes. From CZ-USA.

Price: **$487.00**

CZ REDHEAD

Gauge: 12, 20, 3" chambers. **Barrel:** 28". **Weight:** 7.4 lbs. **Length:** NA. **Stock:** NA. **Features:** Single selective triggers and extractors (12 & 20 ga.), screw-in chokes (12, 20, 28 ga.) choked IC and Mod (.410), coin finished receiver, Schnable forend, multi chokes. From CZ-USA.

Price: **$836.00**

CZ Woodcock

Franchi Renaissance Classic

Franchi Renaissance

Franchi Renaissance

Hoenig Rotary Game

HOENIG ROTARY ROUND ACTION GAME GUN O/U SHOTGUN
Gauge: 20, 28. **Barrel:** 26", 28", solid tapered rib. **Weight:** 6 lbs. and 6-1/4 lbs. **Stock:** English walnut to customer specifications. **Features:** Round action opens by rotating barrels, pulling forward. Inertia extraction system, rotary wing safety blocks strikers. Simple takedown without removing forend. Introduced 1997. Made in U.S.A. by George Hoenig.
Price: **$20,000.00**

KIMBER MARIAS O/U SHOTGUNS
Gauge: 12, 20; 3". **Barrel:** 26", 28", 30". **Weight:** 7.4 lbs. **Length:** NA. **Stock:** Turkish walnut stocks, 24-lpi checkering, oil finish. LOP: 14.75 inches. **Features:** Hand-detachable back-action sidelock, bone-charcoal case coloring. Hand-engraving on receiver and locks, Belgian rust blue barrels, chrome lined. Five thinwall choke tubes, automatic ejectors, ventilated rib. Gold line cocking indicators on locks. Grade I has 28-inch barrels, Prince of Wales stock in grade three Turkish walnut in either 12 or 20 gauge. Grade II shas grade four Turkish walnut stocks, 12 gauge in Prince of Wales and 20 with either Prince of Wales or English profiles. Imported from Italy by Kimber Mfg., Inc.
Price: Grade I . . . . **NA**
Price: Grade II . . . . **NA**

KOLAR SPORTING CLAYS O/U SHOTGUNS
Gauge: 12, 2-3/4" chambers. **Barrel:** 30", 32", 34"; extended choke tubes. **Stock:** 14-5/8"x2-1/2"x1-7/8"x1-3/8". French walnut. Four stock versions available. **Features:** Single selective trigger, detachable, adjustable for length; overbored barrels with long forcing cones; flat tramline rib; matte blue finish. Made in U.S. by Kolar.
Price: Standard. **$8,995.00**
Price: Elite **$12,495.00**
Price: Elite Gold **$15,295.00**
Price: Legend **$15,995.00**
Price: Select **$18,995.00**
Price: Custom . . . . **Price on request**

CZ WOODCOCK
Gauge: 12, 20, 28, .410, 3" chambers. **Barrel:** 26". **Weight:** 7.7 lbs. **Length:** NA. **Stock:** NA. **Features:** Single selective triggers and extractors (auto ejectors on 12 & 20 ga.), screw-in chokes (12, 20, 28 ga.) choked IC and Mod (.410), coin finished receiver, Schnable forend, multi chokes. The sculptured frame incorporates a side plate, resembling a true side lock, embellished with hand engraving and finished wtih color casehardening. From CZ-USA.
Price: **$1,078.00**

FRANCHI RENAISSANCE AND RENAISSANCE SPORTING O/U SHOTGUNS
Gauge: 12, 20, 28, 3" chamber. **Barrel:** 26", 28". **Weight:** 5.0 to 6.0 lbs. **Length:** 42 5/8" to 44 5/8". **Stock:** 14.5" LOP, European oil-finished walnut with standard grade A grade, and AA grade choices. Prince of Wales grip. **Features:** TSA recoil pad, interchangeable chokes, hard case. Introduced 2006. Sporting model : **Gauge:** 12, 3". **Barrel:** 30" ported. **Weight:** 7.9 lbs. **Length:** 46 5/8". **Stock:** 14.5" LOP, A-grade European oil-finished walnut. **Features:** TSA recoil pad, adjustable comb, lengthened forcing cones, extended choke tubes (C, IC, M and wrench), hard case. Introduced 2007. Imported from Italy by Benelli USA.
Price: Field **$1,320.00**
Price: Classic **$1,545.00**
Price: Elite. **$2,110.00**
Price: Sporting **$2,039.00**

Kolar Sporting Clays

Krieghoff K-80 Sporting Clays

Ljutic LM-6 Super Deluxe

Marlin L. C. Smith 12 gauge

Kolar AAA Competition Trap O/U Shotgun
Similar to the Sporting Clays gun except has 32" O/U /34" Unsingle or 30" O/U /34" Unsingle barrels as an over/under, unsingle, or combination set. Stock dimensions are 14-1/2"x2-1/2"x1-1/2"; American or French walnut; step parallel rib standard. Contact maker for full listings. Made in U.S.A. by Kolar.
Price: Over/under, choke tubes, standard **$9,595.00**
Price: Unsingle, choke tubes, standard **$10,195.00**
Price: Combo (30"/34", 32"/34"), standard **$12,595.00**

Kolar AAA Competition Skeet O/U Shotgun
Similar to the Sporting Clays gun except has 28" or 30" barrels with Kolarite AAA sub gauge tubes; stock of American or French walnut with matte finish; flat tramline rib; under barrel adjustable for point of impact. Many options available. Contact maker for complete listing. Made in U.S.A. by Kolar.
Price: Standard, choke tubes **$10,495.00**
Price: Standard, choke tubes, two-barrel set **$12,995.00**

KRIEGHOFF K-80 SPORTING CLAYS O/U SHOTGUN
Gauge: 12. **Barrel:** 28", 30", 32", 34" with choke tubes. **Weight:** About 8 lbs. **Stock:** #3 Sporting stock designed for gun-down shooting. **Features:** Standard receiver with satin nickel finish and classic scroll engraving. Selective mechanical trigger adjustable for position. Choice of tapered flat or 8mm parallel flat barrel rib. Free-floating barrels. Aluminum case. Imported from Germany by Krieghoff International, Inc.
Price: Standard grade with five choke tubes, from **$9,395.00**

KRIEGHOFF K-80 SKEET O/U SHOTGUNS
Gauge: 12, 2-3/4" chambers. **Barrel:** 28", 30", 32", (skeet & skeet), optional choke tubes). **Weight:** About 7-3/4 lbs. **Stock:** American skeet or straight skeet stocks, with palm-swell grips. Walnut. **Features:** Satin gray receiver finish. Selective mechanical trigger. Choice of ventilated 8mm parallel flat rib or ventilated 8-12mm tapered flat rib. Introduced 1980. Imported from Germany by Krieghoff International, Inc.
Price: Standard, skeet chokes **$8,375.00**
Price: Skeet Special (28", 30", 32" tapered flat rib,
skeet & skeet choke tubes) **$9,100.00**

KRIEGHOFF K-80 TRAP O/U SHOTGUNS
Gauge: 12, 2-3/4" chambers. **Barrel:** 30", 32" (Imp. Mod. & Full or choke tubes). **Weight:** About 8-1/2 lbs. **Stock:** Four stock dimensions or adjustable stock available; all have palm-swell grips. Checkered European walnut. **Features:** Satin nickel receiver. Selective mechanical trigger, adjustable for position. Ventilated step rib. Introduced 1980. Imported from Germany by Krieghoff International, Inc.
Price: K-80 O/U (30", 32", Imp. Mod. & Full), from **$8,850.00**
Price: K-80 Unsingle (32", 34", Full), standard, from **$10,080.00**
Price: K-80 Combo (two-barrel set), standard, from **$13,275.00**

Krieghoff K-20 O/U Shotgun
Similar to the K-80 except built on a 20-gauge frame. Designed for skeet, sporting clays and field use. Offered in 20, 28 and .410; 28", 30" and 32" barrels. Imported from Germany by Krieghoff International Inc.
Price: K-20, 20 gauge, from **$9,575.00**
Price: K-20, 28 gauge, from **$9,725.00**
Price: K-20, .410, from **$9,725.00**

LEBEAU-COURALLY BOSS-VEREES O/U SHOTGUN
Gauge: 12, 20, 2-3/4" chambers. **Barrel:** 25" to 32". **Weight:** To customer specifications. **Stock:** Exhibition-quality French walnut. **Features:** Boss-type sidelock with automatic ejectors; single or double triggers; chopper lump barrels. A custom gun built to customer specifications. Imported from Belgium by Wm. Larkin Moore.
Price: From **$96,000.00**

LJUTIC LM-6 SUPER DELUXE O/U SHOTGUNS
Gauge: 12. **Barrel:** 28" to 34", choked to customer specs for live birds, trap, international trap. **Weight:** To customer specs. **Stock:** To customer specs. Oil finish, hand checkered. **Features:** Custom-made gun. Hollow-milled rib, pull or release trigger, push-button opener in front of trigger guard. From Ljutic Industries.
Price: Super Deluxe LM-6 O/U **$19,995.00**
Price: Over/Under combo (interchangeable single barrel, two
trigger guards, one for single trigger, one for doubles) . . . **$27,995.00**
Price: Extra over/under barrel sets, 29"-32" **$6,995.00**

LUGER CLASSIC O/U SHOTGUNS
Gauge: 12, 3" and 3-1/2" chambers. **Barrel:** 26", 28", 30"; Imp. Cyl. Mod. and Full choke tubes. **Weight:** 7-1/2 lbs. **Length:** 45" overall (28" barrel) **Stock:** Select-grade European walnut, hand-checkered grip and forend. **Features:** Gold, single selective trigger; automatic ejectors. Introduced 2000.
Price: Classic (26", 28" or 30" barrel; 3-1/2" chambers) **$919.00**
Price: Classic Sporting (30" barrel; 3" chambers) **$964.00**

Marocchi Conquista Sporting Clay

Merkel Model 2001EL

Merkel Model 303EL

MARLIN L. C. SMITH O/U SHOTGUNS
Gauge: 12, 20. **Barrel:** 26", 28". **Stock:** Checkered walnut w/recoil pad. **Length:** 45". **Weight:** 7.25 lbs. **Features:** 3" chambers; 3 choke tubes (IC, Mod., Full), single selective trigger, selective automatic ejectors; vent rib; bead front sight. Imported from Italy by Marlin. Introduced 2005.
Price: LC12-OU (12 ga., 28" barrel) **$1,416.00**
Price: LC20-OU (20 ga., 26" barrel, 6.25 lbs., OAL 43") **$1,416.00**

MAROCCHI CONQUISTA SPORTING CLAYS O/U SHOTGUNS
Gauge: 12, 2-3/4" chambers. **Barrel:** 28", 30", 32" (ContreChoke tubes); 10mm concave vent rib. **Weight:** About 8 lbs. **Stock:** 14-1/2"-14-7/8"x2-3/16"x1-7/16"; American walnut with checkered grip and forend; sporting clays butt pad. **Sights:** 16mm luminescent front. **Features:** Lower mono-block and frame profile. Fast lock time. Ergonomically-shaped trigger adjustable for pull length. Automatic selective ejectors. Coin-finished receiver, blued barrels. Five choke tubes, hard case. Available as true left-hand model, opening lever operates from left to right; stock has left-hand cast. Introduced 1994. Imported from Italy by Precision Sales International.
Price: Grade I, right-hand **$1,490.00**
Price: Grade I, left-hand **$1,615.00**
Price: Grade II, right-hand **$1,828.00**
Price: Grade II, left-hand **$2,180.00**
Price: Grade III, right-hand, from **$3,093.00**
Price: Grade III, left-hand, from **$3,093.00**

Marocchi Conquista Trap O/U Shotguns
Similar to Conquista Sporting Clays model except 30" or 32" barrels choked Full & Full, stock dimensions of 14-1/2"-14-7/8"x1-11/ 16"x1-9/32"; weighs about 8-1/4 lbs. Introduced 1994. Imported from Italy by Precision Sales International.
Price: Grade I, right-hand **$1,490.00**
Price: Grade II, right-hand **$1,828.00**
Price: Grade III, right-hand, from **$3,093.00**

Marocchi Conquista Skeet O/U Shotguns
Similar to Conquista Sporting Clays model except 28" (skeet & skeet) barrels, stock dimensions of 14-3/8"-14-3/4"x2-3/16"x1-1/2". Weighs about 7-3/4 lbs. Introduced 1994. Imported from Italy by Precision Sales International.
Price: Grade I, right-hand **$1,490.00**
Price: Grade II, right-hand **$1,828.00**
Price: Grade III, right-hand, from **$3,093.00**

MAROCCHI MODEL 99 SPORTING TRAP AND SKEET O/U SHOTGUNS
Gauge: 12, 2-3/4", 3" chambers. **Barrel:** 28", 30", 32". **Stock:** French walnut. **Features:** Boss Locking system, screw-in chokes, low recoil, lightweight Monoblock barrels and ribs. Imported from Italy by Precision Sales International.
Price: Grade I **$2,350.00**
Price: Grade II **$2,870.00**
Price: Grade II Gold **$3,025.00**
Price: Grade III **$3,275.00**
Price: Grade III Gold **$3,450.00**
Price: Blackgold **$4,150.00**
Price: Lodestar **$5,125.00**
Price: Brittania **$5,125.00**
Price: Diana **$6,350.00**

MAROCCHI CONQUISTA USA MODEL 92 SPORTING CLAYS O/U SHOTGUN
Gauge: 12, 3" chambers. **Barrel:** 30"; back-bored, ported (ContreChoke Plus tubes); 10 mm concave ventilated top rib, ventilated middle rib. **Weight:** 8 lbs. 2 oz. **Stock:** 14-1/4"-14-5/8"x 2-1/8"x1-3/8"; American walnut with checkered grip and forend; sporting clays butt pad. **Features:** Low profile frame; fast lock time; automatic selective ejectors; blued receiver and barrels. Comes with three choke tubes. Ergonomically shaped trigger adjustable for pull length without tools. Barrels are back-bored and ported. Introduced 1996. Imported from Italy by Precision Sales International.
Price: **$1,490.00**

MERKEL MODEL 2001EL O/U SHOTGUN
Gauge: 12, 20, 3" chambers, 28, 2-3/4" chambers. **Barrel:** 12-28"; 20, 28 ga.-26-3/4". **Weight:** About 7 lbs. (12 ga.). **Stock:** Oil-finished walnut; English or pistol grip. **Features:** Self-cocking Blitz boxlock action with cocking indicators; Kersten double cross-bolt lock; silver-grayed receiver with engraved hunting scenes; coil spring ejectors; single selective or double triggers. Imported from Germany by GSI, Inc.
Price: 12, 20 . . . . **$7,295.00**
Price: 28 ga. **$7,295.00**
Price: Model 2000EL (scroll engraving, 12, 20 or 28) **$5,795.00**

Merkel Model 303EL O/U Shotgun
Similar to Model 2001EL except Holland & Holland-style sidelock action with cocking indicators; English-style arabesque engraving. Available in 12, 20, 28 gauge. Imported from Germany by GSI, Inc.
Price: **$19,995.00**

Merkel Model 2002EL O/U Shotgun
Similar to Model 2001EL except dummy sideplates, arabesque engraving with hunting scenes; 12, 20, 28 gauge. Imported from Germany by GSI, Inc.
Price: **$10,995.00**

Merkel Model 2002EL

Perazzi MX8

Perazzi MX8/20

Perazzi MX28

Piotti Boss

PERAZZI MX8/MX8 SPECIAL TRAP, SKEET O/U SHOTGUNS
Gauge: 12, 2-3/4" chambers. **Barrel:** Trap: 29-1/2" (Imp. Mod. & Extra Full), 31-1/2" (Full & Extra Full). Choke tubes optional. Skeet: 27-5/8" (skeet & skeet). **Weight:** About 8-1/2 lbs. (trap); 7 lbs., 15 oz. (skeet). **Stock:** Interchangeable and custom made to customer specs. **Features:** Has detachable and interchangeable trigger group with flat V springs. Flat 7/16" vent rib. Many options available. Imported from Italy by Perazzi U.S.A., Inc.
Price: MX Trap Single $10,934.00

Perazzi MX8 Special Skeet O/U Shotgun
Similar to the MX8 Skeet except has adjustable four-position trigger, skeet stock dimensions. Imported from Italy by Perazzi U.S.A., Inc.
Price: From $11,166.00

PERAZZI MX8 O/U SHOTGUNS
Gauge: 12, 2-3/4" chambers. **Barrel:** 28-3/8" (Imp. Mod. & Extra Full), 29-1/2" (choke tubes). **Weight:** 7 lbs., 12 oz. **Stock:** Special specifications. **Features:** Has single selective trigger; flat 7/16" x 5/16" vent rib. Many options available. Imported from Italy by Perazzi U.S.A., Inc.
Price: Standard $12,532.00
Price: Sporting $11,166.00
Price: Trap Double Trap (removable trigger group) $15,581.00
Price: Skeet $12,756.00
Price: SC3 grade (variety of engraving patterns) . . . . $23,000.00+
Price: SCO grade (more intricate engraving, gold inlays) . . . . $39,199.00+

Perazzi MX8/20 O/U Shotgun
Similar to the MX8 except has smaller frame and has a removable trigger mechanism. Available in trap, skeet, sporting or game models with fixed chokes or choke tubes. Stock is made to customer specifications. Introduced 1993. Imported from Italy by Perazzi U.S.A., Inc.
Price: From $11,731.00

PERAZZI MX12 HUNTING O/U SHOTGUNS
Gauge: 12, 2-3/4" chambers. **Barrel:** 26-3/4", 27-1/2", 28-3/8", 29-1/2" (Mod. & Full); choke tubes available in 27-5/8", 29-1/2" only (MX12C). **Weight:** 7 lbs., 4 oz. **Stock:** To customer specs; interchangeable. **Features:** Single selective trigger; coil springs used in action; Schnabel forend tip. Imported from Italy by Perazzi U.S.A., Inc.
Price: From $11,166.00
Price: MX12C (with choke tubes). From $11,960.00

Perazzi MX20 Hunting O/U Shotguns
Similar to the MX12 except 20 ga. frame size. Non-removable trigger group. Available in 20, 28, .410 with 2-3/4" or 3" chambers. 26" standard, and choked Mod. & Full. Weight is 6 lbs., 6 oz. Imported from Italy by Perazzi U.S.A., Inc.
Price: From $11,166.00
Price: MX20C (as above, 20 ga. only, choke tubes). From $11,960.00

PERAZZI MX10 O/U SHOTGUN
Gauge: 12, 2-3/4" chambers. **Barrel:** 29.5", 31.5" (fixed chokes). **Weight:** NA. **Stock:** Walnut; cheekpiece adjustable for elevation and cast. **Features:** Adjustable rib; vent side rib. Externally selective trigger. Available in single barrel, combo, over/under trap, skeet, pigeon and sporting models. Introduced 1993. Imported from Italy by Perazzi U.S.A., Inc.
Price: MX200410 . . . . $18,007.00

PERAZZI MX28, MX410 GAME O/U SHOTGUN
Gauge: 28, 2-3/4" chambers, .410, 3" chambers. **Barrel:** 26" (Imp. Cyl. & Full). **Weight:** NA. **Stock:** To customer specifications. **Features:** Made on scaled-down frames proportioned to the gauge. Introduced 1993. Imported from Italy by Perazzi U.S.A., Inc.
Price: From $22,332.00

Remington Premier Field Grade

Remington Premier Upland Grade

Remington Premier Ruffed Grouse

Remington Premier STS Competition

Remington Premier STS Competition w/adj. comb

Rizzini S790 Emel

PIOTTI BOSS O/U SHOTGUN
Gauge: 12, 20. **Barrel:** 26" to 32", chokes as specified. **Weight:** 6.5 to 8 lbs. **Stock:** Dimensions to customer specs. Best quality figured walnut. **Features:** Essentially a custom-made gun with many options. Introduced 1993. Imported from Italy by Wm. Larkin Moore.
Price: From **$48,000.00**

POINTER O/U SHOTGUN
Gauge: 12. **Barrel:** 28". **Stock:** Walnut. **Features:** Kickeez buttpad, Tru-Glo sight, extractors, barrel selector, engraved receiver, gold trigger and 5 choke tubes. Introduced 2006. Imported by Legacy Sports Int.
Price: **$599.00**

REMINGTON PREMIER FIELD GRADE OVER/UNDER SHOTGUNS
Gauge: 12, 20, 28, 3" chambers; 28 2-3/4" chambers. **Barrel:** 26", 28", 30" in 12 gauge; overbored (.735), polished blue; 7mm vent rib. **Sights:** Ivory front bead, steel mid bead. **Weight:** 6.5 to 7.5 lbs. Length: 43.125" to 45.125" overall. **Stock:** 14.25" LOP; 1.5" drop at comb; 2.4" drop at heel. Walnut, cut checkering, Schnabeled forends. Checkered pistol grip, checkered forend, satin finish, rubber butt pad. Right-hand palm swell. **Features:** Nickel finish receiver, game-scene engraving. Single selective mechanical trigger, selective automatic ejectors; serrated free-floating vent rib. Five flush mount ProBore choke tubes for 12s and 20s; 28-gauge

equipped with 3 flush mount ProBore choke tubes. Hard case included. Introduced 2006. Premier Upland Grade includes engraved game scenes on receiver; 12-, 20- and 28-gauge, 26" or 28" barrels. Oil-finished woodwork, case-colored receiver. Introduced 2006. Ruffed Grouse Edition has Ruffed Grouse Society logo in 14k gold on both sides of the black onyx frame. Gold-script Remington insignia "R" appears on underbelly. 20 gauge, 26" barrel, straight-grip, English-style stock, oil finish. Introduced 2007. STS Series Competition line offers adjustable-comb model with 30" or 32" barrels, and a 32" barrel in non-adjustable stocks. 10mm target-style rib with ivory front bead and steel midpost, gold trigger, engraved receiver. Introduced 2007. Made in Italy, imported by Remington Arms Co.
Price: Premier Field 12 gauge, 26" barrel, 7 lbs. **$2,086.00**
Price: Premier Field 20 gauge, 28" barrel, 6.75 lbs. **$2,086.00**
Price: Premier Field 28 gauge, 27" barrel, 6.75 lbs. **$2,086.00**
Price: Premier Upland **$2,268.00**
Price: Premier Ruffed Grouse **$2,380.00**
Price: Premier STS Series Competition (2007) **$2,540.00**
Price: Premier STS Series Competition Adj. Comb (2007) **$2,890.00**

RIZZINI S790 EMEL O/U SHOTGUN
Gauge: 20, 28, .410. **Barrel:** 26", 27.5" (Imp. Cyl. & Imp. Mod.). **Weight:** About 6 lbs. **Stock:** 14"x1-1/2"x2-1/8". Extra fancy select walnut. **Features:** Boxlock action with profuse engraving; automatic ejectors; single selective trigger; silvered receiver. Comes with Nizzoli leather case. Introduced 1996. Imported from Italy by Wm. Larkin Moore & Co.
Price: From **$9,725.00**

SHOTGUNS — Over/Unders

Ruger Red Label

Ruger Red Label All-Weather Camo

SIGARMS SA5 Field

SKB 85TSS

Rizzini S792 EMEL O/U Shotgun
Similar to S790 EMEL except dummy sideplates with extensive engraving coverage. Nizzoli leather case. Introduced 1996. Imported from Italy by Wm. Larkin Moore & Co.
Price: From **$9,075.00**

RIZZINI UPLAND EL O/U SHOTGUN
Gauge: 12, 16, 20, 28, .410. **Barrel:** 26", 27-1/2", Mod. & Full, Imp. Cyl. & Imp. Mod. choke tubes. **Weight:** About 6.6 lbs. **Stock:** 14-1/ 2"x1-1/2"x2-1/4". **Features:** Boxlock action; single selective trigger; ejectors; profuse engraving on silvered receiver. Comes with fitted case. Introduced 1996. Imported from Italy by Wm. Larkin Moore & Co.
Price: From **$3,350.00**

Rizzini Artemis O/U Shotgun
Same as Upland EL model except dummy sideplates with extensive game scene engraving. Fancy European walnut stock. Fitted case. Introduced 1996. Imported from Italy by Wm. Larkin Moore & Co.
Price: From **$2,100.00**

RIZZINI S782 EMEL O/U SHOTGUN
Gauge: 12, 2-3/4" chambers. **Barrel:** 26", 27.5" (Imp. Cyl. & Imp. Mod.). **Weight:** About 6.75 lbs. **Stock:** 14-1/2"x1-1/2"x2-1/4". Extra fancy select walnut. **Features:** Boxlock action with dummy sideplates, extensive engraving with gold inlaid game birds, silvered receiver, automatic ejectors, single selective trigger. Nizzoli leather case. Introduced 1996. Imported from Italy by Wm. Larkin Moore & Co.
Price: From **$11,450.00**

RUGER RED LABEL O/U SHOTGUNS
Gauge: 12, 20, 3" chambers; 28 2-3/4" chambers. **Barrel:** 26", 28", 30" in 12 gauge. **Weight:** About 7 lbs. (20 ga.); 7-1/2 lbs. (12 ga.). **Length:** 43" overall (26" barrels). **Stock:** 14"x1-1/2"x2-1/2". Straight grain American walnut. Checkered pistol grip or straight grip, checkered forend, rubber butt pad. **Features:** Stainless steel receiver. Single selective mechanical trigger, selective automatic ejectors; serrated free-floating vent rib. Comes with two skeet, one Imp. Cyl., one Mod., one Full choke tube and wrench. Made in U.S. by Sturm, Ruger & Co.
Price: Red Label with pistol grip stock **$1,790.00**
Price: English Field with straight-grip stock **$1,790.00**
Price: Sporting clays (30" bbl.) **$1,790.00**

Ruger Engraved Red Label O/U Shotgun
Similar to Red Label except scroll engraved receiver with 24-carat gold game bird (pheasant in 12 gauge, grouse in 20 gauge, woodcock in 28 gauge). Introduced 2000.
Price: Engraved Red Label, pistol grip only **$1,995.00**

SARSILMAZ O/U SHOTGUNS
Gauge: 12, 3" chambers. **Barrel:** 26", 28"; fixed chokes or choke tubes. **Weight:** NA. **Length:** NA. **Stock:** Oil-finished hardwood. **Features:** Double or single selective trigger, wide vent rib, chrome-plated parts, blued finish. Introduced 2000. Imported from Turkey by Armsport Inc.
Price: Double triggers; mod. and full or imp. cyl.
and mod. fixed chokes **$499.95**
Price: Single selective trigger; imp. cyl. and mod. or mod.
and full fixed chokes **$575.00**
Price: Single selective trigger; five choke tubes and wrench **$695.00**

SIGARMS SA5 O/U SHOTGUNS
Gauge: 12, 20, 3" chamber. **Barrel:** 26-1/2", 27" (Full, Imp. Mod., Mod., Imp. Cyl., Cyl. choke tubes). **Weight:** 6.9 lbs. (12 gauge), 5.9 lbs. (20 gauge). **Stock:** 14-1/2" x 1-1/2" x 2-1/2". Select grade walnut; checkered 20 lpi at grip and forend. **Features:** Single selective trigger, automatic ejectors; hand engraved detachable side plate; matte nickel receiver, rest blued; tapered bolt lock-up. Introduced 1997. Imported by SIGARMS, Inc.
Price: Field, 12 gauge, 20 gauge **$2,670.00**
Price: Sporting clays **$2,800.00**

SKB MODEL 85TSS O/U SHOTGUNS
Gauge: 12, 20, .410: 3"; 28, 2-3/4". **Barrel:** Chrome lined 26", 28", 30", 32" (w/choke tubes). **Weight:** 7 lbs., 7 oz. to 8 lbs., 14 oz. **Stock:** Hand-checkered American walnut with matte finish, Schnabel or grooved forend. Target stocks available in various styles. **Sights:** HiViz competition sights. **Features:** Low profile boxlock action with Greener-style cross bolt; single selective trigger; manual safety. Back-bored barrels with lengthened forcing cones. Introduced 2004. Imported from Japan by G.U. Inc.
Price: Sporting clays, 12 , 20, 28 . . . . **$2,199.00**
Price: Sporting clays, 410 . . . . **$2,899.00**
Price: Sporting clays set, 12 and 20 . . . . **$3,549.00**
Price: Skeet, 12, 20, 28 . . . . **$2,199.00**
Price: Skeet, .410 . . . . **$2,229.00**
Price: Skeet, three-barrel set, 20, 28, .410 . . . . **$5,349.00**
Price: Trap, standard or Monte Carlo **$2,199.00**
Price: Trap adjustable comb **$2,429.00**
Price: Trap Unsingle (2007) **$2,499.00**
Price: Trap Combo (2007) **$3,489.00**

SHOTGUNS — Over/Unders

SKB Model 585 Gold

SKB Model 505 Field

Smith & Wesson Elite Silver

Stoeger Condor Combo

SKB MODEL 585 O/U SHOTGUNS
Gauge: 12 or 20, 3"; 28, 2-3/4"; .410, 3". **Barrel:** 12 ga.-26", 28", (InterChoke tubes); 20 ga.-26", 28" (InterChoke tubes); 28-26", 28" (InterChoke tubes); .410-26", 28" (InterChoke tubes). **Weight:** 6.6 to 8.5 lbs. **Length:** 43" to 51-3/8" overall. **Stock:** 14-1/8"x1-1/2"x2-3/16". Hand checkered walnut with matte finish. **Sights:** Metal bead front (field). **Features:** Boxlock action; silver nitride finish; manual safety, automatic ejectors, single selective trigger. All 12 gauge barrels are back-bored, have lengthened forcing cones and longer choke tube system. Introduced 1992. Imported from Japan by G.U., Inc.
Price: Field **$1,699.00**
Price: Two-barrel field set, 12 & 20 . . . . **$2,749.00**
Price: Two-barrel field set, 20 & 28 or 28 & .410 . . . . **$2,829.00**

SKB Model 585 Gold Package
Similar to Model 585 Field except gold-plated trigger, two gold-plated game inlays, Schnabel forend. Silver or blue receiver. Introduced 1998. Imported from Japan by G.U. Inc.
Price: 12, 20 ga. **$1,899.00**
Price: 28, .410 . . . . **$1,989.00**

SKB Model 505 O/U Shotgun
Similar to Model 585 except blued receiver, standard bore diameter, standard InterChoke system on 12, 20, 28, different receiver engraving. Imported from Japan by G.U. Inc.
Price: Field, 12 (26", 28"), 20 (26", 28") **$1,429.00**

SMITH & WESSON ELITE SILVER SHOTGUNS
Gauge: 12, 3" chambers. **Barrel:** 26", 28", 30", rust-blued chopper-lump. **Weight:** 7.8 lbs. **Length:** 46-48". **Sights:** Ivory front bead, metal mid-bead. **Stock:** AAA (grade III) Turkish walnut stocks, hand-cut checkering, satin finish. **Features:** Smith & Wesson–designed trigger-plate action, hand-engraved receivers, bone-charcoal case hardening, lifetime warranty. Five choke tubes. Introduced 2007. Made in Turkey, imported by Smith & Wesson.
Price: . . . . **NA**

STOEGER CONDOR O/U SHOTGUNS
Gauge: 12, 20, 2-3/4" 3" chambers; 16, .410. **Barrel:** 22", 24", 26", 28", 30" **Weight:** 5.5 to 7.8 lbs. **Sights:** Brass bead. **Features:** IC, M, or F screw-in choke tubes with each gun. Oil finished hardwood with pistol grip and forend. Auto safety, single trigger, automatic extractors.
Price: Condor, 12, 20, 16 ga. or .410 . . . . **$350.00**
Price: Condor Supreme (w/mid bead), 12 or 20 ga. **$599.00**
Price: Condor Combo, 12 and 20 ga. barrels . . . . **$550.00 to $700.00**
Price: Condor Youth, 20 ga. or .410 . . . . **$350.00**
Price: Condor Competition, 12 or 20 ga. **$629.00**
Price: Condor Combo, 12/20 ga., RH or LH (2007) **$749.00**
Price: Condor Outback, 12 or 20 ga., 20" barrel **$410.00**

TRADITIONS CLASSIC SERIES O/U SHOTGUNS
Gauge: 12, 3"; 20, 3"; 16, 2-3/4"; 28, 2-3/4"; .410, 3". **Barrel:** 26" and 28". **Weight:** 6 lbs., 5 oz. to 7 lbs., 6 oz. **Length:** 43" to 45" overall. **Stock:** Walnut. **Features:** Single-selective trigger; chrome-lined barrels with screw-in choke tubes; extractors (Field Hunter and Field I models) or automatic ejectors (Field II and Field III models); rubber butt pad; top tang safety. Imported from Fausti of Italy by Traditions.
Price: Field Hunter: Blued receiver; 12 or 20 ga.; 26" bbl. has IC and Mod. tubes, 28" has mod. and full tubes **$669.00**
Price: Field I: Blued receiver; 12, 20, 28 ga. or .410; fixed chokes (26" has I.C. and mod., 28" has mod. and full) **$619.00**
Price: Field II: Coin-finish receiver; 12, 16, 20, 28 ga. or .410; gold trigger; choke tubes **$789.00**
Price: Field III: Coin-finish receiver; gold engraving and trigger; 12 ga.; 26" or 28" bbl.; choke tubes **$999.00**
Price: Upland II: Blued receiver; 12 or 20 ga.; English-style straight walnut stock; choke tubes **$839.00**
Price: Upland III: Blued receiver, gold engraving; 20 ga.; high-grade pistol grip walnut stock; choke tubes **$1,059.00**
Price: Upland III: Blued, gold engraved receiver, 12 ga. Round pistol grip stock, choke tubes **$1,059.00**
Price: Sporting Clay II: Silver receiver; 12 ga.; ported barrels with skeet, i.c., mod. and full extended tubes **$959.00**
Price: Sporting Clay III: Engraved receivers, 12 and 20 ga., walnut stock, vent rib, extended choke tubes **$1,189.00**

Traditions Field II

Traditions Upland II

Traditions Upland IV

Tristar Silver II

Verona LX501 Hunting Combo

TRADITIONS MAG 350 SERIES O/U SHOTGUNS
Gauge: 12, 3-1/2". **Barrel:** 24", 26" and 28". **Weight:** 7 lbs. to 7 lbs., 4 oz. **Length:** 41" to 45" overall. **Stock:** Walnut or composite with Mossy Oak® Break-Up™ or Advantage® Wetlands ™ camouflage. **Features:** Black matte, engraved receiver; vent rib; automatic ejectors; single-selective trigger; three screw-in choke tubes; rubber recoil pad; top tang safety. Imported from Fausti of Italy by Traditions.
Price: (Mag Hunter II: 28" black matte barrels, walnut stock, includes I.C., Mod. and Full tubes) **$799.00**
Price: (Turkey II: 24" or 26" camo barrels, Break-Up™ camo stock, includes Mod., Full and X-Full tubes) **$889.00**
Price: (Waterfowl II: 28" camo barrels, Advantage Wetlands camo stock, includes IC, Mod. and Full tubes) **$899.00**

TRISTAR SILVER II O/U SHOTGUN
Gauge: 12, 20, .410. **Barrel:** 26" barrel (Imp. Cyl., Mod., Full choke tubes, 12 and 20 ga.), 28" (Imp. Cyl., Mod., Full choke tubes, 12 ga. only), 26" (Imp. Cyl. & Mod. fixed chokes, 28 and .410) automatic selective ejectors. **Weight:** 6 lbs., 15 oz. (12 ga., 26"). **Length:** 45-1/2" overall. **Stock:** 14-3/8"x1-1/2"x2-3/8". Figured walnut, cut checkering; sporting clays quick-mount buttpad. **Sights:** Target bead front. **Features:** Boxlock action with single selective trigger, automatic selective ejectors; special broadway channeled rib; vented barrel rib; chrome bores. Chrome-nickel finish on frame, with engraving. Imported from Italy by Tristar Sporting Arms Ltd.
Price: **$669.00**

VERONA LX501 HUNTING O/U SHOTGUNS
Gauge: 12, 20, 28, .410 (2-3/4", 3" chambers). **Barrel:** 28"; 12, 20 ga. have Interchoke tubes, 28 ga. and .410 have fixed Full & Mod. **Weight:** 6-7 lbs. **Stock:** Matte-finished walnut with machine-cut checkering. **Features:** Gold-plated single-selective trigger; ejectors; engraved, blued receiver, non-automatic safety; coil spring-operated firing pins. Introduced 1999. Imported from Italy by B.C. Outdoors.

Price: 12 and 20 ga. **$878.08**
Price: 28 ga. and .410 . . . . **$926.72**
Price: .410 . . . . **$907.01**
Price: Combos 20/28, 28/.410 . . . . **$1,459.20**

Verona LX692 Gold Hunting O/U Shotguns
Similar to Verona LX501 except engraved, silvered receiver with false sideplates showing gold inlaid bird hunting scenes on three sides; Schnabel forend tip; hand-cut checkering; black rubber butt pad. Available in 12 and 20 gauge only, five Interchoke tubes. Introduced 1999. Imported from Italy by B.C. Outdoors.
Price: **$1,295.00**
Price: LX692G Combo 28/.410 . . . . **$2,192.40**

Verona LX680 Sporting O/U Shotgun
Similar to Verona LX501 except engraved, silvered receiver; ventilated middle rib; beavertail forend; hand-cut checkering; available in 12 or 20 gauge only with 2-3/4" chambers. Introduced 1999. Imported from Italy by B.C. Outdoors.
Price: **$1,159.68**

Verona LX680 Skeet/Sporting/Trap O/U Shotgun
Similar to Verona LX501 except skeet or trap stock dimensions; beavertail forend, palm swell on pistol grip; ventilated center barrel rib. Introduced 1999. Imported from Italy by B.C. Outdoors.
Price: **$1,736.96**

Verona LX692 Gold Sporting O/U Shotgun
Similar to Verona LX680 except false sideplates have gold-inlaid bird hunting scenes on three sides; red high-visibility front sight. Introduced 1999. Imported from Italy by B.C. Outdoors.
Price: Skeet/sporting **$1,765.12**
Price: Trap (32" barrel, 7-7/8 lbs.) **$1,594.80**

Verona LX692G

Verona LX680TC

Verona LX702 GTC

Weatherby Athena Grade V Classic Field

Weatherby Orion
Grade III Field

VERONA LX680 COMPETITION TRAP O/U SHOTGUNS
Gauge: 12. **Barrel:** 30" O/U, 32" single bbl. **Weight:** 8-3/8 lbs. combo, 7 lbs. single. **Stock:** Walnut. **Sights:** White front, mid-rib bead. **Features:** Interchangeable barrels switch from o/u to single configurations. 5 Briley chokes in combo, 4 in single bbl. extended forcing cones, ported barrels 32" with raised rib. By B.C. Outdoors.
Price: Trap Single (LX680TGTSB) $1,736.96
Price: Trap Combo (LX680TC) $2,553.60

VERONA LX702 GOLD TRAP COMBO O/U SHOTGUNS
Gauge: 20/28, 2-3/4" chamber. **Barrel:** 30". **Weight:** 7 lbs. **Stock:** Turkish walnut with beavertail forearm. **Sights:** White front bead. **Features:** 2-barrel competition gun. Color case-hardened side plates and receiver with gold inlaid pheasant. Vent rib between barrels. 5 Interchokes. Imported from Italy by B.C. Outdoors.
Price: Combo $2,467.84
Price: 20 ga. $1,829.12

Verona LX702 Skeet/Trap O/U Shotguns
Similar to Verona LX702. Both are 12 gauge and 2-3/4" chamber. Skeet has 28" barrel and weighs 7-3/4 lbs. Trap has 32" barrel and weighs 7-7/8 lbs. By B.C. Outdoors.
Price: Skeet $1,829.12
Price: Trap $1,829.12

WEATHERBY ATHENA GRADE V CLASSIC FIELD O/U SHOTGUN
Gauge: 12, 20, 3" chambers. **Barrel:** 26", 28", IMC multi-choke tubes. **Weight:** 12 ga., 7-1/4 to 8 lbs.; 20 ga. 6-1/2 to 7-1/4 lbs. **Stock:** Oil-finished American Claro walnut with fine-line checkering, rounded pistol grip and slender forend. **Features:** Old English recoil pad. Sideplate receiver has rose and scroll engraving.
Price: $3,037.00

Weatherby Athena Grade III Classic Field O/U Shotgun
Similar to Athena Grade V, has Grade III Claro walnut with oil finish, rounded pistol grip, slender forend; silver nitride/gray receiver has rose and scroll engraving with gold-overlay upland game scenes. Introduced 1999. Imported from Japan by Weatherby.
Price: 12, 20, 28 ga. $2,173.00

WEATHERBY ORION GRADE III FIELD O/U SHOTGUNS
Gauge: 12, 20, 3" chambers. **Barrel:** 26", 28", IMC multi-choke tubes. **Weight:** 6-1/2 to 8 lbs. **Stock:** 14-1/4"x1-1/2"x2-1/2". American walnut, checkered grip and forend. Rubber recoil pad. **Features:** Selective automatic ejectors, single selective inertia trigger. Top tang safety, Greener cross bolt. Has silver-gray receiver with engraving and gold duck/pheasant. Imported from Japan by Weatherby.
Price: Orion III, Field, 12, IMC, 26", 28" $1,955.00
Price: Orion III, Field, 20, IMC, 26", 28" $1,955.00

Weatherby Orion Grade II Classic Field O/U Shotgun
Similar to Orion Grade III Field except stock has high-gloss finish, and bird on receiver is not gold. Available in 12 gauge, 26", 28", 30" barrels, 20 gauge, 26" 28", both with 3" chambers, 28 gauge, 26", 2-3/4" chambers. All have IMC choke tubes. Imported from Japan by Weatherby.
Price: $1,622.00

Weatherby Orion Upland O/U Shotgun
Similar to Orion Grade III Field. Plain blued receiver, gold W on trigger guard; rounded pistol grip, slender forend of Claro walnut with high-gloss finish; black butt pad. Available in 12 and 20 gauge with 26" and 28" barrels. Introduced 1999. Imported from Japan by Weatherby.
Price: $1,299.00

Weatherby Orion Upland

Weatherby Orion SSC

Winchester Select 101 Field

Winchester Select 101 Sporting

Winchester Select Platinum Field

Winchester Select Platinum Sporting

Winchester Select Deluxe Field

WEATHERBY ORION SSC O/U SHOTGUN
Gauge: 12, 3" chambers. **Barrel:** 28", 30", 32" (skeet, SC1, Imp. Cyl., SC2, Mod. IMC choke tubes). **Weight:** About 8 lbs. **Stock:** 14-3/4"x2-1/4"x1-1/2". Claro walnut with satin oil finish; Schnabel forend tip; sporter-style pistol grip; Pachmayr Decelerator recoil pad. **Features:** Designed for sporting clays competition. Has lengthened forcing cones and back-boring; ported barrels with 12mm grooved rib with mid-bead sight; mechanical trigger is adjustable for length of pull. Introduced 1998. Imported from Japan by Weatherby.
Price: SSC (Super Sporting Clays) $2,059.00

WINCHESTER SELECT O/U SHOTGUNS
Gauge: 12, 2-3/4", 3" chambers. **Barrel:** 28", 30", Invector Plus choke tubes. **Weight:** 7 lbs. 6 oz. to 7 lbs. 12. oz. **Length:** 45" overall (28" barrel). **Stock:** Checkered walnut stock. **Features:** Chrome-plated chambers; back-bored barrels; tang barrel selector/safety; deep-blued finish. Introduced 2000. From U.S. Repeating Arms. Co.
Price: Select Model 101 Field, intr. 2007 . . . . **$2,061.00**
Price: Select Model 101 Sporting, intr. 2007, from **$2,328.00**
Price: Select Platinum Sporting, intr. 2007, from **$2,625.00**
Price: Select Platinum Field, intr. 2007, from **$2,359.00**
Price: Select Deluxe Field, intr. 2007, from **$1,607.00**
Price: Select Energy Trap **$1,948.00**
Price: Select Energy Trap adjustable **$2,112.00**

Variety of models for utility and sporting use, including some competitive shooting.

Bill Hanus Birdgun

Charles Daly Superior Hunter

Charles Daly Empire Hunter AE-MC

Charles Daly Diamond DL

ARRIETA SIDELOCK DOUBLE SHOTGUNS
Gauge: 12, 16, 20, 28, .410. **Barrel:** Length and chokes to customer specs. **Weight:** To customer specs. **Stock:** To customer specs. Straight English with checkered butt (standard), or pistol grip. Select European walnut with oil finish. **Features:** Essentially custom gun with myriad options. H&H pattern hand-detachable sidelocks, selective automatic ejectors, double triggers (hinged front) standard. Some have self-opening action. Finish and engraving to customer specs. Imported from Spain by Wingshooting Adventures.

Price: Model 557, auto ejectors. From $3,250.00
Price: Model 570, auto ejectors. From $3,950.00
Price: Model 578, auto ejectors. From $4,350.00
Price: Model 600 Imperial, self-opening. From $6,050.00
Price: Model 601 Imperial Tiro, self-opening. From $6,950.00
Price: Model 801. From $9,135.00
Price: Model 802. From $9,135.00
Price: Model 803. From $6,930.00
Price: Model 871, auto ejectors. From $5,060.00
Price: Model 872, self-opening. From $12,375.00
Price: Model 873, self-opening. From $8,200.00
Price: Model 874, self-opening. From $9,250.00
Price: Model 875, self-opening. From $14,900.00

AYA MODEL 4/53 SHOTGUNS
Gauge: 12, 16, 20, 28, 410. **Barrel:** 26", 27", 28", 30". **Weight:** To customer specifications. **Length:** To customer specifications. **Features:** Hammerless boxlock action; double triggers; light scroll engraving; automatic safety; straight grip oil finish walnut stock; checkered butt. Made in Spain. Imported by New England Custom Gun Service, Lt.

Price: $2,799.00
Price: No. 2 .... $4,499.00
Price: No. 2 Rounded Action $4,899.00

BILL HANUS BIRDGUNS BY AYA
Gauge: 16, 20, 28. **Barrel:** 27", 20 and 28 ga.; 28", 16 ga. (skeet 1 & skeet 2). **Weight:** 5 lbs., 4 oz. to 6 lbs., 4 oz. **Stock:** 14-3/8"x1-1/2"x2-3/8", with 1/4" cast-off. Select walnut. **Features:** Boxlock action with ejectors; splinter forend, straight English grip; checkered butt; English leather-covered handguard and AyA snap caps included. Made by AyA. Introduced 1998. Imported from Spain by Bill Hanus Birdguns.

Price: $2,995.00

CHARLES DALY SUPERIOR HUNTER AND SUPERIOR MC DOUBLE SHOTGUNS
Gauge: 12, 20, 3" chambers, 28, 2-3/4" chambers. **Barrel:** 28" (Mod. & Full) 26" (Imp. Cyl. & Mod.). **Weight:** About 7 lbs. **Stock:** Checkered walnut pistol grip buttstock, splinter forend. **Features:** Silvered, engraved receiver; chrome-lined barrels; gold single trigger; automatic safety; extractors; gold bead front sight. Introduced 1997. Imported from Italy by K.B.I., Inc.

Price: Superior Hunter, 28 gauge and .410 .... $1,659.00
Price: Superior Hunter MC 26"-28" $1,629.00

Charles Daly Empire Hunter AE-MC Double Shotgun
Similar to Superior Hunter except deluxe wood English-style stock, game scene engraving, automatic ejectors. Introduced 1997. Imported from Italy by K.B.I., Inc.

Price: 12 or 20 .... $2,119.00

CHARLES DALY DIAMOND DL DOUBLE SHOTGUN
Gauge: 12, 20, .410, 3" chambers, 28, 2-3/4" chambers. **Barrel:** 28" (Mod. & Full), 26" (Imp. Cyl. & Mod.), 26" (Full & Full, .410). **Weight:** From 5 lbs. to 7 lbs. **Stock:** Select fancy European walnut, English-style butt, beavertail forend; hand-checkered, hand-rubbed oil finish. **Features:** Drop-forged action with gas escape valves; demi-block barrels with concave rib; selective automatic ejectors; hand-detachable double safety sidelocks with hand-engraved rose and scrollwork. Hinged front trigger. Color case-hardened receiver. Introduced 1997. Imported from Spain by K.B.I., Inc.

Price: .... **Special order only**

Charles Daly Diamond Regent DL

Charles Daly Field II Hunter

CZ Bobwhite

CZ Ringneck

CZ Durango

CZ Hammer Coach

CHARLES DALY DIAMOND REGENT DL DOUBLE SHOTGUN
Gauge: 12, 20, .410, 3" chambers, 28, 2-3/4" chambers. **Barrel:** 28" (Mod. & Full), 26" (Imp. Cyl. & Mod.), 26" (Full & Full, .410). **Weight:** About 5-7 lbs. **Stock:** Special select fancy European walnut, English-style butt, splinter forend; hand-checkered; hand-rubbed oil finish. **Features:** Drop-forged action with gas escape valves; demi-block barrels of chrome-nickel steel with concave rib; selective automatic-ejectors; hand-detachable, double-safety H&H sidelocks with demi-relief hand engraving; H&H pattern easy-opening feature; hinged trigger; coin finished action. Introduced 1997. Imported from Spain by K.B.I., Inc.
Price: Special Custom Order . . . . **NA**

CHARLES DALY FIELD II, AE-MC HUNTER DOUBLE SHOTGUN
Gauge: 12, 20, 28, .410 (3" chambers; 28 has 2-3/4"). **Barrel:** 32" (Mod. & Mod.), 28, 30" (Mod. & Full), 26" (Imp. Cyl. & Mod.) .410 (Full & Full). **Weight:** 6 lbs. to 11.4 lbs. **Stock:** Checkered walnut pistol grip and forend. **Features:** Silvered, engraved receiver; gold single selective trigger in 10, 12, and 20 ga.; double triggers in 28 and .410; automatic safety; extractors; gold bead front sight. Introduced 1997. Imported from Spain by K.B.I., Inc.
Price: 28 ga., .410-bore. **$1,189.00**
Price: 12 or 20 AE-MC **$1,099.00**

CZ BOBWHITE AND RINGNECK SHOTGUNS
Gauge: 12, 20, 28, .410. (5 screw-in chokes in 12 and 20 ga. and fixed chokes in IC and Mod in .410). **Barrel:** 20". **Weight:** 6.5 lbs. **Length:** NA. **Stock:** Sculptured Turkish walnut with straight English-style grip and double triggers (Bobwhite) or conventional American pistol grip with a single trigger (Ringneck). Both are hand checkered 20 lpi. **Features:** Both color case-hardened shotguns are hand engraved.
Price: Bobwhite **$695.00**
Price: Ringneck **$912.00**

CZ DURANGO AND AMARILLO SHOTGUNS
Gauge: 12, 3" chambers. **Barrel:** 20". **Weight:** 6.7 lbs. **Length:** NA. **Stock:** Hand checkered walnut with old style round knob pistol grip. **Features:** The Durango comes with a single trigger, while the Amarillo is a double trigger shotgun The receiver, trigger guard, and forend metal are finished in 19th century color case-hardening.
Price: **$795.00**

CZ HAMMER COACH SHOTGUNS
Gauge: 12, 3" chambers. **Barrel:** 20". **Weight:** 6.7 lbs. **Length:** NA. **Stock:** NA. **Features:** Following in the tradition of the guns used by the stagecoach guards of the 1880's, this cowboy gun features double triggers, 19th century color case-hardening and fully functional external hammers.
Price: **$795.00**

A.H. Fox DE Grade

Garbi Model 100

Kimber Valier Grade I

Kimber Valier Grade II

DAKOTA PREMIER GRADE SHOTGUN
Gauge: 12, 16, 20, 28, .410. **Barrel:** 27". **Weight:** NA. **Length:** NA. **Stock:** Exhibition-grade English walnut, hand-rubbed oil finish with straight grip and splinter forend. **Features:** French grey finish; 50 percent coverage engraving; double triggers; selective ejectors. Finished to customer specifications. Made in U.S. by Dakota Arms.
Price: From $14,950.00

Dakota Legend Shotgun
Similar to Premier Grade except has special selection English walnut, full-coverage scroll engraving, oak and leather case. Made in U.S. by Dakota Arms.
Price: From $19,000.00

E.M.F. OLD WEST HAMMER SHOTGUN
Gauge: 12. **Barrel:** 20". **Weight:** 8 lbs. **Length:** 37" overall. **Stock:** Smooth walnut with steel butt place. **Sights:** Large brass bead. **Features:** Colt-style exposed hammers rebounding type; blued receiver and barrels; cylinder bore. Introduced 2006. Imported from China for E.M.F. by TTN.
Price: $449.90

FOX, A.H., SIDE-BY-SIDE SHOTGUNS
Gauge: 16, 20, 28, .410. **Barrel:** Length and chokes to customer specifications. Rust-blued Chromox or Krupp steel. **Weight:** 5-1/2 to 6-3/4 lbs. **Stock:** Dimensions to customer specifications. Hand-checkered Turkish Circassian walnut with hand-rubbed oil finish. Straight, semi or full pistol grip; splinter, Schnabel or beavertail forend; traditional pad, hard rubber buttplate or skeleton butt. **Features:** Boxlock action with automatic ejectors; double or Fox single selective trigger. Scalloped, rebated and color case-hardened receiver; hand finished and hand-engraved. Grades differ in engraving, inlays, grade of wood, amount of hand finishing. Introduced 1993. Made in U.S. by Connecticut Shotgun Mfg.
Price: CE Grade $13,500.00
Price: XE Grade $15,500.00
Price: DE Grade $18,000.00
Price: FE Grade $23,000.00
Price: Exhibition Grade $36,500.00
Price: 28/.410 CE Grade $15,500.00
Price: 28/.410 XE Grade $17,500.00
Price: 28/.410 DE Grade $20,000.00
Price: 28/.410 FE Grade $25,000.00

GARBI MODEL 100 DOUBLE SHOTGUN
Gauge: 12, 16, 20, 28. **Barrel:** 26", 28", choked to customer specs. **Weight:** 5-1/2 to 7-1/2 lbs. **Stock:** 14-1/2"x2-1/4"x1-1/2". European walnut. Straight grip, checkered butt, classic forend. **Features:** Sidelock action, automatic ejectors, double triggers standard. Color case-hardened action, coin finish optional. Single trigger; beavertail forend; etc. optional. Five additional models available. Imported from Spain by Wm. Larkin Moore.
Price: From $4,850.00

Garbi Model 101 Side-by-Side Shotgun
Similar to the Garbi Model 100 except hand engraved with scroll engraving; select walnut stock; better overall quality than the Model 100. Imported from Spain by Wm. Larkin Moore.
Price: From $6,250.00

Garbi Model 103 A & B Side-by-Side Shotguns
Similar to the Garbi Model 100 except has Purdey-type fine scroll and rosette engraving. Better overall quality than the Model 101. Model 103B has nickel-chrome steel barrels, H&H-type easy opening mechanism; other mechanical details remain the same. Imported from Spain by Wm. Larkin Moore.
Price: Model 103A. From $8,000.00
Price: Model 103B. From $11,800.00

Garbi Model 200 Side-by-Side Shotgun
Similar to the Garbi Model 100 except has heavy-duty locks, magnum proofed. Very fine Continental-style floral and scroll engraving, well figured walnut stock. Other mechanical features remain the same. Imported from Spain by Wm. Larkin Moore.
Price: $11,200.00

KIMBER VALIER GRADE I and II SHOTGUN
Gauge: 20, 3" chambers. **Barrels:** 26" or 28", IC and M. **Weight:** 6 lbs. 8 oz. **Stock:** Turkish walnut, English style. **Features:** Sidelock design, double triggers, 50-percent engraving; 24 lpi checkering; auto-ejectors (extractors only on Grade I). Color case-hardened sidelocks, rust blue barrels. Imported from Turkey by Kimber Mfg., Inc.
Price: Grade I $3,879.00
Price: Grade II $4,480.00

LEBEAU-COURALLY BOXLOCK SIDE-BY-SIDE SHOTGUN
Gauge: 12, 16, 20, 28, .410-bore. **Barrel:** 25" to 32". **Weight:** To customer specifications. **Stock:** French walnut. **Features:** Anson & Deely-type action with automatic ejectors; single or double triggers. Custom gun built to customer specifications. Imported from Belgium by Wm. Larkin Moore.
Price: From $25,500.00

LEBEAU-COURALLY SIDELOCK SIDE-BY-SIDE SHOTGUN
Gauge: 12, 16, 20, 28, .410-bore. **Barrel:** 25" to 32". **Weight:** To customer specifications. **Stock:** Fancy French walnut. **Features:** Holland & Holland-type action with automatic ejectors; single or double triggers. Custom gun built to customer specifications. Imported from Belgium by Wm. Larkin Moore.
Price: From $56,000.00

Marlin L. C. Smith 12 gauge

Merkel Model 47E

Merkel Model 47SL

Merkel Model 280EL/360EL Two-Barrel Set

MARLIN L. C. SMITH SIDE-BY-SIDE SHOTGUN
Gauge: 12, 20. **Stock:** Checkered walnut w/recoil pad. **Features:** 3" chambers, single trigger, selective automatic ejectors; 3 choke tubes (IC, Mod., Full); solid rib, bead front sight. Imported from Italy by Marlin. Introduced 2005.
Price: LC12-DB (28" barrel, 43" OAL, 6.25 lbs) **$2,109.00**
Price: LC20-DB (26" barrel, 41" OAL, 6 lbs) **$2,109.00**

MERKEL MODEL 47E, 147E SIDE-BY-SIDE SHOTGUNS
Gauge: 12, 3" chambers, 16, 2-3/4" chambers, 20, 3" chambers. **Barrel:** 12, 16 ga.-28"; 20 ga.-26-3/4" (Imp. Cyl. & Mod., Mod. & Full). **Weight:** About 6-3/4 lbs. (12 ga.). **Stock:** Oil-finished walnut; straight English or pistol grip. **Features:** Anson & Deeley-type boxlock action with single selective or double triggers, automatic safety, cocking indicators. Color case-hardened receiver with standard arabesque engraving. Imported from Germany by GSI.
Price: Model 47E (H&H ejectors) **$3,295.00**
Price: Model 147E (as above with ejectors) **$3,995.00**

Merkel Model 47SL, 147SL Side-by-Side Shotguns
Similar to Model 47E except H&H style sidelock action with cocking indicators, ejectors. Silver-grayed receiver and sideplates have arabesque engraving, engraved border and screws (Model 47S), or fine hunting scene engraving (Model 147S). Imported from Germany by GSI.
Price: Model 47SL **$5,995.00**
Price: Model 147SL **$7,995.00**
Price: Model 247SL (English-style engraving, large scrolls) **$7,995.00**
Price: Model 447SL (English-style engraving, small scrolls) **$9,995.00**

Merkel Model 280EL, 360EL Shotguns
Similar to Model 47E except smaller frame. Greener cross bolt with double under-barrel locking lugs, fine engraved hunting scenes on silver-grayed receiver, luxury-grade wood, Anson and Deely box-lock action. H&H ejectors, single-selective or double triggers. Introduced 2000. From Merkel.

Price: Model 280EL (28 gauge, 28" barrel, Imp. Cyl. and Mod. chokes) **$5,795.00**
Price: Model 360EL (.410, 28" barrel, Mod. and Full chokes) **$5,795.00**
Price: Model 280/360EL two-barrel set (28 and .410 gauge as above) **$8,295.00**

Merkel Model 280SL and 360SL Shotguns
Similar to Model 280EL and 360EL except has sidelock action, double triggers, English-style arabesque engraving. Introduced 2000. From Merkel.
Price: Model 280SL (28 gauge, 28" barrel, Imp. Cyl. and Mod. chokes) **$8,495.00**
Price: Model 360SL (.410, 28" barrel, Mod. and Full chokes) **$8,495.00**
Price: Model 280/360SL two-barrel set **$11,995.00**

PIOTTI KING NO. 1 SIDE-BY-SIDE SHOTGUN
Gauge: 12, 16, 20, 28, .410. **Barrel:** 25" to 30" (12 ga.), 25" to 28" (16, 20, 28, .410). To customer specs. Chokes as specified. **Weight:** 6-1/2 lbs. to 8 lbs. (12 ga. to customer specs.). **Stock:** Dimensions to customer specs. Finely figured walnut; straight grip with checkered butt with classic splinter forend and hand-rubbed oil finish standard. Pistol grip, beavertail forend. **Features:** Holland & Holland pattern sidelock action, automatic ejectors. Double trigger; non-selective single trigger optional. Coin finish standard; color case-hardened optional. Top rib; level, file-cut; concave, ventilated optional. Very fine, full coverage scroll engraving with small floral bouquets. Imported from Italy by Wm. Larkin Moore.
Price: From **$29,600.00**

Piotti King Extra Side-by-Side Shotgun
Similar to the Piotti King No. 1 except with upgraded engraving. Choice of any type of engraving, including bulino game scene engraving and game scene engraving with gold inlays. Engraved and signed by a master engraver. Other mechanical specifications remain the same. Imported from Italy by Wm. Larkin Moore.
Price: From **$35,000.00**

SHOTGUNS — Side-by-Side

Piotti Lunik

Rizzini Sidelock

Ruger Gold Label

Smith & Wesson Elite Gold

Stoeger Uplander

Piotti Lunik Side-by-Side Shotgun
Similar to the Piotti King No. 1 in overall quality. Has Renaissance-style large scroll engraving in relief. Best quality Holland & Holland-pattern sidelock ejector double with chopper lump (demi-bloc) barrels. Other mechanical specifications remain the same. Imported from Italy by Wm. Larkin Moore.
Price: From **$30,900.00**

PIOTTI PIUMA SIDE-BY-SIDE SHOTGUN
Gauge: 12, 16, 20, 28, .410. **Barrel:** 25" to 30" (12 ga.), 25" to 28" (16, 20, 28, .410). **Weight:** 5-1/2 to 6-1/4 lbs. (20 ga.). **Stock:** Dimensions to customer specs. Straight grip stock with walnut checkered butt, classic splinter forend, hand-rubbed oil finish are standard; pistol grip, beavertail forend, satin luster finish optional. **Features:** Anson & Deeley boxlock ejector double with chopper lump barrels. Level, file-cut rib, light scroll and rosette engraving, scalloped frame. Double triggers; single non-selective optional. Coin finish standard, color case-hardened optional. Imported from Italy by Wm. Larkin Moore.
Price: From **$14,800.00**

REMINGTON PREMIER UPLAND & UPLAND SPECIAL SIDE-BY-SIDE SHOTGUNS
Gauge: 12, 20, 28, .410 bore, 3" chamber; **Barrel:** 28" in 12, 20 gauge; polished blue; vent rib. **Sights:** front bead. **Weight:** 6.5 to 7.5 lbs. Length: 44.125" to 45.125" overall. **Stock:** 14.25" LOP; 1.5" drop at comb; 2.4" drop at heel. Checkered pistol grip, checkered fore-end, oil finish, rubber butt pad. Upland Special has straight grip English-style stock. **Features:** Case-colored receiver, game-scene engraving. Single-selective mechanical trigger, selective automatic ejectors; serrated free-floating vent rib. Five flush-mount ProBore choke tubes for 12s and 20s; 28-gauge equipped with 3 flush mount ProBore choke tubes. Hard case included. Introduced 2007. Made in Italy, imported by Remington Arms Co.
Price: Premier Upland 12 gauge, 28" barrel, 7.5 lbs. **$2,030.00**
Price: Premier Upland 20 gauge, 28" barrel, 6.75 lbs. **$2,030.00**

Price: Premier Upland 28 gauge, 27" barrel, 6.5 lbs. **$2,086.00**
Price: Premier Upland .410, 27" barrel, 6.5 lbs. **$2,086.00**
Price: Premier Upland Special 28 ga. or .410 bore,
27" barrel, 6.5 lbs. **$2,086.00**

RIZZINI SIDELOCK SIDE-BY-SIDE SHOTGUN
Gauge: 12, 16, 20, 28, .410. **Barrel:** 25" to 30" (12, 16, 20 ga.), 25" to 28" (28, .410). To customer specs. Chokes as specified. **Weight:** 6-1/2 lbs. to 8 lbs. (12 ga. to customer specs). **Stock:** Dimensions to customer specs. Finely figured walnut; straight grip with checkered butt with classic splinter forend and hand-rubbed oil finish standard. Pistol grip, beavertail forend. **Features:** Sidelock action, auto ejectors. Double triggers or non-selective single trigger standard. Coin finish standard. Imported from Italy by Wm. Larkin Moore.
Price: 12, 20 ga. From **$66,900.00**
Price: 28, .410 bore. From **$75,500.00**

RUGER GOLD LABEL SIDE-BY-SIDE SHOTGUN
Gauge: 12, 3" chambers. **Barrel:** 28" with skeet tubes. **Weight:** 6-1/2 lbs. **Length:** 45". **Stock:** American walnut straight or pistol grip. **Sights:** Gold bead front, full length rib, serrated top. **Features:** Spring-assisted break-open, SS trigger, auto eject. Five interchangeable screw-in choke tubes, combination safety/barrel selector with auto safety reset.
Price: **$2,650.00**

SMITH & WESSON ELITE GOLD SHOTGUNS
Gauge: 20, 3" chambers. **Barrel:** 26", 28", 30", rust-blued chopper-lump. **Weight:** 6.5 lbs. **Length:** 43.5-45.5". **Sights:** Ivory front bead, metal mid-bead. **Stock:** AAA (grade III) Turkish walnut stocks, hand-cut checkering, satin finish. English grip or pistol grip. **Features:** Smith & Wesson-designed trigger-plate action, hand-engraved receivers, bone-charcoal case hardening, lifetime warranty. Five choke tubes. Introduced 2007. Made in Turkey, imported by Smith & Wesson.
Price: . . . . **NA**

STOEGER UPLANDER SIDE-BY-SIDE SHOTGUNS
Gauge: 16, 28, 2-3/4 chambers. 12, 20, .410, 3" chambers. **Barrel:** 22", 24", 26", 28". **Weight:** 7.3 lbs. **Sights:** Brass bead. **Features:** Double trigger, IC & M fixed choke tubes with gun.
Price: With fixed or screw-in chokes **$350.00**
Price: Supreme, screw-in chokes, 12 or 20 ga. **$485.00**
Price: Youth, 20 ga. or .410, 22" barrel, double trigger **$350.00**
Price: Combo, 20/28 ga. or 12/20 ga. **$649.00**

Stoeger Silverado Coach

Traditions Elite Hunter

Traditions Uplander V

Tristar Brittany

Tristar-Gentry

STOEGER COACH GUN SIDE-BY-SIDE SHOTGUNS
Gauge: 12, 20, 2-3/4", 3" chambers. **Barrel:** 20". **Weight:** 6-1/2 lbs. **Stock:** Brown hardwood, classic beavertail forend. **Sights:** Brass bead. **Features:** IC & M fixed chokes, tang auto safety, auto extractors, black plastic buttplate. Imported by Benelli USA.
Price: Supreme blued finish $410.00
Price: Supreme blued barrel, stainless receiver $430.00
Price: Supreme polished nickel receiver $460.00
Price: Coach Gun black walnut stock, polished nickel receiver $410.00
Price: Nickel Coach Gun synthetic stock, stainless $400.00
Price: Silverado Coach Gun with English synthetic stock $400.00

TRADITIONS ELITE SERIES SIDE-BY-SIDE SHOTGUNS
Gauge: 12, 3"; 20, 3"; 28, 2-3/4"; .410, 3". **Barrel:** 26". **Weight:** 5 lbs., 12 oz. to 6-1/2 lbs. **Length:** 43" overall. **Stock:** Walnut. **Features:** Chrome-lined barrels; fixed chokes (Elite Field III ST, Field I DT and Field I ST) or choke tubes (Elite Hunter ST); extractors (Hunter ST and Field I models) or automatic ejectors (Field III ST); top tang safety. Imported from Fausti of Italy by Traditions.
Price: Elite Field I DT — 12, 20, 28 ga. or .410; IC and Mod. fixed chokes
        (F and F on .410); double triggers . . . . **$789.00 to $969.00**
Price: Elite Field I ST — 12, 20, 28 ga. or .410; same as DT
        but with single trigger . . . . **$969.00 to $1,169.00**

Price: Elite Field III ST — 28 ga. or .410; gold-engraved receiver;
        high-grade walnut stock **$2,099.00**
Price: Elite Hunter ST — 12 or 20 ga.; blued receiver; IC and
        Mod. choke tubes **$999.00**

TRADITIONS UPLANDER SERIES SIDE-BY-SIDE SHOTGUNS
Gauge: 12, 3"; 20, 3". **Barrel:** 26", 28". **Weight:** 6-1/4 lbs. to 6-1/2 lbs. **Length:** 43" to 45" overall. **Stock:** Walnut. **Features:** Barrels threaded for choke tubes (Improved Cylinder, Modified and Full); top tang safety, extended trigger guard. Engraved silver receiver with side plates and lavish gold inlays. Imported from Fausti of Italy by Traditions.
Price: Uplander III Silver 12, 20 ga. **$2,699.00**
Price: Uplander V Silver 12, 20 ga. **$3,199.00**

TRISTAR BRITTANY SIDE-BY-SIDE SHOTGUN
Gauge: 12, 16, 20, 28, .410, 3" chambers. **Barrel:** 12 ga., 20 ga., 26", 28"; 16 ga., 27", 28 ga., 27", .410 ga., 27". All have CT-3 Chokes. **Weight:** 6.2 to 7.2 lbs. **Stock:** Walnut English-style, semi-beavertail forearm with cut checkering, standard semi-gloss finish. **Features:** Boxlock action, engraved case colored frame, auto selective ejectors, single selective trigger.
Price: . . . . **$1,050.00 to $1,069.00**

TRISTAR GENTRY SIDE-BY-SIDE SHOTGUN
Gauge: 12, 16, 20, 28, .410, 3" chambers (16 and 28-ga. @ 2 3/4"). **Barrel:** 12 ga., 27", 20 ga., 28"; 28 ga., 26", 410 ga., 26". All have CT-3 Chokes. **Weight:** 6.2 to 6.8 lbs. **Stock:** Walnut pistol grip stock, semi-beavertail forearm with cut checkering, standard semi-gloss finish. **Features:** Boxlock action, engraved antique silver frame, extractors, single selective trigger with top tang selector.
Price: . . . . **$929.00 to $945.00**

Variety of designs for utility and sporting purposes, as well as for competitive shooting.

Browning BT-99 Trap

H&R Model 928
Ultra Slug Hunter Deluxe

H&R Tamer

H&R Topper

H&R Topper Deluxe

Stock: Walnut. **Features:** Manually cocking single shot bolt, blued receiver.
Price: **$225.95**

BERETTA DT10 TRIDENT TRAP TOP SINGLE SHOTGUN
Gauge: 12, 3" chamber. **Barrel:** 34"; five Optima Choke tubes (Full, Full, Imp. Modified, Mod. and Imp. Cyl.). **Weight:** 8.8 lbs. **Stock:** High-grade walnut; adjustable. **Features:** Detachable, adjustable trigger group; Optima Bore for improved shot pattern and reduced recoil; slim Optima Choke tubes; raised and thickened receiver for long life. Introduced 2000. Imported from Italy by Beretta USA.
Price: **$6,995.00**

BROWNING BT-99 TRAP O/U SHOTGUNS
Gauge: 12. **Barrel:** 30", 32", 34". **Stock:** Walnut; standard or adjustable. **Weight:** 7 lbs. 11 oz. to 9 lbs. **Features:** Back-bored single barrel; interchangeable chokes; beavertail forearm; extractor only; high rib.
Price: BT-99 w/conventional comb, 32" or 34" barrels **$1,396.00**
Price: BT-99 w/adjustable comb, 32" or 34" barrels **$1,584.00**
Price: BT-99 Golden Clays w/adjustable comb,
    32" or 34" barrels **$3,509.00**
Price: BT-99 Micro w/conventional comb, 30" or 32" barrels **$1,396.00**

CHIPMUNK 410 YOUTH SHOTGUN
Gauge: .410. **Barrel:** 18-1/4" tapered, blue. **Weight:** 3.25 lbs. **Length:** 33".

HARRINGTON & RICHARDSON ULTRA SLUG HUNTER/TAMER SHOTGUNS
Gauge: 12, 20 ga., 3" chamber, .410. **Barrel:** 20" to 24" rifled. **Weight:** 6 to 9 lbs. **Length:** 34-1/2" to 40". **Stock:** Hardwood, laminate, or polymer with full pistol grip; semi-beavertail forend. **Sights:** Gold bead front. **Features:** Break-open action with side-lever release, automatic ejector. Introduced 1994. From H&R 1871, LLC.
Price: Ultra Slug Hunter, blued, hardwood **$273.00**
Price: Ultra Slug Hunter Youth, blued, hardwood, 13-1/8" LOP . . . **$273.00**
Price: Ultra Slug Hunter Deluxe, blued, laminated **$273.00**
Price: Tamer .410 bore, stainless barrel, black polymer stock **$173.00**

HARRINGTON & RICHARDSON TOPPER MODEL S
Gauge: 12, 16, 20, .410, up to 3.5" chamber. **Barrel:** 22 to 28". **Weight:** 5-7 lbs. **Stock:** Polymer, hardwood, or black walnut. **Features:** Satin nickel frame, blued barrel. Reintroduced 1992. From H&R 1871, LLC.
Price: Deluxe Classic, 12/20 ga., 28" barrel w/vent rib **$225.00**
Price: Topper Deluxe 12 ga., 28" barrel, black hardwood **$179.00**
Price: Topper 12, 16, 20 ga., .410, 26" to 28", black hardwood **$153.00**
Price: Topper Junior 20 ga., .410, 22" barrel, hardwood **$160.00**
Price: Topper Junior Classic, 20 ga., .410, checkered hardwood . . **$160.00**

H&R Topper Junior

Ljutic Mono Gun

Mossberg SSi One

New England Firearms Standard Pardner

New England Firearms
Pardner Screw-in Choke Model

KRIEGHOFF K-80 SINGLE BARREL TRAP GUN
Gauge: 12, 2-3/4" chamber. **Barrel:** 32" or 34" Unsingle. Fixed Full or choke tubes. **Weight:** About 8-3/4 lbs. **Stock:** Four stock dimensions or adjustable stock available. All hand-checkered European walnut. **Features:** Satin nickel finish. Selective mechanical trigger adjustable for finger position. Tapered step vent rib. Adjustable point of impact.
Price: Standard grade Full Unsingle, from **$10,080.00**

KRIEGHOFF KX-5 TRAP GUN
Gauge: 12, 2-3/4" chamber. **Barrel:** 32", 34"; choke tubes. **Weight:** About 8-1/2 lbs. **Stock:** Factory adjustable stock. European walnut. **Features:** Ventilated tapered step rib. Adjustable position trigger, optional release trigger. Fully adjustable rib. Satin gray electroless nickel receiver. Fitted aluminum case. Imported from Germany by Krieghoff International, Inc.
Price: **$5,395.00**

LJUTIC MONO GUN SINGLE BARREL SHOTGUN
Gauge: 12 only. **Barrel:** 34", choked to customer specs; hollow-milled rib, 35-1/2" sight plane. **Weight:** Approx. 9 lbs. **Stock:** To customer specs. Oil finish, hand checkered. **Features:** Custom gun. Pull or release trigger; removable trigger guard contains trigger and hammer mechanism; Ljutic pushbutton opener on front of trigger guard. From Ljutic Industries.
Price: Std., med. or Olympic rib, custom bbls., fixed choke **$6,995.00**
Price: As above with screw-in choke barrel **$7,395.00**
Price: Stainless steel mono gun **$7,995.00**

Ljutic LTX Pro 3 Deluxe Mono Gun
Deluxe, lightweight version of the Mono gun with high quality wood, upgrade checkering, special rib height, screw-in chokes, ported and cased.

Price: **$8,995.00**
Price: Stainless steel model **$9,995.00**

MOSSBERG SSi-ONE 12 GAUGE SLUG SHOTGUN
Gauge: 12, 3" chamber. **Barrel:** 24", fully rifled. **Weight:** 8 lbs. **Length:** 40" overall. **Stock:** Walnut, fluted and cut checkered; sling-swivel studs; drilled and tapped for scope base. **Sights:** None (scope base supplied). **Features:** Frame accepts interchangeable rifle barrels (see Mossberg SSi-One rifle listing); lever-opening, break-action design; ambidextrous, top-tang safety; internal eject/extract selector. Introduced 2000. From Mossberg.
Price: **$480.00**

Mossberg SSi-One Turkey Shotgun
Similar to SSi-One 12 gauge slug shotgun, but chambered for 12 ga., 3-1/2" loads. Includes Accu-Mag Turkey Tube. Introduced 2001. From Mossberg.
Price: **$459.00**

NEW ENGLAND FIREARMS PARDNER AND TRACKER II SHOTGUNS
Gauge: 10, 12, 16, 20, 28, .410, up to 3.5" chamber for 10 and 12 ga. 16, 28, 2-3/4" chamber. **Barrel:** 24" to 30". **Weight:** Varies from 5 to 9.5 lbs. **Length:** Varies from 36" to 48". **Stock:** Walnut-finished hardwood with full pistol grip, synthetic, or camo finish. **Sights:** Bead front on most. **Features:** Transfer bar ignition; break-open action with side-lever release. Introduced 1987. From New England Firearms.
Price: Pardner, all gauges, hardwood stock, 26" to 32" blued barrel,
    Mod. or Full choke **$140.00**
Price: Pardner Youth, hardwood stock, straight grip,
    22" blued barrel **$149.00**
Price: Pardner Screw-In Choke model, intr. 2006 . . . . **$164.00**
Price: Turkey model, 10/12 ga., camo finish or black . . **$192.00 to $259.00**
Price: Youth Turkey, 20 ga., camo finish or black **$192.00**
Price: Waterfowl, 10 ga., camo finish or hardwood **$227.00**
Price: Tracker II slug gun, 12/20 ga., hardwood **$196.00**

New England Firearms Tracker II

Rossi Single-Shot

Rossi Matched Pair

Savage 210F Slug Warrior

Stoeger Single-Shot

ROSSI SINGLE-SHOT SHOTGUNS
Gauge: 12, 20, .410. **Barrel:** 22" (Youth), 28". **Weight:** 3.75-5.25 lbs. **Stocks:** Wood. **Sights:** Bead front sight, fully adjustable fiber optic sight on Slug and Turkey. **Features:** Single-shot break open, 8 models available, positive ejection, internal transfer bar mechanism, trigger block system, Taurus Security System, blued finish, Rifle Slug has ported barrel.
Price: . . . . **$125.00 to $214.00**

ROSSI MATCHED PAIRS
Gauge/Caliber: 12, 20, .410, .22Mag, .22LR, .17HMR, .223Rem, .243Win, .270Win, .30-06, .308Win, .50 (black powder). **Barrel:** 23", 28". **Weight:** 5-6.3 lbs. **Stocks:** Wood or black synthetic. **Sights:** Bead front on shotgun barrel, fully adjustable front and rear on rifle barrel, drilled and tapped for scope, fully adjustable fiber optic sights (black powder). **Features:** Single-shot break open, 27 models available, internal transfer bar mechanism, manual external safety, blue finish, trigger block system, Taurus Security System, youth models available.
Price: Rimfire/Shotgun . . . . **$169.00 to $253.00**
Price: Centerfire/Shotgun **$297.00**
Price: Black Powder Matched Pair . . . . **$249.00 to $313.00**

ROSSI MATCHED SET
Gauge/Caliber: 12, 20, .22LR, .17HMR, .243Win, .270Win, .50 (black powder). **Barrel:** 33.5"–43". **Weight:** 6.25-6.3 lbs. **Stocks:** Wood. **Sights:** Bead front on shotgun barrel, fully adjustable front and rear on rifle barrel, drilled and tapped for scope, fully adjustable fiber optic sights (black powder). **Features:** Single-shot break open, 4 models available, internal transfer bar mechanism, manual external safety, blue finish, trigger block system, Taurus Security System, youth models available.
Price: . . . . **$319.00 to $398.00**

SAVAGE MODEL 210F SLUG WARRIOR SHOTGUN
Gauge: 12, 3" chamber; 2-shot magazine. **Barrel:** 24" 1:35" rifling twist. **Weight:** 7-1/2 lbs. **Length:** 43.5" overall. **Stock:** Glass-filled polymer with positive checkering. **Features:** Based on the Savage Model 110 action; 60-degree bolt lift; controlled round feed; comes with scope mount. Introduced 1996. Made in U.S. by Savage Arms.
Price: **$475.00**
Price: (Camo) **$513.00**

STOEGER SINGLE-SHOT SHOTGUN
Gauge: 12, 20, .410, 2-3/4", 3" chambers. **Barrel:** 26", 28". **Weight:** 5.4 lbs. **Length:** 40-1/2" to 42-1/2" overall. **Sights:** Brass bead. **Features:** .410, Full fixed choke tubes, screw-in. .410 12 ga. hardwood pistol-grip stock and forend. 20 ga. 26" bbl., hardwood forend.
Price: Blue; Youth **$109.00**
Price: Youth with English stock **$119.00**

Tar-Hunt RSG-20 Mountaineer

Thompson/Center Encore Rifled Slug

Thompson/Center Encore Turkey

TAR-HUNT RSG-12 PROFESSIONAL RIFLED SLUG GUN
Gauge: 12, 2-3/4" or 3" chamber, 1-shot magazine. **Barrel:** 23", fully rifled with muzzle brake. **Weight:** 7-3/4 lbs. **Length:** 41-1/2" overall. **Stock:** Matte black McMillan fiberglass with Pachmayr Decelerator pad. **Sights:** None furnished; comes with Leupold windage or Weaver bases. **Features:** Uses rifle-style action with two locking lugs; two-position safety; Shaw barrel; single-stage, trigger; muzzle brake. Many options available. Right- and left-hand models at same prices. Introduced 1991. Made in U.S. by Tar-Hunt Custom Rifles, Inc.
Price: 12 ga. Professional model, right- or left-hand **$2,585.00**

Tar-Hunt RSG-16 Elite Shotgun
Similar to RSG-12 Professional except 16 gauge; right- or left-hand versions.
Price: **$2,585.00**

Tar-Hunt RSG-20 Mountaineer Slug Gun
Similar to the RSG-12 Professional except chambered for 20 gauge (2-3/4" and 3" shells); 23" Shaw rifled barrel, with muzzle brake; two-lug bolt; one-shot blind magazine; matte black finish; McMillan fiberglass stock with Pachmayr Decelerator pad; receiver drilled and tapped for Rem. 700 bases. Right- or left-hand versions. Weighs 6-1/2 lbs. Introduced 1997. Made in U.S. by Tar-Hunt Custom Rifles, Inc.
Price: **$2,585.00**

THOMPSON/CENTER ENCORE RIFLED SLUG GUN
Gauge: 20, 3" chamber. **Barrel:** 26", fully rifled. **Weight:** About 7 lbs. **Length:** 40-1/2" overall. **Stock:** Walnut with walnut forearm. **Sights:** Steel; click-adjustable rear and ramp-style front, both with fiber optics. **Features:** Encore system features a variety of rifle, shotgun and muzzle-loading rifle barrels interchangeable with the same frame. Break-open design operates by pulling up and back on trigger guard spur. Composite stock and forearm available. Introduced 2000.
Price: **$684.00**

THOMPSON/CENTER ENCORE TURKEY GUN
Gauge: 12 ga. **Barrel:** 24". **Features:** All-camo finish, high definition Realtree Hardwoods HD camo.
Price: **$763.00**

Designs for utility, suitable for and adaptable to competitions and other sporting purposes.

Benelli M3 Convertible

Fabarm FP6

Mossberg Model 500 Persuader

BENELLI M3 CONVERTIBLE SHOTGUN
Gauge: 12, 2-3/4", 3" chambers, 5-shot magazine. **Barrel:** 19-3/4" (Cyl.). **Weight:** 7 lbs., 4oz. **Length:** 41" overall. **Stock:** High-impact polymer with sling loop in side of butt; rubberized pistol grip on stock. **Sights:** Open rifle, fully adjustable. Ghost ring and rifle type. **Features:** Combination pump/auto action. Alloy receiver with inertia recoil rotating locking lug bolt; matte finish; automatic shell release lever. Introduced 1989. Imported by Benelli USA. Price with pistol grip, open rifle sights.

Price: With standard stock, open rifle sights	**$1,255.00**
Price: With ghost ring sight system, standard stock	**$1,335.00**
Price: With ghost ring sights, pistol grip stock	**$1,335.00**

BENELLI M2 TACTICAL SHOTGUN
Gauge: 12, 2-3/4", 3" chambers, 5-shot magazine. **Barrel:** 18.5" IC, M, F choke tubes. **Weight:** 6.7 lbs. **Length:** 39.75" overall. **Stock:** Black polymer. **Sights:** Rifle type ghost ring system, tritium night sights optional. **Features:** Semi-auto intertia recoil action. Cross-bolt safety; bolt release button; matte-finish metal. Introduced 1993. Imported from Italy by Benelli USA.

Price: With rifle sights	**$1,065.00**
Price: With ghost ring sights, standard stock	**$1,175.00**
Price: With ghost ring sights, pistol grip stock	**$1,175.00**
Price: With rifle sights, pistol grip stock	**$1,065.00**
Price: ComforTech stock, rifle sights	**$1,175.00**
Price: Comfortech Stock, Ghost Ring	**$1,280.00**

CROSSFIRE SHOTGUN/RIFLE
Gauge/Caliber: 12, 2-3/4" Chamber: 4-shot/223 Rem. (5-shot). **Barrel:** 20" (shotgun), 18" (rifle). **Weight:** About 8.6 lbs. **Length:** 40" overall. **Stock:** Composite. **Sights:** Meprolight night sights. Integral Weaver-style scope rail. **Features:** Combination pump-action shotgun, rifle; single selector; single trigger; dual action bars for both upper and lower actions; ambidextrous selector and safety. Introduced 1997. Made in U.S. From Hesco.

Price: About	**$1,895.00**
Price: With camo finish	**$1,995.00**

E.M.F. OLD WEST PUMP (SLIDE ACTION) SHOTGUN
Gauge: 12. **Barrel:** 20". **Weight:** 7 lbs. **Length:** 39 1/2" overall. **Stock:** Smooth walnut with cushioned pad. **Sights:** Front bead. **Features:** Authentic reproduction of Winchester 1897 pump shotgun; blue receiver and barrel; standard modified choke. Introduced 2006. Imported from China for E.M.F. by TTN.

Price:	**$474.90**

FABARM TACTICAL SEMI-AUTOMATIC SHOTGUN
Gauge: 12, 3" chamber. **Barrel:** 20". **Weight:** 6.6 lbs. **Length:** 41.2" overall. **Stock:** Polymer or folding. **Sights:** Ghost ring (tritium night sights optional). **Features:** Gas operated; matte receiver; twin forged action bars; over-sized bolt handle and safety button; Picatinny rail; includes cylinder bore choke tube. New features include polymer pistol grip stock. Introduced 2001. Imported from Italy by Heckler & Koch Inc.

Price:	**$999.00**

FABARM FP6 PUMP SHOTGUN
Gauge: 12, 3" chamber. **Barrel:** 20" (Cyl.); accepts choke tubes. **Weight:** 6.6 lbs. **Length:** 41.25" overall. **Stock:** Black polymer with textured grip, grooved slide handle. **Sights:** Blade front. **Features:** Twin action bars; anodized finish; free carrier for smooth reloading. Introduced 1998. New features include ghost-ring sighting system, low profile Picatinny rail, and pistol grip stock. Imported from Italy by Heckler & Koch, Inc.

Price: (Carbon fiber finish)	**$499.00**
Price: With flip-up front sight, Picatinny rail with rear sight, oversize safety button	**$499.00**

MOSSBERG MODEL 500 PERSUADER SECURITY SHOTGUNS
Gauge: 12, 20, .410, 3" chamber. **Barrel:** 18-1/2", 20" (Cyl.). **Weight:** 7 lbs. **Stock:** Walnut-finished hardwood or black synthetic. **Sights:** Metal bead front. **Features:** Available in 6- or 8-shot models. Top-mounted safety, double action slide bars, swivel studs, rubber recoil pad. Blue, Parkerized, Marinecote finishes. Mossberg Cablelock included. From Mossberg.

Price: 12 ga., 18-1/2", blue, wood or synthetic stock, 6-shot	**$353.00**
Price: Cruiser, 12 ga., 18-1/2", blue, pistol grip, heat shield	**$357.00**
Price: As above, 20 ga. or .410 bore	**$345.00**

Mossberg Ghost Ring

Mossberg Model HS410

Remington Model 870 Tactical

Tactical Response TR-870

Mossberg Model 500, 590 Mariner Pump Shotgun
Similar to the Model 500 or 590 Persuader except all metal parts finished with Marinecote metal finish to resist rust and corrosion. Synthetic field stock; pistol grip kit included. Mossberg Cablelock included.
Price: 6-shot, 18-1/2" barrel **$497.00**
Price: 9-shot, 20" barrel **$513.00**

Mossberg Model 500, 590 Ghost-Ring Shotgun
Similar to the Model 500 Persuader except has adjustable blade front, adjustable Ghost-Ring rear sight with protective "ears." Model 500 has 18.5" (Cyl.) barrel, 6-shot capacity; Model 590 has 20" (Cyl.) barrel, 9-shot capacity. Both have synthetic field stock. Mossberg Cablelock included. Introduced 1990. From Mossberg.
Price: 500 Parkerized **$468.00**
Price: 590 Parkerized **$543.00**
Price: 590 Parkerized Speedfeed stock **$586.00**

Mossberg Model HS410 Shotgun
Similar to the Model 500 Persuader pump except chambered for 20 gauge or .410 with 3" chamber; has pistol grip forend, thick recoil pad, muzzle brake and has special spreader choke on the 18.5" barrel. Overall length is 37.5", weight is 6.25 lbs. Blue finish; synthetic field stock. Mossberg Cablelock and video included. Introduced 1990.
Price: HS 410 .... **$355.00**

MOSSBERG MODEL 590 SHOTGUN
Gauge: 12, 3" chamber. **Barrel:** 20" (Cyl.). **Weight:** 7-1/4 lbs. **Stock:** Synthetic field or Speedfeed. **Sights:** Metal bead front. **Features:** Top-mounted safety, double slide action bars. Comes with heat shield, bayonet lug, swivel studs, rubber recoil pad. Blue, Parkerized or Marinecote finish. Mossberg Cablelock included. From Mossberg.
Price: Blue, synthetic stock **$417.00**
Price: Parkerized, synthetic stock **$476.00**
Price: Parkerized, Speedfeed stock **$519.00**

REMINGTON MODEL 870 AND MODEL 1100 TACTICAL SHOTGUNS
Gauge: 12, 2-3/4 or 3" chamber, 7-shot magazine. **Barrel:** 18", 20", 22" (Cyl or IC). **Weight:** 7.5-7.75 lbs. **Length:** 38.5-42.5" overall. **Stock:** Black synthetic, synthetic Speedfeed IV full pistol-grip stock, or Knoxx Industries SpecOps stock w/recoil-absorbing spring-loaded cam and adjustable length of pull (12" to 16", 870 only). **Sights:** Front post w/dot only on 870; rib and front dot on 1100. **Features:** R3 recoil pads, LimbSaver technology to reduce felt recoil, 2-, 3- or 4-shot extensions based on barrel length; matte-olive-drab barrels and receivers. Model 1100 Tactical is available with Speedfeed IV pistol grip stock or standard black synthetic stock and forend. Speedfeed IV model has an 18" barrel with two-shot extension. Standard synthetic-stocked version is equipped with 22" barrel and four-shot extension. Introduced 2006. From Remington Arms Co.
Price: 870, Speedfeed IV stock, 3" chamber, 38.5" overall **$599.00**
Price: 870, SpecOps stock, 3" chamber, 38.5" overall **$625.00**
Price: 1100, synthetic stock, 2-3/4" chamber, 42.5" overall **$759.00**

TACTICAL RESPONSE TR-870 STANDARD MODEL SHOTGUNS
Gauge: 12, 3" chamber, 7-shot magazine. **Barrel:** 18" (Cyl.). **Weight:** 9 lbs. **Length:** 38" overall. **Stock:** Fiberglass-filled polypropolene with non-snag recoil absorbing butt pad. Nylon tactical forend houses flashlight. **Sights:** Trak-Lock ghost ring sight system. Front sight has Tritium insert. **Features:** Highly modified Remington 870P with Parkerized finish. Comes with nylon three-way adjustable sling, high visibility non-binding follower, high performance magazine spring, Jumbo Head safety, and Side Saddle extended 6-shot shell carrier on left side of receiver. Introduced 1991. From Scattergun Technologies, Inc.
Price: Standard model **$815.00**
Price: FBI model **$770.00**
Price: Patrol model **$595.00**
Price: Border Patrol model **$605.00**
Price: K-9 model (Rem. 11-87 action) **$995.00**
Price: Urban Sniper, Rem. 11-87 action **$1,290.00**
Price: Louis Awerbuck model **$705.00**
Price: Practical Turkey model **$725.00**
Price: Expert model **$1,350.00**
Price: Professional model **$815.00**
Price: Entry model **$840.00**
Price: Compact model **$635.00**
Price: SWAT model **$1,195.00**

Dixie Pennsylvania   Harper's Ferry   Kentucky   Le Page   Lyman Plains Pistol

Pedersoli Mang

DIXIE KENTUCKY PISTOL
Caliber: 44 (.430" round ball). **Barrel:** 10", (7/8" octagon). **Weight:** 2-1/2 lbs. **Stocks:** Walnut-stained hardwood. **Sights:** Blade front, open rear drift-adjustable for windage; brass. **Features:** Flintlock only. Brass trigger guard, thimbles, instep, wedge plates; high- luster blue barrel. Imported from Italy by Dixie Gun Works.
Price: Finished flint **$250.00**
Price: Finished percussion **$225.00**
Price: Kit **$195.00**

FRENCH-STYLE DUELING PISTOL
Caliber: 44. **Barrel:** 10". **Weight:** 35 oz. **Length:** 15-3/4" overall. **Stocks:** Carved walnut. **Sights:** Fixed. **Features:** Comes with velvet-lined case and accessories. Imported by Mandall Shooting Supplies.
Price: **$295.00**

HARPER'S FERRY 1806 PISTOL
Caliber: 58 (.570" round ball). **Barrel:** 10". **Weight:** 40 oz. **Length:** 16" overall. **Stocks:** Walnut. **Sights:** Fixed. **Features:** Case- hardened lock, brass-mounted browned barrel. Replica of the first U.S. gov't.-made flintlock pistol. Imported by Navy Arms, Dixie Gun Works.
Price: Dixie Gun Works RH0225 . . . . **$375.00**
Price: Kit (Dixie) **$295.00**

KENTUCKY FLINTLOCK PISTOL
Caliber: 44, 45. **Barrel:** 10-1/8". **Weight:** 32 oz. **Length:** 15-1/2" overall. **Stocks:** Walnut. **Sights:** Fixed. **Features:** Specifications, including caliber, weight and length may vary with importer. Case-hardened lock, blued barrel; available also as brass barrel flintlock Model 1821. Imported by Navy Arms, The Armoury, Dixie Gun Works.
Price: **$300.00**
Price: In kit form. From . . . . **$90.00 to $112.00**
Price: Single cased set (Navy Arms) **$360.00**
Price: Double cased set (Navy Arms) **$590.00**

Kentucky Percussion Pistol
Similar to Flint version but percussion lock. Imported by The Armoury, Navy Arms, CVA (50-cal.).
Price: . . . . **$129.95 to $225.00**
Price: Steel barrel (Armoury) **$179.00**
Price: Single cased set (Navy Arms) **$355.00**
Price: Double cased set (Navy Arms) **$600.00**

LE PAGE PERCUSSION DUELING PISTOL
Caliber: 44. **Barrel:** 10", rifled. **Weight:** 40 oz. **Length:** 16" overall. **Stocks:** Walnut, fluted butt. **Sights:** Blade front, notch rear. **Features:** Single-set trigger. Blued barrel; trigger guard and buttcap are polished silver. Imported by Dixie Gun Works.
Price: PH0310 . . . . **$470.00**

LYMAN PLAINS PISTOL
Caliber: 50 or 54. **Barrel:** 8"; 1:30" twist, both calibers. **Weight:** 50 oz. **Length:** 15" overall. **Stocks:** Walnut half-stock. **Sights:** Blade front, square notch rear adjustable for windage. **Features:** Polished brass trigger guard and ramrod tip, color case-hardened coil spring lock, spring-loaded trigger, stainless steel nipple, blackened iron furniture. Hooked patent breech, detachable belt hook. Introduced 1981. From Lyman Products.
Price: Finished **$244.95**
Price: Kit **$189.95**

PEDERSOLI MANG TARGET PISTOL
Caliber: 38. **Barrel:** 10.5", octagonal; 1:15" twist, **Weight:** 2.5 lbs. **Length:** 17.25" overall. **Stocks:** Walnut with fluted grip. **Sights:** Blade front, open rear adjustable for windage. **Features:** Browned barrel, polished breech plug, remainder color case-hardened. Imported from Italy by Dixie Gun Works.
Price: PH0503 . . . . **$1,100.00**

Queen Anne

Traditions Pioneer

Traditions William Parker

Traditions Buckhunter Pro

QUEEN ANNE FLINTLOCK PISTOL
Caliber: 50 (.490" round ball). **Barrel:** 7-1/2", smoothbore. **Stocks:** Walnut. **Sights:** None. **Features:** Browned steel barrel, fluted brass trigger guard, brass mask on butt. Lockplate left in the white. Made by Pedersoli in Italy. Introduced 1983. Imported by Dixie Gun Works.
Price: RH0211 . . . . $290.00
Price: Kit FH0421 . . . . $225.00

REPLICA ARMS "SEVEN SEAS" DERRINGER
Caliber: 36 cal., smoothbore percussion. **Barrel:** 4-5/8". **Weight:** 21 oz. **Length:** 11" overall. **Grips:** Walnut finished. **Features:** All steel barrel with brass accents. Introduced 2005. Imported by Navy Arms.
Price: $99.95

TRADITIONS BUCKHUNTER PRO IN-LINE PISTOL
Caliber: 50. **Barrel:** 9-1/2", round. **Weight:** 48 oz. **Length:** 14" overall. **Stocks:** Smooth walnut or black epoxy-coated hardwood grip and forend. **Sights:** Beaded blade front, folding adjustable rear. **Features:** Thumb safety; removable stainless steel breech plug; adjustable trigger, barrel drilled and tapped for scope mounting. From Traditions.
Price: With walnut grip $229.00
Price: Nickel with black grip $239.00
Price: With walnut grip and 12-1/2" barrel $239.00
Price: Nickel with black grip, muzzle brake and 14-3/4"
 fluted barrel $289.00
Price: 45 cal. nickel w/bl. grip, muzzle brake and 14-3/4"
 fluted bbl. $289.00

TRADITIONS KENTUCKY PISTOL
Caliber: 50. **Barrel:** 10"; octagon with 7/8" flats; 1:20" twist. **Weight:** 40 oz. **Length:** 15" overall. **Stocks:** Stained beech. **Sights:** Blade front, fixed rear. **Features:** Bird's-head grip; brass thimbles; color case-hardened lock. Percussion only. Introduced 1995. From Traditions.
Price: Finished $139.00
Price: Kit $109.00

TRADITIONS PIONEER PISTOL
Caliber: 45. **Barrel:** 9-5/8"; 13/16" flats, 1:16" twist. **Weight:** 31 oz. **Length:** 15" overall. **Stocks:** Beech. **Sights:** Blade front, fixed rear. **Features:** V-type mainspring. Single trigger. German silver furniture, blackened hardware. From Traditions.
Price: $139.00
Price: Kit $119.00

TRADITIONS TRAPPER PISTOL
Caliber: 50. **Barrel:** 9-3/4"; 7/8" flats; 1:20" twist. **Weight:** 2-3/4 lbs. **Length:** 16" overall. **Stocks:** Beech. **Sights:** Blade front, adjustable rear. **Features:** Double-set triggers; brass buttcap, trigger guard, wedge plate, forend tip, thimble. From Traditions.
Price: Percussion $189.00
Price: Flintlock $209.00
Price: Kit $149.00

TRADITIONS VEST-POCKET DERRINGER
Caliber: 31. **Barrel:** 2-1/4"; brass. **Weight:** 8 oz. **Length:** 4-3/4" overall. **Stocks:** Simulated ivory. **Sights:** Bead front. **Features:** Replica of riverboat gamblers' derringer; authentic spur trigger. From Traditions.
Price: $109.00

TRADITIONS WILLIAM PARKER PISTOL
Caliber: 50. **Barrel:** 10-3/8"; 15/16" flats; polished steel. **Weight:** 37 oz. **Length:** 17-1/2" overall. **Stocks:** Walnut with checkered grip. **Sights:** Brass blade front, fixed rear. **Features:** Replica dueling pistol with 1:20" twist, hooked breech. Brass wedge plate, trigger guard, cap guard; separate ramrod. Double-set triggers. Polished steel barrel, lock. Imported by Traditions.
Price: $269.00

BLACKPOWDER REVOLVERS

Army 1860

Baby Dragoon 1848

Dixie Wyatt Earp

Le Mat Revolver

**New Model
1858 Army Percussion**

ARMY 1860 PERCUSSION REVOLVER
Caliber: 44, 6-shot. **Barrel:** 8". **Weight:** 40 oz. **Length:** 13-5/8" overall.
Stocks: Walnut. **Sights:** Fixed. **Features:** Engraved Navy scene on cylinder; brass trigger guard; case-hardened frame, loading lever and hammer. Some importers supply pistol cut for detachable shoulder stock, have accessory stock available. Imported by Cabela's (1860 Lawman), E.M.F., Navy Arms, The Armoury, Cimarron, Dixie Gun Works (half-fluted cylinder, not roll engraved), Euroarms of America (brass or steel model), Armsport, Traditions (brass or steel), Uberti U.S.A. Inc., United States Patent Fire-Arms.
Price: Dixie Gun Works RH0125 . . . . **$232.00**
Price: Hartford model, steel frame, cartouches (E.M.F.) **$225.00**
Price: Single cased set (Navy Arms) **$300.00**
Price: Double cased set (Navy Arms) **$490.00**
Price: 1861 Navy: Same as Army except 36-cal., 7-1/2" bbl.,
weighs 41 oz., cut for shoulder stock; round cylinder
(fluted available), from Cabela's, CVA (brass frame, 44 cal.),
United States Patent Fire-Arms . . . . **$99.95 to $385.00**
Price: Steel frame kit (E.M.F., Euroarms) . . . . **$125.00 to $216.25**
Price: Colt Army Police, fluted cyl., 5-1/2", 36-cal. (Cabela's) . . . **$229.99**
Price: With nickeled frame, barrel and backstrap,
gold-tone fluted cylinder, trigger and hammer,
simulated ivory grips (Traditions) **$199.00**

BABY DRAGOON 1848, 1849 POCKET, WELLS FARGO
Caliber: 31. **Barrel:** 3", 4", 5", 6"; seven-groove; RH twist. **Weight:** About 21 oz. **Stocks:** Varnished walnut. **Sights:** Brass pin front, hammer notch rear. **Features:** No loading lever on Baby Dragoon or Wells Fargo models. Unfluted cylinder with stagecoach holdup scene; cupped cylinder pin; no grease grooves; one safety pin on cylinder and slot in hammer face; straight (flat) mainspring. From Armsport, Cimarron F.A. Co., Dixie Gun Works, E.M.F., Uberti U.S.A. Inc.
Price: 5.5" barrel, 1849 Pocket with loading lever (Dixie) **$232.00**
Price: 4" (Uberti USA Inc.) **$275.00**

DIXIE WYATT EARP REVOLVER
Caliber: 44. **Barrel:** 12", octagon. **Weight:** 46 oz. **Length:** 18" overall. **Stocks:** Two-piece walnut. **Sights:** Fixed. **Features:** Highly polished brass frame, backstrap and trigger guard; blued barrel and cylinder; case-hardened hammer, trigger and loading lever. Navy-size shoulder stock ($45) requires minor fitting. From Dixie Gun Works.
Price: RH0130 . . . . **$180.00**

LE MAT REVOLVER
Caliber: 44/65. **Barrel:** 6-3/4" (revolver); 4-7/8" (single shot). **Weight:** 3 lbs., 7 oz. **Stocks:** Hand-checkered walnut. **Sights:** Post front, hammer notch rear. **Features:** Exact reproduction with all-steel construction; 44-cal. 9-shot cylinder, 65-cal. single barrel; color case-hardened hammer with selector; spur trigger guard; ring at butt; lever-type barrel release. From Navy Arms and Dixie Gun Works.

Price: Cavalry model (lanyard ring, spur trigger guard) **$675.00**
Price: Army model (round trigger guard, pin-type barrel release) . **$675.00**
Price: Naval-style (thumb selector on hammer) **$675.00**

NEW MODEL 1858 ARMY PERCUSSION REVOLVER
Caliber: 36 or 44, 6-shot. **Barrel:** 6-1/2" or 8". **Weight:** 38 oz. **Length:** 13-1/2" overall. **Stocks:** Walnut. **Sights:** Blade front, groove- in-frame rear. **Features:** Replica of Remington Model 1858. Also available from some importers as Army Model Belt Revolver in 36- cal., a shortened and lightened version of the 44. Target Model (Uberti U.S.A. Inc., Navy Arms) has fully adjustable target rear sight, target front, 36 or 44. Imported by Cabela's, Cimarron F.A. Co., CVA (as 1858 Army, brass frame, 44 only), Dixie Gun Works, Navy Arms, The Armoury, E.M.F., Euroarms of America (engraved, stainless and plain), Armsport, Traditions (44 only), Uberti U.S.A. Inc.
Price: Steel frame, about . . . . **$99.95 to $280.00**
Price: Steel frame kit (Euroarms, Navy Arms) . . . . . **$115.95 to $150.00**
Price: Stainless steel Model 1858 (Euroarms,
Uberti U.S.A. Inc., Cabela's, Navy Arms,
Armsport, Traditions) . . . . **$169.95 to $380.00**
Price: Target Model, adjustable rear sight (Cabela's,
Euroarms, Uberti U.S.A. Inc., Stone Mountain
Arms) . . . . **$95.95 to $399.00**
Price: Brass frame (CVA, Cabela's, Traditions,
Navy Arms) . . . . **$79.95 to $199.99**
Price: As above, kit (Dixie Gun Works) . . . . **$145.00 to $188.95**
Price: Buffalo model, 44-cal. (Cabela's) **$119.99**
Price: Hartford model, steel frame, cartouche (E.M.F.) **$225.00**
Price: Improved Conversion (Cimarron) **$479.00**

BLACKPOWDER REVOLVERS

Navy Arms 1836 Paterson

North American Companion

Rogers & Spencer

Navy Arms Frontiersman

Pocket Police 1862

NAVY ARMS NEW MODEL POCKET REVOLVER
Caliber: 31, 5-shot. **Barrel:** 3-1/2", octagon. **Weight:** 15 oz. **Length:** 7-3/4".
Stocks: Two-piece walnut. **Sights:** Fixed. **Features:** Replica of the
Remington New Model Pocket. Available with polished brass frame or
nickel-plated finish. Introduced 2000. Imported by Navy Arms.
Price: **$300.00**

NAVY ARMS 1836 PATERSON REVOLVER
Caliber: 36. **Barrel:** 9". **Weight:** 2 lbs., 11 oz. **Length:** NA. **Stocks:** Walnut.
Sights: NA. **Features:** Hidden trigger, blued barrel, replica of 5-shooter,
roll-engraved with stagecoach holdup scene.
Price: . . . . **$425.00 to $461.00**

NAVY ARMS 1851 NAVY "FRONTIERSMAN" REVOLVER
Caliber: .36, 6-shot cylinder. **Barrel:** 5". **Weight:** 32 oz. **Length:** 10-1/2"
overall. **Grips:** One piece walnut. **Sights:** Post front, notch rear.
Features: Blued with color case-hardened receiver, trigger and hammer;
German Silver backstrap and triggerguard. Introduced 2005. Imported by
Navy Arms.
Price: **$315.00**

NAVY MODEL 1851 PERCUSSION REVOLVER
Caliber: 36, 44, 6-shot. **Barrel:** 7-1/2". **Weight:** 44 oz. **Length:** 13" overall.
Stocks: Walnut finish. **Sights:** Post front, hammer notch rear. **Features:**
Brass backstrap and trigger guard; some have 1st Model squareback
trigger guard, engraved cylinder with navy battle scene; case-hardened
frame, hammer, loading lever. Imported by The Armoury, Cabela's,
Cimarron F.A. Co., Navy Arms, E.M.F., Dixie Gun Works, Euroarms of
America, Armsport, CVA (44-cal. only), Traditions (44 only), Uberti U.S.A.
Inc., United States Patent Fire-Arms.
Price: Brass frame . . . . **$99.95 to $385.00**
Price: Steel frame . . . . **$130.00 to $285.00**
Price: Kit form . . . . **$110.00 to $142.50**
Price: Engraved model (Dixie Gun Works) **$190.00**
Price: Single cased set, steel frame (Navy Arms) **$280.00**
Price: Double cased set, steel frame (Navy Arms) **$455.00**
Price: Confederate Navy (Cabela's) **$139.99**
Price: Hartford model, steel frame, German silver trim,
cartouche (E.M.F.) **$190.00**
Price: Man With No Name Conversion (Cimarron, 2006) **$459.00**

NORTH AMERICAN COMPANION PERCUSSION REVOLVER
Caliber: 22. **Barrel:** 1-1/8". **Weight:** 5.1 oz. **Length:** 4-1/2" overall. **Stocks:**
Laminated wood. **Sights:** Blade front, notch fixed rear. **Features:** All
stainless steel construction. Uses standard #11 percussion caps. Comes
with bullets, powder measure, bullet seater, leather clip holster, gun rag.
Long Rifle or Magnum frame size. Introduced 1996. Made in U.S. by North
American Arms.
Price: Long Rifle frame **$200.00**

North American Magnum Companion Percussion Revolver
Similar to the Companion except has larger frame. Weighs 7.2 oz., has 1-
5/8" barrel, measures 5-7/16" overall. Comes with bullets, powder
measure, bullet seater, leather clip holster, gun rag. Introduced 1996.
Made in U.S. by North American Arms.
Price: **$215.00**

POCKET POLICE 1862 PERCUSSION REVOLVER
Caliber: 36, 5-shot. **Barrel:** 4-1/2", 5-1/2", 6-1/2", 7-1/2". **Weight:** 26 oz.
Length: 12" overall (6-1/2" bbl.). **Stocks:** Walnut. **Sights:** Fixed.
Features: Round tapered barrel; half-fluted and rebated cylinder; case-
hardened frame, loading lever and hammer; silver or brass trigger guard
and backstrap. Imported by Dixie Gun Works, Navy Arms (5-1/2" only),
Uberti U.S.A. Inc. (5-1/2", 6-1/2" only), United States Patent Fire-Arms
and Cimarron F.A. Co.
Price: About . . . . **$139.95 to $335.00**
Price: Single cased set with accessories (Navy Arms) **$365.00**
Price: Hartford model, steel frame, cartouche (E.M.F.) **$300.00**

ROGERS & SPENCER PERCUSSION REVOLVER
Caliber: 44. **Barrel:** 7-1/2". **Weight:** 47 oz. **Length:** 13-3/4" overall.
Stocks: Walnut. **Sights:** Cone front, integral groove in frame for rear.
Features: Accurate reproduction of a Civil War design. Solid frame; extra
large nipple cut-out on rear of cylinder; loading lever and cylinder easily
removed for cleaning. From Dixie Gun Works, Euroarms of America
(standard blue, engraved, burnished, target models), Navy Arms.
Price: . . . . **$160.00 to 340.00**
Price: Nickel-plated **$215.00**
Price: Engraved (Euroarms) **$430.00**
Price: Kit version . . . . **$245.00 to $360.00**
Price: Target version (Euroarms) . . . . **$239.00 to $270.00**
Price: Burnished London Gray (Euroarms) . . . . **$245.00 to $370.00**

BLACKPOWDER REVOLVERS

Ruger Old Army

3rd U.S. Model Dragoon

Spiller & Burr

Walker

RUGER OLD ARMY PERCUSSION REVOLVER
Caliber: 45, 6-shot. Uses .457" dia. lead bullets or 454 conical. **Barrel:** 5-1/2", 7-1/2" (6-groove; 1:16" twist). **Weight:** 2-7/8 lbs. **Length:** 11-1/2" and 13-1/2" overall. **Stocks:** Rosewood, simulated ivory. **Sights:** Ramp front, rear adjustable for windage and elevation; or fixed (groove). **Features:** Stainless steel; standard size nipples, chrome-moly steel cylinder and frame, same lockwork as original Super Blackhawk. Also stainless steel. Includes hard case and lock. Introduced 1972.
Price: Blued steel, fixed sight (Model BP-5F) **$595.00**
Price: Stainless steel, fixed sight (Model KBP-5F-I) **$685.00**
Price: Stainless steel (Model KBP-7) **$635.00**

SHERIFF MODEL 1851 PERCUSSION REVOLVER
Caliber: 36, 44, 6-shot. **Barrel:** 5". **Weight:** 40 oz. **Length:** 10-1/2" overall. **Stocks:** Walnut. **Sights:** Fixed. **Features:** Brass backstrap and trigger guard; engraved navy scene; case-hardened frame, hammer, loading lever. Imported by E.M.F.
Price: Steel frame **$169.95**
Price: Brass frame **$140.00**

SPILLER & BURR REVOLVER
Caliber: 36 (.375" round ball). **Barrel:** 7", octagon. **Weight:** 2-1/2 lbs. **Length:** 12-1/2" overall. **Stocks:** Two-piece walnut. **Sights:** Fixed. **Features:** Reproduction of the C.S.A. revolver. Brass frame and trigger guard. Also available as a kit. From Dixie Gun Works, Navy Arms.
Price: **$205.00**
Price: Kit form (Dixie) **$155.00**
Price: Single cased set (Navy Arms) **$270.00**
Price: Double cased set (Navy Arms) **$430.00**

UBERTI 1847 WALKER REVOLVERS
Caliber: 36 (.375" round ball), 5-shot engraved cylinder. **Barrel:** 7-1/2" 11 grooves. **Weight:** 2.6 lbs. **Stocks:** One-piece walnut. **Sights:** Fixed. **Features:** Copy of Sam Colt's first commercially-made revolving pistol, loading lever available, no trigger guard. Made in Italy by Uberti, imported by Benelli USA.
Price: Walker with loading lever, 9" barrel, 6 shot **$375.00**

UBERTI 1848 DRAGOON AND POCKET REVOLVERS
Caliber: 44 6-shot engraved cylinder. **Barrel:** 7-1/2" 7 grooves. **Weight:** 4.1 lbs. **Stocks:** One-piece walnut. **Sights:** Fixed. **Features:** Copy of Eli Whitney's design for Colt using Walker parts. Blued barrel, backstrap, and trigger guard. Made in Italy by Uberti, imported by Benelli USA, E.M.F.

Price: 1848 Whitneyville Dragoon, 7-1/2" barrel **$400.00**
Price: 1848 Dragoon, 1st thru 3rd models, 7-1/2" barrel **$350.00**
Price: 1848 Baby Dragoon, 4" barrel **$300.00**

UBERTI 1858 NEW ARMY REVOLVERS
Caliber: 44 6-shot engraved cylinder. **Barrel:** 8" 7 grooves. **Weight:** 2.7 lbs. **Length:** 13.6". **Stocks:** Two-piece walnut. **Sights:** Fixed. **Features:** Blued or stainless barrel, backstrap; brass trigger guard. Made in Italy by Uberti, imported by Benelli USA.
Price: 1858 New Army Stainless 8" barrel **$365.00**
Price: 1858 New Army 8" barrel **$300.00**
Price: 1858 Target Carbine 18" barrel **$475.00**
Price: 1862 Pocket Navy 5.5" barrel, 36 caliber **$300.00**
Price: 1862 Police 5.5" barrel, 36 caliber **$300.00**

UBERTI 1861 NAVY PERCUSSION REVOLVER
Caliber: 36, 6-shot. **Barrel:** 7-1/2", 7-groove, round. **Weight:** 2 lbs., 6 oz. **Length:** 13". **Stocks:** One-piece walnut. **Sights:** German silver blade front sight. **Features:** Rounded trigger guard, "creeping" loading lever, fluted or round cylinder, steel backstrap, trigger guard, cut for stock. Imported by Cimarron F.A. Co., Uberti U.S.A. Inc., Dixie Gunworks.
Price: **$300.00**

1862 POCKET NAVY PERCUSSION REVOLVER
Caliber: 36, 5-shot. **Barrel:** 5-1/2", 6-1/2", octagonal, 7-groove, LH twist. **Weight:** 27 oz. (5-1/2" barrel). **Length:** 10-1/2" overall (5-1/ 2" bbl.). **Stocks:** One-piece varnished walnut. **Sights:** Brass pin front, hammer notch rear. **Features:** Rebated cylinder, hinged loading lever, brass or silver-plated backstrap and trigger guard, color-cased frame, hammer, loading lever, plunger and latch, rest blued. Has original-type markings. From Cimarron F.A. Co., Uberti U.S.A. Inc., Dixie Gunworks.
Price: With brass backstrap, trigger guard . . . . **$240.00 to $310.00**

WALKER 1847 PERCUSSION REVOLVER
Caliber: 44, 6-shot. **Barrel:** 9". **Weight:** 84 oz. **Length:** 15-1/2" overall. **Stocks:** Walnut. **Sights:** Fixed. **Features:** Case-hardened frame, loading lever and hammer; iron backstrap; brass trigger guard; engraved cylinder. Imported by Cabela's, Cimarron F.A. Co., Navy Arms, Dixie Gun Works, Uberti U.S.A. Inc., E.M.F., Cimarron, Traditions, United States Patent Fire-Arms.
Price: About . . . . **$225.00 to $445.00**
Price: Single cased set (Navy Arms) **$405.00**
Price: Deluxe Walker with French fitted case (Navy Arms) **$540.00**
Price: Hartford model, steel frame, cartouche (E.M.F.) **$350.00**

Cabela's Traditional Hawken

Dixie Sharps New Model 1859 Military

ARMOURY R140 HAWKEN RIFLE
Caliber: 45, 50 or 54. **Barrel:** 29". **Weight:** 8-3/4 to 9 lbs. **Length:** 45-3/4" overall. **Stock:** Walnut, with cheekpiece. **Sights:** Dovetailed front, fully adjustable rear. **Features:** Octagon barrel, removable breech plug; double set triggers; blued barrel, brass stock fittings, color case-hardened percussion lock. From Armsport, The Armoury.
Price: .... $225.00 to $245.00

BOSTONIAN PERCUSSION RIFLE
Caliber: 45. **Barrel:** 30", octagonal. **Weight:** 7-1/4 lbs. **Length:** 46" overall. **Stock:** Walnut. **Sights:** Blade front, fixed notch rear. **Features:** Color case-hardened lock, brass trigger guard, buttplate, patchbox. Imported from Italy by E.M.F.
Price: $285.00

CABELA'S BLUE RIDGE RIFLE
Caliber: 32, 36, 45, 50, .54. **Barrel:** 39", octagonal. **Weight:** About 7-3/4 lbs. **Length:** 55" overall. **Stock:** American black walnut. **Sights:** Blade front, rear drift adjustable for windage. **Features:** Color case-hardened lockplate and cock/hammer, brass trigger guard and buttplate, double set, double-phased triggers. From Cabela's.
Price: Percussion $569.99
Price: Flintlock $599.99

CABELA'S TRADITIONAL HAWKEN
Caliber: 50, 54. **Barrel:** 29". **Weight:** About 9 lbs. **Stock:** Walnut. **Sights:** Blade front, open adjustable rear. **Features:** Flintlock or percussion. Adjustable double-set triggers. Polished brass furniture, color case-hardened lock. Imported by Cabela's.
Price: Percussion, right-hand or left-hand $339.99
Price: Flintlock, right-hand $379.99

Cabela's Sporterized Hawken Hunter Rifle
Similar to the Traditional Hawken except has more modern stock style with rubber recoil pad, blued furniture, sling swivels. Percussion only, in 50- or 54-caliber.
Price: Carbine or rifle, right-hand $399.99

CABELA'S KODIAK EXPRESS DOUBLE RIFLE
Caliber: 50, 54, 58, 72. **Barrel:** Length NA; 1:48" twist. **Weight:** 9.3 lbs. **Length:** 45-1/4" overall. **Stock:** European walnut, oil finish. **Sights:** Fully adjustable double folding-leaf rear, ramp front. **Features:** Percussion. Barrels regulated to point of aim at 75 yards; polished and engraved lock, top tang and trigger guard. From Cabela's.
Price: 50, 54, 58 calibers $929.99
Price: 72 caliber $959.99

COOK & BROTHER CONFEDERATE CARBINE
Caliber: 58. **Barrel:** 24". **Weight:** 7-1/2 lbs. **Length:** 40-1/2" overall. **Stock:** Select walnut. **Features:** Re-creation of the 1861 New Orleans-made artillery carbine. Color case-hardened lock, browned barrel. Buttplate, trigger guard, barrel bands, sling swivels and nosecap of polished brass. From Euroarms of America.
Price: $563.00
Price: Cook & Brother rifle (33" barrel) $606.00

CVA OPTIMA PRO 209 BREAK-ACTION RIFLE
Caliber: 45, 50. **Barrel:** 29" fluted, blue or nickel. **Weight:** 8.8 lbs. **Stock:** Ambidextrous Mossy Oak® Camo or black FiberGrip. **Sights:** Adj. fiber-optic. **Features:** Break-action, stainless No. 209 breech plug, aluminum loading rod, cocking spur, lifetime warranty.
Price: Mossy Oak® Camo $399.95
Price: Camo, nickel bbl. $379.95
Price: Mossy Oak® Camo/blued $349.95
Price: Black/nickel $329.95
Price: Black/blued $299.95
Price: Blued fluted bbl. $99.95
Price: Nickel fluted bbl. $115.95

CVA Optima 209 Magnum Break-Action Rifle
Similar to Optima Pro but with 26" bbl., nickel or blue finish, 50 cal.
Price: Mossy Oak® Camo/nickel $310.00
Price: Mossy Oak® Camo/blue $290.00
Price: Black/blued $235.00

CVA Optima Elite
Similar to Optima Pro but chambered for 45, 50 black powder plus 243, 270, 30-06 centerfire cartridges.
Price: Hardwoods Green HD/blue $415.00
Price: Black Fleck/blue $355.00

CVA BUCKHORN 209 MAGNUM
Caliber: 50. **Barrel:** 24". **Weight:** 6.3 lbs. **Sights:** Illuminator fiber-optic. **Features:** Grip-dot stock, thumb-actuated safety; drilled and tapped for scope mounts.
Price: Black stock, blue barrel $145.00

CVA KODIAK MAGNUM RIFLE
Caliber: 50. No. 209 primer ignition. **Barrel:** 28"; 1:28" twist. **Stock:** Ambidextrous black or Mossy Oak® camo. **Sights:** Fiber-optic. **Features:** Blue or nickel finish, recoil pad, lifetime warranty. From CVA.
Price: Mossy Oak® camo; nickel barrel $300.00
Price: Black stock; nickel barrel $255.00
Price: Black stock; blued barrel $225.00

DIXIE EARLY AMERICAN JAEGER RIFLE
Caliber: 54. **Barrel:** 27-1/2" octagonal; 1:24" twist. **Weight:** 8-1/4 lbs. **Length:** 43-1/2" overall. **Stock:** American walnut; sliding wooden patchbox on butt. **Sights:** Notch rear, blade front. **Features:** Flintlock or percussion. Browned steel furniture. Imported from Italy by Dixie Gun Works.
Price: Flintlock FR0838 .... $825.00
Price: Percussion PR0835 .... $825.00

DIXIE DELUXE CUB RIFLE
Caliber: 40. **Barrel:** 28". **Weight:** 6-1/2 lbs. **Stock:** Walnut. **Sights:** Fixed. **Features:** Short rifle for small game and beginning shooters. Brass patchbox and furniture. Flint or percussion. From Dixie Gun Works.
Price: Finished FR0950 .... $520.00
Price: Kit PR0965 .... $430.00
Price: Super Cub (50-caliber percussion) PR0814 ...... $525.00
Price: Super Cub (50-caliber flintlock) FR0803 .... $550.00

DIXIE PEDERSOLI 1857 MAUSER RIFLE
Caliber: 54. **Barrel:** 39-3/8". **Weight:** NA. **Length:** 52" overall. **Stock:** European walnut with oil finish, sling swivels. **Sights:** Fully adjustable rear, lug front. **Features:** Percussion (musket caps). Armory bright finish with color case-hardened lock and barrel tang, engraved lockplate, steel ramrod. Introduced 2000. Imported from Italy by Dixie Gun Works.
Price: PR1330 .... $1,025.00

Euroarms 1861 Springfield

Gonic Model 93 Thumbhole

Harper's Ferry 1803

DIXIE PEDERSOLI 1766 CHARLEVILLE MUSKET
Caliber: 69. **Barrel:** 44-3/4". **Weight:** 10-1/2 lbs. **Length:** 57-1/2" overall. **Stock:** European walnut with oil finish. **Sights:** Fixed rear, lug front. **Features:** Smoothbore flintlock. Armory bright finish with steel furniture and ramrod. Introduced 2000. Imported from Italy by Dixie Gun Works.
Price: PR1045 . . . . **$1,025.00**

DIXIE SHARPS NEW MODEL 1859 MILITARY RIFLE
Caliber: 54. **Barrel:** 30", 6-groove; 1:48" twist. **Weight:** 9 lbs. **Length:** 45-1/2" overall. **Stock:** Oiled walnut. **Sights:** Blade front, ladder-style rear. **Features:** Blued barrel, color case-hardened barrel bands, receiver, hammer, nosecap, lever, patchbox cover and buttplate. Introduced 1995. Imported from Italy by Dixie Gun Works.
Price: PR0862 . . . . **$1,025.00**

DIXIE U.S. MODEL 1816 FLINTLOCK MUSKET
Caliber: 69. **Barrel:** 42", smoothbore. **Weight:** 9.75 lbs. **Length:** 56.5" overall. **Stock:** Walnut with oil finish. **Sights:** Blade front. **Features:** All metal finished "National Armory Bright;" three barrel bands with springs; steel ramrod with button-shaped head. Imported by Dixie Gun Works.
Price: FR0305 . . . . **$1,025.00**

E.M.F. 1863 SHARPS MILITARY CARBINE
Caliber: 54. **Barrel:** 22", round. **Weight:** 8 lbs. **Length:** 39" overall. **Stock:** Oiled walnut. **Sights:** Blade front, military ladder-type rear. **Features:** Color case-hardened lock, rest blued. Imported by E.M.F.
Price: **$600.00**

EUROARMS VOLUNTEER TARGET RIFLE
Caliber: 451. **Barrel:** 33" (two-band), 36" (three-band). **Weight:** 11 lbs. (two-band). **Length:** 48.75" overall (two-band). **Stock:** European walnut with checkered wrist and forend. **Sights:** Hooded bead front, adjustable rear with interchangeable leaves. **Features:** Alexander Henry-type rifling with 1:20" twist. Color case-hardened hammer and lockplate, brass trigger guard and nosecap, remainder blued. Imported by Euroarms of America, Dixie Gun Works.
Price: Two-band. **$910.00**

EUROARMS 1861 SPRINGFIELD RIFLE
Caliber: 58. **Barrel:** 40". **Weight:** About 10 lbs. **Length:** 55.5" overall. **Stock:** European walnut. **Sights:** Blade front, three-leaf military rear. **Features:** Reproduction of the original three-band rifle. Lockplate marked "1861" with eagle and "U.S. Springfield." White metal. Imported by Euroarms of America.
Price: **$730.00**

EUROARMS ZOUAVE RIFLE
Caliber: 54, 58 percussion. **Barrel:** 33". **Weight:** 9-1/2 lbs. **Overall length:** 49". **Features:** One-piece solid barrel and bolster. For 54 caliber, .535

R.B., .540 minnie. For 58 caliber, .575 R.B., .577 minnie. 1863 issue. Made in Italy. Imported by Euroarms of America.
Price: **$469.00**

EUROARMS HARPERS FERRY RIFLE
Caliber: 58 flintlock. **Barrel:** 35". **Weight:** 9 lbs. **Overall length:** 59-1/2". **Features:** Antique browned barrel. Barrel .575 RB. .577 minnie. 1803 issue. Made in Italy. Imported by Euroarms of America.
Price: **$735.00**

GONIC MODEL 93 M/L RIFLE
Caliber: 45, 50. **Barrel:** 26"; 1:24" twist. **Weight:** 6-1/2 to 7 lbs. **Length:** 43" overall. **Stock:** American hardwood with black finish. **Sights:** Adjustable or aperture rear, hooded post front. **Features:** Adjustable trigger with side safety; unbreakable ramrod; comes with A. Z. scope bases installed. Introduced 1993. Made in U.S. by Gonic Arms, Inc.
Price: Model 93 Standard (blued barrel) **$720.00**
Price: Model 93 Standard (stainless brl., 50 cal. only) **$782.00**

Gonic Model 93 Deluxe M/L Rifle
Similar to the Model 93 except has classic-style walnut or gray laminated wood stock. Introduced 1998. Made in U.S. by Gonic Arms, Inc.
Price: Blue barrel, sights, scope base, choice of stock **$902.00**
Price: Stainless barrel, sights, scope base, choice of stock
(50 cal. only) **$964.00**

Gonic Model 93 Mountain Thumbhole M/L Rifles
Similar to the Model 93 except has high-grade walnut or gray laminate stock with extensive hand-checkered panels, Monte Carlo cheekpiece and beavertail forend; integral muzzle brake. Introduced 1998. Made in U.S. by Gonic Arms, Inc.
Price: Blued or stainless **$2,700.00**

HARPER'S FERRY 1803 FLINTLOCK RIFLE
Caliber: 54 or 58. **Barrel:** 35". **Weight:** 9 lbs. **Length:** 59-1/2" overall. **Stock:** Walnut with cheekpiece. **Sights:** Brass blade front, fixed steel rear. **Features:** Brass trigger guard, sideplate, buttplate; steel patchbox. Imported by Euroarms of America, Navy Arms (54- cal. only), Cabela's, and Dixie Gun Works.
Price: . . . . **$495.95 to $995.00**
Price: 54-cal. (Navy Arms) **$625.00**
Price: 54-cal. (Cabela's) **$599.99**
Price: 54-cal. (Dixie Gun Works), FR0171 . . . . **$995.00**
Price: 54-cal. (Euroarms) **$809.00**

HAWKEN RIFLE
Caliber: 45, 50, 54 or 58. **Barrel:** 28", blued, 6-groove rifling. **Weight:** 8-3/4 lbs. **Length:** 44" overall. **Stock:** Walnut with cheekpiece. **Sights:** Blade front, fully adjustable rear. **Features:** Coil mainspring, double-set triggers, polished brass furniture. From Armsport and E.M.F.
Price: . . . . **$220.00 to $345.00**

BLACKPOWDER MUSKETS & RIFLES

J.P. Murray

Kentucky Flintlock

Knight 50 Caliber DISC In-Line

Knight Master Hunter DISC Extreme

J.P. HENRY TRADE RIFLE
Caliber: 54. **Barrel:** 34"; 1" flats. **Weight:** 8-1/2 lbs. **Length:** 45" overall. **Stock:** Premium curly maple. **Sights:** Silver blade front, fixed buckhorn rear. **Features:** Brass buttplate, side plate, trigger guard and nosecap; browned barrel and lock; L&R Large English percussion lock; single trigger. Made in U.S. by J.P. Gunstocks, Inc.
Price: **$965.50**

J.P. MURRAY 1862-1864 CAVALRY CARBINE
Caliber: 58 (.577" Minie). **Barrel:** 23". **Weight:** 7 lbs., 9 oz. **Length:** 39" overall. **Stock:** Walnut. **Sights:** Blade front, rear drift adjustable for windage. **Features:** Browned barrel, color case-hardened lock, blued swivel and band springs, polished brass buttplate, trigger guard, barrel bands. From Euroarms of America.
Price: Dixie Gun Works PR0173 . . . . **$725.00**

KENTUCKY FLINTLOCK RIFLE
Caliber: 44, 45, or 50. **Barrel:** 35". **Weight:** 7 lbs. **Length:** 50" overall. **Stock:** Walnut stained, brass fittings. **Sights:** Fixed. **Features:** Available in carbine model also, 28" bbl. Some variations in detail, finish. Kits also available from some importers. Imported by The Armoury.
Price: About . . . . **$217.95 to $345.00**

Kentucky Percussion Rifle
Similar to Flintlock except percussion lock. Finish and features vary with importer. Imported by The Armoury and CVA.
Price: About **$259.95**
Price: 45 or 50 cal. (Navy Arms) **$425.00**
Price: Kit, 50 cal. (CVA) **$189.95**

KNIGHT 50 CALIBER DISC IN-LINE RIFLE
Caliber: 50. **Barrel:** 24", 26". **Weight:** 7 lbs., 14 oz. **Length:** 43" overall (24" barrel). **Stock:** Checkered synthetic with palm swell grip, rubber recoil pad, swivel studs; black, Advantage or Mossy Oak® Break-Up camouflage. **Sights:** Bead on ramp front, fully adjustable open rear. **Features:** Bolt-action in-line system uses #209 shotshell primer for ignition; primer is held in plastic drop-in Primer Disc. Available in blued or stainless steel. Made in U.S. by Knight Rifles (Modern Muzzleloading).
Price: . . . . **$439.95 to $632.45**

Knight Master Hunter II DISC In-Line Rifle
Similar to Knight 50 caliber DISC rifle except features premium, wood laminated two-tone stock, gold-plated trigger and engraved trigger guard, jeweled bolt and fluted, air-gauged Green Mountain 26" barrel. Length 45" overall, weighs 7 lbs., 7 oz. Includes black composite thumbhole stock. Introduced 2000. Made in U.S. by Knight Rifles (Modern Muzzleloading).
Price: **$1,099.95**

KNIGHT MUZZLELOADER DISC EXTREME
Caliber: 45 fluted, 50. **Barrel:** 26". **Stock:** Stainless steel laminate, blued walnut, black composite thumbhole with blued or SS. **Sights:** Fully adjustable metallic. **Features:** New full plastic jacket ignition system.
Price: 50 SS laminate **$703.95**
Price: 45 SS laminate **$769.95**
Price: 50 blue walnut **$626.95**
Price: 45 blue walnut **$703.95**
Price: 50 blue composite **$549.95**
Price: 45 blue composite **$632.45**
Price: 50 SS composite **$632.45**
Price: 45 SS composite **$703.95**

Knight Master Hunter DISC Extreme
Similar to DISC Extreme except fluted barrel, two-tone laminated thumbhole Monte Carlo-style stock, black composite thumbhole field stock included. Jeweled bolt, adjustable premium trigger.
Price: 50 . . . . **$1,044.95**

Knight American Knight

Knight Wolverine 209

London Armory 1861

Lyman Trade Percussion

KNIGHT AMERICAN KNIGHT M/L RIFLE
Caliber: 50. **Barrel:** 22"; 1:28" twist. **Weight:** 6 lbs. **Length:** 41" overall. **Stock:** Black composite. **Sights:** Bead on ramp front, open fully adjustable rear. **Features:** Double safety system; one-piece removable hammer assembly; drilled and tapped for scope mounting. Introduced 1998. Made in U.S. by Knight Rifles.
Price: Blued, black comp $197.95
Price: Blued, black comp VP $225.45

KNIGHT WOLVERINE 209
Caliber: 50. **Barrel:** 22". **Stock:** HD stock with SS barrel, break-up stock blued, black composite thumbhole with stainless steel, standard black composite with blued or SS. **Sights:** Metallic with fiber-optic. **Features:** Double safety system, adjustable match grade trigger, left-hand model available. Full plastic jacket ignition system.
Price: Starting at $302.45

KNIGHT REVOLUTION
Caliber: 50, 209 primer ignition. **Barrel:** Stainless, 27". **Weight:** 7 lbs., 14 oz. **Stock:** Walnut, laminated, black composite, Mossy Oak® Break-Up™ or Hardwoods Green finish. **Features:** Blued or stainless finish, adjustable trigger and sights.
Price: . . . . NA

LONDON ARMORY 1861 ENFIELD MUSKETOON
Caliber: 58, Minie ball. **Barrel:** 24", round. **Weight:** 7 to 7-1/2 lbs. **Length:** 40-1/2" overall. **Stock:** Walnut, with sling swivels. **Sights:** Blade front, graduated military-leaf rear. **Features:** Brass trigger guard, nosecap, buttplate; blued barrel, bands, lockplate, swivels. Imported by Euroarms of America, Navy Arms.
Price: . . . . $300.00 to $521.00
Price: Kit . . . . $365.00 to $402.00

LONDON ARMORY 2-BAND 1858 ENFIELD
Caliber: .577" Minie, .575" round ball. **Barrel:** 33". **Weight:** 10 lbs. **Length:** 49" overall. **Stock:** Walnut. **Sights:** Folding leaf rear adjustable for elevation. **Features:** Blued barrel, color case-hardened lock and hammer, polished brass buttplate, trigger guard, nosecap. From Navy Arms, Euroarms of America, Dixie Gun Works.
Price: . . . . $385.00 to $563.00

LONDON ARMORY 3-BAND 1853 ENFIELD
Caliber: 58 (.577" Minie, .575" round ball, .580" maxi ball). **Barrel:** 39". **Weight:** 9-1/2 lbs. **Length:** 54" overall. **Stock:** European walnut. **Sights:** Inverted "V" front, traditional Enfield folding ladder rear. **Features:** Recreation of the famed London Armory Company Pattern 1853 Enfield Musket. One-piece walnut stock, brass buttplate, trigger guard and nosecap. Lockplate marked "London Armoury Co." and with a British crown. Blued Baddeley barrel bands. From Dixie Gun Works, Euroarms of America, Navy Arms.
Price: About . . . . $350.00 to $606.00
Price: Assembled kit (Dixie, Euroarms of America) $515.00

LYMAN TRADE RIFLE
Caliber: 50, 54. **Barrel:** 28" octagon;1:48" twist. **Weight:** 8-3/4 lbs. **Length:** 45" overall. **Stock:** European walnut. **Sights:** Blade front, open rear adjustable for windage or optional fixed sights. **Features:** Fast twist rifling for conical bullets. Polished brass furniture with blue steel parts, stainless steel nipple. Hook breech, single trigger, coil spring percussion lock. Steel barrel rib and ramrod ferrules. Introduced 1980. From Lyman.
Price: 50 cal. percussion $581.80
Price: 50 cal. flintlock $652.80
Price: 54 cal. percussion $581.80
Price: 54 cal. flintlock $652.80

LYMAN DEERSTALKER RIFLE
Caliber: 50, 54. **Barrel:** 24", octagonal; 1:48" rifling. **Weight:** 7-1/2 lbs. **Stock:** Walnut with black rubber buttpad. **Sights:** Lyman #37MA beaded front, fully adjustable fold-down Lyman #16A rear. **Features:** Stock has less drop for quick sighting. All metal parts are blackened, with color case-hardened lock; single trigger. Comes with sling and swivels. Available in flint or percussion. Introduced 1990. From Lyman.
Price: 50 cal. flintlock $652.80
Price: 50 or 54 cal., percussion, left-hand, carbine $695.40
Price: 50 or 54 cal., flintlock, left-hand $645.00
Price: 54 cal. flintlock $780.50
Price: 54 cal. percussion $821.80
Price: Stainless steel $959.80

BLACKPOWDER MUSKETS & RIFLES

Lyman Deerstalker

Lyman Great Plains

Markesbery KM Colorado

LYMAN GREAT PLAINS RIFLE

Caliber: 50, 54. **Barrel:** 32"; 1:60" twist. **Weight:** 9 lbs. **Stock:** Walnut. **Sights:** Steel blade front, buckhorn rear adjustable for windage and elevation and fixed notch primitive sight included. **Features:** Blued steel furniture. Stainless steel nipple. Coil spring lock, Hawken-style trigger guard and double-set triggers. Round thimbles recessed and sweated into rib. Steel wedge plates and toe plate. Introduced 1979. From Lyman.

Price: Percussion	**$469.95**
Price: Flintlock	**$494.95**
Price: Percussion kit	**$359.95**
Price: Flintlock kit	**$384.95**
Price: Left-hand percussion	**$474.95**
Price: Left-hand flintlock	**$499.95**

Lyman Great Plains Hunter Model

Similar to Great Plains model except 1:32" twist shallow-groove barrel and comes drilled and tapped for Lyman 57GPR peep sight.

Price: ... **$959.80**

MARKESBERY KM BLACK BEAR M/L RIFLE

Caliber: 36, 45, 50, 54. **Barrel:** 24"; 1:26" twist. **Weight:** 6-1/2 lbs. **Length:** 38-1/2" overall. **Stock:** Two-piece American hardwood, walnut, black laminate, green laminate, black composition, X-Tra or Mossy Oak® Break-Up™ camouflage. **Sights:** Bead front, open fully adjustable rear. **Features:** Interchangeable barrels; exposed hammer; Outer-Line Magnum ignition system uses small rifle primer or standard No. 11 cap and nipple. Blue, black matte, or stainless. Made in U.S. by Markesbery Muzzle Loaders.

Price: American hardwood walnut, blue finish	**$536.63**
Price: American hardwood walnut, stainless	**$553.09**
Price: Black laminate, blue finish	**$539.67**
Price: Black laminate, stainless	**$556.27**
Price: Camouflage stock, blue finish	**$556.46**
Price: Camouflage stock, stainless	**$573.73**
Price: Black composite, blue finish	**$532.65**
Price: Black composite, stainless	**$549.93**
Price: Green laminate, blue finish	**$539.00**
Price: Green laminate, stainless	**$556.27**

Markesbery KM Brown Bear Rifle

Similar to KM Black Bear except one-piece thumbhole stock with Monte Carlo comb. Stock in Crotch Walnut composite, green or black laminate, black composite or X-Tra or Mossy Oak® Break-Up™ camouflage. Made in U.S. by Markesbery Muzzle Loaders, Inc.

Price: Black composite, blue finish	**$658.83**
Price: Crotch Walnut, blue finish	**$658.83**
Price: Camo composite, blue finish	**$682.64**
Price: Walnut wood	**$662.81**
Price: Black wood	**$662.81**
Price: Black laminated wood	**$662.81**
Price: Green laminated wood	**$662.81**
Price: Camo wood	**$684.69**
Price: Black composite, stainless	**$676.11**
Price: Crotch Walnut composite, stainless	**$676.11**

Price: Camo composite, stainless	**$697.69**
Price: Walnut wood, stainless	**$680.07**
Price: Black wood, stainless	**$680.07**
Price: Black laminated wood, stainless	**$680.07**
Price: Green laminate, stainless	**$680.07**
Price: Camo wood, stainless	**$702.76**

Markesbery KM Grizzly Bear Rifle

Similar to KM Black Bear except thumbhole buttstock with Monte Carlo comb. Stock in Crotch Walnut composite, green or black laminate, black composite or X-Tra or Mossy Oak® Break-Up camouflage. Made in U.S. by Markesbery Muzzle Loaders, Inc.

Price: Black composite, blue finish	**$642.96**
Price: Crotch Walnut, blue finish	**$642.96**
Price: Camo composite, blue finish	**$666.67**
Price: Walnut wood	**$646.93**
Price: Black wood	**$646.93**
Price: Black laminate wood	**$646.93**
Price: Green laminate wood	**$646.93**
Price: Camo wood	**$670.74**
Price: Black composite, stainless	**$660.98**
Price: Crotch Walnut composite, stainless	**$660.98**
Price: Black laminate wood, stainless	**$664.20**
Price: Green laminate, stainless	**$664.20**
Price: Camo wood, stainless	**$685.74**
Price: Camo composite, stainless	**$684.04**
Price: Walnut wood, stainless	**$664.20**
Price: Black wood, stainless	**$664.20**

Markesbery KM Polar Bear Rifle

Similar to KM Black Bear except one-piece stock with Monte Carlo comb. Stock in American Hardwood walnut, green or black laminate, black composite, or X-Tra or Mossy Oak® Break-Up™ camouflage. Interchangeable barrel system, Outer-Line ignition system, cross-bolt double safety. Available in 36, 45, 50, 54 caliber. Made in U.S. by Markesbery Muzzle Loaders, Inc.

Price: American Hardwood walnut, blue finish	**$539.01**
Price: Black composite, blue finish	**$536.63**
Price: Black laminate, blue finish	**$541.17**
Price: Green laminate, blue finish	**$541.17**
Price: Camo, blue finish	**$560.43**
Price: American Hardwood walnut, stainless	**$556.27**
Price: Black composite, stainless	**$556.04**
Price: Black laminate, stainless	**$570.56**
Price: Green laminate, stainless	**$570.56**
Price: Camo, stainless	**$573.94**

BLACKPOWDER MUSKETS & RIFLES

Mississippi 1841

Navy Arms 1763 Charleville

Navy Arms Berdan

Navy Arms 1859 Sharps Cavalry Carbine

MARKESBERY KM COLORADO ROCKY MOUNTAIN RIFLE
Caliber: 36, 45, 50, 54. **Barrel:** 24"; 1:26" twist. **Weight:** 6-1/2 lbs. **Length:** 38-1/2" overall. **Stock:** American hardwood walnut, green or black laminate. **Sights:** Firesight bead on ramp front, fully adjustable open rear. **Features:** Replicates Reed/Watson rifle of 1851. Straight grip stock with or without two barrel bands, rubber recoil pad, large-spur hammer. Made in U.S. by Markesbery Muzzle Loaders, Inc.
Price: American hardwood walnut, blue finish **$545.92**
Price: Black or green laminate, blue finish **$548.30**
Price: American hardwood walnut, stainless **$563.17**
Price: Black or green laminate, stainless **$566.34**

MDM BUCKWACKA IN-LINE RIFLES
Caliber: 45, 50. **Barrel:** 23", 25". **Weight:** 7 to 7-3/4 lbs. **Stock:** Black, walnut, laminated and camouflage finishes. **Sights:** Williams Fire Sight blade front, Williams fully adjustable rear with ghost-ring peep aperture. **Features:** Break-open action; Incinerating Ignition System incorporates 209 shotshell primer directly into breech plug; 50-caliber models handle up to 150 grains of Pyrodex; synthetic ramrod; transfer bar safety; stainless or blued finish. Made in U.S. by Millennium Designed Muzzleloaders Ltd.
Price: 50 cal., blued finish **$309.95**
Price: 50 cal., stainless **$339.95**
Price: Camouflage stock . . . . **$359.95 to $389.95**

MDM M2K In-Line Rifle
Similar to Buckwacka except adjustable trigger and double-safety mechanism designed to prevent misfires. Made in U.S. by Millennium Designed Muzzleloaders Ltd.
Price: . . . . **$529.00 to $549.00**

MISSISSIPPI 1841 PERCUSSION RIFLE
Caliber: 54, 58. **Barrel:** 33". **Weight:** 9-1/2 lbs. **Length:** 48-5/8" overall. **Stock:** One-piece European walnut full stock with satin finish. **Sights:**

Brass blade front, fixed steel rear. **Features:** Case-hardened lockplate marked "U.S." surmounted by American eagle. Two barrel bands, sling swivels. Steel ramrod with brass end, browned barrel. From Navy Arms, Dixie Gun Works, Cabela's, Euroarms of America.
Price: Dixie Gun Works PR0870 . . . . **$800.00**

NAVY ARMS 1763 CHARLEVILLE
Caliber: 69. **Barrel:** 44-5/8". **Weight:** 8 lbs., 12 oz. **Length:** 59-3/8" overall. **Stock:** Walnut. **Sights:** Brass blade front. **Features:** Replica of French musket used by American troops during the American Revolution. Imported by Navy Arms.
Price: **$1,020.00**

NAVY ARMS BERDAN 1859 SHARPS RIFLE
Caliber: 54. **Barrel:** 30". **Weight:** 8 lbs., 8 oz. **Length:** 46-3/4" overall. **Stock:** Walnut. **Sights:** Blade front, folding military ladder-type rear. **Features:** Replica of the Union sniper rifle used by Berdan's 1st and 2nd Sharpshooter regiments. Color case-hardened receiver, patchbox, furniture. Double-set triggers. Imported by Navy Arms.
Price: **$1,165.00**
Price: 1859 Sharps Infantry Rifle (three-band) **$1,100.00**

NAVY ARMS 1859 SHARPS CAVALRY CARBINE
Caliber: 54. **Barrel:** 22". **Weight:** 7-3/4 lbs. **Length:** 39" overall. **Stock:** Walnut. **Sights:** Blade front, military ladder-type rear. **Features:** Color case-hardened action, blued barrel. Has saddle ring. Introduced 1991. Imported from Navy Arms.
Price: **$1,000.00**

NAVY ARMS 1861 SPRINGFIELD RIFLE
Caliber: 58. **Barrel:** 40". **Weight:** 10 lbs., 4 oz. **Length:** 56" overall. **Stock:** Walnut. **Sights:** Blade front, military leaf rear. **Features:** Steel barrel, lock and all furniture have polished bright finish. Has 1855-style hammer. Imported by Navy Arms.
Price: **$590.00**

Navy Arms Whitworth

Navy Arms Smith Carbine

New England Firearms Sidekick

New England Firearms Huntsman

New England Firearms Handi-Rifle Combo

NAVY ARMS 1863 C.S. RICHMOND RIFLE
Caliber: 58. **Barrel:** 40". **Weight:** 10 lbs. **Length:** NA. **Stocks:** Walnut. **Sights:** Blade front, adjustable rear. **Features:** Copy of three- band rifle musket made at Richmond Armory for the Confederacy. All steel polished bright. Imported by Navy Arms.
Price: **$590.00**

NAVY ARMS 1863 SPRINGFIELD
Caliber: 58, uses .575 Minie. **Barrel:** 40", rifled. **Weight:** 9-1/2 lbs. **Length:** 56" overall. **Stock:** Walnut. **Sights:** Open rear adjustable for elevation. **Features:** Full-size, three-band musket. Polished bright metal, including lock. From Navy Arms.
Price: Finished rifle **$590.00**

NAVY ARMS PARKER-HALE VOLUNTEER RIFLE
Caliber: .451. **Barrel:** 32". **Weight:** 9-1/2 lbs. **Length:** 49" overall. **Stock:** Walnut, checkered wrist and forend. **Sights:** Globe front, adjustable ladder-type rear. **Features:** Recreation of the type of gun issued to volunteer regiments during the 1860s. Rigby-pattern rifling, patent breech, detented lock. Stock is glass bedded for accuracy. Imported by Navy Arms.
Price: **$905.00**

NAVY ARMS PARKER-HALE WHITWORTH MILITARY TARGET RIFLE
Caliber: 45. **Barrel:** 36". **Weight:** 9-1/4 lbs. **Length:** 52-1/2" overall. **Stock:** Walnut. Checkered at wrist and forend. **Sights:** Hooded post front, open step-adjustable rear. **Features:** Faithful reproduction of Whitworth rifle. Trigger has detented lock, capable of fine adjustments without risk of the sear nose catching on the half-cock notch and damaging both parts. Introduced 1978. Imported by Navy Arms.
Price: **$930.00**

NAVY ARMS SMITH CARBINE
Caliber: 50. **Barrel:** 21-1/2". **Weight:** 7-3/4 lbs. **Length:** 39" overall. **Stock:** American walnut. **Sights:** Brass blade front, folding ladder-type rear. **Features:** Replica of breech-loading Civil War carbine. Color case-hardened receiver, rest blued. Cavalry model has saddle ring and bar, Artillery model has sling swivels. Imported by Navy Arms.
Price: Cavalry model **$645.00**
Price: Artillery model **$645.00**

NEW ENGLAND FIREARMS SIDEKICK
Caliber: 50, 209 primer ignition. **Barrel:** 26" (magnum). **Weight:** 6.5 lbs. **Length:** 41.25". **Stock:** Black matte polymer or hardwood. **Sights:** Adjustable fiber-optic open, tapped for scope mounts. **Features:** Single-shot based on H&R break-open action. Uses No. 209 shotgun primer held in place by special primer carrier. Telescoping brass ramrod. Introduced 2004.
Price: Wood stock, blued frame, black-oxide barrel) **$216.00**
Price: Stainless barrel and frame, synthetic stock) **$310.00**

NEW ENGLAND FIREARMS HUNTSMAN
Caliber: 50, 209 primer ignition. **Barrel:** 22" to 26". **Weight:** 5.25 to 6.5 lbs. **Length:** 40" to 43". **Stock:** Black matte polymer or hardwood. **Sights:** Fiber-optic open sights, tapped for scope mounts. **Features:** Break-open action, transfer-bar safety system, breech plug removable for cleaning. Introduced 2004.
Price: Stainless Huntsman. **$306.00**
Price: Huntsman **$212.00**
Price: Pardner Combo 12 ga./50 cal muzzleloader **$259.00**
Price: Tracker II Combo 12 ga. rifled slug barrel /50 cal. **$288.00**
Price: Handi-Rifle Combo 243/50 cal. **$405.00**

BLACKPOWDER MUSKETS & RIFLES

Peifer TS-93

Prairie River Arms PRA Bullpup

Remington Genesis

C.S. Richmond 1863

New England Firearms Stainless Huntsman
Similar to Huntsman, but with matte nickel finish receiver and stainless bbl. Introduced 2003. From New England Firearms.
Price: **$81.00**

PACIFIC RIFLE MODEL 1837 ZEPHYR
Caliber: 62. **Barrel:** 30", tapered octagon. **Weight:** 7-3/4 lbs. **Length:** NA. **Stock:** Oil-finished fancy walnut. **Sights:** German silver blade front, semi-buckhorn rear. Options available. **Features:** Improved underhammer action. First production rifle to offer Forsyth rifle, with narrow lands and shallow rifling with 1:14" pitch for high-velocity round balls. Metal finish is slow rust brown with nitre blue accents. Optional sights, finishes and integral muzzle brake available. Introduced 1995. Made in U.S. by Pacific Rifle Co.
Price: From **$995.00**

Pacific Rifle Big Bore African Rifles
Similar to the 1837 Zephyr except in 72-caliber and 8-bore. The 72-caliber is available in standard form with 28" barrel, or as the African with flat buttplate, checkered upgraded wood; weight is 9 lbs. The 8-bore African has dual-cap ignition, 24" barrel, weighs 12 lbs., checkered English walnut, engraving, gold inlays. Introduced 1998. Made in U.S. by Pacific Rifle Co.
Price: 72-caliber, from **$1,150.00**
Price: 8-bore, from **$2,500.00**

PEIFER MODEL TS-93 RIFLE
Caliber: 45, 50. **Barrel:** 24" Douglas premium; 1:20" twist in 45; 1:28" in 50. **Weight:** 7 lbs. **Length:** 43-1/4" overall. **Stock:** Bell & Carlson solid composite, with recoil pad, swivel studs. **Sights:** Williams bead front on ramp, fully adjustable open rear. Drilled and tapped for Weaver scope mounts with dovetail for rear peep. **Features:** In-line ignition uses #209 shotshell primer; fast lock time; fully enclosed breech; adjustable trigger; automatic safety; removable primer holder. Blue or stainless. Made in U.S. by Peifer Rifle Co. Introduced 1996.
Price: Blue, black stock **$730.00**
Price: Blue, wood or camouflage composite stock,
or stainless with black composite stock **$803.00**
Price: Stainless, wood or camouflage composite stock **$876.00**

PRAIRIE RIVER ARMS PRA BULLPUP RIFLE
Caliber: 50. **Barrel:** 28"; 1:28" twist. **Weight:** 7-1/2 lbs. **Length:** 31-1/2" overall. **Stock:** Hardwood or black all-weather. **Sights:** Blade front, open

adjustable rear. **Features:** Bullpup design thumbhole stock. Patented internal percussion ignition system. Left-hand model available. Dovetailed for scope mount. Introduced 1995. Made in U.S. by Prairie River Arms, Ltd.
Price: 4140 alloy barrel, hardwood stock **$199.00**
Price: All Weather stock, alloy barrel **$205.00**

REMINGTON GENESIS MUZZLELOADER
Caliber: 50. **Barrel:** 28", 1-in-28" twist, blued or stainless fluted. **Weight:** 7.75 lbs. **Length:** NA. **Stock:** Black synthetic, Mossy Oak New Break-Up. **Sights:** Williams fiber-optic sights, drilled and tapped for scope mounts. **Features:** TorchCam action, 209 primer, up to 150-grain charges. Over-travel hammer, crossbolt safety with ambidextrous HammerSpur (right- and left-handed operation). Buckmasters version has stainless fluted barrel with a Realtree Hardwoods HD camo stock, laser-engraved Buckmasters logo. Aluminum anodized ramrod with jag, front and rear swivel studs, removable 7/16" breech plug; optimized for use with Remington Kleanbore 209 Muzzleloading Primers. Introduced 2006. Made in U.S. by Remington Arms Co.
Price: Genesis ML, black synthetic, carbon matte blued **$293.00**
Price: Genesis MLS Overmold synthetic, stainless satin **$363.00**
Price: Genesis ML Camo Mossy Oak Break-Up,
carbon matte blued (2007) **$405.00**
Price: Genesis ML SF Synthetic Thumbhole, stainless satin **$405.00**
Price: Genesis ML SF Buckmasters (2007) **$419.00**
Price: Genesis ML SF laminate thumbhole, stainless satin **$594.00**

REPLICA ARMS 1863 SHARPS SPORTING RIFLE
Caliber: .54 cal percussion. **Barrel:** 28" Octagonal. **Weight:** 8.82 lbs. **Length:** 45" overall. **Grips:** Walnut checkered at wrist and forend. **Sights:** Blade front, full buckhorn rear. **Features:** Color case-hardened receiver, trigger, hammer and lever. Double-set triggers.
Price: **$939.00**

RICHMOND, C.S., 1863 MUSKET
Caliber: 58. **Barrel:** 40". **Weight:** 11 lbs. **Length:** 56-1/4" overall. **Stock:** European walnut with oil finish. **Sights:** Blade front, adjustable folding leaf rear. **Features:** Reproduction of the three-band Civil War musket. Sling swivels attached to trigger guard and middle barrel band. Lockplate marked "1863" and "C.S. Richmond." All white metal. Brass buttplate and forend cap. Imported by Euroarms of America, Navy Arms, and Dixie Gun Works.
Price: Euroarms **$730.00**
Price: Dixie Gun Works PR0846 .... **$1,025.00**

Rossi Muzzleloader

Savage 10MLSS-IIXP

Second Model Brown Bess

Thompson/Center Encore 209x50 Magnum

Thompson/Center Firestorm

ROSSI MUZZLELOADERS
Caliber: .50. **Barrel:** 20", 23". **Weight:** 5-6.3 lbs. **Stocks:** Wood. **Sights:** Fully adjustable fiber optic sights. **Features:** Black powder break open, 2 models available, manual external safety, Taurus Security System, blue or stainless finish, youth models available. From Rossi USA.
Price: **$199.00**
Price: MiniLoader **$256.00**

SAVAGE MODEL 10ML MUZZLELOADER RIFLE SERIES
Caliber: 50. **Barrel:** 24", 1:24 twist, blue or stainless. **Weight:** 7.75 lbs. **Stock:** Black synthetic, Realtree Hardwood JD Camo, brown laminate. **Sights:** Green adjustable rear, Red FiberOptic front. **Features:** XP Models scoped, no sights, designed for smokeless powder, #209 primer ignition. Removeable breech plug and vent liner.
Price: Model 10ML-II **$531.00**
Price: Model 10ML-II Camo **$569.00**
Price: Model 10MLSS-II Camo **$628.00**
Price: Model 10MLBSS-II **$667.00**
Price: Model 10ML-IIXP **$569.00**
Price: Model 10MLSS-IIXP **$628.00**

SECOND MODEL BROWN BESS MUSKET
Caliber: 75, uses .735" round ball. **Barrel:** 42", smoothbore. **Weight:** 9-1/2 lbs. **Length:** 59" overall. **Stock:** Walnut (Navy); walnut- stained hardwood (Dixie). **Sights:** Fixed. **Features:** Polished barrel and lock with brass trigger guard and buttplate. Bayonet and scabbard available. From Navy Arms, Dixie Gun Works, Cabela's.
Price: Finished . . . . **$475.00 to $950.00**
Price: Kit Navy Arms, Dixie Gun Works, FR0825 . . . **$575.00 to $775.00**
Price: Carbine (Navy Arms) **$835.00**
Price: Dixie Gun Works FR0810 . . . . **$950.00**

THOMPSON/CENTER TRIUMPH MAGNUM MUZZLELOADER
Caliber: 50. **Barrel:** 28" Weather Shield coated. **Weight:** NA. **Length:** NA. **Stock:** Black composite or Realtree AP HD Camo. **Sights:** NA. **Features:** QLA 209 shotshell primer ignition. Introduced 2007. Made in U.S. by Thompson/Center Arms.
Price: . . . . **NA**

THOMPSON/CENTER ENCORE 209x50 MAGNUM
Caliber: 50. **Barrel:** 26"; interchangeable with centerfire calibers. **Weight:** 7 lbs. **Length:** 40-1/2" overall. **Stock:** American walnut butt and forend, or black composite. **Sights:** TruGlo fiber-optic front and rear. **Features:** Blue or stainless steel. Uses the stock, frame and forend of the Encore centerfire pistol; break-open design using trigger guard spur; stainless steel universal breech plug; uses #209 shotshell primers. Introduced 1998. Made in U.S. by Thompson/Center Arms.
Price: Stainless with camo stock **$772.00**
Price: Blue, walnut stock and forend **$678.00**
Price: Blue, composite stock and forend **$637.00**
Price: Stainless, composite stock and forend **$713.00**
Price: All camo Realtree Hardwoods **$729.00**

Thompson/Center Hawken

Traditions Deerhunter

Traditions Pursuit

Traditions PA Pellet

THOMPSON/CENTER FIRESTORM RIFLE
Caliber: 50. **Barrel:** 26"; 1:28" twist. **Weight:** 7 lbs. **Length:** 41-3/4" overall. **Stock:** Black synthetic with rubber recoil pad, swivel studs. **Sights:** Click-adjustable steel rear and ramp-style front, both with fiber-optic inserts. **Features:** Side hammer lock is the first designed for up to three 50-grain Pyrodex pellets; patented Pyrodex Pyramid breech directs ignition fire 360 degrees around base of pellet. Quick Load Accurizor Muzzle System; aluminum ramrod. Flintlock only. Introduced 2000. Made in U.S. by Thompson/Center Arms.
Price: Blue finish, flintlock model with 1:48" twist for round balls, conicals **$436.00**
Price: SST, flintlock **$488.00**

THOMPSON/CENTER HAWKEN RIFLE
Caliber: 50. **Barrel:** 28" octagon, hooked breech. **Stock:** American walnut. **Sights:** Blade front, rear adjustable for windage and elevation. **Features:** Solid brass furniture, double-set triggers, button rifled barrel, coil-type mainspring. From Thompson/Center Arms.
Price: Percussion model **$590.00**
Price: Flintlock model **$615.00**

TRADITIONS BUCKSKINNER CARBINE
Caliber: 50. **Barrel:** 21"; 15/16" flats, half octagon, half round; 1:20" or 1:66" twist. **Weight:** 6 lbs. **Length:** 37" overall. **Stock:** Beech or black laminated. **Sights:** Beaded blade front, fiber-optic open rear click adjustable for windage and elevation or fiber-optics. **Features:** Uses V-type mainspring, single trigger. Non-glare hardware; sling swivels. From Traditions.
Price: Flintlock **$249.00**
Price: Flintlock, laminated stock **$303.00**

TRADITIONS DEERHUNTER RIFLE SERIES
Caliber: 32, 50 or 54. **Barrel:** 24", octagonal; 15/16" flats; 1:48" or 1:66" twist. **Weight:** 6 lbs. **Length:** 40" overall. **Stock:** Stained hardwood or All-Weather composite with rubber buttpad, sling swivels. **Sights:** Lite Optic blade front, adjustable rear fiber-optics. **Features:** Flint or percussion with color case-hardened lock. Hooked breech, oversized trigger guard, blackened furniture, PVC ramrod. All-Weather has composite stock and C-nickel barrel. Drilled and tapped for scope mounting. Imported by Traditions, Inc.
Price: Percussion, 50; blued barrel; 1:48" twist **$189.00**
Price: Percussion, 54 .... **$169.00**

Price: Flintlock, 50 caliber only; 1:48" twist **$179.00**
Price: Flintlock, All-Weather, 50-cal. **$239.00**
Price: Redi-Pak, 50 cal. flintlock **$219.00**
Price: Flintlock, left-handed hardwood, 50 cal. **$209.00**
Price: Percussion, All-Weather, 50 or 54 cal. **$179.00**
Price: Percussion, 32 cal. **$199.00**

Traditions Panther Sidelock Rifle
Similar to Deerhunter rifle, but has blade front and windage-adjustable-only rear sights, black composite stock.
Price: **$129.00**

TRADITIONS PURSUIT BREAK-OPEN MUZZLELOADER
Caliber: 45, 54 and 12 gauge. **Barrel:** 28", tapered, fluted; blued, stainless or Hardwoods Green camo. **Weight:** 8-1/4 lbs. **Length:** 44" overall. **Stock:** Synthetic black or Hardwoods Green. **Sights:** Steel fiber-optic rear, bead front. Introduced 2004 by Traditions, Inc.
Price: Steel, blued, 45 or 50 cal., synthetic stock **$279.00**
Price: Steel, nickel, 45 or 50 cal., synthetic stock **$309.00**
Price: Steel, nickel w/Hardwoods Green stock **$359.00**
Price: Matte blued; 12 ga., synthetic stock **$369.00**
Price: Matte blued; 12 ga. w/Hardwoods Green stock **$439.00**
Price: Lightweight model, blued, synthetic stock **$199.00**
Price: Lightweight model, blued, Mossy Oak® Break-Up™ Camo stock **$239.00**
Price: Lightweight model, nickel, Mossy Oak® Break-Up™ Camo stock **$279.00**

TRADITIONS EVOLUTION BOLT-ACTION BLACKPOWDER RIFLE
Caliber: 50 percussion. **Barrel:** 26", fluted with porting. **Sights:** Steel fiber-optic. **Weight:** 7 to 7-1/4 lbs. **Length:** 45" overall. **Features:** Bolt-action, cocking indicator, thumb safety, aluminum ramrod, sling studs. Wide variety of stocks and metal finishes. Introduced 2004 by Traditions, Inc.
Price: Synthetic stock **$279.00**
Price: Walnut X-wood **$349.00**
Price: Brown laminated **$469.00**
Price: Advantage Timber **$369.00**
Price: Synthetic, TruGlo sights **$249.00**
Price: Mossy Oak® Break-up™ **$279.00**
Price: Nickel finish **$309.00**
Price: Beech/nickel, Advantage/nickel, Advantage 54 cal. **$289.00**

TRADITIONS PA PELLET FLINTLOCK
Caliber: 50. **Barrel:** 26", blued, nickel. **Weight:** 7 lbs. **Stock:** Hardwood, synthetic and synthetic break-up. **Sights:** Fiber-optic. **Features:** Removeable breech plug, left-hand model with hardwood stock. 1:48" twist.
Price: Hardwood, blued **$259.00**
Price: Hardwood left, blued **$269.00**

Traditions Shenandoah

Traditions Tracker 209

TRADITIONS HAWKEN WOODSMAN RIFLE
Caliber: 50 and 54. **Barrel:** 28"; 15/16" flats. **Weight:** 7 lbs., 11 oz. **Length:** 44-1/2" overall. **Stock:** Walnut-stained hardwood. **Sights:** Beaded blade front, hunting-style open rear adjustable for windage and elevation. **Features:** Percussion only. Brass patchbox and furniture. Double triggers. From Traditions.
Price: 50 or 54 . . . . **$299.00**
Price: 50-cal., left-hand **$279.00**
Price: 50-cal., flintlock **$299.00**

TRADITIONS KENTUCKY RIFLE
Caliber: 50. **Barrel:** 33-1/2"; 7/8" flats; 1:66" twist. **Weight:** 7 lbs. **Length:** 49" overall. **Stock:** Beech; inletted toe plate. **Sights:** Blade front, fixed rear. **Features:** Full-length, two-piece stock; brass furniture; color case-hardened lock. From Traditions.
Price: **$279.00**

TRADITIONS PENNSYLVANIA RIFLE
Caliber: 50. **Barrel:** 40-1/4"; 7/8" flats; 1:66" twist, octagon. **Weight:** 9 lbs. **Length:** 57-1/2" overall. **Stock:** Walnut. **Sights:** Blade front, adjustable rear. **Features:** Brass patchbox and ornamentation. Double-set triggers. From Traditions.
Price: Flintlock **$529.00**
Price: Percussion **$519.00**

TRADITIONS SHENANDOAH RIFLE
Caliber: 36, 50. **Barrel:** 33-1/2" octagon; 1:66" twist. **Weight:** 7 lbs., 3 oz. **Length:** 49-1/2" overall. **Stock:** Walnut. **Sights:** Blade front, buckhorn rear. **Features:** V-type mainspring; double-set trigger; solid brass buttplate, patchbox, nosecap, thimbles, trigger guard. Introduced 1996. From Traditions.
Price: Flintlock **$419.00**
Price: Percussion **$399.00**
Price: 36 cal. flintlock, 1:48" twist **$419.00**
Price: 36 cal. percussion, 1:48" twist **$449.00**

TRADITIONS TENNESSEE RIFLE
Caliber: 50. **Barrel:** 24", octagon; 15/16" flats; 1:66" twist. **Weight:** 6 lbs. **Length:** 40-1/2" overall. **Stock:** Stained beech. **Sights:** Blade front, fixed rear. **Features:** One-piece stock has inletted brass furniture, cheekpiece; double-set trigger; V-type mainspring. Flint or percussion. From Traditions.
Price: Flintlock **$339.00**
Price: Percussion **$329.00**

TRADITIONS TRACKER 209 IN-LINE RIFLES
Caliber: 45, 50. **Barrel:** 22" blued or C-nickel finish; 1:28" twist, 50 cal. 1:20" 45 cal. **Weight:** 6 lbs., 4 oz. **Length:** 41" overall. **Stock:** Black, Advantage Timber® composite, synthetic. **Sights:** Lite Optic blade front, adjustable rear. **Features:** Thumb safety; adjustable trigger; rubber butt pad and sling swivel studs; takes 150 grains of Pyrodex pellets; one-piece breech system takes 209 shotshell primers. Drilled and tapped for scope. From Traditions.
Price: (Black composite or synthetic stock, 22" blued barrel) **$129.00**
Price: (Black composite or synthetic stock, 22" C-nickel barrel) . . **$139.00**
Price: (Advantage Timber® stock, 22" C-nickel barrel) **$189.00**

Price: (Redi-Pak, black stock and blued barrel, powder flask,
capper, ball starter, other accessories) **$179.00**
Price: (Redi-Pak, synthetic stock and blued barrel, with scope) . . **$229.00**

ULTRA LIGHT ARMS MODEL 209 MUZZLELOADER
Caliber: 45 or 50. **Barrel:** 24" button rifled; 1:32 twist. **Weight:** Under 5 lbs. **Stock:** Kevlar/Graphite. **Features:** Recoil pad, sling swivels included. Some color options available. Adj. Timney trigger, positive primer extraction.
Price: **$1,100.00**

WHITE MODEL 97 WHITETAIL HUNTER RIFLE
Caliber: 45, 50. **Barrel:** 22", 1:20 twist (45 cal.); 1:24 twist (50 cal.). **Weight:** 7.7 lbs. **Length:** 40" overall. **Stock:** Black laminated or black composite. **Sights:** Marble TruGlo fully adjustable, steel rear with white diamond, red bead front with high-visibility inserts. **Features:** In-line ignition with FlashFire one-piece nipple and breech plug that uses standard or magnum No. 11 caps, fully adjustable trigger, double safety system, aluminum ramrod; drilled and tapped for scope. Hard case. Made in U.S.A. by Split Fire Sporting Goods.
Price: Whitetail w/laminated or composite stock **$499.95**
Price: Adventurer w/26" stainless barrel & thumbhole stock) **$699.95**
Price: Odyssey w/24" carbon fiber wrapped
barrel & thumbhole stock **$1,299.95**

WHITE MODEL 98 ELITE HUNTER RIFLE
Caliber: 45, 50. **Barrel:** 24", 1:24" twist (50 cal). **Weight:** 8.6 lbs. **Length:** 43-1/2" overall. **Stock:** Black laminate wtih swivel studs. **Sights:** TruGlo fully adjustable, steel rear with white diamond, red bead front with high-visibility inserts. **Features:** In-line ignition with FlashFire one-piece nipple and breech plug that uses standard or magnum No. 11 caps, fully adjustable trigger, double safety system, aluminum ramrod, drilled and tapped for scope, hard gun case. Made in U.S.A. by Split Fire Sporting Goods.
Price: Composite or laminate wood stock **$499.95**

White Thunderbolt Rifle
Similar to the Elite Hunter but is designed to handle 209 shotgun primers only. Has 26" stainless steel barrel, weighs 9.3 lbs. and is 45-1/2" long. Composite or laminate stock. Made in U.S.A. by Split Fire Sporting Goods.
Price: **$599.95**

WHITE MODEL 2000 BLACKTAIL HUNTER RIFLE
Caliber: 50. **Barrel:** 22", 1:24" twist (50 cal.). **Weight:** 7.6 lbs. **Length:** 39-7/8" overall. **Stock:** Black laminated with swivel studs with laser engraved deer or elk scene. **Sights:** TruGlo fully adjustable, steel rear with white diamond, red bead front with high-visibility inserts. **Features:** Teflon finished barrel, in-line ignition with FlashFire one-piece nipple and breech plug that uses standard or magnum No. 11 caps, fully adjustable trigger, double safety system, aluminum ramrod, drilled and tapped for scope. Hard gun case. Made in U.S.A. by Split Fire Sporting Goods.
Price: Laminate wood stock, w/laser engraved game scene **$599.95**

WHITE LIGHTNING II RIFLE
Caliber: 45 and 50 percussion. **Barrel:** 24", 1:32 twist. **Sights:** Adj. rear. **Stock:** Black polymer. **Weight:** 6 lbs. **Features:** In-line, 209 primer ignition system, blued or nickel-plated bbl., adj. trigger, Delrin ramrod, sling studs, recoil pad. Made in U.S.A. by Split Fire Sporting Goods.
Price: **$299.95**

BLACKPOWDER MUSKETS & RIFLES

Zouave Percussion

WHITE ALPHA RIFLE
Caliber: 45, 50 percussion. **Barrel:** 27" tapered, stainless. **Sights:** Marble TruGlo rear, fiber-optic front. **Stock:** Laminated. **Features:** Lever action rotating block, hammerless; adj. trigger, positive safety. All stainless metal, including trigger. Made in U.S.A. by Split Fire Sporting Goods.
Price: **$449.95**

WINCHESTER APEX SWING-ACTION MAGNUM RIFLE
Caliber: 45, 50. **Barrel:** 28". **Stock:** Mossy Oak® Camo, Black Fleck. **Sights:** Adj. fiber-optic. **Weight:** 7 lbs., 12 oz. **Overall length:** 42". **Features:** Monte Carlo cheekpiece, swing-action design, external hammer.
Price: Mossy Oak®/stainless **$489.95**
Price: Black Fleck/stainless **$449.95**
Price: Full Mossy Oak® **$469.95**
Price: Black Fleck/blued **$364.95**

WINCHESTER X-150 BOLT-ACTION MAGNUM RIFLE
Caliber: 45, 50. **Barrel:** 26". **Stock:** Hardwoods or Timber HD, Black Fleck, Break-Up™. **Weight:** 8 lbs., 3 oz. **Sights:** Adj. fiber-optic. **Features:** No. 209 shotgun primer ignition, stainless steel bolt, stainless fluted bbl.
Price: Mossy Oak®, Timber, Hardwoods/stainless **$349.95**
Price: Black Fleck/stainless **$299.95**
Price: Mossy Oak®, Timber, Hardwoods/blued **$279.95**
Price: Black Fleck/blued **$229.95**

ZOUAVE PERCUSSION RIFLE
Caliber: 58, 59. **Barrel:** 32-1/2". **Weight:** 9-1/2 lbs. **Length:** 48-1/2" overall. **Stock:** Walnut finish, brass patchbox and buttplate. **Sights:** Fixed front, rear adjustable for elevation. **Features:** Color case-hardened lockplate, blued barrel. From Navy Arms, Dixie Gun Works, E.M.F., Cabela's, Euroarms of America.
Price: Dixie Gun Works PR0835 . . . . **$415.00 to $625.00**

BLACKPOWDER SHOTGUNS

Knight TK2000

CABELA'S BLACKPOWDER SHOTGUNS
Gauge: 10, 12, 20. **Barrel:** 10-ga., 30"; 12-ga., 28-1/2" (Extra-Full, Mod., Imp. Cyl. choke tubes); 20-ga., 27-1/2" (Imp. Cyl. & Mod. fixed chokes). **Weight:** 6-1/2 to 7 lbs. **Length:** 45" overall (28-1/2" barrel). **Stock:** American walnut with checkered grip; 12- and 20- gauge have straight stock, 10-gauge has pistol grip. **Features:** Blued barrels, engraved, color case-hardened locks and hammers, brass ramrod tip. From Cabela's.
Price: 10-gauge **$849.99**
Price: 12-gauge **$719.99**
Price: 20-gauge **$659.99**

DIXIE MAGNUM PERCUSSION SHOTGUN
Gauge: 10, 12, 20. **Barrel:** 30" (Imp. Cyl. & Mod.) in 10-gauge; 28" in 12-gauge. **Weight:** 6-1/4 lbs. **Length:** 45" overall. **Stock:** Hand- checkered walnut, 14" pull. **Features:** Double triggers; light hand engraving; case-hardened locks in 12-gauge, polished steel in 10- gauge; sling swivels. From Dixie Gun Works.
Price: 12 ga. PS0930 . . . . **$685.00**
Price: 12-ga. Kit PS0940 . . . . **$500.00**
Price: 20-ga. PS0334 . . . . **$685.00**
Price: 10-ga. PS1030 . . . . **$685.00**
Price: 10-ga. kit PS1040 . . . . **$500.00**
Price: Coach Gun, 12 ga. 20" bbl PS0914 . . . . **$625.00**

KNIGHT TK2000 MUZZLELOADING SHOTGUN (209)
Gauge: 12. **Barrel:** 26", extra-full choke tube. **Weight:** 7 lbs., 9 oz. **Length:** 45" overall. **Stock:** Synthetic black or Advantage Timber HD; recoil pad; swivel studs. **Sights:** Fully adjustable rear, blade front with fiber-optics. **Features:** Receiver drilled and tapped for scope mount; in-line ignition; adjustable trigger; removable breech plug; double safety system; Imp. Cyl. choke tube available. Made in U.S. by Knight Rifles.
Price: . . . . **$349.95 to $399.95**

KNIGHT VERSATILE TK2002
Gauge: 12. **Stock:** Black composite, blued, Advantage Timber HD finish. Both with sling swivel studs installed. **Sights:** Adjustable metallic TruGlo fiber-optic. **Features:** Full plastic jacket ignition system, screw-on choke tubes, load without removing choke tubes, jug-choked barrel design. Improved cylinder and modified choke tubes available.
Price: . . . . **$349.95 to $399.95**

NAVY ARMS STEEL SHOT MAGNUM SHOTGUN
Gauge: 10. **Barrel:** 28" (Cyl. & Cyl.). **Weight:** 7 lbs., 9 oz. **Length:** 45-1/2" overall. **Stock:** Walnut, with cheekpiece. **Features:** Designed specifically for steel shot. Engraved, polished locks; sling swivels; blued barrels. Imported by Navy Arms.
Price: **$605.00**

NAVY ARMS T&T SHOTGUN
Gauge: 12. **Barrel:** 28" (Full & Full). **Weight:** 7-1/2 lbs. **Stock:** Walnut. **Sights:** Bead front. **Features:** Color case-hardened locks, double triggers, blued steel furniture. From Navy Arms.
Price: **$580.00**

WHITE TOMINATOR SHOTGUN
Caliber: 12. **Barrel:** 25" blue, straight, tapered stainless steel. **Weight:** NA. **Length:** NA. **Stock:** Black laminated or black wood. **Sights:** Drilled and tapped for easy scope mounting. **Features:** Internchangeable choke tubes. Custom vent rib with high visibility front bead. Double safeties. Fully adjustable custom trigger. Recoil pad and sling swivel studs. Made in U.S.A. by Split Fire Sporting Goods.
Price: **$349.95**

ARS HUNTING MASTER AR6 AIR PISTOL
Caliber: 22 (177 +20 special order). **Barrel:** 12" rifled. **Weight:** 3 lbs. **Length:** 18.25 overall. **Power:** NA. **Grips:** Indonesian walnut with checkered grip. **Sights:** Adjustable rear, blade front. **Features:** 6 shot repeater with rotary magazine, single or double action, receiver grooved for scope, hammer block and trigger block safeties.
Price: .... **NA**

BEEMAN P1 MAGNUM AIR PISTOL
Caliber: 177, 20. **Barrel:** 8.4". **Weight:** 2.5 lbs. **Length:** 11" overall. **Power:** Top lever cocking; spring-piston. **Grips:** Checkered walnut. **Sights:** Blade front, square notch rear with click micrometer adjustments for windage and elevation. Grooved for scope mounting. **Features:** Dual power for 177 and 20 cal.: low setting gives 350-400 fps; high setting 500-600 fps. All Colt 45 auto grips fit gun. Dry-firing feature for practice. Optional wood shoulder stock. Imported by Beeman.
Price: **$450.00**

BEEMAN P3 PNEUMATIC AIR PISTOL
Caliber: 177. **Barrel:** NA. **Weight:** 1.7 lbs. **Length:** 9.6" overall. **Power:** Single-stroke pneumatic; overlever barrel cocking. **Grips:** Reinforced polymer. **Sights:** Front and rear fiber-optic sights. **Features:** Velocity 410 fps. Polymer frame; automatic safety; two-stage trigger; built-in muzzle brake.
Price: **$215.00**
Price: **$295.00**

BEEMAN/Feinwerkbau P44
Caliber: 177, single shot. **Barrel:** 9.17". **Weight:** 2.10 lbs. **Length:** 16.54" overall. **Power:** Pre-charged pneumatic. **Grips:** Walnut grip. **Sights:** front and rear sights. **Features:** 500 fps, sighting line adjustable from 360 to 395mm, adjustable 3-d grip in 3 sizes, adjustable match trigger, delivered in special transport case.
Price: **$1,890.00**

BEEMAN/Feinwerkbau P56
Caliber: 177, 5-shot magazine. **Barrel:** 8.81". **Weight:** 2.43 lbs. **Length:** 16.54" overall. **Power:** Pre-charged pneumatic. **Grips:** Walnut Morini grip. **Sights:** front and rear sights. **Features:** 500 fps, match-adjustable trigger, adjustable rear sight, front sight accepts interchangeable inserts, delivered in special transport case.
Price: **$2,280.00**

BEEMAN/FWB 103 AIR PISTOL
Caliber: 177. **Barrel:** 10.1", 12-groove rifling. **Weight:** 2.5 lbs. **Length:** 16.5" overall. **Power:** Single-stroke pneumatic, underlever cocking. **Grips:** Stippled walnut with adjustable palm shelf. **Sights:** Blade front, open rear adjustable for windage and elevation. Notch size adjustable for width. Interchangeable front blades. **Features:** Velocity 510 fps. Fully adjustable trigger. Cocking effort 2 lbs. Imported by Beeman.
Price: Right-hand **$1,805.00**
Price: Left-hand **$1,920.00**

BEEMAN HW70A AIR PISTOL
Caliber: 177. **Barrel:** 6-1/4", rifled. **Weight:** 38 oz. **Length:** 12-3/4" overall. **Power:** Spring, barrel cocking. **Grips:** Plastic, with thumbrest. **Sights:** Hooded post front, square notch rear adjustable for windage and elevation. Comes with scope base. **Features:** Adjustable trigger, 31-lb. cocking effort, 440 fps MV; automatic barrel safety. Imported by Beeman.
Price: **$240.00**

BENJAMIN & SHERIDAN CO2 PISTOLS
Caliber: 177, 22, single shot. **Barrel:** 6-3/8", brass. **Weight:** 1 lb. 12 oz. **Length:** 9" overall. **Power:** 12-gram CO2 cylinder. **Grips:** American Hardwood. **Sights:** High ramp front, fully adjustable notched rear. **Features:** Velocity to 500 fps. Turnbolt action with cross-bolt safety. Gives about 40 shots per CO2 cylinder. Black or nickel finish. Made in U.S. by Crosman Corp.
Price: EB17 (177), EB22 (22) **$185.00**

BENJAMIN & SHERIDAN PNEUMATIC PELLET PISTOLS
Caliber: 177, 22, single shot. **Barrel:** 9-3/8", rifled brass. **Weight:** 2 lbs., 8 oz. **Length:** 12.25" overall. **Power:** Underlever pnuematic, hand pumped. **Grips:** American Hardwood. **Sights:** High ramp front, fully adjustable notch rear. **Features:** Velocity to 525 fps (variable). Bolt action with cross-bolt safety. Choice of black or nickel finish. Made in U.S. by Crosman Corp.
Price: Black finish, HB17 (177), HB22 (22) **$115.00**

Benjamin & Sheridan EB17/EB22

COLT 1911 A1
Caliber: .177, 8-shot pellet. **Barrel:** 5" rifled. **Weight:** 2.4 lbs. **Length:** 9" overall. **Power:** 12g CO2. **Sights:** Fixed front, adjustable rear. **Features:** Velocity of 425 fps. 8-shot rotary clip. Double or single action. Replica of one of the most successful military designs ever developed.
Price: **$216.88**
Price: Nickel **$238.42**

COLT 1911 TACTICAL
Caliber: .177, 8-shot pellet. 5" rifled. **Weight:** 2.9 lbs. 13-3/4" overall. **Power:** 12g CO2. **Sights:** Fixed front, adjustable rear. Velocity of 425 fps. 8-shot rotary clip. Double or single action. Includes Walther Top Point Sight and compensator.
Price: **$320.00**

CROSMAN AUTO AIR II RED DOT PISTOLS
Caliber: BB, 17-shot magazine; 177 pellet, single shot. **Barrel:** 8-5/8" steel, smooth-bore. **Weight:** 13 oz. **Length:** 10-3/4" overall. **Power:** CO2 Powerlet. **Grips:** NA. **Sights:** Blade front, adjustable rear; highlighted system. **Features:** Velocity to 480 fps (BBs), 430 fps (pellets). Semi-automatic action with BBs, single shot with pellets. Black. From Crosman.
Price: AAIIB **$38.00**

CROSMAN MODEL 1008 REPEAT AIR PISTOL
Caliber: 177, 8-shot pellet clip. **Barrel:** 4.25", rifled steel. **Weight:** 17 oz. **Length:** 8.625" overall. **Power:** CO2 Powerlet. **Grips:** Checkered black plastic. **Sights:** Post front, adjustable rear. **Features:** Velocity about 430 fps. Break-open barrel for easy loading; single or double semi-automatic action; two 8-shot clips included. Optional carrying case available. From Crosman.
Price: **$60.00**

CROSMAN MAGNUM AIR PISTOLS
Caliber: 177, pellets. **Barrel:** Rifled steel. **Weight:** 2 lbs. **Length:** 9.38". **Power:** CO2. **Grips:** NA. **Sights:** Blade front, rear adjustable. **Features:** Single/double action accepts sights and scopes with standard 3/8" dovetail mount. Model 3576W features 6" barrel for increased accuracy. From Crosman.
Price: 3576W **$50.00**

DAISY/POWERLINE MODEL 15XT AIR PISTOL
Caliber: 177 BB, 15-shot built-in magazine. **Barrel:** NA. **Weight:** NA. **Length:** 7.21". **Power:** CO2. **Grips:** NA. **Sights:** NA. **Features:** Velocity 425 fps. Made in the U.S.A. by Daisy Mfg. Co.
Price: **$47.99**
Price: With electronic point sight **$57.99**

DAISY MODEL 717 AIR PISTOL
Caliber: 177, single shot. **Weight:** 2.25 lbs. **Length:** 13-1/2" overall. **Grips:** Molded checkered woodgrain with contoured thumbrest. **Sights:** Blade and ramp front, open rear with windage and elevation adjustments. **Features:** Single pump pneumatic pistol. Rifled steel barrel. Crossbolt trigger block. Muzzle velocity 360 fps. From Daisy Mfg. Co.
Price: **$152.99**

DAISY MODEL 747 TRIUMPH AIR PISTOL
Caliber: 177, single shot. **Weight:** 2.35 lbs. **Length:** 13-1/2" overall. **Grips:** Molded checkered woodgrain with contoured thumbrest. **Sights:** Blade and ramp front, open rear with windage and elevation adjustments. **Features:** Single pump pneumatic pistol. Lothar Walther rifled high-grade steel barrel; crowned 12 lands and grooves, right-hand twist. Precision bore sized for match pellets. Muzzle veocity 360 fps. From Daisy Mfg. Co.
Price: **$203.99**

Daisy/Powerline 693

Gamo P-23

DAISY/POWERLINE 693 AIR PISTOL
Caliber: 177, single shot. **Weight:** 1.10 lbs. **Length:** 7.9" overall. **Grips:** Molded brown checkered. **Sights:** Blade and ramp front, fixed open rear. **Features:** Semi-automoatic BB pistol with a nickel finish and smooth bore steel barrel. Muzzle veocity 400 fps. From Daisy Mfg. Co.
Price: **$66.99**

EAA/BAIKAL IZH-M46 TARGET AIR PISTOL
Caliber: 177, single shot. **Barrel:** 10". **Weight:** 2.4 lbs. **Length:** 16.8" overall. **Power:** Underlever single-stroke pneumatic. **Grips:** Adjustable wooden target. **Sights:** Micrometer fully adjustable rear, blade front. **Features:** Velocity about 440 fps. Hammer-forged, rifled barrel. Imported from Russia by European American Armory.
Price: **$349.00**

GAMO P-23, P-23 LASER PISTOL
Caliber: 177, 12-shot. **Barrel:** 4.25". **Weight:** 1 lb. **Length:** 7.5". **Power:** CO2 cartridge, semi-automatic, 410 fps. **Grips:** Plastic. **Sights:** NA. **Features:** Walther PPK cartridge pistol copy, optional laser sight. Imported from Spain by Gamo.
Price: . . . . **$89.95**, (with laser) **$139.95**

GAMO PT-80, PT-80 LASER PISTOL
Caliber: 177, 8-shot. **Barrel:** 4.25". **Weight:** 1.2 lbs. **Length:** 7.2". **Power:** CO2 cartridge, semi-automatic, 410 fps. **Grips:** Plastic. **Sights:** 3-dot. **Features:** Optional laser sight and walnut grips available. Imported from Spain by Gamo.
Price: . . . . **$108.95**, (with laser) **$159.95**
Price: (with walnut grip) **$119.95**

HAMMERLI AP-40 AIR PISTOL
Caliber: 177. **Barrel:** 10". **Weight:** 2.2 lbs. **Length:** 15.5". **Power:** NA. **Grips:** Adjustable orthopedic. **Sights:** Fully adjustable micrometer. **Features:** Sleek, light, well balanced and accurate.
Price: **$1,400.00**

MAGNUM RESEARCH DESERT EAGLE
Caliber: .177, 8-shot pellet. 5.7" rifled. **Weight:** 2.5 lbs. 11" overall. **Power:** 12g CO2. **Sights:** Fixed front, adjustable rear. Velocity of 425 fps. 8-shot rotary clip. Double or single action. The first .177 caliber air pistol with BLOWBACK action. Big and weighty, designed in the likeness of the real Desert Eagle.
Price: **$172.31**

MAGNUM BABY DESERT
Caliber: .177, 15-shot BB. 4" **Weight:** 1.0 lbs. 8-1/4" overall. **Power:** 12g CO2. **Sights:** Fixed front and rear. Velocity of 420 fps. Double action BB repeater. Comes with bonus Picatinny top rail and built-in bottom rail.
Price: **$41.54**

MORINI CM 162 EL MATCH AIR PISTOLS
Caliber: 177, single shot. **Barrel:** 9.4". **Weight:** 32 oz. **Length:** 16.1" overall. **Power:** Scuba air. **Grips:** Adjustable match type. **Sights:** Interchangeable blade front, fully adjustable match-type rear. **Features:** Power mechanism shuts down when pressure drops to a preset level. Adjustable electronic trigger.
Price: **$1,075.00**

PARDINI K58 MATCH AIR PISTOLS
Caliber: 177, single shot. **Barrel:** 9". **Weight:** 37.7 oz. **Length:** 15.5" overall. **Power:** Precharged compressed air; single-stroke cocking. **Grips:** Adjustable match type; stippled walnut. **Sights:** Interchangeable post front, fully adjustable match rear. **Features:** Fully adjustable trigger. Short version K-2 available. Imported from Italy by Larry's Guns.
Price: **$819.00**

RWS 9B/9N AIR PISTOLS
Caliber: 177, single shot. **Barrel:** 8". **Weight:** 2.38 lbs. **Length:** 10.4". **Power:** 550 fps. **Grips:** Right hand with thumbrest. **Sights:** Adjustable. **Features:** Spring-piston powered. Black or nickel finish.
Price: 9B/9N **$150.00**

SMITH & WESSON 586
Caliber: .177, 10-shot pellet. Rifled. **Power:** 12g CO2. **Sights:** Fixed front, adjustable rear. 10-shot rotary clip. Double or single action. Replica revolvers that duplicate both weight and handling.
Price: 4" barrel, 2.5 lbs, 400 fps **$215.34**
Price: 6" barrel, 2.8 lbs, 425 fps **$231.49**
Price: 8" barrel, 3.0 lbs, 460 fps **$247.65**
Price: S&W 686 Nickel, 6" barrel, 2.8 lbs, 425 fps **$253.03**

STEYR LP10P MATCH AIR PISTOL
Caliber: 177, single shot. **Barrel:** 9". **Weight:** 38.7 oz. **Length:** 15.3" overall. **Power:** Scuba air. **Grips:** Adjustable Morini match, palm shelf, stippled walnut. **Sights:** Interchangeable blade in 4mm, 4.5mm or 5mm widths, adjustable open rear, interchangeable 3.5mm or 4mm leaves. **Features:** Velocity about 500 fps. Adjustable trigger, adjustable sight radius from 12.4" to 13.2". With compensator. Recoil elimination.
Price: **$1,400.00**

TECH FORCE SS2 OLYMPIC COMPETITION AIR PISTOL
Caliber: 177 pellet, single shot. **Barrel:** 7.4". **Weight:** 2.8 lbs. **Length:** 16.5" overall. **Power:** Spring piston, sidelever. **Grips:** Hardwood. **Sights:** Extended adjustable rear, blade front accepts inserts. **Features:** Velocity 520 fps. Recoilless design; adjustments allow duplication of a firearm's feel. Match-grade, adjustable trigger; includes carrying case. Imported from China by Compasseco, Inc.
Price: **$295.00**

TECH FORCE 35 AIR PISTOL
Caliber: 177 pellet, single shot. **Weight:** 2.86 lbs. **Length:** 14.9" overall. **Power:** Spring-piston, underlever. **Grips:** Hardwood. **Sights:** Micrometer adjustable rear, blade front. **Features:** Velocity 400 fps. Grooved for scope mount; trigger safety. Imported from China by Compasseco, Inc.
Price: **$39.95**

Tech Force S2-1 Air Pistol
Similar to Tech Force 8 except basic grips and sights for plinking.
Price: **$29.95**

WALTHER LP300 MATCH PISTOL
Caliber: 177. **Barrel:** 236mm. **Weight:** 1.018g. **Length:** NA. **Power:** NA. **Grips:** NA. **Sights:** Integrated front with three different widths, adjustable rear. **Features:** Adjustable grip and trigger.
Price: **$1,800.00**

WALTHER PPK/S
Caliber: .177, 15-shot steel BB. 3-1/2". **Weight:** 1.2 lbs. 6-1/4" overall. **Power:** 12g CO2. **Sights:** Fixed front and rear. Velocity of 295 fps. Lookalike of one of the world's most famous pistols. Realistic recoil. Heavyweight steel construction.
Price: **$71.92**
Price: With laser sight **$94.23**
Price: With BiColor pistol, CO2, targets, shooting glasses, BBs **$84.62**

WALTHER CP99 COMPACT
Caliber: .177, 17-shot steel BB semi-auto. 3". **Weight:** 1.7 lbs. 6-1/2" overall. **Power:** 12g CO2. **Sights:** Fixed front and rear. Velocity of 345 fps. Realistic recoil, blowback action. Heavyweight steel construction. Built-in Picatinny mount.
Price: **$83.08**

AIRGUNS — Long Guns

AIRFORCE CONDOR RIFLE
Caliber: .177, .22 single shot. **Barrel:** 24" rifled. **Weight:** 6.5 lbs. **Length:** 38.75" overall. **Power:** Pre-charged pneumatic. **Stock:** NA. **Sights:** Intended for scope use, fiber-optic open sights optional. **Features:** Lothar Walther match barrel, adjustable power levels from 600-1,300 fps. 3,000 psi fill pressure. Automatic safety. Air tank volume: 490cc. An integral extended scope rail allows easy mounting of the largest air-gun scopes. Operates on high-pressure air from scuba tank or hand pump. Manufactured in the U.S.A by AirForce Airguns
Price: Gun only (.22 or .177) **$589.95**

AIRFORCE TALON AIR RIFLE
Caliber: .177, .22, single-shot. **Barrel:** 18" rifled. **Weight:** 5.5 lbs. **Length:** 32.6". **Power:** Pre-charged pneumatic. **Stock:** NA. **Sights:** Intended for scope use, fiber-optic open sights optional. **Features:** Lothar Walther match barrel, adjustable power levels from 400-1,000 fps, 3,000 psi fill pressure. Automatic safety. Air tank volume: 490cc. Operates on high-pressure air from scuba tank or hand pump. Manufactured in the U.S.A. by AirForce Airguns.
Price: Gun only (.22 or .177) **$479.95**

AIRFORCE TALON SS AIR RIFLE
Caliber: .177, .22, single-shot. **Barrel:** 12" rifled. **Weight:** 5.25 lbs. **Length:** 32.75". **Power:** Pre-charged pneumatic. **Stock:** NA. **Sights:** Intended for scope use, fiber-optic open sights optional. **Features:** Lothar Walther match barrel, adjustable power levels from 400-1,000 fps. 3,000 psi fill pressure. Automatic safety. Chamber in front of barrel strips away air turbulence, protects muzzle and reduces firing report. Air tank volume: 490cc. Operates on high-pressure air from scuba tank or hand pump. Manufactured in the U.S.A. by AirForce Airguns.
Price: Gun only (.22 or .177) **$499.95**

AIRROW MODEL A-8SRB STEALTH AIR RIFLE
Caliber: 177, 22, 25, 9-shot. **Barrel:** 20"; rifled. **Weight:** 6 lbs. **Length:** 34" overall. **Power:** CO2 or compressed air; variable power. **Stock:** Telescoping CAR-15-type. **Sights:** Variable 3.5-10x scope. **Features:** Velocity 1100 fps in all calibers. Pneumatic air trigger. All aircraft aluminum and stainless steel construction. Mil-spec materials and finishes. From Swivel Machine Works, Inc.
Price: About **$2,299.00**

AIRROW MODEL A-8S1P STEALTH AIR RIFLE
Caliber: #2512 16" arrow. **Barrel:** 16". **Weight:** 4.4 lbs. **Length:** 30.1" overall. **Power:** CO2 or compressed air; variable power. **Stock:** Telescoping CAR-15-type. **Sights:** Scope rings only. 7 oz. rechargeable cylinder and valve. **Features:** Velocity to 650 fps with 260- grain arrow. Pneumatic air trigger. Broadhead guard. All aircraft aluminum and stainless steel construction. Mil-spec materials and finishes. A-8S Models perform to 2,000 PSIG above or below water levels. Waterproof case. From Swivel Machine Works, Inc.
Price: **$1,699.00**

ANSCHÜTZ 2002 MATCH AIR RIFLES
Caliber: .177, single shot. **Barrel:** 25.2". **Weight:** 10.8 lbs. **Length:** 42.5" overall. **Stock:** European walnut, blonde hardwood or colored laminated hardwood; stippled grip and forend. Also available with flat-forend walnut stock for benchrest shooting and aluminum. **Sights:** Optional sight set #6834. **Features:** Muzzle velocity 575 fps. Balance, weight match the 1907 ISU smallbore rifle. Uses #5021 match trigger. Recoil and vibration free. Fully adjustable cheekpiece and buttplate; accessory rail under forend. Available in pneumatic and compressed air versions. Imported from Germany by Gunsmithing, Inc., Accuracy International, Champion's Choice.
Price: Right-hand, blonde hardwood stock, with sights **$1,275.00**
Price: Right-hand, walnut stock **$1,275.00**
Price: Right-hand, color laminate stock **$1,300.00**
Price: Right-hand, aluminum stock, butt plate **$1,495.00**
Price: Left-hand, color laminate stock **$1,595.00**
Price: Model 2002D-RT Running Target, right-hand, no sights . . **$1,248.90**
Price: #6834 Sight Set **$227.10**

ARS HUNTING MASTER AR6 AIR RIFLE
Caliber: .22, 6-shot repeater. **Barrel:** 25-1/2". **Weight:** 7 lbs. **Length:** 41-1/4" overall. **Power:** Precompressed air from 3000 psi diving tank. **Stock:**

Indonesian walnut with checkered grip; rubber buttpad. **Sights:** Blade front, adjustable peep rear. **Features:** Velocity over 1000 fps with 32-grain pellet. Receiver grooved for scope mounting. Has 6-shot rotary magazine. Imported by Air Rifle Specialists.
Price: **$580.00**

BEEMAN KODIAK AIR RIFLE
Caliber: .25, single shot. **Barrel:** 17.6". **Weight:** 9 lbs. **Length:** 45.6" overall. **Power:** Spring-piston, barrel cocking. **Stock:** Stained hardwood. **Sights:** Blade front, open fully adjustable rear. **Features:** Velocity to 820 fps. Up to 30 foot pounds muzzle energy. Imported by Beeman.
Price: **$725.00**

BEEMAN GH1050 AIR RIFLE
Caliber: .177 or .22, single shot. **Barrel:** NA. **Weight:** 6.4 lbs. **Length:** 45.67" overall. **Power:** Spring-piston. **Stock:** Anti-shock black synthetic stock w/recoil pad, checkered pistol grip and forend. **Sights:** Fiber optic front & rear sights. **Features:** Velocities 1000 fps in .177 or 812 fps in .22. Dovetail receiver, steel trigger blade, and automatic safety.
Price: .177 or .22 caliber air rifle **$235.00**
Price: .177 or .22 caliber air rile combo **$300.00**

BEEMAN HW100
Caliber: .177 or .22, 14-shot magazine. **Barrel:** 21-1/2". **Weight:** 9 lbs. **Length:** 42.13" overall. **Power:** Pre-charged. **Stock:** Walnut Sporter checkering on the pistol grip & forend; walnut thumbhose with lateral finger grooves on the forend & stippling on the pistol grip. **Sights:** None. Grooved for scope mounting. **Features:** 1140 fps .177 caliber; 945 fps .22 caliber. 14-shot magazine, quick-fill cylinder. Two-stage adjustable match trigger and manual safety.
Price: .177 or .22 caliber Sport Stock **$1,465.00**
Price: .177 or .22 caliber Thumbhole Stock **$1,465.00**

BEEMAN R1 AIR RIFLE
Caliber: .177, .20 or .22, single shot. **Barrel:** 19.6", 12-groove rifling. **Weight:** 8.5 lbs. **Length:** 45.2" overall. **Power:** Spring-piston, barrel cocking. **Stock:** Walnut-stained beech; cut-checkered pistol grip; Monte Carlo comb and cheekpiece; rubber buttpad. **Sights:** Tunnel front with interchangeable inserts, open rear click-adjustable for windage and elevation. Grooved for scope mounting. **Features:** Velocity 940-1000 fps (177), 860 fps (20), 800 fps (22). Non-drying nylon piston and breech seals. Adjustable metal trigger. Milled steel safety. Right- or left-hand stock. Adjustable cheekpiece and buttplate at extra cost. Custom and Super Laser versions available. Imported by Beeman.
Price: Right-hand **$665.00**
Price: Left-hand **$720.00**

BEEMAN R7 AIR RIFLE
Caliber: .177, .20, single shot. **Barrel:** 17". **Weight:** 6.1 lbs. **Length:** 40.2" overall. **Power:** Spring-piston. **Stock:** Stained beech. **Sights:** Hooded front, fully adjustable micrometer click open rear. **Features:** Velocity to 700 fps (177), 620 fps (20). Receiver grooved for scope mounting; double-jointed cocking lever; fully adjustable trigger; checkered grip. Imported by Beeman.
Price: **$370.00**

BEEMAN R9 AIR RIFLE
Caliber: .177, .20, single shot. **Barrel:** NA. **Weight:** 7.3 lbs. **Length:** 43" overall. **Power:** Spring-piston, barrel cocking. **Stock:** Stained hardwood. **Sights:** Tunnel post front, fully adjustable open rear. **Features:** Velocity to 1000 fps (177), 800 fps (20). Adjustable Rekord trigger; automatic safety; receiver dovetailed for scope mounting. Imported from Germany by Beeman Precision Airguns.
Price: **$440.00**

BEEMAN R11 MKII AIR RIFLE
Caliber: .177, single shot. **Barrel:** 19.6". **Weight:** 8.6 lbs. **Length:** 43.5" overall. **Power:** Spring-piston, barrel cocking. **Stock:** Walnut- stained beech; adjustable buttplate and cheekpiece. **Sights:** None furnished. Has dovetail for scope mounting. **Features:** Velocity 910-940 fps. All-steel barrel sleeve. Imported by Beeman.
Price: **$690.00**

BEEMAN RX-2 GAS-SPRING MAGNUM AIR RIFLE
Caliber: .177, .20, .22, single shot. **Barrel:** 19.6", 12-groove rifling. **Weight:** 8.8 lbs. **Power:** Gas-spring piston air; single stroke barrel cocking. **Stock:** Laminated wood stock. **Sights:** Tunnel front, click-adjustable rear. **Features:** Velocity adjustable to about 1200 fps. Imported by Beeman.
Price: .177, .20, .22 regular, right-hand **$798.00**

BEEMAN R1 CARBINE
Caliber: .177,. 20, .22 single shot. **Barrel:** 16.1". **Weight:** 8.6 lbs. **Length:** 41.7" overall. **Power:** Spring-piston, barrel cocking. **Stock:** Stained beech; Monte Carlo comb and checkpiece; cut checkered pistol grip; rubber buttpad. **Sights:** Tunnel front with interchangeable inserts, open adjustable rear; receiver grooved for scope mounting. **Features:** Velocity up to 1000 fps (177). Non- drying nylon piston and breech seals. Adjustable metal trigger. Machined steel receiver end cap and safety. Right- or left-hand stock. Imported by Beeman.
Price: 177, 20, 22, right-hand . . . . **$665.00;** left-hand **$720.00**

BEEMAN/FEINWERKBAU 603 AIR RIFLE
Caliber: .177, single shot. **Barrel:** 16.6". **Weight:** 10.8 lbs. **Length:** 43" overall. **Power:** Single stroke pneumatic. **Stock:** Special laminated hardwoods and hard rubber for stability. Multi-colored stock also available. **Sights:** Tunnel front sight with interchangeable inserts, click micrometer match aperture rear sight. **Features:** Velocity to 570 fps. Recoilless action; double supported barrel; special, short rifled area frees pellet from barrel faster. Fully adjustable match trigger with separately adjustable trigger and trigger slack weight. Trigger and sights blocked when loading latch is open. Imported by Beeman.
Price: Right-hand. **$2,445.00**
Price: Left-hand. **$2,625.00**
Price: Junior. **$2,170.00**

BEEMAN/FEINWERKBAU 700 – ALUMINUM OR WOOD STOCK
Caliber: .177, single shot. **Barrel:** 16.6". **Weight:** 10.8 lbs. Aluminum; 9.9 lbs. Wood. **Length:** 43.3-46.25" Aluminum; 43.7" Wood. **Power:** Pre-charged pneumatic. **Stock:** Aluminum stock – laminated hardwood. **Sights:** Tunnel front sight with interchangeable inserts, click micrometer match aperture rear sight. **Features:** Velocity 570 fps. Recoilless action. Anatomical grips can be tilted and pivoted to the barrel axis. Adjustable buttplate and cheekpiece.
Price: Aluminum 700, precharged, right **$3,000.00**
Price: Aluminum 700, precharged, left **$3,100.00**
Price: Laminated Wood Stock 700, precharged, right **$2,335.00**
Price: Laminated Wood Stock 700, precharged, left **$2,435.00**

BEEMAN/FEINWERKBAU P70 FIELD TARGET
Caliber: .177, single shot. **Barrel:** 24.6". **Weight:** 10.6 lbs. **Length:** 43.3" overall. **Power:** Pre-charged pneumatic. **Stock:** Aluminum stock (red or blue) anatomical grips, buttplate & cheekpiece. **Sights:** None, receiver grooved for scope mounting. **Features:** 870 fps velocity. At 50 yards, this air rifle is capable of achieving 1/2-inch groups. Match adjustable trigger. 2001 US Field Target National Champion.
Price: P70FT, precharged, right (red or blue) **$2,855.00**
Price: P70FT, precharged, left (red or blue) **$2,955.00**

BEEMAN/FEINWERKBAU P700 .177 BASIC AIR RIFLE
Caliber: .177, single shot. **Barrel:** 16.73". **Weight:** 9.04 lbs. **Length:** 43.31" overall. **Power:** Pre-charged pneumatic. **Stock:** Beech wood stock. **Sights:** Tunnel front sight with interchangeable inserts, click micrometer match aperture rear sight. **Features:** Velocity to 570 fps. Recoilless action; match adjustable trigger. Interior absorber.
Price: P700 Basic, .177. . . . . **$1,150.00**

BEEMAN/HW 97 AIR RIFLE
Caliber: .177, .20, single shot. **Barrel:** 17.75". **Weight:** 9.2 lbs. **Length:** 44.1" overall. **Power:** Spring-piston, underlever cocking. **Stock:** Walnut-stained beech; rubber buttpad. **Sights:** None. Receiver grooved for scope mounting. **Features:** Velocity 830 fps (177). Fixed barrel with fully opening, direct loading breech. Adjustable trigger. Imported by Beeman Precision Airguns.
Price: Right-hand only. $625.00

Beretta CX4 Storm

BENJAMIN & SHERIDAN PNEUMATIC (PUMP-UP) AIR RIFLE
Caliber: .177 or .22, single shot. **Barrel:** 19-3/8", rifled brass. **Weight:** 5-1/2 lbs. **Length:** 36-1/4" overall. **Power:** Underlever pneumatic, hand pumped. **Stock:** American walnut stock and forend. **Sights:** High ramp front, fully adjustable notched rear. **Features:** Variable velocity to 800 fps. Bolt action with ambidextrous push-pull safety. Black or nickel finish. Made in the U.S. by Benjamin Sheridan Co.
Price:. $140.95

BERETTA CX4 STORM
Caliber: .177, 30-shot semi auto. 17 1/2", rifled. **Weight:** 5.25 lbs. 30.75" overall. **Power:** 88g CO2. **Stock:** Replica style. **Sights:** Adjustable front and rear. Blowback action. Velocity of 600 fps. Accessory rails.
Price: $276.92

BSA SUPERTEN MK3 AIR RIFLE
Caliber: .177, .22 10-shot repeater. **Barrel:** 17-1/2". **Weight:** 7 lbs., 8 oz. **Length:** 37" overall. **Power:** Precharged pneumatic via buddy bottle. **Stock:** Oil-finished hardwood; Monte Carlo with cheekpiece, cut checkered grip; adjustable recoil pad. **Sights:** No sights; intended for scope use. **Features:** Velocity 1000+ fps (177), 1000+ fps (22). Patented 10-shot indexing magazine, bolt-action loading. Left-hand version also available. Imported from U.K.
Price: $599.95

BSA SUPERTEN MK3 BULLBARREL
Caliber: .177,. 22, .25, single shot. **Barrel:** 18-1/2". **Weight:** 8 lbs., 8 oz. **Length:** 43" overall. **Power:** Spring-air, underlever cocking. **Stock:** Oil-finished hardwood; Monte Carlo with cheekpiece, checkered at grip; recoil pad. **Sights:** Ramp front, micrometer adjustable rear. Maxi-Grip scope rail. **Features:** Velocity 950 fps (177), 750 fps (22), 600 fps (25). Patented rotating breech design. Maxi-Grip scope rail protects optics from recoil; automatic anti-beartrap plus manual safety. Imported from U.K.
Price: Rifle, MKII Carbine (14" barrel, 39-1/2" overall) $349.95

BSA MAGNUM SUPERSPORT™ AIR RIFLE, CARBINE
Caliber: .177, .22, .25, single shot. **Barrel:** 18-1/2". **Weight:** 6 lbs., 8 oz. **Length:** 41" overall. **Power:** Spring-air, barrel cocking. **Stock:** Oil-finished hardwood; Monte Carlo with cheekpiece, recoil pad. **Sights:** Ramp front, micrometer adjustable rear. Maxi-Grip scope rail. **Features:** Velocity 950 fps (177), 750 fps (22), 600 fps (25). Patented Maxi-Grip scope rail protects optics from recoil; automatic anti-beartrap plus manual tang safety. Muzzle brake standard. Imported for U.K.
Price: $194.95
Price: Carbine, 14" barrel, muzzle brake $214.95

BSA METEOR AIR RIFLE
Caliber: .177, .22, single shot. **Barrel:** 18-1/2". **Weight:** 6 lbs. **Length:** 41" overall. **Power:** Spring-air, barrel cocking. **Stock:** Oil- finished hardwood. **Sights:** Ramp front, micrometer adjustable rear. **Features:** Velocity 650 fps (177), 500 fps (22). Automatic anti- beartrap; manual tang safety. Receiver grooved for scope mounting. Imported from U.K.
Price: Rifle $144.95
Price: Carbine $164.95

CROSMAN MODEL POWERMASTER 664SB AIR RIFLES
Caliber: .177 (single shot pellet) or BB, 200-shot reservoir. **Barrel:** 20", rifled steel. **Weight:** 2 lbs. 15 oz. **Length:** 38-1/2" overall. **Power:** Pneumatic; hand-pumped. **Stock:** Wood-grained ABS plastic; checkered pistol grip and forend. **Sights:** Fiber-optic front, fully adjustable open rear. **Features:** Velocity about 645 fps. Bolt action, cross-bolt safety. From Crosman.
Price:. $65.00

AIRGUNS — Long Guns

CROSMAN MODEL PUMPMASTER 760 AIR RIFLES
Caliber: .177 pellets (single shot) or BB (200-shot reservoir). **Barrel:** 19-1/2", rifled steel. **Weight:** 2 lbs., 12 oz. **Length:** 33.5" overall. **Power:** Pneumatic, hand-pump. **Stock:** Walnut-finished ABS plastic stock and forend. **Features:** Velocity to 590 fps (BBs, 10 pumps). Short stroke, power determined by number of strokes. Fiber-optic front sight and adjustable rear sight. Cross-bolt safety. From Crosman.
Price: Model 760 . . . . $40.00

CROSMAN MODEL REPEATAIR 1077 RIFLES
Caliber: .177 pellets, 12-shot clip. **Barrel:** 20.3", rifled steel. **Weight:** 3 lbs., 11 oz. **Length:** 38.8" overall. **Power:** CO2 Powerlet. **Stock:** Textured synthetic or hardwood. **Sights:** Blade front, fully adjustable rear. **Features:** Velocity 590 fps. Removable 12-shot clip. True semi-automatic action. From Crosman.
Price: $68.00
Price: 1077W (walnut stock) $100.00

CROSMAN 2260 AIR RIFLE
Caliber: .22, single shot. **Barrel:** 24". **Weight:** 4 lbs., 12 oz. **Length:** 39.75" overall. **Power:** CO2 Powerlet. **Stock:** Hardwood. **Sights:** Blade front, adjustable rear open or peep. **Features:** About 600 fps. Made in U.S. by Crosman Corp.
Price: $80.00

CROSMAN MODEL CLASSIC 2100 AIR RIFLE
Caliber: 177 pellets (single shot), or BB (200-shot BB reservoir). **Barrel:** 21", rifled. **Weight:** 4 lbs., 13 oz. **Length:** 39-3/4" overall. **Power:** Pump-up, pneumatic. **Stock:** Wood-grained checkered ABS plastic. **Features:** Three pumps give about 450 fps, 10 pumps about 755 fps (BBs). Cross-bolt safety; concealed reservoir holds over 200 BBs. From Crosman.
Price: Model 2100B $55.00

CROSMAN MODEL 2260 AIR RIFLE
Caliber: 22, single shot. **Barrel:** 19", rifled steel. **Weight:** 4 lbs., 12 oz. **Length:** 39.75" overall. **Stock:** Full-size, American hardwood. **Features:** Variable pump power; three pumps give 395 fps, six pumps 530 fps, 10 pumps 600 fps (average). Full-size adult air rifle. From Crosman.
Price: $80.00

DAISY 1938 RED RYDER AIR RIFLE
Caliber: BB, 650-shot repeating action. **Barrel:** Smoothbore steel with shroud. **Weight:** 2.2 lbs. **Length:** 35.4" overall. **Stock:** Walnut stock burned with Red Ryder lariat signature. **Sights:** Post front, adjustable V-slot rear. **Features:** Walnut forend. Saddle ring with leather thong. Lever cocking. Gravity feed. Controlled velocity. From Daisy Mfg. Co.
Price: $44.95

DAISY MODEL 840B GRIZZLY AIR RIFLE
Caliber: .177 pellet single shot; or BB 350-shot. **Barrel:** 19", smoothbore, steel. **Weight:** 2.25 lbs. **Length:** 36.8" overall. **Power:** Single pump pneumatic. **Stock:** Molded wood-grain stock and forend. **Sights:** Ramp front, open, adjustable rear. **Features:** Muzzle velocity 320 fps (BB), 300 fps (pellet). Steel buttplate; straight pull bolt action; cross-bolt safety. Forend forms pump lever. From Daisy Mfg. Co.
Price: $47.99
Price: (840C in Mossy Oak Breakup Camo) $54.99

DAISY MODEL 105 BUCK AIR RIFLE
Caliber: .177 or BB. **Barrel:** Smoothbore steel. **Weight:** 1.6 lbs. **Length:** 29.8" overall. **Power:** Lever cocking, spring air. **Stock:** Stained solid wood. **Sights:** TruGlo fiber-optic, open fixed rear. **Features:** Velocity to 275. Cross-bolt trigger block safety. From Daisy Mfg. Co.
Price: $35.99

DAISY/POWERLINE TARGET PRO 953 AIR RIFLE
Caliber: .177 pellets, single shot. **Weight:** 6.40 lbs. **Length:** 39.75" overall. **Power:** Pneumatic single-pump cocking lever; straight-pull bolt. **Stock:** Full-length, match-style black composite. **Sights:** Front and rear fiber optic. **Features:** Rifled high-grade steel barrel with 1:15 twist. Max. Muzzle Velocity of 560 fps. From Daisy Mfg. Co.
Price: $89.99

DAISY/POWERLINE 880 AIR RIFLE
Caliber: .177 pellet or BB, 50-shot BB magazine, single shot for pellets. **Barrel:** Rifled steel. **Weight:** 3.7 lbs. **Length:** 37.6" overall. **Power:** Multi-pump pneumatic. **Stock:** Molded wood grain; Monte Carlo comb. **Sights:** Hooded front, adjustable rear. **Features:** Velocity to 685 fps. (BB). Variable power (velocity, range) increase with pump strokes; resin receiver with dovetailed scope mount. Made in U.S.A. by Daisy Mfg. Co.
Price: $60.99

DAISY/POWERLINE 901 AIR RIFLE
Caliber: .177. **Barrel:** Rifled steel. **Weight:** 3.7 lbs. **Length:** 37.5" overall. **Power:** Multi-pump pneumatic. **Stock:** Advanced composite. **Sights:** Fiber-optic front, adjustable rear. **Features:** Velocity to 750 fps. (BB); advanced composite receiver with dovetailed mounts for optics. Made in U.S.A. by Daisy Mfg. Co.
Price: $66.99

EAA/BAIKAL MP-512 AIR RIFLE
Caliber: 177, single shot. **Barrel:** 17.7". **Weight:** 6.2 lbs. **Length:** 41.3" overall. **Power:** Spring-piston, single stroke. **Stock:** Black synthetic. **Sights:** Adjustable rear, hooded front. **Features:** Velocity 490 fps. Hammer-forged, rifled barrel; automatic safety; scope mount rail. Imported from Russia by European American Armory.
Price: 177 caliber $49.00

EAA/BAIKAL IZH-61 AIR RIFLE
Caliber: 177 pellet, 5-shot magazine. **Barrel:** 17.8". **Weight:** 6.4 lbs. **Length:** 31" overall. **Power:** Spring-piston, side-cocking lever. **Stock:** Black plastic. **Sights:** Adjustable rear, fully hooded front. **Features:** Velocity 490 fps. Futuristic design with adjustable stock. Imported from Russia by European American Armory.
Price: $99.00

EAA/BAIKAL IZHMP-532 AIR RIFLE
Caliber: 177 pellet, single shot. **Barrel:** 15.8". **Weight:** 9.3 lbs. **Length:** 46.1" overall. **Power:** Single-stroke pneumatic. **Stock:** One- or two-piece competition-style stock with adjustable buttpad, pistol grip. **Sights:** Fully adjustable rear, hooded front. **Features:** Velocity 460 fps. Five-way adjustable trigger. Imported from Russia by European American Armory.
Price: $599.00

GAMO VIPER AIR RIFLE
Caliber: 177. **Barrel:** NA. **Weight:** 7.25 lbs. **Length:** 43.5". **Power:** Single-stroke pneumatic, 1200 fps. **Stock:** Synthetic. **Sights:** 3-9x40IR scope. **Features:** 30-pound cocking effort. Imported from Spain by Gamo.
Price: $299.95

GAMO HUNTER AIR RIFLES
Caliber: 177. **Barrel:** NA. **Weight:** 6.5-10.5 lbs. **Length:** 43.5-48.5". **Power:** Single-stroke pneumatifc, 850-1,000 fps. **Stock:** Wood. **Sights:** Varies by model **Features:** Adjustable two-stage trigger, rifled barrel, raised scope ramp on receiver. Realtree camo model available.
Price: Sport. $219.95
Price: Pro $279.95

HAMMERLI AR 50 AIR RIFLE
Caliber: 177. **Barrel:** 19.8". **Weight:** 10 lbs. **Length:** 43.2" overall. **Power:** Compressed-air. **Stock:** Anatomically-shaped universal and right-hand; match style; multi-colored laminated wood. **Sights:** Interchangeable element tunnel front, adjustable Hammerli peep rear. **Features:** Vibration-free firing release; adjustable match trigger and trigger stop; stainless air tank, built-in pressure gauge. Gives 270 shots per filling. Imported from Switzerland by SIGARMS, Inc.
Price: $1,653.00

HAMMERLI MODEL 450 MATCH AIR RIFLE
Caliber: 177, single shot. **Barrel:** 19.5". **Weight:** 9.8 lbs. **Length:** 43.3" overall. **Power:** Pneumatic. **Stock:** Match style with stippled grip, rubber buttpad. Beech or walnut. **Sights:** Match tunnel front, Hammerli diopter rear. **Features:** Velocity about 560 fps. Removable sights; forend sling rail; adjustable trigger; adjustable comb. Imported from Switzerland by SIGARMS, Inc.
Price: Beech stock $1,355.00
Price: Walnut stock. $1,395.00

Hammerli 850 Airmagnum

RWS 460 Magnum

HAMMERLI 850 AIR MAGNUM
Caliber: .177, 22, 8-shot repeater. 23 1/2", rifled. **Weight:** 5.8 lbs. 41" overall. **Power:** 88g CO2. **Stock:** All-weather polymer, Monte Carlo, textured grip and forearm. **Sights:** Hooded fiber optic front, fiber optic adjustable rear. Velocity of 760 fps (177), 655 (22). Blue finish. Rubber buttpad. Bolt-Action. Scope compatible.
Price: .177, .22 . . . . **$248.08**

HAMMERLI STORM ELITE
Caliber: .177, single shot. 19 1/2", rifled. **Weight:** 6.8 lbs. 45 1/2" overall. **Power:** Spring-air, break-barrel cocking. **Stock:** Synthetic, burled wood look, checkered grip and forearm, cheekpiece. **Sights:** Hooded fiber optic front, fiber optic adjustable rear. Velocity of 1000 fps. 24 lbs. cocking effort. Nickel finish. Rubber buttpad. Scope compatible.
Price: **$222.31**

HAMMERLI RAZOR
Caliber: 177, 22, single shot. **Barrel:** 19", rifled. **Weight:** 17.5 lbs. Length: 45 1/2" overall. **Power:** Spring-air, break-barrel cocking. **Stock:** Vaporized beech wood, checkered grip and forearm, cheekpiece. Sleek curves. **Sights:** Hooded fiber optic front, fiber optic adjustable rear. **Features:** Velocity of 1000 fps (177), 820 (22). 35 lbs. cocking effort. Blued finish. Rubber buttpad. Scope compatible.
Price: **$309.23**

HAMMERLI NOVA
Caliber: .177, single shot. 18", rifled. **Weight:** 7.8 lbs. 45 1/2" overall. **Power:** Spring-air, under-lever cocking. **Stock:** Vaporized beech wood competition, checkered grip and forearm, cheekpiece. **Sights:** Hooded fiber optic front, fiber optic adjustable rear. Velocity of 1000 fps. 36 lbs. cocking effort. Blued finish. Rubber buttpad. Scope compatible.
Price: **$341.92**

HAMMERLI QUICK
Caliber: .177, single shot. 18 1/4", rifled. **Weight:** 5.5 lbs. 41" overall. **Power:** Spring-air, break-barrel cocking. **Stock:** Synthetic impact proof, checkered grip and forearm, cheekpiece. **Sights:** Hooded fiber optic front, fiber optic adjustable rear. Compact, light-weight. Velocity of 620 fps. 18 lbs. cocking effort. Blued finish. Rubber buttpad. Scope compatible. Automatic Safety.
Price: **$102.69**

RWS 460 MAGNUM
Caliber: .177, 22, single shot. 18 7/16", rifled. **Weight:** 8.3 lbs. 45" overall. **Power:** Spring-air, underlever cocking. **Stock:** American Sporter, checkered grip and forearm. **Sights:** Ramp front, adjustable rear. Velocity of 1350 fps (177), 1150 (22). 36 lbs. cocking effort. Blue finish. Rubber buttpad. Top-side loading port. Scope compatible.
Price: .177, .22 . . . . **$480.69**

RWS MODEL 34
Caliber: .177, .22, single shot. **Barrel:** 19 1/2", rifled. **Weight:** 7.3 lbs. Length: 45" overall. **Power:** Spring-air, break-barrel cocking. **Stock:** Wood. **Sights:** Hooded front, adjustable rear. **Features:** Velocity of 1000 fps (177), 800 (22). 33 lbs. cocking effort. Blued finish. Scope compatible.
Price: .177, .22 . . . . **$236.92**

RWS 34 PANTHER
Caliber: .177, .22, single shot. 19 3/4", rifled. **Weight:** 7.7 lbs. 46" overall. **Power:** Spring-air, break-barrel cocking. **Stock:** Synthetic black. **Sights:** Ramp fiber optic front, adjustable fiber optic rear. Velocity of 1000 fps (177), 800 (22). 33 lbs. cocking effort. Blued finish. Scope compatible. Automatic safety.
Price: .177, .22 . . . . **$236.92**

RWS 48
Caliber: 177, 22, single shot. 17", rifled, fixed. **Weight:** 9.0 lbs. 42 1/2" overall. **Power:** Spring-air, side-lever cocking. **Stock:** Wood stock. **Sights:** Adjustable front, adjustable rear. Velocity of 1100 fps (177), 900 (22). 39 lbs. cocking effort. Blued finish. Scope compatible. Automatic safety.
Price: .177, .22 . . . . **$409.23**

TECH FORCE 6 AIR RIFLE
Caliber: 177 pellet, single shot. **Barrel:** 14". **Weight:** 6 lbs. **Length:** 35.5" overall. **Power:** Spring-piston, sidelever action. **Stock:** Paratrooper-style folding, full pistol grip. **Sights:** Adjustable rear, hooded front. **Features:** Velocity 800 fps. All-metal construction; grooved for scope mounting. Imported from China by Compasseco, Inc.
Price: **$69.95**

TECH FORCE 25 AIR RIFLE
Caliber: 177, 22 pellet; single shot. **Barrel:** NA. **Weight:** 7.5 lbs. **Length:** 46.2" overall. **Power:** Spring piston, break-action barrel. **Stock:** Oil-finished wood; Monte Carlo stock with recoil pad. **Sights:** Adjustable rear, hooded front with insert. **Features:** Velocity 1,000 fps (177); grooved receiver and scope stop for scope mounting; adjustable trigger; trigger safety. Imported from China by Compasseco, Inc.
Price: 177 or 22 caliber **$125.00**
Price: Includes rifle and Tech Force 96 red dot point sight **$164.95**

WALTHER LEVER ACTION
Caliber: .177, 8-shot lever action. 18.9", rifled. **Weight:** 7.5 lbs. 38.3" overall. **Power:** two 12g CO2. **Stock:** Wood. **Sights:** Fixed front, adjustable rear. Classic design. Velocity of 630 fps. Scope compatible.
Price: **$269.18**

COMPENDIUM OF STATE LAWS GOVERNING FIREARMS

Since state laws are subject to frequent change, this chart is not to be considered legal advice or a restatement of the law. The following chart lists the main provisions of state firearms laws as of the date of publication. In addition to the state provisions, the purchase, sale, and, in certain circumstances, the possession and interstate transportation of firearms are regulated by the Federal Gun Control Act of 1968 as amended by the Firearms Owners' Protection Act of 1986. Also, cities and localities may have their own gun ordinances in addition to federal and state restrictions. Details may be obtained by contacting local law enforcement authorities or by consulting your state's firearms law digest compiled by the NRA Institute for Legislative Action. All fifty states have passed sportsmen's protection laws to halt harrassment.

Compiled by NRA Institute for Legislative Action; 11250 Waples Mill Road; Fairfax, Virginia 22030

State	Gun Ban	Exemptions to NICS2	State Waiting Period-Number of Days		License or Permit to Purchase or Other Prerequisite		Registration	
			Handguns	Longguns	Handguns	Longguns	Handguns	Longguns
Alabama	—	—	—	—	—	—	—	—
Alaska	—	RTC	—	—	—	—	—	—
Arizona	—	RTC	—	—	—	—	—	—
Arkansas	—	RTC[3]	—	—	—	—	—	—
California	X[1]	—	10[5]	10[5,6]	10,11	—	X	X[13]
Colorado	—	—	—	—	—	—	—	—
Connecticut	X[1]	—	14[5,6]	14[5,6]	X[9,11]	—	—	X[13]
Delaware	—	—	—	—	—	—	—	—
Florida	—	—	3[6]	—	—	—	—	—
Georgia	—	RTC	—	—	—	—	—	—
Hawaii	X[1]	L, RTC	—	—	X[9,11]	X[9]	X[12]	X[12]
Idaho	—	RTC	—	—	—	—	—	—
Illinois	7	—	3	2	X[9]	X[9]	X[14]	X[14]
Indiana	—	—	—	—	—	—	—	—
Iowa	—	L, RTC	—	—	X[9]	—	—	—
Kansas	—	—	7	—	7	—	7	—
Kentucky	—	—	—	—	—	—	—	—
Louisiana	—	—	—	—	—	—	—	—
Maine	—	—	—	—	—	—	—	—
Maryland	X[1]	—	7[5]	7[4,5]	X[10,11]	—	—	—
Massachusetts	X[1]	—	—	—	X[9]	X[9]	—	—
Michigan	—	L	—	—	X[9,11]	—	X	—
Minnesota	—	—	7[9]	X[9]	X[9]	X[9]	—	—
Mississippi	—	RTC3	—	—	—	—	—	—
Missouri	—	—	—	—	X[9]	—	—	—
Montana	—	RTC	—	—	—	—	—	—
Nebraska	—	L	—	—	X	—	—	—
Nevada	—	RTC	7	—	—	—	7	—
New Hampshire	—	—	—	—	—	—	—	—
New Jersey	X[1]	—	—	—	X[9]	X[9]	—	X[13]
New Mexico	—	—	—	—	—	—	—	—
New York	X[1]	L, RTC	—	—	X[9,11]	9	X	X[15]
North Carolina	—	L, RTC	—	—	X[9]	—	—	—
North Dakota	—	RTC	—	—	—	—	—	—
Ohio	7	—	7	—	7	—	7	—
Oklahoma	—	—	—	—	—	—	—	—
Oregon	—	—	—	—	—	—	—	—
Pennsylvania	—	—	—	—	—	—	—	—
Rhode Island	—	—	7[5]	7[5]	X[11]	—	—	—
South Carolina	—	RTC	—	—	—	—	—	—
South Dakota	—	—	2	—	—	—	—	—
Tennessee	—	—	—	—	—	—	—	—
Texas	—	RTC	—	—	—	—	—	—
Utah	—	RTC	—	—	—	—	—	—
Vermont	—	—	—	—	—	—	—	—
Virginia	X[1]	—	—	—	X[10]	—	—	—
Washington	—	—	5[8]	—	—	—	—	—
West Virginia	—	—	—	—	—	—	—	—
Wisconsin	—	—	2	—	—	—	—	—
Wyoming	—	RTC	—	—	—	—	—	—
District of Columbia	X[1]	L	—	—	X[9]	X[9]	X[9]	X

COMPENDIUM OF STATE LAWS GOVERNING FIREARMS

Since state laws are subject to frequent change,
this chart is not to be considered legal advice or a restatement of the law.

All fifty states have passed sportsmen's protection laws to halt harrassment.

State	Record of Sale Reported to State or Local Govt.	State Provision for Right-to-Carry Concealed	Carrying Openly Prohibited	Owner ID Cards or Licensing	Firearm Rights Constitutional Provision	State Firearms Preemption Laws	Range Protection Law
Alabama	—	M	X[19]	—	X	X	X
Alaska	—	R[17]	—	—	X	X[24]	X
Arizona	—	R	—	—	X	X	X
Arkansas	—	R	X[20]	—	X	X	X
California	X	L	X[21]	—	—	X	X
Colorado	—	R	[22]	—	X	X[22]	X
Connecticut	X	M	X	—	X	X[25]	X
Delaware	—	L	—	—	X	X	X
Florida	—	R	X	—	X	X	X
Georgia	—	R	X	—	X	X	X
Hawaii	X	L	X	X	X	—	—
Idaho	—	R	—	—	X	X	X
Illinois	X	D	X	X	X	—	X
Indiana	—	R	X	—	X	X[26]	X
Iowa	—	M	X	—	—	X	X
Kansas	7	D	7	—	X	—	X
Kentucky	—	R	—	—	X	X	X
Louisiana	—	R	—	—	X	X	X
Maine	—	R	—	—	X	X	X
Maryland	X	L	X	—	—	X	X
Massachusetts	X	L	X	X	X	X[25]	X
Michigan	X	R	X[19]	—	X	X	X
Minnesota	—	R[18]	X	—	—	X	—
Mississippi	—	R	—	—	X	X	X
Missouri	X	R	—	—	X	X	X
Montana	—	R	—	—	X	X	X
Nebraska	—	D	—	—	X	—	—
Nevada	—	R	—	—	X	X	X
New Hampshire	—	R	—	—	X	X	X
New Jersey	X	L	X	X	—	X[25]	X
New Mexico	—	R	—	—	X	X	X
New York	X	L	X	X	—	X[27]	X
North Carolina	X	R	—	—	X	X	X
North Dakota	—	R	X[21]	—	X	X	X
Ohio	7	R	7	7	X	—	X
Oklahoma	—	R	X[21]	—	X	X	X
Oregon	X	R	—	—	X	X	X
Pennsylvania	X	R	X[19]	—	X	X	X
Rhode Island	X	L	X	—	X	X	X
South Carolina	X	R	X	—	X	X	X
South Dakota	X[16]	R	—	—	X	X	X
Tennessee	—	R	X[20]	—	X	X	X
Texas	—	R	X	—	X	X	X
Utah	—	R	X[21]	—	X	X	X
Vermont	—	R[17]	X[20]	—	X	X	X
Virginia	—	R	—	—	X	X	X
Washington	X	R	X[23]	—	X	X	—
West Virginia	—	R	—	—	X	X	X
Wisconsin	—	D	—	—	X	X	X
Wyoming	—	R	—	—	X	X	X
District of Columbia	X	D	X	X	NA	—	—

COMPENDIUM OF STATE LAWS GOVERNING FIREARMS

With over 20,000 "gun control" laws on the books in America, there are two challenges facing every gun owner. First, you owe it to yourself to become familiar with the federal laws on gun ownership. Only by knowing the laws can you avoid innocently breaking one.

Second, while federal legislation receives much more media attention, state legislatures and city councils make many more decisions regarding your right to own and carry firearms. NRA members and all gun owners must take extra care to be aware of anti-gun laws and ordinances at the state and local levels.

Notes:

1. "Assault weapons" are prohibited in **Connecticut, New Jersey** and **New York.** Some local jurisdictions in **Ohio** also ban "assault weapons." **Hawaii** prohibits "assault pistols." **California** bans "assault weapons", .50BMG caliber firearms, some .50 caliber ammunition and "unsafe handguns." **Illinois**: Chicago, Evanston, Oak Park, Morton Grove, Winnetka, Wilmette, and Highland Park prohibit handguns; some cities prohibit other kinds of firearms. **Maryland** prohibits "assault pistols"; the sale or manufacture of any handgun manufactured after Jan. 1, 1985, that does not appear on the Handgun Roster; and the sale of any handgun manufactured after January 1, 2003 that is not equipped with an "integrated mechanical safety device." **Massachusetts**: It is unlawful to sell, transfer or possess "any assault weapon or large capacity feeding device" [more than 10 rounds] that was not legally possessed on September 13, 1994. The sale of handguns not on the Firearms Roster. The City of Boston has a separate "assault weapons" law. The **District of Columbia** prohibits new acquisition of handguns and any semi-automatic firearm capable of using a detachable ammunition magazine of more than 12 rounds capacity and any handgun not registered after February 5, 1977. **Virginia** prohibits "Street Sweeper" shotguns. (With respect to some of these laws and ordinances, individuals may retain prohibited firearms owned previously, with certain restrictions.) The sunset of the federal assault weapons ban does not affect the validity of state "assault weapons" bans.

2. **National Instant Check System (NICS) exemption codes:**
   RTC-Carry Permit Holders Exempt From NICS
   L-Holders of state licenses to possess or purchase or firearms ID cards exempt from NICS.

3. **NICS exemption notes: Arkansas**: Those issued on and after 4/1/99 qualify. **Mississippi**: Permits issued to security guards do not qualify.

4. **Maryland** subjects purchases of "assault weapons" to a 7-day waiting period.

5. Waiting period for all sales. **California**: 10 days; sales, transfers and loans of handguns can be made through a dealer or through a sheriff's office. **Maryland**: 7 days; purchasers of regulated firearms must undergo background checks performed by the State Police, either through a dealer or directly through the State Police. **Rhode Island**: 7 days; private sales can be made through a dealer or the seller must follow the same guidelines as a sale from a dealer.

6. The waiting period does not apply to a person holding a valid permit or license to carry a firearm. In **Connecticut**, a certificate of eligibility exempts the holder from the waiting period for handgun purchases; a hunting license exempts the holder for long gun purchasers. **California**: transfers of a long gun to a person's parent, child or grandparent are exempt from the waiting period.

7. In certain cities or counties.

8. May be extended by police to 30 days in some circumstances. An individual not holding a driver's license must wait 60 days.

9. **Connecticut**: A certificate of eligibility or a carry permit is required to obtain a handgun and a carry permit is required to transport a handgun outside your home. **District of Columbia**: No handgun may be possessed unless it was registered prior to Sept. 23, 1976 and re-registered by Feb. 5, 1977. A permit to purchase is required for a rifle or shotgun. **Hawaii**: Purchase permits are required for all firearms **Illinois**: A Firearm Owner's Identification Card (FOI) is required to possess or purchase a firearm, must be issued to qualified applicants within 30 days, and is valid for 5 years. **Iowa**: A purchase permit is required for handguns, and is valid for one year. **Massachusetts**: Firearms and feeding devices for firearms are divided into classes. Depending on the class, a firearm identification card (FID) or class A license or class B license is required to possess, purchase, or carry a firearm, ammunition thereof, or firearm feeding device, or "large capacity feeding device." **Michigan**: A handgun purchaser must obtain a license to purchase from local law enforcement, and within 10 days present the license and handgun to obtain a certificate of inspection. **Minnesota**: A handgun transfer or carrying permit, or a 7-day waiting period and handgun transfer report, is required to purchase handguns or "assault weapons" from a dealer. A permit is valid for one year, a transfer report for 30 days. **Missouri**: A purchase permit is required for a handgun, must be issued to qualified applicants within 7 days, and is valid for 30 days. **New Jersey**: Firearm owners must possess a FID, which must be issued to qualified applicants within 30 days. To purchase a handgun, a purchase permit, which must be issued within 30 days to qualified applicants and is valid for 90 days, is required. An

FID is required to purchase long guns. **New York**: Purchase, possession and/or carrying of a handgun require a single license, which includes any restrictions made upon the bearer. New York City also requires a license for long guns. **North Carolina**: To purchase a handgun, a license or permit is required, which must be issued to qualified applicants within 30 days.

10. A permit is required to acquire another handgun before 30 days have elapsed following the acquisition of a handgun. In **Virginia**, those with a permit to carry a concealed weapon are exempt from this prohibition.

11. Requires proof of safety training for purchase. **California**: Must have Handgun Safety Certificate receipt, which is valid for five years. **Connecticut**: To receive certificate of eligibility, must complete a handgun safety course approved by the Commissioner of Public Safety. **Hawaii**: Must have completed an approved handgun safety course. **Maryland**: Must complete an approved handgun safety course. **Michigan**: A person must correctly answer 70% of the questions on a basic safety review questionnaire in order to obtain a license to purchase. **New York**: Some counties require a handgun safety training course to receive a license. **Rhode Island**: Must receive a state-issued handgun safety card.

12. Every person arriving in **Hawaii** is required to register any firearm(s) brought into the state within 3 days of arrival of the person or firearm(s), whichever occurs later. Handguns purchased from licensed dealers must be registered within 5 days.

13. "Assault weapon" registration. **California** had two dates by which assault weapons had to be registered or possession after such date would be considered a felony: March 31, 1992 for the named make and model firearms banned in the 1989 legislation and December 31, 2000 for the firearms meeting the definition of the "assault weapons in the 1999 legislation. In **Connecticut**, those firearms banned by specific make and model in the 1993 law had to be registered by October 1, 1994 or possession would be considered a felony. A recent law requires registration of additional guns by October 1, 2003. In **New Jersey**, any "assault weapon" not registered, licensed, or rendered inoperable pursuant to a state police certificate by May 1, 1991, is considered contraband.

14. Chicago only. No handgun not already registered may be possessed.

15. New York City only.

16. Purchasers of handguns who do not possess a permit to carry a pistol must file an application for purchase, which will be retained by the chief of police or sheriff for one year.

17. **Vermont** and **Alaska** law respect your right to carry without a permit. **Alaska** also has a permit to carry system to establish reciprocity with other states.

18. Provisions of this law are stayed pending an ongoing dispute in the courts.

19. Carrying a handgun openly in a motor vehicle requires a license.

20. **Arkansas** prohibits carrying a firearm "with a purpose to employ it as a weapon against a person." **Tennessee** prohibits carrying "with the intent to go armed." **Vermont** prohibits carrying a firearm "with the intent or purpose of injuring another."

21. Loaded.

22. Municipalities may prohibit open carry in government buildings if such prohibition is clearly posted.

23. Local jurisdictions may opt of the prohibition.

24. In the Right to Keep and Bear Arms Amendment of the **Alaska** Constitution.

25. Preemption through judicial ruling. Local regulation may be instituted in **Massachusetts** if ratified by the legislature.

26. Except Gary and East Chicago and local laws enacted before January 1994.

27. Preemption only applies to handguns.

Concealed carry codes:

R: Right-to-Carry "Shall issue" or less restrictive discretionary permit system (**Ala., Conn.**) (See also note #21.)

M: Reasonable May Issue; the state has a permissive may issue law, but the authorities recognize the right to keep and bear arms.

L: Right-to-Carry Limited by local authority's discretion over permit issuance.

D: Right-to-Carry Denied, no permit system exists; concealed carry is prohibited.

MANUFACTURER'S DIRECTORY

A

A Zone Bullets, 2039 Walter Rd., Billings, MT 59105 / 800-252-3111; FAX: 406-248-1961

A&W Repair, 2930 Schneider Dr., Arnold, MO 63010 / 617-287-3725

A.A. Arms, Inc., 4811 Persimmont Ct., Monroe, NC 28110 / 704-289-5356 or 800-935-1119; FAX: 704-289-5859

A.B.S. III, 9238 St. Morritz Dr., Fern Creek, KY 40291

A.G. Russell Knives, Inc., 2900 S. 26th St., Rogers, AR 72758 / 800-255-9034; FAX: 479-636-8493 ag@agrussell.com agrussell.com

A.R.M.S., Inc., 230 W. Center St., West Bridgewater, MA 02379-1620 / 508-584-7816; FAX: 508-588-8045

A.W. Peterson Gun Shop, Inc., The, 4255 West Old U.S. 441, Mount Dora, FL 32757-3299 / 352-383-4258; FAX: 352-735-1001

AC Dyna-tite Corp., 155 Kelly St., P.O. Box 0984, Elk Grove Village, IL 60007 / 847-593-5566; FAX: 847-593-1304

Acadian Ballistic Specialties, P.O. Box 787, Folsom, LA 70437 / 504-796-0078 gunsmith@neasolft.com

Accuracy Den, The, 25 Bitterbrush Rd., Reno, NV 89523 / 702-345-0225

Accuracy International Precision Rifles (See U.S.)

Accuracy International, Foster, P.O. Box 111, Wilsall, MT 59086 / 406-587-7922; FAX: 406-585-9434

Accuracy Int'l. North America, Inc., P.O. Box 5267, Oak Ridge, TN 37831 / 423-482-0330; FAX: 423-482-0336

Accuracy Unlimited, 7479 S. DePew St., Littleton, CO 80123

Accuracy Unlimited, 16036 N. 49 Ave., Glendale, AZ 85306 / 602-978-9089; FAX: 602-978-9089 fglenn@cox.net www.glenncustom.com

Accura-Site (See All's, The Jim Tembelis Co., Inc.)

Accurate Arms Co., Inc., 5891 Hwy. 230 West, McEwen, TN 37101 / 931-729-4207; FAX: 931-729-4211 burrensburg@aac-ca.com www.accuratepowder.com

Accu-Tek, 4510 Carter Ct., Chino, CA 91710

Ackerman & Co., Box 133 U.S. Highway Rt. 7, Pownal, VT 05261 / 802-823-9874 muskets@togsther.net

Ackerman, Bill (See Optical Services Co.)

Acra-Bond Laminates, 134 Zimmerman Rd., Kalispell, MT 59901 / 406-257-9003; FAX: 406-257-9003 merlins@digisys.net www.acrabondlaminates.com

Action Bullets & Alloy Inc., RR 1, P.O. Box 189, Quinter, KS 67752 / 785-754-3609; FAX: 785-754-3629 bullets@ruraltel.net

Action Direct, Inc., 14285 SW 142nd St., Miami, FL 33186-6720 / 800-472-2388; FAX: 305-256-3541 info@action-direct.com www.action-direct.com

Action Products, Inc., 954 Sweeney Dr., Hagerstown, MD 21740 / 301-797-1414; FAX: 301-733-2073

Action Target, Inc., P.O. Box 636, Provo, UT 84603 / 801-377-8033; FAX: 801-377-8096 www.actiontarget.com

Actions by "T" Teddy Jacobson, 16315 Redwood Forest Ct., Sugar Land, TX 77478 / 281-565-6977 tjacobson@houston.rr.com www.actionsbyt.com

AcuSport Corporation, William L. Fraim, One Hunter Place, Bellefontaine, OH 43311-3001 / 937-593-7010; FAX: 937-592-5625 www.acusport.com

Ad Hominem, 3130 Gun Club Lane, RR #3, Orillia, ON L3V 6H3 CANADA / 705-689-5303; FAX: 705-689-5303

Adair Custom Shop, Bill, 2886 Westridge, Carrollton, TX 75006

ADCO Sales, Inc., 4 Draper St. #A, Woburn, MA 01801 / 781-935-1799; FAX: 781-935-1011

Advance Car Mover Co., Rowell Div., P.O. Box 1, 240 N. Depot St., Juneau, WI 53039 / 414-386-4464; FAX: 414-386-4416

Advantage Arms, Inc., 25163 W. Ave. Stanford, Valencia, CA 91355 / 661-257-2290

Adventure 16, Inc., 4620 Alvarado Canyon Rd., San Diego, CA 92120 / 619-283-6314

Aero Peltor, 90 Mechanic St., Southbridge, MA 01550 / 508-764-5500; FAX: 508-764-0188

African Import Co., 22 Goodwin Rd., Plymouth, MA 02360 / 508-746-8552; FAX: 508-746-0404 africanimport@aol.com

AFSCO Ammunition, 731 W. Third St., P.O. Box L, Owen, WI 54460 / 715-229-2516 sailers@webtv.net

Ahlman Guns, 9525 W. 230th St., Morristown, MN 55052 / 507-685-4243; FAX: 507-685-4280 www.ahlmans.com

Ahrends Grips, Box 203, Clarion, IA 50525 / 515-532-3449; FAX: 515-532-3926 ahrends@goldfieldaccess.net www.ahrendsgripsusa.com

Aimpoint, Inc., 14103 Mariah Ct., Chantilly, VA 20151-2113 / 877-246-7668; FAX: 703-263-9463 info@aimpoint.com www.aimpoint.com

Aimtech Mount Systems, P.O. Box 223, Thomasville, GA 31799 / 229-226-4313; FAX: 229-227-0222 mail@aimtech-mounts.com www.aimtech-mounts.com

Air Arms, Hailsham Industrial Park, Diplocks Way, Hailsham, E. Sussex, BN27 3JF ENGLAND / 011-0323-845853; FAX: 1323 440573 general.air-arms.co.uk. www.air-arms.co.uk.

Air Venture Airguns, 9752 E. Flower St., Bellflower, CA 90706 / 562-867-6355

AirForce Airguns, P.O. Box 2478, Fort Worth, TX 76113 / 817-451-8966; FAX: 817-451-1613 www.airforceairguns.com

Airrow, 11 Monitor Hill Rd., Newtown, CT 06470 / 203-270-6343

Aitor-Berrizargo S.L., Eitua 15 P.O. Box 26, 48240, Berriz (Viscaya), SPAIN / 43-17-08-50 info@aitor.com www.ailor.com

Ajax Custom Grips, Inc., 9130 Viscount Row, Dallas, TX 75247 / 214-630-8893; FAX: 214-630-4942

Aker International, Inc., 2248 Main St., Suite 6, Chula Vista, CA 91911 / 619-423-5182; FAX: 619-423-1363 aker@akerleather.com www.akerleather.com

AKJ Concealco, P.O. Box 871596, Vancouver, WA 98687-1596 / 360-891-8222; FAX: 360-891-8221 Concealco@aol.com www.greatholsters.com

Alana Cupp Custom Engraver, P.O. Box 207, Annabella, UT 84711 / 801-896-4834

Alaska Bullet Works, Inc., 9978 Crazy Horse Drive, Juneau, AK 99801 / 907-789-3834; FAX: 907-789-3433

Alaskan Silversmith, The, 2145 Wagner Hollow Rd., Fort Plain, NY 13339 / 518-993-3983 sidbell@capital.net www.sidbell.cizland.com

Aldis Gunsmithing & Shooting Supply, 502 S. Montezuma St., Prescott, AZ 86303 / 602-445-6723; FAX: 602-445-6763

Alessi Holsters, Inc., 2465 Niagara Falls Blvd., Amherst, NY 14228-3527 / 716-691-5615

Alex, Inc., 3420 Cameron Bridge Rd., Manhattan, MT 59741-8523 / 406-282-7396; FAX: 406-282-7396

All American Lead Shot Corp., P.O. Box 224566, Dallas, TX 75062

All Rite Products, Inc., 9554 Wells Circle, Suite D, West Jordan, UT 84088-6226 / 800-771-8471; FAX: 801-280-8302 info@allriteproducts.com www.allriteproducts.com

Allard, Gary/Creek Side Metal & Woodcrafters, Fishers Hill, VA 22626 / 540-465-3903

Allen Co., Inc., 525 Burbank St., Broomfield, CO 80020 / 303-469-1857 or 800-876-8600; FAX: 303-466-7437

Allen Firearm Engraving, P.O. Box 155, Camp Verde, AZ 86322 / 928-567-6711 rosebudmulgco@netzero.com rosebudmulgco@netzero.com

Allen Mfg., 2784 Highway 23, Brook Park, MN 55007

Alley Supply Co., P.O. Box 848, Gardnerville, NV 89410 / 775-782-3800; FAX: 775-782-3827 jetalley@aol.com www.alleysupplyco.com

Alliant Techsystems, Smokeless Powder Group, P.O. Box 6, Rt. 114, Bldg. 229, Radford, VA 24141-0096 www.alliantpowder.com

Allred Bullet Co., 932 Evergreen Drive, Logan, UT 84321 / 435-752-6983; FAX: 435-752-6983

Alpec Team, Inc., 1231 Midas Way, Sunnyvale, CA 94085 / 510-606-8245; FAX: 510-606-4279

Alpha 1 Drop Zone, 2121 N. Tyler, Wichita, KS 67212 / 316-729-0800; FAX: 316-729-4262 www.alpha1dropzone.com

Alpha LaFranck Enterprises, P.O. Box 81072, Lincoln, NE 68501 / 402-466-3193

Alpha Precision, Inc., 3238 Della Slaton Rd., Comer, GA 30629-2212 / 706-783-2131 jim@alphaprecisioninc.com www.alphaprecisioninc.com

Alpine Indoor Shooting Range, 2401 Government Way, Coeur d'Alene, ID 83814 / 208-676-8824; FAX: 208-676-8824

Altamont Co., 901 N. Church St., P.O. Box 309, Thomasboro, IL 61878 / 217-643-3125 or 800-626-5774; FAX: 217-643-7973

Alumna Sport by Dee Zee, 1572 NE 58th Ave., P.O. Box 3090, Des Moines, IA 50316 / 800-798-9899

Amadeo Rossi S.A., Rua: Amadeo Rossi, 143, Sao Leopoldo, RS 93030-220 BRAZIL / 051-592-5566 rossi.firearms@pnet.com.br

Amato, Jeff. See: J&M PRECISION MACHINING

AmBr Software Group Ltd., P.O. Box 301, Reisterstown, MD 21136-0301 / 800-888-1917; FAX: 410-526-7212

American Ammunition, 3545 NW 71st St., Miami, FL 33147 / 305-835-7400; FAX: 305-694-0037

American Derringer Corp., 127 N. Lacy Dr., Waco, TX 76705 / 800-642-7817 or 254-799-9111; FAX: 254-799-7935

American Display Co., 55 Cromwell St., Providence, RI 02907 / 401-331-2464; FAX: 401-421-1264

American Gas & Chemical Co., Ltd., 220 Pegasus Ave., Northvale, NJ 07647 / 201-767-7300

American Gunsmithing Institute, 1325 Imola Ave. #504, Napa, CA 94559 / 707-253-0462; FAX: 707-253-7149 www.americangunsmith.com

American Handgunner Magazine, 12345 World Trade Dr., San Diego, CA 92128 / 800-537-3006; FAX: 858-605-0204 www.americanhandgunner.com

American Pioneer Video, P.O. Box 50049, Bowling Green, KY 42102-2649 / 800-743-4675

American Products, Inc., 14729 Spring Valley Road, Morrison, IL 61270 / 815-772-3336; FAX: 815-772-8046

American Safe Arms, Inc., 1240 Riverview Dr., Garland, UT 84312 / 801-257-7472; FAX: 801-785-8156

American Security Products Co., 11925 Pacific Ave., Fontana, CA 92337 / 909-685-9680 or 800-421-6142; FAX: 909-685-9685

American Small Arms Academy, P.O. Box 12111, Prescott, AZ 86304 / 602-778-5623

American Target, 1328 S. Jason St., Denver, CO 80223 / 303-733-0433; FAX: 303-777-0311

American Target Knives, 1030 Brownwood NW, Grand Rapids, MI 49504 / 616-453-1998

Americase, P.O. Box 271, 1610 E. Main, Waxahachie, TX 75165 / 800-880-3629; FAX: 214-937-8373

Ames Metal Products Co., 4323 S. Western Blvd., Chicago, IL 60609 / 773-523-3230 or 800-255-6937; FAX: 773-523-3854 amesmetal@webtv.net

Amherst Arms, P.O. Box 1457, Englewood, FL 34295 / 941-475-2020; FAX: 941-473-1212

Ammo Load Worldwide, Inc., 815 D St., Lewiston, ID 83501 / 800-528-5610; FAX: 208-746-1730 info@ammoload.com www.ammoload.com

Amrine's Gun Shop, 937 La Luna, Ojai, CA 93023 / 805-646-2376

Amsec, 11925 Pacific Ave., Fontana, CA 92337

AMT/Crusader Arms, 5200 Mitchelldale, Ste. E17, Houston, TX 77092 / 800-272-7816 www.highstandard.com

Analog Devices, Box 9106, Norwood, MA 02062

Andela Tool & Machine, Inc., RD3, Box 246, Richfield Springs, NY 13439

Anderson Manufacturing Co., Inc., 22602 53rd Ave. SE, Bothell, WA 98021 / 206-481-1858; FAX: 206-481-7839

Andres & Dworsky KG, Bergstrasse 18, A-3822 Karlstein, Thaya, AUSTRIA / 0 28 44-285; FAX: 0 28 44-28619 andres.dnorsky@wvnet.as

Angelo & Little Custom Gun Stock Blanks, P.O. Box 240046, Dell, MT 59724-0046

Antique American Firearms, Douglas Carlson, P.O. Box 71035, Dept. GD, Des Moines, IA 50325 / 515-224-6552 drearlson@mailstation.com

Antique Arms Co., 1110 Cleveland Ave., Monett, MO 65708 / 417-235-6501

AO Sight Systems, 2401 Ludelle St., Fort Worth, TX 76105 / 888-744-4880; or 817-536-0136; FAX: 817-536-3517

Apel GmbH, Ernst, Am Kirschberg 3, D-97218, Gerbrunn, GERMANY / 0 (931) 707192 info@eaw.de www.eaw.de

Aplan Antiques & Art, James O., HC 80, Box 793-25, Piedmont, SD 57769 / 605-347-5016

AR-7 Industries, LLC, 998 N. Colony Rd., Meriden, CT 06450 / 203-630-3536; FAX: 203-630-3637

ArmaLite, Inc., P.O. Box 299, Geneseo, IL 61254 / 800-336-0184 or 309-944-6939; FAX: 309-944-6949

Armament Gunsmithing Co., Inc., 525 Rt. 22, Hillside, NJ 07205 / 908-686-0960; FAX: 718-738-5019 armamentgunsmithing@worldnet.att.net

Armas Garbi, S.A., 12-14 20.600 Urki, 12, Eibar (Guipuzcoa), SPAIN / 943 20 3873; FAX: 943 20 3873 armosgarbi@euskalnet.n

Armas Kemen S. A. (See U.S. Importers)

Armfield Custom Bullets, 10584 County Road 100, Carthage, MO 64836 / 417-359-8480; FAX: 417-359-8497

Armi Perazzi S.P.A., Via Fontanelle 1/3, 1-25080, Botticino Mattina, ITALY / 030-2692591; FAX: 030-2692594

Armi San Marco (See Taylor's & Co.)

MANUFACTURER'S DIRECTORY

Armi San Paolo, 172-A, I-25062, via Europa, ITALY / 030-2751725

Armi Sport (See Cimarron Firearms, E.M.F., KBI & Taylor's & Co.)

Armite Laboratories Inc., 1560 Superior Ave., Costa Mesa, CA 92627 / 949-646-9035; FAX: 949-646-8319 armite@pacbell.net www.armitelahs.com

Armoloy Co. of Ft. Worth, 204 E. Daggett St., Fort Worth, TX 76104 / 817-332-5604; FAX: 817-335-6517 info@armoloyftworth.com www.armoloyftworth.com

Armor (See Buck Stop Lure Co., Inc.)

Armor Metal Products, P.O. Box 4609, Helena, MT 59604 / 406-442-5560; FAX: 406-442-5650

Armory Publications, 2120 S. Reserve St., PMB 253, Missoula, MT 59801 / 406-549-7670; FAX: 406-728-0597 armorypub@aol.com www.armorypub.com

Arms & Armour Press, Wellington House, 125 Strand, London, WC2R 0BB ENGLAND / 0171-420-5555; FAX: 0171-240-7265

Arms Corporation of the Philippines, Armscor Ave. Brgy. Fortune, Marikina City, PHILIPPINES / 632-941-6243 or 632-941-6244; FAX: 632-942-0682 info@armscor.com.ph www.armscor.com.ph

Arms Craft Gunsmithing, 1106 Linda Dr., Arroyo Grande, CA 93420 / 805-481-2830

Arms, Programming Solutions (See Arms Software)

Armscor Precision, 5740 S. Arville St. #219, Las Vegas, NV 89118 / 702-362-7750

Armscorp USA, Inc., 4424 John Ave., Baltimore, MD 21227 / 301-775-8134 info@armscorpusa.com www.armscorpusa.com

Arratoonian, Andy (See Horseshoe Leather Products)

Arrieta S.L., Morkaiko 5, 20870, Elgoibar, SPAIN / 34-43-743150; FAX: 34-43-743154

Art Jewel Enterprises Ltd., Eagle Business Ctr., 460 Randy Rd., Carol Stream, IL 60188 / 708-260-0400

Artistry in Wood, 134 Zimmerman Rd., Kalispell, MT 59901 / 406-257-9003; FAX: 406-257-9167 merlins@digisys.net www.acrabondlaminates.com

Art's Gun & Sport Shop, Inc., 6008 Hwy. Y, Hillsboro, MO 63050

Aspen Outfitting Co., Jon Hollinger, 9 Dean St., Aspen, CO 81611 / 970-925-3406

A-Square Co., 205 Fairfield Ave., Jeffersonville, IN 47130 / 812-283-0577; FAX: 812-283-0375

Astra Sport, S.A., Apartado 3, 48300 Guernica, Espagne, SPAIN / 34-4-6250100; FAX: 34-4-6255186

Atamec-Bretton, 19 rue Victor Grignard, F-42026, St.-Etienne (Cedex 1, FRANCE / 33-77-93-54-69; FAX: 33-77-93-57-98

Atlanta Cutlery Corp., 2143 Gees Mill Rd., Box 839 CIS, Conyers, GA 30207 / 800-883-0300; FAX: 404-388-0246

Atlantic Mills, Inc., 1295 Towbin Ave., Lakewood, NJ 08701-5934 / 800-242-7374

Atsko/Sno-Seal, Inc., 2664 Russell St., Orangeburg, SC 29115 / 803-531-1820; FAX: 803-531-2139 info@atsko.com www.atsko.com

Austin & Halleck, Inc., 2150 South 950 East, Provo, UT 84606-6285 / 877-543-3256 or 801-374-9990; FAX: 801-374-9998 www.austinhallek.com

Austin Sheridan USA, Inc., 89 Broad St., Middlefield, CT 06455 / 860-346-2500; FAX: 860-346-2510 asusa@sbcglobal.net www.austinsheridanusa.com

Auto Arms, 738 Clearview, San Antonio, TX 78228 / 512-434-5450

Auto-Ordnance Corp., P.O. Box 220, Blauvelt, NY 10913 / 914-353-7770

Autumn Sales, Inc. (Blaser) 1320 Lake St., Fort Worth, TX 76102 / 817-335-1634; FAX: 817-338-0119

Avnda Otaola Norica, 16 Apartado 68, 20600, Eibar, SPAIN

AWC Systems Technology, P.O. Box 41938, Phoenix, AZ 85080-1938 / 623-780-1050; FAX: 623-780-2967 awc@awcsystech.com www.awcsystech.com

Axtell Rifle Co., 353 Mill Creek Road, Sheridan, MT 59749 / 406-842-5814

AYA (See U.S. Importer-New England Custom Gun Serv

B

B&D Trading Co., Inc., 3935 Fair Hill Rd., Fair Oaks, CA 95628 / 800-334-3790 or 916-967-9366; FAX: 916-967-4873

B&P America, 12321 Brittany Cir., Dallas, TX 75230 / 972-726-9069

B.A.C., 17101 Los Modelos St., Fountain Valley, CA 92708 / 435-586-3286

B.C. Outdoors, Larry McGhee, PO Box 61497, Boulder City, NV 89006 / 702-294-3056; FAX: 702-294-0413 jdalton@pmcammo.com www.pmcammo.com

B.M.F. Activator, Inc., 12145 Mill Creek Run, Plantersville, TX 77363 / 936-894-2397; FAX: 936-894-2397 bmf25years@aol.com

Baelder, Harry, Alte Goennebeker Strasse 5, 24635, Rickling, GERMANY / 04328-722732; FAX: 04328-722733

Baer's Hollows, P.O. Box 603, Taft, CA 93268 / 719-438-5718

Bagmaster Mfg., Inc., 2731 Sutton Ave., St. Louis, MO 63143 / 314-781-8002; FAX: 314-781-3363 sales@bagmaster.com www.bagmaster.com

Bain & Davis, Inc., 307 E. Valley Blvd., San Gabriel, CA 91776-3522 / 626-573-4241; FAX: 626-573-8102 baindavis@aol.com

Baker, Stan. See: STAN BAKER SPORTS

Bald Eagle Precision Machine Co., 101-A Allison St., Lock Haven, PA 17745 / 570-748-6772; FAX: 570-748-4443 bepmachine@aol.com baldeaglemachine.com

Ballard, Donald. See: BALLARD INDUSTRIES

Ballard Industries, Donald Ballard Sr., P.O. Box 2035, Arnold, CA 95223 / 408-996-0957; FAX: 408-257-6828

Ballard Rifle & Cartridge Co., LLC, 113 W. Yellowstone Ave., Cody, WY 82414 / 307-587-4914; FAX: 307-527-6097 ballard@wyoming.com www.ballardrifles.com

Ballistic Products, Inc., 20015 75th Ave. North, Corcoran, MN 55340-9456 / 763-494-9237; FAX: 763-494-9236 info@ballisticproducts.com www.ballisticproducts.com

Ballistic Program Co., Inc., The, 2417 N. Patterson St., Thomasville, GA 31792 / 912-228-5739 or 800-368-0835

Ballistic Research, 1108 W. May Ave., McHenry, IL 60050 / 815-385-0037

Ballisti-Cast, Inc., P.O. Box 1057, Minot, ND 58702-1057 / 701-497-3333; FAX: 701-497-3335

Bang-Bang Boutique (See Holster Shop, The)

Bansner's Ultimate Rifles, LLC, P.O. Box 839, 261 E. Main St., Adamstown, PA 19501 / 717-484-2370; FAX: 717-484-0523 bansner@aol.com www.bansnersrifle.com

Barbour, Inc., 55 Meadowbrook Dr., Milford, NH 03055 / 603-673-1313; FAX: 603-673-6510

Barnes Bullets, Inc., P.O. Box 215, American Fork, UT 84003 / 801-756-4222 or 800-574-9200; FAX: 801-756-2465 email@barnesbullets.com www.barnesbullets.com

Baron Technology, 62 Spring Hill Rd., Trumbull, CT 06611 / 203-452-0515; FAX: 203-452-0663 dbaron@baronengraving.com www.baronengraving.com

Barraclough, John K., 55 Merit Park Dr., Gardena, CA 90247 / 310-324-2574 jbarraclough@sbcglobal.net

Barramundi Corp., P.O. Drawer 4259, Homosassa Springs, FL 32687 / 904-628-0200

Barrel & Gunworks, 2601 Lake Valley Rd., Prescott Valley, AZ 86314 / 928-772-4060 www.cutrifle.com

Barrett Firearms Manufacturer, Inc., P.O. Box 1077, Murfreesboro, TN 37133 / 615-896-2938; FAX: 615-896-7313

Bar-Sto Precision Machine, 73377 Sullivan Rd., P.O. Box 1838, Twentynine Palms, CA 92277 / 760-367-2747; FAX: 760-367-2407 barsto@eee.org www.barsto.com

Barta's Gunsmithing, 10231 U.S. Hwy. 10, Cato, WI 54230 / 920-732-4472

Barteaux Machete, 1916 SE 50th Ave., Portland, OR 97215-3238 / 503-233-5880

Bartlett Engineering, 40 South 200 East, Smithfield, UT 84335-1645 / 801-563-5910

Bates Engraving, Billy, 2302 Winthrop Dr. SW, Decatur, AL 35603 / 256-355-3690 bbrn@aol.com www.angelfire.com/al/billybates

Battenfeld Technologies, Inc., 5885 W. Van Horn Tavern Rd., Columbia, MO 65203 / 573-445-9200; FAX: 573-447-4158 battenfeldtechnologies.com

Bauer, Eddie, 15010 NE 36th St., Redmond, WA 98052

Baumgartner Bullets, 3011 S. Alane St., W. Valley City, UT 84120

Bauska Barrels, 105 9th Ave. W., Kalispell, MT 59901 / 406-752-7706

BC-Handmade Bullets, 482 Comerwood Court, S. San Francisco, CA 94080 / 650-583-1550; FAX: 650-583-1550

Bear Archery, RR 4, 4600 Southwest 41st Blvd., Gainesville, FL 32601 / 904-376-2327

Bear Arms, 374-A Carson Rd., St. Mathews, SC 29135

Bear Mountain Gun & Tool, 120 N. Plymouth, New Plymouth, ID 83655 / 208-278-5221; FAX: 208-278-5221

Beartooth Bullets, P.O. Box 491, Dept. HLD, Dover, ID 83825-0491 / 208-448-1865 bullets@beartoothbullets.com beartoothbullets.com

Beaver Park Product, Inc., 840 J St., Penrose, CO 81240 / 719-372-6744

BEC, Inc., 1227 W. Valley Blvd., Suite 204, Alhambra, CA 91803 / 626-281-5751; FAX: 626-293-7073

Beeks, Mike. See: GRAYBACK WILDCATS

Beeman Precision Airguns, 5454 Argosy Dr., Huntington Beach, CA 92649 / 714-890-4808; FAX: 714-890-4808

Beitzinger, George, 116-20 Atlantic Ave., Richmond Hill, NY 11419 / 718-847-7661

Bell & Carlson, Inc., Dodge City Industrial Park, 101 Allen Rd., Dodge City, KS 67801 / 800-634-8586 or 620-225-6688; FAX: 620-225-6688 email@bellandcarlson.com www.bellandcarlson.com

Bell Reloading, Inc., 1725 Harlin Lane Rd., Villa Rica, GA 30180

Bell's Fur & Sport Shop, 3309-19 Mannheim Rd., Franklin Park, IL 60131

Bell's Legendary Country Wear, 22 Circle Dr., Bellmore, NY 11710 / 516-679-1158

Benchmark Knives (See Gerber Legendary Blades)

Benelli Armi S.P.A., Via della Stazione, 61029, Urbino, ITALY / 39-722-307-1; FAX: 39-722-327427

Benelli USA Corp., 17603 Indian Head Hwy., Accokeek, MD 20607 / 301-283-6981; FAX: 301-283-6988 benelliusa.com

Bengtson Arms Co., L., 6345-B E. Akron St., Mesa, AZ 85205 / 602-981-6375

Benjamin/Sheridan Co., Crosman, Rts. 5 and 20, E. Bloomfield, NY 14443 / 716-657-6161; FAX: 716-657-5405 www.crosman.com

Bentley, John, 128-D Watson Dr., Turtle Creek, PA 15145

Beretta Pietro S.P.A., Via Beretta, 18, 25063, Gardone Valtrompia, ITALY / 39-30-8341-1 www.beretta.com

Beretta U.S.A. Corp., 17601 Beretta Dr., Accokeek, MD 20607 / 301-283-2191; FAX: 301-283-0435

Berger Bullets Ltd., 5443 W. Westwind Dr., Glendale, AZ 85310 / 602-842-4001; FAX: 602-934-9083

Bernardelli, Vincenzo, P.O. Box 460243, Houston, TX 77056-8243 www.bernardelli.com

Bernardelli, Vincenzo, Via Grande, 10, Sede Legale Torbole Casaglia, Brescia, ITALY / 39-30-8912851-2-3; FAX: 39-030-2150963 bernardelli@bernardelli.com www.bernardelli.com

Berry's Mfg., Inc., 401 North 3050 East St., St. George, UT 84770 / 435-634-1682; FAX: 435-634-1683 sales@berrysmfg.com www.berrysmfg.com

Bersa S.A., Benso Bonadimani, Magallanes 775 B1704 FLC, Ramos Mejia, ARGENTINA / 011-4656-2377; FAX: 011-4656-2093+ info@bersa-sa.com.dr www.bersa-sa.com.ar

Bert Johanssons Vapentillbehor, S-430 20 Veddige, SWEDEN,

Bertuzzi (See U.S. Importer-New England Arms Co.)

Better Concepts Co., 663 New Castle Rd., Butler, PA 16001 / 412-285-9000

Beverly, Mary, 3969 102nd Pl. N., Clearwater, FL 33762

Bianchi International, Inc., 27969 Jefferson Ave., Temecula, CA 92590 / 951-676-5621; FAX: 951-676-6777 www.customerservice@bianchi-intl.com www.bianchi-intl.com

Big Bore Bullets of Alaska, P.O. Box 521455, Big Lake, AK 99652 / 907-373-2673; FAX: 907-373-2673 doug@mtaonline.net www.awloo.com/bbb/index.

Big Bore Express, 2316 E. Railroad St., Nampa, ID 83651 / 800-376-4010 FAX: 208-466-6927 info@powerbeltbullets.com bigbore.

Big Spring Enterprises "Bore Stores", P.O. Box 1115, Big Spring Rd., Yellville, AR 72687 / 870-449-5297; FAX: 870-449-4446

Bilal, Mustafa. See: TURK'S HEAD PRODUCTIONS

Bilinski, Bryan. See: FIELDSPORT LTD.

Bill Adair Custom Shop, 2886 Westridge, Carrollton, TX 75006 / 972-418-0950

Bill Austin's Calls, Box 284, Kaycee, WY 82639 / 307-738-2552

Bill Hanus Birdguns, LLC, P.O. Box 533, Newport, OR 97365 / 541-265-7433; FAX: 541-265-7400 www.billhanusbirdguns.com

Bill Russ Trading Post, William A. Russ, 25 William St., Addison, NY 14801-1326 / 607-359-3896

Bill Wiseman and Co., P.O. Box 3427, Bryan, TX 77805 / 409-690-3456; FAX: 409-690-0156

Billeb, Stephen. See: QUALITY CUSTOM FIREARMS

Billings Gunsmiths, 1841 Grand Ave., Billings, MT 59102 / 406-256-8390; FAX: 406-256-6530 blgsgunsmiths@msn.com

Billingsley & Brownell, P.O. Box 25, Dayton, WY 82836 / 307-655-9344

Bill's Gun Repair, 1007 Burlington St., Mendota, IL 61342 / 815-539-5786

MANUFACTURER'S DIRECTORY

Billy Bates Engraving, 2302 Winthrop Dr. SW, Decatur, AL 35603 / 256-355-3690 bbrn@aol.com www.angelfire.com/al/billybates

Birchwood Casey, 7900 Fuller Rd., Eden Prairie, MN 55344 / 800-328-6156 or 612-937-7933; FAX: 612-937-7979

Birdsong & Assoc., W. E., 1435 Monterey Rd., Florence, MS 39073-9748 / 601-366-8270

Bismuth Cartridge Co., 3500 Maple Ave., Suite 1650, Dallas, TX 75219 / 214-521-5880; FAX: 214-521-9035

Bison Studios, 1409 South Commerce St., Las Vegas, NV 89102 / 702-388-2891; FAX: 702-383-9967

Bitterroot Bullet Co., 2001 Cedar Ave., Lewiston, ID 83501-0412 / 208-743-5635 brootbil@lewiston.com

BKL Technologies, P.O. Box 5237, Brownsville, TX 78523

Black Belt Bullets (See Big Bore Express)

Black Hills Ammunition, Inc., P.O. Box 3090, Rapid City, SD 57709-3090 / 605-348-5150; FAX: 605-348-9827

Black Hills Shooters Supply, P.O. Box 4220, Rapid City, SD 57709 / 800-289-2506

Black Powder Products, 67 Township Rd. 1411, Chesapeake, OH 45619 / 614-867-8047

Black Sheep Brand, 3220 W. Gentry Pkwy., Tyler, TX 75702 / 903-592-3853; FAX: 903-592-0527

Blacksmith Corp., P.O. Box 280, North Hampton, OH 45349 / 937-969-8389; FAX: 937-969-8399 sales@blacksmithcorp.com www.blacksmithcorp.com

BlackStar AccuMax Barrels, 11501 Brittmoore Park Drive, Houston, TX 77041 / 281-721-6040; FAX: 281-721-6041

BlackStar Barrel Accurizing (See BlackStar AccuMax)

Blacktail Mountain Books, 42 First Ave. W., Kalispell, MT 59901 / 406-257-5573

Blaser Jagdwaffen GmbH, D-88316, Isny Im Allgau, GERMANY

Blount, Inc., Sporting Equipment Div., 2299 Snake River Ave., P.O. Box 856, Lewiston, ID 83501 / 800-627-3640 or 208-746-2351; FAX: 208-799-3904

Blount/Outers ATK, P.O. Box 39, Onalaska, WI 54650 / 608-781-5800; FAX: 608-781-0368

Blue and Gray Products Inc. (See Ox-Yoke Originals)

Blue Book Publications, Inc., 8009 34th Ave. S., Ste. 175, Minneapolis, MN 55425 / 952-854-5229; FAX: 952-853-1486 bluebook@bluebookinc.com www.bluebookinc.com

Blue Mountain Bullets, 64146 Quail Ln., Box 231, John Day, OR 97845 / 541-820-4594; FAX: 541-820-4594

Blue Ridge Machinery & Tools, Inc., P.O. Box 536-GD, Hurricane, WV 25526 / 800-872-6500; FAX: 304-562-5311 blueridgemachine@worldnet.att.net www.blueridgemachinery.com

BMC Supply, Inc., 26051 - 179th Ave. SE, Kent, WA 98042

Bob Allen Sportswear, One Bort Dr., Osceola, IA 50213 / 210-344-8531; FAX: 210-342-2703 sales@bob-allen.com www.bob-allen.com

Bob Rogers Gunsmithing, P.O. Box 305, 344 S. Walnut St., Franklin Grove, IL 61031 / 815-456-2685; FAX: 815-456-2685 3006bud@netscape.com

Bob's Gun Shop, P.O. Box 200, Royal, AR 71968 / 501-767-1970; FAX: 501-767-1970 gunparts@hsnp.com www.gun-parts.com

Bob's Tactical Indoor Shooting Range & Gun Shop, 90 Lafayette Rd., Salisbury, MA 01952 / 508-465-5561

Boessler, Erich, Am Vogeltal 3, 97702, Munnerstadt, GERMANY

Boker USA, Inc., 1550 Balsam Street, Lakewood, CO 80214 / 303-462-0662; FAX: 303-462-0668 sales@bokerusa.com bokerusa.com

Boltin, John M., P.O. Box 644, Estill, SC 29918 / 803-625-2185

Bo-Mar Tool & Mfg. Co., 6136 State Hwy. 300, Longview, TX 75604 / 903-759-4784; FAX: 903-759-9141 marykor@earthlink.net bo-mar.com

Bonadimani, Benso. See: BERSA S.A.

Bonanza (See Forster Products), 310 E. Lanark Ave., Lanark, IL 61046 / 815-493-6360; FAX: 815-493-2371

Bond Arms, Inc., P.O. Box 1296, Granbury, TX 76048 / 817-573-4445; FAX: 817-573-5636 www.bondarms.com

Bond Custom Firearms, 8954 N. Lewis Ln., Bloomington, IN 47408 / 812-332-4519

Bonham's & Butterfields, 220 San Bruno Ave., San Francisco, CA 94103 / 415-861-7500; FAX: 415-861-0183 arms@butterfields.com www.butterfields.com

Boone Trading Co., Inc., P.O. Box 669, Brinnon, WA 98320 / 800-423-1945 or 360-796-4330; FAX: 360-796-4511 sales@boonetrading.com boonetrading.com

Boone's Custom Ivory Grips, Inc., 562 Coyote Rd., Brinnon, WA 98320 / 206-796-4330

Boonie Packer Products, P.O. Box 12517, Salem, OR 97309-0517 / 800-477-3244 or 503-581-3244; FAX: 503-581-3191 customerservice@booniepacker.com www.booniepacker.com

Borden Ridges Rimrock Stocks, RR 1 Box 250 BC, Springville, PA 18844 / 570-965-2505; FAX: 570-965-2328

Borden Rifles Inc., RD 1, Box 250 #BC, Springville, PA 18844 / 717-965-2505; FAX: 717-965-2328

Border Barrels Ltd., Riccarton Farm, Newcastleton, SCOTLAND UK

Borovnik K.G., Ludwig, 9170 Ferlach, Bahnhofstrasse 7, AUSTRIA / 042 27 24 42; FAX: 042 26 43 49

Bosis (See U.S. Importer-New England Arms Co.)

Boss Manufacturing Co., 221 W. First St., Kewanee, IL 61443 / 309-852-2131 or 800-447-4581; FAX: 309-852-0848

Bostick Wildlife Calls, Inc., P.O. Box 728, Estill, SC 29918 / 803-625-2210; or 803-625-4512

Bowen Classic Arms Corp., P.O. Box 67, Louisville, TN 37777 / 865-984-3583 bcacorp@aks.net www.bowenclassicarms.com

Bowen Knife Co., Inc., P.O. Box 802, Magnolia, AR 71754 / 800-397-4794; FAX: 870-234-9005 info@bowen.com www.bowenknife.com

Bowerly, Kent, 710 Golden Pheasant Dr., Redmond, OR 97756 / 541-923-3501 bowerly@bendbroadband.com

Boyds' Gunstock Industries, Inc., 25376 403 Rd. Ave., Mitchell, SD 57301 / 605-996-5011; FAX: 605-996-9878 www.boydsgunstocks.com

Brace, Larry D., 771 Blackfoot Ave., Eugene, OR 97404 / 541-688-1278; FAX: 541-607-5833

Brauer Bros., P.O. Box 2485, McKinney, TX 75070 / 976-548-8881; FAX: 972-548-8886 www.brauerbros.com

Break-Free, Inc., 13386 International Pkwy., Jacksonville, FL 32218 / 800-428-0588; FAX: 904-741-5407 contactus@armorholdings.com www.break-free.com

Brenneke GmbH, P.O. Box 1646, 30837, Langenhagen, GERMANY / +49-511-97262-0; FAX: +49-511-97262-62 info@brenneke.de brenneke.com

Bridgeman Products, Harry Jaffin, 153 B Cross Slope Ct., Englishtown, NJ 07726 / 732-536-3604; FAX: 732-972-1004

Briese Bullet Co., Inc., 3442 42 Ave. SE, Tappen, ND 58487 / 701-327-4578; FAX: 701-327-4579

Brigade Quartermasters, 1025 Cobb International Blvd., Dept. VH, Kennesaw, GA 30144-4300 / 404-428-1248 or 800-241-3125; FAX: 404-426-7726

Briganti, A.J. See: BRIGANTI CUSTOM GUNSMITH

Briganti Custom Gunsmith, A.J. Briganti, 512 Rt. 32, Highland Mills, NY 10930 / 845-928-9573

Briley Mfg. Inc., 1230 Lumpkin, Houston, TX 77043 / 800-331-5718 or 713-932-6995; FAX: 713-932-1043

Brill, R. See: ROYAL ARMS INTERNATIONAL

British Sporting Arms, RR 1, Box 193A, Millbrook, NY 12545 / 845-677-8303; FAX: 845-677-5756 info@bsaltd.com www.bsaltd.com

Broad Creek Rifle Works, Ltd., 120 Horsey Ave., Laurel, DE 19956 / 302-875-5446; FAX: 302-875-1448 bcrw4guns@aol.com

Brockman's Custom Gunsmithing, 445 Idaho St., Gooding, ID 83330 / 208-934-5050 brockman@brockmansrifles.com www.brockmansrifles.com

Broken Gun Ranch, 10739 126 Rd., Spearville, KS 67876 / 316-385-2587; FAX: 316-385-2597 nbowlin@ucom.net www.brokengunranch

Brooker, Dennis, Rt. 1, Box 12A, Derby, IA 50068 / 515-533-2103

Brooks Tactical Systems-Agrip, 279-C Shorewood Ct., Fox Island, WA 98333 / 253-549-2866; FAX: 253-549-2703 brooks@brookstactical.com www.brookstactical.com

Brown Precision, Inc., 7786 Molinos Ave., Los Molinos, CA 96055 / 530-384-2506; FAX: 916-384-1638 www.brownprecision.com

Brownells, Inc., 200 S. Front St., Montezuma, IA 50171 / 800-741-0015; FAX: 800-264-3068 orderdesk@brownells.com www.brownells.com

Browning Arms Co., One Browning Place, Morgan, UT 84050 / 801-876-2711; FAX: 801-876-3331 www.browning.com

Browning Arms Co. (Parts & Service), 3005 Arnold Tenbrook Rd., Arnold, MO 63010 / 617-287-6800; FAX: 617-287-9751

BRP, Inc. High Performance Cast Bullets, 1210 Alexander Rd., Colorado Springs, CO 80909 / 719-633-0658

Brunton U.S.A., 2255 Brunton Ct., Riverton, WY 82501 info@brunton.com www.brunton.com

Bryan & Assoc., R. D. Sauls, P.O. Box 5772, Anderson, SC 29623-5772 / 864-261-6810 bryanandac@aol.com www.huntersweb.com/bryanandac

Brynin, Milton, P.O. Box 383, Yonkers, NY 10710 / 914-779-4333

BSA Guns Ltd., Armoury Rd. Small Heath, Birmingham B11 2PP, ENGLAND / 011-021-772-8543; FAX: 011-021-773-0845 sales@bsagun.com www.bsagun.com

BSA Optics, 3911 SW 47th Ave., Ste. 914, Ft. Lauderdale, FL 33314 / 954-581-2144; FAX: 954-581-3165 4info@basaoptics.com www.bsaoptics.com

B-Square Company, Inc., 8909 Forum Way, Ft. Worth, TX 76140 / 800-433-2909; FAX: 817-926-7012 bsquare@b-square.com www.b-square.com

Buchsenmachermeister, Peter Hofer Jagdwaffen, A-9170 Ferlach, Kirchgasse 24, Kirchgasse, AUSTRIA / 43 4227 3683; or 43 664 3200216; FAX: 43 4227 368330 peterhofer@hoferwaffen.com www.hoferwaffen.com

Buck Knives, Inc., 660 Lochsa St., Post Falls, ID 83854 / 208-262-0500; FAX: 800-326-2825 www.buckknives.com

Buck Stix-SOS Products Co., Box 3, Neenah, WI 54956

Buck Stop Lure Co., Inc., 3600 Grow Rd. NW, P.O. Box 636, Stanton, MI 48888 / 989-762-5091; FAX: 989-762-5124 buckstop@nethawk.com www.buckstopscents.com

Buckeye Custom Bullets, 6490 Stewart Rd., Elida, OH 45807 / 419-641-4463

Buckhorn Gun Works, 8109 Woodland Dr., Black Hawk, SD 57718 / 605-787-6472

Buckskin Bullet Co., P.O. Box 1893, Cedar City, UT 84721 / 435-586-3286

Budin, Dave. See: DEL-SPORTS, INC.

Buehler Custom Sporting Arms, P.O. Box 4096, Medford, OR 97501 / 541-664-9109 rbrifle@earthlink.net

Buenger Enterprises/Goldenrod Dehumidifier, 3600 S. Harbor Blvd., Oxnard, CA 93035 / 800-451-6797 or 805-985-5828; FAX: 805-985-1534

Buffalo Arms Co., 660 Vermeer Ct., Ponderay, ID 83852 / 208-263-6953; FAX: 208-265-2096 www.buffaloarms.com

Buffalo Bullet Co., Inc., 12637 Los Nietos Rd., Unit A, Santa Fe Springs, CA 90670 / 800-423-8069; FAX: 562-944-5054 rdanlitz@verizon.net

Buffalo Gun Center, 3385 Harlem Rd., Buffalo, NY 14225 / 716-833-2581; FAX: 716-833-2265 www.buffaloguncenter.com

Buffalo Rock Shooters Supply, R.R. 1, Ottawa, IL 61350 / 815-433-2471

Buffer Technologies, P.O. Box 105047, Jefferson City, MO 65110 / 573-634-8529; FAX: 573-634-8522 sales@buffertech.com www.buffertech.com

Bull Mountain Rifle Co., 6327 Golden West Terrace, Billings, MT 59106 / 406-656-0778

Bullberry Barrel Works, Ltd., 2430 W. Bullberry Ln., Hurricane, UT 84737 / 435-635-9866; FAX: 435-635-0348 fred@bullberry.com www.bullberry.com

Bullet Metals, Bill Ferguson, P.O. Box 1238, Sierra Vista, AZ 85636 / 520-458-5321; FAX: 520-458-1421 info@theantimonyman.com www.bullet-metals.com

Bullet Swaging Supply, Inc., P.O. Box 1056, 303 McMillan Rd., West Monroe, LA 71291 / 318-387-3266; FAX: 318-387-7779 leblackmon@colla.com

Bull-X, Inc., 411 E. Water St., Farmer City, IL 61842-1556 / 309-928-2574 or 800-248-3845; FAX: 309-928-2130

Burkhart Gunsmithing, Don, P.O. Box 852, Rawlins, WY 82301 / 307-324-6007

Burnham Bros., P.O. Box 1148, Menard, TX 78659 / 915-396-4572; FAX: 915-396-4574

Burris, Inc., P.O. Box 1747, 331 E. 8th St., Greeley, CO 80631 / 970-356-1670; FAX: 970-356-8702

Bushmaster Firearms, Inc., 999 Roosevelt Trail, Windham, ME 04062 / 800-998-7928; FAX: 207-892-8068 info@bushmaster.com www.bushmaster.com

Bushmaster Hunting & Fishing, 451 Alliance Ave., Toronto, ON M6N 2J1 CANADA / 416-763-4040; FAX: 416-763-0623

Bushnell Outdoor Products, 9200 Cody, Overland Park, KS 66214 / 913-752-3400 or 800-423-3537; FAX: 913-752-3550

Buster's Custom Knives, P.O. Box 214, Richfield, UT 84701 / 435-896-5319; FAX: 435-896-8333 www.warenskiknives.com

Butler Creek Corp., 9200 Cody St., Overland Park, KS 66214 / 800-845-2444 or 406-388-1356; FAX: 406-388-7204

Butler Enterprises, 834 Oberting Rd., Lawrenceburg, IN 47025 / 812-537-3584

Buzz Fletcher Custom Stockmaker, 117 Silver Road, P.O. Box 189, Taos, NM 87571 / 505-758-3486

MANUFACTURER'S DIRECTORY

C

C&D Special Products (See Claybuster Wads & Harvester Bullets)

C&H Research, 115 Sunnyside Dr., Box 351, Lewis, KS 67552 / 316-324-5445 or 888-324-5445; FAX: 620-324-5984 info@mercuryrecoil.com www.mercuryrecoil.com

C. Sharps Arms Co. Inc./Montana Armory, 100 Centennial Dr., P.O. Box 885, Big Timber, MT 59011 / 406-932-4353; FAX: 406-932-4443 www.csharpsarms.com

C.S. Van Gorden & Son, Inc., 1815 Main St., Bloomer, WI 54724 / 715-568-2612 vangorden@bloomer.net

C.W. Erickson's Mfg., L.L.C., P.O. Box 522, Buffalo, MN 55313 / 763-682-3665; FAX: 763-682-4328 cwerickson@archerhunter.com www.archerhunter.com

Cabanas (See U.S. Importer-Mandall Shooting Supply

Cabela's, One Cabela Drive, Sidney, NE 69160 / 308-254-5505; FAX: 308-254-8420

Cabinet Mtn. Outfitters Scents & Lures, P.O. Box 766, Plains, MT 59859 / 406-826-3970

Caesar Guerini USA, Inc., 700 Lake St., Cambridge, MD 21613 / 410-901-1131; FAX: 410-901-1137 info@gueriniusa.com www.gueriniusa.com

Cain's Outdoors, Inc., 1832 Williams Hwy., Williamstown, WV 26187 / 304-375-7842; FAX: 304-375-7842 muzzleloading@cainsoutdoor.com www.cainsoutdoor.com

Cali'co Hardwoods, Inc., 3580 Westwind Blvd., Santa Rosa, CA 95403 / 707-546-4045; FAX: 707-546-4027 calicohardwoods@home.com

California Sights (See Fautheree, Andy)

Camdex, Inc., 2330 Alger, Troy, MI 48083 / 810-528-2300; FAX: 810-528-0989

Cameron's, 16690 W. 11th Ave., Golden, CO 80401 / 303-279-7365; FAX: 303-568-1009 ncnoremac@aol.com

Camillus Cutlery Co., 54 Main St., Camillus, NY 13031 / 315-672-8111; FAX: 315-672-8832

Campbell, Dick, 196 Garden Homes Dr., Colville, WA 99114 / 509-684-6080; FAX: 509-684-6080 dicksknives@aol.com

Camp-Cap Products, P.O. Box 3805, Chesterfield, MO 63006 / 866-212-4639; FAX: 636-536-6320 mandrytrc@sbcglobal.net www.langenberghats.com

Cannon Safe, Inc., 216 S. 2nd Ave. #BLD-932, San Bernardino, CA 92400 / 800-242-1055; FAX: 909-382-0707 info@cannonsafe.com www.cannonsafe.com

Canyon Cartridge Corp., P.O. Box 152, Albertson, NY 11507 FAX: 516-294-8946

Cape Outfitters, 599 County Rd. 206, Cape Girardeau, MO 63701 / 573-335-4103; FAX: 573-335-1555

Caraville Manufacturing, P.O. Box 4545, Thousand Oaks, CA 91359 / 805-499-1234

Carbide Checkering Tools (See J&R Engineering)

Carhartt, Inc., 5750 Mercury Dr., Dearborn, MI 48126 / 800-833-3118 www.carhartt.com

Carl Walther GmbH, B.P. 4325, D-89033, Ulm, GERMANY

Carl Zeiss Inc., 13005 N. Kingston Ave., Chester, VA 23836 / 800-441-3005; FAX: 804-530-8481

Carlson, Douglas. See: ANTIQUE AMERICAN FIREARMS

Carolina Precision Rifles, 1200 Old Jackson Hwy., Jackson, SC 29831 / 803-827-2069

Carrell, William. See: CARRELL'S PRECISION FIREARMS

Carrell's Precision Firearms, William Carrell, 1952 W. Silver Falls Ct., Meridian, ID 83642-3837

Carry-Lite, Inc., P.O. Box 1587, Fort Smith, AR 72902 / 479-782-8971; FAX: 479-783-0234

Carter's Gun Shop, 225 G St., Penrose, CO 81240 / 719-372-6240 rlewiscarter@msn.com

Case & Sons Cutlery Co., W R, Owens Way, Bradford, PA 16701 / 814-368-4123 or 800-523-6350; FAX: 814-768-5369 info@wrcase.com www.wrcase.com

Case Sorting System, 12695 Cobblestone Creek Rd., Poway, CA 92064 / 619-486-9340

Cash Mfg. Co./ TDC, P.O. Box 130, 201 S. Klein Dr., Waunakee, WI 53597-0130 / 608-849-5664; FAX: 608-849-5664 office@tdcmfg.com www.tdcmfg.com

Caspian Arms, Ltd., 14 North Main St., Hardwick, VT 05843 / 802-472-6454; FAX: 802-472-6709

Cast Bullet Association, The, 12857 S. Road, Hoyt, KS 66440-9116 cbamemdir@castbulletassoc.org www.castbulletassoc.org

Cast Performance Bullet Company, P.O. Box 1466, Rainier, OR 97048 / 503-556-3006; FAX: 503-556-8037 info@bornhunter.com www.bornhunter.com

Casull Arms Corp., P.O. Box 1629, Afton, WY 83110 / 307-886-0200

Caswell Inc., 2540 2nd St. NE, Minneapolis, MN 55410 / 847-639-7666; FAX: 847-639-7694 www.caswellintl.com

Cathey Enterprises, Inc., P.O. Box 2202, Brownwood, TX 76804 / 915-643-2553; FAX: 915-643-3653

Cation, 2341 Alger St., Troy, MI 48083 / 810-689-0658; FAX: 810-689-7558

Caywood, Shane J., P.O. Box 321, Minocqua, WI 54548 / 715-277-3866

Caywood Gunmakers, 18 Kings Hill Estates, Berryville, AR 72616 / 870-423-4741 www.caywoodguns.com

CBC, Avenida Humberto de Campos 3220, 09400-000, Ribeirao Pires, SP, BRAZIL / 55 11 4822 8378; FAX: 55 11 4822 8323 export@cbc.com.bc www.cbc.com.bc

CBC-BRAZIL, 3 Cuckoo Lane, Honley, Yorkshire HD7 2BR, ENGLAND / 44-1484-661062; FAX: 44-1484-663709

CCG Enterprises, 5217 E. Belknap St., Halton City, TX 76117 / 800-819-7464

CCI/Speer Div of ATK, P.O. Box 856, 2299 Snake River Ave., Lewiston, ID 83501 / 800-627-3640 or 208-746-2351

CCL Security Products, 199 Whiting St., New Britain, CT 06051 / 800-733-8588

Cedar Hill Game Calls, LLC, 238 Vic Allen Rd., Downsville, LA 71234 / 318-982-5632; FAX: 318-982-2031

Centaur Systems, Inc., 1602 Foothill Rd., Kalispell, MT 59901 / 406-755-8609; FAX: 406-755-8609

Center Lock Scope Rings, 9901 France Ct., Lakeville, MN 55044 / 952-461-2114; FAX: 952-461-2194 marklee55044@usfamily.net

Central Specialties Ltd. (See Trigger Lock Division)

Century International Arms, Inc., 430 S. Congress Ave. Ste. 1, Delray Beach, FL 33445-4701 / 800-527-1252; FAX: 561-265-4520 support@centuryarms.com www.centuryarms.com

CFVentures, 509 Harvey Dr., Bloomington, IN 47403-1715 paladinwilltravel@yahoo.com www.caversam16.freeserve.co.uk

CH Tool & Die/4-D Custom Die Co., 711 N. Sandusky St., P.O. Box 889, Mt. Vernon, OH 43050-0889 / 740-397-7214; FAX: 740-397-6600 info@ch4d.com ch4d.com

Chace Leather Products, 507 Alden St., Fall River, MA 02722 / 508-678-7556; FAX: 508-675-9666 chacelea@aol.com www.chaceleather.com

Chadick's Ltd., P.O. Box 100, Terrell, TX 75160 / 214-563-7577

Chambers Flintlocks Ltd., Jim, 116 Sams Branch Rd., Candler, NC 28715 / 828-667-8361; FAX: 828-665-0852 www.flintlocks.com

Champion Shooters' Supply, P.O. Box 303, New Albany, OH 43054 / 614-855-1603; FAX: 614-855-1209

Champion Target Co., 232 Industrial Parkway, Richmond, IN 47374 / 800-441-4971

Champion's Choice, Inc., 201 International Blvd., LaVergne, TN 37086 / 615-793-4066; FAX: 615-793-4070 champ.choice@earthlink.net www.champchoice.com

Champlin Firearms, Inc., P.O. Box 3191, Woodring Airport, Enid, OK 73701 / 580-237-7388; FAX: 580-242-6922 info@champlinarms.com www.champlinarms.com

Chapman Academy of Practical Shooting, 4350 Academy Rd., Hallsville, MO 65255 / 573-696-5544; FAX: 573-696-2266 hq@chapmanacademy.com chapmanacademy.com

Chapman, J. Ken. See: OLD WEST BULLET MOULDS

Chapman Manufacturing Co., 471 New Haven Rd., Durham, CT 06422 / 860-349-9228; FAX: 860-349-0084 sales@chapmanmfg.com www.chapmanmfg.com

Chapuis Armes, Z1 La Gravoux, BP15, 42380 P.O. Box 15, St. Bonnet-le-Chatea, FRANCE / (33)477.50.06.96; FAX: (33)477 50 10 70 info@chapuis.armes.com www.chapuis-armes.com

Charter 2000, 273 Canal St., Shelton, CT 06484 / 203-922-1652

Checkmate Refinishing, 370 Champion Dr., Brooksville, FL 34601 / 352-799-5774; FAX: 352-799-2986 checkmatecustom.com

Cheddite, France S.A., 99 Route de Lyon, F-26501, Bourg-les-Valence, FRANCE / 33-75-56-4545; FAX: 33-75-56-3587 info@cheddite.com www.cheddite.com

Chelsea Gun Club of New York City, Inc., 237 Ovington Ave., Apt. D53, Brooklyn, NY 11209 / 718-836-9422 or 718-833-2704

CheVron Bullets, RR1, Ottawa, IL 61350 / 815-433-2471

Cheyenne Pioneer Products, P.O. Box 28425, Kansas City, MO 64188 / 816-413-9196; FAX: 816-455-2859 cheyennepp@aol.com www.cartridgeboxes.com

Chicago Cutlery Co., 5500 N. Pearl St., Ste. 400, Rosemont, IL 60018 / 847-678-8600 www.chicagocutlery.com

Chicasaw Gun Works, 4 Mi. Mkr., 322 Willow Br. Pluto Rd., Shady Spring, WV 25918-0868 / 304-763-2848; FAX: 304-763-3725

Chip McCormick Corp., P.O. Box 694, Spicewood, TX 78669 / 800-328-2447; FAX: 830-693-4975 www.chipmccormickcorp.com

Chipmunk (See Oregon Arms, Inc.)

Choate Machine & Tool Co., Inc., P.O. Box 218, 116 Lovers Ln., Bald Knob, AR 72010 / 501-724-6193; or 800-972-6390; FAX: 501-724-5873

Christensen Arms, 192 East 100 North, Fayette, UT 84630 / 435-528-7999; FAX: 435-528-7494 www.christensenarms.com

Christie's East, 20 Rockefeller Plz., New York, NY 10020-1902 / 212-606-0406 christics.com

Chu Tani Ind., Inc., P.O. Box 2064, Cody, WY 82414-2064

Chuck's Gun Shop, P.O. Box 597, Waldo, FL 32694 / 904-468-2264

Churchill (See U.S. Importer-Ellett Bros.)

Churchill, Winston G., 2838 20 Mile Stream Rd., Proctorville, VT 05153 / 802-226-7772

Churchill Glove Co., James, P.O. Box 298, Centralia, WA 98531 / 360-736-2816; FAX: 360-330-0151

Cimarron F.A. Co., P.O. Box 906, Fredericksburg, TX 78624-0906 / 830-997-9090; FAX: 830-997-0802 cimgraph@koc.com www.cimarron-firearms.com

Cincinnati Swaging, 2605 Marlington Ave., Cincinnati, OH 45208

Clark Custom Guns, Inc., 336 Shootout Lane, Princeton, LA 71067 / 318-949-9884; FAX: 318-949-9829

Clark Firearms Engraving, 6347 Avon Ave., San Gabriel, CA 91775-1801 / 818-287-1652

Clarkfield Enterprises, Inc., 1032 10th Ave., Clarkfield, MN 56223 / 612-669-7140

Claro Walnut Gunstock Co., 1235 Stanley Ave., Chico, CA 95928 / 530-342-5188; FAX: 530-342-5199 wally@clarowalnutgunstocks.com www.clarowalnutgunstocks.com

Classic Arms Company, Rt 1 Box 120F, Burnet, TX 78611 / 512-756-4001

Classic Arms Corp., P.O. Box 106, Dunsmuir, CA 96025-0106 / 530-235-2000

Classic Old West Styles, 1060 Doniphan Park Circle C, El Paso, TX 79936 / 915-587-0684

Clean Shot Technologies, 21218 St. Andrews Blvd. Ste 504, Boca Raton, FL 33433 / 888-866-2532

Clearview Mfg. Co., Inc., 413 S. Oakley St., Fordyce, AR 71742 / 870-352-8557; FAX: 870-352-7120

Clearview Products, 3021 N. Portland, Oklahoma City, OK 73107

Cleland's Outdoor World, Inc., 10306 Airport Hwy., Swanton, OH 43558 / 419-865-4713; FAX: 419-865-5865 mail@clelands.com www.clelands.com

Clements' Custom Leathercraft, Chas, 1741 Dallas St., Aurora, CO 80010-2018 / 303-364-0403; FAX: 303-739-9824 gryphons@home.com kuntaoslcat.com

Clenzoil Worldwide Corp., Jack Fitzgerald, 25670 1st St., Westlake, OH 44145-1430 / 440-899-0482; FAX: 440-899-0483

Clift Mfg., L.R., 3821 Hammonton Rd., Marysville, CA 95901 / 916-755-3390; FAX: 916-755-3393

Clymer Mfg. Co., 1645 W. Hamlin Rd., Rochester Hills, MI 48309-3312 / 248-853-5555; FAX: 248-853-1530

C-More Systems, P.O. Box 1750, 7553 Gary Rd., Manassas, VA 20108 / 703-361-2663; FAX: 703-361-5881

Cobra Enterprises, Inc., 1960 S. Milestone Drive, Suite F, Salt Lake City, UT 84104 FAX: 801-908-8301 www.cobrapistols@networld.com

Cobra Sport S.R.I., Via Caduti Nei Lager No. 1, 56020 San Romano, Montopoli v/Arno Pi, ITALY / 0039-571-450490; FAX: 0039-571-450492

Coffin, Charles H., 3719 Scarlet Ave., Odessa, TX 79762 / 915-366-4729; FAX: 915-366-4729

Cogar's Gunsmithing, 206 Redwine Dr., Houghton Lake, MI 48629 / 517-422-4591 ecogar@peoplepc.com

Coghlan's Ltd., 121 Irene St., Winnipeg, MB R3T 4C7 CANADA / 204-284-9550; FAX: 204-475-4127

Cold Steel Inc., 3036 Seaborg Ave. Ste. A, Ventura, CA 93003 / 800-255-4716; or 800-624-2363; FAX: 805-642-9727

Cole-Grip, 16135 Cohasset St., Van Nuys, CA 91406 / 818-782-4424

Coleman Co., Inc., 3600 N. Hydraulic, Wichita, KS 67219 / 800-835-3278 www.coleman.com

MANUFACTURER'S DIRECTORY

Collector's Armoury, Ltd., Tom Nelson, 9404 Gunston Cove Rd., Lorton, VA 22079 / 703-493-9120; FAX: 703-493-9424 www.collectorsarmoury.com

Collings, Ronald, 1006 Cielta Linda, Vista, CA 92083

Colonial Arms, Inc., P.O. Box 636, Selma, AL 36702-0636 / 334-872-9455; FAX: 334-872-9540 colonialarms@mindspring.com www.colonialarms.com

Colonial Repair, 47 Navarre St., Roslindale, MA 02131-4725 / 617-469-4951

Colorado Gunsmithing Academy, RR 3 Box 79B, El Campo, TX 77437 / 719-336-4099 or 800-754-2046; FAX: 719-336-9642

Colorado School of Trades, 1575 Hoyt St., Lakewood, CO 80215 / 800-234-4594; FAX: 303-233-4723

Colt Blackpowder Arms Co., 110 8th Street, Brooklyn, NY 11215 / 718-499-4678; FAX: 718-768-8056

Colt's Mfg. Co., Inc., P.O. Box 1868, Hartford, CT 06144-1868 / 800-962-COLT or 860-236-6311; FAX: 860-244-1449

Compass Industries, Inc., 104 East 25th St., New York, NY 10010 / 212-473-2614 or 800-221-9904; FAX: 212-353-0826

Compasseco, Ltd., 151 Atkinson Hill Ave., Bardstown, KY 40004 / 502-349-0910

Competition Electronics, Inc., 3469 Precision Dr., Rockford, IL 61109 / 815-874-8001; FAX: 815-874-8181

Competitive Pistol Shop, The, 5233 Palmer Dr., Fort Worth, TX 76117-2433 / 817-834-8479

Competitor Corp., Inc., 26 Knight St. Unit 3, P.O. Box 352, Jaffrey, NH 03452 / 603-532-9483; FAX: 603-532-8209 competitorcorp@aol.com www.competitor-pistol.com

Component Concepts, Inc., 530 S. Springbrook Road, Newberg, OR 97132 / 503-554-8095; FAX: 503-554-9370 cci@cybcon.com www.phantomonline.com

Concealment Shop, Inc., The, 3550 E. Hwy. 80, Mesquite, TX 75149 / 972-289-8997 or 800-444-7090; FAX: 972-289-4410 theconcealmentshop@msn.com www.theconcealmentshop.com

Concept Development Corp., 16610 E. Laser Drive, Suite 5, Fountain Hills, AZ 85268-6644

Conetrol Scope Mounts, 10225 Hwy. 123 S., Seguin, TX 78155 / 830-379-3030 or 800-CONETROL; FAX: 830-379-3030 email@conetrol.com www.conetrol.com

Connecticut Shotgun Mfg. Co., P.O. Box 1692, 35 Woodland St., New Britain, CT 06051 / 860-225-6581; FAX: 860-832-8707

Connecticut Valley Classics (See CVC, BPI)

Conrad, C. A., 3964 Ebert St., Winston-Salem, NC 27127 / 919-788-5469

Cook Engineering Service, 891 Highbury Rd., Vict 3133, 3133 AUSTRALIA

Cooper Arms, P.O. Box 114, Stevensville, MT 59870 / 406-777-0373; FAX: 406-777-5228

Cooper-Woodward Perfect Lube, 4120 Oesterle Rd., Helena, MT 59602 / 406-459-2287 cwperfectlube@mt.net cwperfectlube.com

Corbin Mfg. & Supply, Inc., 600 Industrial Circle, P.O. Box 2659, White City, OR 97503 / 541-826-5211; FAX: 541-826-8669 sales@corbins.com www.corbins.com

Cor-Bon Inc./Glaser LLC, P.O. Box 173, 1311 Industry Rd., Sturgis, SD 57785 / 605-347-4544 or 800-221-3489; FAX: 605-347-5055 email@corbon.com www.corbon.com

Corkys Gun Clinic, 4401 Hot Springs Dr., Greeley, CO 80634-9226 / 970-330-0516

Corry, John, 861 Princeton Ct., Neshanic Station, NJ 08853 / 908-369-8019

Cosmi Americo & Figlio S.N.C., Via Flaminia 307, Ancona, ITALY / 071-888208; FAX: 39-071-887008

Coulston Products, Inc., P.O. Box 30, 201 Ferry St. Suite 212, Easton, PA 18044-0030 / 215-253-0167 or 800-445-9927; FAX: 215-252-1511

Counter Assault, 120 Industrial Court, Kalispell, MT 59901 / 406-257-4740; FAX: 406-257-6674

Country Armourer, The, P.O. Box 308, Ashby, MA 01431-0308 / 508-827-6797; FAX: 508-827-4845

Cousin Bob's Mountain Products, 7119 Ohio River Blvd., Ben Avon, PA 15202 / 412-766-5114; FAX: 412-766-9354

CP Bullets, 1310 Industrial Hwy #5-6, Southhampton, PA 18966 / 215-953-7264; FAX: 215-953-7275

CQB Training, P.O. Box 1739, Manchester, MO 63011

Craftguard, 3624 Logan Ave., Waterloo, IA 50703 / 319-232-2959; FAX: 319-234-0804

Crandall Tool & Machine Co., 19163 21 Mile Rd., Tustin, MI 49688 / 616-829-4430

Creative Craftsman, Inc., The, 95 Highway 29 N., P.O. Box 331, Lawrenceville, GA 30246 / 404-963-2112; FAX: 404-513-9488

Creedmoor Sports, Inc., 1405 South Coast Hwy., Oceanside, CA 92054 / 800-273-3366; FAX: 760-757-5558 shoot@creedmoorsports.com www.creedmoorsports.com

Creighton Audette, 19 Highland Circle, Springfield, VT 05156 / 802-885-2331

Crimson Trace Lasers, 8090 S.W. Cirrus Dr., Beverton, OR 97008 / 800-442-2406; FAX: 503-627-0166 travis@crimsontrace.com www.crimsontrace.com

Crit' R Calls, P.O. Box 999, La Porte, CO 80535 / 970-484-2768; FAX: 970-484-0807 critrcall@larinet.net www.critrcall.com

Crit'R Call (See Rocky Mountain Wildlife Products)

Crosman Airguns, Rts. 5 and 20, E. Bloomfield, NY 14443 / 716-657-6161; FAX: 716-657-5405

Crosman Blades (See Coleman Co., Inc.)

CRR, Inc./Marble's Inc., 420 Industrial Park, P.O. Box 111, Gladstone, MI 49837 / 906-428-3710; FAX: 906-428-3711

Crucelegui, Hermanos (See U.S. Importer-Mandall)

Cubic Shot Shell Co., Inc., 98 Fatima Dr., Campbell, OH 44405 / 330-755-0349

Cullity Restoration, 209 Old Country Rd., East Sandwich, MA 02537 / 508-888-1147

Cummings Bullets, 1417 Esperanza Way, Escondido, CA 92027

Cunningham, Jerry. See: ORION RIFLE BARREL CO.

Cupp, Alana, Custom Engraver, P.O. Box 207, Annabella, UT 84711 / 801-896-4834

Curly Maple Stock Blanks (See Tiger-Hunt)

Curtis Cast Bullets, 527 W. Babcock St., Bozeman, MT 59715 / 406-587-8117; FAX: 406-587-8117

Curtis Gun Shop (See Curtis Cast Bullets)

Custom Bullets by Hoffman, 2604 Peconic Ave., Seaford, NY 11783

Custom Calls, 607 N. 5th St., Burlington, IA 52601 / 319-752-4465

Custom Checkering Service, Kathy Forster, 2124 S.E. Yamhill St., Portland, OR 97214 / 503-236-5874

Custom Products (See Jones Custom Products)

Custom Shop, The, 890 Cochrane Crescent, Peterborough, ON K9H 5N3 CANADA / 705-742-6693

Custom Single Shot Rifles, 9651 Meadows Lane, Guthrie, OK 73044 / 405-282-3634

Custom Tackle and Ammo, P.O. Box 1886, Farmington, NM 87499 / 505-632-3539

Cutco Cutlery, P.O. Box 810, Olean, NY 14760 / 716-372-3111

CVA, 5988 Peachtree Corners East, Norcross, GA 30071 / 770-449-4687; FAX: 770-242-8546 info@cva.com www.cva.com

Cylinder & Slide, Inc., William R. Laughridge, 245 E. 4th St., Fremont, NE 68025 / 402-721-4277; FAX: 402-721-0263 bill@cylinder-slide.com www.cylinder-slide.com

CZ USA, P.O. Box 171073, Kansas City, KS 66117 / 913-321-1811; FAX: 913-321-4901

D

D&D Gunsmiths, Ltd., 363 E. Elmwood, Troy, MI 48083 / 248-583-1512; FAX: 248-583-1524

D&G Precision Duplicators (See Greenwood Precision)

D&L Industries (See D.J. Marketing)

D&L Sports, P.O. Box 651, Gillette, WY 82717 / 307-686-4008

D.C. Engineering, Inc., 17195 Silver Parkway, Ste. 135, Fenton, MI 48430 / 248-382-1210 guns@rifletech.com www.rifletech.com

D.C.C. Enterprises, 259 Wynburn Ave., Athens, GA 30601

D.J. Marketing, 10602 Horton Ave., Downey, CA 90241 / 310-806-0891; FAX: 310-806-6231

D.L. Unmussig Bullets, 7862 Brentford Dr., Richmond, VA 23225 / 804-320-1165; FAX: 804-320-4587

Daisy Outdoor Products, P.O. Box 220, Rogers, AR 72757 / 479-636-1200; FAX: 479-636-0573 www.daisy.com

Dakota (See U.S. Importer-EMF Co., Inc.)

Dakota Arms, Inc., 130 Industry Road, Sturgis, SD 57785 / 605-347-4686; FAX: 605-347-4459 info@dakotaarms.com www.dakotaarms.com

Dakota Corp., 77 Wales St., P.O. Box 543, Rutland, VT 05701 / 802-775-6062 or 800-451-4167; FAX: 802-773-3919

Daly, Charles/KBI, P.O. Box 6625, Harrisburg, PA 17112 / 866-DALY GUN

Da-Mar Gunsmith's, Inc., 102 1st St., Solvay, NY 13209

damascususa@inteliport.com, 149 Deans Farm Rd., Tyner, NC 27980 / 252-221-2010 damascususa@inteliport.com www.damascususa.com

Dan Wesson Firearms, 5169 Rt. 12 South, Norwich, NY 13815 / 607-336-1174; FAX: 607-336-2730 dwservice@cz-usa.com dz-usa.com

Dangler, Homer. See: DANGLER'S CUSTOM FLINT RIFLES

Dangler's Custom Flint Rifles, Homer L. Dangler, 2870 Lee Marie Dr., Adrian, MI 49221 / 517-266-1997 homerdangler@yahoo.com

Danner Shoe Mfg. Co., 12722 N.E. Airport Way, Portland, OR 97230 / 503-251-1100 or 800-345-0430; FAX: 503-251-1119

Dan's Whetstone Co., Inc., 418 Hilltop Rd., Pearcy, AR 71964 / 501-767-1616; FAX: 501-767-9598 questions@danswhetstone.com www.danswhetstone.com

Danuser Machine Co., 550 E. Third St., P.O. Box 368, Fulton, MO 65251 / 573-642-2246; FAX: 573-642-2240 sales@danuser.com www.danuser.com

Dara-Nes, Inc. (See Nesci Enterprises, Inc.)

D'Arcy Echols & Co., P.O. Box 421, Millville, UT 84326 / 435-755-6842

Darlington Gun Works, Inc., P.O. Box 698, 516 S. 52 Bypass, Darlington, SC 29532 / 803-393-3931

Darwin Hensley Gunmaker, P.O. Box 329, Brightwood, OR 97011 / 503-622-5411

Data Tech Software Systems, 19312 East Eldorado Drive, Aurora, CO 80013

Dave Norin Schrank's Smoke & Gun, 2010 Washington St., Waukegan, IL 60085 / 708-662-4034

Dave's Gun Shop, P.O. Box 2824, Casper, WY 82602-2824 / 307-754-9724

David Clark Co., Inc., P.O. Box 15054, Worcester, MA 01615 / 508-756-6216; FAX: 508-753-5827 sales@davidclark.com www.davidclark.com

David Condon, Inc., 109 E. Washington St., Middleburg, VA 22117 / 703-687-5642

David Miller Co., 3131 E. Greenlee Rd., Tucson, AZ 85716 / 520-326-3117

David R. Chicoine, PO Box 635, Gastonia, NC 28053 / 704-853-0265 bnpress@quik.com www.oldwestgunsmith.com

David W. Schwartz Custom Guns, 2505 Waller St., Eau Claire, WI 54703 / 715-832-1735

Davide Pedersoli and Co., Via Artigiani 57, Gardone VT, Brescia 25063, ITALY / 030-8915000; FAX: 030-8911019 info@davidepedersoli.com www.davide_pedersoli.com

Davis, Don, 1619 Heights, Katy, TX 77493 / 713-391-3090

Davis Industries (See Cobra Enterprises, Inc.)

Davis Products, Mike, 643 Loop Dr., Moses Lake, WA 98837 / 509-765-6178 or 509-766-7281

Daystate Ltd., Birch House Lanee, Cotes Heath Staffs, ST15.022, ENGLAND / 01782-791755; FAX: 01782-791617

Dayton Traister, 4778 N. Monkey Hill Rd., P.O. Box 593, Oak Harbor, WA 98277 / 360-679-4657; FAX: 360-675-1114

D-Boone Ent., Inc., 5900 Colwyn Dr., Harrisburg, PA 17109

Dead Eye's Sport Center, 76 Baer Rd., Shickshinny, PA 18655 / 570-256-7432 deadeyeprizz@aol.com

Deepeeka Exports Pvt. Ltd., D-78, Saket, Meerut-250-006, INDIA / 011-91-121-640363 or ; FAX: 011-91-121-640988 deepeeka@poboxes.com www.deepeeka.com

Defense Training International, Inc., 749 S. Lemay, Ste. A3-337, Ft. Collins, CO 80524 / 303-482-2520; FAX: 303-482-0548 www.defense_training.com

deHaas Barrels, 20049 W. State Hwy. Z, Ridgeway, MO 64481 / 660-872-6308 dehaas@grm.net

Del Rey Products, P.O. Box 5134, Playa Del Rey, CA 90296-5134 / 213-823-0494

Delhi Gun House, 1374 Kashmere Gate, New Delhi 110 006, INDIA / 2940974 or 394-0974; FAX: 2917344 dgh@vsnl.com www.dgh@vsnl.com

Delorge, Ed, 6734 W. Main, Houma, LA 70360 / 985-223-0206 delorge@triparish.net www.eddelorge.com

Del-Sports, Inc., Dave Budin, P.O. Box 685, 817 Main St., Margaretville, NY 12455 / 845-586-4103; FAX: 845-586-4105

Delta Arms Ltd., P.O. Box 1000, Delta, VT 84624-1000

Delta Enterprises, 284 Hagemann Drive, Livermore, CA 94550

Dem-Bart Checkering Tools, Inc., 1825 Bickford Ave., Snohomish, WA 98290 / 360-568-7356 walt@dembartco.com www.dembartco.com

Denver Instrument Co., 6542 Fig St., Arvada, CO 80004 / 800-321-1135 or 303-431-7255; FAX: 303-423-4831

DeSantis Holster & Leather Goods, Inc., 431 Bayview Ave., Amityville, NY 11701 / 631-841-6300; FAX: 631-841-6320 www.desantisholster.com

Desert Mountain Mfg., P.O. Box 130184, Coram, MT 59913 / 800-477-0762 or 406-387-5361; FAX: 406-387-5361

Detonics USA, 53 Perimeter Center East #200, Atlanta, GA 30346 / 866-759-1169

DGR Custom Rifles, 4191 37th Ave. SE, Tappen, ND 58487 / 701-327-8135

MANUFACTURER'S DIRECTORY

DGS, Inc., Dale A. Storey, 1117 E. 12th, Casper, WY 82601 / 307-237-2414; FAX: 307-237-2414 dalest@trib.com www.dgsrifle.com

DHB Products, 336 River View Dr., Verona, VA 24482-2547 / 703-836-2648

Diamond Machining Technology Inc. (See DMT)

Diamond Mfg. Co., P.O. Box 174, Wyoming, PA 18644 / 800-233-9601

Dibble, Derek A., 555 John Downey Dr., New Britain, CT 06051 / 203-224-2630

Dietz Gun Shop & Range, Inc., 421 Range Rd., New Braunfels, TX 78132 / 830-885-4662

Dilliott Gunsmithing, Inc., 657 Scarlett Rd., Dandridge, TN 37725 / 865-397-9204 gunsmithd@aol.com dilliottgunsmithing.com

Dillon Precision Products, Inc., 8009 East Dillon's Way, Scottsdale, AZ 85260 / 480-948-8009 or 800-762-3845; FAX: 480-998-2786 sales@dillonprecision.com www.dillonprecision.com

Dina Arms Corporation, P.O. Box 46, Royersford, PA 19468 / 610-287-0266; FAX: 610-287-0266 dinaarms@erols.com www.users.erds.com/dinarms

Dixie Gun Works, P.O. Box 130, Union City, TN 38281 / 731-885-0700; FAX: 731-885-0440 info@dixiegunworks.com www.dixiegunworks.com

Dixon Muzzleloading Shop, Inc., 9952 Kunkels Mill Rd., Kempton, PA 19529 / 610-756-6271 dixonmuzzleloading.com

DJ Illinois River Valley Calls, Inc., P.O. Box 370, S. Pekin, IL 61564-0370 / 866-352-2557; FAX: 309-348-3987 djcalls@grics.net www.djcalls.com

DKT, Inc., 14623 Vera Dr., Union, MI 49130-9744 / 800-741-7083 orders; FAX: 616-641-2015

DLO Mfg., 10807 SE Foster Ave., Arcadia, FL 33821-7304

DMT-Diamond Machining Technology, Inc., 85 Hayes Memorial Dr., Marlborough, MA 01752 FAX: 508-485-3924

Dohring Bullets, 100 W. 8 Mile Rd., Ferndale, MI 48220

Dolbare, Elizabeth, P.O. Box 502, Dubois, WY 82513-0502 / 307-450-7500 edolbare@hotmail.com www.scrimshaw-engraving.com

Domino, P.O. Box 108, 20019 Settimo Milanese, Milano, ITALY / 1-39-2-33512040; FAX: 1-39-2-33511587

Don Hume Leathergoods, Don Hume, 500 26th Ave. NW, Miami, OK 74354 / 800-331-2686; FAX: 918-542-4340 info@donhume.com www.donhume.com

Don Klein Custom Guns, 433 Murray Park Dr., Ripon, WI 54971 / 920-748-2931 daklein@charter.net www.donkleincustomguns.com

Donnelly, C. P., 405 Kubli Rd., Grants Pass, OR 97527 / 541-846-6604

Doskocil Mfg. Co., Inc., P.O. Box 1246, 4209 Barnett, Arlington, TX 76017 / 817-467-5116; FAX: 817-472-9810

Douglas Barrels, Inc., 5504 Big Tyler Rd., Charleston, WV 25313-1398 / 304-776-1341; FAX: 304-776-8560 www.benchrest.com/douglas

Downsizer Corp., P.O. Box 710316, Santee, CA 92072-0316 / 619-448-5510 www.downsizer.com

DPMS (Defense Procurement Manufacturing Services, Inc.), 13983 Industry Ave., Becker, MN 55308 / 800-578-DPMS or 763-261-5600; FAX: 763-261-5599

Dr. O's Products Ltd., 1177 US Route SW, Selkirk, NY 12158

Dremel Mfg. Co., 4915-21st St., Racine, WI 53406

Dri-Slide, Inc., 411 N. Darling, Fremont, MI 49412 / 616-924-3950

Dropkick, 1460 Washington Blvd., Williamsport, PA 17701 / 717-326-6561; FAX: 717-326-4950

DS Arms, Inc., P.O. Box 370, 27 West 990 Industrial Ave., Barrington, IL 60010 / 847-277-7258; FAX: 847-277-7259 www.dsarms.com

DTM International, Inc., 40 Joslyn Rd., P.O. Box 5, Lake Orion, MI 48362 / 313-693-6670

Duane A. Hobbie Gunsmithing, 2412 Pattie Ave., Wichita, KS 67216 / 316-264-8266

Duane's Gun Repair (See DGR Custom Rifles)

Dubber, Michael W., P.O. Box 312, Evansville, IN 47702 / 812-424-9000; FAX: 812-424-6551

Duffy, Charles E. (See Guns Antique & Modern DBA), 224 Williams Ln., P.O. Box 2, West Hurley, NY 12491 / 845-679-2997 ceo1923@prodigy.net

Du-Lite Corp., 171 River Rd., Middletown, CT 06457 / 203-347-2505; FAX: 203-347-9404

Dumoulin, Ernest, Rue Florent Boclinville 8-10, 13-4041, Votten, BELGIUM / 41 27 78 92

Duncan's Gun Works, Inc., 1619 Grand Ave., San Marcos, CA 92078 / 760-727-0515; FAX: 760-591-9245

DunLyon R&D, Inc., 52151 E. U.S. Hwy. 60, Miami, AZ 85539 / 928-473-9027

Duofold, Inc., RD 3 Rt. 309, Valley Square Mall, Tamaqua, PA 18252 / 717-386-2666; FAX: 717-386-3652

Dybala Gun Shop, P.O. Box 1024, FM 3156, Bay City, TX 77414 / 409-245-0866

Dykstra, Doug, 411 N. Darling, Fremont, MI 49412 / 616-924-3950

Dynalite Products, Inc., 215 S. Washington St., Greenfield, OH 45123 / 513-981-2124

Dynamit Nobel-RWS, Inc., 6007 S. 29th St., Fort Smith, AR 72908

E

E&L Mfg., Inc., 4177 Riddle Bypass Rd., Riddle, OR 97469 / 541-874-2137; FAX: 541-874-3107

E. Arthur Brown Co. Inc., 4353 Hwy. 27 E., Alexandria, MN 56308 / 320-762-8847; FAX: 320-763-4310 www.eabco.com

E.A.A. Corp., P.O. Box 1299, Sharpes, FL 32959 / 407-639-4842 or 800-536-4442; FAX: 407-639-7006

Eagan, Donald. See: EAGAN GUNSMITHS

Eagan Gunsmiths, Donald V. Eagan, P.O. Box 196, Benton, PA 17814 / 570-925-6134

Eagle Arms, Inc. (See ArmaLite, Inc.)

Eagle Grips, Eagle Business Center, 460 Randy Rd., Carol Stream, IL 60188 / 800-323-6144 or 708-260-0400; FAX: 708-260-0486

Eagle Imports, Inc., 1750 Brielle Ave., Unit B1, Wanamassa, NJ 07712 / 732-493-0333; FAX: 732-493-0301 gsodini@aol.com www.bersafirearmsusa.com

E-A-R, Inc., Div. of Cabot Safety Corp., 5457 W. 79th St., Indianapolis, IN 46268 / 800-327-3431; FAX: 800-488-8007

EAW (See U.S. Importer-New England Custom Gun Serv

Ed Brown Products, Inc., P.O. Box 492, Perry, MO 63462 / 573-565-3261; FAX: 573-565-2791 edbrown@edbrown.com www.edbrown.com

Ed Brown Products, Inc., 43825 Muldrow Trl., P.O. Box 492, Perry, MO 63462 / 573-565-3261; FAX: 573-565-2791 edbrown@edbrown.com www.edbrown.com

Edenpine, Inc. c/o Six Enterprises, Inc., 320 D Turtle Creek Ct., San Jose, CA 95125 / 408-999-0201; FAX: 408-999-0216

EdgeCraft Corp., S. Weiner, 825 Southwood Rd., Avondale, PA 19311 / 610-268-0500 or 800-342-3255; FAX: 610-268-3545 www.edgecraft.com

Edmisten Co., P.O. Box 1293, Boone, NC 28607

Edmund Scientific Co., 101 E. Gloucester Pike, Barrington, NJ 08033 / 609-543-6250

Ed's Gun House, Ed Kukowski, P.O. Box 62, Minnesota City, MN 55959 / 507-689-2925

Effebi SNC-Dr. Franco Beretta, via Rossa, 4, 25062, ITALY / 030-2751955; FAX: 030-2180414

Eggleston, Jere D., 400 Saluda Ave., Columbia, SC 29205 / 803-799-3402

Eichelberger Bullets, Wm., 158 Crossfield Rd., King Of Prussia, PA 19406

El Paso Saddlery Co., P.O. Box 27194, El Paso, TX 79926 / 915-544-2233; FAX: 915-544-2535 info@epsaddlery.com www.epsaddlery.com

Electro Prismatic Collimators, Inc., 1441 Manatt St., Lincoln, NE 68521

Electronic Shooters Protection, Inc., 15290 Gadsden Ct., Brighton, CO 80603 / 800-797-7791; FAX: 303-659-8668 esp@usa.net espamerica.com

Eley Ltd., Selco Way Minworth Industrial Estate, Minworth Sutton Coldfield, West Midlands, B76 1BA ENGLAND / 44 0 121-313-4567; FAX: 44 0 121-313-4568 www.eley.co.uk

Ellett Bros., 267 Columbia Ave., P.O. Box 128, Chapin, SC 29036 / 803-345-3751 or 800-845-3711; FAX: 803-345-1820 www.ellettbrothers.com

Ellicott Arms, Inc. / Woods Pistolsmithing, 8390 Sunset Dr., Ellicott City, MD 21043 / 410-465-7979

EMAP USA, 6420 Wilshire Blvd., Los Angeles, CA 90048 / 213-782-2000; FAX: 213-782-2867

Emerging Technologies, Inc. (See Laseraim Technologies, Inc.)

EMF Co. Inc., 1900 E. Warner Ave., Suite 1-D, Santa Ana, CA 92705 / 949-261-6611; FAX: 949-756-0133

Empire Cutlery Corp., 12 Kruger Ct., Clifton, NJ 07013 / 201-472-5155; FAX: 201-779-0759

Empire Rifles, P.O. Box 406, Meriden, NH 03770 info@empirerifles.com www.empirerifles.com

English, Inc., A.G., 708 S. 12th St., Broken Arrow, OK 74012 / 918-251-3399 info@agenglish.com www.agenglish.com

Engraving Artistry, 36 Alto Rd., Burlington, CT 06013 / 860-673-6837

Enguix Import-Export, Alpujarras 58, Alzira, Valencia, SPAIN / (96) 241 43 95; FAX: (96) 241 43 95

Enhanced Presentations, Inc., 3504 Iris St., Wilmington, NC 28409 / 910-799-1622; FAX: 910-799-5004

Ensign-Bickford Co., The, 660 Hopmeadow St., Simsbury, CT 06070

Entreprise Arms, Inc., 5321 Irwindale Ave., Irwindale, CA 91706-2025 / 626-962-8712; FAX: 626-962-4692 www.entreprise.com

EPC, 1441 Manatt St., Lincoln, NE 68521 / 402-476-3946

Erhardt, Dennis, 4508 N. Montana Ave., Helena, MT 59602 / 406-442-4533

Essex Arms, P.O. Box 363, Island Pond, VT 05846 / 802-723-6203; FAX: 802-723-6203

Estate Cartridge, Inc., 900 Bob Ehlen Dr., Anoka, MN 55303-7502 / 409-856-7277; FAX: 409-856-5486

Euber Bullets, No. Orwell Rd., Orwell, VT 05760 / 802-948-2621

Euroarms of America, Inc., P.O. Box 3277, Winchester, VA 22604 / 540-662-1863; FAX: 540-662-4464 mail@euroarms.net www.euroarms.net

Euro-Imports, George Tripes, 412 Slayden St., Yoakum, TX 77995 / 361-293-9353; FAX: 361-293-9353 mrbrno@yahoo.com

European American Armory Corp. (See E.A.A. Corp.)

Eversull Co., Inc., 1 Tracemont, Boyce, LA 71409 / 318-793-8728; FAX: 318-793-5483 bestguns@aol.com

Evolution Gun Works, Inc., 48 Belmont Ave., Quakertown, PA 18951-1347 www.egw-guns.com

Excalibur Electro Optics, Inc., P.O. Box 400, Fogelsville, PA 18051-0400 / 610-391-9105; FAX: 610-391-9220

Excalibur Publications, P.O. Box 89667, Tucson, AZ 85752 / 520-575-9057 excalibureditor@earthlink.net

Excel Industries, Inc., 4510 Carter Ct., Chino, CA 91710 / 909-627-2404; FAX: 909-627-7817 www.excelarms.com or accu-tekfirearms.com

Executive Protection Institute, P.O. Box 802, Berryville, VA 22611 / 540-554-2540; FAX: 540-554-2558 ruk@crosslink.net www.personalprotecion.com

Eze-Lap Diamond Prods., P.O. Box 2229, 15164 W. State St., Westminster, CA 92683 / 714-847-1555; FAX: 714-897-0280

F

F.A.I.R., S.R.L., Via Gitti, 41, 25060 Marcheno (BS), 25060 Marcheno Bresc, ITALY / 030 861162-8610344; FAX: 030 8610179 info@fair.it www.fair.it

F+W Publications, Inc., 700 E. State St., Iola, WI 54990 / 715-445-2214; FAX: 715-445-4087

Fabarm S.p.A., Via Averolda 31, 25039 Travagliato, Brescia, ITALY / 030-6863629; FAX: 030-6863684 info@fabarm.com www.fabarm.com

Fagan Arms, 22952 15 Mile Rd., Clinton Township, MI 48035 / 810-465-4637; FAX: 810-792-6996

Faith Associates, P.O. Box 549, Flat Rock, NC 28731-0549 FAX: 828-697-6827

Falcon Industries, Inc., P.O. Box 1690, Edgewood, NM 87015 / 505-281-3783; FAX: 505-281-3991 shines@ergogrips.net www.ergogrips.net

Farm Form Decoys, Inc., 1602 Biovu, P.O. Box 748, Galveston, TX 77553 / 409-744-0762 or 409-765-6361; FAX: 409-765-8513

Farr Studio, Inc., 17149 Bournbrook Ln., Jeffersonton, VA 22724-1796 / 615-638-8825

Farrar Tool Co., Inc., 11855 Cog Hill Dr., Whittier, CA 90601-1902 / 310-863-4367; FAX: 310-863-5123

Faulhaber Wildlocker, Dipl.-Ing. Norbert Wittasek, Seilergasse 2, A-1010 Wien, AUSTRIA / 43-1-5137001; FAX: 43-1-5137001 faulhaber1@utanet.at

Faulk's Game Call Co., Inc., 616 18th St., Lake Charles, LA 70601 / 337-436-9726; FAX: 337-494-7205 www.faulkcalls.com

Faust Inc., T. G., 544 Minor St., Reading, PA 19602 / 610-375-8549; FAX: 610-375-4488

Fautheree, Andy, P.O. Box 4607, Pagosa Springs, CO 81157 / 970-731-5003; FAX: 970-731-5009

Feather, Flex Decoys, 4500 Doniphan Dr., Neosho, MO 64850 / 318-746-8596; FAX: 318-742-4815

Federal Cartridge Co., 900 Ehlen Dr., Anoka, MN 55303 / 612-323-2300; FAX: 612-323-2506

MANUFACTURER'S DIRECTORY

Federal Champion Target Co., 232 Industrial Pkwy., Richmond, IN 47374 / 800-441-4971; FAX: 317-966-7747

Federated-Fry (See Fry Metals)

FEG, Budapest, Soroksariut 158, H-1095, HUNGARY

Feinwerkbau Westinger & Altenburger, Neckarstrasse 43, 78727, Oberndorf a. N., GERMANY / 07423-814-0; FAX: 07423-814-200 info@feinwerkbau.de www.feinwerkbau.de

Ferguson, Bill, P.O. Box 1238, Sierra Vista, AZ 85636 / 520-458-5321; FAX: 520-458-9125

Ferguson, Bill. See: BULLET METALS

FERLIB, Via Parte 33 Marcheno/BS, Marcheno/BS, ITALY / 00390308610191; FAX: 00390308966882 info@ferlib.com www.ferlib.com

Ferris Firearms, 7110 F.M. 1863, Bulverde, TX 78163 / 210-980-4424

Fieldsport Ltd., Bryan Bilinski, 3313 W. South Airport Rd., Traverse City, MI 49684 / 616-933-0767

Fiocchi Munizioni S.A. (See U.S. Importer-Fiocch

Fiocchi of America, Inc., 5030 Fremont Rd., Ozark, MO 65721 / 417-725-4118 or 800-721-2666; FAX: 417-725-1039

Firearm Brokers, PO Box 91787, Louisville, KY 40291 firearmbrokers@aol.com www.firearmbrokers.com

Firearms Co. Ltd. / Alpine (See U.S. Importer-Mandall

Firearms Engraver's Guild of America, 3011 E. Pine Dr., Flagstaff, AZ 86004 / 928-527-8427 fegainfo@fega.com

Fisher, Jerry A., 631 Crane Mt. Rd., Big Fork, MT 59911 / 406-837-2722

Fisher Custom Firearms, 2199 S. Kittredge Way, Aurora, CO 80013 / 303-755-3710

Fitzgerald, Jack. See: CLENZOIL WORLDWIDE CORP.

Flambeau, Inc., 15981 Valplast Rd., Middlefield, OH 44062 / 216-632-1631; FAX: 216-632-1581 www.flambeau.com

Flayderman & Co., Inc., P.O. Box 2446, Fort Lauderdale, FL 33303 / 954-761-8855 www.flayderman.com

Fleming Firearms, 7720 E. 126th St. N., Collinsville, OK 74021-7016 / 918-665-3624

Fletcher-Bidwell, LLC, 305 E. Terhune St., Viroqua, WI 54665-1631 / 866-637-1860 fbguns@netscape.net

Flintlocks, Etc., 160 Rossiter Rd., P.O. Box 181, Richmond, MA 01254 / 413-698-3822; FAX: 413-698-3866 flintetc@berkshire.rr.com

Flitz International Ltd., 821 Mohr Ave., Waterford, WI 53185 / 414-534-5898; FAX: 414-534-2991

Fluoramics, Inc., 18 Industrial Ave., Mahwah, NJ 07430 / 800-922-0075; FAX: 201-825-7035 pdouglas@fluoramics.com www.tufoil.com

Flynn's Custom Guns, P.O. Box 7461, Alexandria, LA 71306 / 318-455-7130

FN Manufacturing, P.O. Box 24257, Columbia, SC 29224 / 803-736-0522

Folks, Donald E., 205 W. Lincoln St., Pontiac, IL 61764 / 815-844-7901

Foredom Electric Co., Rt. 6, 16 Stony Hill Rd., Bethel, CT 06801 / 203-792-8622

Forgreens Tool & Mfg., Inc., P.O. Box 955, Robert Lee, TX 76945 / 915-453-2800; FAX: 915-453-2460

Forkin Custom Classics, 205 10th Ave. S.W., White Sulphur Spring, MT 59645 / 406-547-2344

Forrest Tool Co., P.O. Box 768, 44380 Gordon Ln., Mendocino, CA 95460 / 707-937-2141; FAX: 717-937-1817

Forster, Kathy (See Custom Checkering)

Forster, Larry L., Box 212, 216 Hwy. 13 E., Gwinner, ND 58040-0212 / 701-678-2475

Forster Products, Inc., 310 E. Lanark Ave., Lanark, IL 61046 / 815-493-6360; FAX: 815-493-2371 info@forsterproducts.com www.forsterproducts.com

Fort Hill Gunstocks, 12807 Fort Hill Rd., Hillsboro, OH 45133 / 513-466-2763

Fort Knox Security Products, 1051 N. Industrial Park Rd., Orem, UT 84057 / 801-224-7233 or 800-821-5216; FAX: 801-226-5493

Forthofer's Gunsmithing & Knifemaking, 5535 U.S. Hwy. 93S, Whitefish, MT 59937-8411 / 406-862-2674

Fortune Products, Inc., 205 Hickory Creek Rd., Marble Falls, TX 78654 / 210-693-6111; FAX: 210-693-6394 randy@accusharp.com

Foster, . See: ACCURACY INTERNATIONAL

Fountain Products, 492 Prospect Ave., West Springfield, MA 01089 / 413-781-4651; FAX: 413-733-8217

Fowler, Bob (See Black Powder Products)

Fox River Mills, Inc., P.O. Box 298, 227 Poplar St., Osage, IA 50461 / 515-732-3798; FAX: 515-732-5128

Fraim, William. See: ACUSPORT CORPORATION

Frank Knives, 1147 SW Bryson St. 1, Dallas, OR 97338 / 503-831-1489; FAX: 541-563-3041

Frank Mittermeier, Inc., P.O. Box 1, Bronx, NY 10465

Franzen International, Inc. (See U.S. Importer-Importer Co.)

Freedom Arms, Inc., P.O. Box 150, Freedom, WY 83120 / 307-883-2468; FAX: 307-883-2005

Fremont Tool Works, 1214 Prairie, Ford, KS 67842 / 316-369-2327

Front Sight Firearms Training Institute, P.O. Box 2619, Aptos, CA 95001 / 800-987-7719; FAX: 408-684-2137

Frontier, 2910 San Bernardo, Laredo, TX 78040 / 956-723-5409; FAX: 956-723-1774

Frontier Arms Co., Inc., 401 W. Rio Santa Cruz, Green Valley, AZ 85614-3932

Frontier Products Co., 2401 Walker Rd., Roswell, NM 88201-8950 / 505-627-0763

Frost Cutlery Co., P.O. Box 22636, Chattanooga, TN 37422 / 615-894-6079; FAX: 615-894-9576

Fry Metals, 4100 6th Ave., Altoona, PA 16602 / 814-946-1611

Fujinon, Inc., 10 High Point Dr., Wayne, NJ 07470 / 201-633-5600; FAX: 201-633-5216

Fullmer, Geo. M., 2499 Mavis St., Oakland, CA 94601 / 510-533-4193

Fulton Armory, 8725 Bollman Place No. 1, Savage, MD 20763 / 301-490-9485; FAX: 301-490-9547 www.fulton-armory.com

Furr Arms, 91 N. 970 West, Orem, UT 84057 / 801-226-3877; FAX: 801-226-3877

G

G&H Decoys, Inc., P.O. Box 1208, Hwy. 75 North, Henryetta, OK 74437 / 918-652-3314; FAX: 918-652-3400

G.C. Bullet Co., Inc., 40 Mokelumne River Dr., Lodi, CA 95240

G.G. & G., 3602 E. 42nd Stravenue, Tucson, AZ 85713 / 520-748-7167; FAX: 520-748-7583 ggg&3@aol.com www.ggg&3.com

G.U., Inc. (See U.S. Importer-New SKB Arms Co.)

G96 Products Co., Inc., 85 5th Ave., Bldg. #6, Paterson, NJ 07544 / 973-684-4050; FAX: 973-684-3848 g96prod@aol

Gage Manufacturing, 20820 W. Kaibab Rd., Buckeye, AZ 85326 / 310-832-3546

Gaillard Barrels, Box 68, St. Brieux, SK S0K 3V0 CANADA / 306-752-3769; FAX: 306-752-5969

Galati International, P.O. Box 10, 616 Burley Ridge Rd., Wesco, MO 65586 / 636-584-0785; FAX: 573-775-4308 support@galatiinternational.com www.galatiinternational.com

Galaxy Imports Ltd., Inc., P.O. Box 3361, Victoria, TX 77903 / 361-573-4867 galaxy06@suddenlink.net

GALCO International Ltd., 2019 W. Quail Ave., Phoenix, AZ 85027 / 623-474-7070; FAX: 623-582-6854 customerservice@usgalco.com www.usgalco.com

Galena Industries AMT, 5463 Diaz St., Irwindale, CA 91706 / 626-856-8883; FAX: 626-856-8878

Gamba Renato Bremec Srl, Via Artigiani 93, 25063 Gardone V.T. BS, ITALY / 30-8910264-5; FAX: 30-8912180 infocomm@renatogamba.it www.renatogamba.it

Game Haven Gunstocks, 13750 Shire Rd., Wolverine, MI 49799 / 616-525-8257

Gamebore Division, Polywad, Inc., P.O. Box 7916, Macon, GA 31209 / 478-477-0669 or 800-998-0669

Gamo (See U.S. Importers-Arms United Corp., Daisy M

Gamo USA, Inc., 3911 SW 47th Ave., Suite 914, Fort Lauderdale, FL 33314 / 954-581-5822; FAX: 954-581-3165 gamousa@gate.net www.gamo.com

Gander Mountain, Inc., 12400 Fox River Rd., Wilmont, WI 53192 / 414-862-6848

GAR, 590 McBride Ave., West Paterson, NJ 07424 / 973-754-1114; FAX: 973-754-1114 garreloading@aol.com www.garreloading.com

Garrett Cartridges, Inc., P.O. Box 178, Chehalis, WA 98532 / 360-736-0702 www.garrettcartridges.com

Garthwaite Pistolsmith, Inc., Jim, 12130 State Route 405, Watsontown, PA 17777 / 570-538-1566 www.garthwaite.com

Gary Goudy Classic Stocks, 1512 S. 5th St., Dayton, WA 99328 / 509-382-2726 goudy@icehouse.net

Gary Reeder Custom Guns, 2601 7th Ave. E., Flagstaff, AZ 86004 / 928-526-3313; FAX: 928-527-0840 gary@reedercustomguns.com www.reedercustomguns.com

Gator Guns & Repair, 7952 Kenai Spur Hwy., Kenai, AK 99611-8311

GDL Enterprises, 409 Le Gardeur, Slidell, LA 70460 / 504-649-0693

Gehmann, Walter (See Huntington Die Specialties)

Genco, P.O. Box 5704, Asheville, NC 28803

Genecco Gun Works, 10512 Lower Sacramento Rd., Stockton, CA 95210 / 209-951-0706; FAX: 209-931-3872

Gene's Custom Guns, P.O. Box 10534, White Bear Lake, MN 55110 / 651-429-5105; FAX: 651-429-7365

Gentex Corp., 5 Tinkham Ave., Derry, NH 03038 / 603-434-0311; FAX: 603-434-3002 sales@derry.gentexcorp.com www.derry.gentexcorp.com

Gentner Bullets, 109 Woodlawn Ave., Upper Darby, PA 19082 / 610-352-9396 dongentner@rcn.com www.gentnerbullets.com

Gentry Custom LLC, 314 N. Hoffman, Belgrade, MT 59714 / 406-388-GUNS gentryshop@earthlink.net www.gentrycustom.com

George & Roy's, P.O. Box 2125, Sisters, OR 97759-2125 / 503-228-5424 or 800-553-3022; FAX: 503-225-9409

George Hoenig, Inc., 4357 Frozen Dog Rd., Emmett, ID 83617 / 208-365-7716; FAX: 208-365-3472 gnhoenig@msn.com

George Ibberson (Sheffield) Ltd., 25-31 Allen St., Sheffield, S3 7AW ENGLAND / 0114-2766123; FAX: 0114-2738465 sales@eggintongroup.co.uk www.eggintongroup.co.uk

Gerber Legendary Blades, 14200 SW 72nd Ave., Portland, OR 97223 / 503-639-6161 or 800-950-6161; FAX: 503-684-7008

Gervais, Mike, 3804 S. Cruise Dr., Salt Lake City, UT 84109 / 801-277-7729

Getz Barrel Company, P.O. Box 88, 426 E. Market St., Beavertown, PA 17813 / 570-658-7263; FAX: 570-658-4110 www.getzbrl.com

Giacomo Sporting USA, 6234 Stokes Lee Center Rd., Lee Center, NY 13363

Gibbs Rifle Co., Inc., 219 Lawn St., Martinsburg, WV 25401 / 304-262-1651; FAX: 304-262-1658 support@gibbsrifle.com www.gibbsrifle.com

Gil Hebard Guns, Inc., 125 Public Square, P.O. Box 3, Knoxville, IL 61448-0003 / 309-289-2700; FAX: 309-289-2233

Gilbert Equipment Co., Inc., 960 Downtowner Rd., Mobile, AL 36609 / 205-344-3322

Gillmann, Edwin, 33 Valley View Dr., Hanover, PA 17331 / 717-632-1662 gillmaned@superpa.net

Gilmore Sports Concepts, Inc., 5949 S. Garnett Rd., Tulsa, OK 74146 / 918-250-3810; FAX: 918-250-3845 info@gilmoresports.com www.gilmoresports.com

Glacier Glove, 4890 Aircenter Circle, Suite 210, Reno, NV 89502 / 702-825-8225; FAX: 702-825-6544

Glaser LLC, P.O. Box 173, Sturgis, SD 57785 / 605-347-4544 or 800-221-3489; FAX: 605-347-5055 email@corbon.com www.safetyslug.com

Glaser Safety Slug, Inc. (see CorBon/Glaser safetyslug.com

Glass, Herb, P.O. Box 25, Bullville, NY 10915 / 914-361-3021

Glimm, Jerome. See: GLIMM'S CUSTOM GUN ENGRAVING

Glimm's Custom Gun Engraving, Jerome C. Glimm, 19 S. Maryland, Conrad, MT 59425 / 406-278-3574 lag@mcn.net www.gunengraver.biz

Glock GmbH, P.O. Box 50, A-2232, Deutsch, Wagram, AUSTRIA

Glock, Inc., P.O. Box 369, Smyrna, GA 30081 / 770-432-1202; FAX: 770-433-8719

Glynn Scobey Duck & Goose Calls, Rt. 3, Box 37, Newbern, TN 38059 / 731-643-6128

GML Products, Inc., 394 Laredo Dr., Birmingham, AL 35226 / 205-979-4867

Goens, Dale W., P.O. Box 224, Cedar Crest, NM 87008 / 505-281-5419

Goergen's Gun Shop, Inc., 17985 538th Ave., Austin, MN 55912 / 507-433-9280; FAX: 507-433-9280 jim_debgoergen@msn.com

GOEX, Inc., P.O. Box 659, Doyline, LA 71023-0659 / 318-382-9300; FAX: 318-382-9303 mfahringer@goexpowder.com www.goexpowder.com

Golden Age Arms Co., 115 E. High St., Ashley, OH 43003 / 614-747-2488

Golden Bear Bullets, 3065 Fairfax Ave., San Jose, CA 95148 / 408-238-9515

Goodling's Gunsmithing, 1950 Stoverstown Rd., Spring Grove, PA 17362 / 717-225-3350

Goodwin, Fred. See: GOODWIN'S GUNS

Goodwin's Guns, Fred Goodwin, 1028 Silver Ridge Rd., Silver Ridge, ME 04776 / 207-365-4451

Gotz Bullets, 11426 Edgemere Ter., Roscoe, IL 61073-8232

Gould & Goodrich Leather, Inc., 709 E. McNeil St., Lillington, NC 27546 / 910-893-2071; FAX: 910-893-4742 info@gouldusa.com www.gouldusa.com

Gournet Artistic Engraving, Geoffroy Gournet, 820 Paxinosa Ave., Easton, PA 18042 / 610-559-0710 ggournet@yahoo. com www.gournetusa.com

Gournet, Geoffroy. See: GOURNET ARTISTIC ENGRAVING

Grace, Charles E., 718 E. 2nd, Trinidad, CO 81082 / 719-846-9435 riflemakerone@yahoo.com

Grace Metal Products, P.O. Box 67, Elk Rapids, MI 49629 / 616-264-8133

Graf & Sons, 4050 S. Clark St., Mexico, MO 65265 / 573-581-2266; FAX: 573-581-2875 customerservice@grafs.com www.grafs.com

Grand Slam Hunting Products, Box 121, 25454 Military Rd., Cascade, MD 21719 / 301-241-4900; FAX: 301-241-4900 rlj6call@aol.com

Granite Mountain Arms, Inc., 3145 W. Hidden Acres Trail, Prescott, AZ 86305 / 520-541-9758; FAX: 520-445-6826

Grant, Howard V., Hiawatha 15, Woodruff, WI 54568 / 715-356-7146

Graphics Direct, P.O. Box 372421, Reseda, CA 91337-2421 / 818-344-9002

Graves Co., 1800 Andrews Ave., Pompano Beach, FL 33069 / 800-327-9103; FAX: 305-960-0301

Grayback Wildcats, Mike Beeks, 5306 Bryant Ave., Klamath Falls, OR 97603 / 541-884-1072; FAX: 541-884-1072 graybackwildcats@aol.com

Great American Gunstock Co., 3420 Industrial Drive, Yuba City, CA 95993 / 800-784-4867; FAX: 530-671-3906 gunstox@ hotmail.com www.gunstocks.com

Green, Arthur S., 485 S. Robertson Blvd., Beverly Hills, CA 90211 / 310-274-1283

Green Head Game Call Co., RR 1, Box 33, Lacon, IL 61540 / 309-246-2155

Green Mountain Rifle Barrel Co., Inc., P.O. Box 2670, 153 W. Main St., Conway, NH 03818 / 603-447-1095; FAX: 603-447-1099 info@gmriflebarrel.com www.gmriflebarrel.com

Greg Gunsmithing Repair, 3732 26th Ave. N., Robbinsdale, MN 55422 / 612-529-8103

Greg's Superior Products, P.O. Box 46219, Seattle, WA 98146

Greider Precision, 431 Santa Marina Ct., Escondido, CA 92029 / 760-480-8892; FAX: 760-480-9800 greider@msn.com

Gre-Tan Rifles, 29742 W.C.R. 50, Kersey, CO 80644 / 970-353-6176; FAX: 970-356-5940 www.gtrtooling.com

Griffin & Howe, Inc., 340 W. Putnam Ave., Greenwich, CT 06830 / 203-618-0270 info@griffinhowe.com www.griffinhowe. com

Griffin & Howe, Inc., 33 Claremont Rd., Bernardsville, NJ 07924 / 908-766-2287; FAX: 908-766-1068 info@griffinhowe.com www.griffinhowe.com

Groenewold, John. See: JG AIRGUNS, LLC

GRS/Glendo Corp., P.O. Box 1153, 900 Overlander St., Emporia, KS 66801 / 620-343-1084 or 800-836-3519; FAX: 620-343-9640 glendo@glendo.com www.glendo.com

Grulla Armes, Apartado 453, Avda Otaloa 12, Eiber, SPAIN

Gruning Precision, Inc., 7101 Jurupa Ave., No. 12, Riverside, CA 92504 / 909-289-4371; FAX: 909-689-7791 gruningprecision@earthlink.net www.gruningprecision.com

GSI, Inc., 7661 Commerce Ln., Trussville, AL 35173 / 205-655-8299

Guarasi, Robert. See: WILCOX INDUSTRIES CORP.

Guardsman Products, 411 N. Darling, Fremont, MI 49412 / 616-924-3950

Gun City, 212 W. Main Ave., Bismarck, ND 58501 / 701-223-2304

Gun Digest (See F+W Publications), 700 E. State St., Iola, WI 54990 / 715-445-2214; FAX: 715-445-4087 www. gundigestmagazine.com

Gun Doc, Inc., 5405 NW 82nd Ave., Miami, FL 33166 / 305-477-2777; FAX: 305-477-2778 www.gundoc.com

Gun Doctor, The, P.O. Box 72817, Roselle, IL 60172 / 708-894-0668

Gun Hunter Books (See Gun Hunter Trading Co.), 5075 Heisig St., Beaumont, TX 77705 / 409-835-3006; FAX: 409-838-2266 gunhuntertrading@hotmail.com

Gun Hunter Trading Co., 5075 Heisig St., Beaumont, TX 77705 / 409-835-3006; FAX: 409-838-2266 gunhuntertrading@ hotmail.com

Gun Leather Limited, 116 Lipscomb, Fort Worth, TX 76104 / 817-334-0225; FAX: 800-247-0609

Gun Room Press, The, 127 Raritan Ave., Highland Park, NJ 08904 / 732-545-4344; FAX: 732-545-6686 gunbooks@ rutgersgunbooks.com www.rutgersgunbooks.com

Gun Room, The, 1121 Burlington, Muncie, IN 47302 / 765-282-9073; FAX: 765-282-5270 bshstleguns@aol.com

Gun Shop, The, 5550 S. 900 East, Salt Lake City, UT 84117 / 801-263-3633

Gun South, Inc. (See GSI, Inc.)

Gun Vault, 7339 E. Acoma Dr., Ste. 7, Scottsdale, AZ 85260 / 602-951-6855

Gun Works, The, 247 S. 2nd St., Springfield, OR 97477 / 541-741-4118; FAX: 541-988-1097 info@thegunworks.com www.thegunworks.com

Gun-Alert, 1010 N. Maclay Ave., San Fernando, CA 91340 / 818-365-0864; FAX: 818-365-1308

Guncraft Books (See Guncraft Sports, Inc.), 10737 Dutchtown Rd., Knoxville, TN 37932 / 865-966-4545; FAX: 865-966-4500 findit@guncraft.com www.guncraft.com

Guncraft Sports, Inc., 10737 Dutchtown Rd., Knoxville, TN 37932 / 865-966-4545; FAX: 865-966-4500 findit@guncraft. com www.usit.net/guncraft

Guncraft Sports, Inc., Marie C. Wiest, 10737 Dutchtown Rd., Knoxville, TN 37932 / 865-966-4545; FAX: 865-966-4500 findit@guncraft.com www.guncraft.com

Guncrafter Industries, 171 Madison 1510, Huntsville, AR 72740 / 479-665-2466 www.guncrafterindustries.com

Gun-Ho Sports Cases, 110 E. 10th St., St. Paul, MN 55101 / 612-224-9491

Gunline Tools, 2950 Saturn St., "O", Brea, CA 92821 / 714-993-5100; FAX: 714-572-4128

Gunnerman Books, P.O. Box 81697, Rochester Hills, MI 48308 / 248-608-2856 gunnermanbks@att.net

Guns Antique & Modern DBA / Charles E. Duffy, 224 Williams Lane, P.O. Box 2, West Hurley, NY 12491 / 845-679-2997 ceo1923@prodigy.net

GUNS Magazine, 12345 World Trade Dr., San Diego, CA 92128-3743 / 619-297-5350; FAX: 619-297-5353

Gunsight, The, 5292 Kentwater Pl., Yorba Linda, CA 92886

Gunsite Training Center, P.O. Box 700, Paulden, AZ 86334 / 520-636-4565; FAX: 520-636-1236

Gunsmithing Ltd., 3 Lacey Place, 2530 Post Rd., Southport, CT 06890 / 203-254-0436; FAX: 203-254-1535

Gunsmithing, Inc., 30 W. Buchanan St., Colorado Springs, CO 80907 / 719-632-3795; FAX: 719-632-3493 www. nealsguns.com

Gurney, F. R., Box 13, Sooke, BC V0S 1N0 CANADA / 604-642-5282; FAX: 604-642-7859

H

H&B Forge Co., Rt. 2, Geisinger Rd., Shiloh, OH 44878 / 419-895-1856

H&P Publishing, 7174 Hoffman Rd., San Angelo, TX 76905 / 915-655-5953

H&R 1871, LLC, 60 Industrial Rowe, Gardner, MA 01440 / 508-632-9393; FAX: 508-632-2300 hr1871@hr1871.com www. hr1871.com

H. Krieghoff Gun Co., Boschstrasse 22, D-89079, Ulm, GERMANY / 731-401820; FAX: 731-4018270

H.K.S. Products, 7841 Founion Dr., Florence, KY 41042 / 606-342-7841 or 800-354-9814; FAX: 606-342-5865

H.P. White Laboratory, Inc., 3114 Scarboro Rd., Street, MD 21154 / 410-838-6550; FAX: 410-838-2802 info@hpwhite. com www.hpwhite.com

Hafner World Wide, Inc., P.O. Box 1987, Lake City, FL 32055 / 904-755-6481; FAX: 904-755-6595 hafner@isgroupe.net

Half Moon Rifle Shop, 490 Halfmoon Rd., Columbia Falls, MT 59912 / 406-892-4409 halfmoonrs@centurytel.net

Hall Plastics, Inc., John, P.O. Box 1526, Alvin, TX 77512 / 713-489-8709

Hallowell & Co., P.O. Box 1445, Livingston, MT 59047 / 406-222-4770; FAX: 406-222-4792 morris@hallowellco.com www.hallowellco.com

Hally Caller, 443 Wells Rd., Doylestown, PA 18901 / 215-345-6354; FAX: 215-345-6354 info@hallycaller.com www. hallycaller.com

Hamilton, Alex B. (See Ten-Ring Precision, Inc.)

Hammans, Charles E., P.O. Box 788, 2022 McCracken, Stuttgart, AR 72160-0788 / 870-673-1388

Hammerli AG, Industrieplaz, a/Rheinpall, CH-8212 Neuhausen, SWITZERLAND / info@hammerli.com www.haemmerli.com

Hammerli Service-Precision Mac, Rudolf Marent, 9711 Tiltree St., Houston, TX 77075 / 713-946-7028 rmarent@webtv.net

Hammerli USA, 19296 Oak Grove Circle, Groveland, CA 95321 FAX: 209-962-5311

Hammond Custom Guns Ltd., 619 S. Pandora, Gilbert, AZ 85234 / 602-892-3437

HandCrafts Unltd. (See Clements' Custom Leathercraft), 1741 Dallas St., Aurora, CO 80010-2018 / 303-364-0403; FAX: 303-739-9824 gryphons@home.com kuntaoslcat.com

Handgun Press, P.O. Box 406, Glenview, IL 60025 / 847-657-6500; FAX: 847-724-8831 handgunpress@comcast.net

Hank's Gun Shop, Box 370, 50 W. 100 South, Monroe, UT 84754 / 435-527-4456 hanksgs@altazip.com

Hanned Line, The, 4463 Madoc Way, San Jose, CA 95130 smith@hanned.com www.hanned.com

Hanned Precision (See The Hanned Line)

Hansen & Co., 244-246 Old Post Rd., Southport, CT 06490 / 203-259-6222; FAX: 203-254-3832

Hanson's Gun Center, Dick, 233 Everett Dr., Colorado Springs, CO 80911

Harford (See U.S. Importer-EMF Co., Inc.)

Harrell's Precision, 5756 Hickory Dr., Salem, VA 24153 / 540-380-2683

Harrington & Richardson (See H&R 1871, Inc.)

Harris Engineering Inc., Dept. GD54, 999 Broadway, Barlow, KY 42024 / 270-334-3633; FAX: 270-334-3000

Harris Enterprises, P.O. Box 105, Bly, OR 97622 / 503-353-2625

Harris Hand Engraving, Paul A., 113 Rusty Ln., Boerne, TX 78006-5746 / 512-391-5121

Harris Publications, 1115 Broadway, New York, NY 10010 / 212-807-7100; FAX: 212-627-4678

Harrison Bullets, 6437 E. Hobart St., Mesa, AZ 85205

Harry Lawson LLC, 3328 N. Richey Blvd., Tucson, AZ 85716 / 520-326-1117; FAX: 520-326-1117

Hart & Son, Inc., Robert W., 401 Montgomery St., Nescopeck, PA 18635 / 717-752-3655; FAX: 717-752-1088

Hart Rifle Barrels, Inc., P.O. Box 182, 1690 Apulia Rd., Lafayette, NY 13084 / 315-677-9841; FAX: 315-677-9610 hartriflebarrels@sbcglobal.net hartbarrels.com

Hartford (See U.S. Importer-EMF Co., Inc.)

Hartmann & Weiss GmbH, Rahlstedter Bahnhofstr. 47, 22143, Hamburg, GERMANY / (40) 677 55 85; FAX: (40) 677 55 92 hartmannundweiss@t-online.de

Harvey, Frank, 218 Nightfall, Terrace, NV 89015 / 702-558-6998

Hastings, P.O. Box 135, Clay Center, KS 67432 / 785-632-3169; FAX: 785-632-6554

Hatfield Gun, 224 N. 4th St., St. Joseph, MO 64501

Hawk Laboratories, Inc. (See Hawk, Inc.), 849 Hawks Bridge Rd., Salem, NJ 08079 / 609-299-2700; FAX: 609-299-2800

Hawk, Inc., 849 Hawks Bridge Rd., Salem, NJ 08079 / 609-299-2700; FAX: 609-299-2800 info@hawkbullets.com www. hawkbullets.com

Hawken Shop, The, P.O. Box 593, Oak Harbor, WA 98277 / 206-679-4657; FAX: 206-675-1114

Hawken Shop, The (See Dayton Traister)

Haydel's Game Calls, Inc., 5018 Hazel Jones Rd., Bossier City, LA 71111 / 318-746-3586; FAX: 318-746-3711 www. haydels.com

Hecht, Hubert J., Waffen-Hecht, P.O. Box 2635, Fair Oaks, CA 95628 / 916-966-1020

Heckler & Koch GmbH, P.O. Box 1329, 78722 Oberndorf, Neckar, GERMANY / 49-7423179-0; FAX: 49-7423179-2406

Heckler & Koch, Inc., 21480 Pacific Blvd., Sterling, VA 20166-8900 / 703-450-1900; FAX: 703-450-8160 www. hecklerkoch-usa.com

Hege Jagd-u. Sporthandels GmbH, P.O. Box 101461, W-7770, Ueberlingen a. Boden, GERMANY

Heidenstrom Bullets, Dalghte 86-3660 Rjukan, 35091818, NORWAY, olau.joh@online.tuo

Heilmann, Stephen, P.O. Box 657, Grass Valley, CA 95945 / 530-272-8758; FAX: 530-274-0285 sheilmann@jps.net www.metalwood.com

Heinie Specialty Products, 301 Oak St., Quincy, IL 62301-2500 / 217-228-9500; FAX: 217-228-9502 rheinie@heinie.com www.heinie.com

Helwan (See U.S. Importer-Interarms)

Henigson & Associates, Steve, P.O. Box 2726, Culver City, CA 90231 / 310-305-8288; FAX: 310-305-1905

Henriksen Tool Co., Inc., 8515 Wagner Creek Rd., Talent, OR 97540 / 541-535-2309; FAX: 541-535-2309

Henry Repeating Arms Co., 110 8th St., Brooklyn, NY 11215 / 718-499-5600; FAX: 718-768-8056 info@henryrepeating. com www.henryrepeating.com

Hensley, Gunmaker, Darwin, P.O. Box 329, Brightwood, OR 97011 / 503-622-5411

Heppler, Keith. See: KEITH'S CUSTOM GUNSTOCKS

Hercules, Inc. (See Alliant Techsystems Smokeless Powder Group)

Heritage Firearms (See Heritage Mfg., Inc.)

MANUFACTURER'S DIRECTORY

Heritage Manufacturing, Inc., 4600 NW 135th St., Opa Locka, FL 33054 / 305-685-5966; FAX: 305-687-6721 infohmi@ heritagemfg.com www.heritagemfg.com

Heritage/VSP Gun Books, P.O. Box 887, McCall, ID 83638 / 208-634-4104; FAX: 208-634-3101 heritage@gunbooks.com www.gunbooks.com

Herrett's Stocks, Inc., P.O. Box 741, Twin Falls, ID 83303 / 208-733-1498

Hesse Arms, Robert Hesse, 1126 70th St. E., Inver Grove Heights, MN 55077-2416 / 651-455-5760; FAX: 612-455-5760

Hesse, Robert. See: HESSE ARMS

Heydenberk, Warren R., 1059 W. Sawmill Rd., Quakertown, PA 18951 / 215-538-2682

Hidalgo, Tony, 12701 SW 9th Pl., Davie, FL 33325 / 954-476-7645

High Bridge Arms, Inc., 3185 Mission St., San Francisco, CA 94110 / 415-282-8358

High North Products, Inc., P.O. Box 2, Antigo, WI 54409 / 715-627-2331; FAX: 715-623-5451

High Performance International, 5734 W. Florist Ave., Milwaukee, WI 53218 / 414-466-9040; FAX: 414-466-7050 mike@hpirifles.com hpirifles.com

High Precision, Bud Welsh, 80 New Road, E. Amherst, NY 14051 / 716-688-6344; FAX: 716-688-0425 welsh5168@aol.com www.high-precision.com

High Standard Mfg. Co./F.I., Inc., 5200 Mitchelldale St., Ste. E17, Houston, TX 77092-7222 / 713-462-4200 or 800-272-7816; FAX: 713-681-5665 info@highstandard.com www.highstandard.com

High Tech Specialties, Inc., P.O. Box 839, 293 E Main St., Rear, Adamstown, PA 19501 / 717-484-0405; FAX: 717-484-0523 bansner@aol.com www.hightech-specialties.com

Highwood Special Products, 1531 E. Highwood, Pontiac, MI 48340

Hill, Loring F., 304 Cedar Rd., Elkins Park, PA 19027

Hill Speed Leather, Ernie, 4507 N 195th Ave., Litchfield Park, AZ 85340 / 602-853-9222; FAX: 602-853-9235

Hinman Outfitters, Bob, 107 N Sanderson Ave., Bartonville, IL 61607-1839 / 309-691-8132

Hi-Performance Ammunition Company, 5231 Greensburg Rd., Apollo, PA 15613 / 304-674-9000; FAX: 304-675-6700 gjrahiperwvo@yahoo.com

HIP-GRIP Barami Corp., P.O. Box 252224, West Bloomfield, MI 48325-2224 / 248-738-0462; FAX: 248-738-2542 hipgripja@aol.com www.hipgrip.com

Hi-Point Firearms/MKS Supply, 8611-A North Dixie Dr., Dayton, OH 45414 / 877-425-4867; FAX: 937-454-0503 www.hi-pointfirearms.com

Hiptmayer, Armurier, RR 112 750, P.O. Box 136, Eastman, PQ J0E 1P0 CANADA / 514-297-2492

Hiptmayer, Heidemarie, RR 112 750, P.O. Box 136, Eastman, PQ J0E 1P0 CANADA / 514-297-2492

Hiptmayer, Klaus, RR 112 750, P.O. Box 136, Eastman, PQ J0E 1P0 CANADA / 514-297-2492

Hirtenberger AG, Leobersdorferstrasse 31, A-2552, Hirtenberg, AUSTRIA / 43(0)2256 81184; FAX: 43(0)2256 81808 www.hirtenberger.ot

HJS Arms, Inc., P.O. Box 3711, Brownsville, TX 78523-3711 / 956-542-2767; FAX: 956-542-2767

Hoag, James W., 8523 Canoga Ave., Suite C, Canoga Park, CA 91304 / 818-998-1510

Hobson Precision Mfg. Co., 210 Big Oak Ln., Brent, AL 35034 / 205-926-4662; FAX: 205-926-3193 cahobbob@dbtech.net

Hodgdon Powder Co., 6231 Robinson, Shawnee Mission, KS 66202 / 913-362-9455; FAX: 913-362-1307

Hodgman, Inc., 1100 Stearns Dr., Sauk Rapids, MN 56379

Hodgson, Richard, 9081 Tahoe Lane, Boulder, CO 80301

Hoehn Sales, Inc., 2045 Kohn Road, Wright City, MO 63390 / 636-745-8144; FAX: 636-745-7868 ron@hoehnsales.com

Hofer Jagdwaffen, P., A9170 Ferlach, Kirchgasse 24, Kirchgasse, AUSTRIA / 43 4227 3683; FAX: 43 4227 368330 peterhofer@hoferwaffen.com www.hoferwaffen.com

Hoffman New Ideas, 821 Northmoor Rd., Lake Forest, IL 60045 / 312-234-4075

Hogue Grips, P.O. Box 1138, Paso Robles, CA 93447 / 800-438-4747 or 805-239-1440; FAX: 805-239-2553

Holland & Holland Ltd., 33 Bruton St., London, ENGLAND / 44-171-499-4411; FAX: 44-171-408-7962

Holland's Shooters Supply, Inc., P.O. Box 69, Powers, OR 97466 / 541-439-5155; FAX: 541-439-2105 bestrifles@aol.com www.hollandguns.com

Hollinger, Jon. See: ASPEN OUTFITTING CO.

Hollywood Engineering, 10642 Arminta St., Sun Valley, CA 91352 / 818-842-8376; FAX: 818-504-4168 cadqueenel1@aol.com

Homak, 350 N. La Salle Dr. Ste. 1100, Chicago, IL 60610-4731 / 312-523-3100; FAX: 312-523-9455

Hoppe's Div. Penguin Industries, Inc., 9200 Cody St., Overland Park, KS 66214 / 800-845-2444

Horizons Unlimited, P.O. Box 426, Warm Springs, GA 31830 / 706-655-3603; FAX: 706-655-3603

Hornady Mfg. Co., P.O. Box 1848, Grand Island, NE 68802 / 800-338-3220 or 308-382-1390; FAX: 308-382-5761

Horseshoe Leather Products, Andy Arratoonian, The Cottage Sharow, Ripon, ENGLAND U.K. / 44-1765-605858 andy@horseshoe.co.uk www.holsters.org

House of Muskets, Inc., The, PO Box 4640, Pagosa Springs, CO 81157 / 970-731-2295

Houtz & Barwick, P.O. Box 435, W. Church St., Elizabeth City, NC 27909 / 800-775-0337 or 919-335-4191; FAX: 919-335-1152

Howa Machinery, Ltd., 1900-1 Sukaguchi Kiyosu, Aichi 452-8601, JAPAN / 81-52-408-1231; FAX: 81-52-401-4999 howa@howa.co.jp http://www.howa.cojpl

Howell Machine, Inc., 815 D St., Lewiston, ID 83501 / 208-743-7418; FAX: 208-746-1703 ammoload@microwavedsl.com www.ammoload.com

H-S Precision, Inc., 1301 Turbine Dr., Rapid City, SD 57701 / 605-341-3006; FAX: 605-342-8964

HT Bullets, 244 Belleville Rd., New Bedford, MA 02745 / 508-999-3338

Hubert J. Hecht Waffen-Hecht, P.O. Box 2635, Fair Oaks, CA 95628 / 916-966-1020

Huebner, Corey O., P.O. Box 564, Frenchtown, MT 59834 / 406-721-7168 bugsboys@hotmail.com

Huey Gun Cases, 820 Indiana St., Lawrence, KS 66044-2645 / 785-842-0062; FAX: 785-842-0062 ketchsailor27@aol.com www.hueycases.com

Hume, Don. See: DON HUME LEATHERGOODS

Hunter Co., Inc., 3300 W. 71st Ave., Westminster, CO 80030 / 303-427-4626; FAX: 303-428-3980 debbiet@huntercompany.com www.huntercompany.com

Hunterjohn, P.O. Box 771457, St. Louis, MO 63177 / 314-531-7250 www.hunterjohn.com

Hunter's Specialties Inc., 6000 Huntington Ct. NE, Cedar Rapids, IA 52402-1268 / 319-395-0321; FAX: 319-395-0326

Hunters Supply, Inc., 1177 Hwy. 96, Regina, NM 87046 / 940-437-2458; FAX: 940-437-2228 hunterssupply@hotmail.com www.hunterssupply.net

Huntington Die Specialties, 601 Oro Dam Blvd., Oroville, CA 95965 / 530-534-1210 or 866-735-6237; FAX: 530-534-1212 buy@huntingtons.com www.huntingtons.com

Hydra-Tone Chemicals, Inc., 7065 Production Coast, Florence, KY 41042 / 859-534-5630; FAX: 859-594-3312 graff-off@hydra-tone.com www.hydra-tone.com

Hydrosorbent Dehumidifiers, P.O. Box 437, Ashley Falls, MA 01222 / 800-448-7903; FAX: 413-229-8743 orders@dehumidify.com www.dehumidify.com

I

I.A.B. (See U.S. Importer-Taylor's & Co., Inc.)

I.D.S.A. Books, 3220 E. Galbraith Rd., Cincinnati, OH 45236 / 513-985-9112; FAX: 513-985-9116 idsabooks@idsabooks.com www.idsabooks.com

I.N.C. Inc. (See Kickeez I.N.C., Inc.)

I.S.W., 106 E. Cairo Dr., Tempe, AZ 85282

IAR Inc., 33171 Camino Capistrano, San Juan Capistrano, CA 92675 / 949-443-3642; FAX: 949-443-3647 sales@iar-arms.com iar-arms.com

Ide, Ken. See: STURGEON VALLEY SPORTERS

IGA (See U.S. Importer-Stoeger Industries)

Image Ind. Inc., 11220 E. Main St., Huntley, IL 60142-7369 / 630-766-2402; FAX: 630-766-7373

Impact Case & Container, Inc., P.O. Box 1129, Rathdrum, ID 83858 / 877-687-2452; FAX: 208-687-0632 bradk@icc-case.com www.icc-case.com

Imperial Magnum Corp., P.O. Box 249, Oroville, WA 98844 / 604-495-3131; FAX: 604-495-2816

Imperial Miniature Armory, 1115 FM 359, Richland, TX 77449 / 800-646-4288; FAX: 832-595-8787 miniguns@houston.rr.com www.1800miniature.com

IMR Powder Co., 1080 Military Turnpike, Suite 2, Plattsburgh, NY 12901 / 518-563-2253; FAX: 518-563-6916

Info-Arm, P.O. Box 1262, Champlain, NY 12919 / 514-955-0355; FAX: 514-955-0357 infoarm@qc.aira.com

Innovative Weaponry Inc., 2513 E. Loop 820 N., Fort Worth, TX 76118 / 817-284-0099 or 800-334-3573

INTEC International, Inc., P.O. Box 5708, Scottsdale, AZ 85261 / 602-483-1708

Inter Ordnance of America LP, 3305 Westwood Industrial Dr., Monroe, NC 28110-5204 / 704-821-8337; FAX: 704-821-8523

Intercontinental Distributors, Ltd., P.O. Box 815, Beulah, ND 58523

International Shooters Service, P.O. Box 185234, Ft. Worth, TX 76181 / 817-595-2090; FAX: 817-595-2090 is_s_@sbcglobal.net www.iss-internationalshootersservice.com

Intrac Arms International, 5005 Chapman Hwy., Knoxville, TN 37920

Ion Industries, Inc., 3508 E Allerton Ave., Cudahy, WI 53110 / 414-486-2007; FAX: 414-486-2017

Iosso Products, 1485 Lively Blvd., Elk Grove Village, IL 60007 / 847-437-8400; FAX: 847-437-8478

Iron Bench, 12619 Bailey Rd., Redding, CA 96003 / 916-241-4623

Ironside International Publishers, Inc., P.O. Box 1050, Lorton, VA 22199 / 703-493-9120; FAX: 703-493-9424

Ironsighter Co., P.O. Box 85070, Westland, MI 48185 / 734-326-8731; FAX: 734-326-3378 www.ironsighter.com

Irwin, Campbell H., 140 Hartland Blvd., East Hartland, CT 06027 / 203-653-3901

Israel Arms Inc., 5625 Star Ln. #B, Houston, TX 77057 / 713-789-0745; FAX: 713-914-9515 www.israelarms.com

Ithaca Classic Doubles, Stephen Lamboy, No. 5 Railroad St., Victor, NY 14564 / 716-924-2710; FAX: 716-924-2737 ithacadoubles.com

Ithaca Guns, LLC, 420 N. Walpole St., Upper Sandusky, OH 43351 / 419-294-4113; FAX: 419-294-9433 service@ithacaguns.com www.ithacaguns-usa.com

Ivanoff, Thomas G. (See Tom's Gun Repair)

J

J J Roberts Firearm Engraver, 7808 Lake Dr., Manassas, VA 20111 / 703-330-0448; FAX: 703-264-8600 james.roberts@angelfire.com www.angelfire.com/va2/engraver

J R Guns, P.O. Box 370, Monticello, NY 12701 / 845-794-2510

J&D Components, 75 East 350 North, Orem, UT 84057-4719 / 801-225-7007 www.jdcomponents.com

J&J Products, Inc., 9240 Whitmore, El Monte, CA 91731 / 818-571-5228; FAX: 800-927-8361

J&J Sales, 1501 21st Ave. S., Great Falls, MT 59405 / 406-727-9789 mtshootingbench@yahoo.com www.j&jsales.us

J&L Superior Bullets (See Huntington Die Specialties)

J&M Precision Machining, Jeff Amato, RR 1 Box 91, Bloomfield, IN 47424

J&R Engineering, P.O. Box 77, 200 Lyons Hill Rd., Athol, MA 01331 / 508-249-9241

J&R Enterprises, 4550 Scotts Valley Rd., Lakeport, CA 95453

J&S Heat Treat, 803 S. 16th St., Blue Springs, MO 64015 / 816-229-2149; FAX: 816-228-1135

J. Dewey Mfg. Co., Inc., P.O. Box 2014, Southbury, CT 06488 / 203-264-3064; FAX: 203-262-6907 deweyrods@att.net www.deweyrods.com

J. Korzinek Riflesmith, RD 2, Box 73D, Canton, PA 17724 / 717-673-8512

J.A. Blades, Inc. (See Christopher Firearms Co.)

J.A. Henckels Zwillingswerk Inc., 9 Skyline Dr., Hawthorne, NY 10532 / 914-592-7370

J.G. Anschutz GmbH & Co. KG, Daimlerstr. 12, D-89079 Ulm, Ulm, GERMANY / 49 731 40120; FAX: 49 731 4012700 JGA-info@anschuetz-sport.com www.anschuetz-sport.com

J.G. Dapkus Co., Inc., Commerce Circle, P.O. Box 293, Durham, CT 06422 www.explodingtargets.com

J.J. Roberts / Engraver, 7808 Lake Dr., Manassas, VA 20111 / 703-330-0448 jjrengraver@aol.com www.angelfire.com/va2/engraver

J.R. Williams Bullet Co., 2008 Tucker Rd., Perry, GA 31069 / 912-987-0274

J.W. Morrison Custom Rifles, 4015 W. Sharon, Phoenix, AZ 85029 / 602-978-3754

J.W. Wasmundt-Gunsmith, Jim Wasmundt, P.O. Box 130, 140 Alder St., Powers, OR 97466-0130 / 541-439-2044 jwasm@juno.com

MANUFACTURER'S DIRECTORY

Jack A. Rosenberg & Sons, 12229 Cox Ln., Dallas, TX 75234 / 214-241-6302

Jack Dever Co., 8520 NW 90th St., Oklahoma City, OK 73132 / 405-721-6393 jbdever1@home.com

Jack First, Inc., 1201 Turbine Dr., Rapid City, SD 57703 / 605-343-9544; FAX: 605-343-9420

Jack Jonas Appraisals & Taki, 13952 E. Marina Dr., #604, Aurora, CO 80014

Jackalope Gun Shop, 1048 S. 5th St., Douglas, WY 82633 / 307-358-3441 wildcatoutfitters@msn.com www.jackalopegunshop.com

Jaffin, Harry. See: BRIDGEMAN PRODUCTS

Jagdwaffen, Peter. See: BUCHSENMACHERMEISTER

James Calhoon Mfg., 4343 U.S. Highway 87, Havre, MT 59501 / 406-395-4079 www.jamescalhoon.com

James Churchill Glove Co., PO Box 298, Centralia, WA 98531 / 360-736-2816; FAX: 360-330-0151 churchillglove@localaccess.com

James Wayne Firearms for Collectors and Investors, 2608 N. Laurent, Victoria, TX 77901 / 361-578-1258; FAX: 361-578-3559

Jamison International, Marc Jamison, 3551 Mayer Ave., Sturgis, SD 57785 / 605-347-5090; FAX: 605-347-4704 jbell2@masttechnology.com

Jamison, Marc. See: JAMISON INTERNATIONAL

Jamison's Forge Works, 4527 Rd. 6.5 NE, Moses Lake, WA 98837 / 509-762-2659

Jantz Supply, Inc., 309 West Main Dept HD, Davis, OK 73030-0584 / 580-369-2316; FAX: 580-369-3082 jantz@jantzusa.com www.knifemaking.com

Jarrett Rifles, Inc., 383 Brown Rd., Jackson, SC 29831 / 803-471-3616 www.jarrettrifles.com

Jarvis, Inc., 1123 Cherry Orchard Lane, Hamilton, MT 59840 / 406-961-4392

Javelina Lube Products, P.O. Box 337, San Bernardino, CA 92402 / 909-350-9556; FAX: 909-429-1211

Jay McCament Custom Gunmaker, Jay McCament, 1730-134th St. Ct. S., Tacoma, WA 98444 / 253-531-8832

JB Custom, P.O. Box 6912, Leawood, KS 66206 / 913-381-2329

Jeff Flannery Engraving, 11034 Riddles Run Rd., Union, KY 41091 / 859-384-3127; FAX: 859-384-2222 engraving@fuse.net www.flannerygunengraving.com

Jeff's Outfitters, 63F Sena Fawn, Cape Girardeau, MO 63701 / 573-651-3200; FAX: 573-651-3207 info@jeffsoutfitters.com www.jeffsoutfitters.com

Jena Eur, P.O. Box 319, Dunmore, PA 18512

Jenco Sales, Inc., P.O. Box 1000, Manchaca, TX 78652 / 800-531-5301; FAX: 800-266-2373 jencosales@sbcglobal.net

Jenkins Recoil Pads, 5438 E. Frontage Ln., Olney, IL 62450 / 618-395-3416

Jensen Bullets, RR 1 Box 187, Arco, ID 83213 / 208-785-5590

Jensen's Arizona Sportsman, 1325 W. Silverlake Rd. Unit 144, Tucson, AZ 85713 / 602-325-3346; FAX: 602-322-5704

Jensen's Firearms Academy, 3975 E. Dripping Springs Rd., Winkelman, AZ 85292 / 602-293-8516

Jericho Tool & Die Co., Inc., 121 W. Keech Rd., Bainbridge, NY 13733-3248 / 607-563-8222; FAX: 607-563-8560 jerichotool.com www.jerichotool.com

Jerry Phillips Optics, P.O. Box L632, Langhorne, PA 19047 / 215-757-5037; FAX: 215-757-7097

Jesse W. Smith Saddlery, 0499 County Road J, Pritchett, CO 81064 / 509-325-0622

Jester Bullets, Rt. 1 Box 27, Orienta, OK 73737

Jewell Triggers, 3620 Hwy. 123, San Marcos, TX 78666 / 512-353-2999; FAX: 512-392-0543

JG Airguns, LLC, John Groenewold, P.O. Box 830, Mundelein, IL 60060 / 847-566-2365; FAX: 847-566-4065 john@jgairguns.biz www.jgairguns.biz

JGS Precision Tool Mfg., LLC, 60819 Selander Rd., Coos Bay, OR 97420 / 541-267-4331; FAX: 541-267-5996 jgstools@harborside.com www.jgstools.com

Jim Blair Engraving, P.O. Box 64, Glenrock, WY 82637 / 307-436-8115 jblairengrav@msn.com

Jim Noble Co., 204 W. 5th St., Vancouver, WA 98660 / 360-695-1309; FAX: 360-695-6835 jnobleco@aol.com

Jim Norman Custom Gunstocks, 14281 Cane Rd., Valley Center, CA 92082 / 619-749-6252

Jim's Precision, Jim Ketchum, 1725 Moclips Dr., Petaluma, CA 94952 / 707-762-3014

JLK Bullets, 414 Turner Rd., Dover, AR 72837 / 501-331-4194

Johanssons Vapentillbehor, Bert, S-430 20, Veddige, SWEDEN

John Hall Plastics, Inc., P.O. Box 1526, Alvin, TX 77512 / 713-489-8709

John J. Adams & Son Engravers, 7040 VT Rt 113, Vershire, VT 05079 / 802-685-0019

John Masen Co. Inc., 1305 Jelmak, Grand Prairie, TX 75050 / 817-430-8732; FAX: 817-430-1715

John Partridge Sales Ltd., Trent Meadows Rugeley, Staffordshire, WS15 2HS ENGLAND

John Rigby & Co., 500 Linne Rd. Ste. D, Paso Robles, CA 93446 / 805-227-4236; FAX: 805-227-4723 jrigby@calinet www.johnrigbyandco.com

John's Custom Leather, 523 S. Liberty St., Blairsville, PA 15717 / 724-459-6802; FAX: 724-459-5996 john'scustomleather@verizon.net www.jclleather.com

Johnson Wood Products, 34897 Crystal Road, Strawberry Point, IA 52076 / 563-933-6504 johnsonwoodproducts@yahoo.com

Jonad Corp., 2091 Lakeland Ave., Lakewood, OH 44107 / 216-226-3161

Jonathan Arthur Ciener, Inc., 8700 Commerce St., Cape Canaveral, FL 32920 / 321-868-2200; FAX: 321-868-2201 www.22lrconversions.com

Jones Custom Products, Neil A., 17217 Brookhouser Rd., Saegertown, PA 16433 / 814-763-2769; FAX: 814-763-4228 njones@mdvl.net neiljones.com

Jones, J. See: SSK INDUSTRIES

Jones Moulds, Paul, 4901 Telegraph Rd., Los Angeles, CA 90022 / 213-262-1510

JP Enterprises, Inc., P.O. Box 378, Hugo, MN 55038 / 651-426-9196; FAX: 651-426-2472 www.jprifles.com

JP Sales, Box 307, Anderson, TX 77830

JRP Custom Bullets, RR2 2233 Carlton Rd., Whitehall, NY 12887 / 518-282-0084 or 802-438-5548

JSL Ltd. (See U.S. Importer-Specialty Shooters Supply)

Juenke, Vern, 25 Bitterbush Rd., Reno, NV 89523 / 702-345-0225

Jungkind, Reeves C., 509 E. Granite St., Llano, TX 78643-3055 / 325-247-1151

Jurras, L. See: L. E. JURRAS & ASSOC.

Justin Phillippi Custom Bullets, P.O. Box 773, Ligonier, PA 15658 / 412-238-9671

K

K&M Industries, Inc., Box 66, 510 S. Main, Troy, ID 83871 / 208-835-2281; FAX: 208-835-5211

K&M Services, 5430 Salmon Run Rd., Dover, PA 17315 / 717-292-3175; FAX: 717-292-3175

K. Eversull Co., Inc., 1 Tracemont, Boyce, LA 71409 / 318-793-8728; FAX: 318-793-5483 bestguns@aol.com

K.B.I. Inc., P.O. Box 6625, Harrisburg, PA 17112 / 717-540-8518; FAX: 717-540-8567

KA-BAR Knives, 200 Homer St., Olean, NY 14760 / 800-282-0130; FAX: 716-790-7188 info@ka-bar.com www.ka-bar.com

Kahles A. Swarovski Company, 2 Slater Rd., Cranston, RI 02920 / 401-946-2220; FAX: 401-946-2587

Kahr Arms, P.O. Box 220, 630 Route 303, Blauvelt, NY 10913 / 845-353-7770; FAX: 845-353-7833 www.kahr.com

Kailua Custom Guns Inc., 51 N. Dean Street, Coquille, OR 97423 / 541-396-5413 kailuacustom@aol.com www.kailuacustom.com

Kalispel Case Line, P.O. Box 267, Cusick, WA 99119 / 509-445-1121

Kamik Outdoor Footwear, 554 Montee de Liesse, Montreal, PQ H4T 1P1 CANADA / 514-341-3950; FAX: 514-341-1861

Kapro Mfg. Co. Inc. (See R.E.I.)

Kasenit Co., Inc., 39 Park Ave., Highland Mills, NY 10930 / 845-928-9595; FAX: 845-986-8038

Kaswer Custom, Inc., 13 Surrey Drive, Brookfield, CT 06804 / 203-775-0564; FAX: 203-775-6872

KDF, Inc., 2485 Hwy. 46 N., Seguin, TX 78155 / 830-379-8141; FAX: 830-379-5420

KeeCo Impressions, Inc., 346 Wood Ave., North Brunswick, NJ 08902 / 800-468-0546

Kehr, Roger, 2131 Agate Ct. SE, Lacy, WA 98503 / 360-491-0691

Keith's Bullets, 942 Twisted Oak, Algonquin, IL 60102 / 708-658-3520

Keith's Custom Gunstocks, Keith M. Heppler, 540 Banyan Circle, Walnut Creek, CA 94598 / 925-934-3509; FAX: 925-934-3143 kmheppler@hotmail.com

Kelbly, Inc., 7222 Dalton Fox Lake Rd., North Lawrence, OH 44666 / 216-683-4674; FAX: 216-683-7349

Kelley's, P.O. Box 125, Woburn, MA 01801-0125 / 800-879-7273; FAX: 781-272-7077 kels@star.net www.kelsmilitary.com

Kellogg's Professional Products, 325 Pearl St., Sandusky, OH 44870 / 419-625-6551; FAX: 419-625-6167 skwigton@sbcglobal.net

Kelly, Lance, 1723 Willow Oak Dr., Edgewater, FL 32132 / 904-423-4933

Kel-Tec CNC Industries, Inc., P.O. Box 236009, Cocoa, FL 32923 / 321-631-0068; FAX: 321-631-1169 www.kel-tec.com

Ken Eyster Heritage Gunsmiths, Inc., 6441 Bisop Rd., Centerburg, OH 43011 / 740-625-6131; FAX: 740-625-7811

Ken Starnes Gunmaker, 15617 NE 324th Circle, Battle Ground, WA 98604 / 360-666-5025; FAX: 360-666-5024 kstarnes@kdsa.com

Keng's Firearms Specialty, Inc., 875 Wharton Dr., P.O. Box 44405, Atlanta, GA 30336-1405 / 404-691-7611; FAX: 404-505-8445 kfs@bellsouth.net www.versa-pod.com

Kennebec Journal, 274 Western Ave., Augusta, ME 04330 / 207-622-6288

Kennedy Firearms, 10 N. Market St., Muncy, PA 17756 / 717-546-6695

Kenneth W. Warren Engraver, P.O. Box 2842, Wenatchee, WA 98807 / 509-663-6123; FAX: 509-665-6123

Ken's Kustom Kartridges, 331 Jacobs Rd., Hubbard, OH 44425 / 216-534-4595

Kent Cartridge America, Inc., P.O. Box 849, 1000 Zigor Rd., Kearneysville, WV 25430

Keowee Game Calls, 608 Hwy. 25 North, Travelers Rest, SC 29690 / 864-834-7204; FAX: 864-834-7831

Kershaw Knives, 18600 SW Teton Ave., Tualatin, OR 97062 / 503-682-1966 or 800-325-2891; FAX: 503-682-7168

Kesselring Gun Shop, 4024 Old Hwy. 99N, Burlington, WA 98233 / 360-724-3113; FAX: 360-724-7003 info@kesselrings.com www.kesselrings.com

Ketchum, Jim (See Jim's Precision)

Keystone Sporting Arms, Inc. (Crickett Rifles), 8920 State Route 405, Milton, PA 17847 / 800-742-2777; FAX: 570-742-1455

Kickeez, I.N.C., Inc., 13715 NE 384th St., La Center, WA 98629 / 877-542-5339; FAX: 954-656-4527 info@kickeezproducts www.kickeez.products.com

Kilham & Co., Main St., P.O. Box 37, Lyme, NH 03768 / 603-795-4112

Kimar (See U.S. Importer-IAR, Inc.)

Kimber of America, Inc., 1 Lawton St., Yonkers, NY 10705 / 800-880-2418; FAX: 914-964-9340

King & Co., P.O. Box 1242, Bloomington, IL 61702 / 309-473-3964 or 800-914-5464; FAX: 309-473-2161

King's Gun Works, 1837 W. Glenoaks Blvd., Glendale, CA 91201 / 818-956-6010; FAX: 818-548-8606

Kirkpatrick Leather Co., P.O. Box 677, Laredo, TX 78040 / 956-723-6631; FAX: 956-725-0672 mike@kirkpatrickleather.com www.kirkpatrickleather.com

KK Air International (See Impact Case & Container Co., Inc.)

Kleen-Bore, Inc., 8909 Forum Way, Ft. Worth, TX 76140 / 413-527-0300; FAX: 817-926-7012 info@kleen-bore.com www.kleen-bore.com

Kleinendorst, K. W., RR 1, Box 1500, Hop Bottom, PA 18824 / 570-289-4687; FAX: 570-289-8673

Klingler Woodcarving, P.O. Box 141, Thistle Hill, Cabot, VT 05647 / 802-426-3811 www.vermartcrafts.com

Knifeware, Inc., P.O. Box 3, Greenville, WV 24945 / 304-832-6878

Knight Rifles, 21852 Hwy. J46, P.O. Box 130, Centerville, IA 52544 / 515-856-2626; FAX: 515-856-2628 www.knightrifles.com

Knight Rifles (See Modern Muzzleloading, Inc.)

Knight's Manufacturing Co., 701 Columbia Blvd., Titusville, FL 32780 / 321-607-9900; FAX: 321-268-1498 civiliansales@knightarmco.com www.knightarmco.com

Knock on Wood Antiques, 355 Post Rd., Darien, CT 06820 / 203-655-9031

Knoell, Doug, 9737 McCardle Way, Santee, CA 92071 / 619-449-5169

Knopp, Gary. See: SUPER 6 LLC

Koevenig's Engraving Service, Box 55 Rabbit Gulch, Hill City, SD 57745 / 605-574-2239 ekoevenig@msn.com

KOGOT, 410 College, Trinidad, CO 81082 / 719-846-9406; FAX: 719-846-9406

Kolar, 1925 Roosevelt Ave., Racine, WI 53406 / 414-554-0800; FAX: 414-554-9093

MANUFACTURER'S DIRECTORY

Kolpin Outdoors, Inc., P.O. Box 107, 205 Depot St., Fox Lake, WI 53933 / 414-928-3118; FAX: 414-928-3687 cdutton@kolpin.com www.kolpin.com

Korth Germany GmbH, Robert Bosch Strasse, 11, D-23909, 23909 Ratzeburg, GERMANY / 4541-84 03 63; FAX: 4541-84 05 35 info@korthwaffen.de www.korthwaffen.com

Korth USA, 437R Chandler St., Tewksbury, MA 01876 / 978-851-8656; FAX: 978-851-9462 info@kortusa.com www.korthusa.com

Korzinek Riflesmith, J., RD 2 Box 73D, Canton, PA 17724 / 717-673-8512

Koval Knives, 5819 Zarley St., Suite A, New Albany, OH 43054 / 614-855-0777; FAX: 614-855-0945 koval@kovalknives.com www.kovalknives.com

Kowa Optimed, Inc., 20001 S. Vermont Ave., Torrance, CA 90502 / 310-327-1913; FAX: 310-327-4177 scopekowa@kowa.com www.kowascope.com

KP Books Division of F+W Publications, 700 E. State St., Iola, WI 54990-0001 / 715-445-2214

Kramer Designs, P.O. Box 129, Clancy, MT 59634 / 406-933-8658; FAX: 406-933-8658

Kramer Handgun Leather, P.O. Box 112154, Tacoma, WA 98411 / 800-510-2666; FAX: 253-564-1214 www.kramerleather.com

Krico Deutschland GmbH, Nurnbergerstrasse 6, D-90602, Pyrbaum, GERMANY / 09180-2780; FAX: 09180-2661

Krieger Barrels, Inc., 2024 Mayfield Rd, Richfield, WI 53076 / 262-628-8558; FAX: 262-628-8748

Krieghoff Gun Co., H., Boschstrasse 22, D-89079 Elm, GERMANY / 731-4018270

Krieghoff International, Inc., 7528 Easton Rd., Ottsville, PA 18942 / 610-847-5173; FAX: 610-847-8691 info@krieghoff.com www.krieghoff.com

Kukowski, Ed. See: ED'S GUN HOUSE

Kulis Freeze Dry Taxidermy, 725 Broadway Ave., Bedford, OH 44146 / 440-232-8352; FAX: 440-232-7305 jkulis@kastaway.com kastaway.com

KVH Industries, Inc., 110 Enterprise Center, Middletown, RI 02842 / 401-847-3327; FAX: 401-849-0045

Kwik-Site Co., 5555 Treadwell St., Wayne, MI 48184 / 734-326-1500; FAX: 734-326-4120 kwiksitecorp@aol.com www.kwiksiteco@aol.com

L

L&R Lock Co., 2328 Cains Mill Rd., Sumter, SC 29154 / 803-481-5790; FAX: 803-481-5795

L&S Technologies Inc. (See Aimtech Mount Systems)

L. Bengtson Arms Co., 6345-B E. Akron St., Mesa, AZ 85205 / 602-981-6375

L. E. Jurras & Assoc., L. E. Jurras, P.O. Box 680, Washington, IN 47501 / 812-254-6170; FAX: 812-254-6170 jurras@sbcglobal.net www.leejurras.com

L.A.R. Mfg., Inc., 4133 W. Farm Rd., West Jordan, UT 84088 / 801-280-3505; FAX: 801-280-1972

L.B.T., Judy Smith, HCR 62, Box 145, Moyie Springs, ID 83845 / 208-267-3588 lbtisaccuracy@imbris.net

L.E. Wilson, Inc., Box 324, 404 Pioneer Ave., Cashmere, WA 98815 / 509-782-1328; FAX: 509-782-7200

L.L. Bean, Inc., Freeport, ME 04032 / 207-865-4761; FAX: 207-552-2802

L.P.A. Inc., Via Alfieri 26, Gardone V.T., Brescia, ITALY / 30-891-14-81; FAX: 30-891-09-51

L.R. Clift Mfg., 3821 Hammonton Rd., Marysville, CA 95901 / 916-755-3390; FAX: 916-755-3393

La Clinique du .45, 1432 Rougemont, Chambly, PQ J3L 2L8 CANADA / 514-658-1144

Labanu Inc., 2201-F Fifth Ave., Ronkonkoma, NY 11779 / 516-467-6197; FAX: 516-981-4112

LaBoone, Pat. See: MIDWEST SHOOTING SCHOOL, THE

LaBounty Precision Reboring, Inc, 7968 Silver Lake Rd., PO Box 186, Maple Falls, WA 98266 / 360-599-2047; FAX: 360-599-3018

LaCrosse Footwear, Inc., 18550 NE Riverside Parkway, Portland, OR 97230 / 503-766-1010 or 800-323-2668; FAX: 503-766-1015 customerservice@lacrossefootwear.com www.lacrossefootwear.com

LaFrance Specialties, P.O. Box 87933, San Diego, CA 92138 / 619-293-3373; FAX: 619-293-0819 timlafrance@att.net lafrancespecialties.com

Lake Center Marina, P.O. Box 670, St. Charles, MO 63302 / 314-946-7500

Lakefield Arms Ltd. (See Savage Arms, Inc.)

Lakewood Products Div of Midwest Textile, PO Box 342, Suamico, WI 54173 / 800-872-8458; FAX: 877-676-3559 info@lakewoodproduct.com www.lakewoodproducts.com

Lamboy, Stephen. See: ITHACA CLASSIC DOUBLES

Lampert, Ron, Rt. 1, 44857 Schoolcraft Trl., Guthrie, MN 56461 / 218-854-7345

Lamson & Goodnow Mfg. Co., 15 Greenfield St., Greenfield, MA 01301 / 800-872-6564; FAX: 413-774-7776 info@lamsonsharp.com www.lamsonsharp.com

Lansky Levine, Arthur. See: LANSKY SHARPENERS

Lansky Sharpeners, Arthur Lansky Levine, P.O. Box 50830, Las Vegas, NV 89016 / 702-361-7511; FAX: 702-896-9511

LaPrade, P.O. Box 250, Ewing, VA 24248 / 423-733-2615

LaRocca Gun Works, 51 Union Place, Worcester, MA 01608 / 508-754-2887; FAX: 508-754-2887 www.laroccagunworks.com

Larry Lyons Gunworks, 29994 M 62 W., Dowagiac, MI 49047 / 616-782-9478

Laser Devices, Inc., 2 Harris Ct. A-4, Monterey, CA 93940 / 831-373-0701; FAX: 831-373-0903 sales@laserdevices.com www.laserdevices.com

Laseraim Technologies, Inc., P.O. Box 3548, Little Rock, AR 72203 / 501-375-2227

Laserlyte, 2201 Amapola Ct., Torrance, CA 90501

LaserMax, 3495 Winton Place, Rochester, NY 14623-2807 / 800-527-3703; FAX: 585-272-5427 customerservice@lasermax-inc.com www.lasermax.com

Lassen Community College, Gunsmithing Dept., P.O. Box 3000, Hwy. 139, Susanville, CA 96130 / 916-251-8800; FAX: 916-251-8838 staylor@lassencollege.edu www.lassencommunitycollege.edu

Lathrop's, Inc., 5146 E. Pima, Tucson, AZ 85712 / 520-881-0266 or 800-875-4867; FAX: 520-322-5704

Laughridge, William R. (See Cylinder & Slide, Inc.)

Laurel Mountain Forge, P.O. Box 52, Crown Point, IN 46308 / 219-548-2950; FAX: 219-548-2950

Laurona Armas Eibar, S.A.L., Avenida de Otaola 25, P.O. Box 260, Eibar 20600, SPAIN / 34-43-700600; FAX: 34-43-700616

Lawrence Brand Shot (See Precision Reloading, Inc.)

Lawrence Leather Co., P.O. Box 1479, Lillington, NC 27546 / 910-893-2071; FAX: 910-893-4742

Lawson, John. See: SIGHT SHOP

Lawson, John G. (See Sight Shop, The)

Lazzeroni Arms Co., P.O. Box 26696, Tucson, AZ 85726 / 888-492-7247; FAX: 520-624-4250

Leapers, Inc., 7675 Five Mile Rd., Northville, MI 48167 / 248-486-1231; FAX: 248-486-1430

Leatherman Tool Group, Inc., 12106 NE Ainsworth Cir., P.O. Box 20595, Portland, OR 97294 / 503-253-7826; FAX: 503-253-7830

Lebeau-Courally, Rue St. Gilles, 386 4000, Liege, BELGIUM / 042-52-48-43; FAX: 32-4-252-2008 info@lebeau-courally.com www.lebeau-courally.com

Leckie Professional Gunsmithing, 546 Quarry Rd., Ottsville, PA 18942 / 215-847-8594

Ledbetter Airguns, Riley, 1804 E Sprague St., Winston Salem, NC 27107-3521 / 919-784-0676

Lee Precision, Inc., 4275 Hwy. U, Hartford, WI 53027 / 262-673-3075; FAX: 262-673-9273 info@leeprecision.com www.leeprecision.com

Lee Supplies, Mark, 9901 France Ct., Lakeville, MN 55044 / 612-461-2114

LeFever Arms Co., Inc., 6234 Stokes, Lee Center Rd., Lee Center, NY 13363 / 315-337-6722; FAX: 315-337-1543

Legacy Sports International, 206 S. Union St., Alexandria, VA 22314 / 703-548-4837 www.legacysports.com

Leica USA, Inc., 1 Pearl Ct., Ste. A, Allendale, NJ 07401 / 201-995-1686 www.leica-camera.com/usa

Leonard Day, 3 Kings Hwy., West Hatfield, MA 01027-9506 / 413-337-8369

Les Baer Custom, Inc., 29601 34th Ave., Hillsdale, IL 61257 / 309-658-2716; FAX: 309-658-2610 www.lesbaer.com

LesMerises, Felix. See: ROCKY MOUNTAIN ARMOURY

Lethal Force Institute (See Police Bookshelf), P.O. Box 122, Concord, NH 03301 / 603-224-6814; FAX: 603-226-3554 ayoob@attglobal.net www.ayoob.com

Lett Custom Grips, 672 Currier Rd., Hopkinton, NH 03229-2652 / 800-421-5388; FAX: 603-226-4580 info@lettgrips.com www.lettgrips.com

Leupold & Stevens, Inc., 14400 NW Greenbrier Pky., Beaverton, OR 97006 / 503-646-9171; FAX: 503-526-1455

Lever Arms Service Ltd., 2131 Burrard St., Vancouver, BC V6J 3H7 CANADA / 604-736-2711; FAX: 604-738-3503 leverarms@leverarms.com www.leverarms.com

Lew Horton Dist. Co., Inc., 15 Walkup Dr., Westboro, MA 01581 / 508-366-7400; FAX: 508-366-5332

Lewis Lead Remover, The (See Brownells, Inc.)

Liberty Mfg., Inc., 2233 East 16th St., Los Angeles, CA 90021 / 323-581-9171; FAX: 323-581-9351 libertymfginc@aol.com

Liberty Safe, 999 W. Utah Ave., Payson, UT 84651-1744 / 800-247-5625; FAX: 801-489-6409

Liberty Shooting Supplies, P.O. Box 357, Hillsboro, OR 97123 / 503-640-5518; FAX: 503-640-5518 info@libertyshootingsupplies.com www.libertyshootingsupplies.com

Lightning Performance Innovations, Inc., RD1 Box 555, Mohawk, NY 13407 / 315-866-8819; FAX: 315-867-5701

Lilja Precision Rifle Barrels, P.O. Box 372, Plains, MT 59859 / 406-826-3084; FAX: 406-826-3083 lilja@riflebarrels.com www.riflebarrels.com

Lincoln, Dean, Box 1886, Farmington, NM 87401

Lindsay Engraving & Tools, Steve Lindsay, 3714 W. Cedar Hills, Kearney, NE 68845 / 308-236-7885 steve@lindsayengraving.com www.handgravers.com

Lindsay, Steve. See: LINDSAY ENGRAVING & TOOLS

Lindsley Arms Cartridge Co., P.O. Box 757, 20 College Hill Rd., Henniker, NH 03242 / 603-995-1267

Linebaugh Custom Sixguns, P.O. Box 455, Cody, WY 82414 / 307-645-3332 www.sixgunner.com

Lion Country Supply, P.O. Box 480, Port Matilda, PA 16870

List Precision Engineering, Unit 1 Ingley Works, 13 River Road, Barking, ENGLAND / 011-081-594-1686

Lithi Bee Bullet Lube, 1728 Carr Rd., Muskegon, MI 49442 / 616-788-4479 lithibee@att.net

"Little John's" Antique Arms, 1740 W. Laveta, Orange, CA 92668

Littleton, J. F., 275 Pinedale Ave., Oroville, CA 95966 / 916-533-6084

Ljutic Industries, Inc., 732 N. 16th Ave., Suite 22, Yakima, WA 98902 / 509-248-0476; FAX: 509-576-8233 ljuticgun@earthlink.net www.ljuticgun.com

Lock's Philadelphia Gun Exchange, 6700 Rowland Ave., Philadelphia, PA 19149 / 215-332-6225; FAX: 215-332-4800 locks.gunshop@verizon.net

Lodewick, Walter H., 2816 NE Halsey St., Portland, OR 97232 / 503-284-2554 wlodewick@aol.com

Lodgewood Mfg., P.O. Box 611, Whitewater, WI 53190 / 262-473-5444; FAX: 262-473-6448 lodgewd@idcnet.com lodgewood.com

Log Cabin Sport Shop, 8010 Lafayette Rd., Lodi, OH 44254 / 330-948-1082; FAX: 330-948-4307 logcabin@logcabinshop.com www.logcabinshop.com

Logdewood Mfg., P.O. Box 611, Whitewater, WI 53190 / 262-473-5444; FAX: 262-473-6448 lodgewd@idcnet.com www.lodgewood.com

Lohman Mfg. Co., Inc., 4500 Doniphan Dr., P.O. Box 220, Neosho, MO 64850 / 417-451-4438; FAX: 417-451-2576

Lomont Precision Bullets, 278 Sandy Creek Rd., Salmon, ID 83467 / 208-756-6819; FAX: 208-756-6824 www.klomont.com

London Guns Ltd., Box 3750, Santa Barbara, CA 93130 / 805-683-4141; FAX: 805-683-1712

Lone Star Gunleather, 1301 Brushy Bend Dr., Round Rock, TX 78681 / 512-255-1805

Lone Star Rifle Company, 11231 Rose Road, Conroe, TX 77303 / 936-856-3363; FAX: 936-856-3363 dave@lonestar.com

Long, George F., 1402 Kokanee Ln., Grants Pass, OR 97527 / 541-476-0836

Lothar Walther Precision Tool Inc., 3425 Hutchinson Rd., Cumming, GA 30040 / 770-889-9998; FAX: 770-889-4919 lotharwalther@mindspring.com www.lothar-walther.com

LPS Laboratories, Inc., 4647 Hugh Howell Rd., P.O. Box 3050, Tucker, GA 30084 / 404-934-7800

Lucas, Edward E, 32 Garfield Ave., East Brunswick, NJ 08816 / 201-251-5526

Lupton, Keith. See: PAWLING MOUNTAIN CLUB

Lyman Instant Targets, Inc. (See Lyman Products Corp.)

Lyman Products Corp., 475 Smith St., Middletown, CT 06457-1541 / 800-423-9704; FAX: 860-632-1699 lymansales@cshore.com www.lymanproducts.com

MANUFACTURER'S DIRECTORY

M

M.H. Canjar Co., 6510 Raleigh St., Arvada, CO 80003 / 303-295-2638; FAX: 303-295-2638

MA Systems, Inc., P.O. Box 894, Pryor, OK 74362-0894 / 918-824-3705; FAX: 918-824-3710

Mac-1 Airgun Distributors, 13974 Van Ness Ave., Gardena, CA 90249-2900 / 310-327-3581; FAX: 310-327-0238 mac1@maclairgun.com www.mac1airgun.com

Machinist's Workshop-Village Press, P.O. Box 1810, Traverse City, MI 49685 / 800-447-7367; FAX: 231-946-6180

Madis Books, 2453 West Five Mile Pkwy., Dallas, TX 75233 / 214-330-7168

Madis, George. See: WINCHESTER CONSULTANTS

MAG Instrument, Inc., 1635 S. Sacramento Ave., Ontario, CA 91761 / 909-947-1006; FAX: 909-947-3116

Magma Engineering Co., P.O. Box 161, 20955 E. Ocotillo Rd., Queen Creek, AZ 85242 / 602-987-9008; FAX: 602-987-0148

Mag-Na-Port International, Inc., 41302 Executive Dr., Harrison Twp., MI 48045-1306 / 586-469-6727; FAX: 586-469-0425 email@magnaport.com www.magnaport.com

Magnum Power Products, Inc., P.O. Box 17768, Fountain Hills, AZ 85268

Magnum Research, Inc., 7110 University Ave. NE, Minneapolis, MN 55432 / 800-772-6168 or 763-574-1868; FAX: 763-574-0109 info@magnumresearch.com

Magnus Bullets, P.O. Box 239, Toney, AL 35773 / 256-420-8359; FAX: 256-420-8360 bulletman@mchsi.com www.magnusbullets.com

MagSafe Ammo, Inc., 4700 S. US Highway 17/92, Casselberry, FL 32707-3814 / 407-834-9966; FAX: 407-834-8185 www.magsafeammo.com

Magtech Ammunition Co. Inc., 248 Apollo Dr. Ste. 180, Linolakes, MN 55014 / 800-466-7191; FAX: 763-235-4004 www.magtechammunition.com

Mahovsky's Metalife, R.D. 1, Box 149a Eureka Road, Grand Valley, PA 16420 / 814-436-7747

Makinson, Nicholas, RR 3, Komoka, ON N0L 1R0 CANADA / 519-471-5462

Mallardtone Game Calls, 10406 96th St., Court West, Taylor Ridge, IL 61284 / 309-798-2481; FAX: 309-798-2501

Marble Arms (See CRR, Inc./Marble's Inc.)

Marent, Rudolf. See: HAMMERLI SERVICE-PRECISION MAC

Mark Lee Supplies, 9901 France Ct., Lakeville, MN 55044 / 952-461-2114; FAX: 952-461-2194 marklee55044@usfamily.net

Markell, Inc., 422 Larkfield Center 235, Santa Rosa, CA 95403 / 707-573-0792; FAX: 707-573-9867

Markesbery Muzzle Loaders, Inc., 7065 Production Ct., Florence, KY 41042 / 859-342-5553; FAX: 859-342-2380 www.markesbery.com

Marksman Products, 5482 Argosy Dr., Huntington Beach, CA 92649 / 714-898-7535 or 800-822-8005; FAX: 714-891-0782

Marlin Firearms Co., 100 Kenna Dr., North Haven, CT 06473 / 203-239-5621; FAX: 203-234-7991 www.marlinfirearms.com

Marocchi F.lli S.p.A, Via Galileo Galilei 8, I-25068 Zanano, ITALY

Marsh, Mike, Croft Cottage, Main St., Derbyshire, DE4 2BY ENGLAND / 01629 650 669

Marshall Enterprises, 792 Canyon Rd., Redwood City, CA 94062

Martin B. Retting Inc., 11029 Washington, Culver City, CA 90232 / 213-837-2412 retting@retting.com

Martini & Hagn, Ltd., 1264 Jimsmith Lake Rd., Cranbrook, BC V1C 6V6 CANADA / 250-417-2926; FAX: 250-417-2928 martini-hagn@shaw.ca www.martiniandhagngunmakers.com

Martin's Gun Shop, 937 S. Sheridan Blvd., Lakewood, CO 80226 / 303-922-2184 rdrnnr74479@peoplepc.com

Martz, John V., 8060 Lakeview Lane, Lincoln, CA 95648 FAX: 916-645-3815

Marvel, Alan, 3922 Madonna Rd., Jarretsville, MD 21084 / 301-557-6545

Marx, Harry (See U.S. Importer for FERLIB)

Maryland Paintball Supply, 8507 Harford Rd., Parkville, MD 21234 / 410-882-5607

Master Lock Co., 2600 N. 32nd St., Milwaukee, WI 53245 / 414-444-2800

Match Prep-Doyle Gracey, P.O. Box 155, Tehachapi, CA 93581 / 661-822-5383; FAX: 661-823-8680 gracenotes@as.net www.matchprep.com

Mathews Gun Shop & Gunsmithing, Inc., 2791 S. Gaffey St., San Pedro, CA 90731-6515 / 562-928-2129; FAX: 562-928-8629

Mauser Werke Oberndorf Waffensysteme GmbH, Postfach 1349, 78722, Oberndorf/N., GERMANY

Maverick Arms, Inc., 7 Grasso Ave., P.O. Box 497, North Haven, CT 06473 / 203-230-5300; FAX: 203-230-5420

Maxi-Mount Inc., P.O. Box 291, Willoughby Hills, OH 44096-0291 / 440-944-9456; FAX: 440-944-9456 maximount454@yahoo.com

Mayville Engineering Co. (See MEC, Inc.)

Mazur Restoration, Pete, 13083 Drummer Way, Grass Valley, CA 95949 / 530-268-2412

McCament, Jay. See: JAY MCCAMENT CUSTOM GUNMAKER

McCann, Tom, 14 Walton Dr., New Hope, PA 18938 / 215-862-2728

McCann Industries, P.O. Box 641, Spanaway, WA 98387 / 253-537-6919; FAX: 253-537-6919 mccann.machine@worldnet.att.net www.mccannindustries.com

McCluskey Precision Rifles, 10502 14th Ave. NW, Seattle, WA 98177 / 206-781-2776

McCombs, Leo, 1862 White Cemetery Rd., Patriot, OH 45658 / 740-256-1714

McDonald, Dennis, 8359 Brady St., Peosta, IA 52068 / 319-556-7940

McFarland, Stan, 2221 Idella Ct., Grand Junction, CO 81505 / 970-243-4704

McGhee, Larry. See: B.C. OUTDOORS

McGowen Rifle Barrels, 5961 Spruce Lane, St. Anne, IL 60964 / 815-937-9816; FAX: 815-937-4024

Mchalik, Gary. See: ROSSI FIREARMS

McKenzie, Lynton, 6940 N. Alvernon Way, Tucson, AZ 85718 / 520-299-5090

McMillan Fiberglass Stocks, Inc., 1638 W. Knudsen Dr. #101, Phoenix, AZ 85027 / 623-582-9635; FAX: 623-581-3825 mfsinc@mcmfamily.com www.mcmfamily.com

McMillan Optical Gunsight Co., 28638 N. 42nd St., Cave Creek, AZ 85331 / 602-585-7868; FAX: 602-585-7872

McMillan Rifle Barrels, P.O. Box 3427, Bryan, TX 77805 / 409-690-3456; FAX: 409-690-0156

McMurdo, Lynn, P.O. Box 404, Afton, WY 83110 / 307-886-5535

MCS, Inc., 166 Pocono Rd., Brookfield, CT 06804-2023 / 203-775-1013; FAX: 203-775-9462

McWelco Products, 6730 Santa Fe Ave., Hesperia, CA 92345 / 619-244-8876; FAX: 619-244-9398 products@mcwelco.com www.mcwelco.com

MDS, P.O. Box 1441, Brandon, FL 33509-1441 / 813-653-1180; FAX: 813-684-5953

Meacham Tool & Hardware Co., Inc., 37052 Eberhardt Rd., Peck, ID 83545 / 208-486-7171 smeacham@clearwater.net www.meachamrifles.com

Measures, Leon. See: SHOOT WHERE YOU LOOK

MEC, Inc., 715 South St., Mayville, WI 53050 reloaders@mayvl.com www.mecreloaders.com

MEC-Gar S.R.L., Via Madonnina 64, Gardone V.T. Brescia, ITALY / 39-030-3733668; FAX: 39-030-3733687 info@mec-gar.it www.mec-gar.it

MEC-Gar U.S.A., Inc., Hurley Farms Industr. Park, 905 Middle St., Middletown, CT 06457 / 203-262-1525; FAX: 203-262-1719 mecgar@aol.com www.mec-gar.com

Mech-Tech Systems, Inc., 1602 Foothill Rd., Kalispell, MT 59901 / 406-755-8055

Meister Bullets (See Gander Mountain)

Mele, Frank, 201 S. Wellow Ave., Cookeville, TN 38501 / 615-526-4860

Menck, Gunsmith Inc., T.W., 5703 S 77th St., Ralston, NE 68127

Mendez, John A., 1309 Continental Dr., Daytona Beach, FL 32117-3807 / 407-344-2791

Men-Metallwerk Elisenhuette GmbH, P.O. Box 1263, Nassau/Lahn, D-56392 GERMANY / 2604-7819

Meopta USA, LLC, 50 Davids Dr., Hauppauge, NY 11788 / 631-436-5900 ussales@meopta.com www.meopta.com

Mercer Custom Guns, 216 S. Whitewater Ave., Jefferson, WI 53549 / 920-674-3839

Merit Corp., P.O. Box 9044, Schenectady, NY 12309 / 518-346-1420 sales@meritcorporation.com www.meritcorporation.com

Merkel, Schutzenstrasse 26, D-98527 Suhl, Suhl, GERMANY FAX: 011-49-3681-854-203 www.merkel-waffen.de

Metal Merchants, P.O. Box 186, Walled Lake, MI 48390-0186

Metalife Industries (See Mahovsky's Metalife)

Michael's Antiques, Box 591, Waldoboro, ME 04572

Michaels of Oregon Co., 9200 Cody St., Overland Park, KS 66214 / 800-845-2444 www.michaels-oregon.com

Micro Sight Co., 502 May St., Arroyo Grande, CA 93420-2832

Microfusion Alfa S.A., Paseo San Andres N8, P.O. Box 271, Eibar 20600, 20600 SPAIN / 34-43-11-89-16; FAX: 34-43-11-40-38

Mid-America Recreation, Inc., 1328 5th Ave., Moline, IL 61265 / 309-764-5089; FAX: 309-764-5089 fmilcusguns@aol.com www.midamericarecreation.com

Middlebrooks Custom Shop, 7366 Colonial Trail East, Surry, VA 23883 / 757-357-0881; FAX: 757-365-0442

Midway Arms, Inc., 5875 W. Van Horn Tavern Rd., Columbia, MO 65203 / 800-243-3220; FAX: 800-992-8312 www.midwayusa.com

Midwest Gun Sport, 1108 Herbert Dr., Zebulon, NC 27597 / 919-269-5570

Midwest Shooting School, The, Pat LaBoone, 2550 Hwy. 23, Wrenshall, MN 55797 / 218-384-3670 shootingschool@starband.net

Midwest Sport Distributors, Box 129, Fayette, MO 65248

Mike Davis Products, 643 Loop Dr., Moses Lake, WA 98837 / 509-765-6178; or 509-766-7281

Mike Yee Custom Stocking, 29927 56 Pl. S., Auburn, WA 98001 / 253-839-3991 miknadyee@comcast.net

Military Armament Corp., P.O. Box 120, Mt. Zion Rd., Lingleville, TX 76461 / 817-965-3253

Millennium Designed Muzzleloaders, P.O. Box 536, Routes 11 & 25, Limington, ME 04049 / 207-637-2316

Miller Arms, Inc., 1310 Industry Rd., Sturgis, SD 57785-9129 / 605-642-5160; FAX: 605-642-5160

Miller Custom, 210 E. Julia, Clinton, IL 61727 / 217-935-9362

Miller Single Trigger Mfg. Co., 6680 Rt. 5-20, P.O. Box 471, Bloomfield, NY 14469 / 585-657-6338; FAX: 585-657-7743 info@turnbullrestoration.com turnbullrestoration.com

Millett Sights, 16131 Gothard St., Huntington Beach, CA 92647 / 714-842-5575 or 800-645-5388; FAX: 714-843-5707 sales@millettsights.com www.millettsights.com

Mills Jr., Hugh B., 3615 Canterbury Rd., New Bern, NC 28560 / 919-637-4631

Minute Man High Tech Industries, 10611 Canyon Rd. E., Suite 151, Puyallup, WA 98373 / 800-233-2734

Mirador Optical Corp., P.O. Box 11614, Marina Del Rey, CA 90295-7614 / 310-821-5587; FAX: 310-305-0386

Mitchell, Jack, c/o Geoff Gaebe, Addieville East Farm, 200 Pheasant Dr., Mapleville, RI 02839 / 401-568-3185

Mitchell Mfg. Corp., P.O. Box 9295, Fountain Valley, CA 92728 / 714-444-2220

Mitchell Optics, Inc., 2072 CR 1100 N, Sidney, IL 61877 / 217-688-2219 or 217-621-3018; FAX: 217-688-2505 mitchell@attglobal.net

Mitchell's Accuracy Shop, 68 Greenridge Dr., Stafford, VA 22554 / 703-659-0165

Mitchell's Mauser, P.O. Box 9295, Fountain Valley, CA 92728 / 714-979-7663; FAX: 714-899-3660

MI-TE Bullets, 1396 Ave. K, Ellsworth, KS 67439 / 785-472-4575; FAX: 785-472-5579

MJK Gunsmithing, Inc., 417 N. Huber Ct., E. Wenatchee, WA 98802 / 509-884-7683

MKS Supply, Inc. (See Hi-Point Firearms)

MMC, 4430 Mitchell St., North Las Vegas, NV 89081 / 800-998-7483; FAX: 702-267-9463 info@mmcsight.com www.mmcsight.com

MOA Corporation, 285 Government Valley Rd., Sundance, WY 82729 / 307-283-3030 www.moaguns.com

Mobile Area Networks, Inc., 2772 Depot St., Sanford, FL 32773 / 407-333-2350; FAX: 407-333-9903 georgew@mobilan.com www.mobilan.com

Modern Gun Repair School, P.O. Box 846, Saint Albans, VT 05478 / 802-524-2223; FAX: 802-524-2053 jfwp@dlilearn.com www.mgsinfoadlifearn.com

Modern Muzzleloading, Inc., P.O. Box 130, Centerville, IA 52544 / 515-856-2626

Moeller, Steve, 1213 4th St., Fulton, IL 61252 / 815-589-2300

Mogul Co./Life Jacket, 500 N. Kimball Rd., Ste. 109, South Lake, TX 76092

Monell Custom Guns, 228 Red Mills Rd., Pine Bush, NY 12566 / 845-744-3021

Moneymaker Guncraft Corp., 1420 Military Ave., Omaha, NE 68131 / 402-556-0226

Montana Armory, Inc., 100 Centennial Dr., P.O. Box 885, Big Timber, MT 59011 / 406-932-4353; FAX: 406-932-4443

MANUFACTURER'S DIRECTORY

Montana Outfitters, Lewis E. Yearout, 308 Riverview Dr. E., Great Falls, MT 59404 / 406-761-0859; or 406-727-4560

Montana Precision Swaging, P.O. Box 4746, Butte, MT 59702 / 406-494-0600; FAX: 406-494-0600

Montana Rifleman, Inc., 2593A Hwy. 2 East, Kalispell, MT 59901 / 406-755-4867

Montana Vintage Arms, 2354 Bear Canyon Rd., Bozeman, MT 59715

Morini (See U.S. Importers-Mandall Shooting Supplies, Inc.)

Morrison Custom Rifles, J. W., 4015 W Sharon, Phoenix, AZ 85029 / 602-978-3754

Morrison Precision, 6719 Calle Mango, Hereford, AZ 85615 / 520-378-6207 morprec@c2i2.com

Morrow, Bud, 11 Hillside Lane, Sheridan, WY 82801-9729 / 307-674-8360

Morton Booth Co., P.O. Box 123, Joplin, MO 64802 / 417-673-1962; FAX: 417-673-3642

Mo's Competitor Supplies (See MCS, Inc.)

Moss Double Tone, Inc., P.O. Box 1112, 2101 S. Kentucky, Sedalia, MO 65301 / 816-827-0827

Mountain Plains Industries, 3720 Otter Place, Lynchburg, VA 24503 / 800-687-3000; FAX: 434-386-6217 MPI_targets@adelphia.net www.targetshandloader.com

Mowrey Gun Works, P.O. Box 246, Waldron, IN 46182 / 317-525-6181; FAX: 317-525-9595

Mowrey's Guns & Gunsmithing, 119 Fredericks St., Canajoharie, NY 13317 / 518-673-3483

MPC, P.O. Box 450, McMinnville, TN 37110-0450 / 615-473-5513; FAX: 615-473-5516 thebox@blomand.net www.mpc-thebox.com

MPI Stocks, P.O. Box 83266, Portland, OR 97283 / 503-226-1215; FAX: 503-226-2661

MSR Targets, P.O. Box 1042, West Covina, CA 91793 / 818-331-7840

MTM Molded Products Co., Inc., 3370 Obco Ct., Dayton, OH 45414 / 937-890-7461; FAX: 937-890-1747

Mulberry House Publishing, P.O. Box 2180, Apache Junction, AZ 85217 / 888-738-1567; FAX: 480-671-1015

Mulhern, Rick, Rt. 5, Box 152, Rayville, LA 71269 / 318-728-2688

Mullins Ammunition, Rt. 2 Box 304N, Clintwood, VA 24228 / 276-926-6772; FAX: 276-926-6092 mammo@extremeshockusa.com www.extremeshockusa.com

Mullis Guncraft, 3523 Lawyers Road E., Monroe, NC 28110 / 704-283-6683

Multiplex International, 26 S. Main St., Concord, NH 03301 FAX: 603-796-2223

Multipropulseurs, La Bertrandiere, 42580, FRANCE / 77 74 01 30; FAX: 77 93 19 34

Mundy, Thomas A., 69 Robbins Road, Somerville, NJ 08876 / 201-722-2199

Murmur Corp., RR 2, Dallas, TX 75241 / 214-630-5400

Murphy, R.R. Murphy Co., Inc. See: MURPHY, R.R. CO., INC.

Murphy, R.R. Co., Inc., R.R. Murphy Co., Inc. Murphy, P.O. Box 102, Ripley, TN 38063 / 901-635-4003; FAX: 901-635-2320

Murray State College, 1 Murray Campus St., Tishomingo, OK 73460 / 508-371-2371 darnold@mscol.edu

Muscle Products Corp., 112 Fennell Dr., Butler, PA 16002 / 800-227-7049 or 724-283-0567; FAX: 724-283-8310 mpc@mpc_home.com www.mpc_home.com

Muzzleloaders Etcetera, Inc., 9901 Lyndale Ave. S., Bloomington, MN 55420 / 952-884-1161 www.muzzleloaders-etcetera.com

MWG Co., P.O. Box 971202, Miami, FL 33197 / 800-428-9394 or 305-253-8393; FAX: 305-232-1247

N

N.B.B., Inc., 24 Elliot Rd., Sterling, MA 01564 / 508-422-7538 or 800-942-9444

N.C. Ordnance Co., P.O. Box 3254, Wilson, NC 27895 / 919-237-2440; FAX: 919-243-9845 bharvey@nc.rr.com www.gungrip.com

Nagel's Custom Bullets, 100 Scott St., Baytown, TX 77520-2849

Nalpak, 1267 Vernon Way, El Cajon, CA 92020

Nammo Lapua Oy, P.O. Box 5, Lapua, FINLAND / 358-6-4310111; FAX: 358-6-4310317 info@nammo.ti www.lapua.com

Nastoff, Steve. See: NASTOFFS 45 SHOP, INC.

Nastoffs 45 Shop, Inc., Steve Nastoff, 1057 Laverne Dr., Youngstown, OH 44511

National Bullet Co., 1585 E. 361 St., Eastlake, OH 44095 / 216-951-1854; FAX: 216-951-7761

National Gun, Inc., 3709 W. Flagler St., Coral Gables, FL 33134 / 305-642-2355

National Target Co., 3958-D Dartmouth Ct., Frederick, MD 21703 / 800-827-7060; FAX: 301-874-4764 www.nationaltarget.com

Nationwide Airgun Repair, 2310 Windsor Forest Dr., Louisville, KY 40272 / 502-937-2614 shortshoestring@insightbb.com

Naval Ordnance Works, 467 Knott Rd., Sheperdstown, WV 25443 / 304-876-0998; FAX: 304-876-0998 nvordfdy@earthlink.net

Navy Arms Company, 219 Lawn St., Martinsburg, WV 25401 / 304-262-9870; FAX: 304-262-1658 info@navyarms.com www.navyarms.com

NCP Products, Inc., 3500 12th St. N.W., Canton, OH 44708 / 330-456-5130; FAX: 330-456-5234

Necessary Concepts, Inc., P.O. Box 571, Deer Park, NY 11729 / 516-667-8509; FAX: 516-667-8588

NEI Handtools, Inc., 10960 Gary Player Dr., El Paso, TX 79935

Neil A. Jones Custom Products, 17217 Brookhouser Road, Saegertown, PA 16433 / 814-763-2769; FAX: 814-763-4228

Nelson, Gary K., 975 Terrace Dr., Oakdale, CA 95361 / 209-847-4590

Nelson, Stephen. See: NELSON'S CUSTOM GUNS, INC.

Nelson's Custom Guns, Inc., Stephen Nelson, 7430 Valley View Dr. N.W., Corvallis, OR 97330 / 541-745-5232 nelsons-custom@attbi.com

Nesci Enterprises Inc., P.O. Box 119, Summit St., East Hampton, CT 06424 / 203-267-2588

Nesika Bay Precision, 22239 Big Valley Rd., Poulsbo, WA 98370 / 206-697-3830

Nettestad Gun Works, 38962 160th Avenue, Pelican Rapids, MN 56572 / 218-863-1338

New England Ammunition Co., 1771 Post Rd. East, Suite 223, Westport, CT 06880 / 203-254-8048

New England Arms Co., Box 278, Lawrence Lane, Kittery Point, ME 03905 / 207-439-0593; FAX: 207-439-0525 info@newenglandarms.com www.newenglandarms.com

New England Custom Gun Service, 438 Willow Brook Rd., Plainfield, NH 03781 / 603-469-3450; FAX: 603-469-3471 bestguns@adelphia.net www.newenglandcustom.com

New Orleans Jewelers Supply Co., 206 Charters St., New Orleans, LA 70130 / 504-523-3839; FAX: 504-523-3836

New SKB Arms Co., C.P.O. Box 1401, Tokyo, JAPAN / 81-3-3943-9550; FAX: 81-3-3943-0695

New Ultra Light Arms, LLC, P.O. Box 340, Granville, WV 26534

Newark Electronics, 4801 N. Ravenswood Ave., Chicago, IL 60640

Newell, Robert H., 55 Coyote, Los Alamos, NM 87544 / 505-662-7135

Newman Gunshop, 2035 Chester Ave. #411, Ottumwa, IA 52501-3715 / 515-937-5775

NgraveR Co., The, 67 Wawecus Hill Rd., Bozrah, CT 06334 / 860-823-1533; FAX: 860-887-6252 ngraver98@aol.com www.ngraver.com

Nicholson Custom, 17285 Thornlay Road, Hughesville, MO 65334 / 816-826-8746

Nickels, Paul R., 2216 Jacob Dr., Santa Clara, UT 84765-5399 / 435-652-1959

Niemi Engineering, W. B., Box 126 Center Rd., Greensboro, VT 05841 / 802-533-7180; FAX: 802-533-7141

Nighthawk Custom, 1306 W. Trimble, Berryville, AR 72616 / 877-268-GUNS; (4867) or 870-423-GUNS; FAX: 870-423-4230 www.nighthawkcustom.com

Nikon, Inc., 1300 Walt Whitman Rd., Melville, NY 11747 / 516-547-8623; FAX: 516-547-0309

Noreen, Peter H., 5075 Buena Vista Dr., Belgrade, MT 59714 / 406-586-7383

Norica, Avnda Otaola, 16 Apartado 68, Eibar, SPAIN

Norinco, 7A Yun Tan N, Beijing, CHINA

Norincoptics (See BEC, Inc.)

Norma Precision AB (See U.S. Importers-Dynamit)

Normark Corp., 10395 Yellow Circle Dr., Minnetonka, MN 55343-9101 / 612-933-7060; FAX: 612-933-0046

North American Arms, Inc., 2150 South 950 East, Provo, UT 84606-6285 / 800-821-5783 or 801-374-9990; FAX: 801-374-9998

North American Correspondence Schools, The Gun Pro, Oak & Pawney St., Scranton, PA 18515 / 717-342-7701

North American Shooting Systems, P.O. Box 306, Osoyoos, BC V0H 1V0 CANADA / 250-495-3131; FAX: 250-495-3131 rifle@cablerocket.com

North Devon Firearms Services, 3 North St., Braunton, EX33 1AJ ENGLAND / 01271 813624; FAX: 01271 813624

North Mountain Pine Training Center (See Executive Protection Institute)

North Star West, Inc., P.O. Box 487, 57 Terrace Ct., Superior, MT 59872 / 406-822-8778 laffindog@msn.com www.northstarwest.com

Northern Precision, 329 S. James St., Carthage, NY 13619 / 315-493-1711

Northside Gun Shop, 2725 NW 109th, Oklahoma City, OK 73120 / 405-840-2353

Northwest Custom Projectile, P.O. Box 127, Butte, MT 59703-0127 www.customprojectile.com

No-Sho Mfg. Co., 10727 Glenfield Ct., Houston, TX 77096 / 713-723-5332

Nosler, Inc., P.O. Box 671, Bend, OR 97709 / 800-285-3701 or 541-382-3921; FAX: 541-388-4667 www.nosler.com

Novak's, Inc., 1206 1/2 30th St., P.O. Box 4045, Parkersburg, WV 26101 / 304-485-9295; FAX: 304-428-6722 www.novaksights.com

Nowlin Mfg. Co., 20622 S 4092 Rd., Claremore, OK 74017 / 918-342-0689; FAX: 918-342-0624 nowlinguns@msn.com nowlinguns.com

NRI Gunsmith School, P.O. Box 182968, Columbus, OH 43218-2968

Nu Line Guns, Inc., 8150 CR 4055, Rhineland, MO 65069 / 573-676-5500; FAX: 573-676-3400 nlg@ktis.net

Null Holsters Ltd. K.L., 161 School St. N.W., Resaca, GA 30735 / 706-625-5643; FAX: 706-625-9392 ken@klnullholsters.com www.klnullholsters.com

Numrich Gun Parts Corporation, 226 Williams Lane, P.O. Box 299, West Hurley, NY 12491 / 866-686-7424; FAX: 877-GUNPART info@gunpartscorp.com www.@e-gunparts.com

O

O.F. Mossberg & Sons, Inc., 7 Grasso Ave., North Haven, CT 06473 / 203-230-5300; FAX: 203-230-5420

Oakman Turkey Calls, RD 1, Box 825, Harrisonville, PA 17228 / 717-485-4620

Obermeyer Rifled Barrels, 23122 60th St., Bristol, WI 53104 / 262-843-3537; FAX: 262-843-2129 www.obermeyerbarrels.com

October Country Muzzleloading, P.O. Box 969, Dept. GD, Hayden, ID 83835 / 208-772-2068; FAX: 208-772-9230 ocinfo@octobercountry.com www.octobercountry.com

Oehler Research, Inc., P.O. Box 9135, Austin, TX 78766 / 512-327-6900 or 800-531-5125; FAX: 512-327-6903 www.oehler-research.com

Oil Rod and Gun Shop, 69 Oak St., East Douglas, MA 01516 / 508-476-3687

OK Weber, Inc., P.O. Box 7485, Eugene, OR 97401 / 541-747-0458; FAX: 541-747-5927 okweber@pacinfo www.okweber.com

Oker's Engraving, P.O. Box 126, Shawnee, CO 80475 / 303-838-6042 engraver@netscape.com

Oklahoma Ammunition Co., 3701A S. Harvard Ave., No. 367, Tulsa, OK 74135-2265 / 918-396-3187; FAX: 918-396-4270

Oklahoma Leather Products, Inc., 500 26th NW, Miami, OK 74354 / 918-542-6651; FAX: 918-542-6653

Olathe Gun Shop, 716-A South Rogers Road, Olathe, KS 66062 / 913-782-6900; FAX: 913-782-6902 info@olathegunshop.com www.olathegunshop.com

Old Wagon Bullets, 32 Old Wagon Rd., Wilton, CT 06897

Old West Bullet Moulds, J. Ken Chapman, P.O. Box 519, Flora Vista, NM 87415 / 505-334-6970

Old West Reproductions, Inc. R.M. Bachman, 446 Florence S. Loop, Florence, MT 59833 / 406-273-2615; FAX: 406-273-2615 rick@oldwestreproductions.com www.oldwestreproductions.com

Old Western Scrounger LLC, 219 Lawn St., Martinsburg, NV 25401 / 304-262-9870; FAX: 304-262-1658 www.ows-ammo.com

Ole Frontier Gunsmith Shop, 2617 Hwy. 29 S., Cantonment, FL 32533 / 904-477-8074

Olson, Myron, 989 W. Kemp, Watertown, SD 57201 / 605-886-9787

Olson, Vic, 5002 Countryside Dr., Imperial, MO 63052 / 314-296-8086

Olympic Arms Inc., 620-626 Old Pacific Hwy. SE, Olympia, WA 98513 / 360-456-3471; FAX: 360-491-3447 info@olyarms.com www.olyarms.com

MANUFACTURER'S DIRECTORY

Olympic Optical Co., P.O. Box 752377, Memphis, TN 38175-2377 / 901-794-3890 or 800-238-7120; FAX: 901-794-0676

One Of A Kind, 15610 Purple Sage, San Antonio, TX 78255 / 512-695-3364

One Ragged Hole, P.O. Box 13624, Tallahassee, FL 32317-3624

Op-Tec, P.O. Box L632, Langhorn, PA 19047 / 215-757-5037; FAX: 215-757-7097

Optical Services Co., P.O. Box 1174, Santa Teresa, NM 88008-1174 / 505-589-3833

Orchard Park Enterprise, P.O. Box 563, Orchard Park, NY 14127 / 616-656-0356

Ordnance Works, The, 2969 Pigeon Point Rd., Eureka, CA 95501 / 707-443-3252

Oregon Arms, Inc. (See Rogue Rifle Co., Inc.)

Oregon Trail Bullet Company, P.O. Box 529, Dept. P, Baker City, OR 97814 / 800-811-0548; FAX: 514-523-1803

Original Deer Formula Co., The, P.O. Box 1705, Dickson, TN 37056 / 800-874-6965; FAX: 615-446-0646 deerformula1@aol.com www.deerformula.com

Orion Rifle Barrel Co., Jerry Cunningham, P.O. Box 130192, Coram, MT 59913 / 406-257-5649

Orvis Co., The, Rt. 7, Manchester, VT 05254 / 802-362-3622; FAX: 802-362-3525

Otis Technology, Inc., RR 1 Box 84, Boonville, NY 13309 / 315-942-3320

Ottmar, Maurice, 920 Timber Trl, Cedar Park, TX 78613

Outa-Site Gun Carriers, 219 Market St., Laredo, TX 78040 / 210-722-4678 or 800-880-9715; FAX: 210-726-4858

Outdoor Connection, Inc., The, 7901 Panther Way, Waco, TX 76712-6556 / 800-533-6076; FAX: 254-776-3553 info@outdoorconnection.com www.outdoorconnection.com

Outdoor Edge Cutlery Corp., 4699 Nautilus Ct. S. Ste. 503, Boulder, CO 80301-5310 / 303-530-7667; FAX: 303-530-7020 www.outdooredge.com

Outdoor Enthusiast, 3784 W. Woodland, Springfield, MO 65807 / 417-883-9841

Outdoor Sports Headquarters, Inc., 967 Watertower Ln., West Carrollton, OH 45449 / 513-865-5855; FAX: 513-865-5962

Outers Laboratories Div. of ATK, Route 2, P.O. Box 39, Onalaska, WI 54650 / 608-781-5800; FAX: 608-781-0368

Ozark Gun Works, 11830 Cemetery Rd., Rogers, AR 72756 / 479-631-1024; FAX: 479-631-1024 ozarkgunworks@cox.net www.geocities.com

P

P&M Sales & Services, LLC, 4697 Tote Rd. Bldg. H-B, Comins, MI 48619 / 989-848-8364; FAX: 989-848-8364 info@pmsales-online.com

P.S.M.G. Gun Co., 10 Park Ave., Arlington, MA 02174 / 781-646-1699; FAX: 781-643-7212 psmg2@aol.com

Pachmayr Div. Lyman Products, 475 Smith St., Middletown, CT 06457 / 860-632-2020 or 800-225-9626; FAX: 860-632-1699 lymansales@cshore.com www.pachmayr.com

Pacific Armament Corp, 4813 Enterprise Way, Unit K, Modesto, CA 95356 / 209-545-2800 gunsparts@att.net

Pacific Rifle Co., P.O. Box 841, Carlton, OR 97111 / 503-852-6276 pacificrifle@aol.com

PAC-NOR Barreling, Inc., 99299 Overlook Rd., P.O. Box 6188, Brookings, OR 97415 / 541-469-7330; FAX: 541-469-7331 chris@pac-nor.com www.pac-nor.com

PACT, Inc., P.O. Box 535025, Grand Prairie, TX 75053 / 972-641-0049; FAX: 972-641-2641

Page Custom Bullets, P.O. Box 25, Port Moresby, NEW GUINEA

Pagel Gun Works, Inc., 2 SE 1st St., Grand Rapids, MN 55744

Pager Pal, P.O. Box 54864, Hurst, TX 76054-4864 / 800-561-1603; FAX: 817-285-8769 info@pagerpal.com www.pagerpal.com

Paintball Games International Magazine Aceville, Castle House 97 High St., Essex, ENGLAND / 011-44-206-564840

Palsa Outdoor Products, P.O. Box 81336, Lincoln, NE 68501 / 402-488-5288; FAX: 402-488-2321

Pansch, Robert F, 1004 Main St. #10, Neenah, WI 54956 / 920-725-8175

Paragon Sales & Services, Inc., 2501 Theodore St., Crest Hill, IL 60435-1613 / 815-725-9212; FAX: 815-725-8974

Para-Ordnance Mfg., Inc., 980 Tapscott Rd., Scarborough, ON M1X 1E7 CANADA / 416-297-7855; FAX: 416-297-1289

Para-Ordnance, Inc., 1919 NE 45th St., Ste 215, Ft. Lauderdale, FL 33308 / 416-297-7855; FAX: 416-297-1289 info@paraord.com www.paraord.com

Pardini Armi Srl, Via Italica 154, 55043, Lido Di Camaiore Lu, ITALY / 584-90121; FAX: 584-90122

Paris, Frank J., 17417 Pershing St., Livonia, MI 48152-3822

Park Rifle Co., Ltd., The, Unit 6a Dartford Trade Park, Power Mill Lane, Dartford DA7 7NX, ENGLAND / 011-0322-222512

Parker & Sons Shooting Supply, 9337 Smoky Row Road, Strawberry Plains, TN 37871 / 865-933-3286; FAX: 865-932-8586

Parker Gun Finishes, 9337 Smokey Row Rd., Strawberry Plains, TN 37871 / 865-933-3286; FAX: 865-932-8586 parcraft7838@netzero.com

Parsons Optical Mfg. Co., PO Box 192, Ross, OH 45061 / 513-867-0820; FAX: 513-867-8380 psscopes@concentric.net

Partridge Sales Ltd., John, Trent Meadows, Rugeley, ENGLAND

Pasadena Gun Center, 206 E. Shaw, Pasadena, TX 77506 / 713-472-0417; FAX: 713-472-1322

Passive Bullet Traps, Inc. (See Savage Range Systems, Inc.)

Paterson Gunsmithing, 438 Main St., Paterson, NJ 07502 / 201-345-4100

Pathfinder Sports Leather, 2920 E. Chambers St., Phoenix, AZ 85040 / 602-276-0016

Patrick W. Price Bullets, 16520 Worthley Drive, San Lorenzo, CA 94580 / 510-278-1547

Pattern Control, 114 N. Third St., P.O. Box 462105, Garland, TX 75046 / 214-494-3551; FAX: 214-272-8447

Paul A. Harris Hand Engraving, 113 Rusty Lane, Boerne, TX 78006-5746 / 512-391-5121

Paul and Sharon Dressel, 209 N. 92nd Ave., Yakima, WA 98908 / 509-966-9233; FAX: 509-966-3365 dressels@nwinfo.net www.dressels.com

Paul Co., The, 27385 Pressonville Rd., Wellsville, KS 66092 / 785-883-4444; FAX: 785-883-2525

Paul D. Hillmer Custom Gunstocks, 7251 Hudson Heights, Hudson, IA 50643 / 319-988-3941

Paul Jones Moulds, 4901 Telegraph Rd., Los Angeles, CA 90022 / 213-262-1510

Paulsen Gunstocks, Rt. 71, Box 11, Chinook, MT 59523 / 406-357-3403

Pawling Mountain Club, Keith Lupton, P.O. Box 573, Pawling, NY 12564 / 914-855-3825

Paxton Quigley's Personal Protection Strategies, 9903 Santa Monica Blvd., 300, Beverly Hills, CA 90212 / 310-281-1762 www.defend-net.com/paxton

Payne Photography, Robert, Robert, P.O. Box 141471, Austin, TX 78714 / 512-272-4554

Peacemaker Specialists, 144 Via Fuchsia, Paso Robles, CA 93446 / 805-238-9100; FAX: 805-238-9100 www.peacemakerspecialists.com

Pearce Grip, Inc., P.O. Box 40367, Fort Worth, TX 76140 / 817-568-9704; FAX: 817-568-9707 info@pearcegrip.com www.pearcegrip.com

PECAR Herbert Schwarz GmbH, Kreuzbergstrasse 6, 10965, Berlin, GERMANY / 004930-785-7383; FAX: 004930-785-1934 michael.schwarz@pecar-berlin.de www.pecar-berlin.de

Pecatonica River Longrifle, 5205 Nottingham Dr., Rockford, IL 61111 / 815-968-1995; FAX: 815-968-1996

Pedersen, C. R., 2717 S. Pere Marquette Hwy., Ludington, MI 49431 / 231-843-2061; FAX: 231-845-7695 fega@fega.com

Pedersen, Rex C., 2717 S. Pere Marquette Hwy., Ludington, MI 49431 / 231-843-2061; FAX: 231-845-7695 fega@fega.com

Peifer Rifle Co., P.O. Box 220, Nokomis, IL 62075

Pejsa Ballistics, 1314 Marquette Ave., Apt 906, Minneapolis, MN 55403 / 612-332-5073; FAX: 612-332-5204 pejsa@sprintmail.com pejsa.com

Peltor, Inc. (See Aero Peltor)

Pence Precision Barrels, 7567 E. 900 S., S. Whitley, IN 46787 / 219-839-4745

Pendleton Woolen Mills, P.O. Box 3030, 220 N.W. Broadway, Portland, OR 97208 / 503-226-4801

Penn Bullets, P.O. Box 756, Indianola, PA 15051

Pennsylvania Gun Parts Inc., RR 7 Box 150, Mount Pleasant, PA 15666

Pennsylvania Gunsmith School, 812 Ohio River Blvd., Avalon, Pittsburgh, PA 15202 / 412-766-1812; FAX: 412-766-0855 pgs@pagunsmith.edu www.pagunsmith.edu

Penrod, Mark. See: PENROD PRECISION

Penrod Precision, Mark Penrod, 312 College Ave., P.O. Box 307, N. Manchester, IN 46962 / 260-982-8385; FAX: 260-982-1819 markpenrod@kconline.com

Pentax U.S.A., Inc., 600 12th St. Ste. 300, Golden, CO 80401 / 303-799-8000; FAX: 303-460-1628 www.pentaxlightseeker.com

Pentheny de Pentheny, c/o H.P. Okelly, 321 S. Main St., Sebastopol, CA 95472 / 707-824-1637; FAX: 707-824-1637

Perazone-Gunsmith, Brian, Cold Spring Rd., Roxbury, NY 12474 / 607-326-4088; FAX: 607-326-3140 bpgunsmith@catskill.net www.bpgunsmith@catskill.net

Perazzi U.S.A. Inc., 1010 West Tenth, Azusa, CA 91702 / 626-334-1234; FAX: 626-334-0344 perazziusa@aol.com

Performance Specialists, 308 Eanes School Rd., Austin, TX 78746 / 512-327-0119

Perugini Visini & Co. SAS, Via Camprelle, 126, 25080 Nuvolera, ITALY / 30-6897535; FAX: 30-6897821 info@peruvisi@visini.com

Pete de Coux Auction House, 14940 Brenda Dr., Prescott, AZ 86305-7447 / 928-776-8285; FAX: 928-776-8276 pdbullets@commspeed.net

Pete Mazur Restoration, 13083 Drummer Way, Grass Valley, CA 95949 / 530-268-2412; FAX: 530-268-2412

Pete Rickard Co., 115 Roy Walsh Rd., Cobleskill, NY 12043 / 518-234-2731; FAX: 518-234-2454 rickard@telenet.net www.peterickard.com

Peter Dyson & Son Ltd., 3 Cuckoo Lane, Honley, Holmfirth, West Yorkshire, HD9 6AS ENGLAND / 44-1484-661062; FAX: 44-1484-663709 peter@peterdyson.co.uk www.peterdyson.co.uk

Peter Hale/Engraver, 997 Maple Dr., Spanish Fork, UT 84660-2524 / 801-798-8215

Peters Stahl GmbH, Stettiner Strasse 42, D-33106, Paderborn, GERMANY / 05251-750025; FAX: 05251-75611 info@peters-stahl.com www.peters-stahl.com

Peterson Gun Shop, Inc., A.W., 4255 W. Old U.S. 441, Mt. Dora, FL 32757-3299 / 352-383-4258; FAX: 352-735-1001

Petro-Explo Inc., 7650 U.S. Hwy. 287, Suite 100, Arlington, TX 76017 / 817-478-8888

Pettinger Books, Gerald, 47827 300th Ave., Russell, IA 50238 / 641-535-2239 gpettinger@lisco.com

Pflumm Mfg. Co., 10662 Widmer Rd., Lenexa, KS 66215 / 800-888-4867; FAX: 913-451-7857

PFRB Co., P.O. Box 1242, Bloomington, IL 61702 / 800-914-5464; FAX: 888-554-8369

Phillippi Custom Bullets, Justin, P.O. Box 773, Ligonier, PA 15658 / 724-238-2962; FAX: 724-238-9671 jrp@wpa.net http://www.wpa.net~jrphil

Phoenix Arms, 4231 Brickell St., Ontario, CA 91761 / 909-937-6900; FAX: 909-937-0060

Piedmont Community College, P.O. Box 1197, Roxboro, NC 27573 / 336-599-1181; FAX: 336-597-3817 www.piedmont.cc.nc.us

Pietta (See U.S. Importers-Navy Arms Co, Taylor's

Pine Technical College, 1100 4th St., Pine City, MN 55063 / 800-521-7463; FAX: 612-629-6766

Pinetree Bullets, 133 Skeena St., Kitimat, BC V8C 1Z1 CANADA / 604-632-3768; FAX: 604-632-3768

Pioneer Arms Co., 355 Lawrence Rd., Broomall, PA 19008 / 215-356-5203

Piotti (See U.S. Importer-Moore & Co., Wm. Larkin)

Piquette, Paul. See: PIQUETTE'S CUSTOM ENGRAVING

Piquette's Custom Engraving, Paul R. Piquette, 511 Southwick St., Feeding Hills, MA 01030 / 413-789-4582 ppiquette@comcast.net www.pistoldynamics.com

Plaza Cutlery, Inc., 3333 Bristol, 161 South Coast Plaza, Costa Mesa, CA 92626 / 714-549-3932

Plum City Ballistic Range, N2162 80th St., Plum City, WI 54761 / 715-647-2539

PlumFire Press, Inc., 30-A Grove Ave., Patchogue, NY 11772-4112 / 800-695-7246; FAX: 516-758-4071

PMC/Eldorado Cartridge Corp., P.O. Box 62508, 12801 U.S. Hwy. 95 S., Boulder City, NV 89005 / 702-294-0025; FAX: 702-294-0121 kbauer@pmcammo.com www.pmcammo.com

Poburka, Philip (See Bison Studios)

Pointing Dog Journal, Village Press Publications, P.O. Box 968, Dept. PGD, Traverse City, MI 49685 / 800-272-3246; FAX: 616-946-3289

Police Bookshelf, P.O. Box 122, Concord, NH 03301 / 603-224-6814; FAX: 603-226-3554 ayoob@attglobal.net www.ayoob.com

Polywad, Inc., P.O. Box 7916, Macon, GA 31209 / 478-477-0669 or 800-998-0669 FAX: 478-477-0666 polywadmpb@aol.com www.polywad.com

Ponsness, Warren, 7634 W. Ohio St., Rathdrum, ID 83858 / 800-732-0706; FAX: 208-687-2233 www.reloaders.com

Pony Express Reloaders, 608 E. Co. Rd. D, Suite 3, St. Paul, MN 55117 / 612-483-9406; FAX: 612-483-9884

Pony Express Sport Shop, 23404 Lyons Ave., PMB 448, Newhall, CA 91321-2511 / 818-895-1231

Powder Horn Ltd., P.O. Box 565, Glenview, IL 60025 / 305-565-6060

Powell & Son (Gunmakers) Ltd., William, 35-37 Carrs Lane, Birmingham, B4 7SX ENGLAND / 121-643-0689; FAX: 121-631-3504 sales@william-powell.co.uk www.william-powell.co.uk

Powell Agency, William, 22 Circle Dr., Bellmore, NY 11710 / 516-679-1158

Power Custom, Inc., 29739 Hwy. J, Gravois Mills, MO 65037 / 573-372-5684; FAX: 573-372-5799 rwpowers@laurie.net www.powercustom.com

Power Plus Enterprises, Inc., P.O. Box 38, Warm Springs, GA 31830 / 706-655-2132

Powley Computer (See Hutton Rifle Ranch)

Practical Tools, Inc., 7067 Easton Rd., P.O. Box 133, Pipersville, PA 18947 / 215-766-7301; FAX: 215-766-8681

Prairie Gun Works, 1-761 Marion St., Winnipeg, MB R2J 0K6 CANADA / 204-231-2976; FAX: 204-231-8566

Pranger, Ed G., 1414 7th St., Anacortes, WA 98221 / 206-293-3488

Precision Airgun Sales, Inc., 5247 Warrensville Ctr. Rd., Maple Hts., OH 44137 / 216-587-5005; FAX: 216-587-5005

Precision Cast Bullets, 101 Mud Creek Lane, Ronan, MT 59864 / 406-676-5135

Precision Delta Corp., P.O. Box 128, Ruleville, MS 38771 / 662-756-2810; FAX: 662-756-2590

Precision Firearm Finishing, 25 N.W. 44th Avenue, Des Moines, IA 50313 / 515-288-8680; FAX: 515-244-3925

Precision Gun Works, 104 Sierra Rd., Dept. GD, Kerrville, TX 78028 / 830-367-4587

Precision Reloading, 124 S. Main St., Mitchell, SD 57301 / 605-996-9984

Precision Reloading, Inc., 124 S. Main St., Mitchell, SD 57301 / 800-223-0900; FAX: 605-996-9987 info@precisionreloading.com www.precisionreloading.com

Precision Shooting, Inc., 222 McKee St., Manchester, CT 06040 / 860-645-8776; FAX: 860-643-8215 www.precisionshooting.com

Precision Small Arms Inc., 9272 Jeronimo Rd., Ste. 121, Irvine, CA 92618 / 800-554-5515 or 949-768-3530; FAX: 949-768-4808 www.tcbebe.com

Precision Specialties, 131 Hendom Dr., Feeding Hills, MA 01030 / 413-786-3365; FAX: 413-786-3365

Precision Sport Optics, 15571 Producer Lane, Unit G, Huntington Beach, CA 92649 / 714-891-1309; FAX: 714-892-6920

Preslik's Gunstocks, 4245 Keith Ln., Chico, CA 95926 / 916-891-8236

Price Bullets, Patrick W., 16520 Worthley Dr., San Lorenzo, CA 94580 / 510-278-1547

Primedia Publishing Co., 6420 Wilshire Blvd., Los Angeles, CA 90048 / 213-782-2000; FAX: 213-782-2867

Primos Hunting Calls, 604 First St., Flora, MS 39071 / 601-879-9323; FAX: 601-879-9324 www.primos.com

PRL Bullets, c/o Blackburn Enterprises, 114 Stuart Rd., Ste. 110, Cleveland, TN 37312 / 423-559-0340

Professional Gunsmiths of America, 1209 South 13 Hwy., Lexington, MO 64067 / 816-529-1337

Professional Hunter Supplies, P.O. Box 608, 468 Main St., Ferndale, CA 95536 / 707-786-9140; FAX: 707-786-9117 wmebride@humboldt.com

ProOlixr;lubricants, P.O. Box 1466, West Jordan, UT 84084-1466 / 801-569-2763; FAX: 801-569-8225 prolix@prolixlubricant.com www.prolixlubricant.com

Pro-Mark Div. of Wells Lamont, 6640 W. Touhy, Chicago, IL 60648 / 312-647-8200

Proofmark Corp., P.O. Box 357, Burgess, VA 22432 / 804-453-4337; FAX: 804-453-4337 proofmark@direcway.com www.proofmarkbullets.com

Pro-Port Ltd., 41302 Executive Dr., Harrison Twp., MI 48045-1306 / 586-469-6727; FAX: 586-469-0425 e-mail@magnaport.com www.magnaport.com

Pro-Shot Products, Inc., P.O. Box 763, Taylorville, IL 62568 / 217-824-9133; FAX: 217-824-8861 www.proshotproducts.com

Protector Mfg. Co., Inc., The, 443 Ashwood Pl., Boca Raton, FL 33431 / 407-394-6011

Protektor Model, 1-11 Bridge St., Galeton, PA 16922 / 814-435-2442 mail@protektormodel.com www.protektormodel.com

Prototech Industries, Inc., 10532 E Road, Delia, KS 66418 / 785-771-3571 prototec@grapevine.net

PWL Gunleather, P.O. Box 450432, Atlanta, GA 31145 / 800-960-4072; FAX: 770-822-1704 covert@pwlusa.com www.pwlusa.com

PWM Sales Ltd., N.D.F.S., Gowdall Lane, Pollington DN14 0AU, ENGLAND / 01405862688; FAX: 01405862622 Paulwelburn9@aol.com

Pyramyd Stone Inter. Corp., 2447 Suffolk Lane, Pepper Pike, OH 44124-4540

Q

Quack Decoy & Sporting Clays, 4 Ann & Hope Way, P.O. Box 98, Cumberland, RI 02864 / 401-723-8202; FAX: 401-722-5910

Quaker Boy, Inc., 5455 Webster Rd., Orchard Parks, NY 14127 / 716-662-3979; FAX: 716-662-9426

Quality Arms, Inc., Box 19477, Dept. GD, Houston, TX 77224 / 281-870-8377 arrieta2@excite.com www.arrieta.com

Quality Cartridge, P.O. Box 445, Hollywood, MD 20636 / 301-373-3719 www.qual-cart.com

Quality Custom Firearms, Stephen Billeb, 22 Vista View Dr., Cody, WY 82414 / 307-587-4278; FAX: 307-587-4297 stevebilleb@wyoming.com

Quarton Beamshot, 4538 Centerview Dr., Ste. 149, San Antonio, TX 78228 / 800-520-8435; FAX: 210-735-1326 www.beamshot.com

Que Industries, Inc., P.O. Box 2471, Everett, WA 98203 / 425-303-9088; FAX: 206-514-3266 queinfo@queindustries.com

Queen Cutlery Co., P.O. Box 500, Franklinville, NY 14737 / 800-222-5233; FAX: 800-299-2618

R

R&C Knives & Such, 2136 Candy Cane Walk, Manteca, CA 95336-9501 / 209-239-3722; FAX: 209-825-6947

R&D Gun Repair, Kenny Howell, RR1 Box 283, Beloit, WI 53511

R&J Gun Shop, 337 S. Humbolt St., Canyon City, OR 97820 / 541-575-2130 rjgunshop@highdesertnet.com

R&S Industries Corp., 8255 Brentwood Industrial Dr., St. Louis, MO 63144 / 314-781-5169 ron@miraclepolishingcloth.com www.miraclepolishingcloth.com

R. Murphy Co., Inc., 13 Groton-Harvard Rd., P.O. Box 376, Ayer, MA 01432 / 617-772-3481 www.r.murphyknives.com

R.A. Wells Custom Gunsmith, 3452 1st Ave., Racine, WI 53402 / 414-639-5223

R.E. Seebeck Assoc., P.O. Box 59752, Dallas, TX 75229

R.E.I., P.O. Box 88, Tallevast, FL 34270 / 813-755-0085

R.E.T. Enterprises, 2608 S. Chestnut, Broken Arrow, OK 74012 / 918-251-GUNS; (4867) FAX: 918-251-0587

R.T. Eastman Products, P.O. Box 1531, Jackson, WY 83001 / 307-733-3217; or 800-624-4311

Rabeno, Martin, 530 The Eagle Pass, Durango, CO 81301 / 970-382-0353 fancygun@aol.com

Radack Photography, Lauren, 21140 Jib Court L-12, Aventura, FL 33180 / 305-931-3110

Radiator Specialty Co., 1900 Wilkinson Blvd., P.O. Box 34689, Charlotte, NC 28234 / 800-438-6947; FAX: 800-421-9525 tkrossell@gunk.com www.gunk.com

Radical Concepts, P.O. Box 1473, Lake Grove, OR 97035 / 503-538-7437

Rainier Ballistics, 4500 15th St. East, Tacoma, WA 98424 / 800-638-8722; FAX: 253-922-7854 sales@rainierballistics.com www.rainierballistics.com

Ram-Line ATK, P.O. Box 39, Onalaska, WI 54650

Rampart International, 2781 W. MacArthur Blvd., B-283, Santa Ana, CA 92704 / 800-976-7240 or 714-557-6405

Ranch Products, P.O. Box 145, Malinta, OH 43535 / 313-277-3118; FAX: 313-565-8536 stevenacrawford@msn.com ranchproducts.com

Randall-Made Knives, P.O. Box 1988, Orlando, FL 32802 / 407-855-8075

Randco UK, 286 Gipsy Rd., Welling, DA16 1JJ ENGLAND / 44 81 303 4118

Randolph Engineering, Inc., Ranger Shooting Glasses, 26 Thomas Patten Dr., Randolph, MA 02368 / 800-541-1405; FAX: 781-986-0337 sales@randolphusa.com www.randolphusa.com

Range Brass Products Company, P.O. Box 218, Rockport, TX 78381

Ransom International Corp., P.O. Box 3845, Prescott, AZ 86302 / 928-778-7899; FAX: 928-778-7993 ransom@cableone.net www.ransomrest.com

Rapine Bullet Mould Mfg. Co., 9503 Landis Lane, East Greenville, PA 18041 / 215-679-5413; FAX: 215-679-9795

Ravell Ltd., 289 Diputacion St., 08009, Barcelona, SPAIN / 34(3) 4874486; FAX: 34(3) 4881394

Ray Riling Arms Books Co., 6844 Gorsten St., Philadelphia, PA 19119 / 215-438-2456; FAX: 215-438-5395 sales@rayrilingarmsbooks.com www.rayrilingarmsbooks.com

Ray's Gunsmith Shop, 3199 Elm Ave., Grand Junction, CO 81504 / 970-434-6162; FAX: 970-434-3452

Raytech Div. of Lyman Products Corp., 475 Smith Street, Middletown, CT 06457-1541 / 860-632-2020 or 800-225-9626; FAX: 860-632-1699 raysales@cshore.com www.raytech-ind.com

RCBS Operations/ATK, 605 Oro Dam Blvd., Oroville, CA 95965 / 800-533-5000; FAX: 530-533-1647 www.rcbs.com

Reardon Products, P.O. Box 126, Morrison, IL 61270 / 815-772-3155

Recoilless Technologies, Inc. (RTI), RTI/High-Low, 2141 E. Cedar #2, Tempe, AZ 85281 / 480-966-7051

Red Diamond Dist. Co., 1304 Snowdon Dr., Knoxville, TN 37912

Redding Reloading Equipment, 1089 Starr Rd., Cortland, NY 13045 / 607-753-3331; FAX: 607-756-8445 techline@redding-reloading.com www.redding-reloading.com

Redfield Media Resource Center, 4607 N.E. Cedar Creek Rd., Woodland, WA 98674 / 360-225-5000; FAX: 360-225-7616

Redman's Rifling & Reboring, 189 Nichols Rd., Omak, WA 98841 / 509-826-5512

Redwood Bullet Works, 3559 Bay Rd., Redwood City, CA 94063 / 415-367-6741

Reed, Dave, Rt. 1, Box 374, Minnesota City, MN 55959 / 507-689-2944

Reimer Johannsen, Inc., 438 Willow Brook Rd., Plainfield, NH 03781 / 603-469-3450; FAX: 603-469-3471

Reloaders Equipment Co., 4680 High St., Ecorse, MI 48229

Reloading Specialties, Inc., Box 1130, Pine Island, MN 55463 / 507-356-8500; FAX: 507-356-8800

Remington Arms Co., Inc., 870 Remington Drive, P.O. Box 700, Madison, NC 27025-0700 / 800-243-9700; FAX: 336-548-8700 info@remington.com www.remington.com

Remington Double Shotguns, 7885 Cyd Dr., Denver, CO 80221 / 303-429-6947

Renegade, P.O. Box 31546, Phoenix, AZ 85046 / 602-482-6777; FAX: 602-482-1952

Renfrew Guns & Supplies, R.R. 4, Renfrew, ON K7V 3Z7 CANADA / 613-432-7080

Reno, Wayne, 2808 Stagestop Road, Jefferson, CO 80456

Republic Arms, Inc. (See Cobra Enterprises, Inc.)

Retting, Inc., Martin B., 11029 Washington, Culver City, CA 90232 / 213-837-2412

RG-G, Inc., P.O. Box 935, Trinidad, CO 81082 / 719-845-1436

RH Machine & Consulting Inc., P.O. Box 394, Pacific, MO 63069 / 314-271-8465

Rhino, P.O. Box 787, Locust, NC 28097 / 704-753-2198

Rhodeside, Inc., 1704 Commerce Dr., Piqua, OH 45356 / 513-773-5781

Rice, Keith (See White Rock Tool & Die)

Richards MicroFit Stocks, Inc., P.O. Box 1066, Sun Valley, CA 91352 / 800-895-7420; FAX: 818-771-1242 sales@rifle-stocks.com www.rifle-stocks.com

Ridgeline, Inc., Bruce Sheldon, P.O. Box 930, Dewey, AZ 86327-0930 / 800-632-5900; FAX: 520-632-5900

Ridgetop Sporting Goods, P.O. Box 306, 42907 Hilligoss Ln. East, Eatonville, WA 98328 / 360-832-6422; FAX: 360-832-6422

Ries, Chuck, 415 Ridgecrest Dr., Grants Pass, OR 97527 / 503-476-5623

Rifles, Inc., 3580 Leal Rd., Pleasanton, TX 78064 / 830-569-2055; FAX: 830-569-2297

Riggs, Jim, 206 Azalea, Boerne, TX 78006 / 210-249-8567

Riley Ledbetter Airguns, 1804 E. Sprague St., Winston Salem, NC 27107-3521 / 919-784-0676

Rim Pac Sports, Inc., 1034 N. Soldano Ave., Azusa, CA 91702-2135

Ringler Custom Leather Co., 31 Shining Mtn. Rd., Powell, WY 82435 / 307-645-3255

Ripley Rifles, 42 Fletcher Street, Ripley, Derbyshire, DE5 3LP ENGLAND / 011-0773-748353

MANUFACTURER'S DIRECTORY

Rizzini F.lli (See U.S. Importers-Wm. Larkin Moore & Co., N.E. Arms Corp.)

Rizzini SNC, Via 2 Giugno, 7/7Bis-25060, Marcheno (Brescia), ITALY

RLCM Enterprises, 110 Hill Crest Drive, Burleson, TX 76028

RMS Custom Gunsmithing, 4120 N. Bitterwell, Prescott Valley, AZ 86314 / 520-772-7626 www.customstockmaker.com

Robar Co., Inc., The, 21438 N. 7th Ave., Suite B, Phoenix, AZ 85027 / 623-581-2648; FAX: 623-582-0059 info@ robarguns.com www.robarguns.com

Robert Evans Engraving, 332 Vine St., Oregon City, OR 97045 / 503-656-5693

Robert Valade Engraving, 931 3rd Ave., Seaside, OR 97138 / 503-738-7672

Robinett, R. G., P.O. Box 72, Madrid, IA 50156 / 515-795-2906

Robinson, Don, Pennsylvania Hse, 36 Fairfax Crescent, W Yorkshire, ENGLAND / 01484-421-362 donrobinsonuk@ yahoo.co.uk www.guns4u2.co.uk

Robinson Armament Co., P.O. Box 16776, Salt Lake City, UT 84116 / 801-355-0401; FAX: 801-355-0402 zdf@robarm. com www.robarm.com

Robinson Firearms Mfg. Ltd., 1699 Blondeaux Crescent, Kelowna, BC V1Y 4J8 CANADA / 604-868-9596

Robinson H.V. Bullets, 3145 Church St., Zachary, LA 70791 / 504-654-4029

Rochester Lead Works, 76 Anderson Ave., Rochester, NY 14607 / 716-442-8500; FAX: 716-442-4712

Rock River Arms, 101 Noble St., Cleveland, IL 61241

Rockwood Corp., Speedwell Division, 136 Lincoln Blvd., Middlesex, NJ 08846 / 800-243-8274; FAX: 980-560-7475

Rocky Mountain Armoury, Mr. Felix LesMerises, 610 Main Street, P.O. Box 691, Frisco, CO 80443-0691 / 970-668-0136; FAX: 970-668-4484 felix@rockymountainarmoury.com

Rocky Mountain Target Co., 3 Aloe Way, Leesburg, FL 34788 / 352-365-9598

Rocky Shoes & Boots, 294 Harper St., Nelsonville, OH 45764 / 800-848-9452 or 614-753-1951; FAX: 614-753-4024

Rogue Rifle Co., Inc./Chipmunk Rifles, 1140 36th St. N., Ste. B, Lewiston, ID 83501 / 208-743-4355; FAX: 208-743-4163 customerservice@roguerifle.com www.roguerifle.com

Rogue River Rifleworks, 500 Linne Road #D, Paso Robles, CA 93447 / 805-227-4706; FAX: 805-227-4723 rrrifles@ calinet.com

Rohner, Hans, 1148 Twin Sisters Ranch Rd., Nederland, CO 80466-9600

Rohner, John, 186 Virginia Ave., Asheville, NC 28806 / 828-281-3704

Rohrbaugh, P.O. Box 785, Bayport, NY 11705 / 631-363-2843; FAX: 631-363-2681 API380@aol.com

Romain's Custom Guns, Inc., RD 1, Whetstone Rd., Brockport, PA 15823 / 814-265-1948 romwhetstone@penn.com

Ron Frank Custom, 7131 Richland Rd., Ft. Worth, TX 76118 / 817-284-9300; FAX: 817-284-9300 rfrank3974@aol.com

Rooster Laboratories, P.O. Box 414605, Kansas City, MO 64141 / 816-474-1622; FAX: 816-474-7622

Rorschach Precision Products, 417 Keats Cir., Irving, TX 75061 / 214-790-3487

Rosenberg & Son, Jack A., 12229 Cox Ln., Dallas, TX 75234 / 214-241-6302

Ross, Don, 12813 West 83 Terrace, Lenexa, KS 66215 / 913-492-6982

Rosser, Bob, 2809 Crescent Ave., Suite 20, Homewood, AL 35209 / 205-870-4422; FAX: 205-870-4421 www.hand-engravers.com

Rossi Firearms, Gary Mchalik, 16175 NW 49th Ave., Miami, FL 33014-6314 / 305-474-0401; FAX: 305-623-7506

Rottweil Compe, 1330 Glassell, Orange, CA 92667

Royal Arms Gunstocks, 919 8th Ave. NW, Great Falls, MT 59404 / 406-453-1149; FAX: 406-453-1149 royalarms@bresnar. net www.lmt.net/~royalarms

Royal Arms International, R J Brill, P.O. Box 6083, Woodland Hills, CA 91365 / 818-704-5110; FAX: 818-887-2059 royalarms.com

Roy's Custom Grips, 793 Mt. Olivet Church Rd., Lynchburg, VA 24504 / 434-993-3470

RPM, 15481 N. Twin Lakes Dr., Tucson, AZ 85739 / 520-825-1233; FAX: 520-825-3333

Rubright Bullets, 1008 S. Quince Rd., Walnutport, PA 18088 / 215-767-1339

Rucker Dist. Inc., P.O. Box 479, Terrell, TX 75160 / 214-563-2094

Ruger (See Sturm Ruger & Co., Inc.)

Ruger, Chris. See: RUGER'S CUSTOM GUNS

Ruger's Custom Guns, Chris Ruger, 1050 Morton Blvd., Kingston, NY 12401 / 845-336-7106; FAX: 845-336-7106 rugerscustom@outdrs.net rugergunsmith.com

Rundell's Gun Shop, 6198 Frances Rd., Clio, MI 48420 / 313-687-0559

Rupert's Gun Shop, 2202 Dick Rd., Suite B, Fenwick, MI 48834 / 517-248-3252 17rupert@pathwaynet.com

Russ Haydon's Shooters' Supply, 15018 Goodrich Dr. NW, Gig Harbor, WA 98329 / 877-663-6249; FAX: 253-857-7884 info@shooters-supply.com www.shooters-supply.com

Russ, William. See: BILL RUSS TRADING POST

Rusteprufe Laboratories, 1319 Jefferson Ave., Sparta, WI 54656 / 608-269-4144; FAX: 608-366-1972 rusteprufe@centurytel. net www.rusteprufe.com

Rutgers Book Center, 127 Raritan Ave., Highland Park, NJ 08904 / 732-545-4344; FAX: 732-545-6686 gunbooks@ rutgersgunbooks.com www.rutgersgunbooks.com

Rutten (See U.S. Importer-Labanu Inc.)

RWS (See U.S. Importer-Dynamit Nobel-RWS, Inc.), 6007 S. 29th St., Fort Smith, AR 72908

S

S&K Scope Mounts, RD 2 Box 21C, Sugar Grove, PA 16350 / 814-489-3091 or 800-578-9862; FAX: 814-489-5466 comments@scopemounts.com www.scopemounts.com

S&S Firearms, 74-11 Myrtle Ave., Glendale, NY 11385 / 718-497-1100; FAX: 718-497-1105 info@ssfirearms.com ssfirearms.com

S.A.R.L. G. Granger, 66 Cours Fauriel, 42100, Saint Etienne, FRANCE / 04 77 25 14 73; FAX: 04 77 38 66 99

S.D. Meacham, 1070 Angel Ridge, Peck, ID 83545

S.I.A.C.E. (See U.S. Importer-IAR Inc.)

Sabatti SPA, Via A Volta 90, 25063 Gandome V.T.(BS), Brescia, ITALY / 030-8912207-831312; FAX: 030-8912059 info@ sabatti.it www.sabatti.com

SAECO (See Redding Reloading Equipment)

Safari Arms/Schuetzen Pistol Works, 620-626 Old Pacific Hwy. SE, Olympia, WA 98513 / 360-459-3471; FAX: 360-491-3447 info@olyarms.com www.olyarms.com

Safari Press, Inc., 15621 Chemical Lane B, Huntington Beach, CA 92649 / 714-894-9080; FAX: 714-894-4949 info@ safaripress.com www.safaripress.com

Safariland Ltd., Inc., 3120 E. Mission Blvd., P.O. Box 51478, Ontario, CA 91761 / 909-923-7300; FAX: 909-923-7400

SAFE, P.O. Box 864, Post Falls, ID 83877 / 208-773-3624; FAX: 208-773-6819 staysafe@safe-llc.com www.safe-llc.com

Sako Ltd. (See U.S. Importer-Stoeger Industries)

Sam Welch Gun Engraving, Sam Welch, HC 64 Box 2110, Moab, UT 84532 / 435-259-8131

Samco Global Arms, Inc., 6995 NW 43rd St., Miami, FL 33166 / 305-593-9782; FAX: 305-593-1014 samco@samcoglobal. com www.samcoglobal.com

Sampson, Roger, 2316 Mahogany St., Mora, MN 55051 / 320-679-4868

San Marco (See U.S. Importers-Cape Outfitters-EMF Co., Inc.

Sandia Die & Cartridge Co., 37 Atancacio Rd. NE, Albuquerque, NM 87123 / 505-298-5729

Sarco, Inc., 323 Union St., Stirling, NJ 07980 / 908-647-3800; FAX: 908-647-9413

Sarsilmaz Shotguns-Turkey (see B.C. Outdoors)

Sauer (See U.S. Importers-Paul Co., The Sigarms Inc.)

Sauls, R. See: BRYAN & ASSOC.

Saunders Gun & Machine Shop, 145 Delhi Rd., Manchester, IA 52057 / 563-927-4026

Savage Arms (Canada), Inc., 248 Water St., P.O. Box 1240, Lakefield, ON K0L 2H0 CANADA / 705-652-8000; FAX: 705-652-8431 www.savagearms.com

Savage Arms, Inc., 100 Springdale Rd., Westfield, MA 01085 / 413-568-7001; FAX: 413-562-7764

Savage Range Systems, Inc., 100 Springdale Rd., Westfield, MA 01085 / 413-568-7001; FAX: 413-562-1152 snailtraps@ savagearms.com www.snailtraps.com

Saville Iron Co. (See Greenwood Precision)

Scansport, Inc., P.O. Box 700, Enfield, NH 03748 / 603-632-7654

Sceery Game Calls, P.O. Box 6520, Sante Fe, NM 87502 / 505-471-9110; FAX: 505-471-3476

Schaefer Shooting Sports, P.O. Box 1515, Melville, NY 11747-0515 / 516-643-5466; FAX: 516-643-2426 robert@ robertschaefer.com www.schaefershooting.com

Scharch Mfg., Inc.-Top Brass, 10325 Co. Rd. 120, Salida, CO 81201 / 800-836-4683; FAX: 719-539-3021 topbrass@ scharch.com www.handgun-brass.com

Scherer, Liz. See: SCHERER SUPPLIES, INC.

Scherer Supplies, Inc., Liz Scherer, Box 250, Ewing, VA 24248 FAX: 423-733-2073

Schiffman, Mike, 8233 S. Crystal Springs, McCammon, ID 83250 / 208-254-9114

Schmidt & Bender, Inc., P.O. Box 134, Meriden, NH 03770 / 603-469-3565; FAX: 603-469-3471 info@schmidtbender. com www.schmidtbender.com

Schneider Bullets, 3655 West 214th St., Fairview Park, OH 44126

Schneider Rifle Barrels, Inc., 1403 W. Red Baron Rd., Payson, AZ 85541 / 602-948-2525

School of Gunsmithing, The, 6065 Roswell Rd., Atlanta, GA 30328 / 800-223-4542

Schroeder Bullets, 1421 Thermal Ave., San Diego, CA 92154 / 619-423-3523; FAX: 619-423-8124

Schulz Industries, 16247 Minnesota Ave., Paramount, CA 90723 / 213-439-5903

Schumakers Gun Shop, 512 Prouty Corner Lp. A, Colville, WA 99114 / 509-684-4848

Scope Control, Inc., 5775 Co. Rd. 23 SE, Alexandria, MN 56308 / 612-762-7295

Score High Gunsmithing, 9812-A, Cochiti SE, Albuquerque, NM 87123 / 800-326-5632 or 505-292-5532; FAX: 505-292-2592 scorehi@scorehi.com www.probed2000.com

Scott Fine Guns Inc., Thad, P.O. Box 412, Indianola, MS 38751 / 601-887-5929

Searcy Enterprises, P.O. Box 584, Boron, CA 93596 / 760-762-6771; FAX: 760-762-0191

Second Chance Body Armor, P.O. Box 578, Central Lake, MI 49622 / 616-544-5721; FAX: 616-544-9824

Seebeck Assoc., R.E., P.O. Box 59752, Dallas, TX 75229

Segway Industries, P.O. Box 783, Suffern, NY 10901-0783 / 914-357-5510

Seligman Shooting Products, Box 133, Seligman, AZ 86337 / 602-422-3607 shootssp@yahoo.com

Sellier & Bellot, USA, Inc., P.O. Box 27006, Shawnee Mission, KS 66225 / 913-685-0916; FAX: 913-685-0917

Selsi Co., Inc., P.O. Box 10, Midland Park, NJ 07432-0010 / 201-935-0388; FAX: 201-935-5851

Semmer, Charles (See Remington Double Shotguns), 7885 Cyd Dr., Denver, CO 80221 / 303-429-6947

Servus Footwear Co., 1136 2nd St., Rock Island, IL 61204 / 309-786-7741; FAX: 309-786-9808

SGS Importer's International, Inc., 1750 Brielle Ave., Unit B1, Wanamassa, NJ 07712 / 732-493-0302; FAX: 732-493-0301 gsodini@aol.com www.firestorm-sgs.com

Shappy Bullets, 76 Milldale Ave., Plantsville, CT 06479 / 203-621-3704

Sharp Shooter Supply, 4970 Lehman Road, Delphos, OH 45833 / 419-695-3179

Sharps Arms Co., Inc., C., 100 Centennial, Box 885, Big Timber, MT 59011 / 406-932-4353

Shaw, Inc., E. R. (See Small Arms Mfg. Co.)

Shay's Gunsmithing, 931 Marvin Ave., Lebanon, PA 17042

Sheffield Knifemakers Supply, Inc., P.O. Box 741107, Orange City, FL 32774-1107 / 386-775-6453; FAX: 386-774-5754

Sheldon, Bruce. See: RIDGELINE, INC.

Shepherd Enterprises, Inc., Box 189, Waterloo, NE 68069 / 402-779-2424; FAX: 402-779-4010 sshepherd@shepherdscopes. com www.shepherdscopes.com

Sherwood, George, 46 N. River Dr., Roseburg, OR 97470 / 541-672-3159

Shilen, Inc., 205 Metro Park Blvd., Ennis, TX 75119 / 972-875-5318; FAX: 972-875-5402

Shiloh Rifle Mfg., P.O. Box 279, Big Timber, MT 59011

Shoot Where You Look, Leon Measures, Dept GD, 408 Fair, Livingston, TX 77351

Shooters Arms Manufacturing, Inc., Rivergate Mall, Gen. Maxilom Ave., Cebu City 6000, PHILIPPINES / 6332-254-8478 www.shootersarms.com.ph

Shooter's Choice Gun Care, 15050 Berkshire Ind. Pkwy., Middlefield, OH 44062 / 440-834-8888; FAX: 440-834-3388 www.shooterschoice.com

Shooter's Edge Inc., 3313 Creekstone Dr., Fort Collins, CO 80525

Shooters Supply, 1120 Tieton Dr., Yakima, WA 98902 / 509-452-1181

Shooter's World, 3828 N. 28th Ave., Phoenix, AZ 85017 / 602-266-0170

MANUFACTURER'S DIRECTORY

Shooters, Inc., 5139 Stanart St., Norfolk, VA 23502 / 757-461-9152; FAX: 757-461-9155 gflocker@aol.com

Shootin' Shack, 357 Cypress Drive, No. 10, Tequesta, FL 33469 / 561-746-2731; FAX: 561-545-4861

Shoot-N-C Targets (See Birchwood Casey)

Shotgun Sports, P.O. Box 6810, Auburn, CA 95604 / 530-889-2220; FAX: 530-889-9106 custsrv@shotgunsportsmagazine.com shotgunsportsmagazine.com

Shotgun Sports Magazine, dba Shootin' Accessories Ltd., P.O. Box 6810, Auburn, CA 95604 / 916-889-2220 custsrv@shotgunsportsmagazine.com shotgunspotsmagazine.com

Shotguns Unlimited, 2307 Fon Du Lac Rd., Richmond, VA 23229 / 804-752-7115

Siegrist Gun Shop, 8752 Turtle Road, Whittemore, MI 48770 / 989-873-3929

Sierra Bullets, 1400 W. Henry St., Sedalia, MO 65301 / 816-827-6300; FAX: 816-827-6300 www.sierrabullets.com

Sierra Specialty Prod. Co., 1344 Oakhurst Ave., Los Altos, CA 94024 FAX: 415-965-1536

SIG, CH-8212 Neuhausen, SWITZERLAND

Sigarms Inc., 18 Industrial Dr., Exeter, NH 03833 / 603-772-2302; FAX: 603-772-9082 customerservice@sigarms.com www.sigarms.com

Sight Shop, The, John G. Lawson, 1802 E. Columbia Ave., Tacoma, WA 98404 / 253-474-5465 parabellum9@aol.com www.thesightshop.org

Sightron, Inc., 1672B Hwy. 96, Franklinton, NC 27525 / 919-528-8783; FAX: 919-528-0995 info@sightron.com www.sightron.com

SIG-Sauer (See U.S. Importer-Sigarms, Inc.)

Silencio/Safety Direct, 3975 Vantech Dr 2, Memphis, TN 38115 / 800-648-1812 or 702-354-4451; FAX: 702-359-1074

Silent Hunter, 1100 Newton Ave., W. Collingswood, NJ 08107 / 609-854-3276

Silhouette Leathers, 8598 Hwy. 51 N. #4, Millington, TN 38053 silhouetteleathers@yahoo.com silhouetteleathers.com

Silver Eagle Machining, 18007 N. 69th Ave., Glendale, AZ 85308

Silver Ridge Gun Shop (See Goodwin Guns)

Simmons, Jerry, 715 Middlebury St., Goshen, IN 46528-2717 / 574-533-8546

Simmons Gun Repair, Inc., 700 S. Rogers Rd., Olathe, KS 66062 / 913-782-3131; FAX: 913-782-4189

Simmons Outdoor Corp., 6001 Oak Canyon, Irvine, CA 92618 / 949-451-1450; FAX: 949-451-1460 www.meade.com

Sinclair International, Inc., 2330 Wayne Haven St., Fort Wayne, IN 46803 / 260-493-1858 or 800-717-8211; FAX: 260-493-2530 sales@sinclairintl.com www.sinclairintl.com

Singletary, Kent, 4538 W. Carol Ave., Glendale, AZ 85302 / 602-526-6836 kent@kscustom www.kscustom

Siskiyou Gun Works (See Donnelly, C. P.)

Six Enterprises, 320-D Turtle Creek Ct., San Jose, CA 95125 / 408-999-0201; FAX: 408-999-0216

SKB Shotguns, 4325 S. 120th St., Omaha, NE 68137 / 800-752-2767; FAX: 402-330-8040 skb@skbshotguns.com www.skbshotguns.com

Skeoch, Brian R., P.O. Box 279, Glenrock, WY 82637 / 307-436-9655 skeochbrian@netzero.com

Skip's Machine, 364 29 Road, Grand Junction, CO 81501 / 303-245-5417

Sklany's Machine Shop, 566 Birch Grove Dr., Kalispell, MT 59901 / 406-755-4257

Slug Site, Ozark Wilds, 21300 Hwy. 5, Versailles, MO 65084 / 573-378-6430 john@ebeling.com john.ebeling.com

Small Arms Mfg. Co., 5312 Thoms Run Rd., Bridgeville, PA 15017 / 412-221-4343; FAX: 412-221-4303 www.ershawbarrels.com

Smires, C. L., 5222 Windmill Lane, Columbia, MD 21044-1328

Smith & Wesson, 2100 Roosevelt Ave., Springfield, MA 01104 / 413-781-8300; FAX: 413-731-8980 qa@smith-wesson.com www.smith-wesson.com

Smith, Art, P.O. Box 645, Park Rapids, MN 56470 / 218-732-5333

Smith, Mark A., P.O. Box 182, Sinclair, WY 82334 / 307-324-7929

Smith, Michael, 2612 Ashmore Ave., Red Bank, TN 37415 / 615-267-8341

Smith, Ron, 5869 Straley, Fort Worth, TX 76114 / 817-732-6768

Smith, Sharmon, 4545 Speas Rd., Fruitland, ID 83619 / 208-452-6329 sharmon@fmtc.com

Smith Abrasives, Inc., 1700 Sleepy Valley Rd., Hot Springs, AR 71902-5095 / 501-321-2244; FAX: 501-321-9232 www.smithabrasives.com

Smith, Judy. See: L.B.T.

Smith Saddlery, Jesse W., 0499 County Road J, Pritchett, CO 81064 / 509-325-0622

Smokey Valley Rifles, E1976 Smokey Valley Rd., Scandinavia, WI 54977 / 715-467-2674

Snapp's Gunshop, 6911 E. Washington Rd., Clare, MI 48617 / 989-386-9226 snapp@glccomputers.com

Sno-Seal, Inc. (See Atsko/Sno-Seal, Inc.)

Societa Armi Bresciane Srl (See U.S. Importer-Jeff's Outfitters)

SOS Products Co. (See Buck Stix-SOS Products Co.), Box 3, Neenah, WI 54956

Sotheby's, 1334 York Ave. at 72nd St., New York, NY 10021 / 212-606-7260

Sound Tech, Box 738, Logan, NM 88426 / 205-999-0416; or 505-487-2277 silenceio@wmconnect.com www.soundtechsilencers.com

South Bend Replicas, Inc., 61650 Oak Rd., South Bend, IN 46614 / 574-289-4500

Southeastern Community College, 1015 S. Gear Ave., West Burlington, IA 52655 / 319-752-2731

Southern Ammunition Co., Inc., 4232 Meadow St., Loris, SC 29569-3124 / 803-756-3262; FAX: 803-756-3583

Southern Armory, The, 25 Millstone Rd., Woodlawn, VA 24381 / 703-238-1343; FAX: 703-238-1453

Southern Bloomer Mfg. Co., P.O. Box 1621, Bristol, TN 37620 / 423-878-6660; FAX: 423-878-8761 southernbloomer@earthlink.net www.southernbloomer.com

Southern Security, 1700 Oak Hills Dr., Kingston, TN 37763 / 423-376-6297; FAX: 800-251-9992

Sparks, Milt, 605 E. 44th St. No. 2, Boise, ID 83714-4800

Spartan-Realtree Products, Inc., 1390 Box Circle, Columbus, GA 31907 / 706-569-9101; FAX: 706-569-0042

Specialty Gunsmithing, Lynn McMurdo, P.O. Box 404, Afton, WY 83110 / 307-886-5535

Specialty Shooters Supply, Inc., 3325 Griffin Rd., Suite 9mm, Fort Lauderdale, FL 33317

Speer Bullets, P.O. Box 856, Lewiston, ID 83501 / 208-746-2351 www.speer-bullets.com

Spegel, Craig, P.O. Box 387, Nehalem, OR 97131 / 503-368-5653

Speiser, Fred D., 2229 Dearborn, Missoula, MT 59801 / 406-549-8133

Spencer Reblue Service, 1820 Tupelo Trail, Holt, MI 48842 / 517-694-7474

Spencer's Rifle Barrels, Inc., 4107 Jacobs Creek Dr., Scottsville, VA 24590 / 804-293-6836; FAX: 804-293-6836 www.spencersriflebarrels.com

SPG, Inc., P.O. Box 1625, Cody, WY 82414 / 307-587-7621; FAX: 307-587-7695 spg@cody.wtp.net www.blackpowderspg.com

Sphinx Systems Ltd., Gesteigtstrasse 12, CH-3800, Matten, BRNE, SWITZERLAND

Splitfire Sporting Goods, L.L.C., P.O. Box 1044, Orem, UT 84059-1044 / 801-932-7950; FAX: 801-932-7959 www.splitfireguns.com

Spolar Power Load, Inc., 17376 Filbert, Fontana, CA 92335 / 800-227-9667

Sport Flite Manufacturing Co., 637 Kingsley Trl., Bloomfield Hills, MI 48304-2320 / 248-647-3747

Sporting Clays Of America, 9257 Buckeye Rd., Sugar Grove, OH 43155-9632 / 740-746-8334; FAX: 740-746-8605

Sports Afield Magazine, 15621 Chemical Lane B, Huntington Beach, CA 92649 / 714-894-9080; FAX: 714-894-4949 info@sportsafield.com www.sportsafield.com

Sportsman Safe Mfg. Co., 6309-6311 Paramount Blvd., Long Beach, CA 90805 / 800-266-7150; or 310-984-5445

Sportsman's Communicators, 588 Radcliffe Ave., Pacific Palisades, CA 90272 / 800-538-3752

Sportsman's Exchange & Western Gun Traders, Inc., 813 Doris Ave., Oxnard, CA 93030 / 805-483-1917

Spradlin's, 457 Shannon Rd., Texas Creek Cotopaxi, CO 81223 / 719-275-7105; FAX: 719-275-3852 spradlins@prodigy.net www.spradlins.net

Springfield Armory, 420 W. Main St., Geneseo, IL 61254 / 309-944-5631; FAX: 309-944-3676 sales@springfield-armory.com www.springfieldarmory.com

Springfield Sporters, Inc., RD 1, Penn Run, PA 15765 / 412-254-2626; FAX: 412-254-9173

Springfield, Inc., 420 W. Main St., Geneseo, IL 61254 / 309-944-5631; FAX: 309-944-3676

Spyderco, Inc., 820 Spyderco Way, Golden, CO 80403 / 800-525-7770; FAX: 303-278-2229 sales@spyderco.com www.spyderco.com

SSK Industries, J. D. Jones, 590 Woodvue Lane, Wintersville, OH 43953 / 740-264-0176; FAX: 740-264-2257 www.sskindustries.com

Stackpole Books, 5067 Ritter Rd., Mechanicsburg, PA 17055-6921 / 717-796-0411 FAX: 717-796-0412 tmanney@stackpolebooks.com www.stackpolebooks.com

Stalker, Inc., P.O. Box 21, Fishermans Wharf Rd., Malakoff, TX 75148 / 903-489-1010

Stalwart Corporation, P.O. Box 46, Evanston, WY 82931 / 307-789-7687; FAX: 307-789-7688

Stan Baker Sports, Stan Baker, 10000 Lake City Way, Seattle, WA 98125 / 206-522-4575

Stan De Treville & Co., 4129 Normal St., San Diego, CA 92103 / 619-298-3393

Star Ammunition, Inc., 5520 Rock Hampton Ct., Indianapolis, IN 46268 / 800-221-5927; FAX: 317-872-5847

Star Custom Bullets, P.O. Box 608, 468 Main St., Ferndale, CA 95536 / 707-786-9140; FAX: 707-786-9117 wmebridge@humboldt.com

Star Machine Works, P.O. Box 1872, Pioneer, CA 95666 / 209-295-5000

Starke Bullet Company, P.O. Box 400, 605 6th St. NW, Cooperstown, ND 58425 / 888-797-3431

Starkey Labs, 6700 Washington Ave. S., Eden Prairie, MN 55344

Starkey's Gun Shop, 9430 McCombs, El Paso, TX 79924 / 915-751-3030

Starlight Training Center, Inc., Rt. 1, P.O. Box 88, Bronaugh, MO 64728 / 417-843-3555

Starline, Inc., 1300 W. Henry St., Sedalia, MO 65301 / 660-827-6640; FAX: 660-827-6650 info@starlinebrass.com http://www.starlinebrass.com

Starr Trading Co., Jedediah, P.O. Box 2007, Farmington Hills, MI 48333 / 877-857-8277; FAX: 248-683-3282 mtman1849@aol.com www.jedediah-starr.com

Starrett Co., L. S., 121 Crescent St., Athol, MA 01331 / 978-249-3551; FAX: 978-249-8495

State Line Gun Shop, 443 Firchburg Rd., Mason, NH 03048 / 603-878-2854; FAX: 603-878-3905 miniguns@empire.net www.statelinegunshop.com

Steelman's Gun Shop, 10465 Beers Rd., Swartz Creek, MI 48473 / 810-735-4884

Steffens, Ron, 18396 Mariposa Creek Rd., Willits, CA 95490 / 707-485-0873

Stegall, James B., 26 Forest Rd., Wallkill, NY 12589

Steve Henigson & Associates, P.O. Box 2726, Culver City, CA 90231 / 310-305-8288; FAX: 310-305-1905

Steve Kamyk Engraver, 9 Grandview Dr., Westfield, MA 01085-1810 / 413-568-0457 stevek201@comcast.net

Steven Dodd Hughes, P.O. Box 545, Livingston, MT 59047 / 406-222-9377; FAX: 406-222-9377

Steves House of Guns, Rt. 1, Minnesota City, MN 55959 / 507-689-2573

Stewart's Gunsmithing, P.O. Box 5854, Pietersburg North 0750, Transvaal, SOUTH AFRICA / 01521-89401

Steyr Arms, P.O. Box 2609, Cumming, GA 30028 / 770-888-4201 www.steyrarms.com

Steyr Mannlicher GmbH & Co. KG, Ramingtal 46, A-4442 Kleinraming, Steyr, AUSTRIA / 0043-7252-896-0; FAX: 0043-7252-78620 office@steyr-mannlicher.com www.steyr-mannlicher.com

STI International, 114 Halmar Cove, Georgetown, TX 78628 / 800-959-8201; FAX: 512-819-0465 www.stiguns.com

Stiles Custom Guns, 76 Cherry Run Rd., Box 1605, Homer City, PA 15748 / 712-479-9945 glstiles@yourinter.net www.yourinter.net/glstiles

Stoeger Industries, 17603 Indian Head Hwy., Suite 200, Accokeek, MD 20607-2501 / 301-283-6300; FAX: 301-283-6986 www.stoegerindustries.com

Stoeger Publishing Co. (See Stoeger Industries)

Stone Enterprises Ltd., 426 Harveys Neck Rd., P.O. Box 335, Wicomico Church, VA 22579 / 804-580-5114; FAX: 804-580-8421

Stone Mountain Arms, 5988 Peachtree Corners E., Norcross, GA 30071 / 800-251-9412

MANUFACTURER'S DIRECTORY

Stoney Point Products, Inc., 9200 Cody St., Overland Park, KS 66214 / 800-845-2444; FAX: 507-354-7236 stoney@newulmtel.net www.stoneypoint.com

Storm, Gary, P.O. Box 5211, Richardson, TX 75083 / 214-385-0862

Stott's Creek Armory, Inc., 2526 S. 475W, Morgantown, IN 46160 / 317-878-5489 stottscrk@aol.com www.Sccalendar.aol.com

Stratco, Inc., P.O. Box 2270, Kalispell, MT 59901 / 406-755-1221; FAX: 406-755-1226

Strayer, Sandy. See: STRAYER-VOIGT, INC.

Strayer-Voigt, Inc., Sandy Strayer, 3435 Ray Orr Blvd., Grand Prairie, TX 75050 / 972-513-0575

Strong Holster Co., 39 Grove St., Gloucester, MA 01930 / 508-281-3300; FAX: 508-281-6321

Strutz Rifle Barrels, Inc., W. C., P.O. Box 611, Eagle River, WI 54521 / 715-479-4766

Stuart, V. Pat, 279 Pilson, Greenville, VA 24440 / 540-377-6187

Sturgeon Valley Sporters, Ken Ide, P.O. Box 283, Vanderbilt, MI 49795 / 989-983-4338 k.ide@mail.com

Sturm Ruger & Co. Inc., 200 Ruger Rd., Prescott, AZ 86301 / 928-541-8820; FAX: 520-541-8850 www.ruger.com

"Su-Press-On", Inc., P.O. Box 09161, Detroit, MI 48209 / 313-842-4222

Sullivan, David S. (See Westwind Rifles, Inc.)

Sun Welding Safe Co., 290 Easy St. No. 3, Simi Valley, CA 93065 / 805-584-6678; or 800-729-SAFE; (7233) FAX: 805-584-6169 sun-welding@sbcglobal.net www.sunwelding.com

Sunny Hill Enterprises, Inc., W1790 Cty. HHH, Malone, WI 53049 / 920-418-3906; FAX: 920-795-4822 triggerguard@sunny-hill.com www.sunny-hill.com

Super 6 LLC, Gary Knopp, 3806 W. Lisbon Ave., Milwaukee, WI 53208 / 414-344-3343; FAX: 414-344-0304

Surecase Co., The, 233 Wilshire Blvd., Ste. 900, Santa Monica, CA 90401 / 800-92ARMLOC

Sure-Shot Game Calls, Inc., P.O. Box 816, 6835 Capitol, Groves, TX 77619 / 409-962-1636; FAX: 409-962-5465

Svon Corp., 2107 W. Blue Heron Blvd., Riviera Beach, FL 33404 / 508-881-8852

Swampfire Shop, The (See Peterson Gun Shop, Inc., A.W.)

Swann, D. J., 5 Orsova Close, Eltham North Vic., 3095 AUSTRALIA / 03-431-0323

Swanson, Mark, 975 Heap Avenue, Prescott, AZ 86301 / 928-778-4423

Swarovski Optik North America Ltd., 2 Slater Rd., Cranston, RI 02920 / 401-946-2220 or 800-426-3089; FAX: 401-946-2587

Sweet Home, Inc., P.O. Box 900, Orrville, OH 44667-0900

Swenson's 45 Shop, A. D., 3839 Ladera Vista Rd., Fallbrook, CA 92028-9431

Swift Bullet Co., P.O. Box 27, 201 Main St., Quinter, KS 67752 / 913-754-3959; FAX: 913-754-2359

Swift Instruments, 2055 Gateway Place, Ste. 500, San Jose, CA 95110 / 800-523-4544; FAX: 408-292-7967 www.swiftoptics.com

Swift River Gunworks, 450 State St., Belchertown, MA 01007 / 413-323-4052

Szweda, Robert (See RMS Custom Gunsmithing)

T

T&S Industries, Inc., 1027 Skyview Dr., W. Carrollton, OH 45449 / 513-859-8414; FAX: 937-859-8404 keith.tomlinson@tandsshellcatcher.com www.tandsshellcatcher.com

T.F.C. S.p.A., Via G. Marconi 118, B, Villa Carcina 25069, ITALY / 030-881271; FAX: 030-881826

T.G. Faust, Inc., 544 Minor St., Reading, PA 19602 / 610-375-8549; FAX: 610-375-4488

T.K. Lee Co., 1282 Branchwater Ln., Birmingham, AL 35216 / 205-913-5222 odonmich@aol.com www.scopedot.com

T.W. Mench Gunsmith, Inc., 5703 S. 77th St., Ralston, NE 68127 guntools@cox.net http://llwww.members.cox.net/guntools

Tabler Marketing, 2554 Lincoln Blvd., Suite 555, Marina Del Rey, CA 90291 / 818-386-0373; FAX: 818-386-0373

Taconic Firearms Ltd., Perry Lane, P.O. Box 553, Cambridge, NY 12816 / 518-677-2704; FAX: 518-677-5974

Tactical Defense Institute, 2174 Bethany Ridges, West Union, OH 45693 / 937-544-7228; FAX: 937-544-2887 tdiohio@dragonbbs.com www.tdiohio.com

Talley, Dave, P.O. Box 369, Santee, SC 29142 / 803-854-5700 or 307-436-9315; FAX: 803-854-9315 talley@diretway www.talleyrings.com

Talon Industries Inc. (See Cobra Enterprises, Inc.)

Tanfoglio Fratelli S.r.l., via Valtrompia 39, 41, Brescia, ITALY / 011-39-030-8910361; FAX: 011-39-030-8910183 info@tanfoglio.it www.tanfoglio.it

Tanglefree Industries, 1261 Heavenly Dr., Martinez, CA 94553 / 800-982-4868; FAX: 510-825-3874

Tank's Rifle Shop, P.O. Box 474, Fremont, NE 68026-0474 / 402-727-1317 jtank@tanksrifleshop.com www.tanksrifleshop.com

Tanner (See U.S. Importer-Mandall Shooting Supplies, Inc.)

Taracorp Industries, Inc., 1200 Sixteenth St., Granite City, IL 62040 / 618-451-4400

Target Shooting, Inc., P.O. Box 773, Watertown, SD 57201 / 605-882-6955; FAX: 605-882-8840

Tar-Hunt Custom Rifles, Inc., 101 Dogtown Rd., Bloomsburg, PA 17815 / 570-784-6368; FAX: 570-389-9150 www.tar-hunt.com

Tarnhelm Supply Co., Inc., 431 High St., Boscawen, NH 03303 / 603-796-2551; FAX: 603-796-2918 info@tarnhelm.com www.tarnhelm.com

Tasco Sales, Inc., 2889 Commerce Pkwy., Miramar, FL 33025

Taurus Firearms, Inc., 16175 NW 49th Ave., Miami, FL 33014 / 305-624-1115; FAX: 305-623-7506

Taurus International Firearms (See U.S. Importer Taurus Firearms, Inc.)

Taurus S.A. Forjas, Avenida Do Forte 511, Porto Alegre, RS BRAZIL 91360 / 55-51-347-4050; FAX: 55-51-347-3065

Taylor & Robbins, P.O. Box 164, Rixford, PA 16745 / 814-966-3233

Taylor's & Co., Inc., 304 Lenoir Dr., Winchester, VA 22603 / 540-722-2017; FAX: 540-722-2018 info@taylorsfirearms.com www.taylorsfirearms.com

TCCI, P.O. Box 302, Phoenix, AZ 85001 / 602-237-3823; FAX: 602-237-3858

TCSR, 3998 Hoffman Rd., White Bear Lake, MN 55110-4626 / 800-328-5323; FAX: 612-429-0526

Techno Arms (See U.S. Importer- Auto-Ordnance Corp.)

Tecnolegno S.p.A., Via A. Locatelli, 6 10, 24019 Zogno, ITALY / 0345-55111; FAX: 0345-55155

Ted Blocker Holsters, 9438 SW Tigard St., Tigard, OR 97223 / 800-650-9742; FAX: 503-670-9692 www.tedblockerholsters.com

Tele-Optics, 630 E. Rockland Rd., P.O. Box 6313, Libertyville, IL 60048 / 847-362-7757; FAX: 847-362-7757

Tennessee Valley Mfg., 14 County Road 521, Corinth, MS 38834 / 601-286-5014 tvm@avsia.com www.avsia.com/tvm

Ten-Ring Precision, Inc., Alex B. Hamilton, 1449 Blue Crest Lane, San Antonio, TX 78232 / 210-494-3063; FAX: 210-494-3066

TEN-X Products Group, 1905 N. Main St., Suite 133, Cleburne, TX 76031-1305 / 972-243-4016 or 800-433-2225; FAX: 972-243-4112

Tepeco, P.O. Box 342, Friendswood, TX 77546 / 713-482-2702

Terry K. Kopp Professional Gunsmithing, 1209 South 13 Hwy., Lexington, MO 64067 / 816-529-1337 tkkopp@earthlink.net

Terry Theis-Engraver, Terry Theis, 21452 FM 2093, Harper, TX 78631 / 830-864-4438

Testing Systems, Inc., 220 Pegasus Ave., Northvale, NJ 07647

Tetra Gun Care, 8 Vreeland Rd., Florham Park, NJ 07932 / 973-443-0004; FAX: 973-443-0263

Tex Shoemaker & Sons, Inc., 714 W. Cienega Ave., San Dimas, CA 91773 / 909-592-2071; FAX: 909-592-2378 texshoemaker@texshoemaker.com www.texshoemaker.com

Texas Armory (See Bond Arms, Inc.)

Texas Platers Supply Co., 2453 W. Five Mile Parkway, Dallas, TX 75233 / 214-330-7168

Thad Rybka Custom Leather Equipment, 2050 Canoe Creek Rd., Springvale, AL 35146-6709

Thad Scott Fine Guns, Inc., P.O. Box 412, Indianola, MS 38751 / 601-887-5929

The Midwest Shooting School, 2550 Hwy. 23, Wrenshall, MN 55797 / 218-384-3670 patrick@midwestshootingschool.com www.midwestshootingschool.com

Theis, Terry. See: TERRY THEIS-ENGRAVER

Thiewes, George W., 14329 W. Parada Dr., Sun City West, AZ 85375

Things Unlimited, 235 N. Kimbau, Casper, WY 82601 / 307-234-5277

Thirion Gun Engraving, Denise, P.O. Box 408, Graton, CA 95444 / 707-829-1876

Thomas, Charles C., 2600 S. First St., Springfield, IL 62704 / 217-789-8980; FAX: 217-789-9130 books@ccthomas.com ccthomas.com

Thompson Bullet Lube Co., 6341 FM 2965, Wills Point, TX 75169 / 866-476-1500; FAX: 866-476-1500 thompsonbulletlube.com www.thompsonbulletlube.com

Thompson Precision, 110 Mary St., P.O. Box 251, Warren, IL 61087 / 815-745-3625

Thompson Target Technology, 4804 Sherman Church Ave. S.W., Canton, OH 44710 / 330-484-6480; FAX: 330-491-1087 www.thompsontarget.com

Thompson Tool Mount, 1550 Solomon Rd., Santa Maria, CA 93455 / 805-934-1281 ttm@pronet.net www.thompsontoolmount.com

Thompson/Center Arms, P.O. Box 5002, Rochester, NH 03866 / 603-332-2394; FAX: 603-332-5133 tech@tcarms.com www.tcarms.com

Thunder Ranch, 96747 Hwy. 140 East, Lakeview, OR 97630 / 541-947-4104; FAX: 541-947-4105 troregon@centurytel.net www.thunderranchinc.com

Tiger-Hunt Longrifle Gunstocks, Box 379, Beaverdale, PA 15921 / 814-472-5161 tigerhunt4@aol.com www.gunstockwood.com

Tikka (See U.S. Importer-Stoeger Industries)

Time Precision, 4 Nicholas Sq., New Milford, CT 06776-3506 / 860-350-8343; FAX: 860-350-6343 timeprecision@aol.com www.benchrest.com/timeprecision

Tinks & Ben Lee Hunting Products (See Wellington Outdoors)

Tink's Safariland Hunting Corp., P.O. Box 244, 1140 Monticello Rd., Madison, GA 30650 / 706-342-4915; FAX: 706-342-7568

Tioga Engineering Co., Inc., P.O. Box 913, 13 Cone St., Wellsboro, PA 16901 / 570-724-3533; FAX: 570-724-3895 tiogaeng@epix.net

Tippman Sports, LLC, 2955 Adams Center Rd., Fort Wayne, IN 46803 / 260-749-6022; FAX: 260-441-8504 www.tippmann.com

Tirelli, Snc Di Tirelli Primo E.C., Via Matteotti No. 359, Gardone V.T. Brescia, ITALY / 0039-030-3912819; FAX: 0039-030-832240 tirelli@tirelli.it www.tirelli.it

TM Stockworks, 6355 Maplecrest Rd., Fort Wayne, IN 46835 / 219-485-5389

Tom Forrest, Inc., P.O. Box 326, Lakeside, CA 92040 / 619-561-5800; FAX: 888-GUN-CLIP info@gunmag.com www.gunmags.com

Tombstone Smoken' Deals, 4038 E. Taro Ln., Phoenix, AZ 85050

Tom's Gun Repair, Thomas G. Ivanoff, 76-6 Rt. Southfork Rd., Cody, WY 82414 / 307-587-6949

Tom's Gunshop, 3601 Central Ave., Hot Springs, AR 71913 / 501-624-3856

Tonoloway Tack Drives, HCR 81, Box 100, Needmore, PA 17238

Torel, Inc./Tandy Brands Outdoors/AA & E, 208 Industrial Loop, Yoakum, TX 77995 / 361-293-6366; FAX: 361-293-9127

TOZ (See U.S. Importer-Nygord Precision Products, Inc.)

Track of the Wolf, Inc., 18308 Joplin St. NW, Elk River, MN 55330-1773 / 763-633-2500; FAX: 763-633-2550 sales@trackofthewolf.com www.trackofthewolf.com

Traditions Performance Firearms, P.O. Box 776, 1375 Boston Post Rd., Old Saybrook, CT 06475 / 860-388-4656; FAX: 860-388-4657 info@traditionsfirearms.com www.traditionsfirearms.com

Trafalgar Square, P.O. Box 257, N. Pomfret, VT 05053 / 802-457-1911

Trail Visions, 5800 N. Ames Terrace, Glendale, WI 53209 / 414-228-1328

Treebone Carving, P.O. Box 551, Cimarron, NJ 87714 / 505-376-2145 treebonecarving.com

Treemaster, P.O. Box 247, Guntersville, AL 35976 / 205-878-3597

Trevallion Gunstocks, 9 Old Mountain Rd., Cape Neddick, ME 03902 / 207-361-1130

Trigger Lock Division / Central Specialties Ltd., 220-D Exchange Dr., Crystal Lake, IL 60014 / 847-639-3900; FAX: 847-639-3972

Trijicon, Inc., 49385 Shafer Ave., P.O. Box 930059, Wixom, MI 48393-0059 / 248-960-7700 or 800-338-0563

Trilby Sport Shop, 1623 Hagley Rd., Toledo, OH 43612-2024 / 419-472-6222

Trilux, Inc., P.O. Box 24608, Winston-Salem, NC 27114 / 910-659-9438; FAX: 910-768-7720

Trinidad St. Jr. Col. Gunsmith Dept., 600 Prospect St., Trinidad, CO 81082 / 719-846-5631; FAX: 719-846-5667

Tripes, George. See: EURO-IMPORTS

Triple-K Mfg. Co., Inc., 2222 Commercial St., San Diego, CA 92113 / 619-232-2066; FAX: 619-232-7675 sales@triplek. com www.triplek.com

Tristar Sporting Arms, Ltd., 1816 Linn St. #16, N. Kansas City, MO 64116-3627 / 816-421-1400; FAX: 816-421-4182 tristarsporting@sbcglobal.net www.tristarsportingarms

Trius Traps, Inc., P.O. Box 25, 221 S. Miami Ave., Cleves, OH 45002 / 513-941-5682; FAX: 513-941-7970 triustraps@ fuse.net www.triustraps.com

Trooper Walsh, 2393 N. Edgewood St., Arlington, VA 22207

Trotman, Ken, P. O. Box 505, Huntingdon, PE 29 2XW ENGLAND / 01480 454292; FAX: 01480 384651 enquiries@ kentrotman.com www.kentrotman.com

Tru-Balance Knife Co., P.O. Box 140555, Grand Rapids, MI 49514 / 616-647-1215

True Flight Bullet Co., 5581 Roosevelt St., Whitehall, PA 18052 / 610-262-7630; FAX: 610-262-7806

Truglo, Inc., P.O. Box 1612, McKinna, TX 75070 / 972-774-0300; FAX: 972-774-0323 www.truglosights.com

Trulock Tool, P.O. Box 530, Whigham, GA 31797 / 229-762-4678; FAX: 229-762-4050 trulockchokes@hotmail.com trulockchokes.com

Tru-Nord Compass, 1504 Erick Lane, Brainerd, MN 56401 / 218-829-2870; FAX: 218-829-2870 www.trunord.com

Tru-Square Metal Products, Inc., 640 First St. SW, P.O. Box 585, Auburn, WA 98071 / 253-833-2310 or 800-225-1017; FAX: 253-833-2349 t-tumbler@qwest.net

Tucker, James C., P.O. Box 366, Medford, OR 97501 / 541-664-9160 jctstocker@yahoo.com

Tucson Mold, Inc., 930 S. Plumer Ave., Tucson, AZ 85719 / 520-792-1075; FAX: 520-792-1075

Turk's Head Productions, Mustafa Bilal, 13545 Erickson Pl. NE, Seattle, WA 98125-3794 / 206-782-4164; FAX: 206-783-5677 info@turkshead.com www.turkshead.com

Turnbull Restoration, Doug, 6680 Rts. 5 & 20, P.O. Box 471, Bloomfield, NY 14469 / 585-657-6338; FAX: 585-657-7743 info@turnbullrestoration.com www.turnbullrestoration.com

Tuttle, Dale, 4046 Russell Rd., Muskegon, MI 49445 / 616-766-2250

U

U.S. Importer-Wm. Larkin Moore, 8430 E. Raintree Ste. B-7, Scottsdale, AZ 85260

U.S. Optics, A Division of Zeitz Optics U.S.A., 5900 Dale St., Buena Park, CA 90621 / 714-994-4901; FAX: 714-994-4904 www.usoptics.com

U.S. Repeating Arms Co., Inc., 275 Winchester Ave., Morgan, UT 84050-9333 / 801-876-3440; FAX: 801-876-3737 www. winchester-guns.com

U.S. Tactical Systems (See Keng's Firearms Specialty, Inc.)

Ugartechea S. A., Ignacio, Chonta 26, Eibar, SPAIN / 43-121257; FAX: 43-121669

Ultra Dot Distribution, P.O. Box 362, 6304 Riverside Dr., Yankeetown, FL 34498 / 352-447-2255; FAX: 352-447-2266

Ultralux (See U.S. Importer-Keng's Firearms Specialty, Inc.)

Uncle Bud's, HCR 81, Box 100, Needmore, PA 17238 / 717-294-6000; FAX: 717-294-6005

Uncle Mike's (See Michaels of Oregon, Co.)

Unertl Optical Co., Inc., 103 Grand Avenue, P.O. Box 895, Mars, PA 16046-0895 / 724-625-3810; FAX: 724-625-3819 unertl@nauticom.net www.unertloptics.net

UniTec, 1250 Bedford SW, Canton, OH 44710 / 216-452-4017

United Binocular Co., 9043 S. Western Ave., Chicago, IL 60620

United Cutlery Corp., 1425 United Blvd., Sevierville, TN 37876 / 865-428-2532 or 800-548-0835; FAX: 865-428-2267 www. unitedcutlery.com

United States Products Co., 518 Melwood Ave., Pittsburgh, PA 15213-1136 / 412-621-2130; FAX: 412-621-8740 sales@ us-products.com www.usporepaste.com

Universal Sports, P.O. Box 532, Vincennes, IN 47591 / 812-882-8680; FAX: 812-882-8680

Upper Missouri Trading Co., P.O. Box 100, 304 Harold St., Crofton, NE 68730-0100 / 402-388-4844 www. uppermotradingco.com

USAC, 4500-15th St. East, Tacoma, WA 98424 / 206-922-7589

Uselton/Arms, Inc., 842 Conference Dr., Goodlettsville, TN 37072 / 615-851-4919

Utica Cutlery Co., 820 Noyes St., Utica, NY 13503 / 315-733-4663; FAX: 315-733-6602

V

V. H. Blackinton & Co., Inc., 221 John L. Dietsch, Attleboro Falls, MA 02763-0300 / 508-699-4436; FAX: 508-695-5349

Valdada Enterprises, P.O. Box 773122, 31733 County Road 35, Steamboat Springs, CO 80477 / 970-879-2983; FAX: 970-879-0851 www.valdada.com

Valtro USA, Inc., 1281 Andersen Dr., San Rafael, CA 94901 / 415-256-2575; FAX: 415-256-2576

VAM Distribution Co. LLC, 1141-B Mechanicsburg Rd., Wooster, OH 44691 www.rex10.com

Van Gorden & Son Inc., C. S., 1815 Main St., Bloomer, WI 54724 / 715-568-2612

Van Horn, Gil, P.O. Box 207, Llano, CA 93544

Van Patten, J. W., 214 Christian Hill Rd., Milford, PA 18337 / 717-296-7069

Vann Custom Bullets, 2766 N. Willowside Way, Meridian, ID 83642

Varmint Masters, LLC, Rick Vecqueray, P.O. Box 6724, Bend, OR 97708 / 541-318-7306; FAX: 541-318-7306 varmintmasters@bendcable.com www.varmintmasters.net

Vecqueray, Rick. See: VARMINT MASTERS, LLC

Vector Arms, Inc., 270 W. 500 N., North Salt Lake, UT 84054 / 801-295-1917; FAX: 801-295-9316 vectorarms@bbscmail. com www.vectorarms.com

Vega Tool Co., c/o T. R. Ross, 4865 Tanglewood Ct., Boulder, CO 80301 / 303-530-0174 clanlaird@aol.com www.vegatool.com

Venco Industries, Inc. (See Shooter's Choice Gun Care)

Venus Industries, P.O. Box 246, Sialkot-1, PAKISTAN FAX: 92 432 85579

Verney-Carron, 54 Boulevard Thiers-B.P. 72, 42002 St. Etienne Cedex 1, St. Etienne Cedex 1, FRANCE / 33-477791500; FAX: 33-477790702 email@verney-carron.com www.verney-carron.com

Vest, John, 1923 NE 7th St., Redmond, OR 97756 / 541-923-8898

VibraShine, Inc., P.O. Box 577, Taylorsville, MS 39168 / 601-785-9854; FAX: 601-785-9874 rdbeke@vibrashine.com www.vibrashine.com

Vibra-Tek Co., 1844 Arroya Rd., Colorado Springs, CO 80906 / 719-634-8611; FAX: 719-634-6886

Vic's Gun Refinishing, 6 Pineview Dr., Dover, NH 03820-6422 / 603-742-0013

Victory Ammunition, P.O. Box 1022, Milford, PA 18337 / 717-296-5768; FAX: 717-296-9298

Vihtavuori Oy, FIN-41330 Vihtavuori, FINLAND, / 358-41-3779211; FAX: 358-41-3771643

Vihtavuori Oy/Kaltron-Pettibone, 1241 Ellis St., Bensenville, IL 60106 / 708-350-1116; FAX: 708-350-1606

Village Restorations & Consulting, Inc., P.O. Box 569, Claysburg, PA 16625 / 814-239-8200; FAX: 814-239-2165 www. villagerestoration@yahoo.com

Vincent's Shop, 210 Antoinette, Fairbanks, AK 99701

Viper Bullet and Brass Works, 11 Brock St., Box 582, Norwich, ON N0J 1P0 CANADA

Viramontez Engraving, Ray Viramontez, 601 Springfield Dr., Albany, GA 31721 / 229-432-9683 sgtvira@aol.com

Viramontez, Ray. See: VIRAMONTEZ ENGRAVING

Virgin Valley Custom Guns, 450 E 800 N. #20, Hurricane, UT 84737 / 435-635-8941; FAX: 435-635-8943 vvcguns@ infowest.com www.virginvalleyguns.com

Vitt/Boos, 1195 Buck Hill Rd., Townshend, VT 05353 / 802-365-9232

Voere-KGH GmbH, Untere Sparchen 56, A-6330 Kufstein, Tirol, AUSTRIA / 0043-5372-62547; FAX: 0043-5372-65752 voere@aon.com www.voere.com

Volquartsen Custom Ltd., 24276 240th Street, P.O. Box 397, Carroll, IA 51401 / 712-792-4238; FAX: 712-792-2542 info@ volquartsen.com www.volquartsen.com

Vorhes, David, 3042 Beecham St., Napa, CA 94558 / 707-226-9116; FAX: 707-253-7334

VSP Publishers (See Heritage/VSP Gun Books), P.O. Box 887, McCall, ID 83638 / 208-634-4104; FAX: 208-634-3101 heritage@gunbooks.com www.gunbooks.com

VTI Gun Parts, P.O. Box 509, Lakeville, CT 06039 / 860-435-8068; FAX: 860-435-8146 mail@vtigunparts.com www. vtigunparts.com

Vulpes Ventures, Inc., Fox Cartridge Division, P.O. Box 1363, Bolingbrook, IL 60440-7363 / 630-759-1229

W

W. Square Enterprises, 9826 Sagedale Dr., Houston, TX 77089 / 281-484-0935; FAX: 281-464-9940 lfdw@pdq.net www. loadammo.com

W. Waller & Son, Inc., 52 Coventry Dr., Sunapee, NH 03782 / 603-763-3320 or 800-874-2247 FAX: 603-763-3225; waller@wallerandson.com www.wallerandson.com

W.B. Niemi Engineering, Box 126 Center Road, Greensboro, VT 05841 / 802-533-7180 or 802-533-7141

W.C. Wolff Co., P.O. Box 458, Newtown Square, PA 19073 / 610-359-9600 or 800-545-0077 mail@gunsprings.com www.gunsprings.com

W.E. Birdsong & Assoc., 1435 Monterey Rd., Florence, MS 39073-9748 / 601-366-8270

W.E. Brownell Checkering Tools, 9390 Twin Mountain Cir., San Diego, CA 92126 / 858-695-2479; FAX: 858-695-2479

W.J. Riebe Co., 3434 Tucker Rd., Boise, ID 83703

W.R. Case & Sons Cutlery Co., Owens Way, Bradford, PA 16701 / 814-368-4123 or 800-523-6350; FAX: 814-368-1736 jsullivan@wrcase.com www.wrcase.com

Wagoner, Vernon G., 2325 E. Encanto St., Mesa, AZ 85213-5917 / 480-835-1307

Waldron, Herman, Box 475, 80 N. 17th St., Pomeroy, WA 99347 / 509-843-1404

Walker Arms Co., Inc., 499 County Rd. 820, Selma, AL 36701 / 334-872-6231; FAX: 334-872-6262

Wallace, Terry, 385 San Marino, Vallejo, CA 94589 / 707-642-7041

Walls Industries, Inc., P.O. Box 98, 1905 N. Main, Cleburne, TX 76033 / 817-645-4366; FAX: 817-645-7946 www. wallsoutdoors.com

Walters Industries, 6226 Park Lane, Dallas, TX 75225 / 214-691-6973

Walters, John. See: WALTERS WADS

Walters Wads, John Walters, 500 N. Avery Dr., Moore, OK 73160 / 405-799-0376; FAX: 405-799-7727 www.tinwadman@ cs.com

Walther America, P.O. Box 22, Springfield, MA 01102 / 413-747-3443 www.walther-usa.com

Walther GmbH, Carl, B.P. 4325, D-89033 Ulm, GERMANY

Walt's Custom Leather, Walt Whinnery, 1947 Meadow Creek Dr., Louisville, KY 40218 / 502-458-4361

WAMCO-New Mexico, P.O. Box 205, Peralta, NM 87042-0205 / 505-869-0826

Ward & Van Valkenburg, 114 32nd Ave. N., Fargo, ND 58102 / 701-232-2351

Ward Machine, 5620 Lexington Rd., Corpus Christi, TX 78412 / 512-992-1221

Wardell Precision, P.O. Box 391, Clyde, TX 79510-0391 / 325-893-3763 fwardell@valornet.com

Washita Mountain Whetstone Co., 418 Hilltop Rd., Pearcy, AR 71964 / 501-767-1616; FAX: 501-767-9598 www.@hsnp. com

Wasmundt, Jim. See: J.W. WASMUNDT-GUNSMITH

Watson Bros., 39 Redcross Way, London Bridge SE1 1H6, London, ENGLAND FAX: 44-171-403-336

Watson Bullets, 231 Allies Pass, Frostproof, FL 33843 / 863-635-7948 cbestbullet@aol.com

Wayne Specialty Services, 260 Waterford Drive, Florissant, MO 63033 / 413-831-7083

WD-40 Co., 1061 Cudahy Pl., San Diego, CA 92110 / 619-275-1400; FAX: 619-275-5823

Weatherby, Inc., 3100 El Camino Real, Atascadero, CA 93422 / 805-466-1767; FAX: 805-466-2527 www.weatherby.com

Weaver Products ATK, P.O. Box 39, Onalaska, WI 54650 / 800-648-9624 or 608-781-5800; FAX: 608-781-0368

Weaver Scope Repair Service, 1121 Larry Mahan Dr., Suite B, El Paso, TX 79925 / 915-593-1005 frank@weaver-scope-repair.com www.weaver-scope-repair.com

Webb, Bill, 6504 North Bellefontaine, Kansas City, MO 64119 / 816-453-7431

Weber & Markin Custom Gunsmiths, 4-1691 Powick Rd., Kelowna, BC V1X 4L1 CANADA / 250-762-7575; FAX: 250-861-3655 www.weberandmarkinguns.com

Webley and Scott Ltd., Frankley Industrial Park, Tay Rd., Birmingham, B45 0PA ENGLAND / 011-021-453-1864; FAX: 0121-457-7846 guns@webley.co.uk www.webley.co.uk

Webster Scale Mfg. Co., P.O. Box 188, Sebring, FL 33870 / 813-385-6362

MANUFACTURER'S DIRECTORY

Weigand Combat Handguns, Inc., 1057 South Main Rd., Mountain Top, PA 18707 / 570-868-8358; FAX: 570-868-5218 sales@jackweigand.com www.jackweigand.com

Weihrauch KG, Hermann, Industriestrasse 11, 8744 Mellrichstadt, Mellrichstadt, GERMANY

Welch, Sam. See: SAM WELCH GUN ENGRAVING

Wellington Outdoors, P.O. Box 244, 1140 Monticello Rd., Madison, GA 30650 / 706-342-4915; FAX: 706-342-7568

Wells, Rachel, 110 N. Summit St., Prescott, AZ 86301 / 928-445-3655 wellssportstore@cableone.net

Wells Creek Knife & Gun Works, 32956 State Hwy. 38, Scottsburg, OR 97473 / 541-587-4202; FAX: 541-587-4223

Wells, Margaret. See: WELLS SPORT STORE

Wells Sport Store, Margaret R Wells, 110 N. Summit St., Prescott, AZ 86301 / 928-445-3655 www.wellssportstore@cableone.net

Welsh, Bud. See: HIGH PRECISION

Wenger North America/Precise Int'l., 15 Corporate Dr., Orangeburg, NY 10962 / 800-431-2996; FAX: 914-425-4700

Wenig Custom Gunstocks, 103 N. Market St., P.O. Box 249, Lincoln, MO 65338 / 660-547-3334; FAX: 660-547-2881 gustock@wenig.com www.wenig.com

Werth, T. W., 1203 Woodlawn Rd., Lincoln, IL 62656 / 217-732-1300; FAX: 217-735-5106

Wescombe, Bill (See North Star West)

Wessinger Custom Guns & Engraving, 268 Limestone Rd., Chapin, SC 29036 / 803-345-5677

West, Jack L., 1220 W. Fifth, P.O. Box 427, Arlington, OR 97812

Western Cutlery (See Camillus Cutlery Co.)

Western Mfg. Co., 550 Valencia School Rd., Aptos, CA 95003 / 831-688-5884 lotsabears@eathlink.net

Western Missouri Shooters Alliance, P.O. Box 11144, Kansas City, MO 64119 / 816-597-3950; FAX: 816-229-7350

Western Nevada West Coast Bullets, P.O. Box 2270, Dayton, NV 89403-2270 / 702-246-3941; FAX: 702-246-0836

Westley Richards & Co. Ltd., 40 Grange Rd., Birmingham, ENGLAND / 010-214722953; FAX: 010-214141138 sales@westleyrichards.com www.westleyrichards.com

Westley Richards Agency USA (See U.S. Importer)

Westwind Rifles, Inc., David S. Sullivan, P.O. Box 261, 640 Briggs St., Erie, CO 80516 / 303-828-3823

Weyer International, 2740 Nebraska Ave., Toledo, OH 43607 / 419-534-2020; FAX: 419-534-2697

Whinnery, Walt (See Walt's Custom Leather)

White Barn Wor, 431 County Road, Broadlands, IL 61816

White Pine Photographic Services, Hwy. 60, General Delivery, Wilno, ON K0J 2N0 CANADA / 613-756-3452

White Rifles, Inc., 234 S. 1250 W., Linden, UT 84042 / 801-932-7950 www.whiterifles.com

White Rock Tool & Die, 6400 N. Brighton Ave., Kansas City, MO 64119 / 816-454-0478

Whitestone Lumber Corp., 148-02 14th Ave., Whitestone, NY 11357 / 718-746-4400; FAX: 718-767-1748 whstco@aol.com

Wichita Arms, Inc., 923 E. Gilbert, Wichita, KS 67211 / 316-265-0661; FAX: 316-265-0760 sales@wichitaarms.com www.wichitaarms.com

Wick, David E., 1504 Michigan Ave., Columbus, IN 47201 / 812-376-6960

Widener's Reloading & Shooting Supply, Inc., P.O. Box 3009 CRS, Johnson City, TN 37602 / 615-282-6786; FAX: 615-282-6651

Wideview Scope Mount Corp., 13535 S. Hwy. 16, Rapid City, SD 57702 / 605-341-3220; FAX: 605-341-9142 wvdon@rapidnet.com www.wideviewscopemount.com

Wiebe, Duane, 1111 157th St. Ct. E., Tacoma, WA 98445 / 253-535-0066; FAX: 253-535-0066 duane@directcom.net

Wiest, Marie. See: GUNCRAFT SPORTS, INC.

Wilcox All-Pro Tools & Supply, 4880 147th St., Montezuma, IA 50171 / 515-623-3138; FAX: 515-623-3104

Wilcox Industries Corp., Robert F. Guarasi, 53 Durham St., Portsmouth, NH 03801 / 603-431-1331; FAX: 603-431-1221

Wild Bill's Originals, P.O. Box 13037, Burton, WA 98013 / 206-463-5738; FAX: 206-465-5925 billcleaver@centurytel.net billcleaver@centurytel.net

Wild West Guns, 7100 Homer Dr., Anchorage, AK 99518 / 800-992-4570 or 907-344-4500; FAX: 907-344-4005 wwguns@ak.net www.wildwestguns.alaska.net

Wilderness Sound Products Ltd., 4015 Main St. A, Springfield, OR 97478

Wildey F. A., Inc., 45 Angevin Rd., Warren, CT 06754-1818 / 860-355-9000; FAX: 860-354-7759 wildeyfa@optonline.net www.wildeyguns.com

Wildlife Research Center, Inc., 1050 McKinley St., Anoka, MN 55303 / 763-427-3350 or 800-USE-LURE; (873-5873) FAX: 763-427-8354 www.wildlife.com

Will-Burt Co., 169 S. Main, Orrville, OH 44667

William E. Phillips Firearms, 38 Avondale Rd., Wigston, Leicester, ENGLAND / 0116 2886334; FAX: 0116 2810644 william.phillips2@tesco.net

William Powell Agency, 22 Circle Dr., Bellmore, NY 11710 / 516-679-1158

Williams Gun Sight Co., 7389 Lapeer Rd., Box 329, Davison, MI 48423 / 810-653-2131 or 800-530-9028; FAX: 810-658-2140 williamsgunsight.com

Williams Mfg. of Oregon, 110 East B St., Drain, OR 97435 / 503-836-7461; FAX: 503-836-7245

Williams Shootin' Iron Service, The Lynx-Line, Rt. 2 Box 223A, Mountain Grove, MO 65711 / 417-948-0902; FAX: 417-948-0902

Williamson Precision Gunsmithing, 117 W. Pipeline, Hurst, TX 76053 / 817-285-0064; FAX: 817-280-0044

Willow Bend, P.O. Box 203, Chelmsford, MA 01824 / 978-256-8508; FAX: 978-256-8508

Wilsom Combat, 2234 CR 719, Berryville, AR 72616-4573 / 800-955-4856; FAX: 870-545-3310 info@wilsoncombat.com www.wilsoncombat.com

Wilson Arms Co., The, 63 Leetes Island Rd., Branford, CT 06405 / 203-488-7297; FAX: 203-488-0135

Wilson Case, Inc., P.O. Box 1106, Hastings, NE 68902-1106 / 800-322-5493; FAX: 402-463-5276 sales@wilsoncase.com www.wilsoncase.com

Wilson Combat, 2234 CR 719, Berryville, AR 72616-4573 / 800-955-4856

Winchester Consultants, George Madis, P.O. Box 545, Brownsboro, TX 75756 / 903-852-6480; FAX: 903-852-5486 gmadis@earthlink.com www.georgemadis.com

Winchester Div. Olin Corp., 427 N. Shamrock, E. Alton, IL 62024 / 618-258-3566; FAX: 618-258-3599

Winchester Sutler, Inc., The, 270 Shadow Brook Lane, Winchester, VA 22603 / 540-888-3595; FAX: 540-888-4632

Windish, Jim, 2510 Dawn Dr., Alexandria, VA 22306 / 703-765-1994

Winfield Galleries LLC, 748 Hanley Industrial Ct., St. Louis, MO 63144 / 314-645-7636; FAX: 314-781-0224 info@winfieldgalleries.com www.winfieldgalleries.com

Wingshooting Adventures, 0-1845 W. Leonard, Grand Rapids, MI 49544 / 616-677-1980; FAX: 616-677-1986

Winter, Robert M., P.O. Box 484, 42975-287th St., Menno, SD 57045 / 605-387-5322

Wise Custom Guns, 1402 Blanco Rd., San Antonio, TX 78212-2716 / 210-828-3388

Wise Guns, Dale, 1402 Blanco Rd., San Antonio, TX 78212 / 210-734-9999

Wiseman and Co., Bill, P.O. Box 3427, Bryan, TX 77805 / 409-690-3456; FAX: 409-690-0156

Wisners, Inc., P.O. Box 58, Adna, WA 98522 / 360-748-4590; FAX: 360-748-6028 parts@wisnersinc.com www.wisnersinc.com

Wolf Performance Ammunition, 2201 E. Winston Rd., Ste. K, Anaheim, CA 92806-5537 / 702-837-8506; FAX: 702-837-9250

Wolfe Publishing Co., 2625 Stearman Rd., Ste. A, Prescott, AZ 86301 / 928-445-7810 or 800-899-7810; FAX: 928-778-5124 wolfepub@riflemag.com www.riflemagazine.com

Wolverine Footwear Group, 9341 Courtland Dr. NE, Rockford, MI 49351 / 616-866-5500; FAX: 616-866-5658

Woodleigh (See Huntington Die Specialties)

Woods Wise Products, P.O. Box 681552, Franklin, TN 37068 / 800-735-8182; FAX: 615-726-2637

Woodstream, P.O. Box 327, Lititz, PA 17543 / 717-626-2125; FAX: 717-626-1912

Woodworker's Supply, 1108 North Glenn Rd., Casper, WY 82601 / 307-237-5354

Woolrich, Inc., Mill St., Woolrich, PA 17701 / 800-995-1299; FAX: 717-769-6234/6259

World of Targets (See Birchwood Casey)

World Trek, Inc., 7170 Turkey Creek Rd., Pueblo, CO 81007-1046 / 719-546-2121; FAX: 719-543-6886

Wright's Gunstock Blanks, 8540 SE Kane Rd., Gresham, OR 97080 / 503-666-1705 doyal@wrightsguns.com www.wrightsguns.com

WTA Manufacturing, P.O. Box 164, Kit Carson, CO 80825 / 719-962-3570 or 719-962-3570 wta@rebeltec.net http://www.members.aol.com/ductman249/wta.html

Wyant Bullets, Gen. Del., Swan Lake, MT 59911

Wyoming Custom Bullets, 1626 21st St., Cody, WY 82414

Wyoming Knife Corp., 101 Commerce Dr., Fort Collins, CO 80524 / 303-224-3454

X

XS Sight Systems, 2401 Ludelle St., Fort Worth, TX 76105 / 888-744-4880; FAX: 800-734-7939

X-Spand Target Systems, 26-10th St. SE, Medicine Hat, AB T1A 1P7 CANADA / 403-526-7997; FAX: 403-528-2362

Y

Yankee Gunsmith "Just Glocks", 2901 Deer Flat Dr., Copperas Cove, TX 76522 / 817-547-8433; FAX: 254-547-8887 ed@justglocks.com www.justglocks.com

Yavapai College, 1100 E. Sheldon St., Prescott, AZ 86301 / 520-776-2353; FAX: 520-776-2355

Yavapai Firearms Academy Ltd., P.O. Box 27290, Prescott Valley, AZ 86312 / 928-772-8262; FAX: 928-772-0062 info@yfainc.com www.yfainc.com

Yearout, Lewis E. (See Montana Outfitters)

York M-1 Conversion, 12145 Mill Creek Run, Plantersville, TX 77363 / 936-894-2397; FAX: 936-894-2397 bmf25years@aol.com

Young Country Arms, William, 1409 Kuehner Dr. #13, Simi Valley, CA 93063-4478

Z

Zabala Hermanos S.A., P.O. Box 97, Elbar Lasao, 6, Elgueta, Guipuzcoa, 20600 SPAIN / 34-943-768076; FAX: 34-943-768201 imanol@zabalahermanos.com www.zabalahermanos.com

Zander's Sporting Goods, 7525 Hwy. 154 West, Baldwin, IL 62217-9706 / 800-851-4373; FAX: 618-785-2320

Zanotti Armor, Inc., 123 W. Lone Tree Rd., Cedar Falls, IA 50613 / 319-232-9650 www.zanottiarmor.com

Zeeryp, Russ, 1601 Foard Dr., Lynn Ross Manor, Morristown, TN 37814 / 615-586-2357

Zero Ammunition Co., Inc., 1601 22nd St. SE, P.O. Box 1188, Cullman, AL 35056-1188 / 800-545-9376; FAX: 205-739-4683 zerobulletco@aoz.com www.zerobullets.com

Ziegel Engineering, 1390 E. Bunnett St. "F", Signal Hill, CA 90755 / 562-596-9481; FAX: 562-598-4734 ziegel@aol.com www.ziegeleng.com

Zim's, Inc., 4370 S. 3rd West, Salt Lake City, UT 84107 / 801-268-2505

Z-M Weapons, 203 South St., Bernardston, MA 01337 / 413-648-9501; FAX: 413-648-0219

NUMBERS

100 Straight Products, Inc., P.O. Box 6148, Omaha, NE 68106 / 402-556-1055; FAX: 402-556-1055

3-Ten Corp., P.O. Box 269, Feeding Hills, MA 01030 / 413-789-2086; FAX: 413-789-1549 www.3-ten.com